MONEY TALKS

MONEY TALKS

Second Edition

by

Bob Rosefsky

McGraw-Hill Publishing Company

New York   St. Louis   San Francisco   Bogotá   Hamburg   Madrid   Mexico
Milan   Montreal   Paris   São Paulo   Tokyo   Toronto

1 2 3 4 5 6 7 8 9   DOC DOC   8 9 2 1 0 9

ISBN 0-07-053699-6

Library of Congress Cataloging-in-Publication Data

Rosefsky, Robert S.
    Money talks / by Bob Rosefsky.—2nd ed.
       p.   cm.
    Includes index.
    ISBN 0-07-053699-6
    1. Finance, Personal.   I. Title.
HG179.R67   1989b
332.024—dc19

Book design by M.R.P. Design.

To my wife, Linda Sue; to my children, Debbie and Mark, Michelle and Paul, Adam and Joshua; and to my grandson, Max. Greater riches no person could ever have.

Contents

Preface

The 1990s are upon us, and all too soon we'll be hearing fanfares about the End of the Century, and even more raucously, The End of the Millennium! In the upcoming years we'll be bombarded with all sorts of lists and perspectives and histories: "The One Hundred Top Tunes of the Second Millennium, A.D." . . . "What the Twentieth Century Meant, and Where the Twenty-first Will Take Us" . . . "Experts Pick the Best Investment Opportunities for the Next Thousand Years" . . . and so on, ad nauseam.

We are also likely to be hearing, with ever greater frequency, the projections of how our nation will become a second-class world citizen; how we're losing our economic clout; how we're failing to keep up with an evermore competitive world market; and how, in the long run, all of that will affect our jobs, our income, our future economic well-being.

Throughout all of this hoopla and doomsaying, we must never overlook one very elemental fact: Life still goes on, one day at a time, and attention must be paid to getting the most out of every day. Perspectives of world history come and go, but we still put on our socks one at a time, we still go to work to earn the bread, and we still struggle to make ends meet.

In short, it's still business as usual, and solid, proven, conservative money-management techniques are as important as ever. This is what *Money Talks* is all about. Stock market crashes may come and go, interest rates may soar and swoon, recessions and recoveries will always be lurking around the next corner, Congress will always be tinkering with tax-law changes, Wall Street will always be dreaming up new investment ideas, inflation may flare and subside—but come what may, the basic common-sense financial skills set forth in *Money Talks* will serve you well.

Numbers and rates and values will continually change. But your tools for success remain the same: prudence, common sense, goal-orientation, and knowledge. These tools make the difference between the confident and successful money manager and the nervous, frightened, insecure individual or family. I want this book to make you more of the former and less of the latter.

One feature I hope you will find particularly useful is the first chapter, which discusses in simple terms how the "economy" works. To help you understand what might otherwise seem so confusing, I've created three whimsical groups of primitive people: the Fish People, the Log People, and the Berry People. Their trials, tribulations, and interrelationships can help you grasp some of the more complex economic factors that shape our lives, for better and for worse.

Make good use of *Money Talks*—as a learning tool today, and as a reference source in the future.

BOB ROSEFSKY
Los Angeles

CHAPTER 1

The Economy: How It Works and What It Means to You

Many factors at work in the world can influence your financial well-being: your work, your budget, your investments, your future security. The more you know about these factors, the better you can cope with them. To ignore them can be dangerous. This chapter explains, in story fashion, the bearing these factors have on your life. In reading it, you'll gain an understanding of such things as

- Why some individuals (or companies, or nations) achieve greater financial success than others
- What makes prices go up and down
- How unexpected forces (such as the weather, international incidents, etc.) can affect your personal situation
- How modern technology can provide you with career advancement and a better life
- How the actions (or inactions) of the government can affect the economic health of the nation, of your employer, and of your family

FORCES THAT SHAPE OUR LIVES

You're looking for a job, and you've had two interesting offers. One is from a firm that manufactures a fancy and expensive sports car. Both the company and the car have an exciting and glamorous image, the working environment is very attractive, and the initial pay is very appealing.

The other offer is from a firm that manufactures a hand-held video camera/recorder. The product has been a smashing success since it was introduced: Lightweight, inexpensive, and virtually foolproof in operation, it has promise of all but wiping out the traditional home movie market and of taking a major share of the home video camera/recorder market. But the company itself lacks the "pizazz" of the sports car firm, the working environment seems rather dull, and the starting pay isn't as good as at the car company. Which do you choose?

Rather than jump at the offer that seems more attractive on the surface, you decide to do some research into the matter. You learn that the sports car manufacturer has very stiff competition from both American and foreign automakers. Further, there was a governmental ban on foreign sports car imports, but that ban has just been lifted and the international competition will become even more threatening. And to top matters off, your research indicates that if business in general slows down—which it seems to be on the verge of doing—fancy sports cars are one of the first products that people will stop buying. And if people stop buying a product that you're involved in making, you could be out of a job.

The picture is quite different with respect to the hand-held video camera/recorder. The company has a huge lead on all of its competitors. Its research department is on the verge of introducing new technology that will bring the price of the product down, thereby making it available to millions more consumers. Moreover, the product offers such wide access to low-cost entertainment and educational material that sales would virtually defy any national recession.

Now you reevaluate the job choices: The higher starting pay and the glamour of the sports car company don't seem quite as important when you consider the future growth opportunities. Indeed, you might conclude, there is very limited future potential with the sports car company. The video company, on the other hand, though stodgy and lower paying at the outset, may well offer a vastly more rewarding future career.

This brief example of choosing between two jobs illustrates some of the economic forces that can shape your future. And as your career is shaped, so is your financial, emotional, and social well-being. These same forces, and others, can also affect the possible success of any investment program you might embark upon. Similarly, your ability to afford such items as a house, a college education for your children, and a comfortable retirement can be definitely influenced by these economic factors.

In short, our financial affairs (and our personal affairs as they are affected by our financial affairs) do not operate in a vacuum. Every day there are elements, some subtle, some direct, that can make our lives better or worse. Some of these elements cannot be avoided, but many of them can be either avoided or countered if we understand them and know what kind of actions to take.

Let's now explore the basic workings of the economic forces and influences that can have a bearing on our lives. This is not intended to be a scientific inquiry into economics but rather a background and a foundation to aid you in putting to best use the specific information you'll learn throughout the balance of this book. Not only will this background information help you to arrive at the best specific financial decisions, but it should also give you an understanding of many of the perplexing and frustrating phenomena you hear about in the news every day. Understanding these phenomena, rather than hiding from them or being misled by them, can allow you to function better at work and at home in both the short and long term.

A SERIOUS GAME

Imagine a football game: two teams of large and garishly costumed gladiators about to bash heads in front of thousands of screaming spectators. Instead of dividing the game into four quarters of fifteen minutes each, let's look at it from a totally different perspective. The game represents certain *forces* at work on the playing field. The effectiveness of these forces is largely controlled by certain *influences* that are brought to bear. The final effect of these forces and the influences acting upon them is that one team wins and one team loses.

☐ *Forces.* The forces at work on the playing field include the brute physical power of the players themselves, plus their individual and collective desire to win.

☐ *Influences.* Many different things can give shape and direction to the basic forces. The *training* and *equipment* available to the players can influence the efficiency with which they use their brute power. The *motivation* imparted by the coach and the *cheering* of the crowd can strongly influence their individual and collective desire to win. And the weather—an uncontrollable influence—can override all of the other factors.

☐ *Effects and results.* The forces clash, shaped and directed as they are by the various influences, and one team emerges the winner, the other the loser.

The economy is similar to this make-believe football game. There are forces at work. There are certain factors that influence the forces. And there are various results that occur depending on which forces have been influenced in what way. The effects, or results, can have a bearing on how you live your life. Further, the same forces and influences can be present in the economy of your family as well as in the economy of your city, state, or nation.

Forces

The basic forces involved in an economic entity are

☐ *Work power.* Work power is the basic capacity of the population to work and produce.

☐ *Human nature.* Comparable to a football team's desire to win (or lack thereof), any given population—be it a family, a company, or government—has certain innate needs and desires: to survive, to compete, to protect, or to expand its territory. Aspects of human nature in the economic sense can be expressed as expectations, greed, desire for power, and concern for the welfare of the citizens that make up the population.

Influences

The influences that can give shape and direction to the basic forces in an economic entity are many and varied. Some of the main influences are listed below, briefly and in no particular order. Compare them with the influences that shape the forces at work in the football game. Later in this chapter we'll take a closer look at these influences.

Information.   Education is to an economic population what training is to a football team. And after basic training, the quality of continuing education further shapes the team's success. In the economic population, continuing education consists of an ongoing awareness of facts and trends obtainable through scrutiny of the news media and specialized publications pertaining to one's pursuits.

Government Policies.   Government policies and philosophies have a tremendous bearing on the forces at work in an economic population. Governmental influences include how the government will tax the people, how the government will spend money, and what relationships the government has with other governments.

Management and Labor.   Within a given company or industry, the quality of management is akin to the quality of coaching on a football team. And the degree to which the workers cooperate with management is comparable to the team spirit or lack thereof on the football team. This can also be viewed as one aspect affecting productivity.

Technology (Research and Development).   Whether it's you examining job opportunities, as illustrated at the start of this chapter, or a company exploring new and better ways to make its products, the importance of the influence of technology cannot be overlooked.

Nature.   A frozen or muddy football field can render the most powerful team harmless. A drought, a flood, an excessively cold winter can cripple the financial well-being of an otherwise healthy family, industry, or region.

Natural Resources.   A family may have a naturally gifted musician, artist, football player, or entertainer who can enrich the whole family's lives, both personally and financially. Likewise, a company may have a file drawer full of exotic and potentially profitable patents. Similarly, a nation may have untapped reserves of petroleum or minerals. Having natural resources is one thing; putting them to productive and profitable use is another.

Marketing.   Some people are better salespersons than others. The skills with which a product or service is packaged, advertised, and sold have a bearing on the economic strength of a given entity.

Capital Investment.   If an economic entity seems attractive enough to outsiders, the outsiders might be willing to invest in that entity. Such investments, put to proper use, can further enhance the well-being of the entity. An entity that is unattractive to outsiders can suffer accordingly.

The Law of Supply and Demand.   The law of supply and demand is one of the most basic concepts of economics and of the world in general. It can exert a profound influence on your attempts to succeed economically. If you grow watermelons and the harvest is too bountiful, you may bring more melons to the market than people are willing to buy. You may then have to drop your price to avoid taking home unsold watermelons, and you could end up a big loser. If the harvest is just right but the weather is cold when you come to the market with your melons, people may not be interested in buying the thirst-quenching fruit at all, and again you may end up a loser. In the former case, the supply exceeds the usual demand. In the latter case, the supply is customary, but the demand is low. On the other hand, if your harvest is just right and the demand is high because the weather is hot and dry, you could reap a tremendous profit on your melons.

Luck.   Luck is, to be sure, a very unscientific aspect of the science of economics. But it is ever-present in virtually every one of the other influences. Whether good or bad, it's unpredictable and unavoidable. The ability to take advantage of good luck and avoid the ravages of bad luck can make a distinct difference between success and failure in an economic endeavor.

As noted, these influences are not stated in any particular order. In many cases they overlap, intertwine, and influence one another. But whether taken individually, in combination, or as an aggregate, they do shape and give direction to the human forces that constitute an economic population.

Effects and Results

The forces go to work and are influenced one way or another by the various factors mentioned above. Here's a summary of some of the potential effects we'll explore in the course of this chapter:

- Inflation or deflation (rising or falling prices and wages)
- Employment or unemployment (good jobs or lack thereof)
- Economic growth or recession
- Survival or termination of an economic entity
- An attractive or an unattractive investment climate
- Surpluses or deficits (having money in the bank or being excessively in debt)

Many of these effects and results can become influences in their own right. The football team suffers a loss, and the score against them is so lopsided that the players are humiliated. This effect—humiliation—lowers their morale to such a point that they lose their next game, which they had been heavily favored to win. The effect has become a cause in its own right. Or a company develops a highly touted product only to have the public ignore it because of a poorly designed advertising campaign. Not only does the company lose money because of the high costs of introducing the new product, but some of the top managers leave in protest over the marketing program. The company suffers even further as a result. The effect—poor sales—has become an influence in its own right on the future of the company.

FISH, BERRIES, AND LOGS

To get a better idea of how these forces and influences interact in an economic population, let's examine the history of three fictional primitive tribes: the Fish People, the Berry People, and the Log People. Any similarities between the economic concerns of these ancient folk and your own family's, your employer's, or your nation's are not coincidental.

Where It All Began

The Fish People lived at the water's edge. They had learned to make spears, and they harvested a bounty from the sea. Their work was not physically demanding, but it required patience, cunning, and long hours. As long as they were willing to work, there were fish to be caught. An endless supply of fish seemed assured, and their leader, Mug, told them that they could indeed become rich through hard work and through the expansion of their fishing grounds along the shoreline and out to sea. What fish they didn't need for their own purposes they traded with the Berry People for berries and with the Log People for logs. Men, women, and children all worked. They saw no limit to the amount of fish they could catch and thereby no limit to the amount of berries and logs they could acquire from their neighbors. Their energies and their expectations were high. They desired to expand and to become ever wealthier.

A few miles inland, on a plateau blessed by constant sunshine and fresh ocean breezes, lived the Berry People. The plateau was covered with thousands of wild berry bushes of all kinds—black, huckle, rasp, straw, and goose. These sweet, delicious berries were always in demand by the Log People and the Fish People. Nature blessed the Berry People: The berries grew in abundance with little need for care. The only work that the Berry People had to do was to pick their crop. What they didn't keep for themselves, they packaged to deliver to the neighboring tribes in return for their products. With the sun, the rain, and the soil doing most of their work for them, the Berry People tended to be lazy and greedy. Their leader, Wump, assured them that everything was going their way, and that while they should appreciate their good furtune, they should also take advantage of it and live the good life. Wump saw no need to plan for the future. The future, it appeared, would take care of itself.

Beyond the plateau the land rose into wooded hills. This was the domain of the Log People. They had devised tools to cut down the plentiful trees that surrounded them, and they traded the logs to their neighbors for fish and berries. The neighbors found the logs necessary for building fires, creating shelters, and fashioning additional tools for their own uses. Work for the Log People was very demanding physically. Cutting the trees down and chopping them into pieces with their primitive tools was bone-wearying. It had become custom among the Log People for only the men to work since their physical prowess was greater than that of the women. The women tended to the home and to the needs of their men, who returned exhausted from their work at day's end. They were content with their modest lot and aspired to neither wealth nor power. Their leader, Theodore, had told them, "This is the way it has always been with us, and this is the way it probably always will be."

By mutual agreement, the three tribes had decided that for trading purposes one fish equal in length to Mug's forearm would be equal to one basket of berries the size of Wump's head, which in turn would be equal to one log the length of Theodore's leg. Thus, if the Fish People wanted to acquire ten logs, they would have to deliver ten appropriately sized fish to the Log People, and so on.

The three tribes lived in relative harmony, trading among themselves as their needs and desires dictated, and otherwise leaving each other alone. The following, in no particular order of importance, are some of the occurrences that shaped the lives and welfare of these tribes. As you read, bear in mind the economic influences outlined above.

The Empty Forest

As long as the Log People had ever known, the big trees had always been there. Many years before, when all the tribes were much smaller, all of their needs had been filled by chopping down just two or three trees a year. But in recent years the tribes had all expanded considerably and were demanding much more wood than they had formerly needed. The Berry People were building ever-more elaborate log huts; the Fish People needed logs to make rafts; and all three tribes were making ever-more furniture, tools, fences, and fires for heat and for cooking.

Whereas the big trees used to be just a few minutes' walk from the Log People's village, the choppers now had to walk farther to get to the available trees.

Theodore had done too little calculating, and he had done it too late. Never having been faced before with the problem of not having trees readily available close at hand, the thought of planting new trees had never dawned on him. And when he finally did realize that new plantings were needed, he was dismayed to discover that it took many years for the seedlings to grow into mature trees. Meantime, it was now taking the choppers three hours to get to the mature trees and six hours to drag the logs back to the village. The amount of time to create a single log had multiplied many times over what it had been before. This meant that it was costing the Log People dearly to acquire one fish or one basket of berries. Mankind was suffering its first energy crisis.

Although blessed with a natural resource that could be renewed, the Log People had failed to do so, and they were suffering accordingly. Further, by failing to anticipate an ever-increasing cost of acquiring the natural resource, their problems were compounded. Eventually, Theodore would invent the wheel, which would make possible the creation of a wagon. This would sharply cut down the time and energy needed to get to and retrieve the logs. But in the meantime, waiting for their new plantings to mature, the Log People settled into an era of economic distress.

All Dried Up

As far as the Berry People ever knew, it always rained when it was supposed to. How shocking it must have been to them, then, when one year it did not rain. The first known drought in the history of the Berry People was devastating. Many of the berry bushes produced no fruit at all, some bushes withered and died, and the berries that did grow were puny and withered. The Log People and the Fish People would no longer accept one basket of berries in equal trade for a fish or a log because the berries were of such poor quality. They insisted on two baskets for one fish or one log, and the Berry People found themselves with no choice. Until they could remedy the problems caused by the drought, they would have to do with fewer fish and fewer logs. The unpredictable forces of nature had seriously undercut the life of the Berry People, and Wump, their leader, vowed to do something about it.

Wump searched the surrounding countryside and finally discovered what he felt would be the solution to their problem—an underground spring of fresh water. He told his people that if the drought continued, their only salvation would be to carry buckets to the spring and bring water back for the bushes. Indeed, the drought continued into the next season, but the Berry People had grown so lazy throughout the fat years that they were unwilling to work hard carrying water to save themselves. Many of them refused to accept Wump's warnings about the ultimate consequences if they failed to work hard, believing that the rains would come the next day, or the next, or the next. But the rains didn't come, and the Berry People were on the edge of extinction.

Fearing the worst, Wump retired to his private quarters to concentrate all of his thought powers on how to save his people. It came to him in a flash! The head of the underground spring was at a point of land higher than the Berry People's plateau. "Why not," Wump reasoned, "fashion a trench leading from the spring to our plateau? We could then direct the water to flow through the trench and onto our parched berry bushes."

He announced his plan to the people, telling them that it would take a lot of hard work to dig the trench, but that once it was completed abundant water would flow to their bushes. Faced with the ultimate crisis, the Berry People agreed to do the necessary work. Within a few weeks, the trench had been dug and properly lined, and the water began to flow. Soon the bushes would be blooming again, and they'd be back to one basket of berries for each fish or each log. Prosperity was just around the corner.

Wump had researched the problem and had developed a means of coping with it. Wump's technology—the first irrigation canal—had overcome the adverse forces of nature, as well as the weak spirit of his people. Wump also knew that they should never again take for granted that the rains would fall. Planning for the future was something that had to be done, for, Wump admitted to himself in his private moments, it *was* possible for the spring to dry up someday.

The Disappearing Fish

Just as the trees had always been there for the Log People, and the rain had always fallen for the Berry People, the fish always swam close to the shore settlement of the Fish People—until one strange day when the fish disappeared. Disbelief quickly spread throughout the village, and each man, woman, and child ran into the water to see if it was really a fact. The fish were gone! In panic, they ran up and down the shore and put rafts out to sea. Far from their village the fish still swam, but why did they no longer swim near the village, where it was so convenient to catch them? Mug stood knee-deep in the water in front of the village and tried to reason the answer. It came through his nose. There was a strange and offensive odor to the water. Mug sniffed and sniffed again until the odor could be identified. It was the odor of human waste.

Mug realized immediately why the fish had disappeared. For as long as he could remember, the Fish People had disposed of their waste in the water near the village, relying on the tides to carry it out to sea. But little by little over the years, the saturation of the water had become so dense that the tides could no longer wash the water clean. Simply enough, the fish were repelled by the polluted water and sought other grounds.

Mug disclosed his findings to the village council and told them that unless drastic action was taken immediately, their hopes and dreams would quickly fade. It would be necessary, he suggested, for the waste to be carried to some distant inland point and buried. He realized that this would drain the work power of the people, but only by doing so would the water eventually cleanse itself and allow the fish to return. The Fish People were motivated to realize their expectations. So they commenced an energetic program of waste disposal.

In just a few months the water had cleansed itself and the fish had returned. Even though it was more costly to the Fish People in terms of their time to remove the waste from the village, they were willing to do the necessary work.

They had realized that their well-being could be affected by polluting their environment, and they were willing to pay the price to correct the problem. That price had been reasonable enough. Had the price been much higher, Mug worried, the people might have objected to paying it, and the village could have been split into factions moving up the coast and down the coast, thus destroying the entity of the Fish People.

The First Price Wars

It had taken many years for the Log People to recover from their first energy crisis. To insure that it would not happen again, they planted as many trees as they possibly could as close to their village as space allowed. But during the time it took for these new plantings to become mature trees, the Fish People and Berry People had taken their own steps to avoid being caught in a shortage of logs from the Log People. The Fish People had started to collect driftwood and found that it was very suitable for repairing their huts. The Berry People found that dead bushes made excellent fuel for their fires—better, in fact, than the Log People's logs. The Fish People and the Berry People began an active trade between each other in driftwood and dead berry bushes. That was the situation when the Log People's new trees came to maturity. Not only did they have more logs available than the other tribes needed, but there was now an added factor: competition. Berry bushes burned better, and driftwood was more decorative. The supply of logs was too great, and the demand too little. The Log People were again facing poverty. They literally had logs to burn.

Faced with stiff competition from their neighbors and being on the losing side of the law of supply and demand, the Log People had no choice but to cut the price of their logs if they were to survive. Instead of trading one log for one fish or one basket of berries, they traded two logs. In effect, the cost to the Log People of one fish or one basket of berries had doubled. Since berries and fish were still relatively scarce—at least compared with the supply of logs—the Log People saw no end to their dilemma. If by some chance the fish crop doubled or the berry crop doubled, the Log People could return to their one-for-one trading basis. But for the time being they had too many logs available to buy too few fish or berries. This dilemma—otherwise referred to as "too much money chasing too few goods"—has come to be known as one of the basic causes of a phenomenon called *inflation*. Another historical first for the Log People!

The Value of Good Hard Work

The horror of the drought stayed in the minds of the Berry People for many years. Adding to this the constant reminder that the underground spring could someday dry up, Wump succeeded in creating a force of energetic workers out of what had been lazy playboys and playgirls.

Wump organized the workers into efficient squadrons. One squadron tended the underground spring and continually looked for new sources of water. Another squadron tended to the irrigation canal to make sure it had no leaks or diversions. Another squadron dug catch basins to store excess water, and yet another tended to the pruning and fertilizing of the berry bushes. The Berry People knew that their crop would grow only on that particular plateau. They had no desire to plant in other areas, but they realized that by improving the specific yield on the plateau berry bushes, they could become more wealthy.

Wump urged the workers on to exert themselves, and he congratulated them lavishly for jobs well done. The workers appreciated Wump's concern for their welfare, and they cooperated with his plans to the best of their ability.

The fruits of their labors were soon evident: Some of the bushes grew twice as many good berries as they had in the past; still others grew fewer berries, but they were much larger, much sweeter, and much more desirable. Because of this cooperation between Wump, the manager, and the workers, the Berry People had become more efficient. They were turning out more goods and better goods for a given amount of labor. Building upon his earlier technological advance (the irrigation canal), Wump had succeeded in increasing the productivity of the population.

Smoking a Fish

After the Fish People had implemented their waste disposal program, they eventually found that there were more fish than ever in the waters off their village. Now they faced a curious dilemma: They could catch more fish than they could trade to the other tribes. Still keenly motivated by their desire for wealth and expansion, they deliberated on what to do with this excess of natural resource. At the heart of the problem was the fact that there was no way to keep a fish after it had been out of the water for a day or so. It simply rotted and had to be thrown away.

If only there was some way that fish could be kept for an indefinite period. The village council met in Mug's hut to deliberate on the matter. They threw some fish over the fire for that evening's meal and commenced their discussions. Someone suggested that a freezer be invented, but Mug noted that they did not as yet have a place to plug it into. Other ideas flowed freely, with discussion and debate ensuing. The proceedings became so intense that the council forgot about the fish that were on the dying fire. Many hours later, still not having reached a conclusion, hunger got the best of them. They were dismayed to find that the fish had been *too* thoroughly cooked. The juices were dried out and the meat smelled of the wood smoke.

Thus they all had to go to bed without any supper that evening. But, on a hunch, Mug did not throw away the overcooked fish. He put them into a box to see what might happen to them in the next few days.

Three days later, Mug sniffed at the box of overcooked fish. To his amazement, they did not smell rotten. He picked off a piece of flesh and tasted it. It was dry and smoky tasting, but curiously appealing. Mug said nothing of his discovery and three days later tried it again. It still tasted good. Then Mug announced the great breakthrough to a general meeting of the Fish People.

Purely by accident, technology had created a new product: smoked fish. Experiments began with different kinds of fish and different kinds of woods to find the combination that would extend the usefulness of smoked fish for the longest possible time. In the ensuing weeks the techniques were refined and perfected.

The Log People and the Berry People were at first skeptical of this new edible item, but on tasting it and testing it they found it satisfying. The popularity of the smoked fish spread rapidly among the tribes. In addition to providing a new taste sensation, it also solved two other important problems that the tribes faced. One problem was that the people could never travel more than one day from their village, because they couldn't carry a supply of fish that would last them that long. If they could carry a supply of fish that would last them many days, they could explore realms far beyond their villages and expand their universe accordingly.

The other problem was that there were occasional shortfalls in the amount of fish needed to satisfy their daily appetites. By laying in a supply of smoked fish, they could get through those brief shortages comfortably. Needless to say, all of these factors meant more sales for the Fish People. Here, technology (albeit accidental) as applied to the natural resources of the Fish People allowed them to gain some control over the law of supply and demand. No matter how high or unexpected the demand, they could meet it with either fresh or smoked fish. And if demand should drop, they could either smoke the fish or leave it in the water until needed. And by insuring themselves of a market for one form of fish or another during all seasons, the Fish People were able to keep their village budget on an even keel.

Bad News, Good News

Meanwhile, back in the Log People's village, Theodore and his advisors were trying to figure out a way to avoid the problem of an oversupply of logs. They reviewed the factors that had caused the problem in the first place. Their major mistake, they discerned, was that they had relied on false or incomplete information in deciding how many new trees to plant. It had all happened so long ago that they couldn't remember precisely, but they felt that they had either been told or had let themselves believe that there was a market for as many trees as they could produce. Thus, the overplanting. Now, in retrospect, they realized how detrimental that information had been.

Theodore explained that they must, from that time on, seek out proper and correct information upon which to base their planting decisions. "Let's determine," he urged his people, "just how many logs we can really sell at a fair price, and we'll plant accordingly." This was no easy task, for they all well knew that it took many years between the planting and the cutting of the trees. Theodore assigned people to ferret out the facts: How large will the populations of the tribes be when today's plantings mature? What kind of demand will they have for logs at that time? What kind of competition can be expected at that time from driftwood and dead bushes? Are there other kinds of trees that can be planted that will be more salable? Can farming techniques be developed to make the trees grow taller and faster while still retaining the quality of the wood, if not improving it?

Theodore sent his people out to study these intricate questions. They worked hard at their tasks and returned a year later with their recommendations. Theodore acknowledged that specific answers were elusive, but he felt much more confident in guiding his people with this researched information than he had with the suppositions, guesses, and impulsive thinking that had guided them in the past. He took the conclusions to each of the clusters in the village who tended their own groves. He gave them lessons in how to plant, how much to plant, and how to properly tend the growing trees.

It took a full generation for all of this effort to pay off, but the rewards were worth the wait. The Log People had utilized education, market research, and the proper dissemination of information to stabilize and strengthen their economic well-being.

A Crushing Blow

Many years had passed since Wump had stirred the Berry People to new heights of productivity. Things were going perhaps a bit too well for the Berry People, and the old ways of laziness and greed had begun to seep back into the population. Wump was much older now, and his influence on the people was not as direct. His apparent successor, Terwilliger, was intrigued by tales of the good old days when the Berry People had to do little work and were richly rewarded by nature.

In his zeal, Terwilliger cast about for ways that the Berry People could do less work, at less expense, and nevertheless earn more fish and logs. He hit upon an idea that was greeted with unanimous approval by his followers. They would double the size of the berry baskets. Despite the cost and time involved in making the new larger baskets, they were confident that the investment would be well worth it. By using the double-sized baskets, they would save considerably on their packing costs, on replacing baskets, and on overall handling. In short, there would be less work, less expense, and more net income.

Terwilliger was delirious with the prospects for his new plan, and his enthusiasm spread rapidly. So confident was everyone in Terwilliger's ideas that nobody bothered to question him. Terwilliger sent messengers out to the Log People's village and the Fish People's village to inform them of the forthcoming event: ''New, bigger, better berry baskets for all!'' He posted signs on hundreds of trees to extol the virtues of the new baskets and promised discounts for advance orders of the new product.

Terwilliger was even able to obtain a personal audience with Mug of the Fish People and Theodore of the Log People to tell them of the new advanced product. Both Mug and Theodore responded politely, saying that it sounded very interesting and that they'd certainly be willing to give the new baskets a try. Terwilliger interpreted their remarks as an enthusiastic endorsement of the new baskets, and he returned to the Berry village with orders to put the entire current crop into the new baskets at once. He was so sure that the demand would be great that he risked putting the entire crop on the market all at once.

The pickers worked tirelessly to fulfill Terwilliger's orders. Thousands and thousands of double-sized baskets were laid out on the delivery wagons. Terwilliger himself escorted the first wagon to the Fish People's village and presented the first basket to Mug. Mug was flattered by the gift and poured the double basket of berries into a large bowl for his family to taste. Then, to everyone's shock, they discovered that the berries on the bottom of the basket had been crushed by the weight of the berries on the top of the basket. Fully one-third of all the berries in the basket were damaged, and Mug expressed his feeling that he had been cheated by this new means of packaging.

''You told me I'd be getting two baskets' worth of berries in one, and in fact

I only have a little more than one basket's worth of usable berries! You led me to believe that I was getting fair value for my two fish! I've been cheated!''

Stunned and embarrassed, Terwilliger apologized. He admitted that they had never tested to see whether the double-sized baskets would create any crushing problems. They had just assumed that if a single-sized basket did not result in crushing, neither would a double-sized basket.

But it was too late for Terwilliger and the Berry People. Bad word of mouth quickly spread from Mug to the entire village and then to the Log People's village. Terwilliger had put the entire current crop on the line and now found it difficult even to give it away. The bulk of the crop rotted in the double baskets, and the Berry People were flung into all but instant poverty. Their underlying force—greed—had been thrown back in their faces by dreadful marketing procedures. Despite the quality of the product, the lack of research, poor packaging, and misleading advertising had resulted in a disaster for the people in the Berry village.

Help Wanted

One aspect of the smoked fish development brought unexpectedly good results: Loaded with a multi-day supply of fish, all of the tribes were able to venture out of their villages into previously unexplored areas. They found numerous other tribes specializing in their own products. To the north were tribes that produced wheat, chickens, and apples. To the south were tribes that produced barley, bananas, and a strange bubbling fermented beverage that the natives called *beer*. None of these tribes had ever seen a fish—either fresh or smoked. The Fish People were anxious to take advantage of this vast new market for their product. But they had some serious problems. All of the available population was already working overtime to supply fish to the Berry and Log tribes. And the leadership of the Fish People had long ago determined that no one but the Fish People should work the teeming waters by the village. How then could they catch more fish to sell to these outlying tribes?

First, the leaders had to agree that the basic tradition of the Fish People should be changed and that outsiders should be allowed to work in their village. Second, they had to create a reason for outsiders to *want* to work in the fishing village. Passing the law to allow outsiders to work was relatively easy. But how could they induce the members of the other tribes to want to work there? They decided to allow any such outsiders a share of profits generated by the sale of fish to the outlying tribes, in addition to a basic wage for their labor. The women of the Log People, who hitherto had not been accustomed to working, found this an attractive proposition. By this time much of the log cutting had become easier because of improved tools, and the women were freer to explore other opportunities for themselves. They welcomed the chance to be productive in their own right and were further satisfied that their village would benefit from the added wealth that they would bring home. Even some of the more energetic Berry People found the offer intriguing, and thus the first export business was created.

Governmental policy, coupled with the creation of an incentive to invest (in this case, time rather than money), was responsible for bringing a new era of prosperity to the three tribes.

Making Munny

The discovery of the outlying tribes and the commencement of trading with them brought great changes to the Fish, Berry, and Log Peoples. Steps were taken to improve the efficiency of their internal trading. As the populations of the three tribes had grown, it was becoming ever more cumbersome to handle fish, berries, and logs each time a transaction occurred. The leaders of the tribes agreed to create small tokens, made of stones, that would represent either a fish, a basket of berries, or a log. Thus, instead of trading the goods themselves, they could trade the tokens that represented the goods. Each token was referred to, in their primitive language, as a *Munny*. Now, if a Fish Person sold a large quantity of fish, he could take Munnies in exchange, rather than load himself up with berries and logs that he might not need at that time. Later, if that Fish Person wanted to acquire a basket of berries, he could trade a Munny for it rather than having to carry a fish clear across town.

Before long, the more entrepreneurial members of the tribes began to accumulate large quantities of Munnies, and to protect themselves against thieves they asked the leaders of the tribes to oversee the creation of a bank that would hold their Munnies for them.

In addition to their Munny tokens, the three tribes had many other things in common. They were physically close to one another; they had many similar traditions and beliefs because of their centuries of living near and trading with one another; and they felt a common need to help defend one another against any outside attacks. Eventually, they decided to formalize their communal interests by creating a pact that was to bind them together in an alliance called the United Tribes. Meanwhile, and in similar fashion, the tribes in the north had joined together as the Wheat/Apples/Chicken Alliance. And the southerly producers of barley, bananas, and beer had joined together as the 3-B Federation. Each of these two other groups had created their own tokens representing their products, and the Alliance tokens, the 3-B tokens, and the Munny tokens were freely interchanged as the groups traded actively among one another. For many years all the peoples of these nations regarded one Alliance token as being equal to one Munny token, which was equal to one 3-B token. And for all those years the amount of trade among the nations was equal. Each nation bought and sold the same amount from the other nations year in and year out.

The Building Binge

Then some unusual things began to happen in the United Tribes, which until now had been the biggest and most powerful of the nations. The government of the United Tribes decided to build a series of magnificent roads connecting each of the three villages. Many citizens objected because the project promised to be very expensive and there was serious doubt that such magnificent roads were in fact needed. Further, it was noted, the government didn't have any Munny with which to build such roads. The government countered the arguments by saying, "We are here to decide what is best for our people. If we don't need the roads today, we'll certainly need them in the future as our population grows. Further, with roads like the ones we have in mind, we will be the envy of the Alliance and the 3-B Federation. Our national pride is at stake. And there's no problem about Munny. We will simply borrow it from our citizens. If they lend us ten Munnies for one year, we will repay them with eleven Munnies at the end of the year. That will get us all the Munny we need."

But, critics asked the government, how will the citizens be repaid? "Again, easy," the government replied. "Since each and every citizen of the United Tribes will benefit from these magnificent new roads, we will require each and every citizen to pay one Munny per year until all the loans have been repaid to our investors. We will call this a *tax*."

The program got underway, and the government announced its plans to borrow Munnies from the citizens. The opportunity to earn one extra Munny per year for each ten invested was too good for most citizens to resist. They rushed to the bank to take out their unused Munny to lend it to the government. This shocked the bank managers deeply. "We can't survive under such competitive pressure from the government," they claimed. "And if we don't survive you'll have no place to store your Munny." The bankers were told by the government that the matter would be attended to at some other time.

The magnificent roads were barely completed when the government, proud of itself, announced plans to build lovely gardens and rest stops along the roadways. Again, they would borrow and again they would tax the citizens to pay for the improvements.

Some of the citizens began to complain that they could never use the magnificent roadways because they didn't have enough of their own Munny to buy a wagon. Heeding their plight, the government assisted these people in the purchase of wagons, again borrowing and again taxing the citizens to pay for these expenses.

There seemed to be no end in sight to the government's spending. And the more they spent, the more they borrowed, and the deeper in debt they went. The citizens—taxpayers—finally rebelled. "We've had enough! We're paying a lot of Munny in taxes and we're not getting benefits in return! Something has to change, and it has to change quickly!"

This incident describes what is known as *fiscal policy*. Fiscal policy has to do with how a government decides to spend money and how it raises the money it does spend—normally through taxation. If a government's income from taxation and outgo through expenses are equal, it is said that the government has a balanced budget, just like a family's or a business's. If a government takes in more money than it spends, it is said to have a surplus; if it spends more than it takes in, it is said to have a deficit. The fiscal policy of a government as determined by its population and by its leaders can thus have many influences on the well-being of the people.

The other unusual development in the United Tribes was the insatiable craving for beer, available only through the 3-B Federation.

The Beer Bust

For a long time, the trade between the United Tribes and the 3-B Federation was equal. But for inexplicable reasons, the United Tribes thirst for beer began to increase at a rapid pace. The United Tribes citizens were hooked on beer. Despite the warnings of the government, the citizens continued to consume beer in ever-greater quantities.

The rulers of the 3-B Federation saw a unique opportunity. "First," they said, "the United Tribes will consume all the beer we can produce, and seemingly at whatever price we decide to charge. Second, one day we're liable to run out of the pure mountain spring water we use to make our beer. And by the time that day comes, either the United Tribes or the Alliance may have discovered their own pure mountain spring water and we'll be bankrupt. We ought to charge all we can for our product now while we have it to sell. We can stash away all the surplus tokens we make and use them when our own supply of water runs out."

So it was that the 3-B Federation quadrupled the price of beer to the United Tribes. The citizens of the United Tribes were, to say the least, shocked. But they insisted on having their beer. The government told them that there was not enough Munny floating about to pay for the beer. But the citizens were not to be denied their beverage. Rather than risk being thrown out of office, the leaders of the government agreed to create new pieces of Munny. "But you can't do that," critics argued. "A piece of Munny can be created only when there is a fish, a basket of berries, or a log available to back it up. You can't carve more Munnies than there are fish or berries or logs!"

"Oh no? Watch us!" replied the government. And they proceeded to create vast stockpiles of additional Munnies, which they made available to the citizens of the United Tribes by allowing the bank to lend more Munnies to individuals.

This enabled the United Tribes to buy all the beer they wanted with reckless abandon. The citizens of the 3-B Federation, meanwhile, were being flooded with Munnies. They in turn used the Munnies to buy chickens and wheat and apples from the Alliance. But the Alliance grew cautious about accepting so many Munnies. "It used to be," they said, "that one Munny was equal to one fish or one log or one basket of berries. But there are so many Munnies floating about these days that we are not sure exactly what they are worth. Perhaps they're worth only half a fish or a log or a basket of berries. If that's the case, then we're going to double the price in Munnies for our wheat, chicken, and apples."

Very soon thereafter, the beer-guzzling citizens of the United Tribes found that products they purchased from the Alliance cost twice what they used to. They were at an impasse: either continue paying double the price for their wheat, chickens, and apples; or give up beer; or revamp their own internal policies to improve their economic strength in the three-nation marketplace.

The foregoing incident reflects what is known as governmental *monetary policy*. Monetary policy is that part of a government's program that regulates the amount of money flowing throughout the economy. As the case of the beer bust illustrates, creating too much money can cause economic disruptions; creating too little money can prevent an economy from growing. Perhaps the greatest economic debates of the past century have been with regard to monetary policy. There is no sure-fire, long-lasting formula that is guaranteed to work. But the farther away a government is from the ''right'' formula, the more effect it can have on the financial well-being of its citizens.

HERE AND NOW

The adventures and misadventures of these primitive peoples are meant to illustrate some of the most basic economic influences that we live with on a day-to-day basis. All of these various influences intertwine, overlap, and bounce back and forth on one another. Let's now put these phenomena into a more modern perspective by examining again, in no particular order, some incidents in recent American and world history that illustrate the workings of the various influences and the results that they can cause.

Productivity

Productivity is a measurement of efficiency: How much output can be generated by a given individual or group, considering the cost of raw materials, labor, capital, and overhead? Here are some examples:

☐ You work in a factory that makes farnolas. At your average pace, you are capable of turning out ten farnolas an hour. But your foreman is a mean and nasty person, and every time he makes the rounds you get so irritated that your efficiency drops, and for the next four hours you're capable of turning out only nine farnolas an hour. The same is true for all of your co-workers.

☐ The owner of the factory finally learns of the morale problem that's being caused by the foreman. He replaces the foreman with a much more friendly person, and you find yourself able to turn out eleven farnolas an hour. Your productivity has improved by a change in management, at no extra cost to the factory owner. This can mean greater profits for the owner and any stockholders of the company. And if you are paid on an incentive basis, it can also mean an increase in your pay.

☐ The owner of the factory installs an improved lighting system and better air conditioning. The improved visibility and comfort for the workers enable them to become more efficient. The productivity of the factory has been increased as a result of capital investment.

☐ The owner of the factory is willing to pay the price for skilled labor in the manufacturing end of his business. But he is not willing to pay more than the minimum wage in his shipping department. As a result, he is unable to keep an adequate work force in the shipping department, and thus shipments of farnolas to customers are unduly delayed. The overall productivity of the factory is thereby undermined: The efficiency of the workers in the manufacturing sector is being offset by inadequate labor in the shipping department. Customers become disgruntled, and the factory loses business as a result.

Examine the various aspects of productivity in your home and workplace. Where and how can matters be improved? Is the cost of making these improvements justifiable? Be your own efficiency expert. It could mean extra money in your pocket.

Government

The stories of the primitive tribes have already illustrated how government policies can affect the economic status of individuals and entire nations. The activities of our own government in recent years further illustrate this phenomenon in very real terms.

Throughout the 1980s the U.S. government continued to increase spending on defense and social programs, while at the same time cutting taxes in many areas. The result—as can be expected when one is spending more than one takes in— was a series of huge budget deficits, topping $200 billion in some years. Where did the money that was spent come from? Most of it was borrowed and will eventually have to be repaid. Some of it was borrowed from American individuals and institutions, but ever-increasing amounts of it was borrowed from foreigners. When a government owes money to its own citizens, it's relatively easy to adjust to a repayment schedule that everyone can agree to. But when a government owes money to foreign individuals and institutions, the government becomes more at the mercy of those foreign entities, and a repayment plan is not as flexible.

The heavy government spending programs did provide jobs and benefits to millions of American citizens. But the repayment of the borrowed money that provided those jobs and benefits could well mean sharply higher future taxes to the citizenry. Increased taxation could in turn cause people to diminish their other spending, which in turn can slow down the entire economy, resulting in lost jobs and lost benefits.

How have specific government actions affected your individual economic well-being for better or for worse? How can you anticipate future government actions that could affect you, and what defensive actions can you take to protect yourself?

Strategies for Success

Keeping Up to Date Can Pay Off

It's difficult indeed to accurately predict the long-term fluctuations in our nation's economy. But by keeping up to date with certain key statistics, you can gain a good sense of short-term trends, and you can better plan your investments and other economic activities accordingly. Each month the government publishes the Index of Leading Indicators, which tends to be the most reliable gauge of expected growth or shrinkage in the economy over the next months. Also major borrowings by the U.S. Treasury Department tend to set trends for interest rates throughout the nation. The Credit Markets section of the *Wall Street Journal* carries news and analyses about these borrowings on a regular basis. Keeping up with these matters will help you better manage your own personal finances.

International Matters

Heading into the 1990s, and no doubt well into the next century, our involvement in the international marketplace could be the factor that has the most direct influence on our economic well-being. Earlier in this chapter we referred to football teams and how various forces and influences can affect the outcome of the game. Imagine now that two football teams met on a field and played by different rules. One team, for example, gets five downs to make a first down. The other team is allowed to play with thirteen players instead of eleven. It would indeed be a crazy game.

We face a similar situation in the international marketplace. Different nations embark upon international trade using different rules to govern what they can and cannot do. Some nations might provide financial assistance to companies wanting to make products for export. This assistance could be in the form of low interest loans or tax breaks. The effect is to give those exporting companies a great advantage in competing with other companies in other nations that are not being subsidized. Some nations might keep tight controls on the value of their currency in order to better manipulate their import and export activities. Other nations, on the other hand, might not attempt to exert such controls over their currencies, and they are thus more at the mercy of international currency speculators and other market forces.

Throughout the 1980s, the United States found itself lagging behind many other nations in such matters. The Japanese government, for example, which plays a very active role in assisting its industries in the export trade, enabled the Japanese to take a very large share of the market for many popular goods, such as electronics, video equipment, cameras, and the like. By promoting exports, the Japanese government thus continues to help provide jobs for its workers, and American jobs suffer accordingly. Could your job be threatened by foreign imports? What could you do to protect yourself against this possibility?

Technology

The irrigation canal that the Berry People built and the fish-smoking technique that the Fish People developed were examples of technological development that improved conditions for the respective populations. Advancing technology, based on research and development, plays an extraordinary role in our economy. Technological advancement directly relates to productivity in most cases. And lack of technological advancement can mean stagnation.

Probably the most stunning example of technological advancement has been in the area of electronics. The cost of doing calculations today is a tiny fraction of what it was just a few years ago. Consider the effect on your checking account, for example. Every day millions of checks are processed throughout the American banking system. This massive flow of paper would slow down drastically—and our overall economy with it—if we didn't have the sophisticated computers we have today. You may pay a few dollars a month in service charges for your checking account. Lacking the electronic marvels that process all the checks, your monthly costs for those same services rendered by individual human beings might be $20, $30, $40 a month, or even more. There's no way to calculate actual figures, but the productivity of that industry has increased almost infinitely as a result of electronic advancements. The same is true for virtually every major industry that processes information—insurance, stock brokerage, government, education, manufacturing, retailing, and so on.

Another emerging area of technological advance is in the field of super conductors. Major breakthroughs beginning in the late 1980s hold the promise of new materials that will permit electricity to flow with virtually no resistance. In time, this could result in computers that are vastly more efficient than the fastest ones now in existence; medical diagnostic equipment that will make X-rays and scanning look primitive by comparison; electric-generating facilities that will be much more efficient than those we have today; trains that can travel up to 300 miles per hour floating an a magnetic force field; and similar wonders that scientists once only dreamed about.

What technological advances have affected you in your home life or work life in recent years? Are they for better or worse? How might advancing technology affect your job in the foreseeable future?

Information

Information in the general sense is gathered both from education (basic and advanced) and from what we learn through the media (print and broadcast, general and specialized). To the extent that we do or don't take advantage of the information available to us, we can improve our lots considerably, or not at all.

Sometimes the creation and implementation of information can work apparent miracles. In the late 1950s, the Russians put the first man into orbit around the earth. Americans were caught flat-footed—we were years away from being able to duplicate that feat. We seemed to lack both the sense of purpose and the skilled people needed to carry out such a mission. When John F. Kennedy was inaugurated president in 1961, he urged the nation to move forward to put a man on the moon by the end of that decade. The nation was stirred by his encouragement and commitment to that project, but it seemed an impossibility. Given the necessary support by the government, however (and here again we see the interweaving of various intangible influences), our educational facilities immediately began supplying skilled technicians who, indeed, succeeded in putting more than one man on the moon by the end of the decade. It will be up to future historians to determine whether the effort was worthwhile, but the space program illustrates that, given information (as well as government support), seemingly impossible goals can become realities.

The creation and flow of information will have a major impact on the U.S. economy during the 1990s and onward as the undeveloped nations of the world learn, grow, and become consumers of products that we will manufacture for sale to them. Roughly three-quarters of the earth's population is still considered undeveloped. In those nations 60 to 90 percent of the population still works at agriculture to create enough food to feed the population. (In the United States, only about 2 percent of the population feeds the other 98 percent.) As the citizens of these undeveloped nations learn more about agriculture and health, they will become more self-sufficient and secure. As they learn basic trades and skills, they will become better able to support themselves and their families. As they continue to improve their lot—largely through education and training—they will have money to spend on such things as tools, medicines, books, and teachers. This in turn will beget more information, greater skills, and more income. Sooner than later, these billions of people will be buying things that we've long since been accustomed to buying: tennis shoes and blue jeans, tape recorders and tennis rackets, furniture and television sets, movie tickets, and so on. For many generations to come, these billions of people will look to the existing industrial nations to provide most of these goods—and our economies will boom. Eventually, those nations will be self-sufficient in most of those goods, and whole new trends of international economy will emerge. But for the next twenty to fifty years, information will be the seeds planted abroad that will bear fruit back home.

Capital Investment

Even with all the skills, enthusiasm, and technology that an individual or business can muster, money is still needed to make things happen. Every large business—even a General Motors, an IBM, an Exxon, or the like—started as a small business. And small businesses grew because they were able to attract capital investors. A company whose management, product, and profitability are attractive to investors will be able to raise more capital to improve and enlarge itself. And working for such a company can, simply put, mean career advancement for you.

Not all capital investment comes from outsiders. Specific businesses must also have reason to believe that they can invest their own money internally and reap rewards accordingly. Here again we see the intertwining of various economic influences: The government can create incentives for a business to invest in its own future. For many years, the U.S. government offered a variety of tax credits to businesses that invested in new technology and equipment. These tax credits gave businesses incentive to improve their ability to create and sell products and services and thus to earn even greater profits and create more jobs in the future. But the Tax Reform Act of 1986 removed those tax breaks. It might be years before we can measure the impact of this disincentive for capital investment. But analysts have speculated that by removing the tax credits, businesses will be less inclined to take the more risky types of capital investments that they previously would have taken.

Strategies for Success

Biblical Wisdom Helps You Manage Your Money

Remember the Biblical account about the Egyptian Pharaoh's dream of the seven lean years and the seven fat years? Simply put: When times are good, put away something for the lean years. Any economy —your nation's or your family's—goes through times of relative prosperity alternated with times of relative austerity. When times are good, when income is high, it can be tempting to spend everything you're earning. But better to heed the ancient wisdom: Put some aside when the putting is good. You'll be happy you did when times aren't so rosy. A dollar put away during the fat years can be worth $1.25, $1.50, or more during the lean years.

Marketing

Everybody is selling something. When you apply for a job, you are selling yourself. The "package" that you present to the employer can determine whether you get the job. In addition to looking at your résumé and application, the employer will observe how you dress, how you speak, how you move about. He may or may not be impressed by your level of enthusiasm, your knowledge of his company and industry, and your overall personality. Applying for a job is, in short, a marketing effort that you make on your own behalf. The better you market yourself, the better chance you'll have for your own individual success.

Similarly, the employer must make efforts to market his own product. Those efforts include knowing the marketplace, learning what the competition is and will be doing, designing a package that will appeal to the public, informing the public of the benefits of the product (advertising), and establishing a price structure for the product that the public will accept. Just as your employer must continually seek newer and better ways to market his products or services, so must you if you are to achieve your fullest potential. How can you better market yourself today in your work situation? And how can you assist your employer in better marketing the products or services that are created?

Nature and Natural Resources

Until we discover or invent some new kind of energy source to power our vehicles, our factories, and our homes, we will be living in the age of petroleum. Petroleum is a natural resource found in some of the most unreachable places on the planet: miles beneath the ocean, in the frozen wastelands of the polar icecaps, and in the middle of hostile deserts. Nature has given us the gift of petroleum as a fuel. But nature has also seen to it that access to this gift can be costly and challenging.

As the Log People found it necessary to go farther and farther away to chop down their trees, we too might soon find it necessary to go to ever-increasing expense to acquire our basic fuel commodities, as well as other important natural resources. Sometimes ingenuity replaces one natural resource with another that is more readily available. Nuclear fusion might, for example, someday replace petroleum as our primary source of energy. But what about clean water and clean air? As those natural resources—which we take for granted—become more scarce, what might there be to replace them? The economic and social well-being of everyone on the planet will be affected by our ultimate need to modify or replace some of these resources.

THE RESULTS

It has not been the intent here to give you textbook definitions of such things as inflation, recession, deficits, surpluses, and other economic phenomena. Rather, it is hoped that the foregoing discussion will help you understand the influences at work in the world, in our nation, and in your own individual environment, as all these things can affect you as an individual. It is also hoped that the trials and tribulations of the Fish People, the Log People, and the Berry People—and all the ramifications thereof—will give you a workable understanding of why prices go up and down, why wages go up and down, why job opportunities come and go, why taxes must be raised (and sometimes lowered), and why our government sometimes intervenes in our own daily lives—for better or for worse.

Further, it is hoped that this basic introduction into the forces that shape our economic well-being will assist you in understanding and putting to practical use the information you'll need to become a smart shopper, a wise investor, a sensible homeowner or tenant, and an overall efficient manager of your financial affairs.

How Do You React?

As this chapter has illustrated, a great many matters—both close-at-hand and remote—can have an effect on your personal financial well-being. An awareness of these matters should alert you to defensive or corrective actions that you might take to protect yourself. Consider the following list of incidents that may have had a bearing on you in the past year. Think deeply about the not-so-obvious effects. What reactions did you have, or could you have had, either to fend off harmful effects or take advantage of good effects?

Incident	*Effects on you, directly or indirectly*	*Your reactions— actual or possible*
☐ Strikes (local, regional, or national)		
☐ Weather conditions		
☐ Business conditions for your employer		
☐ Business conditions in your city, in the nation		
☐ Your own health		
☐ Health of your family		
☐ Changes in tax laws		
☐ Changes in working conditions		
☐ International incidents		
☐ Your acquiring more education		

The Asian Connection:
Customers or Competitors?

Let's say you work in a factory where you earn $5, $10, $15 an hour, maybe even more. How do you think you'd compete with other workers who were willing to earn 15¢ to 20¢ an hour? That's the challenge that faces the U.S. economy as the People's Republic of China moves away from its socialist economy and more toward a free market economy, a trend that began in the mid-1980s.

For centuries the industrialized nations of the world have looked at China as a phenomenal potential source of customers: currently more than one billion people, who sooner or later will be in a position to afford the commodities in life that we take for granted: cameras, video recorders, fancy running shoes, electric carving knives, and the entire spectrum of such toys, gadgets, and necessities.

Today, the Chinese worker cannot possibly afford to buy typical American-made products because of the extremely low wage scale in China. Nevertheless, everyone is willing to (or has to) work for less in China; everything accordingly costs less. However, as the workers begin to accumulate wealth, they will, little by little, begin to buy from abroad things that are not manufactured in China. In the meantime, the growing Chinese economy—unless it's disrupted by political upheavals—poses a threat to all of the manufacturing elements in the world's economy. Indeed, hundreds of companies in the industrialized world have already begun assembly operations in China, using the cheap labor there to prepare goods for the marketplace. This has already begun to take a toll on the work force in those nations that would otherwise be utilized to assemble those items.

If Chinese workers can make good tennis balls or typewriters or transistors—and they can—how will we be able to continue competing with them as their industrial universe expands? The development of Chinese industry can be the most powerful force in the world's economy in the years ahead. No one can afford to ignore what is happening and what could happen in that oldest and largest society on earth.

CHAPTER 2

Work and Income

If your work is pleasant, challenging, and financially rewarding, you will feel fulfilled and satisfied. But if your work is none of the above, everything in your life can turn sour. Nobody ever said it would be easy to find the right combination of elements for your working hours, but the goal is worth striving for. Along the way there will have to be compromises with respect to money, opportunities for advancement, working environment, getting along with your bosses and co-workers, and so on. Seeking the right balance among those compromises is a challenge in itself. This chapter discusses the more important aspects of work and income and will help you to evaluate many of the decisions you'll have to make, such as:

☐ Based on your aptitudes and attitudes, what type of work would be most rewarding to you?

☐ What is a given job really worth: putting a dollar sign on the basic wage, the fringe benefits, and the future potential?

☐ What are the best methods you can use to acquire the jobs that are right for you?

☐ What actions can you take if your legal or financial rights as an employee are infringed upon?

THE ROLE OF WORK IN YOUR LIFE

Work is perhaps the single most powerful force in shaping your life. It is your work that creates the vast bulk of all your income. It is that income, put to proper use, that allows you to be self-sufficient. It provides you with the necessities of life as well as whatever luxuries may be within your reach. Income that isn't needed for current uses can be invested for your future welfare.

Work is a form of training ground. The job you do today gives you experience. That experience should enable you to accept future work tasks that will be more challenging, more rewarding, and more promising of greater benefits.

And work can—for better or for worse—play an important role in many of the nonfinancial aspects of your life. The type of work you do can clearly shape a great deal of your social life, leading you into friendships and activities that generate from the working environment.

Your work can also influence the uses you make of leisure time—not only weekends and vacations during your working years, but also that vast expanse of leisure time that befalls you when you retire. Some of you may engage in leisure-time activities and involvements directly related to your work activity. Others may charge off in the opposite direction, seeking activities as remote from work as possible. And still others, because of their psychological involvement with their work, may be unable to find any leisure activities that offer any ongoing sense of pleasure or reward. For this group, leisure time can be frustrating and retirement bleak: "It takes me the first half of my vacation to unwind from work and during the second half I'm gearing myself up to go back to work. I didn't really relax at all." Or, "I worked so hard all my life that I never generated any outside activities. Now here I am with all the time in the world and nothing to do with it."

As a well-planned working career progresses, it should create increasing leisure time along with increasing dollars to spend in that leisure time. If you are to cope with, and make the most of, this powerful force that shapes so much of your life, it's necessary to look at work in a broader perspective than simply a means of filling the hours from nine to five. You must look at not only what you might be doing today, tomorrow, or next week, but where your aspirations and abilities can lead you. You must examine the many ways by which you can prove yourself so that you can maximize the rewards and pleasures available to you through work. Finally, you must consider how you can most efficiently use the fruits of your labor—your income—to satisfy current and future needs and desires.

FACTORS IN CHOOSING YOUR WORK

You have an extraordinary range of opportunity available to you in choosing your work. In every part of the country, there is access to community colleges and state universities that offer relatively low-cost educational opportunities that can lead to virtually any type of career. The economy of our nation is dynamic and expanding in a multitude of directions, thus offering new types of work opportunity and ever-increasing chances for advancement within a chosen field of endeavor.

The vastness and diversity of the United States make possible a range of work activities unparalleled by any other nation: We farm lobsters in New England, peanuts in Georgia, timber in Washington. From "Silicon Valley" in California, through the breadbasket of the Midwest, and on to Wall Street, we lead the world in the production of such things as microelectronics, edible grains, and investment opportunities. We are at the forefront of many new technologies and sciences that will in turn create challenging new opportunities: genetic engineering, laser technology, satellite communications, space exploration, weapons and defense systems, and much more. Even our leisure activities generate tens of billions of dollars per year worth of jobs for our citizens, ranging from neighborhood health clubs to professional sports teams to our worldwide exporting of movies and television programs.

In short, your ability to achieve your fullest potential in your work has very few limitations. Achieving full potential is often interpreted as "success"—a term that generally implies making a lot of money. That's not necessarily an accurate description of achieving full potential. Indeed, there are many people who work so hard and so long to make a lot of money that they never find themselves with the *time* available in which to enjoy the *money* they've made. They may consider themselves failures.

There are important criteria other than money. Consider such rewards as a sense of self-satisfaction; the pride and pleasure that one can feel from being creative, from being innovative, from being part of a winning team; a sense of personal growth and development that enhances your social, family, and community life. These matters are often referred to as aspects of "psychic income"—you can't spend them, but they can be invaluable. People must determine their own proper balance of the various rewarding aspects of work: money, leisure time, advancement, personal pleasures derived from the work environment, camaraderie, and pride in their own achievements or the achievements of the team they're working with. This sense of balance is not easily achieved. Many people work for years or decades before sensing that they have achieved the right balance. Many people never find it. Many give up prematurely because they feel it's beyond their grasp. And many others never strive to achieve it at all.

No easy formula or rule of thumb can guide you toward achieving the balance that is right for you. It's an ongoing quest, subject to change as your own individual needs and desires change. Your own ability to achieve the right sense of balance depends on your own desire to do so and on a number of other factors, which we'll now examine.

Attitudes and Aspirations

Your choice of work and your pursuit of success will be shaped not only by your own attitudes and aspirations but also by those of others as well. Evaluate for yourself the extent to which each of the following influences might affect your choice of work and career goals.

- ☐ Your own individual, self-formulated ideas of what you want to achieve for yourself.

- ☐ The degree to which you mold your own ideas of success based on what you perceive in other people. For example, "My friend Pat seems to have everything going just right. If I could achieve the same things that Pat has achieved, I'd be very satisfied."

- ☐ The degree to which you are directly influenced by others in your choice of work. For example, a teacher may sense that you have certain aptitudes, and without your being aware of it, she may motivate you to seek a career that you might not have otherwise considered. Or parents or other well-meaning relatives may either gently nudge or emphatically push you in one career direction or another, perhaps for their own sense of self-satisfaction more than for yours.

☐ The extent to which you are influenced by traditional social values. Will you be satisfied with adopting the type of life that our general society has typically offered: a good job, a nice family, living in a pleasant neighborhood, and becoming part of the community? Do you aspire to more than that? Or do you rebel against those values?

☐ The extent to which a change in your immediate family circumstances can reshape your attitudes. For example, on the one hand, you might say, "I had great dreams for myself, but now I must make them secondary to the demands of my family." Or, on the other hand, you might say, "I had great dreams for myself, and now with the help and support and encouragement of my family, I can begin to achieve those goals."

☐ The extent to which you are encouraged or discouraged by the support, or lack thereof, of your employer. Can you profit from the support you receive from your employer? Can you overcome the lack of support from your employer?

☐ The extent to which you view your current work as merely a "job" or as one step on the ladder of a long-range career.

How do you really feel about all of these elements? Are you satisfied? Can you distinguish between the positive influences and the negative influences as they affect your own attitude? Can you take advantage of the good influences? And can you walk away from the bad influences?

Education

It's generally acknowledged that education is the major foundation upon which a successful career is built. As Table 2-1 illustrates, the more education people receive, the greater the income they'll receive throughout their work career and throughout their life. If you project the figures in Table 2-1 over the length of a full working career, you can readily see that the college graduate will earn roughly double what the high school graduate earns. However, as attractive as the college graduate's lifetime earnings seem to be, relative to the high school graduate's, the cost of obtaining that education creates a serious dilemma for many individuals.

Table 2-1 **Income and Education**

Education of householder	*Annual income (August 1984 dollars)*
Elementary school	$23,447
High school (4 years)	31,892
College (4 or more years)	60,417

Source: U.S. Bureau of the Census, 1987.

Table 2-2 Rising College Costs

If you started a 4-year college career in . . .	. . . your cost for 4 years (room, board, tuition) would be . . .
1988	$31,000
1989	34,000
1990	37,500
1991	41,000
1992	45,000

Source: U.S. Department of Education, 1986.

Table 2-2 illustrates the rising trends in obtaining a college education. The amounts given in Table 2-2 represent the costs at an average state (public) university. For private universities, the amounts are roughly double. For students who do not live at college, the costs can be much less. A variety of scholarships, loans, grants, and other forms of financial aid are available to qualified students.

College offers more than simply career training opportunities. Students have access to educational opportunities beyond those strictly required for career matters; and the broader one's background, the better equipped one may be to take advantage of future opportunities, both for personal enrichment and for career advancement. Also available are the opportunities to interact with people from different backgrounds and cultures and having different attitudes—a life experience difficult to duplicate in an on-the-job situation.

The debate over the value of *college* may never be resolved, but there can be very little argument as to the point that *education*—college, on-the-job training, or self-education—plays an integral role in career advancement and achieving one's fullest potential. Learning job skills, in whatever fashion, can provide entree into the job market, where further skills can be learned and further advancement obtained. Sharpening existing skills can also help provide more rapid advancement. Moreover, acquiring outside skills that aren't necessarily related to current employment can broaden one's entire career horizon and income potential.

In short, educational facilities *alone* do not necessarily equip a person for a bigger or better or more rewarding career. It's *what one does* with the educational facilities available that makes all the difference.

Aptitudes

Aptitude, in the career sense, generally means what you're best suited for. But what one is best suited for may not necessarily be the thing one enjoys most or that from which one can generate the level of income commensurate with the desired life style. For example, a young man worked in his father's clothing store after school hours and during vacations. During those years, his father innocently, but persuasively, convinced the young man that he should take over the clothing store when he graduated from college. Because of the extensive on-the-job training, the young man had an aptitude for retailing; security and income seemed assured by following his father's advice. But the young man never really liked retailing; and he always resented—though never questioned overtly—his father's persuasions; and while the income and security were comfortable enough, he swiftly felt stifled, unproductive, discontented. By common methods of measurement, his aptitude was for retailing. But for him it was the wrong career.

What, then, is aptitude? It's a very precarious balance of a number of personal elements, some of which can be measured, some of which defy measurement. Few and fortunate are those who have a good grasp of all the various elements, for they might enjoy fulfilling careers in every sense of the word. Most of us have to compromise on one or more points, but this doesn't mean a rich and active career can't be attained. Guidance counseling can be of some help in sorting out these various elements if a clear focus isn't available at any point. The personal elements, in brief, are as follows:

☐ What do you enjoy doing?

☐ What do you do well? (This is not the same as the element above. Many of us do things well but don't necessarily enjoy doing them. And many of us enjoy doing certain things that, regrettably, we don't do very well. The difference should be noted.)

☐ What can you do that will generate a desirable level of income, security, and future potential income and security?

☐ To what extent, if any, are you seeking to satisfy, or must you satisfy, the expectations of others? Many people, such as the young retailer noted earlier, embark on careers that are not necessarily those of their own choosing, but because others—parents, spouses, in-laws—expect it of them.

Personal Experience

Your own personal experiences, both at work and in your private life, can affect your career choice and the success you might achieve in a chosen career. Any prior work experience you may have had, whether paid or volunteer, can indicate whether you like a particular type of work, whether you are good at it, and whether the general field interests you. Furthermore, any prior work experience that you have performed well can lead to personal references that you can later put to use in seeking more permanent employment.

Other personal experiences—at work, in leisure activities, in social or civic involvements—can help you determine if you enjoy working with people or if you're more of a loner; if you tend to be a leader or a follower; if you're content being confined to a specific location for extended periods of time, or if you feel a strong need to be out and around in different locations; if your span of concentration on menial tasks is long or short; if you accept criticism constructively or if you rebel against it; if you're a fast or a slow learner; if you're aggressive or shy with others; if your ambitions are greater or less than your peers; if your energies can be sustained for long periods or if they come and go in spurts; and if you are basically a patient or impatient person.

Examine your personality traits as they have been evidenced by your experiences. Which will be helpful in your work and which will be detrimental? Which might be enhanced, which might be corrected, and which might worsen? Overall, which kind of work opportunities will most happily blend with these traits to provide you with maximum satisfaction without having to go through painful compromises?

Changing Composition of the Work Force

Patterns of work life in America are changing. In the years to come, very few individuals will be left untouched by some of these continuing changes. To be aware of the emerging trends that can affect your career is to be prepared to cope and to adjust. Let's briefly examine some of these trends.

Age and Sex. The percentage of males participating in the work force is diminishing, while the percentage of females is sharply increasing. As Table 2-3 illustrates, the participation rates for men of all ages was 76.3 percent in 1985; it is

Table 2-3   **Labor Force Participation Rates (1985–1995)**

		Participation rates (%)		
Sex	*Age*	*1985*	*1990 (Projected)*	*1995 (Projected)*
Male	16–19	56.8	57.6	57.9
	20–24	85.0	86.3	87.3
	25–34	94.7	94.1	93.7
	35–44	95.0	94.7	94.3
	45–54	91.0	90.8	90.4
	55–64		64.4	62.6
	65+		13.2	11.0
Total		76.3	75.8	75.3
Female	16–19	52.1	51.8	51.2
	20–24	71.8	73.8	76.3
	25–34	70.9	76.2	81.1
	35–44	71.8	75.9	80.5
	45–54	64.4	67.8	71.3
	55–64	42.0	41.9	42.7
	65+	7.3	6.4	5.5
Total		54.5	56.6	58.9

Source: U.S. Bureau of Labor Statistics, 1985.

projected to decline to 75.3 percent by 1995. For females of all ages, the participation rate was 54.5 percent in 1985 and is expected to climb to 58.9 percent by 1995.

Men are entering the work force later in life than in past years due to longer schooling, and they are leaving the work force sooner because of earlier retirement programs. Improvements in disability and health-care benefits in recent years have also enabled men to leave the labor market when health problems have arisen; in past years the limited availability of such benefits tended to keep men tied to their jobs longer.

Further, a drastic drop in the birth rate—from 23.7 births per thousand population per year in 1960 to 15.7 births per thousand population per year in 1985 —has resulted in more women being able to work uninterrupted by childbearing. Expanded day-care facilities and increased tax benefits for child-care expenses have also motivated many more women to enter the work force.

These factors, plus rapid gains by women in achieving equal educational and job opportunities, are resulting in dramatic shifts in the roles assigned to men and women. Role separation is being replaced by role sharing within the marriage structure for vast numbers of married couples. In addition, the increase in the number of working wives provides some protection to a married couple in the event of a layoff—compared with previous situations when the family unit depended predominantly on the man's income.

In the years ahead the competition will continue to heighten between males and females for comparable jobs and comparable pay. The number of two-income families (slightly more than 50 percent of all married couples) will continue to increase. What had been traditionally ''male jobs'' and ''female jobs'' will begin to intermix, and with rare exceptions sexual distinctions in the work force will all but disappear. How will these shifting demographic trends work to your advantage? To your disadvantage?

Geography. Major shifts in the nation's population have also been dramatic and will continue to be so for many years. The mass migration from the Snow Belt to the Sun Belt began shortly after World War II. Since that time, cities in the southern half of the nation have tended to boom, while many metropolitan areas in the northern half of the nation have actually dwindled in population. But the trend is not necessarily permanent. The population explosion in the nation's southwestern quadrant has begun to severely drain that arid area's water resources. Also, since most of that region depends on hydroelectric sources for most of its energy needs, the cost of household and industrial energy has begun to rise at an alarming rate and is likely to continue to do so. Many migrants to the sunny Southwest, when faced with air conditioning bills in their modest dwellings of $200 to $300 per month, are likely to return to the Snow Belt to take their chances with the winter heating bills.

Many northern communities, debilitated by population losses over the past decades, are beginning to show signs of a rebirth. Inner-city land, vacant or in disuse, is being converted into new industrial parks and residential complexes. These attractive new facilities, designed to lure jobs and incomes back into the decaying cities, might not reverse the trend to the Sun Belt, but they could definitely slow it down by the 1990s. Finally, as improved energy sources—nuclear, solar, and as yet undeveloped means—become more commonplace by the end of the century, shifting population trends will become even more unpredictable.

In considering your work opportunities, you can't afford to ignore the implications of population shifts. Your location can affect your company's ability to attract the kinds of workers it needs to enable it to prosper. Lacking that ability, the company—and your career—could flounder. It isn't just the old cities that may find themselves having difficulty attracting population. Many Sun Belt cities have grown so rapidly that housing costs have skyrocketed, making it difficult for employers to import workers who can afford the housing in the area. They're faced, in effect, with a form of Catch-22: ''Things got *so* bad here because they were *so* good.''

Financial Rewards

The line of least resistance in choosing one's work is to go for the job that offers the best pay. Of all the factors that might affect your choice of work, perhaps none is as persuasive as money. But, as the vignette at the start of Chapter 1 indicated, this can be a mistake. As you may recall, the choice there was between (1) higher income today but little advancement opportunity in the future and (2) less pay today with much more rewarding future potential. You must, of course, scrutinize the promised potential with great care. There's a critical difference between a well-researched analysis of a company's future possibilities and succumbing to fast-talking exaggerations of a personnel interviewer. If a company seems overly anxious to hire you at a lower-than-ordinary starting wage, but with overblown promises of future advancement and salary raises, you should be cautious and undertake judicious research before accepting such an offer.

Beyond the base earnings that you may be offered, it's essential that you carefully evaluate the full range of fringe benefits that may be available. In a 1981 survey by the U.S. Chamber of Commerce, the average value of fringe benefits for the American worker was put at approximately $5600 per year. Inflationary trends since then boost the total to close to $10,000 per year. Here is a rundown of the major fringe benefits you should know about. The Personal Action Checklist at the end of this chapter will allow you to evaluate and compare fringe-benefit packages at various places of employment.

Pension Plans. When a company offers a pension plan to its employees, the employer puts aside a certain sum of money for the benefit of eligible employees every year. In accordance with what is known as the *vesting plan*, you must work for the company for a given number of years before the benefits are locked up on your behalf. Normally, you don't receive the money in the pension plan until you retire. Pension plan benefits vary considerably from one company to another. (See Chapter 20 for a more detailed discussion of pensions and vesting.)

Profit-Sharing Plans. Profit-sharing plans are similar to pension plans. A certain percentage of the company's annual profits is divided up among employees, and employees are entitled to their share in accordance with the vesting plan. Commonly, the vested interest will not be paid out until the employee quits or retires. A particularly attractive aspect of pension and profit-sharing plans is that one doesn't have to pay income taxes on the employer's contributions during the years in which that money is credited to one's pension or profit-sharing account.

Investment Programs. A popular new fringe benefit is an investment program known as the 401(k) plan. A part of the employee's pay is placed in the plan. This portion of pay is not subject to income taxes until money is eventually withdrawn by the employee. The earnings of this plan are also tax-deferred. Employees generally have a choice of different types of investments, including a guaranteed income plan, which is similar to a savings program; a mutual fund type of plan which invests in a variety of stocks; and a stock plan, which invests in the stock of the employer company. It's generally possible to mix and match among the different plans, and the mix can be changed at various intervals. It's also common for the company to contribute a certain amount of its money for each dollar the employee puts in. For example, for every dollar an employee puts in, the company might contribute an additional 25¢ or 50¢.

Health-Insurance Plans. Health-insurance plans are among the most common type of fringe benefits offered to employees. Because the employer purchases this insurance on a group basis—covering many employees under a single contract—it's far less expensive protection than what it would cost to buy it individually. Health-insurance protection through an employer may be minimal—covering little more than a certain percentage of one's doctor and hospital bills—or it may be very extensive, including virtually all medical costs incurred, plus such additional items as a percentage of dental bills, prescription costs, psychiatric care, and physical examinations.

Life Insurance Plans. Life insurance is not as common a benefit as health insurance, but its prevalence is growing. As with group insurance, the employer is able to purchase the coverage for many employees at a lower cost than one could obtain on his own. Group life insurance might be a flat, fixed sum or might vary in relation to one's earnings at the company.

Educational Programs. Many employers will pay all, or a part of, the cost of courses and seminars that either it recommends or you wish to take in the furtherance of your career. Education is an asset you can take with you wherever you go.

Paid Vacations, Holidays, and Sick Leave. Although paid time off may not be as important as some of the fringe benefits mentioned above, its availability should obviously be considered in evaluating employment opportunities. How much paid time off is available to you as a starting employee, and how much does that paid time off increase over the years?

Sick-pay benefits, coupled with disability payments in the event of an extended absence from work, can be much more important than paid vacations. Determine how much regular pay you'd receive in the event of absence due to sickness or accident, and find out how long it would continue. When the sick-pay benefits run out, does the employer offer any kind of long-term disability program that would pay you all or a portion of your income?

Miscellaneous. There is no limit to the types of fringe benefits employers can offer. Depending on the company, you might find particular advantage in the dining facilities available to employees; recreation and entertainment facilities on or off the premises; the availability of parking; the scheduling of retirement and financial-planning seminars; maternity benefits; and access to counseling for drug abuse, alcohol abuse, and family problems.

In addition to evaluating the fringe benefits *before* you commence employment, you must also evaluate the benefits you've acquired at the time you're considering *leaving* a job. If you leave before your pension rights are fully vested, you could be giving up tens of thousands of dollars that would ultimately be yours if you remained with the company for just a few more months or years. You may be giving up a medical-insurance program that won't be available to you at a new place of employment. You may be giving up a substantial amount of life insurance protection that might be quite costly to obtain on your own.

In some cases, you can maintain the health-care or life insurance programs on your own if you leave the company by making the premium payments yourself, affording you at least some measure of protection if your new employer doesn't offer such plans. It may also be possible for you to transport your vested pension benefits from a former employer to a new one. Under the Employee Retirement Income Security Act of 1974, the portability of vested pension rights is permitted if the new employer is willing to accept these benefits into its plan. But you must see to it that these arrangements are made on your behalf. If you don't do it for yourself, it's doubtful that the employer will do it for you.

Job Availability

Obviously, one important factor that will affect your work choice is the availability of jobs in your chosen field in your community at the time you're seeking employment. If you live in Lincoln, Nebraska, and you're anticipating a career in marine biology, you're going to have to think about moving. The same goes for the would-be lumberjack growing up in Miami, Florida, the aspiring movie star whose home is Duluth, Minnesota, and so on. As the completion of your education and the commencement of work get closer, you should begin a careful analysis of desired job opportunities in your home community. It would be wise to explore such opportunities in neighboring communities as well. And if you're inclined to

Table 2-4 **Job Opportunities in the 1990s**

Fastest-growing fields of work, 1984–1995 (projected)		Fastest-declining fields of work, 1984–1995 (projected)	
	Change (%)		Change (%)
Computer programmers	+72	Stenographers	−40
Computer systems analysts	+69	Private household workers	−18
Medical assistants	+62	Telephone installers and repairers	−17
Electrical and electronics engineers	+53	Sewing machine operators	−17
Electrical and electronics technicians	+50	Textile machine operators	−16
Computer operators	+40	Industrial truck and tractor operators	−12
Lawyers	+36	Farm workers	−11
Correction officers, jailers	+35	College and university faculty	−11
Accountants, auditors	+35	Postal service clerks	−9
Mechanical engineers	+34		
Registered nurses	+33		

Source: U.S. Bureau of Labor Statistics, 1987.

leave the homestead altogether, there's no limit to your potential. The placement office at your school will give you guidance. If your career interests lie in a different city or state, you should contact the respective state department of employment to learn what career opportunities exist in your new residence.

By way of a very broad national projection, the U.S. Department of Labor has prepared employment estimates in a variety of job descriptions. Table 2-4 is an excerpt from the U.S. Department of Labor study. It's important to note that these figures are only projections subject to considerable possible change from unforeseen economic shifts and other trends that could reshape various occupational groupings. The figures are also based on a total national count; there's no attempt to break down job figures on a local basis. Thus, these figures should be used only as a very broad and general guideline.

THE JOB QUEST

Seeking a job that will lead to a career is a matter of selling. If a prospective employer is to buy your services on terms you are seeking, she must be convinced that your services will be able to generate a profit once you have acquired the necessary training, if any specialized instruction is needed.

Any successful salesperson knows that preparation is essential if a sale is to be concluded on favorable terms. In the selling process that we call seeking employment, preparation is most critical. Your "sales kit" consists of a number of different elements:

☐ ***Résumé.*** Your résumé is the history of your experience in school and at work. It should accurately and succinctly inform your prospective employer of all the various forms of training you've had that would be appropriate to the employment, as well as personal and social activities that would establish your broader profile as an individual. The value of an employee lies not just in getting a specific task accomplished. The employer wants the tasks accomplished by individuals who will get along well with their fellow workers; who will exhibit constructive and productive attitudes; and who will be, in general, well-rounded members of the community.

☐ ***References.*** Written references from anyone you've been involved with in terms of work or responsibility are important. This includes not just full-time work situations but also part-time and charitable work and involvement with civic, religious, or social organizations. The thicker your file of references, the more easily you'll be able to establish your reputation for trustworthiness, integrity, and industriousness. Lack of references may not necessarily mean that you won't get a job. But an accumulation of honest references from responsible individuals can enhance your opportunities for current employment and future advancement.

☐ ***Presentation.*** Résumés and references may depict the experience you've had, but they don't necessarily tell a prospective employer what you can do with this experience. This is perhaps the most critical aspect of your "sales pitch": what you can do for the employer that other applicants for the job might not be able to do. Applicants normally have an opportunity to make their presentation during the job interview.

Strategies for Success

Prepare Yourself Well for Job Interviews

The better prepared you are for a job interview, the better your chances of getting the position you want. Dress and groom yourself well. Learn as much about the company as you can: Talk to current employees and obtain any literature about the company. If the firm is large, check to see if their name appears in the *Standard and Poor's Register* at your local library. Also inquire at your local newspaper for recent items that may have discussed the company. Be prepared to tell your interviewer how you think you can help the company, and have convincing reasons why you want to work there. Don't ask about what kind of pay, hours, and benefits you'll have. Don't smoke or chew gum, and try not to fidget. Rehearse interviews with a close friend to help get over your nervousness.

Experience: An Invaluable Teacher

Job seekers are often disappointed when they don't find exactly what they're looking for. You may be distressed in thinking that you have to settle for second best or third or fourth best. But in reality, such a decision need not be detrimental to your long-term career goals. In fact, choosing other occupational activities could enhance your ultimate career.

Experience is an invaluable teacher. Even though a given work activity may not directly coincide with your chosen career goals, you can learn from it. You can learn added skills that may be of value in the future. You can learn about people, about corporate intrigue, about the workings of the hierarchy; you can learn about the kind of energy it takes to improve yourself and how its lack can set a person back. The experiences of learning, observing, and always doing your best at whatever task is assigned will be to your ultimate credit.

For many people, career goals may not come into clear focus until they have gone through a variety of work experiences. Over a period of perhaps many years, certain work activities that seem pleasurable and profitable may evolve from the varied background one has gone through. Job hopping in search of instant gratification is certainly not recommended. But reasonable job experimentation with an eye toward choosing a permanent (or even semi-permanent) career could be effective.

Changing Careers

A 1977 study by the U.S. Department of Labor based on census surveys indicates that nearly one-third of all American workers may be changing their *careers*—not just their *jobs*—over a given five-year period. A job change implies going from one employer to another but doing the same work. A career change is much more drastic: altering virtually the total mode of one's work, whether with the same employer, with a new one, or on one's own.

Although there are no valid statistics concerning the success quotient in career changes (did the change bring the money, the happiness, the challenge, the contentment you were seeking?), it seems to be an infectious phenomenon that will attract increasingly larger numbers of people.

Children have been reared from their earliest days to think in terms of "What do you want to be when you grow up?" They are seldom asked, "How many different things would you like to be when you grow up?" Many individuals choose a career at an early age with the assumption that it will be their one and only career and that they will learn, grow, and flourish in that endeavor. Little if any thought is ever given to the possibility that the chosen career may be limited in its overall satisfactions. Many people are poorly prepared for the day that often arrives when they find their careers have reached a dead end. They acquired neither the skills nor the outside interests nor the sense of flexibility that could assist them in a career change. Many may recognize the need or value of making such a change but may be reluctant to move for fear of giving up the security of what they have already accomplished. They may thus resign themselves to continuing an unsatisfying career without ever knowing the consequences of a change.

Many others, though, acquire other skills, other interests, and a sense of flexibility that can broaden their perspective and allow them to easily adapt to a new career situation.

You may never have the slightest notion about changing your career until you encounter one of the various factors that can motivate you to begin to seek a change. Figure 2-1 illustrates the typical flow patterns of a career-change experience. Look at the far left column, "Motivating Factors." Any one of these factors or others not included in this chart may prompt you to begin exploration, which can include diagnosis and testing as well as counseling and referral. Many people will opt for the "trial-and-error" aspect of exploration, which can be costly, time consuming, and frustrating.

Evita and Mickey. Let's briefly trace the career-change patterns of Evita and Mickey. Evita started as a salesperson in a large chain of shoe stores, and within a few years she had become assistant manager of one of the chain's most important stores. But the owner's son, who was about to graduate from college, had expressed a desire to be the manager of Evita's store, and Evita began to fear that she might find herself suddenly unemployed. She had long enjoyed the hobby of assembling electronic kits, and she wondered if there might not be some better career opportunities in that field.

The motivating factors—suspected unemployment and an enjoyable hobby— led Evita to do some exploring. She had her aptitude in electronics tested and made

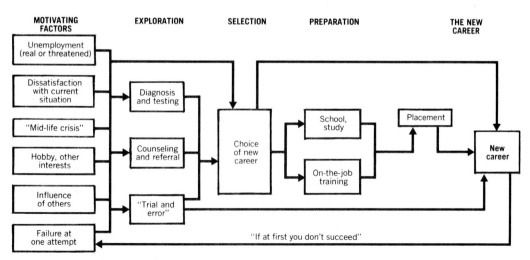

Figure 2–1 Typical flow patterns in a career change
Source. Adapted from a study by the Rand Corporation, "Mid-life Career Redirections, 1975."

careful inquiry in the community about job opportunities that would put her skills and interests to best use. After due exploration she made a selection. She would train herself to work on the development of new game cartridges for the popular video games that were capturing the nation's imagination, attention, and money. She took some appropriate courses in electronics at a local community college and did some apprentice work for a company that was manufacturing the game cartridges. She was able to do this in the evening while maintaining her flow of income from the shoe store. In the few months it took Evita to prepare for her new career, the game cartridge company developed a successful new device and hired Evita to develop variations on it. Her new career began with great promise. And, as it is said, Evita hit the ground running.

Mickey was not as successful. He had been relatively happy and successful as a musician, playing in a combo at local nightclubs. The life suited him, but his family was appalled. They nagged at him constantly to seek out a more respectable profession—to work in a bank, to sell insurance, to be a stockbroker, anything that would enable him to wear a suit and tie to work.

The family's nagging was the main motivating force in Mickey's career change. He just wanted to get it over and done with and get them off his back. So he didn't bother with any diagnosis or counseling. He just looked through the want ads for the first opportunity he could find in a "white-collar" position, and within a week he was involved in a training course for life insurance sales. "I'll try it," he said, "and if I don't like it, I'll start all over again." To be sure, his first few weeks in the new career were disastrous. He liked neither the work, the people he dealt with, the hours, nor the need to sell life insurance to unwilling, unsuspecting, and often unfriendly prospects. Mickey then took the "if at first you don't succeed" route back to the beginning, where the failure at his first attempt motivated him to seek some professional counseling. The counselor told him that he'd do best as a musician and that his family would just have to learn to live with it. With newfound confidence in himself, Mickey went back to his old job with the combo.

YOUR WORK AND INCOME: PROTECTION AND REGULATION

Your financial and legal rights as an employee are regulated and protected by a variety of federal and state laws. It's important that you be aware of how these laws can affect your work and income. Following is a brief summary of the most important laws governing these areas.

Your Paycheck

The Internal Revenue Service requires that your employer withhold a certain amount from your pay to be applied toward your income tax obligations for the year.

Additional amounts are withheld to be applied toward your social security taxes and other state and local income taxes. It's then the employer's responsibility to forward these amounts to the appropriate taxing authorities.

The amount that is withheld from your pay should approximate as closely as possible your actual income tax obligation for the year. The majority of workers have more withheld than is actually necessary to pay their taxes. The result is that they get a refund for the amount that has been overpaid when they file their federal tax return the following year. The average refund check is in excess of $800. These workers are, in effect, paying about $67 a month into an account with the government on which they earn no interest at all. The government has the use of their money all year without paying anything for the privilege.

Garnishment.   If you do not pay your legal debts, your creditors can sue you and obtain a judgment against you. The judgment may entitle them to garnish your wages. In other words, your employer could be legally required to send a portion of your wages to the judgment creditors.

Under the Consumer Credit Protection Act (1968), also known as the Truth in Lending Law, there are limits to how much of your pay can be garnished by a creditor. Most states have similar laws. Check to determine local regulations.

Aside from the financial aspects of a garnishment, such an event can be extremely embarrassing to the garnished employee. Federal law prohibits an employer from discharging an employee just because his wages have been garnished. If, however, an employee's credit performance becomes so improper that the employer is overloaded with garnishment claims, the employer could make a good case for dismissing the employee.

W-4 Form

The amount that is withheld from your pay is based upon your total pay before any deductions, that is, your gross earnings, and is adjusted by the number of *allowances* you claim on the W-4 form you file with your employer when you begin work. The more allowances you claim on your W-4 form, the less withheld from your pay, and thus the higher your take-home amount. You are entitled to claim as many allowances as are reasonable as long as the total amount withheld during the year approximates your true tax obligation. You can claim allowances for yourself and for members of your family; this number is usually the same number as the exemptions you claim on your federal tax return. You can also claim additional special allowances if, for example, you itemize your income tax deductions and if you are entitled to certain income tax credits. A worksheet accompanying the W-4 form explains these special allowances in detail.

Many workers have gotten into the habit of receiving their annual refund check. It's like an extra bonus to them; some view it as a form of forced savings. But the fact remains that they are earning no interest on that money. W-4 forms can be amended simply and quickly by paying a visit to your personnel office. You can amend it to reflect the proper number of allowances so that you will receive more take-home pay each week and less or no refund at tax time. Amending your W-4 form to the correct amount needed to pay your taxes can enable you to have more money to spend or invest as you see fit throughout the year, rather than allowing the government to spend or invest your money as it sees fit without rewarding you accordingly.

W-2 Form

By the end of January of each year you should receive a set of W-2 forms from your employer. These forms reflect the total amount you were paid for the prior year and the total amounts that were withheld for federal and state taxes and for social security. The information on the W-2 form will assist you in completing your annual 1040 or 1040A form, and a copy of the W-2 should be attached to your federal and state returns. One copy should be kept for your own records. The W-2 form enables the Internal Revenue Service to verify your total pay and the amount that was withheld.

1040ES Form

If you receive income that is not subject to withholding and you expect that your federal tax obligation will be more than $500, you are expected to pay an estimated tax quarterly during the year. The federal form 1040ES contains a worksheet that will assist you in estimating your total tax obligation from income not subject to withholding. You are expected to pay one-fourth of the total estimated tax each quarter, accompanied by the appropriate 1040ES papers. Your state may also require you to file a similar form for state estimated taxes. Income that is not subject to withholding can include such items as money received from independent contract work, tips, and investment income.

Workers' Compensation

If you suffer injuries in conjunction with your employment, you are entitled to certain benefits under the work compensation law of your state. These laws differ from state to state, but all states do have such laws. You may be entitled to benefits even if an injury occurs as the result of your own fault. But if you injured yourself deliberately, or if you were drunk or under the influence of drugs, you might not be entitled to benefits.

Workers' compensation benefits can include both medical expenses and reimbursement for lost income. Both types of benefits have limitations depending on the state program.

In general, if you accept workers' compensation benefits from your employer, you might not be able to bring a lawsuit against him for loss or damages you may have suffered. If a situation arose in which it appeared that the workers' compensation benefits and other medical insurance would not adequately compensate you, it would be advisable to consult an attorney at the earliest possible time. Each state has workers' compensation review boards, which evaluate claims and pass judgments accordingly.

It's not prudent to wait until after an injury has occurred to find out what workers' compensation benefits are available to you. Check now with your employer to determine the extent of possible coverage.

Unemployment Insurance

If you are discharged from a job that is covered by unemployment insurance, you are entitled to a weekly check to tide you over until you find satisfactory employment with another company. The unemployment-insurance program is administered separately by each state. Funds for unemployment insurance are generally paid in by employers, with some additional subsidy from the federal government.

If you are discharged, you should immediately file a claim with your nearest state unemployment office. You will have to appear in person each week to claim your check. You will be expected to be ready, willing, and able to accept any suitable full-time job that becomes available to you. If the employment office offers you such a job and you refuse to take it, you could lose your unemployment benefits.

If you are discharged from a full-time job, you can take on a part-time job and still receive *partial* unemployment benefits. If, after discharge, you receive workers' compensation income, severance pay, or a pension from the former employer, you may be ineligible for unemployment-insurance benefits. If your claim for benefits is turned down, you are entitled to file an appeal with the unemployment-insurance office.

If you leave a job voluntarily, you will not likely be eligible for any unemployment benefits. The following dilemma can occur: Michelle worked at a job that was covered by unemployment insurance. But the company was having hard times, and Michelle feared that her job was in jeopardy. She quit the job in order to have time to seek another, more secure job. One week later she learned that had she remained on the job, she indeed would have been discharged because of a mass layoff in the company. It took her two months to find another suitable job. During those two months she did not receive a penny of unemployment insurance because she had quit voluntarily. Had she remained on the job for one more week and been discharged, she could have been entitled to unemployment insurance for almost two full months.

Many workers wrongly view unemployment insurance as a form of welfare. It is not that at all. It is insurance. If you had a fire in your home, you certainly wouldn't refuse the payments from the insurance company. If you were ill, you certainly wouldn't refuse payments from the health-insurance company. Unemployment insurance is the same type of thing: Premiums are paid for your protection, and the benefits should not be turned down because of pride or lack of knowledge of the situation.

Strategies for Success

How to Leave a Job the Smart Way

When you want to quit a job, your emotions can easily overcome your common sense. In this type of situation, costly mistakes can happen. Before you hand in your resignation, find out *specifically* what will happen to your fringe benefits if you quit now or if you wait till later: Will you lose vesting rights on your retirement plan? Can you take over your health-insurance protection so that you don't go uninsured until the coverage from your new job kicks in? What about the other group plans—life insurance, dental insurance, and so on? If you're worried about being laid off, don't quit in anticipation. If you do, you could lose your right to future unemployment-insurance benefits.

Employee Retirement Income Security Act (ERISA)

Also known as the Pension Reform Law of 1974, the Employee Retirement Income Security Act established a variety of protections for your rights under any pension or profit-sharing plan that your employer may offer. A more detailed discussion of ERISA is contained in Chapter 20. One of the most important requirements of ERISA is that all employees covered by such plans be provided with a description of their benefits under the plans at least once a year. A great deal of your financial welfare—particularly for the future—may depend on your expected benefits under a pension or profit-sharing plan. The description you receive should not be treated lightly. Read it carefully, and if any part of it is not clear, seek clarification from your personnel office.

The individual retirement account (IRA) was also created as part of ERISA. Effective for tax year 1987, all employees are eligible for IRA accounts, although some employees can receive greater benefits than others. See Chapter 20 for further details.

Your Right to Work, and Discrimination

The Constitution of the United States does *not* contain any guarantees of your right to work. Historically, employment in the United States has been based on the concept of the employers being willing to hire workers when they see fit and firing workers when they no longer want to keep them. But in recent years a number of federal and state laws have been passed to protect workers from discriminatory hiring and firing practices. These laws don't necessarily guarantee that you'll get a job or that you won't be fired. If you are denied a job or fired from a job in violation of these laws, you still have to pursue your own rights through the appropriate state or federal agencies. But at least some protection now exists where little once did.

Here's a rundown on the major federal laws. Most states have adopted parallel laws and have established agencies to administer them. If you have specific questions or problems, contact the nearest office of the U.S. Department of Labor or your state labor department for assistance.

Fair Labor Standards Law.   The Fair Labor Standards Law protects minors from being employed in "oppressive" jobs such as those that are hazardous or detrimental to the health and well-being of minors. Laws adopted by individual states may further protect minors. In most states, minors under fourteen years of age are not allowed to take jobs, and work permits are required for minors until they reach a prescribed age, depending on state law. These laws also limit the number of hours and times of day during which minors can work.

The Age Discrimination in Employment Law.   The Age Discrimination in Employment Law of 1967 applies to workers between the ages of forty and sixty-five. It is a violation of the law for covered employers to refuse to hire or wrongfully discharge individuals in that age bracket because of age alone. Other discriminatory practices are also barred except where good cause is shown.

Fair Employment Practices Law.   Also known as the Civil Rights Act of 1964, the Fair Employment Practices Law, as amended through the years, provides perhaps the broadest antidiscriminatory measures. Under this law, "It is unlawful for an employer to fail or refuse to hire or to discharge any individual, or otherwise to discriminate against any individual with respect to compensation, terms, conditions or privileges of employment because of such individual's race, color, religion, sex or national origin." Sections of the law apply such prohibitions to employment agencies and labor unions as well as employers.

There are some exceptions under this law. For example, religious groups are not required to hire members of other religions. A Japanese restaurant has the right to hire a Japanese chef without fear of violating the law. An employer cannot be required to hire a worker of one sex when a job reasonably requires that a member of the other sex is more appropriate, such as a restroom attendant. Furthermore, distinctions in pay and in other employment matters can be allowed if the company has a good faith seniority system; a system that bases pay and promotions on merit, quantity, or quality of production; or a system that distinguishes among employees who work in different locations.

The Equal Employment Opportunity Commission (EEOC), created as a part of this law, has power to begin actions in court to correct or eliminate violations of the law. Parallel state or local agencies may, however, provide a complainant with more efficient means of resolving a problem.

Wage and Hour Laws

The federal wage and hour laws derive from the Fair Labor Standards Law and basically apply to people whose work is in any way involved with interstate or foreign commerce. If your work doesn't fall into one of these categories, you'll likely be protected by your state wage and hour law as administered by your state labor department. These laws generally set a maximum number of hours you can be required to work each week and, further, establish a minimum wage to which you are entitled. These limits have been subject to change in recent years. Check what current regulations are in force on your job.

Health and Safety Regulations

State and local building and industry codes require building owners and employers to be responsible for the safety conditions within work areas covered by the laws.

The Occupational Safety and Health Act (OSHA) sets standards to protect the health and safety of workers in their working environment. If an unsafe condition exists as specified by the act, an employee can complain to the U.S. Department of Labor, which in turn can require the employer to correct the condition.

As a general rule, if you as an employee complain about an employer, under OSHA or the other federal employment laws, it is illegal for the employer to retaliate against you for your having made a complaint.

Union Matters

Tens of millions of workers are members of labor unions. Labor unions negotiate wages and other benefits for members and can act on behalf of members if unfair employment practices occur.

The National Labor Relations Act of 1935 and the Labor-Management Relations Act of 1947 (also known as the Taft-Hartley Law) govern relations between management and labor with respect to unions. Under the National Labor Relations Act employers are prohibited from

☐ Unreasonably interfering with employees who are attempting to organize a union or to bargain collectively

☐ Discriminating against workers by imposing hiring conditions that discourage union membership

☐ Interfering with a labor union in its formation or administration

☐ Refusing to bargain collectively with appropriately elected representatives of the employees

☐ Discriminating against any worker because she has complained against the employer under the law

The Labor-Management Relations Act generally prohibits employees and unions from

☐ Forcing workers into joining a union

☐ Refusing to bargain collectively with an employer once the employer has received proper certification of the union's status as the employee's bargaining agent

☐ Becoming involved in illegal work stoppages

☐ Requiring an employer to pay for work that was not performed

☐ Charging excessive initiation fees or union dues to employees belonging to the union

The National Labor Relations Board (NLRB) is the agency that oversees these laws relating to unions and management.

Employment Policies and Contracts

The terms and conditions of many workers' employment situations are covered by contracts, either directly between employer and employee or between employer and union. These contracts should spell out all pertinent matters relating to employment, including pay, raises, fringe benefits, vacation privileges, sick-pay provisions, and causes for rightful termination. If your employment is covered by such a contract, it is your duty to acquaint yourself with all of these various provisions and to act accordingly. When the term of the contract expires, either you or your union representative must renegotiate all of the appropriate terms. Such renegotiation should commence many months before the actual termination date to avoid possible failure to agree on new terms, which could result in your termination.

Most workers are not covered by contracts but by the ongoing employment policies of the employer. Except where state or federal law prevails, many of these policies can be changed at the sole discretion of the employer. Such changes could occur with respect to fringe-benefit programs, sick-pay benefits, hours and place of employment, and pay-raise schedules. To the extent possible, you should protect yourself by obtaining the current policies in written form and by obtaining whatever promises you can from the employer to give you ample advance notice of any intended changes in the policies.

SUCCESS IS WHAT YOU MAKE IT

Your success, your achievements, your advancements in your work and career depend on more than just fulfilling your basic duties as an employee. Your awareness of and participation in your employer's striving for improvement can enhance your value to the employer. Your initiative, your creativity, and your willingness to cooperate can all help move you up the ladder toward higher pay, greater recognition, and career advancement. Your current job may not be what you have in mind for a lifetime career, but every good experience can build your knowledge, and every good performance can result in a positive reference that will help you achieve the ultimate potential you are seeking for yourself.

Viewed positively and patiently, your work can provide you with an ongoing sense of challenge and achievement. Viewed negatively and impatiently, your work and your personal life can end up in a rut. The choice is yours.

What Is Your Real Income?

Real money income consists of both wages and fringe benefits. Wages are visible every time you get your paycheck, but fringe benefits are difficult to evaluate. Following is a list of common fringe benefits. Note the ones you now enjoy. If your employer doesn't make them available to you, estimate how much it would cost you to obtain them on your own. Tally the total value of all your current fringe benefits. Compare the value of the current package with what may be available from another employer you may be thinking of transferring to.

Benefit	*Value or cost of obtaining benefit on your own (per year)*
☐ Health insurance	$_____
☐ Disability insurance	_____
☐ Life insurance	_____
☐ Pension contributions	_____
☐ Profit-sharing contributions	_____
☐ Investment-fund contributions	_____
☐ Automobile	_____
☐ Uniform allowance	_____
☐ Educational programs, seminars	_____
☐ Dental insurance	_____
☐ Legal insurance	_____
☐ Club membership	_____
☐ Use of athletic and other facilities	_____
☐ Scholarship program for your children	_____
☐ Retirement counseling	_____
☐ Personal financial counseling	_____
☐ Medical and psychological counseling	_____
☐ Other _____	_____
_____	_____
_____	_____

Career "Opportunities" Can Prove Costly

"NOW . . . LEARN AT HOME IN YOUR SPARE TIME . . . START AN EX-CITING NEW CAREER AS A BRAIN SURGEON/GENETIC ENGINEER/MOVIE STAR/ASTRONAUT/U.S. SENATOR/NOVELIST!!! . . . . etc.''

Advertisements appear everywhere—inside matchbook covers, on bulletin boards, in newspapers and magazines. Most of the so-called career opportunity ads are more mundane than those noted above, but the appeal is just as compelling: Get out of your rut and start making *big* money.

Great care should be taken before embarking on a mail-order education that promises you more than you can reasonably expect. Abuses in the field of mail-order education include the following:

- Excessively high costs
- Promises of future high-paying jobs that in fact can't be delivered
- Restrictive contracts that make it difficult to get a refund if you're not satisfied

If you do aspire to learning new skills or to embarking on a new career, first find out whether appropriate training is available through local high school extension courses, community colleges, or universities. If so, you might be able to receive better training at a far lower cost than you could through mail order. Many such programs are scheduled so that they will not conflict with your regular work routine. Second, talk to local employers to determine whether, in fact, there are job openings in the field you're considering. Learn also whether they offer on-the-job training for such careers. It might be possible to get paid while you learn.

If you do think that mail-order education is the way you want to go, investigate the school very carefully before you sign any contracts.

CHAPTER 3

Creating a Workable Plan: Goal Setting and Budgeting

Many people—perhaps too many—spend all of their income with little thought for the future. When the future arrives, they find themselves ill-prepared to cope with it. They might not be able to buy the house they had yearned for, or educate their children, or look forward to a secure retirement. On the other hand, there are people who can enjoy the present and yet still know that their future desires will be met. They are the ones who have set goals and who have embarked on a well-disciplined plan to meet those goals. This chapter explores the ways and means you can set and reach the goals that are right for you, including the following:

☐ How to sort out the high-priority and low-priority goals you may have for yourself

☐ How to identify the specific sources of money that, if properly funded over the years, will allow you to meet your goals

☐ How to use some simple tools that can tell you whether your goal achievement program is proceeding on target

☐ How to adjust your current spending program to help assure that you can meet your ultimate future goals

SETTING GOALS

To cope with your personal finances efficiently and to manage your money most productively, you must have a plan. This plan should set forth as clearly as possible your goals, current and future, and the steps you'll take to meet these goals. Further, for the plan to be truly functional, it must be reexamined periodically and revised when necessary. Personal circumstances change over the years, and as they do, so will many of your needs, desires, and long-range aspirations.

The essential elements of any personal financial plan include the following: How should I distribute income to best accomplish current and future needs and desires? How much will I spend today, and how much will I put away for the future?

To answer these questions, let's look at the specific uses to which your dollars will be put in terms of goals or objectives. Let's further break down your spendable money into two broad categories: "Today" Dollars and "Tomorrow" Dollars. Today Dollars are those applied toward meeting current and continuing needs and goals. Tomorrow Dollars are those that, while available today, aren't spent for current needs but are put away in one form or another for future use.

Tomorrow Dollars can be accumulated directly; we put aside a portion of our spendable Today Dollars into savings plans and other forms of investment. Or Tomorrow Dollars may be accumulated indirectly; deductions are made from our paychecks for pension plans, profit-sharing plans, and social security. Also, some of our spent Today Dollars may come back to us in the future: A portion of our mortgage payments on our homes will theoretically come back to us when we later sell or refinance the home; and a portion of our ordinary life insurance premiums may be available to us in the future should we wish to cash in or convert our policies.

SORTING OUT GOALS

An efficient financial plan demands that we maintain a focus as clear as possible on our specific goals. Obviously, it will be much easier to focus on the more immediate goals than it will be on the longer-term ones. Many long-term goals may not really have taken complete shape yet, and some will arise that we may not have fully anticipated. Not only do we have to attach numbers to our goals (how much will we need for what purpose, and when will we need it?), but we also must assign *priorities* to our goals: Which are more important, and which must we strive more deliberately to accomplish?

There are two main sorting processes. The first is to determine current and continuing goals on the one hand and the future goals (near-term and far-term) on the other. The other sorting process concerns the priorities of our goals. Some goals naturally demand a higher priority than others, although each individual and family must make such determinations.

Let's look at an example of the difference between "Must" and "Maybe" goals with regard to one family's future aspirations. Howard and Hedda have an eight-year-old child, and it is their fervent desire that the child receive a college education on graduation from high school some ten years hence. When that day arrives, Howard and Hedda don't want to say, "We're sorry, but you can't go to college just now. We don't have enough money."

They know that they must have either the money or the ability to borrow or generate the money for their child's college education at a specific future point. For them this is a Must goal. If they don't reach their goal at the appointed time, the results will be most unsatisfactory.

On the other hand, Howard and Hedda have also dreamed of taking a trip to

Europe. They'd like to do it within about five years if they could, but it's not that critical. If circumstances dictate that they never take the trip, they'll be disappointed but not devastated. This aspiration falls into the Maybe goal category: If they don't ever achieve it, not that much has been lost in the trying.

Although each individual and family sets its own goals based on desires and needs, there is one particular goal that has a Must quality for almost everybody: having enough money to live on when work ceases, that is, upon retirement.

If, on reaching retirement, we find we don't have adequate funds, we can't go back ten, twenty, or thirty years and accumulate the necessary nest egg that will provide us with the retirement life style we were hoping for. We must have the needed funds at that appointed time. It's all too easy at the age of twenty or thirty or even forty to ignore the importance of this Must goal because it's too far off to warrant thinking about. But sound financial planning, even at a very young age, requires that this Must goal be kept in mind and planned for at the earliest possible time.

Common sense suggests that the prudent person create a well-disciplined plan that will allow her to reach the Must destination at the appointed time. This generally entails putting away Tomorrow Dollars in such a form as to give the highest degree of assurance that the needed money will be available at the right time. The techniques that offer the highest level of assurance for this program are "fixed income investing" techniques.

Once a well-disciplined program is underway to meet the Must goals, the prudent individual might begin planning for the Maybe goals, using more speculative techniques, such as the stock market, to achieve them. These various investment techniques are discussed in later chapters, along with other matters relating to our spending programs.

CHANGING AND TRADING OFF GOALS

It would indeed be attractive if, at any age, we could program all of our financial needs and desires into a computer and let the machine create and maintain a plan that would help us achieve our various goals. But, alas, technology cannot yet take into account the shifting patterns of human activity. As we grow and mature, old goals are accomplished or abandoned, and new ones arise, perhaps unexpectedly. These shifts, whether drastic or imperceptible, require a revision of our financial plan. Further, as we pass old goals and strive toward new ones, we may have to make certain trade-offs—adjustments in priority to allow us to accomplish something that may not have been necessary yesterday.

In short, a workable financial plan is only as valid as its revisions. In addition to developing the disciplines of saving wisely and spending prudently, one must also develop the habit of periodically reviewing and, where needed, revising the overall plan that will most clearly satisfy the sought-after life style. For the family it may be a yearly meeting at which everyone sits down to discuss, analyze, evaluate, and make plans for the future regarding family finances. For the individual it may be an annual meeting with a banker, accountant, lawyer, or other advisor to do the same. An important part of such a review is to go step by step through each expense and each item of future needs and ask, "Am I doing it right; am I getting bogged down in unproductive spending habits; will I arrive at my appointed destination on time with the right amount of dollars in my pocket?"

CURRENT NEEDS:
A GOAL WORKSHEET

Table 3-1 is designed as a worksheet. It lists all the common immediate and continuing goals that we must be continually achieving, and it contains spaces for inserting the amounts you are currently spending (or setting aside) to meet these goals, as well as projected amounts that you will be spending one and two years from now. The exercise of filling out the worksheet serves several purposes: It can help to provide a clearer picture of your actual current financial situation; it will aid you in anticipating future goals as your needs may change; and it can help you determine what expenses might be modified to supply more spendable dollars in another area.

Each of the items contained in the worksheet is discussed here in more detail. For your own purposes, you might want to break down any of these items into its more specific components.

As you calculate each monthly expense, whether current or anticipated, include within the expense any debt repayment that may be a part of the total expense. In other words, any payments on an automobile loan would apply toward your overall transportation expense. Try also, to the best of your ability, to separate from debt payments that portion attributable toward interest, and include those interest items under the category "cost of credit." It's important to get a clear-cut picture of what all of your credit is actually costing you. It may come as quite a surprise.

1. ***Food and beverage.*** This category includes food and beverages consumed at home and at restaurants. Don't overlook alcoholic beverages, lunch money, snack money, and the tips you might leave when dining or drinking out.

2. ***Shelter.*** Your overall shelter costs should be broken down into various components, to include the following:

   Basic expense: rent or mortgage payment. If you are an owner, remember that a portion of your mortgage payment applies to the reduction of your debt. This portion, referred to as the *principal*, will theoretically be recovered at some future time when you sell or refinance the property. But because that future time is probably unknown at present, the total mortgage payment should be considered as a current expense.

   Property taxes. In most communities, property owners are billed twice each year for property taxes. The tax bill may include separate allocations to the

Table 3-1 **Goal Worksheet: Current and Ongoing Expenses**

Item	*Current estimated monthly expenses*	*Estimated monthly expenses one year from now*	*Estimated monthly expenses two years from now*
1. Food and beverage			
2. Shelter			
3. Clothing and other textile needs			
4. Protection against risk (insurance)			
5. Entertainment			
6. Education			
7. Medical and health-care costs			
8. Transportation			
9. Little "rainy day" funds			
10. Cost of credit			
11. Travel and recreation			
12. Personal business matters			
13. Children's allowances			
14. Miscellaneous personal expenses			
15. Luxuries			
16. Charity and religious expenses			
17. Income taxes			

city, the county, the school district, and any other jurisdictions having the power to tax local properties.

Property insurance. Commonly, property insurance includes forms of protection in addition to the basic coverage of your dwelling and its contents, such as public liability coverage and medical payments coverage for costs incurred by people who may be injured on your premises, plus specially scheduled protection for loss or theft of valuable property.

Utilities. In an ever-increasingly energy-conscious world, the cost of utilities (electricity, heat, water) is no longer taken for granted. In evaluating current and future utility costs, it would be wise also to evaluate how these costs can be reduced by various energy-saving techniques. Ample literature on these techniques is generally available from utility company offices, home improvement supply dealers, and your local library or bookstore.

Telephones are another form of utility. A simple evaluation of your telephone service could result in substantial cost savings. If you're paying for more telephones than you realistically need or for "fancy" equipment, you might be able to eliminate the extras and realize extra dollars in your pocket instead. If your local calls are measured on a time basis, how much a month could you save by reducing each conversation by simply a minute or two? If you make frequent long-distance calls, are you taking full advantage of the nighttime and weekend discounts available?

Maintenance and repairs. Typically, maintenance and repair costs, although paid in small amounts, can become a substantial sum over the course of a year. Further, there is always the possibility of minor disasters, some of which are preventable through an alert maintenance system; others are totally unpredictable. A program of preventive maintenance can be decidedly less costly than one of after-the-fact maintenance.

Renovation and improvements. Whether you renovate your dwelling cosmetically (painting, landscaping, etc.) or functionally (adding new equipment, rooms, etc.), you as a prudent homeowner should consider how much of the improvement expenses can be recaptured when the house is sold at a later date. Costs for improvements that are excessively personal and may not appeal to a later would-be buyer and for those that are too expensive—that is, that would cause the house to be priced too much higher than other homes in the neighborhood—will not likely be recaptured. Discuss any such major improvements with local real estate people before you proceed to determine the potential value of the improvements on a subsequent resale.

Appliances and reserves for replacements. A number of major items in your home can be costly to replace: the water heater, dishwasher, refrigerator, furnace, and other major appliances. Rather than wait for these items to die and then have to scramble to find the money to replace them, it's wiser to put aside a few dollars each month well in advance; in this way you will have established a replacement fund that will allow you to buy new items at the appropriate time without doing serious harm to your budget.

3. **Clothing and other textile needs.** Clothing expenses tend to be based on two predominant factors: need (function) and style (frivolity). No guidelines are suggested other than prudence and the caution that all too many budgets are thrown into disarray due to excessive purchases of clothing and accessories.

    Other textile needs include sheets, towels, and blankets. Although these may be relatively minor budget items, shopping with an eye toward durability and washability can keep replacements at a minimum.

4. **Protection against risk (insurance).** Your program, for individual or family, of protecting your cash flow against the risks of illness, accident, and the unexpected premature death of the breadwinners must be carefully considered. Health insurance, disability income insurance, and life insurance are discussed in more detail in later chapters. But as current and continuing expenses, actual costs must be carefully calculated and allocated in your overall budget and

goal program. Much of this protection may be available to you in the form of fringe benefits at work, and you may not actually incur out-of-pocket expenses.

5. *Entertainment.*   Much of the money we spend on entertainment tends to be spent impulsively. This is natural; when we get the urge to escape, we don't always stop to examine how the expenses might affect our normal budgetary program. The frequent result is a severe budget "leak." Make a detailed listing of all entertainment expenses so that you can determine where excesses might lie.

6. *Education.*   Expenses for education should include any costs for private school tuition, religious education tuition, adult education expenses, and all reading materials related to such schooling or used apart from normal schooling activities. Include also the expenses of tutors as well as fees and expenses for school clubs, uniforms, equipment, and printed materials.

7. *Medical and health-care costs.*   Over and above any premiums you may pay for health insurance, include here any costs you incur that are not reimbursable by any insurance program. In addition to costs for doctor visits, include expenses for prescriptions, dental care, eye glasses, ambulatory devices (e.g., crutches), hearing aids, therapeutic equipment, and any other special treatments or devices needed.

8. *Transportation.*   Costs for transportation should include the cost of both privately owned vehicles and public transit. Don't overlook the cost of motorcycles and bicycles and their maintenance, repairs, and parts. Chapter 6 discusses transportation costs in greater detail.

9. *Little "rainy day" funds.*   We should distinguish little "rainy day" funds to be used in your immediate and continuing budget program from big "rainy day" funds for your long-range budget program. The little rainy day fund is a handy source of money—perhaps kept in a savings account—that can be used to equalize some of the inevitable fluctuations that occur in a month-to-month spending program. It should be added to regularly and tapped as little as possible. The more it can grow, the better off your big rainy day fund will be, should major future needs arise.

10. *Cost of credit.*   Apart from interest that you may be paying on your home mortgage, which is included in the shelter category, you should distinguish what costs you are incurring for all your other credit uses. These include revolving charge accounts at department stores; interest on loans at banks, credit unions, and consumer finance companies; interest on credit card lines; interest on overdraft checking lines; interest on personal loans payable to other individuals; interest on second mortgages you may have taken out on your home; and interest on insurance premiums, which may be charged to you if you are paying monthly or quarterly instead of annually. The cost of credit is too easily buried in your overall payments, and not enough attention is paid to this cost, which can add from 10 to 30 percent to the cost of the goods and services you're purchasing, depending on the sources of credit. Only by de-

termining a clear picture of the actual dollar cost of your credit will you be able to decide whether you are using credit excessively. The use of credit is discussed in more detail in later chapters.

11. *Travel and recreation.* Considered as a category separate from your normal transportation and entertainment expenses, primarily travel and recreation expenses refer to travel on vacations, to family for visits, to attend out-of-town weddings and other functions. The cost of children's activities, such as summer camp, should also be included. Expenses in this category include costs for transportation, lodging, meals, entertainment, tips, shopping (souvenirs, etc.), car rentals, baby-sitting services, special clothing and equipment, and maintaining your dwelling while you are away.

12. *Personal business matters.* Into the personal business category fall all those expenses you incur in keeping your personal and family matters under control: legal fees, accounting fees, income tax preparation charges, investment advisory expenses, safety deposit box rentals, checking account costs, and the purchase of necessary equipment and supplies related to these matters (a calculator, stationery, filing equipment, etc.).

13. *Children's allowances.* Factors to be considered in establishing allowances are the following: the degree of control over children's spending habits that parents wish to exert, the amount of allowance received by your children's peers (peer group pressure can be stronger than you might think), the amount that the children themselves contribute to family needs (housework, odd jobs). The size and conditions under which an allowance is given can have a considerable effect on a child's ability to establish a sense of self-sufficiency and self-worth. The matter should not be regarded lightly, even when children are very young.

14. *Miscellaneous personal expenses.* The miscellaneous category is something of a catchall, but it can't be ignored. Experience has shown that individuals and families with financial problems will have an excessively large and unspecified ''miscellaneous'' category in their expense program. If all the miscellaneous expenses are carefully noted, it's much easier to bring a runaway budget under control.

Among myriad other common miscellaneous expenses, you should include the following: money for snacks, cosmetic expenses (haircuts, beauty parlor costs, and all related accessories, salves, etc.), gifts purchased for others or for yourself, pet supplies and veterinarian fees, tobacco costs, various toys and trinkets purchased for your children, your spouse, or yourself, equipment and supplies for hobbies. Another miscellaneous expense is gambling, whether for state lottery tickets or for other forms of betting.

15. *Luxuries.* Luxuries is an optional category designed for those who genuinely have a goal of acquiring certain luxuries as a part of their immediate and continuing expense program. What are such luxuries? It all depends on the individual. Obviously, what one person might consider a luxury, another might view as an ordinary acquisition. Luxuries must be designated in terms of priority

with regard to all your other expenses, that is, what would you be willing to give up in order to acquire them?

16. *Charity and religious expenses.* This category includes membership in religious organizations and contributions to them, as well as other ongoing charitable contributions made during the year, such as the local United Fund, Red Cross, medical-oriented charities (heart fund, cancer association, muscular dystrophy fund), and so on.

17. *Income taxes.* Most of us never see the money we pay to the government (federal, state, and local, where applicable). It's simply deducted from our paychecks. If we have instructed our employers to withhold the proper amount, the annual withholding sum will cover our total tax obligation. If we have underwithheld, we will have a tax bill to pay each April. If we have over-withheld, we have a refund coming. By completing a W-4 form in which we list our exemptions and dependents, we are controlling how much is withheld from our regular salary. Some people may prefer to overwithhold, looking forward to a ''bonus'' when their tax refund comes each year. In a sense, this is a form of enforced saving, except that you don't get any interest on your money.

If you are self-employed, you have to make quarterly payments of your estimated income tax due, as well as of your self-employment tax (the parallel to social security for the employed). Because estimated tax payments are due only four times each year, it might be overly tempting not to worry about them until they fall due. But coming up with one-fourth of your annual income tax bill at those appointed times might be difficult if you have not embarked on a well-disciplined program to set aside the money for meeting those payments. One method is to set aside the necessary amount each week in a separate ''untouchable'' fund; in this way you won't have to throw your budget out of joint each quarter (see Table 3-2).

Strategies for Success

Use Annual Meeting to Plan Family Finances

Businesses have annual planning meetings without fail, and so should you. Conduct a family annual meeting to review and plan your family's finances. For your agenda include any successes and failures you have had in the past year. Discuss how you can take advantage of the successes, and how you can avoid future failures. Then talk over your specific goals for the year ahead—how much you want to save, your spending limits, the major expenses and/or borrowings you want to undertake this year or put off until another year. Keep detailed notes so that you can review them from year to year. Everyone in the family should attend, even the children. It's a good habit for them to observe.

Table 3-2 **Annual Budget for 4-Person Families**[a]

	Spendable income		
Item	*Under $15,000* *(%)*	*$15,000–$30,000* *(%)*	*Over $30,000* *(%)*
Food	31.2	24.7	21.1
Housing	19.0	22.2	22.9
Transportation	7.4	8.8	8.0
Clothing	6.9	6.9	6.1
Personal care	2.6	2.2	2.1
Medical care	9.7	6.1	4.3
Miscellaneous and other items	8.3	9.1	10.6
Personal income taxes	8.0	14.7	20.6
Social security and disability	6.3	6.3	5.1

[a]All figures represent percent of totals. Totals may not add up to 100 percent because of rounding.
Source: U.S. Department of Labor, 1987.

COORDINATING CURRENT NEEDS WITH FUTURE NEEDS

Once you've established what the spending patterns are in meeting immediate and continuing needs, you'll next have to assign priority to each goal. But first you must get the broad picture of your future goals, both near- and long-term. If, after making all the appropriate adjustments in your immediate goal program, you can find excess dollars available, you must choose whether to apply these dollars to other immediate goals or perhaps to more important, longer-term goals.

Discretionary income—the excess dollars available once your basic needs are met—now enters the picture. How will you spend the excess dollars? They could be spent on frivolities that might be quickly forgotten. Or they could be allocated to future needs, to provide pleasures whose values may be much more treasured.

Your ability to meet long-term goals is largely shaped by the demands of your immediate goals. Only you can determine what each of the sets of goals will be. You are unique. A budgetary program should serve as a discipline in meeting the goals that you individually have set. Individuals and families often adopt rule-of-thumb budget programs to keep their spending habits in line. Such programs may work to an extent, but if they haven't been created with the individual's or individual family's own particular needs in mind, the ultimate result can be a high level of dissatisfaction.

SHAPING FUTURE GOALS

Table 3-3 lists some of the more common major goals that most individuals and families anticipate. These goals are not listed in any order of priority; this is for you to determine. If you can complete the columns accompanying the goals, even in rough fashion (since many may be several years away for you), you'll begin to get a better idea about what priorities you want to attach to them.

Bear in mind that this exercise is to help you establish priorities, not specific dollar amounts. It's very difficult to take inflation into account, since no one knows what the inflation factor will be over the years. However, the rate of personal income runs on a parallel track with the rate of inflation. The more your expenses go up, the more your income goes up, as a general rule. Thus, for purposes of establishing boundaries in this exercise, assume that the *percentage* of your income that you set aside for future goals remains the same regardless of income or inflationary trends. In other words, if you're now earning $20,000 a year and are able to put aside 5 percent ($1000) after all expenses have been met, and if some years from now you're earnings are $30,000 and you're still able to put aside 5 percent ($1500), your annual savings and investments will be growing at a constant rate. Thus you'll be able to meet your future higher-priced goals.

Let's now take a closer look at each of the suggested items in the future goal list.

Education. Higher education for children, in the light of current trends, can be a most foreboding goal. Educational costs are increasing rapidly in both public and private school sectors. College education is a goal that traditionally must be met at a fairly fixed point.

Preparations to meet this goal must begin at the earliest possible time.

Table 3-3 **Major Future Goals**

Item	How much will be needed?	When will it be needed?	How much per year?
Education	_____	_____	_____
Housing (new shelter)	_____	_____	_____
Retirement	_____	_____	_____
"Stake" for your children	_____	_____	_____
"Stake" for yourself	_____	_____	_____
Care of elderly or disabled	_____	_____	_____
"One-shot" expenses	_____	_____	_____
Big "rainy day" fund	_____	_____	_____

These preparations can include a savings and investment program; acquiring an awareness of loan, grant, and scholarship programs; and communications between parents and child regarding the child's own contribution to the financial needs, such as through work.

Housing (new shelter). The individual or family currently owning a home and anticipating buying a bigger and better one in the future have an advantage over those currently renting: They are building some equity in their existing home, which can be applied toward the purchase of a new one. Current renters must accumulate a large enough down payment to enable them to obtain their first home. The home, once acquired, can become a growing asset that will assist them in meeting other goals later in life. Later chapters on housing provide assistance in working out the arithmetic of buying versus renting and focus on this particular priority and how it can be accomplished.

Retirement. With rare exceptions, this is the most predominant "must" goal for everyone. You don't have a chance to do it over if you reach a point when work ceases and there's not enough to live on. Whatever your aims, it's not too early to begin focusing on this important goal. Chapter 21 contains more guidelines to help you achieve that focus.

Stake for your children. Many families have a goal of acquiring enough money to provide their children with a stake to help them get started in life. The stake might be used to help them buy a home, to get them started in business or professional practice, or just to provide a cushion to assist them in coping with the world's vagaries. If this is one of your goals, you must give it priority in line with other goals.

Stake for yourself. As discussed in Chapter 2, career changing is becoming a more prevalent phenomenon in our society. Many of these changes involve going into business for oneself, and very often a substantial stake is needed. Unfortunately, the concept of going to work for oneself does not always loom clearly on the horizon, and so it's difficult to put a priority on such a goal. Consider it accordingly, and keep it in mind each time you renew and revise this list of goals and priorities.

Care of elderly or disabled. This should perhaps be called a "need" rather than a "goal," since we all hope that those near and dear to us will be able to maintain themselves throughout their lifetime. But it doesn't always work out that way. Parents and other close relatives may, through circumstances beyond anyone's control, become dependent on us for a measure of support. If this likelihood can be anticipated, it can be planned for and better coped with.

"One-shot" expenses. These might be "must" goals, or they could be "maybe" goals. They can include such items as a once-in-a-lifetime trip, a large wedding for one's child, a major purchase of jewelry or luxury items, or a generous gift to a charity or other institution. These are voluntary goals, and their priority

may be high or low, depending on you. The higher the priority, the earlier the planning must be done.

Big "rainy day" fund. In the discussion of current and continuing goals and needs, we mentioned the little "rainy day" fund. The big "rainy day" fund is directed more to major unanticipated expenses that any individual or family might confront—uninsured medical expenses and recuperative costs; extended periods of lay-off from work; emergency needs of other family members of various purposes; uninsured losses; and so on. Generally, this is an item of fairly high priority. Proper insurance programs can minimize much of the risk, and there's always the possibility that the fund will never be needed and that it can, at some point, be allocated into other goal requirements.

Strategies for Success

Keeping Up with the Joneses Can Be Trouble

Are your financial goals really your own? Or are you just trying to mimic your spendthrift neighbors or friends by "keeping up with the Joneses." Carefully examine your goals. This self-examination can be critical to your happiness. Do you spend money on things you really need? Do you spend money to show off? To impress others? To "look good"? Your own goals should reflect what's right for you, not what others might think about you. Just ask yourself, "What if I actually *caught up* with the Joneses, only to find that I didn't like them? Where would I be then?" Take care of your own and your family's needs. Let the Joneses take care of their own.

ACCOMPLISHING FUTURE GOALS: AVAILABLE SOURCES

In addition to keeping a careful watch on your goals and their shifting priorities, it's also important to maintain a careful vigil on the sources of money that will allow you to accomplish these goals. They, too, might be subject to change over the years, and it's obviously important to be able to adjust goals and priorities in line with adjustments in the sources of money.

Income from Work

Employment, obviously, is the primary source from which your current and continuing goals will be met. To the extent that you don't use all your current income in meeting your current goals, the remainder will be put aside to meet future goals.

Savings and Investments

Income you earn in your savings and investment plans and the principal might ultimately be used to meet various goals. Depending on the manner of placement of these funds, you may have a reliable or an unreliable source of dollars. Prudence can assure your future; speculation can demolish it. Be well aware of possible consequences before you make any decisions in this extremely important area.

Equities

Homeowners are building a source of future funds as they reduce their mortgage debt. Owners of ordinary life-insurance policies likewise are building a source of future funds. Both forms of equity—your share of ownership—can amount to substantial sums. If they are tapped too early, by refinancing your home or prematurely cashing in your life-insurance policies, the ability to meet future goals may be seriously impaired. Know what these values are and what they can amount to in the future. Later chapters on housing and life insurance will assist you in determining these future values.

Borrowing

Borrowing can provide a most convenient way of meeting goals. Certainly with regard to housing, transportation, and such other major items as college tuition, borrowing allows you to accomplish what otherwise may take many years of accumulating. But borrowing is little more than a means of accelerating the use of future income, with an added cost factor of 10 to 30 percent, depending on the credit source used. It should also be well noted that funds that are borrowed and have to be repaid in the future will probably affect the budget flow when the funds are being repaid. Prudent borrowing can enhance your current, continuing life style; imprudent borrowing can devastate your future life style.

Enforced Savings: Pensions, Social Security, Profit-sharing Plans

Enforced savings represent a form of what would otherwise be current income, shifted to future accessibility. To many people, these forms of enforced savings represent all, or a substantial part, of the sources for meeting long-range goals, particularly retirement. But a danger exists in overestimating the total of these sources. Many people may find that their reliance on these sources has been in error—there simply isn't as much as expected. Even though access to these sources may be many years off, it's vital that a reasonably close estimate of what will be available is maintained on a continuing basis.

Inheritances, Gifts, and Other Windfalls

For most of us this category may be a complete imponderable. But if you have any reasonable assurance that inheritances or gifts will be coming your way, it would be wise to try to determine the amount involved; this can have a considerable effect on your other ongoing financial plans. Whenever an inheritance can be anticipated, be sure you understand the impact of the tax laws on it. Federal taxes can take a substantial bite out of inherited property if it is sold at a gain. It's the net amount; not the gross amount, that you should assimilate into your budget.

THE FINANCIAL STATEMENT

Can you imagine buying an automobile with no dashboard indicators on it? No speedometer, no gas gauge, no mileage indicator, no oil, brake, or battery warning lights? And to top it off, the hood is sealed shut, requiring two days in the shop every time you want to check your oil, battery, and other innards.

It might be O.K. for an occasional spin down to the supermarket, but to take it out on the highway would be risky, to say the least.

In much the same sense, any individual, family, or business needs a proper set of financial indicators plus easy access to the inner workings, so that periodic tuneups can be done quickly and simply.

A thoughtfully prepared and *regularly updated* financial statement is a neat and invaluable package of gauges, meters, and warning lights. It can tell you how fast you're going, how your fuel is holding out, how much fuel you'll need in the future, and how smooth your ride is.

Financial statements provide a picture, at any given time, of the exact financial condition of the person or business involved. But it's important to remember that these financial statements reflect the condition only on the given day. The value of a single statement is limited. The true value comes in comparing it with past statements, so that changes in growth and strong and weak points can be spotted and evaluated.

Elements of a Financial Statement

The financial statement consists of three major elements: assets, liabilities, and net worth.

Assets. *Assets* are the sum total of everything you own, plus everything owed to you. The value of assets is figured as of the date of the statement. Because the value of many assets can and does change, it's essential to evaluate them anew each time a statement is prepared, if it's to be accurate.

Included among your assets are your house; cars; personal property; bank accounts; and cash value of life insurance, stocks, and other securities. Also included are money or property due you as a result of a pending inheritance, personal debts owed to you, property settlements, and so on.

Liabilities.   Liabilities are debts—everything you owe. As with assets, these are figured as of the date of the statement, and values must be updated accordingly to insure the accuracy of your statement.

Included among liabilities will be the mortgage on your home, amounts owed on personal loans, amounts owed on contracts, and other personal debts. A detailed financial statement will break down financial liabilities into long term and short term. This can aid an analysis of your condition by distinguishing which debts will fall due within, say, one year and which will fall due at some more distant point.

Net Worth.   Your net worth is the difference between assets and liabilities, it should be on the plus side. You arrive at net worth by subtracting liabilities from assets. The business executive regards it this way: If he wanted to close up shop altogether, he would sell off all assets and use the money to pay off all liabilities. What's left would be his net worth.

Here's a simple example of how net worth is calculated on one particular item. Louise has a car valued at $6000. However, she still owes the bank $2000. Therefore, her net worth in this asset is $4000. The asset (car, $6000) minus the liabilities (debt to bank, $2000) equals net worth, $4000.

Uses of a Financial Statement

Simple personal financial statements have many uses. They can include a brief summary of your annual earnings and living expenses, as well as schedules of your life-insurance holdings, your investments, and your property, both real and personal.

From time to time you might be required to provide personal financial information to obtain credit or other services. In such instances, you'll probably have to sign a statement that says, in essence, that the information you have given is accurate, that you have given the information with the intent that the other party can act in reliance on it, that you have not withheld any pertinent information, and that you agree to notify the other party of any adverse changes in your circumstances. In providing this information and then signing the statement, you are legally binding yourself to the accuracy of the information given. If you give false or incomplete information, and the other party acts on it, you may be putting yourself in jeopardy. An insurance policy can conceivably be voided, a loan can be declared in default, a debt can be refused discharge in bankruptcy proceedings. Although such happenings may be rare, they can occur, and the proper way to avoid them is to be certain that the information on any kind of financial statement is accurate. Figure 3-1 illustrates a typical financial statement provided by financial institutions (usually at no cost). After you have filled it out, consider the uses to which it can be put.

As a Safety Valve.   An ongoing program of updated financial statements can help you spot troubles before they get out of hand. A financial mess can be lurking beneath the surface for years before it begins to hurt. For example, you may be involved in a gradual buildup toward becoming overly extended with debts. By tracing your indebtedness over the years via your financial statement, the signals might become evident early enough to warn you to correct the situation. Or your nest egg may not be growing as rapidly as it should be, and this can be spotted by comparing a series of annual financial statements. It's all a matter of "keeping track," and the financial statement program can be a most important tool for this.

To Keep the Reins on Your Credit. Good credit, wisely used, can be of immense value. Knowing well in advance your borrowing needs and your borrowing capabilities helps assure the wise use of credit. Through your financial statements, you can maintain a close vigil on your current debts, your depreciating assets (items that need replacement in the future, such as a car), and your anticipated future income (your ability to afford tomorrow's obligations). Of course, you realize without looking at some figures that you'll need a new car two years from now. But considering what other things you might have to borrow for between now and then, how will that car loan fit into your overall plans at that time? The financial statement gives you the current data that can help you cope with the future.

To Help Protect You against Loss. If you keep your financial statements up to date—at least yearly—you'll be forcing yourself to keep accurate current valuations on all your property. The value of any property is subject to change, and only by knowing true current values can you be sure of obtaining the necessary insurance to protect you against loss.

To Maintain a Sensible Life Insurance Program. Sound planning dictates that provision be made to maintain comforts in the event of the premature death of a breadwinner. Life insurance is the most common means of providing for this. A life insurance program should be planned in conjunction with the availability of other assets that can be cashed in to provide for needs. The financial statement provides a reliable current indicator of available assets that can be converted readily into cash without undue sacrifice should the necessity arise. This can help you tailor your life insurance program to your specific needs rather than guessing what that program should consist of.

To Help Establish a Worry-Free Estate Plan. Your progressive financial statements provide the best possible at-a-glance gauge of how much and what type of estate planning you need. Prudent estate planning requires a regular checkup of your net worth: Which assets and liabilities are increasing and decreasing? At what rate? Until what time? Which assets and liabilities can be shifted out of the estate to obtain maximum tax benefits and assure a proper distribution to survivors? Which assets have actual earnings or income potential and to what extent? A concise inventory and evaluation of these factors can be gained from your financial statements.

Santa Monica Bank

PERSONAL FINANCIAL STATEMENT

SMB

As of _____ 19 ____

Purpose of Loan: _____

Source of Repayment: _____

Name in Full	Soc. Sec. No.	Age	☐ Married ☐ Unmar. ☐ Sep.	No. of Dep.

Residence Address (No., Street, City, State, Zip Code)	Phone No. (Inc. Area Code)	Yrs. at Address	☐ Rent ☐ Own

Previous Addresses If at above address less than 5 years (No. and Street, City, State, Zip Code)

Employer	Position	No. Yrs.	Address (No. and Street)	City	Phone & Ext.

If You Are Married, You May Apply for a Separate Account.

Complete this part only if: 1. Your spouse will also be contractually liable for the account, OR 2. You are relying on alimony, child support or maintenance as income, OR 3. You want us to consider your spouse's income or other community property for the purpose of this application for credit.

Name and Address of Spouse or Former Spouse	Soc. Sec. No.	Age	Area Code-Bus. Phone ( )

Name and Address of Spouse's or Former Spouse's Employer	Position	How Long Yrs. ___ Mos. ___	Mo. Earnings $

ASSETS			DOLLARS		LIABILITIES			DOLLARS
CASH	Santa Monica Bank	Office		NOTES PAYABLE TO BANKS	Santa Monica Bank	Office		
	Other Banks				Other (Itemize)			
STOCKS AND BONDS	Listed (Schedule A)							
	Unlisted (Schedule A)							
ACCOUNTS AND NOTES RECEIVABLE	Relatives, Friends and Business			OTHER NOTES AND ACCOUNTS PAYABLE	Real Estate Loans (Schedule B)			
					Contracts payable (Itemize)			
LIFE INSURANCE	Cash Surrender Value				Loans on Cash Surrender Value			
REAL ESTATE	Improved (Schedule B)							
	Unimproved (Schedule B)							
	Trust Deeds and Mortgages (Schedule C)			OTHER LIABILITIES				
OTHER PERSONAL PROPERTY	Automobile							
	Other (Itemize)			NET WORTH	TOTAL LIABILITIES			
					(TOTAL ASSETS MINUS TOTAL LIABILITIES)			
	TOTAL ASSETS				TOTAL			

ANNUAL INCOME	(Refer to Federal Income Tax Returns for Previous Year)	ANNUAL EXPENDITURES	(Refer to Federal Income Tax Returns for Previous Year)
Salary or Wages		Real Estate Loan Payments	
Dividends and Interest		Payments on Contracts and other Notes	
Rentals (Gross)		Property Taxes and Assessments	
Business or Professional Income (Net)		Federal and State Income Taxes	
Other Income		Insurance Premiums	
(You do not have to list income from alimony, child support or maintenance unless you want the Bank to consider it for the purpose of this application for credit.)		Estimated Living Expenses	
		Other	
TOTAL INCOME		**TOTAL EXPENDITURES**	

LESS — TOTAL EXPENDITURES

NET CASH INCOME

INSURANCE:

Insurance on Buildings $ _____ Accident/Health Insurance $ _____

Automobiles: Coll. $ _____ Ded. $ _____ Comp. $ _____

Life Insurance Co. Name _____ Amount _____

Beneficiary of Life Insurance _____

N-123 (Rev. 5-77)   (PLEASE READ IMPORTANT STATEMENT ON REVERSE BEFORE SIGNING)

Figure 3–1 New financial statement

SCHEDULE A: LISTED AND UNLISTED STOCKS AND BONDS OWNED

No. of Shares or Par Value	Description	Issued in name of (as joint tenants, community or separate property)	Cost	Market Value
Listed:				
			Total Listed	
Unlisted:				
			Total Unlisted	

Are any of the above Securities pledged to secure a debt? (If yes describe)

SCHEDULE B: REAL ESTATE

Address (Also Give Brief Phys. Descrip.)	* Title in Name of:	Purch. Date	Cost	Market Value	Trust Deed, Mortgage or Other Liens				
					Unpaid Balance	Rate	Monthly Payment	Held By	
		TOTAL							

Is any of above Real Estate subject to declaration of homestead?
Yes   No

*Indicate how title is held in above real properties by following abbreviations:
J/T - Joint Tenancy; T/C - Tenancy in Common;
S/P - Separate Property; C/P - Community Property

Are you leasing any Real or Personal Property?
Yes   No
If yes, give details as to terms of leases

SCHEDULE C: TRUST DEEDS AND MORTGAGES OWNED

Name of Payer	Street Address, & Type of Improvements	Unpaid Bal.	Terms	1st or 2nd Lien	Market Value of Prop.
	TOTAL		x x x	x x x x	

GENERAL INFORMATION

Have you ever failed in business or compromised debts with your creditors?   Yes   No
If yes, give details

Are any of your assets pledged, or in any other manner unavailable for paying debts?   Yes   No
If unavailable or pledged, give details

Are there any suits, judgments, executions of attachments against you pending?   Yes   No
If yes, give details

DO YOU HAVE A WILL?
YES   NO

Are any of your assets held in Joint Tenancy, Tenancy in Common or Community Property?   Yes   No
If yes, give details _____

Are you contingently liable for any Endorsements or Guarantees?   Yes   No
If yes, give details _____

For the purpose of procuring and establishing credit from time to time with you, each of the undersigned furnish this statement as being true and accurate.

The undersigned agree to and will notify you immediately in writing of any material change in the financial condition of the undersigned and in the absence of such notice or of a new and full written statement, this may be considered as a continuing statement and substantially correct; and it is hereby expressly agreed that upon application for further credit, this statement shall have the same force and effect as if delivered as an original statement of the financial condition of the undersigned at the time such further credit is requested. In consideration of the granting of such credit the undersigned and each of them agree that if the undersigned or any or either of them, or any endorser or guarantor of the obligations of the undersigned or any or either of them at any time fail or become insolvent or commit an act of bankruptcy, or if any deposit account of the undersigned or any or either of them with you, or any other property of the undersigned or any or either of them held by you be attempted to be obtained or held by writ of execution, garnishment, attachment, or other legal process, or if any of the representations made above prove to be untrue or if the undersigned or any or either of them fail to notify you of any material change as above agreed, or if any such material change occurs, then and in either case all obligations of the undersigned or any or either of them held by you shall immediately become due and payable without demand or notice. All sums at any time in any deposit account shall be subject to Bank's right to set-off for liabilities owed to the Bank by any of the undersigned, to the fullest extent permissible by applicable law, and upon any other personal property of the undersigned or any or either of them in your possession, from time to time, to secure all obligations of the undersigned and each of them, either as borrower or guarantor, held by you, and further agree that all obligations or any part thereof, of the undersigned or any or either of them held by you, both matured and unmatured, may at any time be charged against the balance of any deposit account of the undersigned or any or either of them with you, without notice to the undersigned, unless required by applicable law.

I hereby certify that I have carefully read the above statement, including the reverse side, and it is a complete, true and correct statement of the undersigned to the best of my knowledge and belief.

Applicant's Signature _____ Date _____

Co-applicant's Signature — If this is to be a joint account. _____ Date _____

Your spouse's signature is not required if this is to be your separate account. If you want us to consider your spouse's income or credit history in making our credit decision, your spouse's authorization is needed.

Spouse's Signature — To authorize verification of income or credit history ONLY. _____ Date _____

To Help Plan Your Long-Range Budget. The financial statement, regularly updated, is a simple device to keep your current and future goals in clear focus and to provide an ongoing measurement of the sources from which those goals will be met.

To Aid in Borrowing. If a financial statement is required as a condition to getting a loan, you'll expedite matters considerably if you are prepared with a current statement as well as those of recent years. It will speed up application processing and will serve as evidence of your financial good housekeeping.

SPENDING HABITS: THEIR IMPORTANCE

It's the object of this chapter and this book to help guide you in establishing financial habits that will allow you to accomplish your individual goals. But all too often we are waylaid from those ultimate goals by strange and often inexplicable outside circumstances. We live in an age of instant gratification, constantly bombarded by commercial messages urging us to acquire products that will provide happiness and satisfaction in almost every phase of our day-to-day life.

Spending habits born out of impulse, gullibility, or low sales resistance can be extremely counterproductive to one's financial welfare. To some degree, we are all subject to impulsive spending, but the more aware we can become of this susceptibility, the more readily we'll be able to control it.

Spending habits may have been unconsciously dictated to us by our observations of our parents. We should evaluate what spending habits are inherited and determine their good and bad points. Peer group pressure—"keeping up with the Joneses"—can also influence our spending habits, and succumbing to it can be costly and unsatisfying.

Spending habits can be a powerful force in shaping your overall financial well-being, which in turn can have a considerable effect on your social, psychological, and personal well-being. To the extent that spending habits control you, you'll have a much more difficult time achieving your own personal potential; when *you* control these habits, you will indeed be the master of your fate.

Taking the "Dollar Diet"

Do you have too much month left at the end of the money? When budgets fail to balance, it's generally because too many dollars have dribbled away in unnoticed fashion. Big items—utility costs, rent, mortgage payment, car payment, and so forth—are fairly easy to trace. But the variety of "miscellaneous" expenses are too easily gone and forgotten. This results in the "Miscellaneous Bulge," and a good cure may be the "Dollar Diet." Using this page, or a separate notebook, keep track of every nickel, dime, quarter, and dollar that you spend for the next month. At the end of that time you should be able to identify the spending habits that are causing the problem, and corrective action can be instituted. Sample items usually found in the Miscellaneous Bulge include the following. Keep track of them.

Miscellaneous budget items	*List your expenses and dates thereof for one full month*			
☐ Cigarettes	____	____	____	____
☐ Gum, candy, other sweets	____	____	____	____
☐ Magazines, newspapers	____	____	____	____
☐ Liquor, beer, wine—both for at-home and outside uses	____	____	____	____
☐ Gasoline, other car care	____	____	____	____
☐ Movies, other entertainment tickets	____	____	____	____
☐ Records, tapes (music, video)	____	____	____	____
☐ Hair care and cosmetics	____	____	____	____
☐ Carfare, taxis	____	____	____	____
☐ Restaurants	____	____	____	____
☐ Minor clothing items	____	____	____	____
☐ Laundry, dry cleaning	____	____	____	____
☐ Gifts, greeting cards	____	____	____	____
☐ Adornments for person or home	____	____	____	____

Goals Should Satisfy You, Not Others

Linda and Gary faced a dilemma common to many young married couples. "We both have good jobs with a lot of potential, and we're confident that we can afford to buy a home in the near future. We've found a funky old cottage about twenty miles out of town right on the lake. It's run down and would need a lot of work, but the price is right, and we love the location. Even with improvements, it would still be funky, but it's 'our thing.'

"This is where the problem arises. Our folks and a lot of our friends have been hounding us to buy a place in a certain neighborhood that's the 'in' place for up-and-coming career couples.

"But to us it's stuffy and phony. However, we can't deny that it does offer contact opportunities and whatever advantages may come from living in the 'right' neighborhood. It would cost a lot more than our funky bungalow, and we'd really be strapped to make the monthly payments. But, then, our friends and family say, 'You'll reap a bigger profit when you sell the "right" place, compared with what you might gain when you sell the bungalow.'

"When we boil it all down, it's the two of us against a lot of them. We know we're young and naive. We respect the experience of others. But we've come to feel guilty: If we buy the bungalow we're being self-indulgent and foolish; if we buy into the 'right' area, we're being sensible and mature—supposedly. Just who are we supposed to be trying to please anyway?"

The ending, at least for Linda and Gary, was a happy one. They bought the bungalow, fixed it up, and eventually their friends and family admitted that they had done the right thing.

As Linda later put it, "The final decision came down to this: Do we strive toward goals that we ourselves have set, or do we live our lives as others want us to? Well-meaning though the others may have been, we have to express our own independence and live our own lives. Fortunately, we made the right choice. Other couples in the same boat might have done better to listen to the others. To each his own—as long as you know what your own is."

CHAPTER 4

The Smart Shopper

You can be better off by $1000 a year, maybe even more! That's how much you, as a Smart Shopper, can save in your routine shopping for food, pharmaceuticals, clothing, and the like. Not all the techniques outlined in this chapter will work for all people. But if you don't try them, you'll never know. Smart Shopper techniques that you'll learn about in this chapter include

☐ How to recognize your built-in bad shopping habits and replace them with good, money-saving habits

☐ How to cut 10 percent, 20 percent, and even more from your food and pharmaceutical expenses

☐ How to look good without spending excessively at the clothing store

☐ How to get the best values for your money when shopping for furniture, appliances, and other big-ticket items

SHOPPING FOR FOOD

Bad Shopping Habits

Every day we are bombarded with hundreds if not thousands of advertising messages: on television, radio, billboards, newspapers, magazines, and in our mail. Millions of dollars are spent every day on market research and advertising to create the most effective pursuasions. Advertising can be a very good thing insofar as it can educate us regarding the choices we have for various products and services in the marketplace. But advertising must also be approached with caution: Aside from the relatively infrequent instances when advertising may be misleading (see Chapter 5), advertising can create buying habits that can prove costly. It can motivate us to buy on impulse, spending dollars that we might have otherwise put to better use. It can induce us to stick with one specific product when other comparable products might be less costly and equally satisfying. It can prompt us to pay more money for a product that promises certain benefits, when comparable products offer the same benefits at a lower cost.

Advertising isn't all to blame. No ad ever reached out and twisted anyone's arm to buy a particular product. We also must blame our own tendencies to be impulsive and unwilling to take a few extra moments during each shopping decision to pick the product that can satisfy our needs at the best possible price.

If you have any doubts about the general tendency toward poor shopping habits by the average American, conduct a simple experiment *after* you've read this chapter: Be a supermarket spy. Push a cart so as not to raise suspicion, and follow other shoppers up and down the aisles of the supermarket. Notice how they succumb to impulse, brand favoritism, and lack of doing adequate comparisons. After a short time, you'll be tempted to tap your fellow shopper on the shoulder and suggest, "You know, you really could save money by buying X instead of Y, and I'm sure you'll be just as happy with it." If you're not emboldened enough to do that, you'll at least feel confident that *you* know how to save as much as 20 percent on the bulk of your shopping—and for a family that spends an average of $100 a week on such items, or over $5000 a year, that's a savings of about $1000 per year.

Good Shopping Habits

Let's now examine some of the specific Smart Shopper techniques, particularly those that can be employed at the supermarket, where the majority of our normal shopping budget is spent. (All price comparisons referred to in the following material are based on regular prices, not on specials or discounts.)

Unit Pricing. A 14-ounce bottle of Heinz ketchup at 79¢ is a lot cheaper than a 44-ounce bottle at $1.59. Correct? Yes and no. The smaller bottle is cheaper than the big bottle, but the ketchup inside, *per ounce*, is much more expensive in the smaller bottle. The ketchup in the small bottle is 5.64¢ per ounce (79 divided by 14 equals 5.64). The ketchup in the big bottle is 3.61¢ per ounce (1.59 divided by 44 equals 3.61). In other words, the exact same product—Heinz ketchup—is 2.03¢ per ounce cheaper when bought in a big bottle compared with a small bottle (5.64 minus 3.61 equals 2.03). Put another way, an ounce of ketchup from the big bottle is 30 percent cheaper than an ounce of ketchup from the small bottle.

This is what's known as *unit pricing*: calculating the price of a product by the unit (ounce, pound, etc.) rather than by the container it comes in.

A substantial number of commonly purchased products—food, cosmetics, pharmaceuticals, and the like—are packaged in a variety of different-sized containers. With few exceptions, very attractive savings can be realized by buying the larger-sized containers. And also, with very few exceptions, the products in the larger containers can remain every bit as fresh if properly stored. Many shoppers, in an effort to keep their weekly expenses down, will choose the smaller containers without giving the matter a second thought. This can be a costly mistake.

Table 4-1 illustrates a number of other unit pricing comparisons. Experiment with your hand-held calculator the next time you go shopping. Determine which products you can save money on by using unit pricing without sacrificing quality.

Table 4-1 **Unit Pricing Comparisons**

Product	Size (Ounce)	Cost per package ($)	Cost per ounce ($)[a]	Savings per ounce in larger package (%)
Taster's Choice coffee	8	5.49	.69	35
	2	2.09	1.05	
Mott's apple sauce	36	1.59	.04	10
	16	.79	.05	
Del Monte corn	17	.59	.04	27
	12	.57	.05	
Johnson's baby shampoo	15	3.69	.25	21
	7	2.19	.31	
Phillips milk of magnesia	26	4.89	.19	29
	12	3.19	.27	
Tree Sweet apple juice	128	4.19	.03	11
	32	1.19	.04	
Best Foods mayonnaise	32	1.85	.06	19
	16	1.15	.07	
Del Monte peach halves	29	.99	.03	39
	16	.89	.06	

[a]These figures have been rounded to the nearest cent.

Brand Name versus Generic Products.   A ten-ounce jar of Welch's grape jelly costs $1.09. A ten-ounce jar of a grape jelly with the market's own label costs 83¢, a difference of 26¢ or 24 percent. Unless you or your children are true connoisseurs of grape jelly, the difference in taste may be insignificant, especially after you've covered it with a layer of peanut butter and sandwiched the whole gooey mass between two slabs of bread. But even if there is a distinguishable difference in taste, is it worth the sacrifice for the 24 percent savings?

Brand-name products are those regional or national items whose names are known to us through advertising and general familiarity. Generic products are those that are privately labeled for specific stores or chains of stores. In many cases, the quality of generic products is equal to their brand-name counterparts. Indeed, many are made by the same manufacturers and to the same specifications. Some generic products may not have the same quality as their brand-name counterparts, but the difference may be so slight as to justify buying them for the savings that can be realized. At the very least, a trial of the generic products is certainly warranted. If you're dissatisfied, you're always free to go back to the brand label. But if you're satisfied with the generic label, you can reap substantial savings.

Table 4-2 **Brand Label versus Generic Label**

Product	Size of package	Cost of package ($)	Cost per unit ($)[a]	Savings per unit in generic label (%)
Betty Crocker pancake mix	32 oz.	1.43	.05	40
Generic equivalent	32 oz.	.87	.03	
Q-tip cotton swabs	300 ct.	1.94	.07[b]	29
Generic equivalent	300 ct.	1.37	.05[b]	
Diaparene baby wash cloths	150 ct.	3.55	.02	42
Generic equivalent	150 ct.	2.09	.01	
Heinz vinegar	32 oz.	1.35	.04	71
Generic equivalent	128 oz.	1.55	.01	
Lipton tea bags	100 ct.	3.09	.03	52
Generic equivalent	100 ct.	1.49	.02	
Carnation coffee creamer	22 oz.	2.69	.12	53
Generic equivalent	22 oz.	1.25	.06	
Vlasic's pickles	22 oz.	1.49	.07	24
Generic equivalent	22 oz.	1.15	.05	

[a]Figures have been rounded to the nearest cent.

[b]Figure indicates cost per hundred.

Pharmaceuticals and prescriptions

Generic products also offer considerable savings in the drugstore. Table 4-2 compares some common supermarket items, plus some drugstore items that can be purchased without a prescription. Many prescription items are also available in generic fashion, and considerable savings can be realized on these as well. If your doctor gives you a brand-name prescription, ask whether there is a generic equivalent that would be satisfactory. Very often the doctor will be satisfied with the generic equivalent and will prescribe it for you instead of the brand name. But you must ask. If you don't ask the doctor at the time he writes the prescription, ask the pharmacist at the time you order the prescription. If he knows of a generic equivalent, he may call the doctor himself and ask the doctor's approval to substitute the generic prescription for the brand-name prescription.

Bulk Buying.   Many stores offer substantial discounts—10 to 20 percent—if you buy by the case. Indeed, in many cities there is a growing phenomenon of "warehouse" supermarkets that specialize in by-the-case merchandising, where you can purchase goods at much lower prices than at regular markets. In addition to the discounts you can obtain, buying in bulk quantity protects you against inflationary price increases on those products. If you buy a year's supply of, say, paper towels, you've insulated yourself against a price increase in paper towels for a year. That might be as much as an additional 10 percent. Further, by buying enough staples in bulk quantity, you might be able to cut down on the number of trips you make to the market.

Most common nonfood products have a virtually infinite shelf life—you can keep them in storage almost forever without there being any deterioration in their quality. Most canned, boxed, and bottled foodstuffs have shelf lives that can stretch for years. Here's a sampling of common products that can be stored for long times. If your market doesn't advertise bulk savings, ask the manager. You might be surprised at the bargains you can obtain.

☐ Paper products, such as napkins, towels, toilet tissue

☐ Soap products, including detergents

☐ Storage products, such as wax paper, aluminum foil, plastic bags for both food and garbage disposal

☐ Pharmaceuticals, such as toothpaste, powders, rubbing alcohol, bandages, shaving creams, razors and razor blades, colognes and lotions, deodorants, shampoos, makeup, and so on

☐ "Instant" powdered items, such as coffee, tea, juice products

☐ Dehydrated products, including milk, eggs, and so on

☐ Food items in cans, bottles, and jars can have a shelf life of at least one year. Check with your store manager for specifics on each item.

☐ Frozen foods: individual taste, plus the cost and availability of a freezer, may dictate how much bulk food you'd want to buy for frozen storage. Most food items, when frozen, will eventually undergo some deterioration. The U.S. Department of Agriculture recommends the following limits for these common products. Check with your store manager for details on other products.

Beef and lamb roasts and steaks, 8 to 12 months

Veal and pork roasts, 4 to 8 months

Chops and cutlets, 3 to 6 months

Ground beef, veal, lamb, and stew meats, 3 to 4 months

Chicken and turkey, 12 months

Duck and goose, 6 months

Fresh fish, 6 to 9 months

Fruits and vegetables (most), 8 to 12 months

To take advantage of the savings that can be gained through bulk shopping, you must, of course, provide proper storage facilities. A cool, dark, dry place is best for virtually all items. There's hardly a house or apartment that can't clear away a few cubic feet of space to store bulk-purchased items. If you really feel cramped for space, see the later discussion on ''rummaging,'' by which you can gain not only added space but tax savings as well.

Convenience Foods versus Fresh Foods. *The experiment:* Compare Aunt Jemima frozen French toast with French toast made from scratch. A 9-ounce box of the Aunt Jemima product contains six pieces of premade frozen French toast at a cost of $1.13. We allocated $1.13 of raw products: milk, bread, eggs, and butter. We made two teams: the fresh and the frozen. At the starting bell the fresh team began mixing the batter, dunking the bread, and placing it on the griddle. At the same time the team making the frozen product started inserting the frozen pieces into the toaster, two pieces at a time. We wanted to determine not only the quantity that could be made for the same amount of money but the time it took to make it.

The results: The fresh team made twelve full-size pieces of French toast in the same time (give or take a minute) that it took for the toaster to defrost and heat six pieces of frozen product. The fresh product looked, smelled, and tasted delicious. The frozen pieces had no aroma and looked and tasted a bit like cardboard. The only drawback to the fresh side was that more cleanup had to be done, but that was well worth doing in view of the fact that there was twice as much finished product, and it was vastly more satisfying.

This was not what might be called the most scientifically controlled experiment ever conducted, but it serves to illustrate very important points: Convenience can be expensive, not altogether satisfying, and not even time saving!

The extent to which you may choose to use convenience foods is a very individual matter depending on taste, your willingness to exert some of your own energy, the season of the year, and the whim of the moment. The only rule of thumb that can be proposed is to compare the ''inconvenient'' do-it-yourself way with the convenience-food way and determine whether the savings are worth it to you. In many instances the savings will be considerable. For example, a 12-ounce package of frozen Ore Ida French fries costs 79¢, about 6.6¢ per ounce. A 10-pound sack of fresh potatoes costs $1.99, about 1.2¢ per ounce. The frozen costs more than five times more than the fresh on a per-ounce basis. If peeling and slicing your own potatoes is not a hardship, why not take advantage of the extensive savings and enjoy the freshness as well?

As noted, the season can make a difference. A summertime purchase of fresh strawberries was 79¢ for 12 ounces. The same amount of frozen strawberries cost exactly the same. Given the choice, which would you prefer? Obviously, during eight or nine months of the year fresh strawberries aren't available, so the frozen style is all you have to choose from. But when fresh products are available, compare their cost with the frozen variety, and compare the satisfaction you get from each.

Frozen vegetables may come with a conveniently packed pat of butter in the container, and the cost may be only a penny or two more than similar frozen vegetables without a pat of butter. The convenience element is that the packers have saved you the trouble of putting your own butter onto the vegetables. But that little pat of butter, at a penny or two, will actually be costing you about $5 a pound.

The same goes for things like presugared cereals and a variety of other seasoned foods. If you're willing to pay the price to have the manufacturer do your buttering, your sugaring, and your seasoning for you, that's your choice. The extra pennies or nickels you spend on these products may seem invisible to you at the time you spend them, but they do mount up.

The Smart Shopper will get into the habit of using unit pricing, comparing brands with generic labels, buying bulk quantities when the best deals are available, and avoiding costly convenience foods. In addition, here are some other ways that the Smart Shopper will save money.

Coupons and Specials.   Cents-off coupons are offered by both manufacturers and stores. Coupon offerings are abundant in your daily newspaper, particularly in the Wednesday and Thursday editions. Coupons may also be found in magazines, in your mail, on the market shelves, and on the products themselves. The main purpose of coupons is to motivate you to try a new product. You can determine for yourself whether the experiment is worth it. But if you don't use coupons on products that you *regularly* buy, you're throwing money away. The Smart Shopper will take perhaps an hour per week to scour the newspaper and magazine ads looking for coupons offering discounts on all products he commonly buys. Appropriate coupons will be clipped, sorted, and taken on the next trip to the market. The savings can be many dollars per week—an hour well spent.

The Wednesday and Thursday daily newspapers also contain the special offerings from your local markets for the coming week. These specials can be particularly attractive to the bulk buyer and may even justify driving a few extra miles to take advantage of them. If you shop during the latter part of the week, you are most likely to find the broadest selection of specially advertised items. Considering the cost of getting from one market to another, it may not pay you to buy a quart of milk here, a pound of apples there, a loaf of bread somewhere else. But if you prepare a careful shopping list containing all of your weekly needs, a careful study of the advertised specials can lead you to specific savings that might justify some extra travel.

Shopping on a Full Stomach.   If you shop while you're hungry, you're more likely to load up your basket with nonessentials, snack foods, impulse items, and so on. Shop only after you've had a filling meal, so you'll be less susceptible to wasting your shopping dollars on such items.

Shopping with a List.   Shopping without a list can lead to purchasing items you don't really need and forgetting those you do need. Carefully plan your needs in advance, and write them down on a list. Stick to the list if you want to keep your budget in line. Once you've developed a habit of shopping from a list, your shopping trips will be that much more efficient in both time and money saved.

Avoiding Snack Foods.   Avoid snack foods. They tend to be very costly, and the nutritional value you get for your money is questionable. The following case history best illustrates this warning:

"I came home from work early one afternoon and found my children and a few of their neighborhood friends sitting around our kitchen table eating DingDongs. DingDongs are chocolate-covered pastries enveloping a blob of white substance that to me looks like shaving cream, tastes like wet tissue paper, and seems to have the nutritional value of soap bubbles. As I stood there and watched an entire box of DingDongs disappear before my eyes, I realized that our household went through $5 worth of DingDongs and similar snack foods per week. That's more than $250 per year! I immediately ordered an end to all DingDongs in our house. My children looked at me aghast. I didn't want to interfere with their after-school snacking, so I told my young teenage daughters that rather than spend money on DingDongs, they could make cookies and cakes from scratch on their own. The prospect thrilled them, and the next day they began their baking adventures. This not only satisfied them, but it delighted them for three or four days. Then the task of cleaning up after themselves began to get too much for them. The baking tapered off and so did the snacking. Not only did our food budget go down noticeably, but I'm sure I detected a drop in our dental bills as well."

Bending a Little.   In general, supermarkets stock their highest profit margin items on the eye-level shelves. The better bargains for you—in terms of unit price and generic availability—tend to be on the lower shelves. A little bit of bending will save you a lot of money.

Searching out Extra Bargains.   Many markets discount bread, pastries, and produce after it has been on display for a day or so. If the market doesn't advertise these items, ask your manager what she has available. If you're going to consume these products in the very near future, they can be every bit as satisfying as the fresher product with a distinct savings to you. Many markets also have a "thrift" shelf where slightly damaged nonconsumable items are placed. These can represent substantial savings; it's worth at least a look to see whether there are any products there that you'd otherwise buy at full price.

Knowing Your Local Markets.   Habit often finds us shopping at the same market most of the time. That's not necessarily a bad thing, but it's wise to get to know the other markets that are conveniently close to you. You might find that they offer a better price on most of the products you commonly buy. You won't know until you've spent a few shopping trips at most of them. Also, get to know the individual managers at each of the markets. Public relations is important in the supermarket (and drugstore) business. The managers are there to try to please the public, and the better they know you, the more likely they are to offer you that extra special little item: a better choice in the produce department or the meat department, a whispered tip that a certain item you're buying will be going on sale the next day, an offer to sell you an overstocked item at a discount.

SHOPPING FOR CLOTHING AND ACCESSORIES

". . . That looks absolutely smashing on you. Wear it anywhere, and you'll have the opposite sex enthralled."

". . . Your taste is excellent. I can tell that you're a real fashion leader."

". . . That's what absolutely everybody is wearing today. If you want to be with it, you'll buy it now before we run out of stock."

". . . As long as you're buying the slacks, you ought to get some nice things to go with it. Here's a nice matching sweater."

Vanity, thy name is clothing shopper. Young or old, male or female, few of us are immune to the flattering persuasions of the clothing salesperson. But Smart Shopper *is* immune. Smart Shopper keeps a firm grip on his common sense, never letting it succumb to moods, to ego, to fads, or to impulse. Smart Shopper has carefully studied his practical needs for clothing and accessories and is willing to take the time to shop for those items that offer the best value (appearance considered) for the money.

Personal appearance is, needless to say, very personal. Clothing is the most costly and the most visible element of your overall personal appearance. Only you can decide how you want to look or how you should look. There's little argument that the well-dressed and well-groomed person can enjoy certain advantages over the poorly groomed or slovenly dressed person. To that extent, appropriately attractive clothing and accessories can be considered an investment in one's social and business well-being.

On the other hand, excessive spending on clothing will not necessarily produce commensurate results. The overly dressed person can be looked upon by her peers as extravagant, excessive, or even in poor taste. Given your own individual circumstances—at school, at work, in social activities—you must find the balance that's right for you. And that balance must include both the desired appearance *and* the cost of creating that appearance. It's not the province of this book to suggest how you should look, but the following material can help you with the budget-balancing tricks of affording the look you do want to have.

Controlling Ego and Impulse

The brief quotes at the beginning of this section are samples of just a few of the tricks of the clothing trade. But long before we enter the clothing stores, our brains and our egos have been preconditioned. With the possible exception of the automobile, no product that we commonly buy is more lavishly and glamorously advertised than clothing. The advertising lets us believe that we can look like models in *Vogue* or *Gentleman's Quarterly*, and the salesperson confirms it.

Nothing can cripple a budget more quickly and more devastatingly than our vanity and our impulsive natures. You can't fit designer jeans on a nondesigner body. But we spend ourselves silly trying. True, many otherwise aggressive salespersons will sometimes be honest enough to tell you that a particular outfit makes you look like a hippopotamus. But that's the exception. The rule is that they are there to sell clothing, and they know well that nothing sells clothing more rapidly than flattery. Arm yourself accordingly: Don't act on impulse; shop around for comparable items before you make a decision.

Strategies for Success

Impulsive Shopping Can Cost You Plenty

One study revealed that shoppers often pay two to three times more for a given item if a credit card sign is visible near the cash register. "Oh, what the heck, let's buy the better version; we can use our plastic!" they say. And a psychologist reports that certain symbols and visual cues, such as signs claiming Discount and Last Day of Sale, can prompt impulsive and unnecessary spending. Stores know this, and they use every trick they can to move their merchandise. Don't let your impulses get the best of your common sense, lest you spend more than you can reasonably afford.

Embellishing the Simple

You can stretch your clothing dollars farther by sticking to basically simple outfits and embellishing them with attractive accessories—as opposed to buying more decorative and more costly basic units. For example, a common men's outfit—navy blue blazer and gray slacks—can take on a variety of appearances depending on the accessories. Shirt and tie, open-neck shirt, turtleneck shirt—all give the basic unit a totally different look. Similar combinations are possible with basic women's outfits. A variety of simple accessories can offer much more diversity for the money in a wardrobe than can a variety of basic outfits.

Finding the Good Buys

Check the advertising carefully in your local newspapers and go where the good buys are. Don't be embarrassed to shop at discount stores or through catalogues (Sears, Wards, etc.). You could save considerably through such outlets, particularly on such items as underclothing, pajamas, socks, stockings, and the like.

Factory outlets can be an excellent source for buying stylish clothing at considerable discounts. Such outlets commonly buy overstocks from other stores and overruns from clothing manufacturers. You won't find the personalized attention that you do in specialty shops or boutiques, and you may not be able to open a charge account, but the savings may be well worth giving up those costly frills.

Thrift shops and "next-to-new" stores offer exceptional bargains if you're willing to spend the time rummaging around. And no one will know where you bought it if you don't tell.

Department stores and specialty shops often have special sales for their charge account customers. If what they have to offer meets your clothing needs at the time, good bargains can be had.

Timing Your Purchases

Use the calendar to your advantage. Buying clothing and accessories off season can represent substantial savings. Buy winter clothes in the spring and summer (when they are usually on sale); buy summer clothes in the fall and winter. You won't have an abundant choice of fashions or styles, but you can pick up bargains that will be well worth your shopping trip.

Seasonal sales are common with most large clothing and department stores. Major sales are usually after Christmas and after Easter. Shop early for the best selection.

Buying Seconds

Seconds (or irregulars) are items of clothing with minor flaws in them. The price of a second can be well below the price of an otherwise identical item. And the flaw itself may be so minor that no one would really notice it; or you could simply pass it off as a minor snag. With a lot of casual clothing, a minor flaw is not uncommon anyway. Factory outlets and discount stores are good sources of seconds.

Considering Cleanability and Durability

How readily soiled will a particular garment get, and what will be required to clean it? Is it hand washable or must it be dry-cleaned? The care labels on the garments indicate the recommended cleaning techniques. The durability and cleanability—or lack thereof—represent an important element of your overall clothing investment. The cost of cleaning your clothing or replacing worn clothing is also directly related to your personal habits and the care you take to protect and preserve your clothing.

Avoiding Counterfeits

It has become very fashionable to wear clothing and carry accessories that have other people's names and initials on them. Presumably this is a sign of affluence, prestige, good taste, or an inability to resist a fad. There seem to be no other reasons why one person would want to wear the clothing that carries the initials of another person. But people do, and they are willing to pay heavily for the privilege. This fact has not been overlooked by manufacturers who are happy to create counterfeit versions of the designer-initialed items, but these versions may be woefully inferior to the genuine articles. So beware: If you find yourself obsessed with an opportunity to buy "genuine" Pucci-Gucci at a price that seems too good to be true, don't be disappointed if it falls into shreds after the first or second wearing. The counterfeit designer-clothing industry has reached multimillion dollar proportions. You're most likely to get stung buying such articles at swap meets, from street vendors, or from stores that seem to open one week and close the next.

Knowing Store Policies

If you buy a garment and take it home, will you be able to return it if it doesn't suit you? Will the store refund your cash, or will they simply allow you a credit against other purchases? Or will they refuse to take it back altogether? If the store does allow return privileges, how long does that privilege last? Many sales items might be purchased on an as-is basis, thereby preventing you from getting any kind of refund or exchange privilege. You must know this before you buy if you want to avoid disappointment. In any case, you can safely assume that if you want to return any items, you must bring in your sales receipt in order to get credit or refund.

Buying for Children

As a general rule most children will outgrow most clothing before it has had a chance to deteriorate. Except for one or two "dress" outfits, it can be false economy to buy top-of-the-line clothing for children. Look to the same factory outlets, discount stores, and special sales for the best bargains on children's clothing.

Rummaging

In the earlier discussion on buying in bulk, we noted that you might be hard-pressed for space to store those products. You can kill two birds with one stone by having an annual rummaging through your closets and dressers to get rid of excess, unusable, or unneeded clothing and other personal items. If you don't know a worthy hand-me-down recipient, you can donate your used clothing to any one of a number of thrift shops or charities in your community. If you itemize your income tax deductions, you can claim a deduction for the donated clothing. Itemize everything specifically, and make sure you get a signed receipt for the clothing from the thrift shop. You create added storage space, you save a few tax dollars, and you provide inexpensive clothing for someone in need—a good project all the way around.

SHOPPING FOR MAJOR HOME FURNISHINGS

Your overall budget can be drastically affected by your need—or lack thereof—of major home furnishings: furniture, carpeting, appliances. Your budgetary capacity to buy furnishings may, in turn, influence the type of dwelling you choose to live in: large versus small, furnished versus unfurnished, shared versus alone. And, in weighing your housing and furnishing considerations, you must also take into account the following:

▫ How long will you be living in the given dwelling? If you're settling in for the foreseeable future, a bigger investment in furnishings is more easily justified. If you'll be living in the particular dwelling for only a year or so, it might not make sense to burden yourself with major expenses for furnishings. Realistically determine whether your job, your marital status, or the growth of your family will dictate a likely move in the near future.

▫ Are there youngsters (or pets) on the scene? Children (and dogs and cats) can wreak havoc on furnishings. A jelly spot on a sofa; a urine stain on a carpet; plus assorted tears, smudges, scratches, and other blemishes have to be expected when little ones are about. The family with young children and active pets must evaluate how its furnishings will withstand the onslaught. If you buy ''fancy'' and expensive furnishings while the children are very young, you may be faced with expensive cleaning and repair costs, or the furnishings could look a shambles by the time the children are grown and more responsible. It might make more sense to buy more modest furnishings while the children are young, then dispose of them later in favor of the more elaborate items.

▫ Will your tastes change? Major furnishings—particularly furniture and carpeting—are available in a wide variety of styles, ranging from conservative to what some people would call outlandish. Tastes do change, make no mistake about it. Will your selections today still please you one year, five years, ten years from now? There's no way of knowing for certain, of course, but it can be foolhardy to be overindulgent in choosing highly personalized furnishings with respect to either design or color.

   For example, today you might be very excited about strong pastel colors in your upholstery and carpeting, accented by chrome and glass tables and accessories. It might indeed look beautiful. But say you weary of it within a few years. Or say your marriage terminates and King Solomon's wisdom can't help you and your divorced spouse divide up the furnishings. Or you move to a new location where the furniture absolutely clashes with your new surroundings. The market for used furniture is rather sparse, and the more highly personalized the individual items, the fewer buyers there may be for them. You may then look back on your original choice as money wasted, money that could tally many hundreds, if not thousands, of dollars.

   You might be better off choosing a more conservative design and color range for the major items and accenting those pieces with relatively inexpensive accessories—throw pillows, lamp shades, area rugs, and the like. These can be changed easily and inexpensively and can give your premises a very different look at a much lower cost than a whole new truck full of furnishings.

▫ What is the focal point of your social life? Will you be doing a lot of entertaining at home, for either personal or business purposes? Or do you prefer to go out a lot for your social life? It may not be possible to afford both fine home furnishings and a lavish outside entertainment budget. Many people don't realize this until after they've invested heavily in furnishings and then find themselves in a budgetary crisis. Examine your preferences before you make your furnishing decisions. If you'll be spending a major portion of your social life at home, you can more easily justify more expense for the furnishings. If you'll be doing business entertaining at home, the expense may even prove to be a worthwhile investment. On the other hand, however, if you're not a homebody, you should structure your budget more to suit your ''going out'' needs and less to satisfy the at-home needs.

This book isn't intended to influence your taste, your sense of comfort, or your desire for convenience in home furnishings. Those are matters that you must determine for yourself. But the following guidelines may be helpful in getting you the best value for the home furnishing dollars you do decide to spend.

Furniture

Shop with great care! There can be vast differences in quality—both construction and upholstery—and you can't tell quality just by looking at the furniture. Shop at a number of stores before you make any decision. At each store ask the salesperson to go over the following points with you.

- ☐ *Wood furniture.* (tables, cabinets, dressers, etc.). How are the parts joined together? Is the piece all wood, or does it utilize less expensive fiber board in unseen places? Does it stand firm and solid? Do moving parts (doors, drawers) fit and operate properly? What is the quality of the hardware (hinges, knobs, etc.), and how is it attached to the wood? What is the quality of the finish and any decorative elements? Bear in mind that for tables, a synthetic surface (such as formica) can wear more durably than wood.

- ☐ *Upholstered furniture.* (sofas, chairs, matching pillows and cushions). Pay attention to the construction elements as with the wood furniture noted above. How is the fabric anchored to the piece? Do the patterns and colors match properly? How durable is the fabric? What are the sun- and soil-resistance factors of the fabric? What is the stuffing made of, and how long will it hold its shape? How does it sit? Test it for firmness, comfort, clothing against fabric. The more carefully you shop, the more readily you'll see that better quality costs more. Only you can decide whether the better quality is affordable and worth the price for you.

- ☐ *Bargain items.* If you're handy with a paintbrush, you might find that unfinished wood furniture offers you better value for your money. Secondhand furniture in good condition and ''seconds'' (new furniture with minor flaws) can also be feasible alternatives in furnishing your dwelling.

Guarantees.   What protection do you have if something goes wrong: a leg comes unglued, fabric comes detached from the frame, cabinet door hinges fall off? Better furniture dealers will usually guarantee to fix or replace defects not due to normal wear and tear. Determine how long such a guarantee lasts. ''Cash and carry'' stores may offer little or no guarantee; you may be totally on your own if something goes wrong. To erase any possible doubts, ask about the guarantee before you decide on your purchase, and then have it put in writing.

Delivery and setup charges.   Some furniture dealers will deliver and set up your furniture at no additional charge. (The cost of doing so is no doubt built into the price of the furniture.) Other dealers may charge. Still other dealers, such as the warehouse and factory outlets, may not offer delivery service at all. Depending on where you live and how easy the access is to the rooms into which the furniture will be placed, delivery and setup charges can add considerably to your overall cost. Shop these charges as carefully as you do the furnishings themselves. Naturally, if you have access to a truck and some strong-armed helpers, you can save considerably by arranging for your own delivery and setup.

Shopping tips.   Don't guess on color or size. If you guess wrong, you could end up with an expensive purchase that doesn't suit you. If you are buying pieces to go into an already partially furnished room, take color samples of the carpet, wallpaper, paint, and drapes with you to furniture stores. If that's not convenient, ask the furniture dealer whether he can give you a color swatch of the pieces you are interested in to take home and match against the existing room. Take careful measurements before you shop. Draw your room to scale on graph paper and test out different arrangements. Most large stationery stores sell plastic cut-out templates showing various sizes and types of furniture. This can be a handy tool to help you determine what pieces of what size can go where in any given room. If you are considering buying ''movable'' furniture—convertible sofas, reclining chairs, expanding tables—make sure you measure properly for both the basic and expanded versions of each piece.

Take your time. Acting on impulse can be dangerous, as it is with any kind of shopping. Visit many stores, looking for those whose reputation and inventory suit your budget. Scour the ads for sales: The home furnishing market is very sale-prone, and the best buys are available to those who are patient and willing to hunt.

Bedding (Springs and Mattresses)

The general consensus of consumer testers is that quality pays in bedding. A well-constructed box spring and mattress can last twenty years, perhaps even longer, without deterioration in support or comfort. An off-brand product may cost 20 to 30 percent less than a major brand, but it may last only half as long. Evaluate the choice accordingly. Major manufacturers and dealers often offer sales on bedspring and mattress items that are similarly constructed but do not have matching covers.

Since you see the mismatched covers only when you take off the sheets, there's no reason not to take advantage of these special buys when available.

Carpeting and Other Flooring

The varieties and price ranges of carpeting and floor coverings are limitless. Area rugs, bare polished wood, linoleum, vinyl tile, brick, fake brick, stone, fake stone, ceramic tile, adobe tile, and carpeting ranging from synthetic grass to luxuriously thick wool represent but a sampling of the possible types of flooring that you can obtain.

Personal taste, budget, durability, and cleanability must all be taken into account when choosing flooring. Of particular concern in making a decision on flooring is the length of time you'll be in the premises. Most types of flooring, once installed, can't be taken with you from place to place. The obvious exception is area rugs. Carpeting, of course, can be removed, but it's usually difficult to install it in a new dwelling: Wear patterns from the original dwelling will be quite evident and perhaps very unsatisfactory. Further, the cost of lifting, moving, recutting, and reinstalling old carpeting in a new dwelling can come close to the cost of new carpeting.

All carpeting and other flooring materials should be shopped for as carefully as furniture. Review all the tips and precautions stated above with respect to furniture. In addition, note that medium shades tend to be the best with respect to not showing soil and dirt, that patterned and multicolored carpeting tends not to show wear patterns as readily as solid-color carpeting, and that different types of carpet fabric have distinctly different levels of soil resistance and cleanability. Check all of these items with the salesperson as you shop. In addition to pricing the carpeting, determine the cost of padding and installation. And check the reputation of the dealer with the Better Business Bureau for reliability and willingness to adjust complaints.

Appliances

What you *need*, what you would *like*, and what you can *afford* are all up to you. Before you make buying decisions, bear in mind the following:

Installation. Will the items (particularly such things as dishwashers, disposals, trash compactors) fit into your existing space? Or will extensive work have to be done to accommodate them? If so, how much will that added work cost? Will any special installation be necessary for any given appliance? An electric clothes dryer may require special wiring. A gas clothes dryer will require a gas line. Both will require a venting outlet. Will you need special drain capacity for a dishwasher or disposal? Is your existing wiring suitable to carry window air-conditioning units? Central air conditioning? A refrigerator with a built-in ice cube maker will require a water line to the site. A gas water heater must be properly vented, as must a kitchen exhaust fan. Determine these special requirements from the dealer, and get cost estimates of the special requirements before you make your buying decision.

Service and Warranties. On major items (clothes washers and dryers, dishwashers, freezers, refrigerators, and room air conditioners) a one-year warranty for parts and labor is common. Additionally, the sealed systems in such units may have warranties for as long as five years. Examine the written warranty before you make a buying decision. Don't be content with just the salesperson's representations. Determine whether the dealer offers warranty service or whether it must be obtained from another source. Determine the reliability of the service source. Check with the local office of the Better Business Bureau.

With smaller units (television sets, food processors, radios and phonographs, video recorders) much shorter warranties are common. With most television sets, the warranty for labor is ninety days, but some may be as long as one year. The warranty on the picture tube and other parts is commonly one to two years. The source of service is again very important. Will the dealer or a nearby service center be able to correct warranty problems? Or will servicing involve time, money, and inconvenience for you?

For example, a comparison of two similar brand-name food processors revealed the following: Though the warranties were identical, one brand had to be sent to a distant state for any warranty servicing, whereas the other could be repaired locally. Should a breakdown have occurred in the first unit, the cost of packing and shipping it, plus the return postage that was required under the warranty, represented more than 10 percent of the original purchase price of the unit. The latter unit could be serviced simply by delivering it to the original dealer, who in turn would arrange to have it sent to and picked up from the local service center.

With most such appliances, you can obtain a service contract to take care of problems once the original warranty has expired. Such service contracts may be worthwhile with more temperamental items that have short initial warranties, such as color television sets; but products such as refrigerators and freezers are constructed to last decades, and any major defects will usually show up during the initial warranty period. For products such as these, extended service contracts may not be worth the money. For items with durability somewhere between that of a refrigerator or freezer and of the more defect-prone color television set, you could almost flip a coin to determine the value of an extended service contract. The cost of an extended service contract for an automatic clothes washer or dryer or a dishwasher or room air conditioner may be less than the cost of one service call. If you're the type that's subject to having mechanical things break down all around you, you might feel more comfortable with the service contract. If you have a knack for being able to lubricate moving parts and the like, you might find a service contract an unnecessary expense.

Periodic servicing of some major appliances is definitely worthwhile if for no other reason than preventive maintenance. Furnaces and central air-conditioning units should be checked and lubricated periodically, filters should be changed, and the entire systems should be checked for leaks. Checkups prior to the heating and cooling seasons, respectively, can be far less expensive, not to mention less inconvenient, than repairing a major breakdown.

Strategies for Success

Consider Renting Instead of Buying

In many circumstances, it might be wiser to rent rather than buy costly household items, particularly furniture. For example, if you'll probably be doing a lot of moving within the next few years, moving your own furniture can become a costly proposition. Most cities have furniture rental companies that can furnish an apartment or house from top to bottom in a few hours and in a wide variety of styles and colors. Also look into rental plans that give you an option to purchase the items.

Buying on Credit

If you haven't yet established credit or if you've had credit problems, you'll likely be attracted to furnishing stores that offer ''easy credit terms . . . no down payments . . . past credit history no problem. . . .'' What appears in the advertising to be ''easy credit'' may indeed be costly. If a merchant or a lender is taking a risk on you, you will be charged accordingly.

Home furnishings represent major budget items, and credit is commonly used to obtain them. Follow the guidelines set forth in Chapter 14, and shop for the best terms available. Consider what financing terms a dealer might offer, and compare those terms with banks and savings and loans in your area. For buyers with no credit or with credit problems, it might be far cheaper to obtain a co-signer for credit purchases rather than get involved with credit companies that charge exorbitant interest rates and that ply their wares at the ''easy credit'' emporiums.

Consumer Information Sources

Consumer Reports magazine is the best single source for learning about and comparing home furnishing items. Visit your local library and review the issues for the last year or two, or go back as far as you have to to find valid comparisons of the item you're planning on buying. Kiplinger's *Changing Times* magazine is another excellent source, though its ratings are not usually as extensive as those in *Consumer Reports*.

With most appliances you can obtain specification sheets from the manufacturer or dealer. These give you abundant information about each product. You should read and compare different brands before you make your decision. Your best source of information is yourself: The more time you're willing to take to compare, to study, and to shop, the better equipped you'll be to make the right buying decision.

Unit Pricing: Prove It to Yourself

See for yourself what savings can be realized by taking advantage of unit pricing. While you're at it, compare brand-name products with private label or generic products. Following are commonly purchased items at markets and drugstores. Add in any other items you often buy. Take a pocket calculator with you to make the exercise simpler.

| | Brand name | | Private label | |
| | Price per ounce | | Price per ounce | |
Item	*Smallest container*	*Largest container*	*Smallest container*	*Largest container*
☐ Mustard				
☐ Ketchup				
☐ Mayonnaise				
☐ Grape jelly				
☐ Peanut butter				
☐ Vegetable oil				
☐ White vinegar				
☐ Tomato juice				
☐ Cornflakes				
☐ Milk				
☐ Cottage cheese				
☐ Sliced cheeses				
☐ Crackers (saltines)				
☐ Canned peas				
☐ Canned pears				
☐ Gelatin				

	Brand name		Private label	
	Price per ounce		Price per ounce	
Item	*Smallest container*	*Largest container*	*Smallest container*	*Largest container*
□ Sugar	————	————	————	————
□ Flour	————	————	————	————
□ Salt	————	————	————	————
□ Aspirin	————	————	————	————
□ Cotton balls	————	————	————	————
□ Witch hazel	————	————	————	————
□ Milk of magnesia	————	————	————	————
□ Antacid tablets	————	————	————	————
□ Toothpaste	————	————	————	————
□ Vitamin E	————	————	————	————
□ Disposable diapers	————	————	————	————
□ Other ————	————	————	————	————
————	————	————	————	————
————	————	————	————	————
————	————	————	————	————

Beating the High Price of Water

Would you pay $4.00 for a gallon of ordinary water? Of course not, you say, but you may have already done so many times. Let's look at an example. The local supermarket offers a six-pack of canned iced tea for $2.29. Six cans of 12 ounces each totals 72 ounces. At $2.29 (not including any sales taxes), that works out to 3.18¢ per ounce. There are 128 ounces in a gallon, so at 3.18¢ per ounce you are effectively paying $4.07 per gallon for canned iced tea. But all you are really getting is ordinary water, with a few cents worth of tea, or tea flavoring, added to it.

Another similar example is juice in cans or in concentrate form. How many quarts of Hawaiian Punch can you make from a jar of the concentrated product? Compare the cost of doing so with buying regular canned Hawaiian Punch. What other products offer you the same choice? If you've been buying the canned instead of the concentrate, how much extra have you been paying to buy water and haul it home from the market?

Paying $4.00 per gallon for ordinary water is, obviously, absurd. It's bad enough to pay $1.50 or so for a gallon of gasoline—but at least that product is capable of propelling a 4000-pound vehicle twenty to thirty miles at speeds in excess of fifty miles per hour. What will the water do by comparison?

It won't do to say that nobody is foolish enough to spend $4.00 for a gallon of water. The product wouldn't be on the market shelves if nobody bought it.

Calculate how much money you might have paid in the last year to buy water at the supermarket. From now on, be a Smart Shopper. Buy the concentrates and use your own tap water. Think of what can be saved, in both money and energy.

CHAPTER 5

Frauds and Swindles: How to Avoid Them

"There's a sucker born every minute," said P. T. Barnum decades ago. And the statement is as true today as it was in his time. Despite all of the consumer-education material available today, there is still an abundance of shady, misleading, and illegal business going on in every community every day. There are schemes that can relieve the unwary and the greedy from a few dollars or from many thousands of dollars. And more often than not, the swindlers get away with their schemes and skip from one city to the next, laughing at their victims all the way. Chances are good that someday you may be a victim of consumer fraud. But you'll have a strong defense against this possibility if you heed the techniques in this chapter:

☐ Spotting and avoiding the deals that sound too good to be true; that promise something for nothing; that promise instant wealth, health, or success

☐ Knowing whom to inform if you discover a fraudulent scheme in the works

☐ Knowing where you can get help if you find yourself the apparent victim of a swindle

BARNUM WAS RIGHT

There are no reliable statistics on the extent of consumer fraud in America today. Neither victims nor swindlers tend to report very much about their transactions. But the Council of Better Business Bureaus has estimated that in one area alone—home improvements—more than $1 billion a year is taken in by swindlers!

Why are there so many victims, and why isn't something more being done about it? No one is immune from the wiles of the con artist or the shady business operator. Young and old, rich and poor, all succumb to one scheme or another at one time or another. Because most business activities are indeed legitimate, we tend to trust people. We believe what we're told. We believe what we read in advertisements. And despite the ever-constant rule of *caveat emptor*, we are not wary enough. If we are led to believe that we are getting something that sounds too good to be true, or something for nothing, we tend to believe it. And we part with our money without even asking questions. Sometimes it's nothing more than our own greed that does us in. Sometimes we are simply gullible—believing all sorts of preposterous statements. And sometimes a salesperson wins our confidence so totally that we act as if we're hypnotized when we write out our checks.

Consumer fraud will never go away. Indeed it may never even diminish. It's not a violent crime. And in many instances it's not even that serious in terms of an individual's financial loss. Thus the citizens of our various cities and states may not be willing to pay the taxes needed to hire adequate police enforcement bureaus to deal with the problem. Further, according to a presidential crime commission study, more than 90 percent of the victims of consumer fraud never do anything about it. The majority of the victims are not even *aware* of the fact that they've been defrauded until it's far too late to do anything about it. Those who may be aware of having been defrauded are reluctant to report it to the police, either out of embarrassment or out of belief that the police won't do anything about it. And that's often the case—not because the police don't want to, but because their available manpower is allocated toward more serious matters. Thus, with few exceptions, promoters and swindlers run free throughout our society, taking advantage of our weaknesses, our greed, our gullibility, and our basically trusting nature.

This chapter explores some of the more common types of consumer fraud. Each type of fraud has endless variations, so don't for a moment think that the schemes described here are the only ones that you might fall victim to. In any kind of transaction, you must be aware of certain *basic patterns* that can indicate that you might be involved in a fraudulent setup. The basic patterns appear in the following situations:

☐ You're led to believe that you're getting something for nothing or are offered a deal that sounds too good to be true. There is no such thing as "something for nothing," and any deal that sounds too good to be true is usually neither good nor true.

☐ A salesperson (or even a stranger) tries to sell you something with such vigor or with such cleverness that you find yourself on the verge of spending money for something that you might otherwise have ignored. In such cases you must immediately ask yourself, "If this thing he's selling is so good and so beneficial, why is he willing to sell it to me? Could it be that he'll get more benefit out of it by selling it to me than I can by buying it from him?"

☐ The advertising or the salesperson tells you that you can obtain something that is not otherwise available through normal channels. This may be a miracle cure for some ailment, a chance to get rich quick, or a chance to become famous. These offerings will do nothing but deplete your bank account.

One final warning before we embark on tales of the wild and woolly world of consumer fraud: While most advertising media (newspapers, magazines, radio, television) attempt to police the advertising that they present to the public, there are definitely flaws in the system. Some policing efforts are not adequate, and misleading advertising can slip past the censor's scrutiny. Further, misleading advertising that appears in an otherwise legitimate medium takes on an aura of legitimacy. "It must be so if it appeared in the daily paper. If it weren't legitimate, the newspaper wouldn't run it." Being constantly alert is no guarantee that you'll never get stung. But *lack* of constant alertness will almost guarantee that you *will* get stung.

BAIT AND SWITCH

Bait and switch is probably the oldest game of all. The bait, very simply, is an extremely attractive enticement to lure you into a store in a buying frame of mind. The switch occurs when you are in the store ready, willing, and able to buy. The clever salesperson diverts you from the bait item and switches you to another item that offers the store a higher profit. The switch can happen in many ways, and even otherwise legitimate merchants often find themselves slipping into this form of deception.

For instance, you're sitting up with insomnia watching the late, late show on television, and here comes good old Gideon Gotcha "out here in automobile land ready to sell you folks some real zing-doozies of some beautiful cars of all makes and models. Here's a 1980 Cadillac with only 1600 miles on it, in perfect condition, with brand-new radial-ply-biased-steel-double-whitewall-hand-autographed tires and a built-in Hammond organ in the back seat! And how much would you expect to pay for this beautiful car? About $15,000? Maybe at some other place, but not at Gideon Gotcha's! Would you believe only $3995!''

Right then you rush down to Gideon Gotcha's where, of course, you find that the lot is closed for the night. You camp on the doorstep until morning, and when Gideon comes in to open up the shop, you hand him an envelope full of cash and tell him you want to buy the $3995 Cadillac you saw on television just a few hours ago.

"Oh, I'm really sorry," says Gideon, "but we sold it during the night. I got a call at my house from an old customer out in the country who insisted on having that very car, and he sent a courier at 4:00 A.M. with the cash. But now that you're here, maybe I can interest you in a brand-new Caddie whose classic beauty will withstand the years better than the Mona Lisa. And since you came down so early in the morning, I could make a special deal for you. . . .''

Or you see an ad in the newspaper for a wholesale meat firm offering an entire side of beef, cut and trimmed to your specifications, for only 79¢ a pound. A fantastic deal! You rush to the place, and the butcher is happy to show you the particular side of beef that they had advertised.

"Of course," he points out, "it's got some funny green spots here and there, but maybe we can cut them out. Anyway, if you boil the meat for fifteen or twenty minutes, it should kill any contamination that may have gone deeper. Now, if you don't like that particular side, we've got some regular sides over here in the cooler for $3.99 a pound.''

Bait-and-switch tactics are outlawed by the Federal Trade Commission as well as by many state and local laws. But they still occur in abundance, and your best protection against getting involved is your own careful scrutiny of the advertising, your willingness to shop around for similar products, and your ability to resist the temptation in the first place.

Distinction should be made between bait and switch on the one hand and "loss leaders" on the other. A *loss leader* is a product offered by a merchant at a lower-than-normal price to entice you into the store where, it's hoped, you'll buy other merchandise as well as the loss leader. Supermarkets and discount stores use loss leaders all the time, and there's nothing wrong with this practice if you are getting the goods as represented and not a cheap replacement.

Where loss-leader advertising is employed, legitimate merchants will note in their advertising any catches in their offering, such as a limited supply, or will make clear that the offer is good only at certain stores or at certain hours. The Federal Trade Commission says that if a loss leader or other kind of promotional product is offered, the merchant is expected to have a sufficient amount on hand to meet what she reasonably expects to be the demand. Many merchants, realizing the value of pleasing their customers, offer rainchecks if they run out of the supply of a loss leader. It might be worth inquiring of the merchant whether rainchecks will be given out should you get to the store and find that the loss-leader items are sold out.

If you detect a bait-and-switch operation in action in your community, alert the newspaper (or radio or TV station) where the advertising was placed. You may also want to notify the local Better Business Bureau and the police department. Very likely, nothing much will be done to the merchant who employed these tactics, but he'll be warned, and he may even promise not to do it again. Until next time.

MAIL-ORDER MADNESS

In terms of both dollar volume and number of incidents, the U.S. Mail probably is the single biggest carrier of fraudulent activity. Although many billions of dollars worth of perfectly satisfactory goods are sold through the mail each year, the level of abuse also runs very high. Mail-order swindlers owe their success not just to the greed and gullibility of victims, but also to the fact that the fraud inspection division of the U.S. Post Office is woefully understaffed. A false or misleading advertisement can cover the country for many months before the postal inspectors are able to gather enough evidence to put a stop to it. In the meantime, the promoters will have made their fortune and disappeared, only to reappear shortly thereafter using a different name and selling a slightly different product. And the chase begins again, with the promoters always the winners.

For purposes of this discussion, mail-order can consist of either an advertisement seen in print, heard in a broadcast, or received in the mail. Either way you are dealing with unknown people, probably in a different city; and if something goes wrong, you're not able to get it corrected as simply as if you were dealing with a local merchant. Many mail-order problems, as opposed to fraud, are simply the result of the wrong product or a defective product being shipped. If you're dealing with legitimate mail-order purveyors, those problems should be fairly easy to correct.

But if you find yourself in the hands of a mail-order swindler, it is safe to assume that there's virtually no chance of your ever getting satisfaction or your money back.

Following is a brief sampling of mail-order swindles, based on actual experience. To determine how cleverly the promoters toy with the minds and bank accounts of potential victims, I became an intentional victim of a number of offerings. The results should speak for themselves.

Vanity Rackets

The price of an ego trip can be high indeed. The vanity rackets prey on the common desire in so many people to be recognized. Ads offer to publish your book, your song, your poem, even your baby's picture in a directory sent to television producers.

Anyone who has ever tried to have a song or a book published through normal channels knows how frustrating it can be: Rejection slips pour in, and it seems as though there's no way ever to achieve success. How wondrous it is, then, when you see an ad by a publisher soliciting your work. "Authors wanted." "Songwriters wanted." Technically the ads may not be illegal—they promise nothing specifically, but the high hopes of victims-to-be lead them to believe that fame and fortune are just around the corner.

In the legitimate publishing world, most books and songs are created by established artists under contract to the publisher. In those rare instances when a publishing company acquires your work, it pays you for the rights to publish.

In the vanity publishing world, the publishers will publish virtually anything, provided you pay them enough money. They may actually deliver printed copies of your book manuscript or produce recordings of your song, but the veiled promises of fame and fortune will never materialize. You will have paid a high price to have your ego massaged.

Do vanity publishers really seek quality? Or will they publish anything that comes in attached to a big enough check? To seek an answer to this question, I wrote an intentionally atrocious song and sent it off to three different vanity music publishers. If they were looking for any kind of quality, they would have rejected my lyrics instantly. They were as follows:

ETHEL IS MY ONLY LOVE
(sing slowly)

Oh oh oh oh Ethel
Ethel Ethel will you be my blessing
Cuz when I look at you and sigh,

It makes me feel high. Oh me oh my.
It seems like only yesterday that we were in high school together.
I can't believe how old we are now, forever.
Oh oh oh oh Ethel
I feel just lousy without you
You are my only love—not Rita anymore.
Seriously, I mean it.
Oh oh Ethel. Yeah yeah yeah.

This drivel was accepted, not once, not twice, but all three times by the vanity publishers. Here is a sample of the letters they sent me:

Dear Mr. Rosefsky:

We have good news for you! Your song has been rated #5 on our top 30 evaluation chart. We sincerely believe that your song poem, with the proper servicing, has the potential for a hit song. We have already contacted nearby publishers, and the response to it was positive. Publishers acceptance seems assured. If you have as much faith in your song as we have, you will want to take advantage of our offer.

Each of the three acceptances requested that I send in approximately $80 to $90 for "servicing" of the song. I inquired what might follow that initial servicing and was told that the next step would be to pay them $200 to $300 for complete scoring or orchestration. Following that, the sky was the limit. I could pay for as many records to be pressed as I wished to, they would distribute them, and I would receive royalties. Legitimate music publishers assured me that the normal channels of distribution were so clogged with the outpouring from legitimate producers that a product from a vanity publisher stood virtually no chance of even having the envelope opened, let alone being played on a radio station or distributed to record stores.

Tabloid newspapers found in supermarkets are perhaps the primary source of potentially fraudulent advertising. It was in one of these publications that I found a small classified ad offering $300 for my baby's picture. On inquiring, I learned that if the baby picture was acceptable, it would be published in a magazine that was distributed to movie and television producers who might be looking for child talent. I sent in a picture of my thirty-year-old cousin, Herbie, who at the time weighed well in excess of 200 pounds. The photo was taken in the midst of an attack of indigestion. The movie magazine accepted the picture for publication provided I send them $12.95. Responsible people in the motion picture and television industries assured me that they had never heard of the magazine, nor would they ever hire talent through such a publication. Yet it's likely that many thousands of checks for $12.95 each were sent to this publication by parents eager to have their children achieve fame and fortune.

Get-Rich-Quick Schemes

How far wrong can you go? You send away $10 or $15 for a book that promises to make you rich almost overnight. And if you don't like it, they promise to send you your money back. These types of ads abound because it's difficult to prove them illegal. You will indeed receive a book. Judging from all those I've seen, it will be a cheaply produced paperback, worth perhaps 50¢, which will attempt to motivate you to think great thoughts, and then instruct you in the ways of becoming rich, for instance, write a similar book of your own, take out full-page ads in newspapers and magazines, and let people send *you* money. You'll also get your name on dozens of other mailing lists, one of which is likely to hit you for big money in the future.

Other types of get-rich-quick schemes are nothing more than blatant chain letters. On inquiring into such ads, you'll receive a letter instructing you to send $30 to a name at the top of an enclosed list. You're then to duplicate this letter five times and put your own name at the bottom of the list. Within weeks, the promoters promise, thousands of people all over the country will be sending you $30. Chain letters, under whatever guise, are illegal: They violate federal postal laws and most state postal laws. They proliferate faster than postal authorities can eliminate them. Not only do such schemes never produce money for you, but they could involve you in a federal lawsuit.

Work-at-Home Schemes

Promises of work at home are more modest versions of the get-rich-quick promotions. They don't promise instant riches but merely a way to supplement your income by working at home in your spare time. They appeal to people who can least afford to lose money—the elderly, the invalid, the poor. Some of these schemes are nothing more than chain letters as described above. Other formats are discussed below.

Addressing Envelopes. You send $20 or so to the promoter and receive a kit instructing you how to address envelopes. You might even receive a sampling of blank envelopes to practice on. You also receive instructions describing how to approach local businesses to sell them your services as an envelope addresser. If you're clever enough and energetic enough, you may be able to acquire some business in this manner. But the fact is you are competing with the business's existing secretarial staff and with professional mailing houses that can turn out thousands of addressed envelopes in the time it would take you to do a few dozen.

Handicraft Kits. For your $10 or $20 you'll receive a kit of materials with instructions on how to turn them into baby booties, key chains, and the like. The promise is that once you've made the finished product, the company will buy it back from you in finished form at a profit to you. You make the seemingly simple product, send it back to the company, only to be told that it's not up to their standards. They're very sorry, they'll say, but perhaps you'd like to try again by ordering another kit.

The postal fraud authorities and the Council of Better Business Bureaus agree: They have never seen a work-at-home scheme that worked, except for the promoters.

Quackery

Do these enticements sound familiar: "Lose weight . . . cure baldness . . . look younger . . . live longer . . . straighten curly hair . . . curl straight hair . . . increase your bust line . . . grow taller . . . improve your sex life"? Sounds like shades of Snake Oil Sam, who sold caramel-flavored alcohol to the gullible from his traveling sideshow wagon.

For example, I once saw an ad that told me that I could grow taller. The cost was $15 with a money-back guarantee if I wasn't satisfied. How far wrong could I go? For my money I received a single sheet of paper with a program of exercises entitled "Erecto-Dynamics." I was instructed to do these simple calisthenics for at least twenty minutes every day for a full year. But most important to the growing taller program was that I should stand up straighter. As for the money-back guarantee, it was contingent upon my having my height verified by a doctor before the start of the year program and at the end. Needless to say, the expense of having a doctor verify my height would be more than the money I'd get back from the promoter.

This type of mail-order business particularly concerns the postal fraud authorities, for, as they point out, not only can you lose money, but your health can be endangered by some of the devices sold. In some cases, people will fail to seek proper medical attention, relying instead on the pufferies of Snake Oil Sam's great-grandchildren. If your condition can't be helped by a doctor, a physical therapist, or a program of exercise under the guidance of a coach, you certainly won't be helped by these mail-order offerings.

FRAUDS ON THE STREET

When you respond to an advertisement, you have at least a few moments to think about the wisdom of doing so. But when you're confronted by a stranger on the street, the surprise element alone can often be enough to embroil you in a money-losing proposition.

The Pigeon Drop

The pigeon drop is a classic scheme having dozens of variations. In a typical operation, an elderly person is approached by a stranger in a shopping center or on a street corner. The stranger chats with the victim for a few minutes to win his friendship and confidence. Then the stranger announces that he has just found a wallet on a nearby bench, and the wallet contains a lot of money but no identification.

The stranger usually suggests that the law of "finders keepers" prevails in such cases and offers to split the finding with the newfound friend, the victim. At this point the victim is so taken in by the con artist's friendship and generosity that the victim will do almost anything the con artist advises. The con artist then quickly suggests that before they split the loot, they should double-check the legality with a lawyer, and that the victim, in order to show good faith, should put up an equal amount of cash and let the lawyer hold it while a decision is made concerning who is entitled to the money.

At this point it sounds totally ludicrous that the victims would put up the cash, but they do time and time again—and it's often thousands of dollars that are involved. As soon as the victim delivers the cash, the whole package is left with the con artist's "lawyer," who promptly disappears. The victim's money? Gone in a flash. Why elderly people? They tend to be more easily won over by the confidence game, they're more likely to have a substantial amount of cash in a savings account, and they're less likely to give chase. But no one is excluded from the potentials of the pigeon drop.

Phony Goods

Peddling phony merchandise is done mostly during the Christmas season, but it can pop up at any time, in any place. The scheme is decisive in its swiftness and simplicity. You're approached by a stranger on the street offering to sell you anything from watches to jewelry to perfume to a color TV set "still in the carton." The price is too good to be true, a real steal. It won't be until you get the item home, or until after the salesperson has disappeared, that you find that the watch has no innards, the perfume is kerosene, the jewelry is cut glass, and the color TV set still in the carton is nothing more than a wooden box. Similar shenanigans can take place at flea markets and swap meets.

If you do fall prey to such a scheme, you can be certain that you will not be able to get your money back. If you are able to find the seller, she'll deny ever having seen you, and it's unlikely that the police will bother to assist you in what they would consider a relatively petty matter.

FRAUDS IN THE HOME

You don't always have to go out seeking con artists. Sometimes they'll come to you, either knocking on your door or calling on the telephone. As with street schemes, the element of surprise works in favor of con artists. They are prepared to sell you something, and you're totally unprepared for their pitch. And since they are coming to you rather than you going to their place of business, you have no way of knowing if you can ever find them again if things go wrong.

Bank Examiner Swindle

You receive a call or a visit from someone who represents himself to be a bank examiner, a bank officer, or some type of governmental official looking into a problem at your bank. You might be told, for example, that the bank suspects one of the tellers of embezzling money. You're asked if you would cooperate with the authorities, go to the bank, withdraw a substantial sum of cash, give it to the so-called official, who will then redeposit it immediately into your account. They assert that in so doing, they can tell whether the accused teller is guilty of embezzlement. If you fall for such a swindle, you will never see your money again. Banking and law enforcement officials state most emphatically that representatives of banks or governmental agencies *never* call on the public in matters of this type, nor would they ever suggest that money be withdrawn from an account. If you are approached by anyone suggesting that you do so, contact the police immediately.

A close cousin of the bank examiner scheme is the social security inspector scheme. The so-called inspector comes to your house to inquire whether you have enough money to live on. She wants to help you in case you don't. She may request that she see the money you have. If you've got some put away in the cookie jar and give it to her for even a moment to count, say goodbye to it. She'll either use her nimble fingers to switch your money for a phony packetful, or she'll simply run out the door and be gone.

In any of these cases, don't be fooled by seemingly official-looking credentials. They are easily forged, and you wouldn't know what the real ones looked like in the first place.

Dump-and-Run Tactics

A truck pulls into your driveway, and the driver offers to spread a layer of slick new blacktop coating on your driveway for a modest sum of money—perhaps only $50 to $100. He tells you that he's just done the same for the supermarket parking lot a few blocks away and that he has a little of the goop left over. Then he says he wants to pass on a good deal to the local neighbors. If you fall for such a trick, he'll indeed put the black goop on your driveway, where it will look nice and slick until the next rain. It will wash off onto your lawn and remain there throughout the following seasons. You'll have paid an excessive sum of money for a few dollars worth of oil. And it will be a costly nuisance to get it out of your lawn. Bulk fertilizer is another commodity used in the dump-and-run scam.

A fast-moving dump-and-run operator can clear $1000 in an easy working day, and he's on to the next neighborhood. In a week he can earn $5000, and he's off to the next town. These facts alone should serve as clear warning.

Home Improvement Swindles

Our homes are our castles. They're also among the favorite targets for swindlers. Not only are the stakes quite large in home improvement frauds, but the confusion and legal consequences can be devastating. Note the similar patterns that emerge in the following three case histories—stories that might almost be amusing if, in fact, they were not true.

The Squirrels. An elderly widow lived alone in a large three-story house surrounded by old overhanging oak trees. Though she was financially secure, the loneliness of her days left her an easy mark for the person who could win her confidence.

The home improvement salesperson who appeared at her door was trained to win her confidence instantly; in this instance he succeeded by complimenting her on her beautiful grandchildren, whose pictures were on her fireplace mantle. She soon told him of a grave concern of hers: She had antique furniture stored in her attic, and she was worried that the squirrels living in the overhanging oak trees would gain access to her attic and gnaw the furniture into ruins. The salesperson had a ready solution: He would install "squirrel deflectors" on her roof. These would be aluminum panels that would reflect the sunlight. He told her that when the squirrels tried to jump from the trees to the roof, they would be blinded by the reflected light and would fall to the ground. The elderly widow couldn't sign the contract fast enough, and indeed the deflectors were installed. The price: $1500. The installation turned out to be defective; serious damage was done to the roof; and a legitimate roofer had to repair the damage at considerable additional cost. Needless to say, the whole idea of squirrel deflectors was rather insane, but the widow couldn't resist, since she had such a sense of confidence in the salesperson.

Strategies for Success

Listen for the "Uh-oh" Music

Film makers use this gimmick to increase your sense of anticipation: Just before the monster leaps out of the closet, or just before the bad guys ambush the good guys, you'll hear "uh-oh" music, that is, music that signals that something bad or frightening is about to happen. Most of us, if we're reasonably cautious, have a sixth sense that plays "uh-oh" music in our minds before we find ourselves on the brink of being swindled. The melody may differ from time to time, but the lyrics are generally the same: "This sounds like something too good to be true. How far wrong can I go?" Listen for the "uh-oh" music. It's telling you to beware. And most of the time it's right on cue.

The Furnace. An innocent homeowner was approached by a succession of rip-off artists as follows:

Day one: A young lad offers to clean out his furnace for a very minimal sum of money. The homeowner agrees, the work is done, and the lad is paid.

Day two: A "work inspector" asks the homeowner if he could see the furnace. He is supposedly checking up on the work that his furnace-cleaning crew has been doing in the neighborhood.

Day three: A man representing himself to be a "furnace inspector" asks to see the furnace, having been recommended by the person who appeared the previous day. The furnace inspector flashes credentials to verify his status. Needless to say, he's a phony. He tells the homeowner that the furnace has serious cracks in it and that he must "condemn" the furnace.

Day four: The man from day two returns, telling the homeowner that he is sorry to hear that his furnace has been condemned. But he has a wonderful deal on a new furnace that can be installed immediately at a price that's too good to be true.

The homeowner was confused and distraught over this sequence of events, but he bought the whole scam, hook, line, and sinker. He signed a contract for the new furnace. The contract was immediately sold to a finance company. The furnace installers left the old furnace in the homeowner's yard prior to removal, and the homeowner had it checked by another furnace company. It was then that he learned that there was nothing at all wrong with the original furnace, but by that time he had no energy to fight the matter any further.

He did not take the time to learn that if merchandise is faulty or defective, Federal Trade Commission regulations permit the buyer to withhold payment to a third party, such as a finance company.

The Model Home. The quick-talking salesperson knocked at the door and told the gullible young couple that their house had been chosen as part of an advertising program. They would receive a "free" aluminum siding job on the house. All they had to do was tell their friends and neighbors and any passersby who had done this magnificent work. Thereby, the home improvement company would receive many referrals, and everybody would be happy. The young couple couldn't sign the contract fast enough.

The work was done, and a month later, to the couple's amazement, they received a bill from a finance company for the first installment on a very expensive contract. Then—too late—they read the contract in detail. It stated quite clearly that they were obliging themselves to pay for the entire siding installation, but that they would receive a discount for every referral they made that resulted in another installation for the company. If they made enough referrals that resulted in enough contracts, then presumably their own job would have cost them nothing.

Is this fraud or not? The contract was explicit but the young couple failed to read it or understand it. It could be said that this was a fair business deal and if the couple didn't understand the terms, they should legally bear the consequences. However, after the end of the second month, the siding began to peel and their ''model home'' began to look a shambles. They called the improvement company to repair the shoddy work, but the company's phone had been disconnected, and they were nowhere to be found. The finance company that had purchased their contract was demanding payment. The couple had to hire a lawyer at considerable cost to attempt to void the allegedly fraudulent contract. They were successful, but they were still out of pocket many hundreds of dollars and had to repair the house at their own expense.

Warning Signals. In addition to the ''too-good-to-be-true'' and ''something-for-nothing'' appeals of the home improvement salesperson, there are some other aspects of the sales presentation that should cause you to be wary.

- ☐ **The ''perfect'' guarantee.** The materials and their installation might be accompanied by an ''unconditional lifetime money-back'' guarantee. The guarantee is only as good as its written statements and the ability of the guarantor to perform. If there is to be a guarantee, it should be spelled out in explicit detail, and you should understand exactly what is and is not guaranteed. Even though the guarantee might appear to be ironclad, how about the ability of the firm to honor it? If they're not in business a month or a year after your job is completed, the best guarantee in the world is meaningless.

- ☐ **Big savings.** There may be representations that the work will save you many hundreds of dollars over what it would cost through other contractors. You can never know this for sure unless you have properly drawn plans and specifications and obtained bids from reputable local contractors. Until you have done that, the salesperson's words are nothing more than puffery.

- ☐ **''Will last forever.''** The salesperson may make representations that the materials, such as aluminum siding, are ''maintenance free forever.'' No substance yet discovered by science and affordable to the average homeowner is maintenance free forever.

- ☐ **''Sign up now or never.''** The salesperson is very anxious to get you to sign a contract right away. She knows that if you don't, and if you have time to think about the deal, she may lose you. This is when the pressure begins. She may try to convince you that getting other prices will be a waste of your time; that her price is certainly the lowest; and that if you don't sign right now, the low price won't be available later. This ''now-or-never'' kind of pressure may sound convincing. When you're dealing with legitimate contractors, there's no job that can't be contracted for a day or so later as well as it can at that moment. If you feel that by not signing right away you're losing out on something special, you had best begin preparing yourself for the worst.

- ☐ **Credentials.** A reputable home improvement contractor's past history will speak for itself. You can visit his place of business, and you can talk to customers who have used his services. The shady home improvement promoter will make a big fuss about his credentials. He may have become a member of the Chamber of Commerce and the Better Business Bureau in your community, and he may well have established a bank account and lines of credit with local suppliers. But all of these credentials don't necessarily mean that he can get the job done properly or that you're getting good value for your money. It can indeed be difficult to spot the credential-laden con artist from the honest businessperson since such credentials apply equally to both. It's necessary for you to look beyond the credentials and to try to spot the other warning signals.

☐ *Brand names.* Another ploy used to gain respectability involves the use of major brand names by the promoters. There have been hundreds of cases in recent years involving improvement swindlers using the names of national firms to convince customers that they themselves are legitimate. The impression given is that the promoter is in direct alliance with the manufacturer, with the implication being that such national firms certainly wouldn't condone anything but the highest quality workmanship with regard to their products and that the salesperson must thus be of the highest repute.

In fact, anyone can go out and buy most of these name-brand products. Many homeowners have been bilked, believing that the contractor will use such brand-name products, only to find when the job is done that inferior brands were used.

Avoiding Home Improvement Rackets. Unless you are absolutely certain of a contractor's reputation and integrity, you must follow the following steps if you want to avoid being swindled on a major home improvement project:

1. Do not sign any home improvement contracts unless you have prepared or received firm, clear, detailed plans and specifications.

2. Do not sign any home improvement contracts until you have received comparable bids from local reputable contractors based on those plans and specifications.

3. Do not sign any home improvement contracts until you have had the documents checked by an attorney.

4. Do not sign any home improvement contracts until you have discussed with your banker the overall financing of the project.

If you want the job done right and if you want to get the most for your money, there are no shortcuts around these steps. It might seem like a lot of work, but when you consider that you may be spending thousands of dollars and risking damage to your house should you hire unqualified people, it should be worth the effort.

INVESTMENT SCHEMES

"Here's the deal, with a rock solid guarantee: You give me your money—$1000 . . . $5000 . . . $10,000 . . . whatever—and if at any time you're unsatisfied with what I'm doing with it, just let me know, and I'll immediately return the unused portion thereof."

Who would fall for an offer like that? You'd be surprised. When it comes to the area of investments—making your money grow—greed and gullibility reach their peak. The opportunities for fraudulent activities are infinite. The fast-buck artists promise instant fortunes and huge tax savings in stocks, commodities, gold, silver, gemstones, land, and virtually anything else that might capture a victim's attention. You might be solicited through the mail or through advertising, but one of the most common and insidious media used by investment promoters is the telephone.

Strategies for Success

Protect Yourself with Second, Third Opinion

If someone is trying to sell you something, no matter how convincing the sales pitch may sound, you must remember that the seller stands to benefit from making the sale. Maybe the seller will benefit more than you, the buyer. This can be especially so if what's being pitched is a fly-by-night investment scheme. Before you part with your money or before you sign a contract, get a second opinion on the matter from someone who is not selling anything and who has no axe to grind. Protect yourself even more by getting a third opinion. The more money at stake, the more this strategy will save you.

Boiler Room Operations

In a typical boiler room operation, a fleet of fast-talking, hard-driving salespersons telephone would-be victims all across the country, offering their latest and greatest miracle for getting wealthy. How will they have gotten your name? Very likely from mailing lists: If you subscribe to any financial periodicals or if you have bought any money-related products such as books or other investment offerings, your name will be on those lists and will be sold by the list owner to all comers.

Following is a replica—with little exaggeration—of what you're likely to hear if you receive a telephone call from a boiler room operation:

"Good morning, Mr. Rosefsky. This is J. Fairly Nicely of Mammoth Investments on Wall Street. If you can give me just three minutes of your time, I'd like to tell you about a way that you can double your money within six months. Would you be interested in hearing about that? . . . Mammoth has been authorized to sell a private placement of stock in Amalgamated International—you've heard of them, of course—they've just discovered one of the world's largest linoleum deposits, and mining of the linoleum is expected to start next week. I'm authorized to offer you 500 shares at $10 per share, but the offer is good only for the next hour. Now get this: We know for a fact that the big brokerage firm—Merrill-Lynch-Hutton-Shearson-Bache-Webber—is going to the market with a public offering six months from now, and we have just confirmed that the offering price will be $20 per share. You'll double your money in six months, but you've got to buy now. Could you hold on just a moment, my other phone is ringing. [You now hear him supposedly talking on another phone.] Yes, Mr. Rockefeller, we still have some shares left in the linoleum venture. How many would you like? . . . Yes, Mr. Rockefeller . . . 200 shares at $10 apiece . . . that'll be fine, I'll have the paperwork in the mail before the end of the day. Now, Mr. Rosefsky, as I was saying, I just sold 200 shares, so I can offer you only 300, but if you really want the 500, maybe I can arrange for it. . . . You seem hesitant; is there any reason why you wouldn't want to double your money in six months?''

Yes, people do run to their checkbooks and send money to J. Fairly Nicely and his ilk without hesitation or fear. And that's probably the last they'll ever see of it. But that's not the last they'll hear of J. Fairly Nicely, for he'll sell their name to other boiler room operations, and some other day, in some other way, they'll be offered a partnership in a veal farm, a future interest in a grove of tarantula trees, or syndication rights on a herd of prize-winning Naugahydes.

The con artist's spiel is so frenetic that it doesn't give the victims time to think about anything other than doubling their money. If the would-be victim did stop to think, the first thought that might cross her mind would be: ''If this deal is so good, how come you're selling it to me? Why don't you just keep it all yourself?'' If that question is asked of the salesperson, the answer will be: ''I've hocked my house, my family, and my gold fillings to raise every penny I could to buy into this. And with every penny I make on my commissions, I'm buying more. I can't buy enough of it. In six months I'll retire on my fortune. I can't buy it all, but I'm buying all I can.'' He may even sound all choked up at this point.

Your best defense against the wiles of the boiler room operator is to take advantage of a technical device built into your telephone. Alexander Graham Bell, in his great wisdom, saw fit to include this item for the benefit of those being pestered by boiler room operators. It's called the hang-up button. It works like a charm.

Ponzis and Pyramids

Charles Ponzi was a hustler who plied his skills in Boston during the 1920s. He so popularized an ancient scheme that it has carried his name ever since—the Ponzi scheme. It was simple, straightforward, and attracted victims like a magnet. It worked like this:

Ponzi told victims, ''You give me $100 today and in thirty days I'll give you back $120.'' Thirty days later he did just that. His own initial investment of $20 paid off, since he now had avid believers who would do exactly what he said. ''Want to try it again for another thirty days?'' The first wave of investors took the plunge again. Ponzi had no trouble soliciting a second wave of investors, and he used their money to pay off the first wave. Then he would solicit a third wave and use their money to pay off the second wave, and so on, until one day Ponzi simply took the money and ran.

A Ponzi scheme, then, is in essence a plan whereby new investors are constantly solicited and their money is used to pay off older investors. Keeping the investors happy keeps the money pouring in, but at some time the promoter will skip.

Closely related to the Ponzi scheme is the pyramid scheme, which is the basis for chain letters and multilevel distributorships. The promoters who start these schemes can make money, but at the risk of jail sentences, for the schemes can be illegal and in many states a criminal offense. Here's how the concepts work: You have to pay money to someone to get in on the action. You are then entitled to seek money from others, who would be below you in the pyramid. As each of these new players pays you, they, in turn, solicit others below them. This might involve a simple exchange of money. Or it might involve a business venture in which participants receive territories or licensing rights for the money they have paid out.

Each participant's success in such schemes depends on her ability to enlist an array of subparticipants. If you carry the concept to its logical conclusion, you can quickly see how foolish it is. For example, you buy into a scheme. Then, in order to recoup your investment and make a profit, you have to enlist ten other people. Each of these ten people must then enlist ten additional people, and on it goes. If you carry this out mathematically to the tenth level down, you'll see that ten billion people will have to be involved in the pyramid for everyone to be satisfied. That's double the population of the entire earth.

Pyramid schemes collapse because they run out of people who are willing to participate, and the victims find that their names never move up high enough on the list to recoup their often heavy investment.

Land Frauds and Time Sharing

Will Rogers once said, "Land is the best investment there is cuz they ain't going to print no more of it." Tens of thousands of people have taken that remark seriously and have lost uncounted hundreds of millions of dollars on land swindles. They may not have realized that Will Rogers was a comedian. A lot of his remarks were said in jest, and this statement may have been one of his biggest jokes.

Rogers' statement, amplified by land salespersons, implies that we all ought to rush out and buy land before there is no more left to buy. A prudent purchase of land for investment or future building purposes takes time and careful study and does involve some risk. (See Chapter 18 for a more detailed discussion.) But a rush to buy land—as urged by the salesperson—means impulse, and impulse means a high probability of mistakes. If you don't buy this week, this month, or this year, there's going to be plenty still available next year or next decade. Yes, the price might be going up, but so does the price of everything. So does your income. The price can also go down. It happens every day.

Land fraud schemes flourished in the 1970s and then slowed down as the impact of a newly created federal agency—the Office of Interstate Land Sales Regulation—began to be felt. Unscrupulous salespeople sold unwitting victims worthless swampland in Florida and barren desert in Arizona under the guise of ''future retirement communities,'' ''vacation rancheros,'' and just plain double-your-money-in-a-hurry investment opportunities.

But the swindlers didn't stop their activities just because of the creation of a new federal agency. Many of the land salespeople switched their energies to a new concept that emerged in the 1970s and early 1980s called *time sharing*. The concept of time sharing is certainly legitimate, and indeed there are many reputable time-sharing opportunities throughout the nation. However, abuses have been numerous. In a typical time-sharing situation, you buy the right to use a resort or hotel facility for one or two or more weeks per year. The sales pitches, which are generally very high-pressure affairs, make it appear that this is the bargain of the century.

Abuses occur when the promised facilities are not built in accordance with the original promises, when they are never built at all, or when they are so poorly managed that you can't enjoy them. Sometimes you learn that six other families have purchased the same room for the same time you were to have its exclusive use. Promoters lure would-be buyers to the sales meetings by promising what seem to be expensive gifts, such as television sets, automobiles, and free travel opportunities. Often, however, after sitting through a two-hour presentation, the gift turns out to be a cheap, perhaps worthless, electronic gadget or a travel opportunity that you have to pay a considerable amount of money for. (Chapter 7 contains more information on time sharing.)

All That Glitters . . .

Gold, silver, and precious gems have been the subject of many fraudulent investment schemes in the 1980s, a situation that will likely continue throughout the 1990s. The following are the most common schemes:

- *Counterfeit coins.* Many thousands of counterfeit South African Krugerrands were circulated out of Los Angeles all across the nation. Eager speculators in the gold market snapped them up without making any attempt to determine their legitimacy. In years to come, when these speculators dig out the phony coins to sell, they're in for severe disappointment when potential buyers, smarter than the owners, recognize that the coins are phony.

- *Gold-painted lead.* Tens of millions of dollars are lost by eager gold investors who deal with companies that promise future delivery of gold bullion. Of course, the investors are expected to pay up front. The future deliveries never take place. In a number of cases, when law enforcement agencies stepped in, they found that the bars of supposed gold sitting on shelves in the gold promoters' vaults were nothing more than lead covered with gold paint. The ''gold'' was there to convince curiosity seekers that the bullion was available to the investors.

- *Junk gems.* Countless tons of worthless stones are passed off to gullible buyers as valuable rubies, sapphires, emeralds, and diamonds. Intriguing ads in newspapers and magazines make it appear that phenomenal bargains can be had in these stones. Little do gullible buyers know that they are buying pure junk. Not only that, but once they complete their mail-order transactions, their names are sold to countless other mailing lists. The more mailing lists their names appear on, the more inevitable it is that sooner or later they'll fall for yet another scheme.

New High-Tech Opportunities

In this modern era, hardly a month goes by without some startlingly new technological development. Swindlers prey on gullible, innocent investors, luring them into investing in franchises or distributorships that will market the new high-tech items. One such high-tech advancement that was exploited was the cellular car telephone. Investors were offered opportunities to take their chances in a lottery that would award them exclusive territories in which they could sell cellular telephones. Another such venture used the name and endorsement of a popular television personality to lure investors. The whole venture proved a sham, but not until millions of dollars' worth of investors' money was down the drain.

ADVANCE LOAN SCHEMES

In periods of rising interest rates, Snake Oil Sam is adept at filling his pockets through a pitch known as the advance loan scheme. Individuals and businesspeople who are in need of money and who may be having a difficult time borrowing from their normal banking sources are easy prey for this rip-off. In a nutshell, the advance loan scheme promises that you will receive the loan you need if you pay a sizable amount of money up front. In effect, the swindler is telling you that this is his commission for getting you the loan. All too often, once the up-front money is paid, the swindler disappears into the night with your money, neither one to be seen again.

CREDIT REPAIR CLINICS

People who have fallen for the advance loan scheme are just as likely to fall for the credit repair clinics. These appeal to people who have more debt than they can handle or who have bad credit histories that hinder their getting credit when needed. Unscrupulous credit repair clinics promise to relieve you of your debt problems and restore your credit-worthiness, for a large sum of money, of course. As you can no doubt guess at this point, the up-front money you pay can readily disappear without your getting any benefit from it.

SOURCES OF HELP
FOR FRAUD VICTIMS

The sad fact is that if you do become a victim of a fraudulent scheme, there's little chance you'll get your money back unless you're willing to spend a lot of time and a lot more money on legal fees. And even if you are willing to spend money on legal fees, you can't sue someone you can't find: The con artist knows how to disappear quickly and totally.

Even though the chances of getting your money back may be slim, you still should take action if you believe you've been defrauded. If nothing else, your action may help put a stop to certain fraudulent practices, thus benefiting your fellow citizens. And if they do the same, their actions will benefit you. Here are the main sources of possible help:

Federal Trade Commission

This is a governmental agency charged with many areas of responsibility including deceptive business practices. The FTC is based in Washington and has regional branches in Atlanta, Boston, Chicago, Cleveland, Dallas, Kansas City, Los Angeles, New Orleans, New York, San Francisco, and Seattle. FTC officials emphasize, however, that they are not in a position to represent individual consumers.

Information regarding possible deceptive practices can come to the attention of the FTC in a number of ways. Complaints from individual consumers are probably the predominant way. In addition, newspaper clippings and complaints from other businesspeople also supply information.

The FTC does not have the staff or the funds to investigate every complaint that comes to its attention. When there is enough frequency of a certain type of complaint against a given company, the investigative staff may look into it. If, after due investigation, the FTC has reason to believe that a deceptive practice has occurred, the agency will call this to the attention of the alleged offender and attempt to work out what is called a *consent order*. A consent order is a rather curious document in which the alleged offender promises not to do what he has been accused of doing but in which he does not admit that he was guilty of doing it. In other words, in effect, he's not guilty but he promises he won't do it again. If he does violate the consent order, serious punishment can follow. If the offender does not feel he has done anything wrong and does not want to sign a consent order, the matter must proceed to the law courts.

From the time that consumer complaints start trickling in until the time a consent order or court determination is obtained, many months can elapse. If an out-and-out fraudulent activity has been underway, the perpetrator may have long since vanished by the time the consent order is issued.

If the FTC is limited in its powers, it is even more limited by a closed-mouth public. This federal agency can function only if it gets the input from the public. Lacking that input, it has nothing to go on. While it may serve little purpose in your own situation to alert the FTC to a deceptive business practice, doing so could aid the agency on the broader scale of bringing such practices to an end.

U.S. Postal Service

Contact the Mail Fraud Division of the U.S. Postal Service if you suspect that the U.S. mails have been used to perpetrate a fraud. As with the FTC, the postal service is limited due to a lack of available money and employees to track down every complaint, but it does what it can. The more complaints there are on a given matter, the better chance the postal service has of obtaining a satisfactory conclusion.

State and Local Governmental Agencies

All fifty states have some form of consumer-protection office. Frequently it's associated with the attorney general's office. Many large cities also have consumer-protection agencies. As with the aforementioned federal agencies, lack of money and available staff deter these agencies from being able to assist you in getting satisfaction in a fraudulent situation, but they should be immediately contacted anyway, and given all pertinent details. If there seems to be any hope at all of apprehending the promoters, your local police or sheriff's office should also be contacted.

In addition to governmental agencies, there are a number of nongovernmental sources of possible assistance.

Your Local Newspapers and Broadcast Services

Newspapers, radio stations, and television stations throughout the nation have been doing an ever-expanding job of surveillance and reporting on consumer fraud. These columns and reports are provided at considerable expense by the media as a public service. Very often they're able to resolve matters right on the spot.

Better Business Bureaus

Better Business Bureaus can be helpful before the fact: A call to your local BBB prior to entering into a transaction might disclose whether the person you're dealing with has a record of complaints with the bureau. BBB personnel might also be able to give you general guidelines concerning certain types of suspect business endeavors. The BBB might also be able to provide arbitration services to help you iron out a dispute you have with a local business. If you're dealing with a business located in another city, you would be well served to contact the Better Business Bureau in that city to determine whether the firm has a clean record. Understand that if a business has a clean record with the BBB, it does not necessarily mean that all is on the up and up. The clever con artist knows how to keep his BBB record clear. He also knows how to time his activities cleverly enough so that he can be out of town before the complaints begin hitting the BBB office.

Financial Institutions

Banks, savings and loan associations, credit unions, and consumer finance companies are all actively involved on a day-to-day basis with the flow of IOUs generated from all kinds of business activities. If a deceptive practice is under way, alerting these institutions could help bring an end to the activity. Such institutions might be involved in buying fraudulently induced IOUs. Tens of thousands of dollars' worth of paper can be generated before anyone is aware that a fraud is in the works. The sooner the institutions know of it, the sooner they can stop buying the IOUs, and that can be the death knell for the fraudulent endeavor.

Your financial institution can also be of help to you if you consult them regarding your own financial situation before you get involved in signing any contracts. The astute loan officer might spot trouble in a situation that you might not otherwise be aware of.

Small Claims Court

Your local small claims court can be of assistance in settling a claim of fraudulent or improper business practices, *if* you can locate the party who has wronged you. Small claims courts differ from place to place, but in general you do not need a lawyer to represent you. If the amount of money involved in a claim exceeds a certain limit (perhaps $750 or $1000, depending on the court), the small claims court will not hear your case. Contact your local court to determine their rules and procedures.

Common Sense: A Tasty Recipe

Take one heaping enticement of ''get rich quick!'' or ''earn big money fast!'' or ''something for nothing!''

Add one flickering reaction of ''how far wrong can I go?'' or ''what have I got to lose?''

Fold in one prevailing attitude of ''it can't happen to me!''

Simmer well.

This is the recipe upon which the wild and wooly world of consumer fraud is based. No one is immune. Your common sense is your best defense against getting involved and losing money. If you are to be a successful consumer and manager of your finances, heed the following cautions:

1. Analyze your needs and desires before you make a commitment to buy anything.
2. Obtain a basic knowledge of the product you're seeking to buy.
3. Compare the product you're interested in with that offered by other manufacturers and retailers.
4. Study carefully the guarantee behind the product, as well as the reputation of the manufacturer and retailer.
5. Realistically analyze your financial ability to obtain the item, and shop carefully for financing arrangements.
6. Take prompt and appropriate action in the event that the product or service does not live up to your expectations or up to the representations made by the seller.

Fraud-Avoidance Techniques

This is a two-part exercise. First, ask yourself the following questions—and jot down reasonable answers—before you enter into any dealing with persons whose reputations are uncertain or unknown. Having read this chapter and answered the questions honestly, your choice should be clear.

Second, obtain and write down for future reference the local telephone numbers of the indicated consumer-protection sources.

1. If I'm not satisfied with the product or service I get from this person, what assurance do I have that I'll be able to get my money back?

2. Does this deal sound too good to be true, or does it seem that I'm going to be getting something for nothing?

3. Am I being pressured to sign up or to buy right away, lest I lose the chance forever?

4. If the secret method (or investment technique, etc.) is so good, why is the salesperson selling it to me? Could it be that she will make more money by selling it to me than I can make by buying it?

5. Have I checked with the appropriate consumer-protection sources to learn what I can about the company?

6. Do I really need the product or service that's being sold? And can I get it through other sources without any worry about satisfaction?

Telephone Numbers:

Better Business Bureau

City, State Consumer Protection Agency

Small claims court

Consumer journalists (radio, TV, newspaper)

Federal Trade Commission (nearest office)

Learning to Say No
Can Save $$$$$$$$

While many good products are sold door to door, there are also many flimflams conducted in that mode. Your best protection is to learn how to say no. An old friend, best known as Sybil the Intrepid, had a way of saying no with such style and flair that anyone can benefit from her tactics. Here is how Sybil the Intrepid once handled a door-to-door vacuum cleaner salesperson:

Sybil: Oh, I've heard about your product, and I understand it's simply marvelous. I'd like you to give me a demonstration right now, but first I must see your identity card.

Salesperson: (enthusiastically) No problem. Here's my card from the company.

Sybil: No, that's not what I meant. I meant your *identity* card.

Salesperson: (now slightly flustered and confused) Well, here's my driver's license . . . my voter registration card . . . my library card. . . .

Sybil: (deceptively calmly) No, no. Those aren't what I mean. I mean your *identity* card. Your card that verifies you aren't a member of the Communist Party.

Salesperson: (now almost apoplectic) But I've never heard of such a thing. I don't have such a card.

Sybil: (with a straight face that would make your hair curl) There, there now. That's all right. You just come back anytime with your proper identity card, and I'd love to have you demonstrate your vacuum cleaner. We just can't let Communists in the house. You understand, I'm sure. Bye now. (the door closes ever so gently)

CHAPTER 6

Transportation

"Urban sprawl" is a very accurate way of describing today's typical American city, whether large or small. We have a lot of space to use, and we've used it. In the process, we've put a lot of distance between our homes, our places of work, our shopping centers, our recreational facilities. "Getting there" used to be no problem in the days when cars, gasoline, and mass transit were relatively inexpensive (pre-1973). But today the cost of moving about is a serious matter and must be taken into account in anyone's financial planning. This chapter will help you solve the common problems you face in trying to keep your transportation expenses in line.

☐ Should you buy a car, and if so, what kind is right for you?

☐ How do you deal with car dealers?

☐ What kind of financing arrangement is best for you?

☐ How much car insurance should you have, and how much will it cost?

☐ What is your car warranty worth?

☐ What are your alternatives to buying a car?

CARS: AN EVER-INCREASING EXPENSE

The average cost of owning, financing, operating, and insuring an automobile is now about 35¢ for each mile driven, and it is rising. This means

☐ If you drive a mile or two to pick up a loaf of bread at the supermarket, the cost of getting to the market and back will be higher than the cost of the bread itself.

☐ If you drive around the block a few times looking for a parking space, you could spend as much money as you would have if you had parked in a paid lot.

□   That inexpensive treat of not so many years ago—the weekend drive in the country—can now cost you $20, $30, $40.

□   If you drive a twenty-mile round-trip commute to work, it's costing you $35 per *week* to get to your job and back.

In short, getting from point A to point B—particularly by automobile—is an expensive proposition. If you were driving before October 1973—when a gallon of gas was less than 50¢ and a well-equipped, medium-sized car could be purchased for about $4000—today's high costs are still difficult to comprehend. If you didn't start driving until after October 1973, you won't remember how much driving used to be taken for granted.

That fateful date—October 1973—was when the oil-exporting countries began doubling, tripling, and quadrupling oil prices. Not only did that cause the price of gas at the pump to begin a crazy upward spiral, but it also did the same to the cost of manufacturing cars. The cost of delivering the raw materials (steel, rubber, glass, etc.) to the manufacturing site increased proportionately, as did the cost of delivering the finished car to the dealership. And as manufacturing and delivery costs skyrocketed, so did the cost of the cars themselves, as did the financing costs for both the dealer and the buyer.

Yet, while the auto becomes more and more of a luxury, decades of conditioning have patterned much of our lives around it: Getting to work, shopping, school, recreation all depend largely on the availability of a car. In many cities, mass transit provides a less costly (and often less convenient) alternative. To the more adventuresome, motorcycles and mopeds provide a less costly (and less safe) alternative. To the energetic, bicycling, walking, and jogging may be the best alternatives of all.

The cost of driving cannot be taken for granted any longer. For most, it's a major budget item, and an increase or decrease in your driving can have a definite bearing on the rest of your budget. If you are choosing a dwelling or seeking a job, the cost of commuting must definitely be calculated. As noted above, a twenty-mile daily round trip commute can cost $35 a week, or $150 per month. That $150 per month in commuting costs is the same that you'd pay on $18,000 worth of mortgage at a 10 percent fixed annual interest rate. In other words, if you didn't have to drive to and from work, the $150 per month in commuting costs could be used to pay off an $18,000 higher mortgage on your home.

Your overall ability to make ends meet and manage your money prudently requires that you keep your driving to a minimum and that you utilize all means of less expensive transportation whenever possible (car pooling, mass transit).

Operating Costs

Of course 35¢ per mile is an approximation. It's based on a small-sized car being driven 15,000 miles per year and kept for four years. Because so much depends on individual circumstances, it's very difficult to arrive at an exact figure for the cost of a car, but the 35¢ price can be used as a fairly reliable average guideline. It takes into account the following:

□ The depreciation (difference between the purchase price and what it might be worth when you later sell it or trade it in)

□ Operating and maintenance costs (including tuneups, oil, tires, lubrication, and average necessary repairs)

□ Interest (presuming that the car is financed for an average of three years)

□ Taxes and fees (including sales tax, property taxes, registration, titling fee, license costs, necessary inspections)

□ Insurance (public liability, collision, comprehensive)

□ Gasoline (the amount of which can vary considerably depending on your driving habits and your maintenance of the automobile)

The following factors affect the cost per mile of driving your car:

Equipment. The cost, the weight, and the usage of optional equipment can have a distinct bearing on your overall operating costs. Example: An air-conditioning unit is one of the more expensive optional extras that can be installed in a car. The cost can exceed $700. In addition, the cost of registration, insurance, and interest will increase accordingly. And further, the use of the air conditioning can decrease your gas mileage by as much as 12 percent (see Table 6-1).

Maintenance. Proper regular tuneups can improve your gas mileage by almost 13 percent (see Table 6-1). Proper tire inflation and rotation can also improve gas mileage as well as the overall ridability of the car. And a periodic "trouble-shooting" checkup by a reliable garage can help prevent costly problems before they occur.

Table 6-1   **How Speed, Air Conditioning, and Tuneups Can Affect Gas Mileage**

	Speed				
Miles per gallon	*30 mph*	*40 mph*	*50 mph*	*60 mph*	*70 mph*
With air conditioner on	18.14	17.51	16.42	15.0	13.17
With air conditioner off	20.05	19.71	18.29	16.23	14.18
MPG increase with air conditioner off	10.5%	12.6%	11.4%	8.33%	7.7%
Before tuneup	19.3	18.89	17.29	15.67	13.32
After tuneup	21.33	21.33	18.94	17.40	15.36
MPG increase after tuneup	10.5%	12.9%	9.54%	11.04%	15.3%

Source: U.S. Department of Transportation, 1984.

Insurance. The number of cars on your auto insurance policy, the number of drivers, and the safety record of the drivers can have a major effect on your car insurance costs. The section on car insurance later in this chapter explores these matters in greater detail.

Driving habits. Hot-rodding, drag racing, excessive speeding, and jack-rabbit starting can diminish your gas mileage and also create more wear and tear on the basic mechanical aspects of the car. It may seem like fun, but it's going to cost you.

Knowledge. Knowing how to buy right, finance right, and insure right can definitely save you money. The more you know about the care and maintenance of your car, and the more of it that you can do yourself, the more money you'll save. A car care book or a short course in basic car maintenance can be an investment that pays for itself many times over each year.

BUYING A CAR

Individual tastes, habits, needs, and budgets being as different as they are, there is no fast rule of thumb that describes the "best" buy for anyone's dollars. And with an almost infinite variety of cars to choose from—differing in age, condition, size, equipment, and cost—even general guidelines are difficult to set forth. The following considerations, however, weighed carefully as you shop, can help you find the vehicle that's right for your needs and for your budget.

Needs versus Desires

You must clearly distinguish between your automotive *needs* and your automotive *desires*. The difference between the two can cost you thousands of dollars with little to show for that money but some chrome, vinyl, and extra things that can go wrong in the car. For generations, American car buyers have been conditioned into believing that the automobile is a reflection of an individual's power, prestige, sex appeal, and success. If you can afford to succumb to that kind of hypnosis, feel free. The other side of the coin—never advertised by automotive manufacturers— is that when people find themselves in a financial jam, very often it's because they're paying far more for their car than their budget realistically can allow them to. If you're willing to sacrifice in other areas (housing, clothing, food, future savings, recreation) for the sake of a more luxurious car, that's your choice. Just be aware of the potential consequences.

In examining your automotive needs, be honest with yourself and with your budget. There are three factors that can boost the price of an automobile, and you must be careful that the price of your automobile does not exceed your ability to pay. These three factors are size, "flair," and optional extras.

☐ How big a car do you really need for the bulk of your driving purposes? Larger cars cost more than comparably equipped smaller cars and can consume considerably more fuel. Can you justify a larger car because of your needs, such as extensive traveling for business purposes or extensive hauling of children, cargo, or other items that take up a lot of space? If you don't need a large vehicle much of the time, consider purchasing a smaller car and renting a large vehicle for those rare occasions when you might need one.

□ "Flair" refers to the sportiness, the "muscle," the luxurious aspects of driving that many people crave. Make no mistake—"flair" is very expensive, and it won't get you from point A to point B more safely or quickly than a basic set of wheels will. It's your choice and your money.

□ Optional extras, in fact, aren't really optional. They're already built into the car, and you can't have them taken out. Optional extras can add $3000 and more to the basic cost of the car, and many of them may be of marginal value. Racing stripes, fancy wheel covers, vinyl roofs, luxurious upholstery, and an assortment of electronic gadgets provide very little in the way of essential transportation. In many cases, they're just something extra to break down, usually after the warranty has expired.

New versus Used

A used car in good mechanical condition can provide you with decent transportation for many years and many tens of thousands of miles at a much lower cost than a similar new model. Note the qualification: "In good mechanical condition." A prerequisite to buying a used car is a thorough analysis by a responsible mechanic. The buyer of a used car has no way of knowing what accidents or operating problems the car had in the past. The seller—whether dealer or private—may not be inclined to divulge all that is known about the car's history. Indeed, if the car has had more than one prior owner, the current owner may not have any idea about the car's complete history. The cost of a thorough inspection can be a very inexpensive way of finding out whether you're getting a good or a bad deal. The bad deal will end up costing you many times what the inspection will cost.

If you buy a used car from a private individual, you'll take it on an as-is basis, unless the seller agrees to some sort of private warranty. If she does, have her put it in writing. If you buy a used car from a dealer, the typical warranty runs for only thirty days, and even with that, the buyer may have to absorb part of any repair costs. That warranty should also be expressed in writing.

Warranties

New-car warranties used to be fairly cut and dried: They were good for twelve months or 12,000 miles, whichever came first. In recent years, however, competition has created a lot of confusion regarding new-car warranties. Many manufacturers now offer limited warranties extending for five, six, or seven years. But it's important to note that these are *limited* warranties. The extended warranties generally cover the basic drive train and transmission in the car. Many other items such as power windows, windshield wipers, radio, dashboard circuits, and so forth may still be restricted to the twelve months or 12,000-mile limitation.

The matter is further confused by the availability of additional warranties that extend beyond the basic manufacturer's warranty. Some of these plans are offered by the manufacturers themselves, and others are offered by private insurance companies. These extra warranties can cost many hundreds of dollars depending on the extent of coverage and on how many miles (or months) they run. Often the price of these warranties can be negotiated along with the price of the automobile. If you are mechanically inclined, or if you know a good, trustworthy mechanic, the extended warranties may be of less value to you. If you're a novice when it comes to dealing with a broken-down automotive function, the warranty might give you peace of mind. The best solution is to take a course in automotive repair at your local community college. A second-best alternative is to buy one of the many good guide books on automotive repair. Taking a course or buying a book might not enable you to do your own repairs, but at least you'll be able to determine whether an item can be fixed at minimal cost or whether the $700 estimate the garage gives you is reasonable.

Shopping Criteria

Since this book is devoted to money handling and not car handling, we'll leave the details of road testing and comfort testing up to the individual reader.

After you've decided what pleases you with respect to size, color, equipment, and handling, refer to the Personal Action Checklist at the end of this chapter for a guide to what you'll get for your money. The checklist contains space for three comparisons. If you compare more than three cars, simply use extra paper to fill in the comparisons. In addition to the base price, list each optional extra and the cost thereof separately. This will cause you to stop and think twice about the value of those extras and will also give you a better comparison of the total product that you're getting for your money.

Very likely the dealer will quote you a price that's different from the total sticker price. That price will take into account the value of any car you are trading in. Haggling over the price of a new car is still one of the great old American traditions. The dealers almost expect that you'll haggle, and if you don't, you could be spending hundreds of dollars more than you have to.

Don't guess: Be precise with each dealer's offerings with respect to warranty, extended service contracts, insurance (if the dealer will offer it), and financing terms.

To the extent possible, check the dealer's reputation in the community for service and adjustment of complaints. With respect to service, determine whether the dealer will pick up and drop off your car when it needs work and whether the dealer has loan cars available and at what price, should you have to leave your own car there for an extended period.

Games Dealers Play

The automobile business is extremely competitive. Competitiveness breeds anxiety, and that in turn may cause car salespeople and dealerships to now and then bend the ethics of good business practices in order to win a sale. Some of these practices are illustrated in the following tale. Try to spot the pitfalls as they occur.

You're planning to buy a car, and you've set your heart on a Rammer-Jammer XJKB. You've priced it at two dealerships, who are within a few dollars of each other: About $4000 in cash will be required over your old trade-in. You want to try one more dealership, which advertises heavily that they will ''meet or beat any deal in town.''

You and your spouse take a drive to that dealership one evening after dinner. A pleasant young chap takes you under his wing and suggests that you test drive the model you've been admiring. While you're driving around, you're very impressed with the seeming honesty and candor of this nice fellow, and you're particularly intrigued when he suggests that the trade-in value of your old car might be $1000 more than what other dealers have quoted you! He explains that this dealer's inventory of used cars is very low, and he's offering better deals on trade-ins to build up his inventory. What's more, the salesman confides, he thinks the boss has been overcharging too many customers, and he, as a bright honest young man, doesn't like people to get a raw deal. Thus, he tells you, he's going to take it upon himself to see that you get the best possible deal available, and the boss won't know the difference.

Back at the showroom, he takes you into his little office to do some calculating. After a few moments, he looks up at you with a smile. ''If I can get the boss to agree on a deal that would take $3000 plus your trade-in, would you sign the contract tonight?''

Wow! $3000! You were almost willing to pay $4000 for exactly the same car at a different showroom. Of course you'd be willing to take a deal for $3000 if the boss will go along with it. The well-trained salesman spots your enthusiasm and proceeds.

''Look,'' he says, ''the boss doesn't like me to approach him with proposed deals unless they're sure that the customer will take the deal. He doesn't like to waste his time haggling back and forth. If he knows he has a firm deal right at the outset, that means he's saving time and he'll give you a better price. Let me do this: Let me fill out the contract showing a $3000 trade difference, and you give me a good faith check for $50. That way, he knows he's got a firm deal *if* he signs the contract. If he doesn't go for the deal, he won't sign the contract and you're not obligated for anything. If he doesn't go for it, I'll give you back the contract and your check, and you can rip them both up. What have you got to lose?''

You've got nothing to lose, or so you think. You're sitting there planning on how you can spend the $1000 you've just saved and itching to get behind the wheel of the new car that's just a signature away. You review what the salesman has just said. He's right. If the owner doesn't sign the contract, there's no deal.

''O.K.,'' you say, ''fill out the contract and I'll sign it.''

He leaves the room with the signed contract and the check, and you and your spouse sit and snicker over the tremendous deal you're getting. "I was ready to pay $4000, and we're stealing it for $3000," you say. (There's a little bit of larceny in all of us.)

You sit and wait for ten, then twenty minutes. You're getting impatient because you want that contract to come back signed by the owner so you can hop in your new Rammer-Jammer and be off, before they realize how you've taken them.

Just as you're about out of patience, the young man sticks his head in the door, smiles at you, and says, "I think everything is going to be O.K. I'm going to take the car around to the service department and get it ready for you so you can take it home tonight if you want."

Your motor starts racing, and you lean back to wait some more. Another ten minutes pass, and an older man enters the room. He tells you he is the assistant boss. Very understandingly, he tells you that he appreciates how anxious you are to get into that new car. But, sadly, there seems to have been a snag. The pleasant young man whom you were so fond of, it seems, has been doing a lousy job for the dealer. He makes mistakes on his estimates, and he's trying to cut the prices lower than the dealer can afford. Very likely, the young man isn't long for this kind of business. As a matter of fact, the assistant boss continues, it seems as though the young man was off by $1000 on your deal. He vastly overestimated the value of your trade-in. "We'd love to have you in this car, because I know you want to be in it," the assistant boss says, "but we've just got to talk about a $4000 trade difference, not $3000." The bubble has burst.

"In the first place," the assistant boss goes on, "we didn't even give your trade car a test drive. Let me have the keys to it so our service manager can check it out and give you a fair trade-in price." Bewildered, you hand over your keys and he disappears with them.

You're confused and dejected. You want to get back the contract and your check, and though some suspicions are beginning to grow in your mind, there's still a glimmer of hope that you can correct this foul-up and still get the deal that you had already set your heart on. You and your spouse debate the matter in the privacy of the closing room and tentatively agree that if you can strike a deal somewhere between $3500 and $4000, maybe you'd still go for it since it would be better than any of the other quotes you'd been given.

The assistant boss reappears momentarily with your contract, which he hands over to you; and you tear it up. "Where's my $50 check?" you ask. He looks a little bewildered and guesses that it must still be in the boss's office. "Don't worry about it," he says, "I'll get it for you in just a few minutes. Now about your deal," he begins. "We've given your trade-in a good look, and it needs a lot of work and new tires. A good deal for us would be $4300 plus your trade-in, but since you've been here so long and have been so patient, and since you were misled by the young fellow, we can bend some and let you have the new Rammer-Jammer for $4100."

You've been there over an hour already, and the grind is beginning to wear you down. You finally concede, "$3900, not a penny more," knowing that he's winning. You're starting to wonder when you're going to get your $50 check back and what they are doing with your old car. You finally tell him that you think you had best go home and talk about the matter before making a decision, and you demand your check and your car keys. He promises that he will try to locate them right away, and he leaves the room. You're getting tense now, but you still feel that you can get the deal for $3900, which is still a $100 better than the next best deal. You discuss it with your spouse and decide that since you've been here this long you might as well hang around a little longer and hope the deal can be wrapped up for $3900.

A few minutes later, salesman number three comes in. This is the boss, and he's high pressure all the way. The hour is getting later and you're getting more and more tired. The boss now is pushing hard to close you at $4050, which, as he says, "I'm losing money on."

Then comes the clincher. You again demand your check and your keys, and he comes back from a quick search to inform you sadly that the cashier has left for the night and the check has been locked up in the register. "Don't worry, it's perfectly safe there. If we don't close the deal tonight, you can come back and pick it up in the morning."

Furthermore, the used car appraiser has also left for the night and thinking that your old car had been accepted as a trade-in, he parked it in the lot and locked up the keys in his office. "Don't worry," says the boss, "we can give you a ride home tonight and pick you up in the morning to get your old car. I assure you, there's absolutely no problem. Now about this deal. . ."

The final thrust: "Look folks, I know how late it's getting, and I want to get out of here as badly as you do. Let me ask you this—if I give you the deal for $4000, will you take it, then we'll all go out and have a drink?" Resignation has finally set in, and you agree to the deal. After all, it's still as good as the best deal you had any other place. Wearily, you reach for your pen.

Interwoven throughout this intrigue are four types of sales tactics (Did you recognize them?) that have brought a poor reputation to a small segment of the automobile sales industry.

The Highball Trick.   The first salesman used the highball trick, in which he quoted a much higher trade-in value on your old car than was reasonable. Indeed, it sounds too good to be true, which causes the first strong opening pull on your purse strings. The opposite of the highball is the lowball, where the salesperson looks at the sticker price on the new car and suggests a too-good-to-be-true discount from that price. The obvious tactic here is to lead you to believe that you're going to get a better deal than you thought possible, all the quicker to get you into the showroom where the heavy pressure can be applied.

The Takeover Operation.   The "takeover" ploy involves a succession of salespersons ranging from low pressure to high pressure. The first one's job is to soften you and win your confidence. Subsequent salespeople increase the pressure until the closer takes over. The process is designed to wear down your resistance grad-

---

Strategies for Success

Get Price Quotes in Writing

If you're quoted a price on an automobile, have the salesperson put it in writing. Make sure it's adequately detailed, including any extras, financing terms, down payment, and so on that may be part of the deal. And be certain to have the salesperson indicate—again, in writing—how long this price quote will last. If you leave to do some comparison shopping and return to the original dealer two hours later, you don't want to be told, "Sorry, that price quote was good for only ten minutes." If you don't get the quote in writing, you have nothing to go on later. And if they won't put it in writing, maybe it's because they don't intend to honor it. What does this tell you?

---

ually. The first salesperson's job is accomplished when he gets you to sit down in the closing office, not just in a mood to buy, but with a raging desire to buy, albeit at a price that would later turn out to be impossible. The success of the takeover operation depends on the next tactic.

The Bugged Closing Room.   Unless you are an electronics whiz, you would probably not be able to determine whether a room is bugged. This indeed is a devious trick not generally employed by a legitimate dealer, but you never know what you're up against. By listening in on your conversations, the salespeople know just where your soft spots are and how far they can take you. If they determine that you are really thick skinned and have strong sales resistance, they can always fall back on the next sales tactic.

The "Disappearing Check" Trick or the "Keys Are Locked up for the Night" Gambit.   This is the last straw. By claiming to have "misplaced" something of value, such as a check or car keys, they are, in effect, nailing you to the wall until your resistance finally breaks. The best way to avoid being trapped in this manner is not to write any checks and to stand by as they test your trade-in car so you can retain the keys until the deal is either made or not made.

If you spot any of the tactics noted above in operation in your car shopping, you can be relatively sure that you're in for a high-pressure pitch that might lead you to signing a contract you otherwise wouldn't sign. Even though, in the above case, you thought you got away with the same deal you could have had elsewhere, that isn't necessarily so. Had you gone back to the other dealers for a follow-up bargaining session, you might have gotten a still better deal. Awareness of these tricks and a willingness to walk away from shady tactics when you spot them are necessary weapons when shopping for a car. Dealers sell hundreds of cars each month. You buy only one every few years. They know a lot more about the tricks of bargaining and striking a deal than you do. They're entitled to a fair profit for whatever work they're involved in, just as you are, but that doesn't give them the right to take advantage of you—all of which leads back to the most important point: Know whom you are dealing with. There's no substitute for a reputation of integrity.

Strategies for Success

Alternate Sources for Good Used Car Buys

Used-car dealers and private parties are commonly the sources of used cars for sale. The dealers can be expensive. The private parties might not reveal hidden defects. Dealers might also hide hidden defects, but reputable ones often offer at least some type of warranty that can give you minimal protection. You could do better on a used-car purchase at a car rental agency's disposal lot. Major agencies such as Hertz and Avis sell rental cars to the public after they've been driven a certain amount of miles. They might have been better maintained than privately owned cars, and they might have decent warranties. Also check car wholesalers who take trade-ins from new-car dealers and sell them to used car lots. Don't expect any warranties, but the price might be right.

Your Old Car: Selling It Yourself versus Trading It In

It's difficult to determine whether you can do better by selling your own used car or by using it as a trade-in on a new purchase. First, check the used-car price directory and used-car lots to see what cars similar to yours are selling for (see Table 6-2). The directory is available at all dealerships and at most banks. Bear in mind that the prices on cars at lots are the asking prices, not necessarily the selling prices. If you can find a buyer who's ready, willing, and able to pay your price, it may be wise to make a deal. But before you can determine the wisdom of such a deal, you must go to various dealers to determine the different price that you'd be expected to pay with and without a trade-in.

If you can't find a ready, willing, and able buyer quickly, you might be in for more headaches than the project is worth. You'll have to advertise the car for sale, and you'll have to be available when interested buyers want to come around to take it for a test drive. Not only can this be inconvenient; you could feel quite uncomfortable having a stranger take your car for a half-hour or so test spin.

Sales tax is another important factor to take into account. Customarily, when you offer an old car as a trade-in, you pay a sales tax on the difference between the selling price and the trade-in value. If you pay all cash for a car, you pay a sales tax on the total amount. Assuming a 6 percent sales tax rate, the tax on a $10,000 cash purchase would be $600. If you offer a trade-in valued at $4000,

Table 6-2 Abbreviated Listing from Typical Used-Car Price Directory (as of Spring 1988).

1986 Chevrolet model	List price[a]	Average wholesale price	Average retail price
Cavalier Sedan, 4-door	$ 8,695	$5,400	$ 7,005
Celebrity Wagon, 4-door	10,735	6,850	8,670
Camaro V6, Sport Coupe	10,914	7,150	9,015
Monte Carlo, LS Coupe	11,974	7,300	9,185
Caprice Classic Brougham	12,654	8,450	10,505

[a]Price refers to original suggested retail price of the car, including standard equipment. Optional extras, destination charges, preparation charges, taxes and licensing fees are not included. Average wholesale and retail prices are for clean reconditioned cars ready for sale. See separate listings in directory for increases/decreases in price due to equipment, condition, and mileage.

your cash difference is $6000 with a resulting sales tax of $360. In short, you save $240 by going the trade-in route. That alone might offset any better deal you could get by selling the car on your own. Check in your locality to determine current regulations on this matter.

How Much Haggling Room Do You Have?

Again, no rule of thumb can determine how much bargaining room you have with a dealer, but there are some broad guidelines. Your haggling room largely depends on the value of your trade-in, whether you're financing through the dealer (see section on financing), and how anxious the dealer is to move his current inventory. Very generally speaking, dealers work on a markup of about 20 percent. Thus, depending on the foregoing conditions, it might not be unreasonable to expect a discount of 5 to 10 percent off the sticker price. To get much more than 10 percent is going to take some hard bargaining, but if you don't ask for it, they're not going to volunteer it. *Consumer Reports* magazine publishes an annual price listing of new model cars, which can serve as a more specific guideline to your bargaining powers. Consult these lists before you go shopping.

The Best Time to Buy

Although some change in traditional patterns has been creeping into the industry, late summer and early fall still tend to be the times when dealers are clearing out their old inventory to make room for the new model cars shipped from the factories. While there may be a smaller assortment of cars to choose from at this time of year, there's a strong chance that you will get a better price than you might have earlier in the model year.

This is also a time when dealers tend to sell their demonstrator models—cars that have been driven by employees of the dealership. Demos can be very good bargains. They tend to be well-equipped and well taken care of, and many dealerships offer them with full warranty, even though they have been driven for a few thousand miles or more.

FINANCING A CAR

Assuming you have the necessary trade-in or down payment and acceptable credit, most dealers can arrange financing for you right on the spot. You can also make your own financing arrangements through your bank (and in many instances, your automobile-insurance company). Which is better?

It can be very convenient to have the dealer arrange for the financing. It saves you time, but it can cost you extra money. Determine the annual percentage rate (APR) that the dealer will charge you for the financing. (See Chapter 14 for a more detailed discussion of interest rates and installment loans.) Compare the dealer's APR with that offered by other lenders. The APR is the only means of comparing interest rates. Have any APR quote put in writing and signed by the salesperson. If the dealer is charging more for the financing he's arranging for you, obviously it wouldn't pay to deal with him, unless there are other extenuating circumstances, such as the fact that you don't want to extend your credit any further at your regular bank.

Virtually all dealers will receive a rebate from the lender; it can be as much as a few hundred dollars, depending on the amount of financing involved. Thus, dealers are eager to arrange financing for you. If you play the game advantageously, you'll let the dealer believe that you're going to do the financing through him before you make a commitment to purchase the car. The dealer is liable to quote you a lower price for the car, since he anticipates additional profit through the financing. He may, if he suspects your wise purchasing tactics, give you two prices for the car—one if you finance with him, one if you don't. Act accordingly.

One important advantage—in addition to saving on interest—in dealing with your own bank is that you are dealing with people who know you and who can be accommodating to you should problems arise. If the dealer arranges the financing for you, it may be with a bank or finance company you've never dealt with; it might even be with an out-of-town institution. In such a case, if you run into problems with lateness or other financial distress, the institution is liable to regard you as little more than a number in their computer and any accommodation may be hard to come by.

In recent years car manufacturers have been offering incentive plans involving either extremely low interest rates for financing or so-called cash rebates that reduce the price of the car. When such opportunities are available, it can be wise to examine their benefits. Be aware the availability of such low financing does not necessarily mean you're getting the best all-around deal. The low financing rate might be available only on a limited number of models, which might not include the model you would normally buy. And there may be little or no room for haggling over the price on such models. In short, you might end up spending more for a car than you otherwise would have or should have in order to get a lower interest rate on the financing. The net savings in such a case may not truly exist.

Wherever you arrange your financing, it's essential that you do not allow the loan to last longer than you expect to own the car. If you expect to trade every three years, you shouldn't finance for more than three years. (See the section on Credit Abuses in Chapter 14 on how this timing of your loans can be important to you.)

BUYING VERSUS LEASING

Leasing has become very popular in the last few years. It tends to be more advantageous for business than for individual purposes, but you might want to entertain the possibility of leasing.

If you do explore leasing, first be aware that the credit requirements for a lease tend to be much more stringent than for outright financing. This is because you are putting very little down payment into the deal and because leases tend to involve more expensive automobiles. With a lease, as noted, there's a fairly small down payment. Also monthly payments are lower than they normally would be on a straight financing. At the end of the lease term, you have the right to buy the car at a pre-agreed-upon price, or you can simply turn the car back over to the dealer and walk away, assuming the car is in acceptable condition. For example, on a three-year lease, the residual value at the end of the lease might be approximately 50 percent of the original purchase price. Thus, on a $20,000 car, the residual value might be $10,000. This is the price at which you can then buy the car. If it happens to be worth more than that on the open market, you can turn around and sell it and reap a profit. If it happens to be less than that on the open market, you have to make up the difference to the dealer. Customarily, at the end of a lease, the customer either renews the lease at a lower monthly rental or starts a new lease with a new car.

Note well that when you turn in a car at the end of a lease, you will be charged for any defects in the condition of the car, except for normal wear and tear. You will be charged for dents, scratches, stains, and any other blemish. The cost of fixing these defects can quickly add up to many hundreds of dollars. If you had originally thought that leasing was preferable to buying, this cost reckoning at the end of the lease might change your mind.

Tax law changes that went into effect in 1987 can have considerable impact on your choice of buying versus leasing. If you buy and finance a car, and the car is used for personal purposes, only a portion of the interest you pay is tax deductible: 40 percent for tax year 1988, 20 percent for 1989, 10 percent for 1990, and none in 1991 and onward. If the car is used as a business vehicle, the interest expense on the financing can be more fully deductible. If you lease the car for personal purposes, the lease payments are not deductible. If a leased car is used for business purposes, the lease payments can be deductible. If a car is used for a combination of personal and business purposes, the portion of interest or lease payment that is deductible would generally be prorated according to the extent the car is used for each purpose. A visit with an accountant would be highly advised before you make a buying versus leasing decision.

CAR INSURANCE

An adequate package of automobile insurance protects you against the hazards inherent in owning and using an automobile: damage to the machine itself and damage that it may cause others for which you might be responsible. Each state has imposed a requirement that motorists must maintain a minimum level of financial responsibility in the event that they are involved in an automobile accident. Most commonly, this minimum responsibility is met by obtaining an automobile-insurance policy, which includes the all-important public liability protection.

Types of Insurance

The typical automobile-insurance policy packages many different types of insurance. The types of coverage are given below.

Public Liability for Bodily Injury. This is the single most important financial aspect of your automobile-insurance policy and possibly of your entire insurance program. Should your car injure or kill other people, this coverage will defend you against claims and will pay any claims for which you're found to be legally responsible. Coverage is generally broken down into two phases: one for injury to a single individual involved in an accident and a second phase for all individuals involved. The limits of coverage are usually expressed as follows: $10,000/$20,000. This coverage would protect you for up to $10,000 worth of claims from any single individual and for up to $20,000 for all parties injured in an accident. The amount of protection you choose is up to you. You may have to comply with a minimum required by your state, which may be as low as $10,000/$20,000 (more commonly expressed as 10/20). Or, if you are prudent and aware of the potential circumstances, you may choose much higher limits, perhaps as high as $100,000/$300,000, or even higher if it's available. The difference in cost between the minimal coverage and the more extensive coverage is only a few dollars per month—an investment that many would have a hard time turning down.

Public Liability for Property Damage. If your automobile causes damage to the property of others, property liability coverage will defend you against claims and will pay claims for which you are found to be legally responsible. The limit of coverage is usually expressed as a number following the limits for bodily injury liability. For example, overall public liability limits of 25/50/10 would mean that your property damage liability limits are $10,000 (following the bodily injury limits of $25,000 and $50,000). In this case, if you caused injury to the property of others, you would be protected for up to $10,000 of such damage.

Property damage liability covers damage to the property of *others*—not to your own property. It can include damage to the automobiles of others when involved in an accident or damage caused to buildings if a driver hits one. Property damage coverage will usually not be less than $5000, and a ceiling of $50,000 should be adequate in most situations. It's difficult to conceive of an auto accident causing much more physical damage to property than that, although it is possible if you crash into a new Rolls-Royce or career through the lobby of a modern retail building.

Your public liability protection for bodily injury and property damage will cover you in your own car or if you're driving someone else's car, as well as covering other persons who drive your car with your permission. It also provides legal defense for claims made against you.

Medical Payments.   If you or members of your household or guests who are driving in your car are injured while driving (or even if struck while walking), the medical payments provision will reimburse all reasonable actual medical expenses arising out of the accident up to the limits of the policy. Generally, the payments will be made regardless of who was at fault. The minimum may be as low as $500, but much greater coverage than that can be obtained at a reasonable added annual cost. As with the public liability portions of the coverage, the prudent motorist would do well to consider taking much higher than minimal limits on the medical payments provisions, for the added extra cost is small indeed compared with the immediate protection obtained.

Uninsured Motorists.   Regrettably, not everyone who drives an automobile is insured or is adequately insured. You might be caused serious harm by a motorist having little or no insurance protection. You could be out tens of thousands of dollars in medical expenses and lost income, and the party at fault may have little or no money with which to reimburse you for the damage caused. (Generally, too, property damage is not covered.) Although the courts may find the person legally responsible for making payments to you, he may not be financially responsible, and you may never be able to recover. Uninsured motorist protection is designed to take care of this problem, providing you with reimbursement for your losses through your own insurance company.

Unfortunately, we don't have a choice as to who might cause us harm in an automobile. It could be a perfectly adequately insured individual, or it could be the uninsured individual or a hit-and-run driver whom we will never see again. This form of protection is quite inexpensive, and the motorist is assuming an unnecessary risk by not having it.

Comprehensive Insurance.   Comprehensive insurance is a broad form of protection for loss caused other than by collision. It includes damage to your car due to fire, glass breakage, riots, windstorm, hail, loss due to theft, and other types of miscellaneous damage. Limited protection on contents is also available. Deductibles are common in such policies. If the deductible is, for example, $50, the motorist has to pay the first $50 worth of any such loss, and the insurance company has to pay for damages over the deductible amount. You should check your policy to determine whether you are protected against theft if you leave your car unattended or unlocked. Some policies will not protect the motorist under these circumstances.

Collision Insurance.   Collision insurance protects you against damage done to your own car should you be in a collision with another car or an object such as a telephone pole or a building. Collision insurance also usually carries a deductible amount. If car A and car B collide and the accident is the fault of the driver of car A, her property liability insurance will pay for the damage to the owner of car B, and car A's owner's collision insurance will pay for the damage to car A. Compared with the other forms of automobile insurance, collision protection tends to be fairly expensive. If you're driving a car more than five or six years old, the cost of the collision protection might be high enough to discourage you from obtaining that protection in view of the limited recovery you can expect on an older car. Weigh the cost and the protection accordingly.

Cost of Insurance

The cost of automobile insurance can vary considerably depending on the age, safety record, and occupation of the owner and the purposes for which the car is used. It's common knowledge that younger drivers have to pay a higher rate for their automotive insurance, primarily because those drivers have a generally bad statistical record when it comes to accidents and claims. Some companies will offer discounts for drivers with safe records and for younger persons who have taken certain driver education courses. Other discounts may be available if more than one car is insured or if compact cars are involved. In shopping around for the best automobile-insurance package, all available discounts should be inquired about from each agent.

The amount of the various deductibles can also have a bearing on the total premium cost. As with deductibles in other forms of personal insurance, you are assuming a higher risk in exchange for paying a lower premium. The premium saved is an actual savings, whereas the higher risk may never occur.

If You Are in an Accident

If you are involved in an automobile accident, you should obtain the following information from the other driver: his name, his driver's license number, his automobile's license number, name of his insurance company, and the number of his insurance policy. In all likelihood the other driver will expect the same information from you. Depending on the extent of personal injury or property damage, a police report may or may not be taken. You should also determine whether your state law requires a detailed report to be filed with the Department of Motor Vehicles. You should notify your insurance company at the earliest possible time. Your own insurance company can arrange for you to have your car repaired; they will later recover the amount for the repairs from the other driver's insurance company, if, in fact, the other driver was at fault.

If the accident was your fault, and if the other driver is paid for a claim against your insurance policy, your insurance rates might increase. Depending on the amount of damages, you might prefer to pay for the other party's costs yourself, rather than incur higher insurance premiums for the next few years. Discuss this possibility with your own insurance agent before you proceed either way.

If injuries or damages in an accident are extensive, one driver may bring a lawsuit against the other. Some states have "no-fault" laws that determine who can receive what payments, regardless of who might have been at fault in the accident. In other states, a jury trial determines who was at fault and what damages should be paid to the injured party. It could take years before such claims are heard by a jury. In reality, most claims are settled out of court by the parties within a few months after the accident.

Personal injury lawyers who represent injured parties usually take 30 to 40 percent of recoveries as their fee, plus out-of-pocket expenses. These fees are based on the amount you receive over and above your own out-of-pocket medical and repair expenses. In other words, if you retain a lawyer who is able to get you an award of $10,000 for your pain and suffering, you may end up netting $6000. It might take you many months before you can get that much. On the other hand, you might be able to negotiate on your own with the other insurance company for $3000 to $5000, depending, of course, on the extent of injuries. This would be cash in hand right on the spot, compared with an unknown amount that you might or might not receive many months later. In short, the personal injury lawyer can be helpful when circumstances indicate more severe injuries, lost work time, extensive suffering, and so on. When the injured party pursues a claim based more on inconvenience and annoyance, it's less likely that the costly lawyer can be of much value.

Automobile Clubs

Another form of worthwhile insurance can be obtained through automobile clubs. For a modest annual fee these clubs provide towing insurance, which will get your car to a service station at no out-of-pocket cost to you should it break down on the road. Auto club insurance can also provide you with bail in the event of arrest; travel services are an added plus included with the price of the annual premium.

CAR POOLING

Comfort and convenience aside, it can definitely pay to become involved in a car pool. Whether it's to work, to pick up and deliver children at school, or even to a supermarket, there can be considerable savings in the cost of operating your au-

Table 6-3 **Annual Car-Pool Savings**

Round-trip commute (Miles)	Type of car	Cost of driving alone	Cost of shared driving in a car pool	
			2 persons	4 Persons
20	Subcompact	$ 726	$ 398	$ 217
20	Standard	1,062	582	316
40	Subcompact	1,262	718	398
40	Standard	1,857	1,053	582
80	Subcompact	2,194	1,250	718
80	Standard	3,251	1,844	1,053

tomobile. Table 6-3, based on a 1980 U.S. Department of Transportation study, gives some examples of the annual savings that can be realized by continuous participation in a car pool.

RENTING A CAR

Renting cars is an ever-growing business. Aside from the commonplace airport and hotel car rental agencies used in conjunction with business travel and tourism, car renting is increasingly popular with residents of highly populated urban centers where ownership and parking of automobiles are costly and inconvenient. There are a number of major national rental firms with computerized reservation services and garage facilities well located in most major cities. These include Hertz, Avis, National, Dollar, Budget, and Thrifty. There are hundreds of smaller regional or local firms, which, because they don't have the high advertising and rental over-heads, can offer much lower prices on rentals. Another recently popular concept is "renting a wreck," which offers drivable vehicles at a low price, if you don't mind that they may be covered with dents, scratches, rips, and tears. If appearance is no object, this might be a most inexpensive way to rent a car. But if long-distance travel is in your plans, you may prefer a larger agency where better mechanical service is assured.

Whatever your rental needs, it definitely pays to shop around for the best deal. Many rental firms regularly offer discounts at special times of the week, month, or year. Discounts are also available through magazine ads and through a corporate account that your company may have with one of the major rental firms.

Rental plans can vary considerably. Most popular are those that charge a fixed amount per day plus a fixed amount per mile driven; alternatively, you may pay a fixed amount per day with a set number of miles included as part of that charge. In both cases the customer pays for gasoline used. If you can reasonably determine the number of miles you expect to drive the car, you can easily figure which of these two plans would be cheaper for you.

The major rental firms also offer the capability of picking up a car in one city and leaving it in another. Depending on the cities involved, there may or may not be a drop-off charge. Determine in advance exactly what drop-off charges would be connected with inter-city usage.

Car rental firms will also offer you two different types of protection: collision and medical. The typical car rental contract states that you will be responsible for the first $1000 or $2000 or more of any damage to the car as a result of a collision, for example, running the car into a tree. The rental company will offer you a *collision damage waiver* (CDW) for roughly $8 to $12 per day. If you pay for this collision damage waiver you are no longer obligated to pay the initial amount should there be a collision. However, in order for the CDW to be effective, you must be using the car in accordance with the strict terms of the rental agreement. If the collision occurs when an unauthorized driver is at the wheel or if an unauthorized use of the car is being made, you might lose the advantage of the collision damage waiver. Your own automobile-insurance policy may cover you for some of these expenses. Check with your insurance agent to be sure.

Also talk to your agent to determine the extent of your protection for medical expenses should you be injured while driving a rental car. If you feel comfortable with the extent of protection you already have, either on your automobile policy or your own health-insurance program, it may not be wise to spend the extra money for the car rental company's medical-insurance protection.

ELECTRONIC COMMUTING

America's dependence on the automobile will be with us for many years to come, but little by little the picture is changing, with electronics the wave of the future. Already, tens of thousands of workers are able to do their work at home via computer terminals that can relay all necessary information between the worker's home and the central place of business (or central computer). This number will grow to hundreds of thousands in a few years and eventually to millions. Most of the people affected by this revolution will be those who deal in information and services: stock brokers, insurance employees, bookkeepers, accountants, and so on. They will simply find it not necessary to "go to work" in the traditional sense. By working at home or at some nearby neighborhood facility to which they can walk, they'll eliminate the need for an automobile.

Similarly, as Chapter 7 notes, many other common functions that now depend on the automobile will be taken over by electronics. We'll do our banking through a computerized hookup to our telephone/television complex. We'll be able to order our goods from the supermarket by means of the same device, and the market will send one truck to deliver what fifty or one hundred cars used to have to go and pick up. Large-screen television sets in the home will replace driving to the movies.

Two-way video telephones will replace countless business meetings, commutes, and conferences.

In short, the electronics revolution can be a step in the right direction toward solving the energy crisis. These changes—which are inevitable—will allow you (or require you) to change many of your habits and ways of thinking, ways that affect your financial welfare and your work/leisure cycle. People will have to determine for themselves whether resistance to change hurts more than acceptance of change.

Car Shopping Comparison

Use this checklist to compare offerings from various dealers. Remember, the price of a car itself is not the only factor that determines how good a deal is.

Item	*Dealer A*	*Dealer B*	*Dealer C*
☐ Base price of car	_____	_____	_____
☐ Cost of optional extras (list items separately)	_____	_____	_____
	_____	_____	_____
	_____	_____	_____
	_____	_____	_____
☐ Dealer preparation and delivery charges	_____	_____	_____
☐ Total sticker price	_____	_____	_____
☐ Trade allowance on your old car	_____	_____	_____
☐ Trade difference: new car cost less trade-in	_____	_____	_____
☐ Sales tax and license cost	_____	_____	_____
☐ How long will this offer be good?	_____	_____	_____
☐ Financing: What APR is offered?	_____	_____	_____
☐ Insurance: If offered, terms and cost	_____	_____	_____
☐ Reputation for fair dealing	_____	_____	_____
☐ Reputation for service and adjustment of complaints	_____	_____	_____
☐ Convenience in getting to and from when service is needed	_____	_____	_____
☐ If buying a used car: physical condition	_____	_____	_____
mechanical condition	_____	_____	_____
extent of warranty	_____	_____	_____
☐ Treatment by salesperson	_____	_____	_____

Service Station Sharpies Commit Highway Robbery

Most service station operators are honorable and reliable businesspeople. Sad, then, that a small scattering of sharpies smudge the reputation of an otherwise honest industry.

Long-distance travelers are particularly vulnerable to the following money-gouging tactics when they are far from home and in strange territory or when they stop for gas:

- *Tire "honking."* While you're not looking, a swift kick at your tire, with a boot that has a sharp nail point embedded in the toe, gives you a sudden flat and a sales pitch to buy a costly new tire.

- *Slashing.* A few quick slices with a well-hidden razor blade can destroy a fan belt or a radiator hose in an instant.

- *"White smoke" trick.* The attendant sprays a few drops of a chemical on your hot engine, and a cloud of white smoke erupts. It's actually harmless, but you're then susceptible to a pitch for costly engine repairs, which, of course, aren't needed in the first place.

- *Bubbling battery.* Drop a few grains of Alka-Seltzer, or the like, into a battery, and watch it bubble over. The unwary will find themselves paying for a new battery before they have time to say, "Plop, plop, fizz, fizz."

- *Shocking shocks.* A few dribbles of oil under one's shock absorbers are enough to convince many drivers that the absorbers are shot and need replacement. The same can hold true for the transmission and so on.

The common ploy following any of these tactics is a stern and concerned statement by the attendant to the effect that "you ought not drive more than a few hundred feet with your car in this condition. . . ."

The best protection against such events is to know the operation of your car; have it properly serviced before you set off on a long trip; never leave the car while it's being serviced; keep your eye on the attendant at all times. If you really do suspect a problem, take it to another station for a second opinion. Better still, you might want to take it to a dealer who sells your make of car.

CHAPTER 7

Leisure and Recreation

"All work and no play makes Jack a dull boy . . . and Jill a dull girl." How true those words can be. And how easy it is for our workaday routine to get the best of us, so that we spend the bulk of our leisure time—evenings, weekends, vacations—doing little more than sitting and staring at a television set. Sometimes it doesn't even matter if the set is turned on.

Our work week is growing shorter—from about fifty hours at the start of this century to about thirty-five hours currently. Less work time means more leisure time. And more leisure time gives every individual a choice: vegetation or recreation. This chapter is intended to stimulate you to plan how you can combine your spendable dollars and your spendable leisure time in the most rewarding way. You'll learn how to

☐ Seek out vacation and holiday activities that you can affordably enjoy

☐ Make use of the professional services of a travel agent

☐ Evaluate the opportunities to buy, rent, or share vacation facilities

☐ Shop for the best values in at-home electronic leisure equipment

☐ Make yourself aware of no-cost or low-cost personal enrichment activities that can enhance your life

How much of your disposable income should you devote to recreation and leisure? This is a very personal decision that each individual and family must make for themselves. Some people go overboard on their leisure expenses, leaving them in a budgetary bind. Some people consciously choose to curtail other types of expenses—living in a more modest dwelling, driving a more modest car—in order to enjoy their leisure freely. And still others forgo their leisure activities so that they can live in the more elaborate dwelling and drive the more elaborate car. To each his own. No one can dictate the proper balance for someone else. If you're overspending on leisure, you can either make adjustments or suffer the consequences. The same holds true if you are not partaking of any meaningful leisure activities. This chapter will help you think about the balance that you'd like to achieve and may motivate you to take action. We will explore two broad basic areas of leisure and the important financial considerations relating to them. These areas are (1) vacation and travel, and (2) recreation at home.

VACATION AND TRAVEL

From the weekend camping trip to the elaborate cruise or European junket, you want to be certain that everything goes just right. It's a shame to waste money, but it's even more disappointing to have wasted time. You can always go out and make more money, but you can never go out and make more time. Careful planning is essential if you want to make the most of your time and money.

Using a Travel Agent

Throughout this book we discuss the importance of using professional help to best protect your financial interests: the real estate agent in buying and selling a home, the accountant in working on your taxes, the lawyer for a variety of purposes, and so on. The proper professional to assist you with your vacation and travel plans is a travel agent.

A well-trained and experienced travel agent has many tools at her disposal to assist you in getting the most out of your vacation dollars. Among these tools are the following:

☐ The *Official Airline Guide (OAG)* gives updated flight information on virtually every commercial flight in the United States, as well as many international flights. Included in the *OAG* are arrival and departure times, fare structures, type of equipment flown on each route, and meals and other services offered on the flight. The *OAG* is an excellent device for getting an overview of all the different ways you can get from point A to point B and back again. (But as Table 7-1 points out, some further checking may be in order to verify and update *OAG* information.)

☐ Directories of hotels, resorts, car rental agencies, and cruises are available at most major travel agencies. These directories provide abundant detailed information on costs, facilities, reservation requirements, and often the quality of the various services and facilities. The directories also contain maps of the communities in question, showing locations of hotels; amusements; and air, bus, and train terminals.

☐ Brochures are in abundance at every travel agency. These are publications by airlines, resorts, states, nations, and tour-packaging companies. They provide an excellent means to familiarize oneself with various travel opportunities, price ranges, available dates, and other useful information.

☐ All of the information above is supplemented by the travel agent's own personal experiences and the experiences of her colleagues at the agency. Travel agents normally travel extensively to examine resort facilities, convention facilities, and other matters of concern to their clientele. They can provide worthwhile recommendations on hotels, restaurants, sightseeing, and basic dos and don'ts in given cities or resort areas. A well-equipped travel agency also has up-to-date travel books for customer browsing.

☐ The age of electronics has indeed arrived at the travel agency. Many agencies today are equipped with computers that can instantly show the agent the availability and times of flights, data on hotel rooms, rental car prices, and even weather reports in most cities of destination. The computer acts as an instant update of all the other material at the agent's disposal.

A travel agent can give you advice and guidelines on choosing a vacation that will satisfy your interests and budget. The agent, furthermore, can make all necessary reservations for travel and accommodation. The more advance time you give the agent to work on your plans, the wider choice you'll have of flights, hotel rooms, rental cars, and the like. Visiting a travel agent at the last minute will likely prove frustrating, but even in such cases the agent can probably do more for you than you could on your own.

What does a travel agent cost? Travel agents will not charge you for their services except, perhaps, for long-distance phone calls and other out-of-pocket expenses made on your behalf. Travel agents are paid on a commission basis by the airlines, hotels, cruise operators, and tour packagers that they book for you. In some cases, travel agents may actually be able to save you money. They may be aware of a group package tour whose itinerary virtually matches the travel you are planning. By making arrangements to take part in the group tour, you could cut your travel costs considerably. If the agent doesn't volunteer such information, ask about any such possibilities.

Choosing a travel agent is like choosing any other kind of professional advisor. Personal recommendations are always worth seeking out. The neatness and efficiency of the travel agent's office can also often be a giveaway to the quality of her work or lack thereof. The agent should be a member of the American Society of Travel Agents (ASTA) and should have credentials from the International Air Transport Association (IATA).

A Wealth of Information

In addition to the printed material a travel agent can offer you, there is an abundance of literature on travel that you should take advantage of at the earliest possible planning stages. Whether you're traveling on your own or with a guided tour group, the more you can learn about your places of destination, the more choice you'll have concerning what you want to see and do. Visit your local bookstore, and choose from among the following worthwhile publications:

☐ Good travel guide books are available in increasing numbers every year. The following travel guides cover major travel destinations throughout the United States and around the world. The Fodor Modern guides and Baedeker guide series are directed more toward the adult and affluent traveler. The Birnbaum guides seem more appropriate to younger travelers in their thirties and forties who do not have to pinch pennies. The *Let's Go* and *Frommer* series appeal to younger travelers, as well as to those who have to mind their travel budgets carefully.

☐ The Mobil *Travel Guides* cover various segments of the United States and are very detailed with respect to hotels, motels, and sightseeing facilities. They also contain discount coupons at various amusements and attractions.

☐ Sunset Guides publishes an extensive series of travel books covering the western part of the United States, Canada, and Mexico.

☐ Michelin guides provide excellent information on many major European cities and countries.

☐ Magazines also abound. *Travel and Leisure*, published monthly by American Express Company, contains in-depth articles on a wide variety of travel destinations. So-called city magazines, which are published in and about major American cities such as Los Angeles, New York, Chicago, and many more, offer up-to-date travel, sightseeing, and dining possibilities in those cities. Write to the Chamber of Commerce in the cities you plan to visit, and ask them how you can obtain these city magazines and any other tourist information they may have available.

Public libraries have many of these publications available but not always the latest editions. Particularly in the case of the books noted, it might be better to spend the money to get the most recent edition rather than rely on out-dated information that might be in the older library books.

Air Fares

The price of airline tickets is an incredible jumble. If you want to fly from point A to point B, the price of your ticket depends on how far in advance you make your reservations, how far in advance you pay for the ticket, the day of the week you're traveling, how long you're staying at your destination, and the class of service in which you choose to travel. The matter is further complicated by *frequent flyer plans* and by special discounts for air travel made available by many resort and cruise lines. And, depending on the type of plan you choose, you may or may not receive a refund of all or part of your ticket if you have to cancel your travel plans before your date of departure.

The best guide through the maze of air travel costs is a travel agent, who has access to all of these fare structures in a computer. Each airline will likely quote you only its specific prices for a given trip. The travel agent, however, can quickly determine all possible choices between points A and B. Table 7-1 illustrates the spectrum of fares available for short and long flights.

Table 7-1 Air Fares: A Comparison[a]

City	Type of Price	Restrictions	Price
Phoenix/Los Angeles	Lowest	Special excursion, must stay over a Saturday night, 7-day advance booking	$ 38
	Middle	No restrictions, but limited seats per flight; coach class	138
	Highest	First class, no restrictions	310
Los Angeles/New York	Lowest	Special excursion, must stay over a Saturday night, 7-day advance booking	238
	Middle	7-day advance booking, 50% penalty for cancellation	318
		Special excursion with 25% penalty for cancellation	508
	Highest	Coach class, no restrictions	1,120
		First class, no restrictions	1,676

[a]The fares represent the range of possible prices one would pay for a round-trip ticket between the destinations. All fares are quoted for the same flight dates.

Frequent Flyer Plans.   Most major airlines offer frequent flyer plans that enable you to accumulate points for distance traveled on a given airline. Once you've accumulated the necessary number of points, you are entitled to either free travel on the airline or discounts on future flights. Many airlines also cooperate with hotels and car rental agencies, which in turn provide lodging and car rentals at discounts. In short, the more you use the services of designated companies, the more benefits you'll accumulate. If you're certain that you'll be traveling given routes frequently enough to take advantage of the frequent flyer plans, it can be worth paying the nominal fee that's often required to join the plan. Be sure you know in advance, however, what restrictions and limitations there are on the plan. For example, is there a set time during which you must accumulate a given number of points? How long do you have to use the bonuses that you win? Are there any exclusions, such as certain days on which you cannot travel using your bonus points?

Note also that there has been a secondary market developing in the sale and exchange of frequent flyer bonus points. One traveler may have accumulated enough points to win a free trip to Europe, for example. Rather than take the trip, the traveler may sell the bonus points to another person, often through a broker who deals in such matters. A serious problem has arisen in this regard: Airlines have been declining to honor frequent flyer bonus points except to the individual who actually accumulated them. Thus you might find yourself having paid for someone else's bonus points, only to have the airline refuse to honor them and require that you pay full price for your ticket.

Charters and Discounts. If you shop carefully, you might achieve substantial savings on international travel by using charter companies or ''wholesalers'' who make sharp price reductions available. Both types of companies advertise in the travel sections of major newspapers, particularly the *Los Angeles Times*, the *New York Times*, and the *Chicago Tribune*. If you can't find these papers at your local newsstand, check with your local library. The biggest selection of ads are in the travel sections of the Sunday newspapers.

Wholesalers are companies that commit themselves to purchase a number of seats on given transoceanic flights. They buy the seats from the airline at a sharp discount, and they pass part of the savings on to their customers. Many of the wholesalers also offer discounts on hotel packages in destination cities. Before you book flights with these companies, check how long they have been in business and the manner in which they conduct their business. Also be aware of the fact that these discounted tickets are usually nonrefundable should you alter or cancel your travel plans. Wholesalers, as a rule, offer a wide selection of regularly scheduled flights to different destinations on different airlines.

Charter operators sometimes work in conjunction with regularly scheduled airlines; sometimes they hire planes for specific large-group travel arrangements. Many charter flights have extra seats available, which can be sold to the general public. These companies also advertise in the newspapers mentioned above.

A fairly new phenomenon for the adventuresome traveler is the *around-the-world special package*. Wholesalers offer these plans. For one fixed price, ranging from roughly $1000 to $2000, you can fly around the world stopping at designated cities along the way. The price of the ticket varies, depending on how many stops you make along the way. These tickets are generally good for a one-year period, and you must continue traveling in the same direction for the duration of your expedition. You use regularly scheduled airline flights, and you can stay over as long as you like in each city, taking as many side trips as you like. You can return home at any time during the year, provided you follow the established itinerary.

Strategies for Success

How to Get Free Travel

How would you like to take a free ski trip, or cruise, or guided tour of Europe, or whatever else suits your fancy? Many travel packagers, including wholesalers, cruise lines, and resorts, are willing to give away one free arrangement with every fifteen sold. If you can put together a group of fifteen people—friends, co-workers, club members, whoever —who are willing to pay full price for the arrangements, you might be able to get yours free. Or, if you prefer, you can pass your discount on to the members of your group. It'll take some work on your part, but it can be well worth the energy. Talk to a friendly travel agent to get details and to get the ball rolling.

Seasonal Bargains

Perhaps the best way to stretch your travel dollar farthest is to take advantage of the seasonal bargains in many major resort areas. You may not have the best possible weather, but the low prices may more than make up for the climatic situation. Off-season hotel prices in many major resort and tourist areas can be as little as one-half to one-third the high-season price. Samples include resorts in Las Vegas, Arizona, and Florida, where summertime prices are a fraction of wintertime hotel rates. Similarly, England and Europe in the winter can be much cheaper than during the hot and crowded summer months. If the weather is of secondary concern to you and you primarily want to see the sights and partake of the tourist opportunities, ask your travel agent to explain the off-season fare alternatives that are available. You could see more of the world for less money than you may have imagined.

Near-Home Vacations

If air, bus, or train fares threaten to use up too much of your vacation budget, consider the travel opportunities within an easy day's drive of your own home. How many New Yorkers have never been to Boston or Washington, or vice versa? How many San Franciscans have never been to Los Angeles, and vice versa? And so it goes throughout the nation. Close-to-home opportunities for fun, adventure, and enrichment are abundant no matter where you live. Not to take advantage of these opportunities is to deny yourself recreation.

Package Tours and Resorts

If you're not inclined to hassle over travel details, there are thousands of "package trips" available to you. Whether you're traveling within the United States or abroad, a package trip offers an almost all-inclusive price for your vacation, including travel, accommodations, sightseeing, the services of a guide where appropriate, and some meals and extras. Package tours are available through resorts, airlines, travel tour companies (such as American Express), and major travel agencies. Sometimes, but not necessarily always, package tours can save you money. It's always wise to compare what the same travel would cost if you bought each separate component (air, hotel, rental car, etc.) separately. The experienced traveler will probably prefer to create her own package. The novice might appreciate the convenience and possible cost savings of the package.

   If you are considering a package tour, whether to a resort or to another continent, study and evaluate the brochure that details what you get for your money. Pay attention to the following:

□ Most packages are advertised as costing "from" a certain amount of dollars. That little word *from* is vitally important. It describes the *lowest* possible price for the package, and that price might include lesser hotel rooms and restaurants. If you would prefer better accommodations or meals, you might, on carefully examining the brochure, find that your true price is considerably more than the minimum price. You also might find, on inquiring about booking, that the minimum accommodations are sold out and the only ones available are the higher-priced ones. This can be very disappointing, because you will have already set your desires, only to find out that you can't achieve them without paying substantially more money. The earlier packages are booked, the better chance you'll have of getting the minimum price, if that's what you prefer.

□ Many of the advertised "extras" may not represent a true travel bargain, but on the surface they seem appealing. A "free welcoming cocktail" or a "free bottle of champagne" in your room may sound alluring, but it's worth only a few dollars at most. The more important things to evaluate in terms of cost are the basic room accommodations and meals, if any.

□ If meals are included as a part of the package, determine what kind of menu and what kind of choices will be available to you. The basic package price might include minimal food service with anything extra being at an added cost. You can avoid disappointment by finding this out in advance.

□ If recreational facilities are included as part of the package, such as tennis or golf privileges, determine whether these facilities are available at any time you want them or only at certain fixed times, which may be inconvenient for you.

□ If the package includes transportation, when will the flights leave? Night flights can knock your body clock awry and render you incapable of enjoying your destination.

□ How much free time will you have, particularly on a multi-city guided tour? There are always horror stories coming out of some tour groups, indicating that the travelers were herded around like sheep. After a few days of that, you might not know whether you're in Athens, Greece or Athens, Georgia. To protect yourself, make sure you examine the day-to-day itinerary, which should be included in the travel brochure published by the package company. Too little free time can leave you exhausted; too much free time can mean that you'll be out spending money on your own, and that can leave you broke. Look for the happy balance with your travel agent as your guide.

Do-It-Yourself Tours and Vacations :

The more adventuresome or more experienced traveler will probably prefer to make his own arrangements. This means more time spent in the detailed planning stages, but more free time during the trip itself to do what one wishes, rather than do what the tour guide says it's time to do. Careful research is the key to arranging a successful do-it-yourself trip to other cities or even to a resort. Refer to the list of books and magazines mentioned earlier in this chapter to start your homework.

One of the chores that the do-it-yourselfer has to face that the package traveler needn't be concerned about is how do you get around once you've arrived at your destination? If it's to be by rental car, make your reservations well in advance. Popular tourist cities and resort areas often have a slim choice of cars, particularly during busier seasons. (Review the discussion on rental cars in Chapter 6 for further advice on getting good value for your money.)

For inter-city travel, particularly on a foreign trip, rail and bus travel passes may be available. These passes offer unlimited travel within a certain area and for a specific length of time. They can represent a considerable savings over booking individual travel from city to city. Keep in mind that some of these passes for European travel must be purchased in the United States.

When booking do-it-yourself travel, it's essential that you get all of your reservations confirmed in writing from the hotels, car rental agencies, and any other facilities you'll be using. Make certain that these confirmations spell out exactly what you are getting for your money: the type of room, the price of the room, the arrival and departure dates, and the type and price of the car you may be reserving. Take these written confirmations with you. If you get into an argument with a desk clerk over the facilities you've ordered, your written confirmation will go a long way toward assuring that you will get what you have bargained for. Also, if you pay any deposit in advance, be certain to get a receipt for that deposit; and make sure when you make final payment for your stay that you are given the proper credit for that deposit.

Cruises

Cruises have often been thought of as an indulgence only for the wealthy. But when you consider that for one all-inclusive price you receive your room, your meals, entertainment, all facilities of the ship, and transportation from port to port, the price of a cruise may not be much different from a stay of comparable length at a resort or a moderate, budgetwise trip abroad. If, that is, you plan far enough in advance.

Cruises, like tour packages, are advertised on a "from" basis. The price quoted in the advertising is the minimum price. For this price you will get the least desirable stateroom on the ship. It will probably be on the lowest deck, inside (as opposed to an outside room with a porthole), and at the far end of the ship (either fore or aft) where the motion of the boat will be more noticeable than in the center. But aside from the stateroom, all passengers have equal use of all facilities on the ship at all times. The food is the same, the entertainment is the same, the access to all facilities is the same. Experienced cruisers know that these minimum staterooms can't be all that bad: They are the first ones to be sold out on virtually every cruise. If a minimum stateroom isn't available to you, the price of better staterooms escalates rapidly. Since life on a cruise ship is spent predominantly in the public rooms and on shore—the stateroom is used for little else than to sleep and change clothes in—the booking of a minimum stateroom should not prove a hardship to most travelers.

The all-inclusive price means just that: elaborate meals, snacks, and midnight buffet; nightly professional entertainment and dancing to live bands; daily movies; plus lectures and lessons on a wide variety of subjects. Not included are alcoholic beverages, laundry, tips, and onshore expenses. All of these expenses are, of course, up to the individual. With respect to tipping, though, the cruise lines generally recommend a tipping formula, which most passengers customarily observe. The formula suggests tips ranging from $1 to $3 per person per day for your room steward and your dining room waiter. Additional tips for deck stewards, maitre d', and wine stewards are warranted as services are received from them. The traveler is the final judge on whether to tip and how much.

With respect to onshore expenses, travelers should be cautious of acquiring things (jewelry, perfume, watches, etc.) that they could obtain at home for a similar price. When shopping in foreign ports, it's always important to ask, "If I'm not satisfied with this when I get it home, how can I get the matter corrected?" It's one thing to visit a local jewelry store where you bought a watch that stopped working. It can be quite something else to try to get a watch fixed if you bought it in a tiny shop on some exotic Caribbean island.

In planning a cruise, your travel agent can provide you with schedules of all ships leaving from accessible ports. Many cruise bookings also offer substantial air fare discounts to get you from your home town to the port city. The travel agent or the cruise line can provide you with deck plans of ships you may be interested in. Study the deck plans carefully. Notice where the minimum-rate rooms are and where higher-rate rooms are. Make your choice for adequate comfort, cost considered.

Many cruise lines offer discounts if you pay for your passage in advance. If you know that you are definitely going to be taking a cruise, it can make very good sense to take advantage of these discounts. For example, a cruise ticket will cost $3000. The discount plan says that if you pay for the ticket in full twelve months in advance you will get a discount of $300, or 10 percent of the full price. If you invested the money in a bank, you might not be able to earn that much in twelve months. Further, since this is a discount, not money you've actually earned, there would be no income tax implications. In effect, you would be $300 ahead without having to pay income tax on it. If the money was earned in a bank account, the earnings would be taxable.

Trip Insurance

Whether you're going on a cruise, a package trip, or a do-it-yourself trip, it may be possible for you to buy insurance that will provide a refund if you or a member of your family becomes ill and thus is unable to travel. Such insurance may also provide that if a close member of your family who was not planning on taking the trip becomes ill, with the result that you have to cancel your trip to be with that relative, you can also get a refund. Ask your travel agent for details on trip insurance. The more members of your family planning the trip, the more sense such insurance makes. It's not inexpensive, but if you have to forfeit a substantial deposit in the event of illness, it may be worthwhile.

Travel Scams

The travel industry is not without its fair share of con artists. The problem has become more severe in recent years, as telephone solicitations have blanketed the country offering all varieties of supposedly free travel to innocent and gullible victims. Operating on the theory that ''there's no such thing as a free lunch,'' you'd be wise to avoid such tempting inducements as free flights to Hawaii, Europe, Rio de Janeiro, and other exotic destinations. Intriguing though the offers may sound, if you give your credit card number to the caller, you might be in for a rude shock when phony charges appear on your credit card statement some months later.

Home-Exchange Programs

If you're the trusting type, a home-exchange program can offer you the best of both worlds—the chance to live in a distant city at very little expense. The idea behind a home exchange is that you swap residences with a family in another city, either in the United States or abroad. In addition to eliminating hotel bills, you also have kitchen facilities at your disposal so that you can save considerably on food costs. In some cases it is even possible to swap the use of each other's automobile.

Ask your travel agent for the names and addresses of various home-exchange programs. Sponsors of these programs usually charge a modest fee for either putting you in touch with other persons interested in swapping or providing you with a subscription to a swapping listing. When you've found a good match, that is, someone who lives in a place where you'd like to visit and who wants to come to where you live—you should correspond in detail with them to make certain that you both know enough about the home and facilities to satisfy each other. To the extent possible, get personal references on the other individuals so that you can feel a sense of trust, since they will be living in your home. But the fact that you are living in each other's homes does help keep the level of trust elevated. You needn't own a house to get involved in an exchange; apartments and condominiums can be just as acceptable as a single-family home.

Pocket Money

Traveler's checks are the best way to carry money with you on a vacation. Personal checks and credit cards might not be accepted at restaurants, shops, and hotels (though most such facilities in most tourist areas do accept common credit cards). Cash is convenient, but if lost, it's gone forever. For a very modest cost, traveler's checks offer a virtually universal acceptability and protection against loss. If traveler's checks are lost, the issuing company can arrange for an immediate refund.

Traveler's checks are available at most major banks and through some travel agencies. They are issued by such companies as American Express, Bank of America, Citicorp, Visa, and MasterCard. The cost of traveler's checks is about $1 per

$100 worth of checks. Many banks and savings and loan associations will make traveler's checks available to their customers at no charge.

Foreign Money

If you are traveling to another country, you'll have to convert at least some dollars into the currency of that country. You'll likely be able to charge hotel bills and restaurant bills on most major credit cards, but you'll need local currency for such things as taxis, minor purchases, tips, and the like. Unless you've established a bank account in the foreign country, it will be extremely difficult for you to cash a personal check. Traveler's checks are, again, the best way to carry money. Cash your traveler's checks at local banks. You'll obtain a much better rate of exchange than you will at hotels, shops, or restaurants. Another alternative is to buy foreign-denominated traveler's checks before you leave the United States. You can buy traveler's checks issued in pounds, French francs, German marks, and Japanese yen at major banks' international departments or through American Express facilities. In so doing, you pay the exchange rate at the time you obtain the traveler's checks rather than at the time you cash them in the foreign country.

Precautions Before You Leave Home

Before you leave home on a vacation, secure your financial interests and peace of mind by taking a few simple precautions. If you don't have a trustworthy person to stay at your home while you're away, make certain that all valuables are out of harm's way. Either put them in a safety deposit box at your bank or leave them with someone you trust. Be certain to stop all mail and newspaper deliveries by contacting the post office and newspaper circulation office. For less than $10 you can buy time clocks that turn your lights on and off at various times of the day and night to make it appear that someone is living in the home. Ask neighbors to keep an eye out for any strange persons around your home. If you leave your car in the driveway, it will accumulate dust and tip off a would-be burglar that the home is empty. Leave a car key with a neighbor or friend and ask her to move the car around every few days and to keep it dusted off. Check with your property insurance agent to determine what coverage, if any, you have for valuables you plan to take with you. What additional coverage might be advisable? Alert your local police that you will be away; very often they will keep an extra eye on the property for you. Consider hiring a private patrol service to provide surveillance on your home while you're away. Check with your local telephone company to see whether they have a call-forwarding service that will inform callers how you can be reached if you do, in fact, wish to be reached.

Make arrangements for all payments falling due during your absence to be made. If that's not feasible, explain to your creditors that you will be gone for a while, and ask them if they can waive any late charges or make other accommodations in your absence. If you neglect to take care of such matters, you risk having late payments show on various accounts, which could be detrimental to your credit rating. If you have an investment program with a stockbroker, determine what action, if any, you might want the broker to take in your absence, depending on the ebbs and flows of the stock market. If that's not practical, leave word with the broker how you can be reached if the need arises. If you have any savings certificates or other securities maturing during the time you'll be absent, make arrangements with the bank or broker accordingly. The better you take care of such details before you leave, the better time you'll be able to have.

Know Your Rights

If you are traveling on a common carrier—particularly an airplane—make certain you know in advance what your rights are in the event you get bumped from your flight or in the event your luggage is lost or damaged. Bumping means that you have had your reservation canceled; there's no room for you on the plane. The Federal Aviation Administration requires that airlines make payments to passengers who are bumped. Determine what the current regulations are at the time you make your flight reservations. There are limitations on how much an airline is responsible for in the event of lost or damaged luggage. Determine current regulations in that matter as well. (As a matter of general precaution, never pack valuables in luggage that is to be checked. Rather than risk the anguish of even a temporary loss, carry those valuables with you onto the plane.)

Buying Big-Ticket Vacation Items

It's a curious facet of human nature: Most people are not in their "right minds" when they are planning a vacation or when they are actually on the vacation. During the planning stages, there's an aura of excited anticipation that surrounds the family, and common sense does not always penetrate that aura. That's the time when one is likely to say, with a burst of wild enthusiasm, "Let's go for broke and *buy* that camper we've always been talking about, or that speedboat we've always been talking about!" Or while on the vacation itself, a similar loss of reality can occur, in response to which one might say, "It's foolish to spend money *renting* a place here—let's *buy* a place!"

Then, in the rosy glow of a vacation mentality, you find that you've plunked down a few thousand dollars and signed a whopping contract for the balance of payments on the new motor home, speedboat, or vacation home.

Remember, before you write that check or sign that contract, that you've read these paragraphs and consider the following:

☐ On a minimal purchase of any of those items—say $20,000—the interest alone that you will pay on your debt will be in the neighborhood of $2000 to $3000 per year. That amount, in itself, can pay for one or more very nice vacations. Is it worth it?

☐ For the first year or two, or maybe even three, you'll get great enjoyment out of your purchase. But human nature being what it is, we tend to want to change the scene every few years for our vacations. Three years from now will you still want to go traveling in your van, or boating in your boat, or spending your vacation in a place that by now may have become boring to you? Your thoughts at the time you made the purchase may be, "We'll love it forever!" But a few years later you may wish you'd never taken the plunge. The time to think of that is *before* you take the plunge.

If you're contemplating a big-ticket vacation expenditure, such as a van, a boat, or your own vacation home or condominium, the best precaution is to proceed on a test basis. Rent for a year or two and see if it's really your style. The rental will probably cost you less than the interest alone on a purchase, and if you don't like it, you're able to walk away with no obligation trailing behind you. Contrary to what many salespersons may tell you, it's *not* always that easy to unload an unwanted camper, boat, or home in a distant resort area.

Time Sharing: An Easy Solution?

Time sharing is a recent phenomenon. Simply stated, time sharing means that you buy the right to use a specific apartment, condominium, or resort facility for one or two or more specific weeks during the year. Part of the time-sharing concept is that you can exchange your specific location for one of many others each year. If you weary of your condo in Waikiki after a few years, you can swap it for a villa in Switzerland or a resort in Miami or a castle in Spain.

Strategies for Success

Condominium Rentals Can Mean Big Vacation Savings

Staying in a motel or a resort can be expensive. The bigger your family and the longer you stay, the more expensive it gets. In most resort areas it's possible to rent condominiums for a lot less than you'd pay for a hotel room. Condominium owners often use the condo for their own vacations during part of the year and then put them up for rent when they're not using them. Condos usually come fully equipped (kitchen, linens, towels, etc.), and many have nice amenities, such as tennis courts, a swimming pool, and the like. If you don't need the services of a hotel (room service, telephone operator, etc.), the condo can give you a lot more vacation for a lot less money. Check with the Chamber of Commerce or Visitor's Bureau in the city you plan to visit for references on condo rentals.

It all sounds very attractive. Indeed, the concept is plausible, and some people have found great satisfaction in it. But the time-sharing phenomenon is also rife with misrepresentation and outright fraud. Many people have purchased time-sharing interests in resorts that were never built. Many find that the facilities are vastly inferior to the way in which the salesperson represented them. Many find that the so-called guaranteed cost is not guaranteed at all—that increasing assessments on owners boost the cost much higher than was anticipated. And, to make matters worse, many find that the exchange privileges are not as represented or are not available at all.

Time-sharing sales pitches are very high pressure. (See the discussion of land frauds and time sharing in Chapter 5.) The most prudent approach to a time-share sales offering is to visit the place in person to be certain that it is as it is represented to be. Study your contract carefully to determine what your exchange privileges, if any, might be and what added costs you might have to incur in the future. If you're not certain what the contract states in these matters, hire an attorney to review it for you. It may be many years before there is adequate governmental regulation of the abuse-ridden time-sharing industry. In the meantime, all due caution is worthwhile.

RECREATION AT HOME

Major vacation travel may occur only once every few years, and only a few weekends may be devoted to camping, traveling, or sightseeing. But every day, day in and day out, there are excess hours of leisure time to fill at home or within your community. Following are some considerations—financial and otherwise—on some of those predominant modes of filling your leisure time at home.

Electronics

It wasn't so long ago—in the late 1940s—that television was an infant. For a few hours a day, on one or two channels, you had your choice of watching pie-in-the-face comedians, grunt-and-groan wrestlers, slap-dash roller derby, and a smattering of news. It was all done in black and white on very small and very expensive screens.

In the space of just a single generation, television became the most pervasive and most influential medium for entertainment, news, and information in the history of mankind. And it's all in living color, on big screens that cost less than the early sets did a few decades ago.

In the 1990s, we'll start looking back on television as we knew it as a quaint antique compared with the newly emerging electronic phenomena that will become one of our predominant leisure-time fillers.

Electronics offers ever-increasing sophistication and capability at ever-decreasing costs. By the end of this decade, virtually every home in America will have one or more of the following: cable television offering dozens of channels; dish antennas capable of receiving scores, if not hundreds, of television channels from satellites hovering in space; video player/recorders; wide screen television sets that are five feet or more across; and home-computer terminals capable of interacting with the television for educational purposes, for work purposes, and for game playing.

And commonplace by the year 2000 will be video/computerized facilities that will print newspapers and magazines on recyclable plastic sheets right in our living rooms, that will allow us to work at home and interact with our home offices, that will serve as mail-order catalogues and banking facilities, and that will permit us access to virtually everything that's ever been filmed or printed via giant computers reached through satellite connections.

In short, we're at the early stages of the electronics revolution, and the emergence of new techniques and equipment will shape our leisure lives to a great extent.

With so many electric marvels due in the future, it can be frustrating to deliberate here and now what investments should be made in electronic leisure equipment. "Should I buy something today only to have it become obsolete next month by a more advanced model?" The point is well taken. But whatever you do invest in today, you can still enjoy for many years, while planning the next investment in more advanced equipment. Let's examine some of the specific items that may be tempting you currently.

Video Player/Recorders. Probably the most popular of the new electronic wonders are the video player/recorders. There are two basic types: cassette and disc. The cassette players can record, whereas the disc players can play only prerecorded material that the user buys or rents. Let's take a closer look at the pertinent details, all of which are, of course, subject to rapid change as technology advances.

☐ *Cassette players.* As noted, these can be used to record anything that is broadcast through your television set, including incoming cable and pay TV signals. There are two cassette systems: Beta and VHS. Each system uses a slightly different technology and tape. The two systems are not compatible; you cannot play or record a Beta tape on a VHS machine and vice versa.

When cassette player/recorders were first introduced in the early 1970s, they were priced at about $2000 and had very little flexibility. Currently, you can obtain top-quality equipment in either Beta or VHS for well under $500, and the machines are equipped with internal computers that allow you to set them to turn on, record, and turn off many days in advance. Other common features in both systems include fast forward, slow motion, and freeze-frame capability.

Prerecorded tapes, including movies, sporting events, and instructional material, can be purchased or rented. Many video shops in larger cities offer membership plans for tape rentals. By paying an annual fee, the daily rental rate for cassette tapes can be as low as $1. Compare that with the cost of taking the family to a movie theater. Blank recording tapes with a capacity of upward of six hours can be purchased for $5 to $10.

In shopping for a cassette player/recorder, bear in mind the following criteria: Will you really benefit from the costly optional extras included in many sets, or will you be better off with a lower cost, no-frills set? What type of warranty comes with the set? Parts? Labor? If service is needed, can it be done locally, or must the set be sent away to a service bureau? Competition is very keen with these products, so it will pay to shop around and seek discounts at local dealers.

☐ *Disc players.* Just as there are two types of noncompatible cassette players, there are two types of noncompatible disc players. One uses a tiny laser beam to scan the grooves on the disc; the other uses a stylus, or needle, just as a regular phonograph does. Because of their inability to record, disc players are less appealing for general home use. They are, though, less costly than the cassette machines. Both players and prerecorded discs are 20 to 30 percent less than the cassette machines and tapes.

In addition to stores that sell and rent prerecorded material, many public libraries are now offering prerecorded discs and cassettes to their local communities.

Video Cameras. The newest technological fad in the home electronic market is the video camera, which bodes to replace the now old-fashioned movie camera that uses film. It might even cut sharply into the market for still film cameras. While the price of a good quality video camera is on the high side ($700 to $1200), the long-range cost of capturing images can be much lower with a video camera. An hour's worth of video tape, in color and sound, costs less than $10. There are no developing or processing costs with the video tape. One hour's worth of movie film, including processing, could cost more than $100 and perhaps as much as $200. As with all other electronic gadgets, technology moves rapidly. This year's best deal might be obsolete hours after you get it home. But if you let yourself worry about that, you'll never enjoy using the machine. So make your best purchase after doing the necessary homework, and don't look back on what you might have bought had you only waited another week or two.

Computers. Technology is advancing so rapidly with these devices that it's difficult to predict what will be available to the public next month, let alone next year. The basic component is the typewriter-sized home computer that attaches to a television set, a printing machine, and your telephone. The cost of these units ranges from a few hundred dollars to thousands of dollars depending on their capabilities.

Popular uses of the home computer include budgeting and financial planning, instructional programming, and a wide variety of games. Many more sophisticated uses are available to the small businessowner and the professional person, including billing, inventory control, and a host of other bookkeeping and calculating functions.

Shopping for a home computer and the accompanying programs and games takes a lot of careful homework. How much will you really use the equipment?

Can you justify the cost of doing the projected work on the computer, or can you get it done as simply and more inexpensively using more traditional methods? Rapid change is expected in the home-computer market, so you must decide whether you will be buying something that will too quickly become obsolete or that will serve justifiable purposes for at least three to five years. And as with the video player/recorders, you must determine the extent of warranty as well as availability and cost of service for computer units. Finally, beware of what has befallen many home-computer buyers: After the novelty wears off, it is relegated to the expensive toy status, gathering dust in a forgotten corner of your family room.

High-Tech Television.   Technology never sleeps with respect to new developments in television sets. The allure of spending many hundreds, or even thousands, of dollars on the latest TV advances may be hard to resist. As with computers, today's "state of the art" television sets could be outmoded before tonight's programs become reruns. Study your needs, your budget, and the most up-to-date consumer guides available before you take the plunge on:

□ Large screen TV

□ "HDTV" (High definition television), the newest advance in making your picture more crisp, but for which you'll have to pay a handsome price

□ Hand-held mini-TV/VCRs, introduced by Japanese manufacturers in late 1988; these engineering marvels (at under $1,000) could prove useful as business and educational tools, in addition to their entertainment capabilities

Personal Enrichment

A great deal of your leisure time can be put to rewarding and productive use without spending much money. Look into the activities that may be available at your local library, college, church or synagogue, or community center, often at no charge. You're likely to find a delightful assortment of concerts, art exhibits, theatrical presentations, and lectures.

Carefully examine the continuing-education catalogs of your local community college or university. It's not all dry academic matter. Such programs are usually liberally sprinkled with a variety of courses and seminars that can amuse, entertain, and stimulate as well as educate. These programs are generally offered on weekends and evenings so that you can take advantage of them without interfering with your work.

Volunteer work—through religious and civic organizations—can be a very rewarding use of your leisure time. Volunteers are eagerly sought, and by helping others you can help yourself.

Sports, Hobbies, and Out-on-the-Town Activities

Whether it's an individual activity such as jogging, or a group activity such as joining a softball team, sports and athletics are among the most popular modes of spending leisure time, and they generally have minimal cost. There are, though, some areas where financial considerations should be taken into account.

☐ *Health spas and athletic clubs (tennis, golf, racquetball, etc.).* Membership at a health spa or an athletic club can be very expensive, and you must determine whether the cost is justifiable for you. You may be subjected to a rigorous sales pitch designed to convince you that you'll spend every waking nonworking hour on the premises becoming a better person. And in all likelihood, you will be expected to sign a long-term contract committing you to monthly payments for your membership. If it's at all possible, take a trial membership to see whether this particular facility is really right for you. Will you use it as much as the salesperson tells you? And will the benefits to you be as delightful as the sales brochure suggests? Determine how long the facility has been in business, and talk with current members to ascertain their level of satisfaction. Be aware that many such facilities run into financial problems. This can result in a sharp increase in cost to members; or at worst (and not that uncommon), the facility simply closes down and disappears along with the money you've paid.

☐ *Individual sports and hobbies.* Many activities, such as skiing, sailing, scuba diving, and photography, can involve considerable investment on your part. If you are already committed to such activities, you know well what it is costing you. If you are contemplating embarking on any of these activities, calculate in advance the cost of getting set up. Then, as with the health spas and athletic clubs, give it a trial run first to see if it's really right for you. Once you've spent many hundreds of dollars, if not more, on gear and equipment, if you then find that it's not your cup of tea, you might be hard pressed to sell all that used equipment.

☐ *Professional sports.* If you're a "sports nut" and you live in a major league city (for baseball, football, hockey, basketball, soccer), you know how expensive it can be to satisfy your cravings. If you're a frequent devotee of any of these sports, consider buying and sharing season tickets with other fans. The total cost to you over the full season might be considerably less for the same number of admissions as if you were buying tickets individually for each event. Also, inquire periodically at the respective ticket offices to determine when discount plans and group plans may be available. Your employer or union may also offer discount packages to sporting events.

☐ *A night on the town.* Dining out and attending movies or concerts are regular items on many people's leisure-time schedule. That's all well and good, but bear in mind that the expenses for these activities are often not inconsiderable. They are also the expenses that tend to get forgotten about in budget calculations.

Since we often do such things on impulse, and since part of the activity itself finds us under the influence of external substances, it can become all too easy to ignore what the particular activity is costing. When you say, ''Sure let's have another bottle of wine'' enough times in a month, you could unwittingly be impairing your ability to buy necessities the following month. And since a very high percentage of dining out is paid for by credit card instead of hard cash, the temptation to spend more than what is reasonable is easily succumbed to. Further, if the credit card bill isn't paid in full by the end of the month, you'll start building up interest costs, which can end up increasing the price of that meal or that bottle of wine by 20 percent, 50 percent, or even 100 percent if you wait long enough to get the bill paid.

Out-on-the-town expenses should be budgeted in advance and whenever possible paid for by cash or check. Nobody is telling you not to have a good time. You just must be careful of having too good a time right now at the expense of not being able to afford a good time some months hence.

THE ULTIMATE LEISURE

The poet William Wordsworth wrote these lines:

The world is too much with us; late and soon,
Getting and spending, we lay waste our powers.
Little we see in nature that is ours;
We have given our hearts away, a sordid boon!

With these words, Wordsworth bemoaned the fact that we get so caught up in the day-to-day business of life that we neglect to take advantage of the beauties and pleasures that nature has provided. We have, as he says, ''given our hearts away,'' sold out to the daily tumult of our regular work routine, and while that may have its own rewards, we may be missing out on other things more valuable. A more modern (and anonymous) philosopher put it more succinctly on a popular poster: ''Don't run so fast that you can't smell the flowers.''

Vacation Planner

No worksheet can help you determine how much pleasure you'll have on a vacation. But this planner can aid you in calculating and comparing the costs of various leisure holidays. Estimate each item carefully. A travel agent can be of great help, at no additional cost to you. Bon voyage!

Item	Estimated cost		
	Vacation 1	*Vacation 2*	*Vacation 3*
☐ Getting there			
Airplane			
Bus			
Train			
Car			
Meals, lodging en route			
☐ Getting about			
Rental car			
Buses, tours, excursions			
☐ Room and board			
Hotel, motel (are any meals included?)			
Meals (not included in hotel price)			
Snacks, drinks			
☐ Activities			
Equipment usage and rental (boats, skis, lifts, horses, etc.)			
Amusements (movies, amusement parks, concerts, plays, etc.)			
☐ Miscellaneous			
☐ Total estimated expense			
☐ Amount of money available to pay for vacation			
☐ Amount to be financed (loans, credit cards, etc.)			
☐ Interest cost on amount financed (assuming you pay it all off in 12 monthly installments)			

Troubles with Time Sharing

Time sharing is a relatively new concept for vacationing. For a fixed amount of money, you obtain the right to use a resort facility for one or two weeks per year. But many emerging abuses in the time-sharing industry illustrate the old adage, "the big print giveth, the small print taketh away." Some examples are as follows:

What the big print in the ad says or what the salesperson tells you	*What the small print in the contract says*
Time-sharing interests start at only $1000 down for one week per year. . . .	At that minimum price, if it's a ski resort, your week will be in July. If it's a condo in the Caribbean, your time is hurricane season. In-season rates start at $5000.
Low monthly payments, never to exceed $100. . . .	. . . except for miscellaneous assessments for repairs, added taxes, promotion, advertising, and such sundry items as the managers may from time to time determine they need or want.
If during any year you don't wish to use your facilities, you can swap the use for any of our 126 other resort facilities throughout the world.	Of course, since you bought the cheapest unit in the package, you can swap only for a one-week stay at the Thrifty Motel in Pittsburgh during January. Or you can have a lovely villa in Tasmania, but you have to get there at your own expense.
If you don't sign up for this fabulous deal within 60 minutes, you may have forever passed up the chance of a lifetime.	. . . unless you come back tomorrow, or next week, or next month, when the same deal will be available.

Time-sharing sales tactics are traditionally high pressure, and the contracts control your rights, not what the salesperson tells you. Resist impulsive buying. Study the offering carefully before you sign. Better still, visit the resort first to make sure it's really there and really has the facilities that it's represented to have.

CHAPTER 8

Buying a Home

Where to live? House, apartment, condominium? Central city, suburban, or somewhere in between? How much of your available budget should be devoted to housing, at the possible expense of other needs or desires? Scrimp now for the sake of something better in the future? Or spend now and not worry about the future?

There are no easy answers to these questions. Each individual or family must decide what will best suit their own specific needs and desires taking into account the applicable financial, geographical, architectural, and personal factors involved. This chapter will help you evaluate these factors and will also help you resolve these other common problems:

□ How to find a dwelling in the right price range

□ How to make the best use of real estate agents

□ How to handle the contracts and other documents involved in a housing transaction

□ How to get ready for the closing when you buy a house or condominium

□ How to know your legal rights as a home buyer

FINANCIAL FACTORS

A house (or condominium) is the single largest purchase that most individuals will ever make, and they generally have to live with it longer than most other purchases. A mortgage loan is the biggest debt most people will ever incur, and monthly payments (including utility costs and maintenance obligations) represent a major portion of most budgets.

If you have the down payment available to allow you to purchase a home and if you can meet the monthly payments without unduly crippling your budget, owning a home can offer very attractive financial benefits. The interest you pay on your mortgage, as well as the property taxes, will provide substantial deductions on your income tax return. This can result in a substantially lower federal income tax, and the money saved on taxes can be applied toward your housing costs. Through these tax breaks, the government, in effect, subsidizes homeownership.

The Tax Reform Act of 1986 placed some restrictions on the deductibility of interest paid on home loans. These restrictions are discussed at greater length in Chapters 9 and 22.

Homeownership also offers the possibility of attractive profits. Home values have been rapidly accelerating in most parts of the country, and the trend seems likely to continue. Not only are the profit potentials attractive, but tax laws favor those who sell their homes at a profit. When a home is sold at a profit, it is possible to postpone the payment of capital gains taxes for an indefinite period. And for home sellers over fifty-five years of age, a substantial portion of their profit can be excluded from taxes altogether. These aspects of taxation on the sale of a home are discussed in more detail in Chapter 12.

GEOGRAPHICAL FACTORS

You cannot afford to overlook the cost involved in getting to and from work, shopping, schools, and other places, whether by private automobile or by mass transit.

Travel Time and Cost Worksheet

Consider, for example, having to choose between house A and house B, which are identical in all respects, including price. The only difference between them is that house A is closer to work, schools, shopping, and entertainment facilities. You estimate that if you bought house A, your overall transportation costs would be $100 per month less than if you bought house B. Furthermore, if you bought house B, you'd have to spend, on the average, an extra twenty hours a month commuting than if you bought house A. You must consider these factors when choosing a house.

Use the worksheet in Table 8-1 to calculate your travel time and costs, including both minutes of driving time and miles driven per month for houses A and B.

Neighborhood

The condition of the neighborhood must also be evaluated. A stable, declining, or improving neighborhood can affect not only your state of mind and comfort level but can also be of great importance with respect to the future resale value of your house. For example, assume you are evaluating two identical houses. One costs less than the other. The less costly house is in a declining neighborhood. Today the less expensive house might seem to be the better buy, but what about in the future?

Table 8-1   **Travel Time Worksheet**

Destination	To and from House A (Minutes/Miles)	To and from House B (Minutes/Miles)
School(s)	_____	_____
Major shopping places	_____	_____
Church/synagogue	_____	_____
Major entertainment places	_____	_____
Work (husband)	_____	_____
Work (wife)	_____	_____
Car pooling	_____	_____
Other	_____	_____

ARCHITECTURAL FACTORS

When making a house-purchasing decision, consider the house's architectural aspects: design, layout, size, and physical condition. They all have a bearing on getting the best value for your money.

- ☐ *Design.*   Design is largely a matter of taste, but it comes at a price. To what extent can you justify what could be costly design elements? If you expect to do business entertaining in your home, however, the extra investment in decor might pay off.

- ☐ *Layout and size.*   The size and layout of the house should suit your family needs as they exist today and as you expect them to be in the foreseeable future. It's uncomfortable when a house is too small, and it can be very costly to expand later.

- ☐ *Physical condition.*   Invest in a professional evaluation of all the physical aspects of the house: roof, walls, foundation, heating system, plumbing, and so on. Any contract to purchase should be contingent upon your approval of an inspection.

PERSONAL FACTORS

All too often we make major financial decisions based on what others think best for us, not on what we ourselves prefer. (Reread the Consumer Beware section at the end of Chapter 3.) Following others' advice rather than your own desires can be a sorry mistake. A house defines your life style. You and your family have to live in it, deal with it, enjoy it. Consider the following personal factors in your search for a house:

☐ *Privacy.* A house offers considerably more privacy than a condominium or an apartment. If, however, you prefer the closeness and camaraderie of others, a condominium or an apartment may be the best choice.

☐ *Leisure activities.* Assuming that house A and condominium A are similar in size, type of neighborhood, and structural quality, the house will cost more than the condominium. If most of your leisure activities are at home, spending the extra money on the house can be a worthwhile investment. On the other hand, if most of your leisure activities are outside the home (skiing, fishing, hiking, traveling), purchasing the condominium might make more sense. Then you'll have more money available for your leisure activities.

☐ *Future considerations.* Spending less on housing now than you can otherwise afford will allow you to have more money to spend for future needs. Evaluate this possibility if it applies to you.

The Personal Action Checklist at the end of this chapter will help you evaluate these factors.

TYPES OF HOUSING

Inflation has pushed the cost of new homes skyward. Along with the sharply escalating costs of building a home come the comparable expenses of financing it. Interest rates on home loans, which had been in the 5 to 6 percent range through the 1950s and into the 1960s, shot to as high as 18 percent in the early 1980s. By the late 1980s, rates had fallen back below 10 percent. This recent history of fluctuation in interest rates indicates that long-term stability for this important element of housing is not likely in the years ahead.

Houses

Although it is possible to rent a house, outright ownership is the more common means of acquiring this type of dwelling. The usual mode of purchasing involves a cash down payment that might represent as little as 5 percent of the purchase price, up to a more common range of 20 to 30 percent. The balance of the purchase price is paid over an extended period of time, frequently running as long as twenty to thirty years. The buyer's promise to repay the remaining balance is secured by signing an IOU commonly referred to as a *mortgage*. (In some states this is referred to as a *trust deed*.)

During times of high home-buying costs and high interest rates, many would-be home buyers find themselves priced out of the market. But there are some innovative techniques that could allow you to buy a house in spite of the high costs.

Shared Housing. Two or more individuals or families can chip in to buy a house, a condominium, or a co-op. They will split the down payment and the monthly payments in accordance with whatever agreement they reach among themselves. Indeed, many builders throughout the country have embarked on construction of houses designed for sharing. Typically, these houses will have private bedroom suites for each owner and a common living room, dining room, and kitchen area that the owners share. Shared housing is comparable to having a roommate in a rental situation, with the important difference being that you own your share of the dwelling and can reap the financial benefits therefrom.

Shared Equity. Although shared ownership can be a good way to acquire an equity interest in a home, it is not without its problems. The partners must agree on how the down payment and monthly payments are to be split between them, how the operating and maintenance costs are to be shared, and what percent of ownership each person is entitled to. If you are considering a shared-equity partnership, it's essential that you obtain legal advice before signing any documents.

Land Leasing. In a land leasing situation, the buyer buys only the house and leases the land upon which the house sits for a long term (upward of fifty years). Ownership of the land is retained by the former owner. The new buyer agrees to pay a set monthly rental to the seller for the land lease and arranges his own mortgage financing for the purchase of the house. The advantage to the buyer in this arrangement is that the purchase price is lower than it would be had the land as well as the house been purchased.

Both shared housing and land leasing can have legal intricacies, and the advice of a lawyer is essential before entering into either type of arrangement.

Condominiums and Cooperatives

Condominiums and cooperatives are a relatively new form of dwelling ownership. They are somewhat similar and are often confused, but their differences should be well understood. Both refer to multiple-housing complexes, and in each case an individual resident has a form of ownership. In a *cooperative*, each resident owns what's called an undivided percentage of the total building. In a *condominium*, the resident owns only a specific dwelling unit.

Here's how they both work. Picture what you would call an apartment house, five stories high, with four apartments on each floor. All of the apartments are of equal size and value. On a cooperative basis, each of the twenty residents own an undivided one-twentieth of the total building. In effect, it's like twenty partners owning the whole project, each having an equal vote. The cooperative owners enter into an agreement that sets forth what type of vote is necessary to take various actions. For example, it may require a simple majority vote—eleven out of the twenty—to commit the group to improvements or repairs of a certain value. It might take a three-quarters vote, or fifteen out of the twenty, to commit all of the members to major expenses. And it may take a unanimous vote to reach an agreement to sell the project. Each cooperative group determines its own rules and regulations.

Each member or family belonging to the cooperative has an individual lease agreement with the cooperative for the premises they occupy. If there is not an actual lease, there is some form of agreement in the cooperative documents permitting a particular member of the cooperative to occupy a particular apartment within the building. This master agreement among all the cooperative members also spells out such matters as the right to sublease their own apartments to nonmembers of the cooperative, the right to sell their own interests in the cooperative to outsiders, and the right to sell or bequeath interest in the cooperative to members or nonmembers of their own families. Not unlikely, any members of the cooperative who wish to dispose of their interest in one way or another may first be required to offer it back to the other members of the cooperative, perhaps at a previously agreed price, or based on a previously agreed formula for setting a price.

The business affairs of the cooperative may be run by a volunteer member of the group or by a hired professional, depending on the size and complexity of the building management. The cooperative, as principal owner (and its members indirectly) is responsible for all the building occupancy costs, including property taxes, property insurance, utilities, and maintenance. In all likelihood, the cooperative will have borrowed money—a mortgage—to make the property purchase (or construction) in the first place. Each of the individual members will have signed the mortgage to individually insure payment.

In a *condominium* each of the twenty occupants, individuals or families, own their own separate and distinct unit. As in a cooperative, all of the individual owners enter into agreement with all of the others regarding basic management of the property, maintenance of the common areas, and rights of the individual owners to sublease and sell to parties of their own choosing. Each owner is responsible for individual property taxes and property insurance, and, as with a cooperative, each is additionally responsible for taxes and insurance as they apply to the common areas of the building.

Condominiums and cooperatives can come into being in one of two ways: An existing building can be converted into condominium or cooperative ownership, or a new structure may be developed and sold to occupants on a condominium or cooperative basis. When apartments are converted, the contractual consent of all occupants is required in advance. Occupants who don't want to go along with the conversion might have to move. When new structures are built, there can be many potential pitfalls until the building is completed and all units are sold. During the construction period there is dual ownership: The developer owns all of the unsold units, and new buyers own their separate units. If the developer is not able to sell the units at a favorable price, he may rent the unsold units to tenants, which can cause serious friction between the tenants and those who have already purchased their units. If the developer's lawyer has drawn a tight contract, the individual unit owners have very little recourse in such a situation.

Other problematic situations that can occur in new condominium developments include the following:

□ The developer reserves ownership of the recreational facilities, for which the occupants are charged a use fee. If the developer is not contractually limited concerning the amount of the charge, the fee can become outrageous.

□ The developer may scrimp on construction, knowing that once each individual unit is sold, the owner is responsible for the unit's maintenance. This can eventually cause costly maintenance and renovation headaches for individual owners.

□ A developer may run into financial problems before completing a project, thus putting owners who have already bought units in financial jeopardy. The financial condition of the developer should be carefully checked before a purchase contract is signed.

Homeowners can do as they please as long as they don't break any laws or create any nuisances. They can sell their homes when they like, to whom they like, and at the price the market will bear. However, owners of condominiums and cooperatives have limited rights subject to the contract with the association and possibly with the original developer. Although many have regarded condominiums as the best of both worlds—the convenience of apartment living with the advantages of homeownership—the contractual agreements they necessitate often prove that life in a condominium is not without its own problems.

Mobile Homes

A mobile home dwelling customarily involves a combination of ownership and rental. The unit itself is purchased from a dealer and is often financed with a long-term installment loan. The unit is then shipped to the owner's destination, usually at the owner's expense, where it is moored on its pad and hooked up to the available water, gas, and electricity. The owner pays a rental for the pad to the park management and is responsible for individual insurance and utility costs. In some instances, of course, mobile home purchasers may have their unit installed on property they already own, thus avoiding the rental fee.

Although mobile homes may really not be as mobile as they were a generation ago, an owner does have some limited degree of flexibility in moving the dwelling from one site to another. The farther the distance, the higher the cost, so long-range moves may not be feasible. If there's a slight possibility that a mobile home may be moved to a different location, the would-be buyer must understand explicitly what the costs may be.

Because mobile homes are not of the same permanent construction as regular houses, an owner must be alert to the possibility of a depreciation in value, compared with the more customary increase in value that permanent homes enjoy. In shopping for a new mobile home, one should compare the prices of similar *used* mobile homes to get an idea about the likely future of the current purchase. In making a final decision, this depreciation should be carefully evaluated.

It's also important to consider the rental arrangements for the site upon which a mobile home is placed. Commonly, such sites are rented on a month-to-month basis. If the owner of the park decides to sell the entire property, that could mean eviction on short notice for the site renters, requiring a costly move of the mobile home. It may be advantageous to try to negotiate a long-term ground lease for a mobile home to eliminate or minimize the possibility of having to move on short notice.

Multiple Units

Other forms of dwellings are represented by multiple-unit buildings and townhouses. The latter are called *row houses* in some parts of the country. The multiple-unit housing is most commonly the *duplex*, where two dwelling units occupy the same building, either side by side or one above the other. Some structures may even house three units (a *triplex*) or four units (a *fourplex*). Buildings having more than four units are normally referred to as apartment houses, although there is no precise legal definition of an apartment house. One may buy a duplex, a triplex, or a fourplex with the intention of living in one of the units and renting out the others. This situation can prove to be attractive if the style of living is suitable to you, for the rental income can offset your own dwelling costs and even provide an attractive tax shelter. (A more detailed discussion of the tax-shelter benefits of rental real estate is provided in Chapter 18.) It's also possible for the occupants of a multiple-housing complex to own their units on a condominium basis or as a cooperative.

Town houses, or *row houses*, are a series of connected dwelling units sharing common walls. These walls allow economy in construction, and the higher density of units on a given piece of property can also result in cost efficiencies. Town houses, which may be owned individually as condominiums or cooperative units or which may be rented, offer a combination of house and apartment living that is attractive to many. They can provide more space than an apartment at a lower price than a comparably sized single-family home. If the walls between the adjoining units are well insulated, a homelike privacy can be maintained.

BUYING THE RIGHT DWELLING AT THE RIGHT PRICE

Buying a dwelling—and whether it's a cooperative, a condominium, or a house, we'll use the all-encompassing term *house* for simplicity—will be the largest and most complicated transaction you'll probably ever enter into. It's worth doing it right even if it means spending a lot of time and energy in the process.

The two critical elements in buying a house are

1. Determining how much you can comfortably afford to pay (down payment and monthly payments); and

2. Finding the right house, at that affordable price, in a neighborhood that will suit you. A real estate agent can be of considerable value in this respect.

There are many considerations that have a bearing on the elements listed above, including the following:

☐ Satisfying your personal needs

☐ Finding comparable values

☐ Evaluating the age of the dwelling and consequent advantages or disadvantages

☐ Warranties that may be available

☐ Financing terms

☐ Utility costs

☐ Financing costs

☐ Resale potential

Your Price Range

You must take into account the amount of both the down payment available and the monthly payments. The higher your down payment, the lower your monthly payments, and vice versa. As a starting exercise—before you even begin to look at houses—visit one or more local home financing institutions (banks, savings and loan associations, savings banks, mortgage brokers), and determine what *they* think you can afford. Their guidelines, even though they may be vague, will at least give you a starting point. It is reasonable to assume that monthly housing costs for most families are in excess of 40 percent of their after-tax income. For many families, it may take two incomes to allow them to buy a house. (For more details on financing, see Chapter 9.)

Strategies for Success

Shop for Financing Before Shopping for a Home

If you're planning on buying a home, shop for the financing before you shop for the property itself. Most lenders can give you at least a tentative commitment about how much of a loan you can get. (Some lenders will even prequalify you for a loan, subject only to their appraisal of the property you select.) Knowing in advance how much of a loan you can get allows you to zero in on the right price range from the start. Thus, you won't go over your head, nor will you undercut yourself. More important, knowing that you can get a loan in advance puts you in a better bargaining position with a seller. You're talking from a position of financial strength. The seller knows he won't have to wait a month or two to find out if you can get the financing you need. Cash talks.

Using a Real Estate Agent

In addition to scouring the classified ads in your local newspaper and visiting open houses at every opportunity, you should consider the value in finding a good real estate agent to help you in your housing quest. Many people think of using a real estate agent only when they sell a house. But there are many advantages to using a real estate agent when you are buying.

Most agents belong to an association of local real estate professionals called the *multiple listing service*. This service publishes a directory, usually weekly, of all houses in the area that are for sale. The listings contain extensive information on each house, including its physical features and its costs. By using the listings, a real estate agent has access to the vast majority of all houses on the market. The listings provide considerably more information than you can glean from the classified ads. By using the listings, a real estate agent can help you locate the right house in the right neighborhood at a considerable savings to you of your time and energy.

A good agent is a skilled negotiator and should be able to help you bargain for the best possible price. And good agents are in constant touch with the financial markets so that they can help you obtain the financing you'll need. Furthermore, the services of a real estate agent cost the buyer nothing: The agent's commission is paid by the seller.

It's not easy to find a good real estate agent to represent you as a buyer. Many agents are leery, and perhaps rightfully so, of would-be buyers who are really just ''lookers.'' They can't afford to spend much of their time unless they know that a would-be buyer is really serious. If an agent feels that a buyer is serious and that the buyer will, in fact, work with the agent all the way, the agent is more likely to work hard on the buyer's behalf. A contract between the real estate agent and the buyer is customarily not necessary; the agent acts on good faith between the parties.

If you do find an agent who is willing to work for you, be sure that she is willing to show you properties that are listed by firms other than her own. You want to be sure that you are getting a good look at all available properties in the community.

Timing

Timing can be critical in the purchase of a house. To the extent possible, make certain that your financing arrangements for your new home will coincide with the expected closing date. Also arrange as far in advance as possible for your departure from your current dwelling. If you're living in an apartment, be certain to give proper and timely notice of your departure to your landlord. If you're living in another house or condominium, do as much as you can to assure that that dwelling will be sold as close as possible to the time you take possession of the new dwelling. If you fail to coordinate these transactions, you could become an anxious seller of the dwelling you now occupy. As the next paragraphs indicate, the plight of the anxious seller is not a happy one.

Looking for the Anxious Seller

The anxious seller is the person from whom you are most likely to get a good buy and who accordingly is worth seeking out. A real estate agent can be of considerable help in locating anxious sellers. The listings referred to earlier often contain information that can help identify this type of seller.

Here are the most typical situations confronting the anxious seller:

□ The house has been on the market for a particularly long time. The seller realizes that each month that goes by costs an extra month's worth of payments. The sooner he can unload the house, the quicker he can stop the drain on his funds.

□ The house is already vacant. The seller has moved into a new dwelling— perhaps because of a job transfer—and is making payments on both. Nothing can make a seller more anxious to sell than making monthly payments on two dwellings.

□ There has been a major change in the family such as divorce or death. In either instance, the owner may be more anxious than usual to wrap up the sale of the property, if for no other reason than to be relieved of the legal complications that go with such situations.

Strategies for Success

Pros and Cons of Buying Foreclosures

No one likes to capitalize on someone else's misfortunes. But the fact is that you might be able to buy a home that has been foreclosed for a much lower price than it would sell for on the regular market. Check with local lenders—such as banks, savings institutions, and so forth to find out what's available in their portfolio of properties that they have taken over in foreclosure. Better still, a friendly banker or real estate agent might know of properties about to go into foreclosure. You might be able to get first crack at a nice house before the general public does. Beware, though, of the dangers of taking over foreclosed property: The physical condition of the home may be sorely neglected and in need of costly repairs. Also, there may be other liens on the property. Don't buy anything without a thorough inspection and a title search. Legal services are also advised.

Driving a Hard Bargain

It's traditional that a seller will ask one price, the buyer will offer a lower price, and they will ultimately settle for something in between. Unless the demand for houses vastly exceeds the supply, this type of bargaining is almost taken for granted when buying a house. It may seem distasteful to you to bargain over the price, but be well forewarned that when *you* sell a house, buyers will haggle with *you* over the price. The real estate agents representing the buyer and the seller will generally convey the offers and counter-offers back and forth, so that you don't actually have to come face to face with the seller on this matter. All the more reason to consider using a real estate agent when you buy: The agent is better able to handle this delicate phase of the purchase than you might be.

OTHER CONSIDERATIONS

Let's now examine some of the other considerations that can have a bearing on your purchase of a house.

Personal Needs

A good price on a house that's too small today may prove to be a regrettable decision if, in a few years, you have to either enlarge the house or tolerate the inconvenience of inadequate space. Similarly, if a house later proves to be too large for your needs, you may look back at the original purchase as having been more costly than necessary. Although changes in household size aren't always predictable, the possibilities must be considered, particularly when you're putting out many thousands of dollars for a down payment and signing an IOU for many more thousands.

Comparable Values

Assuming you've located an area in which you want to live, and taking into full account the costs of commuting to work, shopping, schools, and other facilities, you should try to determine if a specific house you're interested in is priced in a range comparable to others in the vicinity. Your real estate agent can help you by examining the records of recent sales in the area. All other things (size, quality, location) being equal, comparable houses should sell for comparable prices. You may be fortunate in finding an anxious seller who is disposing of property at a comparably lower price than what otherwise might be obtained. Likewise, you may find someone who is asking the maximum they think the traffic will bear. Unless you, the buyer, do some checking, you may succumb to the asking price, when in fact you could have perhaps obtained a better buy if you were armed with knowledge of comparable sales in the neighborhood.

Age of the Dwelling

Be careful not to compare apples with oranges. This is particularly true concerning houses that otherwise are equal in size and quality but differ in age. The age of a house can have a distinct bearing on the value you may or may not be getting for your money. Aside from elements of decor, you have to evaluate the physical deterioration that may have occurred regarding either the old or the new house. In certain neighborhoods the old saying "They don't build them like they used to" may be perfectly true. Certain older homes may have been built with better quality materials and greater craftsmanship than more recent homes. However, the reverse can also be true. Only a detailed inspection by a qualified contractor can reveal the current condition and need for maintenance and replacement of such things as foundation, sidewalls, roof, heating system, plumbing, wiring, and specific appliances.

One advantage of purchasing an older home may be an older home loan that carries a lower rate of interest. Another advantage can be that as you make payments on the older mortgage, you build up your equity at a faster rate. The older a mortgage gets, the greater portion of each monthly payment goes to principal, as illustrated by Table 8-2. Possibly offsetting this advantage of the older mortgage will be the likely requirement for a larger down payment. Careful analysis is called for.

Warranties

Unless warranties are specifically spelled out in a contract and agreed to by the parties, they might not be enforceable. Customarily, brand-new homes are sold with a one-year warranty by the builder. (It is not customary for used homes to have warranties, but in recent years many real estate brokerage firms have been offering limited warranties to buyers of used homes.) New home warranties generally cover the premises with respect to cracks, leaks, and breakdowns of mechanical equipment. In addition to such warranties, the buyer and seller might agree to specific clauses that should be included in the contract of sale. A seller may warrant, for example, that the roof is in excellent condition and that if it leaks within the first twelve months, it will be repaired at the seller's own expense. This is an agreement between the two parties, and if properly drawn and executed, it

Table 8-2 **Rate of Debt Reduction on Mortgage**

$60,000 Mortgage	*30-Year term*	*9% Fixed interest rate*	
During	*% of Debt paid off*	*Dollars paid off*	*Dollars still owed at end*
1st 10 years	10.6	$ 6,360	$53,640
2nd 10 years	25.9	15,540	38,100
3rd 10 years	63.5	38,100	–0–

Example: During the first 10 years of this loan, you pay off 10.6% of the debt, or $6360. But during the second 10 years, you reduce the original debt by 25.9%, or $15,540. Thus, if you step into a seasoned mortgage, as opposed to a brand-new mortgage, and you own the dwelling for 10 years, a much larger portion of your payments will come back to you when you sell.

binds the seller to perform his promise should the roof leak. A seller may offer such warranties as an inducement to a buyer, or a buyer may request such warranties from the seller as part of the overall bargain. It's strictly a matter to be negotiated between the parties. There is no legal requirement that a seller offer such warranties, and lacking anything in writing, the buyer has little protection.

Another form of warranty that may accrue to the buyer's benefit is the warranty on specific mechanical equipment. For example, a water heater may be installed with a seven-year guarantee. During the seven-year period, the house changes hands. The remaining guarantee on the water heater could accrue to the benefit of the new buyer. The same might be true of any other mechanical equipment.

In the purchase of a new house, the buyer should take care to determine whether mechanical equipment warranties are included in the builder's overall warranty and, if they are not, exactly what one's protection may be. For example, the warranty on a water heater may begin as of the date of installation. The unit may actually have been installed one year prior to the sale of the house to the ultimate buyer. Thus, one full year of the warranty may have already elapsed before the buyer even begins to use the appliance.

Any warranty—be it on a house, an appliance, or any other product or service—is only as good as its specific legal statements, and it's only as good as the ability of the warrantor to perform.

Financing Costs

"How much down, and how much a month?" These are the predominant questions asked when considering any kind of financing. It's not always as simple as that, though. You have to determine how much of a down payment you can make, relative to the money you have access to, without interfering with your other predictable financial needs. Bear in mind that once money has been used for a down payment on a house, that money can't be retrieved unless you either refinance or sell the house. Both transactions can be costly and time-consuming, if in fact they're feasible at all. Before you commit your down payment dollars, evaluate if and when you might need that money for other purposes, such as emergency medical expenses or other personal matters.

The monthly payments must similarly be in line with your overall budget. Examine the terms of the proposed mortgage to determine if the payments can change in future months or years. This can be the case if you have an adjustable-rate mortgage or another plan that allows the lender to alter the interest rate, and thus the monthly payments, at some future time. These escalation possibilities are discussed in more detail in Chapter 9.

To your advantage will be the tax breaks given to homeowners: The interest you pay on your mortgage is deductible on your tax return (as are the property taxes you pay). This can result in a sharply lower income tax bill each year. You can realize these tax savings immediately, instead of having to wait until you get your tax refund. By amending your W-4 form at work to reflect your deductions, you can increase your take-home pay accordingly and use that extra spendable money to meet your mortgage payments.

Utility Costs

Heating and electrical costs have risen drastically in most parts of the country in recent years. A generation ago, a home buyer may have paid little attention to utility costs, for they were a relatively small portion of the total out-of-pocket expenses involved in homeownership. Not so any longer. Energy conservation is not just a patriotic slogan; it's an economic necessity and must be considered carefully during the home-buying decision-making process. If you're buying a used home, it's necessary to determine the utility costs that the former owners incurred. Obviously, not all families will utilize energy in the same way, but the amounts the former owner incurred serve at least as a beginning guideline to help you determine the costs you'll be facing. If you're buying a new home, this task is more difficult. But if the same builder has erected comparable homes in the immediate vicinity, you might attempt to visit the owners of those homes and inquire about their utility expenditures. A visit to the local utility companies might also be helpful in getting these preliminary estimates. Also, a physical examination of the insulation in the house can be important. If there's adequate insulation, you'll be realizing a better bargain. If insulation is inadequate, you should evaluate the cost of bringing it up to standard compared with the cost of additional fuel you'll use because of its lack. Your local utility company and local building contractors can assist you in these considerations.

Furnishing Costs

Beyond the cost of the house itself, the cost of financing the house, and the cost of utilities, you must also consider the cost of furnishing the house to suit your desires. If the decor is not satisfactory, how much will it cost to repaint, repaper, and otherwise change it? Other items that can run into considerable expense include carpeting, draperies, and cabinetry. You'll also want to determine how much of your existing furniture can be used in the new dwelling, and how much additional furniture you may need to complete the interior satisfactorily. Two houses, with all other things being equal, can differ considerably with regard to the furnishings that may be included or may have to be added. Evaluating these elements is part of your initial buying decision. Where will the money come from to provide the necessary furnishings and changes in decor? Do you have the cash available? Will you finance these purchases over the customary three- to five-year term of a home improvement installment loan? Can you add the cost of these purchases to your overall cost of the home and include them in the mortgage? Whichever step you take, or whichever combination of steps, how will it affect the balance of your regular budget?

The bulk of the money you spend on furnishings cannot be recaptured. Used furniture has very little resale value. Changes in decor, including carpeting and draperies, may enhance the value of the property on a subsequent resale, but if they are too deteriorated or out of style, they could detract from the price. In other words, before you commit dollars to furnishing expenses on the new home, you must carefully evaluate the effect of such expenses on your overall budget.

Resale Potential

When buying a house, it may seem foolish to exercise your brain in estimating what you might be able to sell it for five or ten or fifteen years in the future. Granted, there's no way to assuredly predict what any property in any community might bring even a year or two after purchase. But it may be foolish to ignore the question altogether. As previously discussed, some neighborhoods evidence signs of slow and gradual deterioration, while others seem to have a fairly assured future of increase in property values. There may be subtle changes underway in the neighborhood characteristics. This can have a decreasing effect on the value of property. If you envision the possibility of reselling the home within a relatively short period of time—say, four to seven years—your real estate agent should be able to help you estimate the possibility of increase or decrease in value. If you'll be in the home for longer than that, you'd probably do best to put your thoughts into the hunch category and hope for the best.

Once you've made all the necessary evaluations, you're ready to visit your attorney and discuss the terms of the sale.

MAKING THE PURCHASE

You've found a house that is desirable and affordable. You've made an offer on it, which the seller has accepted. What happens next? Commonly, the seller's real estate agent prepares a brief memorandum of agreement setting forth the basic terms of the deal. Both parties sign this memorandum, and the buyer may be asked to pay some "earnest money" to bind the deal. The memorandum controls the situation until a more formal purchase contract is entered into.

Purchase Contracts

The purchase contract is a very important aspect of a real estate transaction. It sets forth the names of the parties involved, describes the property, dictates the terms and conditions of the sale, stipulates the kind of deed that the seller will deliver to the buyer, and states where and when the closing is to take place. Generally, a purchase contract is prepared by the seller's representative, either a real estate agent or an attorney. One of the primary rules in the world of financial and legal trans-actions is that if the other party's representative has prepared a contract for your signature, you can and should assume that the contract is structured to favor the other party. Only by having your own representative review the document can you be assured of the fullest protection of your own interests.

Parties to the Contract. The names and addresses of the buyers and the sellers are set forth in the contract. Customarily, a married couple will acquire a house in joint names, or what is referred to as *tenants by the entirety.* Although complications concerning the names of the parties may be rare, they nevertheless can occur. For example, the house may originally have been in the name of Mr. and Mrs. Jones. Since they bought the house, though, they have become divorced. By the terms of the divorce settlement, Mrs. Jones still retains a one-half interest in the house, even though she is no longer Mrs. Jones. In order for Mr. Jones to properly and legally sell the house, he must get his ex-wife's signature on the contract and deed. Lacking her signature, the contract may not be valid. If Mrs. Jones is unwilling to go along with the deal, the buyers could end up in a muddle. They'd probably be able to get back any money they had paid in, but they could have sacrificed considerable time in the process. Similar situations could result if one of the owners had died.

What if the buyers sign a contract and before the actual closing decide that they don't want to buy the house? Perhaps a job transfer has been cancelled. Perhaps the would-be buyers have found another couple who wish to buy the house at a price higher than what they are paying for it. If the contract permits a "right of assignment," the buyers can transfer their interest in the contract to another party.

For example, the Smiths, having been told of a job transfer, contract to buy the Joneses' house for $80,000. Shortly thereafter the job transfer is cancelled, and the Smiths no longer have any need or desire to buy the Joneses' house. But in the meantime they have met the Whites, who would be willing to pay $85,000 for the Joneses' house. The Smiths, under the right of assignment clause, can assign their rights in the contract to the Whites and the Smiths could profit by $5000 as a result. In effect, then, the names of the buying parties would be changed in the contract. The Smiths would have to notify the Joneses that they were assigning their rights to the Whites. Unless the Joneses had reserved the right to approve of any such assignments, the Whites would then legally stand in the shoes of the Smiths as contractual buyers of the property.

Description of the Property. The purchase contract should contain the full legal description of the property, not just the street address. The proper legal description should be either a surveyor's description or a subdivision description. The surveyor's description generally indicates the boundaries, their length, and the angle measurements between the boundary lines, all relating to a particular starting point. The subdivision description may refer to a specific parcel within a larger subdivision, whose map has been filed under local legal requirements by the original developer of the property. Such a description might refer to a lot as "lot #17 of the XYZ subdivision, which is registered in the county recorder's book of maps #576, at page 148."

Title to the Property.   Your title to a piece of property represents the rights you have regarding that property. There may be certain restrictions concerning how you can use any given piece of property; and your use of the property may be subject to the rights of other people. Purchase contracts commonly state that you are receiving "title free and clear of all liens and encumbrances, except as otherwise noted." What does this mean? It means that you are receiving the property without any restrictions and subject to no other rights of other people, unless such other restrictions or rights are specifically spelled out. If your contract says that you are receiving the right to use the property "free and clear," when in fact you are not, you may have the right to get out of the contract. Your lawyer or your title insurance company will search the appropriate records to determine whether, in fact, any other such rights or restrictions do exist. If you take title to property without being aware of other persons' rights or restrictions on you, you could find yourself in a difficult position when it comes to financing the property or later selling the property. It could also mean lawsuits to resolve whether the rights and restrictions are in fact valid. Restrictions on your use of the property and rights that others may have to use your property are referred to as *blots on the title*. The most common forms of blots are easements, liens, and restrictive covenants.

☐ *Easements.*   Many years ago the owner of a piece of property may have given a neighbor the right to lead cattle across the property to a watering hole. The neighbor may have paid for this right and in return received a document setting forth that right. Later, when the owner of the property sold to another buyer, the neighbor's right to cross the property was included as a part of the deal. Thus, the new buyer acquired the property subject to the neighbor's right to use it. Unless and until the owners of the respective adjoining properties agree to terminate this right, making whatever payments and exchanging whatever documents are necessary, this right would continue down through all subsequent owners of the property.

This is a form of easement, and it exists today in many forms. It's not uncommon for a utility company to have easements across residential property for the purpose of installing utility lines and underground piping. These rights may have been reserved, but not yet exercised by the utility company. The fact that they have not yet exercised their rights does not mean that their easement has expired. Easements may have been created many years or many decades before, yet they will continue to run with the property until they are terminated by mutual agreement.

☐ *Liens.*   Laws on the subject of liens differ from state to state. A lien on the property comes into being when the owner of the property has a debt that has not been paid, and the creditor takes legal action to collect the debt. If the legal action is successful, the creditor may wind up with the right to force the owner to sell the property (real estate and personal) in order to satisfy the debt.

For example, John had borrowed $10,000 from Mary and could not repay it when the debt became due. Mary began legal action, but John still refused to pay. Mary won a judgment against John that technically gave her the right to force a sale of John's house to satisfy the debt. Mary, in effect, had a lien on John's house. The lien was properly recorded according to state law. Anyone then buying John's house would own it subject to Mary's right to force a sale in order to satisfy John's debt to her.

Other liens can arise out of a property owner's failure to pay taxes, in which case the government will have a lien. Or if a property owner has failed to pay contractors or workers who have performed work on the property, what's known as a *mechanic's lien* can arise.

Note that a debt alone does not give rise to a lien. The creditor must pursue the legal requirements set forth in the state in order to "perfect" the lien. Not until the lien is legally perfected does the creditor have any claim on the property. Because there are often many months between the signing of a purchase contract and the final closing of a real estate transaction, a lawsuit could occur in the meantime and result in a lien coming into being prior to the actual date of closing. Thus, it's common for a title search to occur both on the signing of the purchase contract and again just before the closing to make certain that no liens have arisen in the interim. A proper purchase contract should disclose the existence of any actual liens. If the contract does not disclose actual liens, the seller is promising to sell something that he cannot in fact deliver—a "free and clear" title. In such a case the buyer should have the right to bow out of the contract and recoup any monies paid in. The buyer might possibly also be entitled to damages suffered as a result of entering into the contract.

☐ **Restrictive covenants.**   Restrictive covenants may prevent you from doing certain things on your property. For example, a restrictive covenant may state that you may not build a house of less than a certain value. Such a covenant, or promise, may have originated with the subdivider of the property who wanted to insure that the subdivision was developed with homes of at least a minimum quality. He would do so to protect the financial interests of all those persons buying his lots, for they would want to know that their investment in a house would not be tarnished by the construction of buildings of lesser values.

☐ **Title insurance.**   Even though all of the proper record books have been searched and no blots against the title have appeared, someone can still make a claim against the property. Any such claim may be invalid, but it can be a costly nuisance to prove that it's invalid. Or in very rare cases, such an outside claim against a title may prove to be valid, and the owner could stand to lose a substantial sum of money, if not the property itself.

To prevent such problems and losses, homeowners acquire an insurance policy known as *title insurance*. This insurance policy protects both the homeowner and the mortgage lender against such claims. A title-insurance policy does not establish the *value* of your property. It sets forth the maximum amount of monetary damages that can be recovered if a claim is made against the title.

Deed to the Property.   The deed is the legal document by which the title to the property passes from the seller to the buyer. It's the actual symbol of ownership. The purchase contract should spell out when you will get it.

The contract should also stipulate that the deed will be transferred at the time of closing. If the contract does not call for the deed to be delivered at the closing, you should receive an explanation before consenting to sign the contract.

There are different kinds of deeds, and they convey different interests in a piece of property. The highest and most complete form of deed is called a *full warranty deed*. In such a deed, the seller warrants that he has clear title to the property (subject to any stated exceptions), that he is conveying the title to you, and that he will protect you against any outside claims made against the property.

The lowest form of deed is called a *quitclaim deed*. By this document the seller conveys to you whatever interest she may have in the property, with no further assurance as to title. By virtue of a quitclaim deed the seller is saying, in effect, "I hereby quit, or give over to you, the buyer, any claim I may have to this property." If in fact the seller has full and complete title to the property, this is what is conveyed to the buyer. If in fact she has no claim whatever to the property, that too is what she is conveying to the buyer. In other words, a seller could convey to a buyer via a quitclaim deed "all of my right, title, and interest in the Grand Canyon." The seller has no interest whatsoever in the Grand Canyon, but it's still a valid deed. She is simply giving over any rights that she may have, and it's up to the buyer to determine the worth of those rights.

Once a buyer takes title to a property, he can convey only the title that he has received. He can't convey more than he actually owns. If he receives a quitclaim deed to a piece of property and later wants to sell it, he can't give anything more than a quitclaim deed, unless it's been otherwise legally established that he does, in fact, have free and clear title.

The buyer should demand the highest form of deed that the seller is capable of delivering. If your purchase contract calls for you to receive a certain type of deed, and at the closing the seller does not deliver the type of deed he has committed himself to deliver, you technically might be able to void the deal or bargain for better terms.

There's a type of property transaction that is known as a *land contract*. In this type of transaction, the right to use the property transfers to the buyer, but the buyer does not obtain a deed until certain contractual terms have been complied with. This might take many years. This type of transaction is discussed in greater detail in Chapter 9.

Manner of Payment.   The purchase contract sets forth the manner in which the buyer pays the seller for the property. See Chapter 9 for a more detailed discussion of where the buyer obtains the money with which to pay the seller. If a buyer is planning to obtain his own financing for the purchase, he should make certain that a *financing contingency* clause is inserted in the contract. This clause states, in effect, that if the buyer is not able to obtain financing at an agreeable rate of interest by the date of the closing, he can back out of the deal with little or no penalty.

Closing Date. The purchase contract should set forth the date and the place of the closing. The *closing* is the official event at which the transfer of deeds, checks, and IOUs takes place. When a closing date is fixed, both parties must perform by that date or risk forfeiture. Of course, the parties can subsequently agree to amend the date of closing. This is often done, particularly when financing arrangements have been delayed or when personal circumstances unavoidably alter the plans of either or both of the parties.

In some states the signed contracts and other documents are held by a third party pending completion of all the buyer's and seller's obligations. This is known as *escrow*, and it is commonly performed by a title insurance company, an attorney, an escrow company, or the escrow department of a bank. The party holding the papers in escrow (the escrow agent) has been instructed by both buyer and seller not to release the papers for the ultimate closing until all of the various obligations of buyer and seller are performed as agreed. When an escrow agent is used, the *close of escrow* is the same as the closing date referred to above.

The parties usually agree to have the closing date (close of escrow) from one to three months after the signing of the purchase contract, although any other agreement is possible if the parties are willing.

Seller's Obligations. As part of the negotiations, the seller may agree to perform certain services or work on the property. For example, the seller might have agreed to have the house painted for the buyer's benefit. If the seller fails to perform as agreed, what recourse does the buyer have? It all depends on how carefully the seller's obligation was worded in the original purchase contract. If the buyer was careful enough and fussy enough to protect herself to the fullest, the seller's obligations would have been spelled out in detail, including the nature of the paint to be used, the number of coats to be put on, and specific damages should the seller not perform in accordance with the contract.

Default and Recourse. What if either of the parties fails to perform in accordance with the agreement? What are the rights of the other party? Much depends on the nature of the default and how serious it is in relation to the overall transaction.

For example, if the seller has agreed to paint the house at her own expense and has done so substantially but has omitted some minor touchup, this type of default would probably not destroy the entire transaction. In such a case, the parties could likely negotiate a quick and simple settlement. But more serious defaults— by either party—can create serious questions as to the rights of the parties. The broadest remedy to either party is to bring a lawsuit against the other for ''specific performance.'' A judgment of specific performance would require the defaulting party to perform in accordance with the specific terms of the original contract.

Perhaps a simpler way of resolving disputes and defaults is for the buyer and seller to agree to arbitration proceedings in the event that one of them does not perform as promised. Arbitration could provide a quicker and less expensive means of resolving disputes than would lawsuits.

The Closing

Depending on what the parties have agreed to, the closing may take place at the offices of the mortgage lender, at one of the attorney's offices, at the title insurance office, or at the offices where the recording of the documents takes place. The signed deed, in accordance with the purchase contract, is delivered to the buyer, and the appropriate monies or IOUs are delivered to the seller. Also, the appropriate "adjustments" are made, and payment passed accordingly.

Adjustments and Closing Costs. The adjustments are a prorating of any expenses incurred on the property by the seller. For example, property taxes on the house total $800 per year, payable in installments on January 1 and July 1. The closing between the buyer and the seller takes place on April 1. The seller will have previously paid a $400 property tax installment on January 1. This covers the first six months of the year. Thus, the buyer must reimburse the seller for $200 worth of property taxes, representing the period from April 1 to July 1, during which the buyer will have occupancy of the property.

By the time of the closing, the buyer should have also made arrangements with his insurance agent to have the property insurance in effect in his own name. He should also arrange with the local utility companies—gas, electricity, water—to have the meters changed over to his name effective as of the date of the closing. Even though the new buyer may not take occupancy until sometime after the closing, he will be responsible for these costs from the time of closing onward.

Other substantial sums of money can change hands at the closing. The closing is the appropriate time for the seller to pay any real estate commissions to the agent who represented him. The lawyers for the two parties involved and the company insuring the title will also receive payments due to them. Perhaps the single biggest closing cost will be the fee that the borrower has to pay to the lender who made home financing arrangements. Under a federal law, the Real Estate Settlement Procedures Act (RESPA), a lender is required to give advance notice to a borrower of the closing costs, or a reasonable estimate thereof. The specifics of this law are discussed in more detail in Chapter 9.

With all of these payments changing hands at the closing, it's wise for the buyer to determine in advance how much cash will be required of him so that all payments can be made without embarrassment.

Recording. Individual state laws govern the recording requirements for the appropriate documents. The recording of the mortgage agreement is the responsibility of the lender, and the recording of the deed is the responsibility of the buyer. Recording these documents in the fashion required by state law puts the world on notice that the lender has a mortgage lien on the property and that the owner has ownership of the property. The buyer's attorney or company insuring the title will theoretically have searched the title to the property up to the time of closing. But if the search was concluded days, or even hours, prior to the closing, it is possible for a lien to have snuck in against the property. Although this rarely happens, it can cause tremendous problems. Thus, the ultimate precaution is to have a search conducted at the time of closing to be certain that no liens have attached themselves to the property prior to the actual moment of transfer.

The material in this chapter has provided guidelines to finding a house and the steps one must take to legally obtain ownership of it. The following chapter discusses a matter equally important to the hunting for and contracting for a house—paying for it.

Homebuyer's Guidelines

The following evaluations can be helpful in your quest to buy a home or condominium. Seek the aid of a real estate agent in doing this analysis.

Factors	*Home 1*	*Home 2*	*Home 3*
□ Condition of neighborhood (present and future trends)	———	———	———
□ Approximate miles driven per month to			
Work	———	———	———
Schools	———	———	———
Routine shopping	———	———	———
Other	———	———	———
□ Transportation costs per month	———	———	———
□ Physical condition of building, including			
Walls, foundation	———	———	———
Roof	———	———	———
Plumbing	———	———	———
Wiring	———	———	———
Heating, air conditioning	———	———	———
Landscaping	———	———	———
Appliances	———	———	———
Insulation	———	———	———
□ Estimated refurbishing costs, interior and exterior	———	———	———
□ Asking price	———	———	———
□ Down payment	———	———	———
□ Terms offered by seller	———	———	———
□ Price seller will probably accept	———	———	———
□ Monthly mortgage payments, including interest, assuming seller accepts your offer	———	———	———
□ Property taxes	———	———	———
□ Estimated utility costs	———	———	———
□ General maintenance and upkeep	———	———	———
□ Closing costs	———	———	———

Check and Double-Check Statements by Sellers

A home seller, or his real estate agent, might be tempted to stretch the truth when discussing certain features of a house or condominium. If you're a buyer, the following precautions might be helpful in clarifying matters that would otherwise not be spelled out in the contract:

If the seller, or his real estate agent, says . . .	You should . . .
"Our utility bills are amazingly low . . . this home is really energy efficient."	Ask to see the last year's worth of actual bills. If seller doesn't have them, check with the utility companies. Understand, though, that different families will consume different amounts of energy.
"That water stain on the ceiling is from an old leak. We had it patched up watertight years ago."	Get a garden hose, and—with the owner's permission, of course—simulate a heavy rain on the roof. You'll find out soon enough whether the leak is still there.
"The basement is dry as a bone, winter and summer."	Check with a flashlight for watermarks around the basement wall. Better still, hire a contractor, who'll know better what to look for.
"Oh, we're just a quick 5 (10, 20) minutes from the school (freeway, airport) . . . etc."	If time spent traveling is important to you, drive these routes yourself, at various times of day, to find out just what is involved.
"You'll just love the neighbors."	Go knock on the doors. Find out for yourself. They won't be there forever, but they can make a difference.

If conditions are found which you agree the seller is to correct, make certain that these corrections are clearly spelled out in the contract. And then make certain that the corrections are completed before the deal is consummated.

CHAPTER 9

Financing a Home

The great American dream has long been to own one's own home. Is the dream now beyond reach? Not necessarily. This chapter will acquaint you with methods of home financing and will equip you with the knowledge you'll need to pursue your own dream of owning a home. Among the techniques you'll learn are

☐ How to distinguish among and evaluate different types of home financing plans

☐ Where you can shop for home financing

☐ What home financing terms are negotiable

☐ How to structure a financing package that will best match your housing budget

A WHOLE NEW BALL GAME

If you were shopping for a home loan as recently as the late 1970s, you might have visited a dozen different lenders and found very little difference among their home financing plans. Most lenders would have quoted approximately the same interest rate, which would remain fixed for the entire term of the loan, usually thirty years. This is not true any longer. The age of the adjustable-rate (or variable-rate) loan is upon us, and if you visited a dozen different lenders today, you'd likely find a dozen different plans. Sorting them all out would make your head spin.

A home loan is the largest IOU you probably will ever sign, and it will be with you for years, perhaps even decades. A difference of one-quarter of a percent in interest can mean a difference of many thousands of dollars over an extended period of time. If you want to get the best arrangement for your money, it's essential to do the necessary homework before you make a commitment on any home loan.

The home financing arena is further complicated by some major tax law changes that were put into effect as a result of the Tax Reform Act of 1986. Prior to this tax law, virtually all interest paid on any home loan was deductible on the income tax return. Under the 1986 law, interest paid on a loan incurred to buy a house is still fully deductible. However, if you refinance a home loan, some of the interest you pay on the new loan may not be deductible.

Let's take a quick look at the major provisions of the Tax Reform Act of 1986 as it affects the deductibility of interest on home loans. For any home loan in place on or before August 16, 1986, all interest is deductible, regardless of the size of the loan or the purpose for which the loan was obtained. But for loans written after this date, there are restrictions concerning the deductibility of interest. In the latter case, the amount of deductible interest is determined by the price you paid for the home, plus allowable improvements and certain educational and medical expense borrowings that may be included in your home loan.

Let's look at an example. You bought your home in 1980 for $40,000, using $10,000 as a down payment and taking a loan of $30,000. In 1981, you added on a room at a cost of $5000. In 1985, your home's value had increased to $65,000, so you refinanced your loan in 1985 up to a total of $55,000. Since you completed the refinancing before the cutoff date of August 16, 1986, you continue to deduct all of your interest on the full $55,000 debt. But if you had refinanced the original loan after August 16, 1986, you would only be able to deduct interest on a debt of $45,000—the total of the original cost of the home ($40,000) plus the improvements ($5000).

Tax laws are always subject to change. Before you refinance a home loan, check with a tax advisor to learn the extent of deductibility of your interest costs at that time.

THE MORTGAGE

Let's say that you're interested in buying a house that costs $80,000. You've saved up $10,000 of your own money, but that's all you have. How can you buy the house? You can borrow the other $70,000. You can go to a bank, a savings and loan association, or any other lender that offers home financing and make arrangements to borrow the needed amount. If your application for the loan is approved and the loan is made, you will sign a document promising to repay the full amount to the lender over a period of time, plus an agreed amount of interest. This document is commonly called a *mortgage*. (In some states—notably California—the document is referred to as a *trust deed* or *deed of trust*. There are some minor technical differences between a mortgage and a trust deed, but the basic concept is the same.) The mortgage is also referred to as a *purchase money mortgage* or a *first mortgage*. With a purchase money mortgage, as in this case, you borrow the money to purchase the property. The designation of the mortgage as ''first'' means that the lender stands first in line to take back your property in the event you default in your obligation to make the payments.

Perhaps there is already a mortgage on the property that you might be able to ''assume.'' Say that there is a mortgage on the property for $70,000. You could become the owner of the property by paying the seller your $10,000 in cash and then stepping into his shoes as the person responsible for making the payments on the existing mortgage. In effect, you assume the seller's debt. You take it over. What if the existing mortgage on the property is only $65,000? After paying the seller your $10,000 in cash, you'll still be shy the total purchase price by $5000.

In such a case, the seller may be willing to take your IOU for the $5000. Your IOU would be known as a *second mortgage*. The terms of payment would be whatever you and the seller agreed to, and the seller, holding your second mortgage, would stand second in line behind the holder of the first mortgage to get paid off in the event that you defaulted on your obligations.

See Table 9-1 to determine how large a home loan you can get. A mortgage contains two very important legal considerations. First, you are legally committing yourself to make the payments to the lender as agreed. Second, you are giving the lender the right to take steps to take back the property from you if you fail to make the payments. In other words, you have given the lender a security interest in the property as collateral for the loan.

If a borrower fails to make payments as agreed, the lender can begin a legal action known as a *foreclosure proceeding*. Foreclosure proceedings differ somewhat from state to state, but basically they allow the lender to cause the property to be sold at public auction. The lender recovers whatever money is owed on the debt out of the proceeds of the auction sale. The first mortgage holder gets first crack at the auction proceeds. Any money left over after the first mortgage holder is paid off goes to a second mortgage holder, and so on. For example, William owes $60,000 on a first mortgage and $10,000 on a second mortgage. William defaults and the property is foreclosed. The property is sold at auction, and after foreclosure

Table 9-1   **How Large a Home Loan Can You Get?**

Amount of Principal for 30-Year, 12% Fixed-Rate Loan

Lender's limit (% of gross monthly income)	Gross monthly income							
	$2,500	$3,000	$3,500	$4,000	$4,500	$5,000	$5,500	$6,000
25	$63,200[a]	$ 72,900	$ 85,000	$ 97,200	$109,300	$121,500	$133,600	$145,800
	$ 625	$ 750	$ 875	$ 1,000	$ 1,125	$ 1,250	$ 1,375	$ 1,500
30	72,900	87,500	102,000	116,600	131,200	145,800	160,300	175,000
	750	900	1,050	1,200	1,350	1,500	1,650	1,800
35	85,000	102,000	119,000	136,080	153,000	170,100	187,100	204,100
	875	1,050	1,225	1,400	1,575	1,750	1,925	2,100

Example: Your monthly income is $3,500, and your lender will only approve a loan on which your monthly payments do not exceed 30% of your gross monthly income. You could thus get a loan of $102,000, with monthly payments of $1,050. This assumes a down payment of 20% or a total purchase price of about $125,000 and a 30-year, 12% fixed-rate loan. Income tax implications are not taken into account, but you could calculate your own.

[a]The upper figure is the amount of the loan; the lower figure is the monthly payment.

expenses are taken out, $65,000 remains. The first mortgage lender will recapture the entire $60,000. The remaining $5000 goes to the second mortgage holder. This means, obviously, that the second mortgage holder suffers a $5000 loss on the transaction.

The basic elements of a mortgage are the same whether the mortgage has a fixed interest rate or a variable interest rate: interest, acquisition fees, and insurance costs.

Interest

In the standard fixed-rate mortgage, your interest cost is calculated on the unpaid amount of the debt, or principal balance, at each given monthly point. For example, on a $70,000 mortgage, set to run for thirty years at a 12 percent interest rate, the monthly payments for interest and principal total $720. During the first month of the mortgage loan, the debt that the borrower owes is the full $70,000. Since 12 percent of $70,000 is $8400, this would be the total interest for the full year if the debt did not change.

But we're interested now only in the first month, which is the first one-twelfth of the year. One-twelfth of the full year's interest is $700 (one-twelfth of $8400 equals $700). Therefore, $700 is the amount of interest due for the first full month of the mortgage. Thus, in that first month, the total payment of $720 is broken down as follows: $700 for the interest and $20 for the debt.

Going into the second month, the debt due has been reduced by $20, from the original $70,000 to $69,980. During the second month of the mortgage the interest is calculated on this new debt of $69,980. One-twelfth of 12 percent of that amount equals $699.80. That's the amount of interest due during the second month. In the second month, therefore, your total payment of $720 is broken down as follows: $699.80 for interest and $20.20 to reduce the debt.

The debt has now been reduced by an additional $20.20, leaving a full balance owing of $69,959.80 going into the third month. In the third month, the interest due is one-twelfth of 12 percent of $69,959.80, or $699.60. The payment for the third month is broken down as follows: $699.60 for interest and $20.40 to reduce the debt. A breakdown of the first three payments is as follows:

Month	*Interest*	*Principal*	*Debt remaining*
First	$700.00	$20.00	$69,980.00
Second	699.80	20.20	69,959.80
Third	699.60	20.40	69,939.40

Succeeding months' interest is based on the balance remaining after the debt reduction in the previous month. As each month goes by and the amount of the debt shrinks, the amount of interest paid for subsequent months gets smaller and smaller. As the interest portion of the total monthly payment decreases, the principal portion obviously increases. As you can see from this example and from Table 9-2 the payments during the early years of a mortgage are mostly interest. It's not until many years into the mortgage that the interest and principal portions of each monthly payment equal each other. In the last few years of a mortgage, the principal portion is substantially greater than the interest portion.

Adjustable-Rate Loans. An adjustable-rate loan, most simply stated, means that your interest rate can be adjusted up or down over the months and years. By adjusting the interest rate, your monthly payments might also change. In recent years, the standard interest rates for home loans have fluctuated wildly, ranging from under 10 percent to almost 20 percent. Future trends are uncertain. But if you are concerned that interest rates might get even higher than they are now, you might feel uncomfortable with an adjustable-rate loan.

In order to make a prudent choice between a fixed-rate loan and an adjustable-rate loan, you have to understand the jargon of the adjustable loan and how it works. The following statements may not make any sense to you when you first read them, but they're not far from what you might be told by a lending officer at a home loan institution when you apply for an adjustable-rate loan.

> Your initial rate will be 8 percent. The base rate will be 9 percent, with semiannual adjustments. The index will be the floating treasury bill rate, which is now 6.8 percent, and there will be a margin of 3 points over that. You'll have an annual cap of 1 percentage point, a lifetime cap of 5 percentage points, and you can avoid negative amortization by making the full payment upon each adjustment.

Did reading this jargon make your head spin? Let's discuss one item at a time.

☐ *Initial rate.* The initial rate might be an attractively low interest rate, designed to lure you into getting your mortgage at a given institution. When an initial rate is used (and not all institutions do this), it will last only until the first interest adjustment occurs, which is usually after six months.

☐ *Base rate.* The base rate is the interest rate upon which the lifetime cap is calculated. If you have a lifetime cap of 5 percent, your interest rate over the entire life of the loan cannot exceed 5 percentage points above the base rate. To continue our example, the base rate is 9 percent, and the lifetime cap is 5 percent. Thus the interest rate over the life of the loan cannot exceed 14 percent. Borrowers can be easily confused by thinking that the lifetime cap is calculated from the initial rate, which in this example is 8 percent. If that were the case, the maximum interest would be 13 percent. It's essential that you determine the exact terms and conditions of these items before you commit to a loan.

☐ *Index.* The index is an arbitrary number, beyond the control of the lender, that is used to determine interest rate adjustments. One common index is the so-called cost of funds for savings institutions in your region. Another could

Table 9-2 Typical Mortgage-Reduction Schedule: $60,000, 12% Fixed-Rate, 30-Year Mortgage. Monthly Payments = $617.40. Annual Payments = $7,410.00 (rounded).

Years elapsed	Percentage of original balance remaining (%)	Balance due	Appropriate portion of annual payments applied to	
			Principal	Interest
1	99.6	$59,760	$ 238	$7,172
2	99.2	59,520	239	7,171
3	98.8	59,280	240	7,170
4	98.3	58,980	300	7,110
5	97.7	58,620	360	7,050
6	97.0	58,200	418	6,992
7	96.3	57,780	420	6,990
8	95.4	57,240	538	6,872
9	94.5	56,700	540	6,870
10	93.4	56,040	660	6,750
11	92.2	55,320	720	6,690
12	90.9	54,540	780	6,630
13	89.4	53,640	900	6,510
14	87.6	52,560	1,080	6,330
15	85.7	51,420	1,140	6,270
16	83.5	50,100	1,320	6,090
17	81.1	48,660	1,440	5,970
18	78.3	46,980	1,680	5,730
19	75.2	45,120	1,860	5,550
20	71.7	43,020	2,100	5,310
21	67.7	40,620	2,400	5,010
22	63.3	37,980	2,640	4,770
23	58.3	34,980	3,000	4,410
24	52.6	31,560	3,420	3,990
25	46.2	27,720	3,840	3,570
26	39.1	23,460	4,260	3,150
27	31.0	18,600	4,860	2,550
28	21.9	13,140	5,460	1,950
29	11.6	6,960	6,180	1,230
30	–0–	–0–	6,960	450

Note: Apparent discrepancies in some years because of rounding.

interest rate renegotiated) at a set future time. If you're not aware that such a clause exists in your mortgage, it could indeed come as a shock if the lender exercised its privileges.

Assumption Clause.   An assumption clause in a mortgage means that the owner of a house can sell the house to another party and that new buyer can assume the existing debt. The new buyer, in other words, steps into the shoes of the former owner and becomes liable for the remaining balance on the debt as well as all other terms and conditions of the mortgage. Assumption privileges are subject to the right of approval of the lender. The lender might, for example, refuse to allow a person with a known bad credit history to assume an existing mortgage. If you are contemplating buying a house that has an assumable mortgage, you should determine in advance whether you will be permitted to assume the mortgage. If you are entering into a new mortgage, the existence or absence of an assumption clause can have an effect on your ability to sell the house later.

Prepayment Clause.   You might come into a sum of money and wish to make advance payments on your mortgage, either wholly or partially. Do you have the right to do so, and if so, will it cost you anything? Some mortgages contain prepayment privilege clauses that allow you to make such advance payments on your debt without suffering any penalty. On the other hand, some mortgages have prepayment penalty clauses stating that you must pay a penalty if you do pay early.

Open-End Clause.   An open-end clause is rare but might be negotiated if requested. A typical open-end clause permits the borrower to borrow back up to the original amount of the mortgage at the same original interest rate, perhaps without paying any costs or fees in the process.

SHOPPING FOR HOME FINANCING

If you're buying a house with an existing mortgage that you plan to assume, you're more or less locked into its terms. This doesn't mean that you can't discuss revision of any of the terms with the lender. It might be worth your while to do so to help tailor a different payment program that would be better suited to your financial circumstances.

If you're buying a house and seeking your own original financing, the following shopping list, tables, and Personal Action Checklist at the end of this chapter can help you to work out a deal that's best suited to your needs.

Where to Shop

The major sources of home financing are savings and loan associations and mutual savings banks (the latter appearing predominantly in the northeastern states). Many commercial banks also offer home financing plans, as do some credit unions and insurance companies. There are also private mortgage brokers in most communities who act as intermediaries in finding mortgage loans for home buyers. They usually obtain the needed funds through institutional or private investors. Mortgage brokers charge a fee for their services. Before entering into any commitment with a private mortgage broker, the terms of such an arrangement should be explicitly understood.

Insured and Noninsured Loans

The differences between fixed-rate and variable-rate loans have already been discussed. There's another broad distinction that should be considered, for it can have an effect on the amount of down payment you'll be required to make. This distinction is between insured loans and noninsured loans.

Lenders don't really want to foreclose on properties if the borrower defaults. Foreclosure is a messy, costly, and irritating proceeding. A lender would much rather have some form of guarantee that all or a portion of the payments will be made as agreed. And, indeed, lenders *can* obtain insurance that will offer these guarantees. There are two main sources of this insurance: the U.S. government and private insurance companies.

The U.S. government offers two types of insurance plans. One is offered through the Federal Housing Administration (FHA); the other is through the Veterans Administration (VA). FHA insures certain mortgage loans if both the buyer of the property and the property itself meet certain governmental requirements. The VA also guarantees certain loans made to eligible military veterans, again providing that all qualifications are met. Because the government is guaranteeing repayment of these FHA and VA loans—at least in part—lenders are willing to take a greater risk with such loans than they are if there are no such guarantees. In short, lenders are willing to make these loans to borrowers with smaller down payments. If you can meet either the FHA or VA restrictions, you might be able to obtain home financing with a smaller down payment than you may have suspected. Check with local lenders for current requirements.

Lenders can also obtain insurance through private companies. As with the FHA and VA loans, the private insurance plan means lower risks for lenders, and they will therefore approve a lower down payment on an insured loan than on a noninsured loan. Borrowers might have to pay a slightly higher monthly payment as a result of their loans being insured, but the cost can be well worth it if it allows them to purchase a house with a relatively small down payment.

One relatively new type of insured loan is the FHA-245, also known as the *graduated payment plan*. This type of loan is geared toward younger couples who might not otherwise be able to meet the high monthly payment requirements currently called for. In the graduated payment plan, the monthly payments for the first few years of the loan are lower than they would be under a regular plan. As the years go by, and as the borrower's income presumably increases, the payments increase accordingly.

Noninsured loans, whether fixed- or variable-rate, generally require a down payment of roughly 20 percent of the purchase price of the property.

Acquisition Costs

What points and other fees will you have to pay in order to get the financing you're seeking? Under the federal Real Estate Settlements Procedures Act (RESPA), lenders are required to give you a copy of a government booklet, *Settlement Costs*, not later than three days after you have made your loan application. The information in this booklet is very important to you. It describes your rights under the federal law and contains helpful advice on completing your property transaction. The law also requires that the lender give you a good-faith estimate of all settlement costs (or *closing costs*, as they're often called) that will be charged. You should also determine whether the closing costs are to be paid in cash at the time of the transaction or whether those costs can be added into the mortgage and spread out over the life of the mortgage.

Interest Rates

What will be the original interest rate, and what fluctuations might it be subject to in the future? Table 9-3 is a handy guide to help you find the monthly payment for any size mortgage at various interest rates and terms of repayment. Table 9-4 illustrates how different interest rates can affect your actual costs on a mortgage. These cost differentials can be tremendous, as the table illustrates.

Table 9-3   **Monthly Payment Finder for Fixed-Rate Mortgage (per $1,000)**

Annual fixed interest rate (%)	Length of mortgage (years)			
	15	20	25	30
10	10.75	9.66	9.09	8.78
10½	11.06	9.99	9.45	9.15
11	11.37	10.33	9.81	9.53
11½	11.69	10.67	10.17	9.91
12	12.01	11.02	10.54	10.29
12½	12.33	11.37	10.91	10.68
13	12.66	11.72	11.28	11.07
13½	12.99	12.08	11.66	11.46
14	13.32	12.44	12.04	11.85
14½	13.66	12.80	12.43	12.25
15	14.00	13.17	12.81	12.65

Example: What is the monthly payment (interest and principal) on a $50,000 mortgage for 25 years at 13% interest? Find the factor where the 13% line meets the 25-year line. The factor is 11.28. Multiply 11.28 by 50. The result is 564. The monthly payment, then, is $564.

Table 9-4   **Effect of Interest Rates on Cost: $60,000, 30-Year Mortgage**

Fixed rate (%)	Monthly payment	Total amount paid out after			
		5 years	10 years	20 years	30 years[a]
10	$526.80	$31,608	$63,216	$126,432	$189,648
10½	549.00	32,940	65,880	131,760	197,640
11	571.80	34,308	68,616	137,232	205,848
11½	594.60	35,676	71,352	142,704	214,056
12	617.40	37,044	74,088	148,176	222,264
12½	640.80	38,448	76,896	153,792	230,688
13	664.20	39,852	79,704	159,408	239,112
13½	687.60	41,256	82,512	165,024	247,536
14	711.00	42,660	85,320	170,640	255,960
14½	735.00	44,100	88,200	176,400	264,600
15	759.00	45,540	91,080	182,160	273,240

Example: What would be the difference in cost to you on a $60,000 mortgage between an interest rate of 13% and an interest rate of 13½%? On the 13% loan, your monthly payments would be $664.20, and after 10 years you would have made payments totaling $79,704. On the 13½% loan, your monthly payments would be $687.60, and after 10 years you would have made payments totaling $82,512. The 13½% loan would have cost you $2808 more than the 13% loan over the first 10 years. To compare mortgages of any other amounts, use Table 9-3 to figure the monthly payments. Multiply the payments by the number of months in question.

[a]To find the total interest paid over the full 30-year life of the loan, subtract the original amount borrowed ($60,000) from each of the figures.

How Much Down Payment Is Required?

The amount of the down payment required and the amount that you may have available for down payment may not jibe. If you have more than enough, you're in good shape, but then you'll have to decide *how much* of your available funds you want to use as a down payment. (Bear in mind that available money that is not used for your down payment can be invested to earn more money for you.) If you have less than the required amount, how will you raise the difference? If one lending institution requires a higher down payment than another, its interest rate may be lower or its other terms may be more favorable. These must be compared.

   Table 9-5 illustrates how the amount of the down payments can affect your total mortgage expense over a period of years. There is no easy solution to the

Table 9-5   **Effect of Down Payments on Costs: $80,000, 30-Year, 12% Fixed-Rate Mortgage**

Down payment		*Amount of mortgage*	*Monthly payment*	*Total payments after*		
% of Cost	*Amount*			*10 years*	*20 years*	*30 years*
5	$ 4,000	$76,000	$782.04	$93,844	$187,689	$281,534
10	8,000	72,000	740.88	88,905	177,811	266,716
15	12,000	68,000	699.72	83,966	167,932	251,899
20	16,000	64,000	658.56	79,027	158,054	237,081
25	20,000	60,000	617.40	74,088	148,176	222,264
30	24,000	56,000	576.24	69,148	138,297	207,446

Example: What will be the difference in cost to you if you make a 10% down payment versus a 20% down payment on an $80,000 purchase, assuming a fixed annual interest rate of 12%? With the 10% down payment, your monthly payment will be $740.88, and after 20 years you will have made payments totaling $177,811. With the 20% down payment you will have a monthly payment of $658.56, and after 20 years you will have made payments totaling $158,054, a difference of $19,757. (But by making the smaller down payment, you could have had $8,000 extra money to invest or spend.)

dilemma concerning how much of a down payment one should make. It must be resolved based on your own personal circumstances as they are now and as you expect them to be in the future.

How Long Should the Mortgage Run?

The longer the mortgage, the lower the monthly payment. But this means a higher interest expense over the long term. However, it's unlikely that you'll stay with the same mortgage for more than ten or twelve years, for the average American changes houses and moves on within that time. Table 9-6 illustrates the different cost factors involved for mortgages of varying terms.

Services from Lender

You should try to determine what additional kinds of financial services might be available to you from prospective lenders. Some may offer nothing more than friendly and helpful advice. Don't underestimate the value of this service. Advice can come in handy and may be the deciding factor in your choice of lender for your home financing.

Table 9-6 **Effect of Length of Mortgage on Costs: 12% Fixed-Rate Mortgage**

Original amount of mortgage	*Number of years to run (Full term)*	*Monthly payment*		*Amount paid after*					
				5 Years	*10 Years*	*15 Years*	*20 Years*	*25 Years*	*30 Years*
$60,000	15	$720.60	Int.	33,456	58,872	69,708			
			Prin.	9,780	27,600	60,000			
			Total	43,236	86,472	129,708			
60,000	20	661.20	Int.	34,692	65,364	88,716	98,688		
			Prin.	4,980	13,980	30,300	60,000		
			Total	39,672	79,344	119,016	158,688		
60,000	25	632.40	Int.	35,364	68,568	97,872	120,156	129,720	
			Prin.	2,580	7,320	15,960	31,620	60,000	
			Total	37,944	75,888	113,832	151,776	189,720	
60,000	30	617.40	Int.	35,664	70,128	102,552	131,196	152,940	162,264
			Prin.	1,380	3,960	8,580	16,980	32,280	60,000
			Total	37,044	74,088	111,132	148,176	185,220	222,264
80,000	15	960.80	Int.	44,608	78,496	92,944			
			Prin.	13,040	36,800	80,000			
			Total	57,648	115,296	172,944			
80,000	20	881.60	Int.	46,256	87,152	118,288	131,584		
			Prin.	6,640	18,640	40,400	80,000		
			Total	52,896	105,792	158,688	211,584		
80,000	25	843.20	Int.	47,152	91,424	130,496	160,208	172,960	
			Prin.	3,440	9,760	21,280	42,160	80,000	
			Total	50,592	101,184	151,776	202,368	252,960	
80,000	30	823.20	Int.	47,552	93,504	136,736	174,928	203,920	216,532
			Prin.	1,840	5,280	11,440	22,640	43,040	80,000
			Total	49,392	98,784	148,176	197,568	246,960	296,532

Example: Compare a 25-year term and a 30-year term on an $80,000 mortgage at a 12% fixed interest rate. With the 25-year term, you will have made total payments during the first 15 years of $151,776, compared with a lesser amount—$148,176—during the first 15 years of the 30-year term. The difference in total payments between the two is $3,600. However, during that first 15 years you will have reduced your total debt by $21,280 on the 25-year plan, and only by $11,440 on the 30-year plan, a difference of $9,840. In other words, if you sold the house after 15 years, you'd get $9,840 more cash from the 25-year plan than from the 30-year plan. But you would have paid out $3,600 in extra payments with the 25-year plan. Subtract that from the extra gain on the sale, and you have a net advantage of $6,240 as a result of using the 25-year plan, mainly because you've reduced your debt at a faster rate, and in doing so you reduced the interest accordingly.

Strategies for Success

Shorter Home Loans Are Better, If You Can Afford Them

The average home loan runs for a thirty-year term. But if you can afford to make higher monthly payments, you would be much better off taking a shorter term on your home loan. For example, on a fixed-rate, 12 percent loan of $100,000, the monthly payments on a thirty-year term are $1029. For a fifteen-year loan, the payments are $1201—a difference of $172 per month. If you can handle the higher payments, you'll be considerably happier after ten years, at which time you'll still owe about $54,000 on the fifteen-year loan. But after ten years into the thirty-year loan, you'll still owe over $93,000. Why? On the longer loan, most of your payment goes toward interest, which means that very little goes toward actually reducing your debt. Discuss these alternatives with your lender before you make a commitment.

APPLYING FOR HOME FINANCING

After you've done your shopping for rates, terms, and other clauses, you will decide which institution or broker you want to make formal application to. Before you make your final application, it would be wise to spend a few dollars to examine your credit file at your local credit bureau to make sure that everything is in order. Erroneous information can find its way into your credit file, and you have rights under the Fair Credit Reporting Law to have false information corrected. See Chapter 13 for more details on your rights under this law. The lender will do a credit check on you, and if false information has not been corrected in your file, it will cause delays in processing your application.

In addition to obtaining detailed financial information on you—including your income and your debts—the lender will also reserve the right to appraise the property you are buying. A title search will also be called for to assure the lender that the property is properly secured if a loan is made. Depending on the lender, these processing steps can take from a few days to a few weeks and might entail some fees that you will be expected to pay whether the loan is approved or not. You should determine in advance just how long the processing will take and at what cost to you.

If your application is approved, you should obtain a copy of the lender's commitment in writing, so that there is no mistake about the terms of the arrangement. It's very likely that any commitment will extend for only a limited time at the given interest rate. If the purchase transaction is not completed within that specified time, the lender could back out of the commitment, at least at the quoted interest rate. If you suspect that the transaction will not be completed within the time of the lender's commitment, you should move quickly to attempt to get it extended.

It could happen that a lender will approve your application, but with the contingency that you provide a co-signer; or the loan may be approved for a lesser amount than you had requested. In the event a co-signer is required, the lender is asking you to find someone else who will sign the IOU with you. This shouldn't be taken as an insult. It may merely mean that the lender doesn't feel comfortable with your age, the amount of job experience you've had, or your credit history. After payments on the loan have been made for perhaps one or two years, it's perfectly acceptable to request that the co-signer be removed from the obligation. If, at that time, the lender feels that you have been performing well on the obligation, your request may be granted. Discuss this possibility in advance with the lender.

Creative Financing

When interest rates go up, home financing becomes more difficult to obtain. When lenders evaluate a loan application, they compare your income with the amount of the monthly payment you would be required to pay for the loan you're seeking. High interest rates could boost your monthly payment over the level that the lender feels comfortable with. And as a result you may be denied the loan.

In times of high interest rates, lenders, brokers, buyers, and sellers have put their heads together to come up with unique ways of accomplishing everyone's desires. These unique methods generally fall under the category of "creative financing." Following are some examples of creative financing techniques. It is absolutely essential before you commit yourself to any such technique that you get adequate legal advice. These arrangements can be very complex and can create legal pitfalls that you might not be aware of. Protect yourself before you sign anything.

Land Contracts. A land contract can be anything that a willing buyer and a willing seller agree to. For example, Sam and Roberta are negotiating the terms of a potential deal. Sam is asking $80,000 for his house. Roberta has no money for a down payment but is willing to pay $90,000—$10,000 more than Sam is asking. Both Sam and Roberta know that a normal lender would not consider financing such an arrangement with no down payment. But if Sam is willing to accept Roberta's terms, they can enter into a contract accordingly.

It's customary in a land contract that the deed not be delivered to the buyer until an agreed amount of time has elapsed, during which time the buyer will presumably have proven his ability to make the payments in timely fashion.

The Sleeping Second. Selma is asking $80,000 for her house. She wants $10,000 as a down payment, and she's willing to carry the buyer's IOU in the form of a first mortgage for $70,000. Bernice has the $10,000 down payment, but she doesn't have enough income to make the monthly payments on a $70,000 first mortgage.

She does, though, have enough to make the payments on a $50,000 first mortgage. Selma and Bernice agree that Selma will carry a $20,000 "sleeping second." Bernice will make the payments she promises on the first mortgage. The second mortgage will have no payments required for the first three years—or whatever length of time the parties agree to. Interest will accrue on the sleeping second, likely at a higher rate than a normal second mortgage, since Selma is being very accommodating to Bernice. At the end of the agreed time, either the second mortgage has to be paid off, which means refinancing the entire deal, or payments must begin on the sleeping second as the parties previously agreed.

Buying Down. Buying down, as a type of creative financing, is more commonly used for financing new housing during times of high interest rates. Say, for example, that the current prevailing rate is 15 percent, but buyers cannot afford home loans having more than 12 percent interest. A hungry developer might contribute the 3 percent differential out of his own pocket in order to sell the homes. As a rule, he might do this only for the first few years of the loan. At the end of this time, the buyer takes over the higher monthly payments. This enables a buyer to get into a home at a lower monthly payment, banking on the fact that after a few years his income will have increased enough to allow him to live comfortably with the higher payment.

Shared Appreciation Loans. If a buyer cannot afford either the price of the home, the amount of the down payment, or the monthly payments, the seller or any other third party might enter into an agreement with the buyer to provide a portion of the down payment or the monthly payments. In return, the outside partner or seller shares in any future appreciation in the value of the house. This kind of arrangement offers very attractive potentials, but it is not without risk. It most definitely requires the assistance of a knowledgeable attorney from the very outset.

TIMING HOME FINANCING

A final word to those who embark on the stormy seas of home loan shopping: A great deal depends on getting your loan at the exact time you need it. Delays in processing loan applications can cause a domino effect with wide repercussions. If your loan processing is delayed for any reason, the closing date might have to be delayed. Technically, such a delay might give the seller the right to cancel the whole transaction, although most sellers will go along with moderate delays if they are approached properly at the earliest possible time. A delay in your closing means that you'll have to continue living where you are for another month or two, resulting in added cost and inconvenience. If you live in an apartment and have already given notice to your landlord that you expect to leave on November 1, and you find that your home loan application won't be completed until December 15, you're in a pickle.

To the best of your ability make certain that you establish a workable schedule with the lender from the very outset. Be certain that you know what paper work has to be completed and within what time frame. There's little you can do to prevent delays caused by the lender, but the more open and thorough your communications with the lender, the more you'll be able to anticipate and deal with any possible delays.

Financing Comparisons

It's expected that most home financing plans will be based on a variable interest rate—a rate that can be adjusted upward or downward from time to time. Since it's impossible to know what future rate fluctuations will be, there's no way a borrower can accurately predict the costs of the actual mortgage over a long period of time. The dilemma is further compounded by the fact that different lenders use different formulas to vary the rate, thus making a comparison between lenders very difficult. The following checklist is not designed as an accurate cost comparison chart; rather, it's designed to help you ask the right questions in evaluating variable-rate financing plans. The more you know about how the plans work, the more judicious your decision can be.

Question	*Plan A*	*Plan B*	*Plan C*
☐ What is the starting interest rate?	_____	_____	_____
☐ How often can the rate be changed?	_____	_____	_____
☐ How much can the rate be raised at any given interval?	_____	_____	_____
☐ How much can the rate be raised over the life of the loan?	_____	_____	_____
☐ How much can the rate be lowered at any given interval?	_____	_____	_____
☐ How much can the rate be lowered over the life of the loan?	_____	_____	_____
☐ By what outside index are the rate changes to be measured? (Consumer Price Index? Cost of funds? Prime rate?)	_____	_____	_____
☐ Is there a prepayment penalty? If so, how much?	_____	_____	_____
☐ If the rate is increased at any given interval, do you, the borrower, have the option of keeping the monthly payment the same (in which case the final maturity of the loan will be extended)?	_____	_____	_____
☐ If the answer to question above is yes, what limits are there, if any, to the option?	_____	_____	_____

Perils of Creative Financing

Quark wanted to buy Neutrino's house. The asking price was $120,000, with $20,000 to be paid down. The buyer, Quark, was to obtain his own financing for the remaining $100,000. But Quark couldn't afford conventional financing, so he convinced Neutrino to "carry back" an IOU for the $100,000. Quark agreed to pay Neutrino interest at a rate 2 percent higher than the going rate at local banks, which at that time was 14 percent.

Neutrino had an old existing mortgage with a balance of $90,000 having an interest rate of 9 percent. The deal between Quark and Neutrino was a "land contract": The title to the property was to remain in Neutrino's name for three years; Neutrino would continue to make payments on the original mortgage; after three years Quark was to get his own financing and pay off whatever was then owed to Neutrino. The bank that held the original mortgage was never notified that Quark now had a vested interest in the property, by way of the land contract.

Neutrino turned nasty. Though he received Quark's payments regularly and promptly, he stopped making payments on the old mortgage to the bank. Quark never knew of this, for the delinquency notices were sent directly to Neutrino's office.

It wasn't until the bank started foreclosure proceedings and sent an appraiser to look at the house that Quark learned he was being victimized.

Neutrino had skipped town with Quark's $20,000 cash down payment, content to let that be his profit on the deal. Quark was left with having to pay off all back payments (duplicating all those he had already made), plus late charges, to prevent the house from being sold out from under him. And when the original three years had elapsed, Neutrino reappeared and refused to deliver the deed to Quark unless Quark paid him the remaining $10,000 that was owed him.

When Quark asked about the double payments and late charges he had had to make to avoid the foreclosure, Neutrino simply replied, "So sue me!"

Better to have a lawyer construct a creative financing deal properly from the outset, when the cost will be relatively small, rather than have to pay heavily later when the mess is piled so high that it smells.

CHAPTER 10

Housing Costs and Regulations

The cost of maintaining a dwelling does not end with writing your monthly mortgage or rent check. Home or condominium owners in particular will feel a constant drain on their budget from such expenses as property taxes, property insurance, utilities, and maintenance. All of these items must be properly anticipated if you are to keep your financial affairs on an even keel. In addition to costs, your dwelling situation can be affected by local rules and regulations that must be complied with.

This chapter is designed to assist you in planning sensibly to meet your overall dwelling costs and to alert you to the legal rights and responsibilities that pertain to dwellings. You'll learn how to

- ☐ Choose the right type and amount of property insurance
- ☐ Take action to cut your property taxes if they are wrongfully too high
- ☐ Get control of your utility and maintenance costs
- ☐ Protect yourself and your property if neighbors or landlords violate housing rules and regulations

PROPERTY INSURANCE

As with automobile insurance, discussed in Chapter 6, property insurance provides two forms of protection. First, the insurance provides reimbursement for loss or damage to the physical premises and the contents and furnishings. Second, the insurance protects you in the event that harm comes to other people or to the property of other people. This latter form of protection is known as *public liability insurance*. As an owner or tenant of property, you can be responsible to others if they are harmed as a result of your negligence in maintaining the property. The law does not require you to maintain public liability insurance on your house or apartment, as it does on automobiles in most states. But the law does require that you pay damages should a court find that you were in fact responsible for injuries suffered by another. A lack of proper insurance on either the physical premises or for public liability can prove financially catastrophic.

In general, homeowner's insurance reimburses you in the amount needed to replace or repair lost or damaged property, based on its value at the time of loss. Some kinds of property tend to increase in replacement cost, such as a house or jewelry. Other types of property tend to decrease in value, such as furniture and carpeting. These changes in value are known as *appreciation* and *depreciation*. In spite of the fluctuations in replacement costs, it should be relatively easy to determine what these costs are from year to year.

For those who rent, there is a special type of policy called the *tenant's policy*. It provides protection against loss or damage to furnishings and personal items as well as public liability protection.

The cost of your homeowner's or tenant's insurance depends on a number of factors: the company you deal with, the risk rating of your property, the amount of protection you seek, and the type of policy and coverage you decide on.

The Company You Deal With

As with all other forms of insurance, property insurance is competitive. Rates for similar coverage can differ from company to company. The cheapest protection is not necessarily the best. You must try to gauge the extent of service you'll get from a company, their response to claims, and the possibility of increased premiums when claims have been submitted.

The Risk Rating of the Property

Each property insured is rated by the insurance companies according to relative risk factors. These factors can include location, proximity to fire departments and fire hydrants; construction (for example, brick as opposed to wood frame); proximity to other buildings; and fire and crime statistics in the neighborhood in which the building is located. Check with your agent to determine what precautions you might take to keep your property-insurance premiums as low as possible. Such precautions might include the installation of fire extinguishers and fire-retardant materials, the cleanliness of attics and basements (piles of combustible rubbish or souvenirs do not please insurance raters), security devices such as smoke detectors and burglar alarms, as well as the locking mechanisms used throughout the premises.

The Amount of Coverage You Desire

If you have a mortgage on your house, the lending institution requires that you carry at least enough fire insurance to protect its interest in the event the building is destroyed. This may be all the fire insurance you care to have; you've decided to take your chances, come what may. On the other hand, you may insure your property against virtually any hazard conceivable with the possible exceptions of earthquakes, landslides, and tidal waves. (Flood protection may not be obtainable in some areas; but check with your local agent regarding the federal flood-insurance program that may provide protection for you against that hazard.) The amount and extent of coverage can affect your insurance costs considerably for obvious reasons.

Prudent individuals will carry enough insurance to see to it that their routine is not materially disrupted by most foreseeable hazards. They are likely to be willing to take certain chances that some hazards won't occur or if they do, they are confident they can get by without reimbursement for particular losses.

The Homeowner's Types of Policies

Homeowner's insurance comes in three primary forms: the basic form, or "Homeowner's 1" (HO1); the broad form, or "Homeowner's 2" (HO2) (the tenant's form is similar to the Homeowner's 2 and is known as the "Homeowner's 4" [HO4]); and the comprehensive form, known as "Homeowner's 5" (HO5). A special form, "Homeowner's 3" (HO3), combines the broad form (HO2) coverage on personal property with the comprehensive form (HO5) coverage on the dwelling itself.

Basic Form (HO1).   With HO1 your premise is protected against the most common risks, including the following:

- Fire
- Lightning
- Windstorms
- Hail storms
- Explosions
- Riots
- Aircraft
- Vehicles
- Smoke damage
- Vandalism and malicious mischief
- Theft (except for certain exempt items, among which are credit cards)
- Breakage of glass in the building
- Loss suffered to personal property that you removed from endangered premises (e.g., the building next door to you is on fire, and you flee into the night clutching some private possessions that are later lost or damaged—they are covered under your basic form policy)

Broad Form (HO2).   The broad form (HO2) and the tenant's form (HO4) provide protection against additional risks at a nominal extra cost, including the following:

- Falling objects
- Collapse of the building
- Damage to the building due to the weight of ice or snow
- Certain damage caused by escape of steam and water from a boiler, radiator, or similar device

☐ Certain accidents involving electrical equipment, such as an overloaded circuit that blows out an appliance

Comprehensive Form (HO5).   The comprehensive form is sometimes referred to as an *all-risk policy*. But the comprehensive form generally excludes certain risks from coverage, such as earthquakes, tidal waves, sewer backups and seepages, landslides, floods, war, and nuclear radiation. See each specific policy to determine what exceptions do exist on the comprehensive form. Even though flood may be excluded from coverage, the federal government has acted to make flood insurance more easily available to homeowners in flood-prone areas. Your agent can give you details on this coverage and its cost. The added cost of the comprehensive protection may not be worthwhile to many homeowners, but must examine his or her own circumstance to determine what kind of protection is best for the dollars available.

The Types of Coverage

Protecting Other Property.   The basic insurance applies to loss or damage occurring to the building itself. In addition, the typical homeowner's policy also provides extended coverage for other forms of property. For example, auxiliary buildings such as garages and storage sheds are customarily covered for 10 percent of the full value on the main building. In other words, if the main building is covered for $80,000, the auxiliary buildings are covered for a total of $8000. Your personal property within the home is covered for 50 percent of the coverage on the house itself. Personal property that you take with you while away from home, with the possible exception of jewelry and securities, are protected for 10 percent of the primary value. In the comprehensive and special plans, the protection for personal property away from home may be as much as 100 percent of primary value on the house itself.

If your home or apartment suffers damage and you are required to live elsewhere while the damage is repaired, the typical homeowner's and tenant's policies provide additional living expenses, usually 10 percent on the basic HO1 policy and 20 percent on the broad and comprehensive policies. The percentages are calculated on the total primary value. In addition, your trees, plants, and shrubs are covered for up to 5 percent of the primary value in the event they are damaged.

Public Liability.   Homeowner's policies also contain public liability protection. Commonly, the homeowner's policy has up to $25,000 liability protection per occurrence, $500 in medical expenses payable to others, and $250 in property damages. For example, a guest in your house slips on a banana peel that you have negligently left lying in the hallway. The guest is unable to walk, and an ambulance is summoned. X-rays reveal that he has fractured his hip and has also broken his wristwatch in the fall. Your homeowner's policy will pay the injured guest up to $500 in medical expenses, which will probably be required in such a case. They will reimburse him for up to $250 in property damages, which will likely cover the expense of replacing the watch. The injured guest then learns that he will be unable to work for a number of months and makes a claim against your homeowner's policy. The public liability provision will pay him up to $25,000 in damages—loss of income—as a result of the accident, assuming that all facts proved that you were legally liable.

If you live in an apartment or a condominium, the issue of public liability protection is a bit more complicated. You should maintain coverage to protect yourself for anything that may occur within your premises. The apartment building owner or the condominium owners' association should also maintain adequate coverage to protect all interested parties in the event of an injury in a common area, such as a parking lot, a hallway, or an elevator shaft. As a tenant or condominium owner, you should make certain that the coverage on the common areas is adequate to protect you in the event someone is hurt in a common area and sues everyone in sight for as much as possible.

The limits on public liability coverage can be increased considerably by paying an added premium. Vastly higher limits for public liability can be obtained at a fairly modest increase in premium, and the prudent homeowner might do well to consider obtaining a much higher level of protection than the basic policy offers.

Valuables. Valuable personal property, may *not* be adequately covered for theft or loss under your homeowner's or tenant's policies. Valuable personal property can include such items as jewelry, paintings, sculptures, china, silver, cameras, projectors, collections (stamps, coins, medallions), golf clubs, furs, securities, cash, and credit cards. In order to be fully covered for loss of these items—whether at home or away—you may have to obtain a separate "personal floater." The cost of this added insurance can be considerable. You should seek the assistance of your agent in determining exactly what personal property is covered under your homeowner's policy and under what circumstances you may wish additional protection for your valuables.

The Deductible

The amount of your premium varies in relation to the deductible that you choose. The deductible is the amount you pay out of pocket for any losses before the insurance company becomes responsible. Some policies have a no-deductible clause, which means that the insurance company is responsible for the first dollar onward. A $50 deductible means that in any given occurrence, you must pay the first $50 worth of expense before the insurance company becomes responsible. Deductibles may be obtained for as much as $250 or $500. In choosing the higher deductibles you are exposing yourself to more potential risk in return for a lower premium. However, the premium is not lowered as much as the risk is enlarged. For example, the difference in premium cost between a $50 deductible and a $250 deductible may only be $20 or $30, but you're exposing yourself to $200 more potential risk. However, the premium expense is an actual out-of-pocket cost that you can save, whereas the added risk is only a possible expense that you may never incur.

The Co-Insurance Clause

The co-insurance clause can be extremely important. It states generally that if you wish to receive full replacement value for any damage to the premises, you must insure the premises for at least 80 percent of its replacement cost. For example, a house has a current replacement cost (not counting the land and foundation) of $80,000. This means that at current prices, it would cost $80,000 to duplicate the house in its depreciated condition on the existing foundation. (The land and the foundation are not included in figuring costs for insurance coverage because theoretically they cannot be destroyed.) But the owner has insured the building for only $56,000, which is $8000 shy of the 80 percent level of $64,000. The owner has a fire in the house that results in an actual loss of $16,000. But because he has not insured the house up to the 80 percent co-insurance level, the company will only pay $14,000 instead of the full $16,000. Why? Because the owner's coverage is only seven-eighths of what it should have been under the co-insurance clause ($56,000 is seven-eighths of $64,000). Thus, the owner will receive only seven-eighths of the actual damages ($14,000 is seven-eighths of $16,000). If the owner had insured the property for the full 80 percent co-insurance value ($64,000), he would have recovered the full $16,000 on the loss. The difference in premium between the full 80 percent value and the lesser value would have been so relatively small that the owner could be accused of having been woefully imprudent for not obtaining the balance of the 80 percent coverage.

Keeping up with Change

The prudent homeowner or tenant will make a careful inventory of all furnishings, appliances, and personal property and evaluate current market or replacement costs of those items in order to determine whether she is adequately covered by a basic homeowner's policy. The owner or renter will also be aware of the effects of inflation in most areas of the country; the value of housing is steadily increasing and, in order to maintain the proper level of insurance protection, continual upward adjustments must be made. Many policies offer clauses that automatically increase the amount of coverage in line with inflation: As the replacement value of the house increases, so does the amount of coverage. Policies may also be available that pay you the full amount needed to rebuild your home no matter what the cost.

If a homeowner or tenant acquires new property such as personal items or disposes of old items that have been insured, the owner must notify the insurance company so that the new acquisitions can be properly covered and the old dispositions properly deleted. When the insurance company is notified, they issue an endorsement amending the policy, which should be checked for accuracy and then attached to the policy itself.

Filing a Claim

In the event you do suffer a loss or damage, notify your insurance agent immediately. Even if you don't think that the loss is covered by insurance, you should still discuss the matter with your agent. It may, in fact, be covered. Depending on the extent of damage, the agent may require that you obtain estimates for the proper repair or replacement of damaged items. If a burglary or theft has occurred, it may be necessary to obtain copies of the police report. If someone is hurt on your property, you should report it immediately to your agent, because a public liability claim may arise. Under the public liability provisions of your homeowner's policy, the insurance company is obliged to provide legal defense for you against such claims as well as to pay any claims that are found to be valid. Delay in reporting to your agent could jeopardize your rights under your homeowner's policy.

PROPERTY TAXES

Property taxes (also called *real estate taxes*) provide the money that allows your local government to operate. Owners of all nonexempt kinds of property are required to pay these taxes, in return for which the city provides services. A portion of the property taxes may also be allocated to the county and state jurisdictions within which the city is located to enable them to provide their respective services.

How are property taxes calculated? The residents of each city, at least in theory, determine the amount and type of services they wish. In order to meet the expenses of these services, the city must generate income from taxation. The city officials determine what types of property will carry what share of the overall tax burden. The city, through its assessor's office, undergoes a program by which each property in the city is evaluated. Representatives of the assessor's office visit each property in the city periodically to determine the actual value of each parcel. When the current value of every property is known, the *assessment rate* is applied. For example, a given city may determine that residential property will be assessed at 20 percent of market value, while commercial property will be assessed at 25 percent, and industrial property at 30 percent. (Business and industrial areas frequently contribute a heavier share of tax dollars because they are using the property for income-producing purposes.) Thus, a house with a market value of $60,000 may be assessed at $12,000. In theory, all properties of the same type with equal market values are assessed equally.

Once the assessment rates are established, the city officials look at the outgo side of their budget and determine how much money is needed on the income side. They then determine the *tax rate*. Based on their budgetary needs, they may determine that the tax rate for a given year will be $100 for each $1000 of assessed valuation. Thus, the house with the $60,000 current value, which has an assessment of $12,000 (20 percent of the current market value according to the formula) will pay taxes of $1200 for the year.

The tax rate is adjusted annually to keep the city's income and expenses as close to equal as possible. Periodically, depending on local law and custom, all properties in the city, or a selection of properties in the city, may be reassessed to make sure that they are in line with the prevailing assessment program.

Commonly, homeowners are billed for their property taxes in two installments six months apart. If the homeowner has a mortgage escrow account, the tax bills will be sent to the mortgage lender, who will then pay the taxes. They will be paid out of this account to which the owner has made payments each month in addition to interest and principal.

Tenants are also indirectly paying a share of the tax because a portion of their rent is applied by the landlord to the tax bill on the property.

If a property owner defaults in the payment of property taxes, the city can take steps to force the property to be sold at public auction to satisfy the unpaid taxes due.

Protesting Your Assessment

Local laws provide measures by which property owners can protest the assessment on their property and, if successful, reduce the assessment and thereby the taxes. Tenants, who have an indirect stake in the taxation on the property they occupy, can also take steps to have the assessment reduced. They can act as a group in conjunction with the landlord in the same way that individual property owners can.

Although each local assessor's office attempts to value equal properties equally, errors can occur. Equal properties are those comparable in size, location, age, and quality of construction. For example, your house and your next-door neighbor's house are as identical as two houses can be. They were built at the same time by the same builder, and they are identical in size and room layout. Both houses have been maintained equally, and except for different decor, they are virtual twins. However, there is one exception: Your house is assessed for $15,000 while your neighbor's house is assessed for only $12,000. His annual tax bill, therefore, is roughly 20 percent lower than yours.

If an error exists concerning property that you own or occupy, nobody will take steps to correct that error other than you. An improper assessment can mean hundreds of dollars lost each year, year in and year out, so it behooves any property owner to examine the local assessment rolls every few years to determine that the property is, in fact, being properly assessed.

The steps to take to examine local assessment rolls are relatively simple. Visit your local assessor's office, and compare the assessment rolls for the buildings in your immediate neighborhood. Ask the assessor's office for assistance in determining how properties are valued. If you determine that your property is appraised at too high a level, ask the assessor to explain the steps you must take to file a protest. It's not necessary to have an attorney, but it might help if there is enough at stake. Regulations differ from one community to the next, but there is usually a cutoff date each year, after which assessments cannot be protested until the following year.

Figure 10-1 illustrates a typical neighborhood. Assume that all houses were built at the same time and are equal in size and condition. Houses A and C are assessed for $20,000 each; house B is assessed at $25,000; houses D and E are each assessed for $30,000. Why the discrepancy? Since A, B, and C are indeed

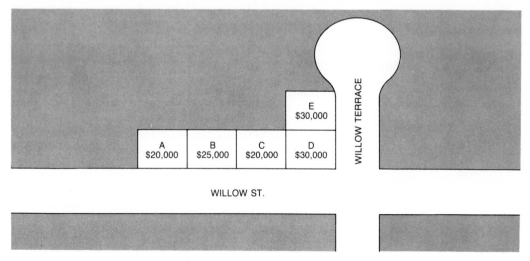

Figure 10–1   Property tax assessments

equal, it is likely that house B is overassessed by $5000. House D might be rightfully assessed at $30,000, since it is a corner lot, and in many communities a corner lot is considered more valuable than an interior lot. House E might be properly assessed at $30,000 if the street on which it fronts is considered to be a "better" street, such as a cul-de-sac, than the street on which the other houses front. Whoever owns houses B, D, and E would be wise to inquire at the local assessor's office.

UTILITIES

The owner of a house must make arrangements with the local utility companies to obtain gas, electricity, and telephone service. The individual owner is responsible for paying for the utilities used. Utility bills, particularly for heating, can vary considerably throughout the seasons. Some utility companies offer budget payment programs in which the estimated annual total cost is broken down into relatively even payments allowing the homeowner to maintain a program that does not disrupt other budget elements.

Not enough mention can be made of the importance of energy conservation. In addition to keeping your energy usage at a minimum—commensurate with your personal comfort needs—many states as well as the federal government offer attractive tax credits for energy-saving improvements to your property. Explore these possibilities with your local utility companies.

Strategies for Success

Energy Audit Can Save $$$$$

Your local utility company—gas, electric, or water company—might be willing to examine your home to see if you are wasting energy. Wasted energy is wasted money. In addition the utility company might publish literature on money-saving techniques from time to time. Such an energy "audit" can be particularly worthwhile if you are thinking of installing new, major energy-using devices, such as a water heater, furnace, oven, or air conditioner.

MAINTENANCE AND REPAIRS

Human nature being what it is, we often don't get around to doing preventive maintenance for a house, such as seasonal lubrication and servicing of a heating plant, until we hear the creaks and rattles and one thing or another is about to self-destruct. Unexpected maintenance costs can be a severe jolt to any budget.

To the homeowner, a periodic inspection is an inexpensive insurance policy, alerting you to potential dangers and expenses. In addition to paying for current ongoing maintenance costs, the wise homeowner will set aside a reserve fund for replacements to take care of these costs without having to interfere with borrowing lines, savings account, or ongoing regular budget.

Strategies for Success

Be Wise on Home Improvement Expenses

Adding major improvements to your home can increase the value of the home accordingly. But take care not to overdo it, or you won't be able to recapture the expense when you later sell. There are two problems you must consider before embarking on home improvement: (1) improving your house so much that you price it out of the range of similar homes in the neighborhood, and (2) "personalizing" improvements to such a degree that a later would-be buyer might find them frivolous or unnecessary. For example, adding new kitchen cabinets and bathroom fixtures are considered safe improvements. You'll likely get back the cost of them, maybe even more, when you sell. However, having an observatory in your attic or a waterfall in your yard might not appeal to a later buyer. Chances are you won't get your money back on such highly personalized items. Plan accordingly.

HOUSING LAWS

There are a number of laws that can affect the rights and obligations of both property owners and tenants. These laws differ from state to state and from city to city, and you should make inquiry in your own locality regarding any laws that might affect you.

Zoning

Cities commonly specify that certain areas may have only certain kinds of uses permitted on them. The city map will be divided into zones according to the uses allowed in those zones. The broad categories in zoning regulations are residential, commercial, industrial, and agricultural. Within each category there may be sub-categories. For example, within a residential category there may be zones for single-family housing only and zones in which multiple housing is permitted. Each specific zone may carry within it certain regulations applicable to that zone. In a commercial zone, for example, there may be a requirement that so many off-street parking places are available for each thousand square feet of building space.

Generally, zoning regulations are like a pyramid: higher uses are permitted in any of the lower use zones, but lower use of zones may not be permitted in the zones above them. Figure 10-2 provides an illustration. In most cities, the highest use is for single-family homes, often designated as R-1 (residential zone 1). In areas zoned R-1, therefore, only single-family homes are permitted. The next zone down may be designated R-2. R-2 zones would permit R-1 uses (single-family homes) plus low-rise multiple dwellings. The next zone down might be called R-3, and it would permit all R-2 uses, plus high-rise multiple dwellings.

Zoning laws can restrict you or protect you in an effort to maintain the quality of your neighborhood. For example, you wish to set up a beauty parlor in your home. You hang a simple sign on your front porch and accept clientele. If your home is in a zone that prevents businesses from being operated in the home, any neighbors who object to this activity could have your business stopped because it is in violation of the zoning ordinances. Likewise, you could do the same if a neighbor similarly violates the zoning ordinances.

Residents of any municipality should make themselves aware of current zoning regulations and be on the alert for the possibility of any change in the immediate vicinity that could affect the value of their residence. Zoning hearings are usually open to the public, and customarily there are appeals that can be taken from unfavorable zoning rulings. If many people are affected by the possibility of a zoning ordinance change, they can group together and hire an attorney to represent all of their joint interests.

Nuisances

Your next-door neighbor keeps a rooster that crows at dawn each morning, or plays a stereo at high volume each night into the wee hours, or burns strange or noxious

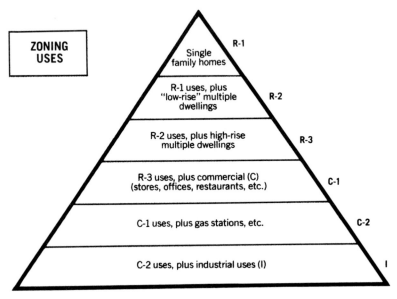

Figure 10–2 Zoning uses.

chemicals at odd hours, or permits dangerous conditions to exist. These actions and scores of others like them fall into the general category known as *nuisances*. If you're located in a multi-unit building, such as an apartment house or a condominium, you may be able to get some assistance from a sympathetic landlord or from the condominium owners' association. If you're a homeowner, you may have to resort to the local police or to your own attorney to get some satisfaction. Nuisance laws exist in almost every city, but enforcing them can involve feats of diplomacy that the local magistrates may be incapable of carrying out to your satisfaction. Some nuisances fall under the jurisdiction of other laws. For example, opening a business in premises where businesses are not permitted could be in violation of zoning laws. Matters relating to health and safety could fall under the multiple-housing laws or health and safety codes of the city. If a nuisance exists within your immediate vicinity, it might be better for you to explore the possibility that laws other than nuisance laws control the situation.

Eminent Domain

The law of eminent domain permits a local government—perhaps city, county, or state—to acquire private property where it can prove that the need exists for the public welfare. The process is generally known as *condemnation*, and it occurs where new highways and bridges are to be constructed, where urban-renewal programs take place, and where other public uses are called for. Owners of property threatened by condemnation are entitled to fair payment for their property. Procedures vary as to how property owners are compensated. Often there is a hearing at which property owners present their claims for fair compensation. If owners aren't satisfied with the offer, they may appeal, and if the appeal does not satisfy, they may take the matter into the courts. The aid of a lawyer and a competent real estate appraiser is necessary in any condemnation situation.

The law of eminent domain can also affect your property indirectly, without actually taking any portion of it. For example, a new highway nearby may create noise and pollution problems for your house. None of your property has actually been taken, but the value of the property may suffer as a result. You may be entitled to some claim for damages as a result.

Anyone who is either buying or already owns property, whether residential, commercial, or industrial, should be aware of any possible eminent domain that could take place within the proximity of your property. Knowledge of an impending condemnation might discourage you from buying certain property, and that knowledge can also permit you to take early action to best protect your interests if a condemnation threatens currently owned property.

Rent Control and Condominium-Conversion Regulations

If you live in a multiple-dwelling unit, rent control ordinances and condominium-conversion regulations can have a very important effect on your rights. These laws are discussed in more detail in the following chapter.

Insurance Inventory

Whether you're a renter or an owner, it's important that your valuable personal possessions be adequately insured against damage or loss. Insurance coverage is generally advisable if the damage or loss of personal property would cause you financial distress. (Insuring items of sentimental value may be an unwise expense.) Too little coverage or too much coverage can be costly. This checklist will help you determine the right amount of coverage.

Items[a]	Current protection	Replacement cost	Cost to fully insure	Most recent appraisal
☐ Jewelry	_____	_____	_____	_____
☐ Collections (coins, stamps, etc.)	_____	_____	_____	_____
☐ Art	_____	_____	_____	_____
☐ Chinaware	_____	_____	_____	_____
☐ Silverware	_____	_____	_____	_____
☐ Cash, securities kept at home	_____	_____	_____	_____
☐ Musical instruments	_____	_____	_____	_____
☐ Electronic items (TV, stereo, video recorder)	_____	_____	_____	_____
☐ Sports equipment (skis, scuba gear, golf clubs)	_____	_____	_____	_____
☐ Furniture and furnishings	_____	_____	_____	_____

[a]Do you have a color photo of each valuable item?

Mortgage Insurance
Can Be Confusing

There's one kind of insurance related to homeownership that really doesn't insure the property itself. Rather, it insures that your mortgage payments will be made in the event of the death or disability of the primary breadwinner in the family. Technically, it's a form of life or disability insurance and could really be considered a part of the subjects discussed in Chapters 19 and 20. However, because it relates to homeownership and because it is often sold by affiliates of banks and savings associations that also provide the home financing, let's examine the pros and cons of this protection briefly here.

Since your overall mortgage debt is the largest you'll likely ever face and since your monthly mortgage payments represent one of your major monthly obligations, it can be prudent to protect yourself against a catastrophe that could affect your ability to meet your home loan debt.

Life insurance on your mortgage is generally of the "decreasing term" variety. The amount of protection decreases monthly as the amount of your debt decreases. Depending on your age and family circumstances, you might want to explore a level-term or ordinary life policy instead of the decreasing term type. You might be able to obtain better long-term protection without greatly increasing the cost.

In the event of the death of the breadwinner, proceeds of mortgage life insurance are commonly paid directly to the lender. This may not be best for you. It might be preferable to obtain a policy that would pay the proceeds to your named beneficiary (spouse, children) to do with as they please. Rather than have the mortgage paid off, they might prefer to continue making payments or to sell the house with the original mortgage intact. If the interest rate on the mortgage is lower than the current rate, it could prove costly later if the survivors needed to refinance the property.

Disability policies make your monthly payments for you if you are unable to work due to illness or accident. Many will have a thirty- or sixty-day "waiting period" before payments commence. Compare the terms and costs of such policies, bearing in mind other sources of income that might be available to help you make your payments during a period of disability. Your own insurance agent might be able to provide better coverage at a lower cost than the lender.

CHAPTER 11

Renting

Tens of millions of Americans rent their dwellings. Many do so because they've not been able to accumulate enough money to purchase a house or condominium. Others do so because they simply prefer the freedom and flexibility that come with renting. Whether you're making a choice between renting and buying or whether you have no choice in the matter, the rental of a dwelling entails many important legal and financial considerations. This chapter will make you aware of those considerations and will help you resolve common problems that come with renting. They include the following:

□ What factors you should evaluate in deciding whether to rent or buy

□ How to understand the terms of a lease and how to negotiate a rental arrangement that's best for you

□ How you might be able to obtain the right to buy the place you've been renting or want to rent

□ What to do if your rights as a tenant are violated

If you are a renter, you are paying another person—the owner of property or the landlord—a fee for the privilege of living in his property. You may rent a person's house, or you may rent in a multiple-unit dwelling such as a duplex, a condominium complex, or an apartment house. Mobile home rentals are also not uncommon.

A renter occupies a dwelling in one of two ways: on a month-to-month basis or on a fixed-term basis. On a month-to-month basis, both the landlord and the tenant have the right to terminate the arrangement upon giving thirty days' notice to the other party. Commonly, the landlord expects the tenant to comply with certain rules and regulations that are spelled out in a written agreement. On a fixed-term basis, the landlord and tenant agree in a written document that the tenant has the right to occupy the premises for a specific amount of time, such as one or two years. The agreement between the two parties is called a *lease*.

RENTING: THE PROS AND CONS

Many people, particularly in larger cities, are dyed-in-the-wool renters. They simply prefer the apartment mode of living—being close to other people and being free of the cares that often go with ownership. To them, rental is a way of life, and the thought of buying a home may never enter their minds.

Many other people have no choice: They do not have the money available to make a down payment on a home, and thus they must be renters. This latter group is further broken down into two categories. (1) There are those who prefer to spend their money on other things rather than accumulate it for a down payment. These people are likely to remain permanent renters. (2) There are other renters who desire to eventually become owners and who will structure their budget to accumulate the necessary down payment. As they struggle to accumulate the down payment, they often ponder the dilemma: Is it worth it to own a home, or should we just be content as renters?

There is no simple answer to the dilemma. Homeownership has long been considered one of the great American dreams. In decades gone by, this dream was reasonably attainable by a large segment of the population. But today, with housing costs as high as they are and with so many other temptations upon which to spend one's money, this great American dream may be fading.

Traditionally, homeownership has long been considered a wise step financially. Over the long run, this probably has remained true. But ownership is not necessarily the right answer for everybody.

To help you make a decision best suited to your own individual needs, (see Figure 11-1), desires, and abilities, let's now examine some of the pros and cons of renting.

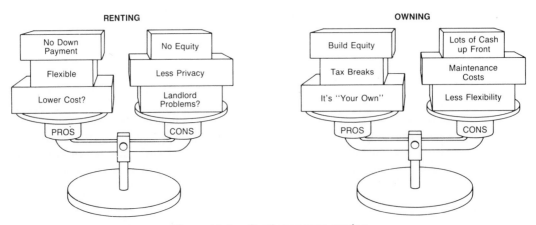

Figure 11-1   Renting versus owning

Flexibility

One of the primary advantages of renting—whether it's a house or an apartment—is the flexibility available. When a lease expires, the tenant is free to move on (or renew, assuming she and the landlord agree on renewal terms). There's no need to worry about selling and no danger of getting caught with making payments on two dwellings, such as when a sale is not completed by a homeowner prior to the time of moving out. The flexibility is even greater when furnished units are rented, for the chores of physically moving are considerably minimized. Largely for this reason, renting is often preferable for younger persons who have not yet settled into their chosen life style or career and who may not yet know what ultimate size their family will be. The same is true for older persons at or near retirement who may wish to be able to come and go as they please without the concerns of ownership.

No Money Tied Up

With very few exceptions, ownership requires a substantial sum of money to be tied up in the property. When one buys a house or condominium, it's necessary to make a substantial down payment. Further, as you make your monthly mortgage payments, a portion of which goes to reduce your mortgage debt, these additional sums are effectively tied up in the property. Money that's tied up in property ownership is money you do not have direct access to. It's money that could otherwise be earning income for you if it were invested. Until you sell or refinance the property—either of which could be time consuming and costly—you cannot get at your money. In a rental situation, there's no need to tie up any large sums of money. A rental deposit, usually not in excess of two months' rent, will frequently be called for, but this is not a large enough sum to create any noticeable disadvantage.

Income Tax Implications

Ownership provides certain income tax advantages that are not available to renters. Tax laws allow owners to take deductions for the interest they pay on their mortgage and the property taxes they pay. This can mean a substantial savings in taxes. Further, if you sell your home and realize a profit, the profit is subject to favorable tax laws. (See Chapter 12 for a more detailed discussion.)

These tax advantages have often been the deciding factor for many people to purchase a home rather than to rent. But a closer look at the situation reveals that in many cases the advantages may not necessarily be as attractive as they seem on the surface.

For example, the Alpers have saved $20,000 to use as a down payment for the purchase of a house. Considering the interest they pay on their mortgage and their property taxes and their particular tax bracket, the ownership of the home results in an income tax savings of $2000 per year. Had the Alpers *not* bought a home, but instead invested the $20,000 at 12 percent interest, they would have earned $2400 per year, before income tax considerations. In this particular case, careful arithmetic indicates that they may not be better off financially on a year-to-year basis as a result of buying instead of using their available funds for investment and renting their dwelling.

When analyzing specific financial advantages in owning versus renting, this income tax factor should be carefully calculated based on your own tax situation. The numbers will differ from person to person, from deal to deal, and from year to year. The more costly the house and the higher the interest rate, the more favorable the tax advantage can be to an owner. But it's not an automatic bonanza. Many years ago, when the standard deduction was much smaller than it is today, the tax advantage of ownership was much more obvious. But in recent years the standard deduction has grown to such a relatively high percentage of income that careful arithmetic is necessary before final decisions are made.

The Tax Reform Act of 1986 leaves these considerations basically intact. But a careful analysis made with professional help can still be very important in reaching the best possible conclusion.

No Chance of Profit, No Risk of Loss

One of the attractions of ownership is the chance that one may profit on a later resale. The tenant, of course, has no such chance for profit, but he faces no risk of loss either.

Indeed, the lure of profit often bears fruit. But profit is often the direct result of inflation, and although you may profit on the sale of your existing home, you'll soon realize that you have to live somewhere else, and the cost of acquiring new housing will have likely risen in step with the price of your old housing. Thus, your profit can easily be absorbed by simply changing from one dwelling to another.

Profit can also be reduced by two other factors: real estate commissions and income taxes. In all likelihood you will have used a real estate agent to help you sell your house, and a commission of 6 or 7 percent of the selling price goes to the agent. Further, if you sell your house at a profit, the profit is subject to federal income taxes. (If you sell your house at a loss, the loss is not deductible on your income tax return.) See Chapter 12 for further details.

No Protection against Inflation

Neither owning nor renting can insure you of protection against inflation. For a month-to-month tenant, the rental can be increased on thirty days' notice. For a tenant on a lease, the rental can be increased upon a renewal of the lease (subject to any rent control ordinances that may exist in the community). The homeowner can expect increasing expenses for property taxes, property insurance, maintenance, repairs, and utilities. And if the homeowner is making payments on a variable-rate mortgage, her basic monthly payments can be subject to increases as well. The homeowner with a fixed-rate mortgage has much greater protection against inflation because the monthly payments for interest and principal remain constant as long as he remains owner of the property.

Overall, homeowners do have a better chance to protect themselves from inflation, because as prices rise over the years, so will the value of their home. The only problem with this, as noted earlier, is that the prices of all other homes will have risen comparably, so any profit realized on the sale may be illusory when another house is purchased.

This particular advantage to homeownership is based on the assumption that housing values will continue to rise. But this phenomenon is by no means guaranteed. Housing markets are definitely subject to fluctuations from time to time and from place to place. If your timing is unfortunate enough to find you buying when the market is high and wanting to sell when the market is low, this inflation-proofing advantage of homeownership may not exist. Indeed, you might have been better off renting.

No Building Equity

"Why rent and collect worthless rent receipts when we can own and be building a hefty equity in our home?" Fact or myth? Although it's true that rent receipts have no tangible value, the other side of the question can be misleading. The average stay in a dwelling by a typical American family is from seven to ten years, and during the early years of the common thirty-year mortgage, the reduction of mortgage debt is very small indeed.

Equity is the difference between what your house is worth and what is owed on it. Part of each mortgage payment you make reduces your debt, and theoretically, when you later sell your property, you recapture the equity plus any appreciation in the value of your house.

You have seen in Chapter 9 how interest is figured on mortgages. For the moment, note that during the first seven years of a 12 percent, thirty-year morgage, the reduction of debt on the mortgage is only about 5 percent of the total original mortgage.

For example, during the first seven years of a $70,000 mortgage that is set to run for thirty years at a 12 percent interest rate, the portion of your mortgage payments allocated to reducing the debt totals 5 percent of the total original mortgage, or $3500. In other words, after seven years of making payments on such a mortgage, you will have reduced your mortgage indebtedness from $70,000 to $66,500.

No Added Expenses

If you're a tenant, the cost of certain repairs may be borne by the landlord, depending on the terms of the lease. If you're an owner, you'll usually have to bear most of these costs yourself, except in certain condominium or cooperative situations. As a tenant, you're probably limited in the number of alterations and modifications you can make to the premises. The lease controls what you can and cannot do. Unless you're willing, on terminating your lease, to correct any personal modifications that you might have installed, you will be very limited in what you can do in a rental unit. As an owner, you're free to do as you please—paint the walls purple and pink if you like—as long as you're aware of the implications of such modifications when it comes time to sell the house or condominium. You run the risk of overpersonalizing your premises and scaring away would-be buyers. You can also run the risk of overimproving the premises and thus pricing the dwelling out of the market for comparable units within that neighborhood. But bearing these factors in mind, the freedom of modifying your dwelling is vastly greater in an ownership situation than with a rental.

A Case History

Let's examine a situation in which a family is debating between buying and renting. This example does not presume to answer the dilemma. It's merely intended to serve as a guide, a framework, to help you know what arithmetic you should consider in trying to find the right answer for your own personal situation.

The Browns have found a condominium, and they have the opportunity of either buying or renting it. The purchase price is $80,000, and the monthly rental is $900, which includes all utilities, maintenance, and association dues.

If the Browns buy, they have $10,000 in cash to use as a down payment. The property has an existing $70,000 mortgage with an annual interest rate of 12 percent. The mortgage can be assumed. Monthly payments on interest and principal total $720. Property taxes are $120 per month, property insurance is $40 per month, and utilities and maintenance total $100 per month. Thus, if they buy, their total monthly cash outlay would be $980.

The Browns estimate that based on their current tax bracket, ownership will result in a tax savings to them of $2000 in the first year or $166 per month.

On the other hand, if they decide not to buy but to rent and if they invest their $10,000 at 12 percent return, they will take in $1200 during the first year (before income taxes), or $100 per month. After taxes, they estimate that the $100 per month would shrink to $76 per month. Thus as Table 11-1 shows, they are looking at a difference of $10 per month net savings should they buy instead of rent. This alone might convince them to buy, particularly if they felt that they'd be living in the condominium for a period of years and had an opportunity to reap a profit upon a later sale.

But the Browns know their own circumstances very well: They suspect that within a year Mr. Brown's job might require them to move to a different city. They've also examined the local housing market and have found that prices are flat and seem likely to remain so for at least many months. Looking one year ahead, they realize that if they have to sell the condominium and find themselves without a buyer for just one month after they've been transferred, they will be out of pocket over $900. That would more than wipe out the monthly savings they'd have realized during that year by being owners instead of renters.

The Browns, it appears, are almost at a "toss the coin" situation. Table 11-1 illustrates the arithmetic of the Browns' dilemma. As their case illustrates, resolving the matter can depend basically on personal circumstances. How long might they stay in a given dwelling? How wisely might they invest their funds if they decide

Table 11-1 **The Browns: Renting versus Owning**

Monthly costs			
As owners		*As renters*	
Mortgage	$720	Base rent (including utilities)	$900
Property tax	120	Net earning on invested $10,000	76
Property insurance	40	Out-of-pocket cost	$824
Utilities and maintenance	100		
	980		
Tax savings	166		
Out-of-pocket cost	$814		

to rent instead of buy? Which way will the housing market turn? The case of the Browns is not intended to convince you to become a renter or a buyer but merely to show you the arithmetic and the ''crystal-ball gazing'' that you must do in order to reach a conclusion best suited to your own circumstances. The table illustrates the actual cash flow differences in the choices the Browns have.

SHOPPING FOR RENTALS

Many of the same considerations apply to looking for a dwelling to rent as we discussed in the section on buying a dwelling in Chapter 8. How close will it be to your place of work, to shopping, to schools, to entertainment? What is the condition of the building and of the neighborhood? How large are the premises, and will they suit your foreseeable needs for the time you'll be living there?

There are additional matters to be considered if you are looking for an apartment. You should talk to other tenants in the building and try to determine the level of service and care provided by the landlord. Are reasonable requests by tenants taken care of promptly and courteously? Is the building well maintained, both esthetically and mechanically? What has been the history of rent increases? Are there any local rent control ordinances that apply to the building? The renters' checklist at the end of this chapter will help you in your quest for an apartment.

Depending on your community, the classified ads in your local newspaper may be all you need to direct you to available apartments. In larger communities, you might find it desirable to seek the services of a rental agent. It's not uncommon for a rental agent to charge the tenant a fee for finding an apartment. Before you contract with a rental agent, determine what fees, if any, will be expected from you. Also get personal references from other individuals who have used the services of the rental agent.

When you buy a house, you can reasonably expect that a real estate agent who is working for you will escort you from one house to another. But don't expect the same kind of service from a rental agent. In all likelihood, you will be given the address and instructions on how to view the apartment, and you'll be on your own to take care of yourself.

Depending on the supply of apartments in your community and on the demand for them, you might find it necessary to leave a deposit with a landlord immediately if you find a place you like. If the demand is high and the supply low, a landlord will rent to the first interested party who puts up the necessary deposit. On the other hand, if the demand is low, the landlord might be willing to "hold" a given apartment for you for a day or two, perhaps even longer. In such a case it would be to your advantage to get the promise in writing from the landlord.

When you examine an apartment, determine whether the landlord expects you to rent on a month-to-month basis or to sign a lease. Examine the premises carefully to determine if everything is in proper working order (appliances, plumbing, electrical outlets). If you have children or pets or expect to have them, make sure they will be acceptable to the landlord. And in addition to finding out what the monthly rental will be, find out what kind of deposit the landlord expects.

Strategies for Success

How to Compete for Rental Space

You want to rent an apartment, and it's just your luck that there are more lookers than apartments on the market. The competition for a good apartment in your price range is tough. How can you win? Assuming that any prudent landlord will want to check your credit and see references, particularly from your current landlord and from your employer, get a copy of your credit history. A call to a local credit bureau can help; so can your banker. Get copies of these references, and have them in hand to give to the landlord when you apply. This saves the landlord time and trouble. Another way to beat the competition is to offer to give the landlord a cash deposit on the spot—maybe $50 or so—if he'll take the apartment off the market while he checks you out. Make it refundable if he doesn't accept you, nonrefundable if *you* bow out. You're risking some money, but if you're sure you want the unit, this strategy can help you get it.

THE LEASE AND ITS KEY CLAUSES

Renting a dwelling—be it a house, a mobile home, or an apartment—involves numerous rights and obligations between the landlord and the tenant. These rights and obligations may be spelled out in a full-fledged contract called a *lease*. A lease is not of the same financial magnitude as the mortgage that corresponds to the purchase of a house, but it can entail many thousands of dollars that you will be paying, and you want to make sure you're getting what you bargained for.

The lease, basically, entitles you to occupy certain premises for a certain period of time at an agreed price. Here are some of the key clauses that could well affect the nature and cost of your occupancy.

Expenses

The lease should set forth exactly who is responsible for what expenses in connection with the property. If the landlord is responsible for all utilities and all real estate taxes, the lease should so state. If the tenant is responsible for individual utilities, will the tenant be separately metered so that the true utility costs can be exactly measured? If the tenant is paying based on a certain percentage of the total building occupancy and is not separately metered, will the tenant be getting a fair shake, or will she be paying more than actual utility usage?

Repairs

Who will be responsible for *making* which repairs? And perhaps more important, who will be responsible for *paying* for the repairs that are made? The landlord may be responsible for seeing to it that repairs are made, but some repairs may be done at the tenant's expense, others at the landlord's. Generally, the landlord is responsible for repairing structural defects and for keeping the central heating unit in proper working order. The tenants may be responsible for attending to their own repairs on minor items within the premises, including but not limited to plumbing leaks and defective appliances. If you have examined the premises before you sign a lease, you should be able to determine what possible repair bills you might be facing during your occupancy. If you or the contractor you hire to assist you in your evaluation determine that you would be more than normally vulnerable to repair costs, you might want to renegotiate the repair clause of your lease with the landlord before you sign.

Quiet Enjoyment

Quiet enjoyment is a legal term that assures you of the right to privacy and quiet in your occupancy of the premises. If the landlord fails to deliver quiet enjoyment, that is, fails to keep the adjoining neighbors from playing air hockey next to your bedroom wall at 4 A.M.,—you will have the right to either withhold your rent payment or get assistance in the courts in upholding your rights.

Extra Fees

Does your monthly rental include all of the features of your occupancy, or will added costs be hidden in the small print on the back page of the lease, such as

<hr>

Strategies for Success

Good Public Relations with Landlord Can Pay Off

Relations between landlords and tenants are seldom sweet and happy, but they can be more positive than negative if you, as a tenant, maintain a good sense of public relations with your landlord. It isn't necessarily your obligation to do so, but it can pay off for you. Paying your rent promptly can win a good reference for your credit file. This can always be of value. If minor repairs or replacements are needed, volunteer to do them yourself. This could be a lot better than going through the irritation of hassling the landlord and waiting for him to do it. It's appropriate that you ask to be reimbursed for any out-of-pocket expenses that the landlord would normally incur. And you can ask a proper sum to cover your own labor. A decent-minded landlord will appreciate this, and you might be able to negotiate a more favorable renewal as a result.

<hr>

parking fees, use of recreational facilities, and assessments for improvements in the common areas? All rental costs and fees should be clearly understood prior to the signing of any lease.

Renewal Options

Will you have a right to renew your lease on the expiration of the original term? Not all leases contain this privilege, and it may be one worth bargaining for. Without a renewal option, the landlord can ask whatever the market will bear when the original lease term expires. If the tenant is not willing to pay what the landlord is asking, the landlord has the right to have the tenant move out. A renewal option is for the protection of the tenant: She has the right either to stay on at the agreed rental or to move out. It's reasonable to expect that the rental rate on a renewal will be higher than on the original term, so the landlord can be protected against rising costs. Even at a higher rent, though, the renewal option does offer the tenant flexibility and choice, things often worth paying for.

Some leases may contain an automatic renewal clause. When such a clause exists, the lease may automatically renew for another term unless the tenant gives written notice to the landlord that she does not wish to have the lease renewed. If you have such a lease and you fail to give the proper notice, you could become responsible for lease payments for an additional term. For example, if the original term was for one year and the automatic renew clause goes into effect, you could become responsible for an additional year's rent.

Sublease Privileges

You may be subleasing *from* another party, or you may wish to sublease *to* another party. If you are subleasing from the original tenant, you will be subject to the terms of his lease. Prior to subleasing from another party, you might want to determine if in fact that party has the right to sublease to you, if the landlord has given his consent, and if such a consent is included in the original lease. If you sublease from another party, and the party does not have the legal right to sublease to you, the landlord technically could evict you and perhaps the main tenant as well, because the lease has been violated.

On the other hand, if you wish to have the right to sublease to other parties while you are the main tenant, you had best make certain that the lease contains this privilege. In the sublease clause, the landlord may or may not reserve the right to approve of any sublessee, generally for reasons of credit-worthiness. Unless the landlord consents, the fact that you sublease to another party does not relieve you of the obligation to pay the rent.

A sublease privilege is one that favors the tenant. It gives the tenant the flexibility of being able to move out before the lease has expired and to defray obligations by allowing another party to live in the apartment or house. If you do sublease to another party, you must make certain in advance that the party is credit-worthy and reliable. It would pay to obtain a credit history on the party to whom you're subleasing to determine these factors.

Security Deposits

There are three possible types of security deposits that you might be required to pay: deposits to insure the payment of the rent, cleaning deposits, and breakage deposits. The rental deposit is usually designated to cover the last month's rent of the lease. This gives the landlord some protection in the event that you move out early. The fact that you do move out early does not necessarily relieve you of your remaining obligations under the lease. Technically, if you move out after eighteen months of a twenty-four-month lease, you'll be liable for the remaining six months. The landlord will apply the one month's deposit that you have paid toward that six months' obligation and will be able to commence legal proceedings to collect the remaining five months' worth of rent from you.

If the premises does need cleaning after you've moved out, the landlord can be expected to apply the cleaning deposit to cleanup. If damage or breakage has occurred, the damage deposit will be applied to making the necessary repairs, but the tenant's obligation may not be limited to the amount of the breakage deposit. If the breakage or damage exceeds the amount of the deposit, and the lease stipulates that the damages aren't limited to that amount, the landlord can pursue the tenant for the excess needed to make the appropriate repairs.

For the fullest protection of the tenant, both parties should closely examine all aspects of the premises before the tenant takes occupancy to determine the condition of cleanliness and what damages exist at the time the tenant takes occupancy. For example, there may be a crack in a wall that would normally be covered by a piece of furniture or a wall hanging. If it's there when the tenant takes occupancy, the fact should be noted on the lease document so that no one can claim that the tenant caused the damage during her period of occupancy. The tenant and the landlord may trust each other implicitly, but the tenant has to remember that when she moves out there may be a different landlord who will not remember that the crack was there at the time the tenant moved in. Color photos of the premises can be particularly helpful in this regard.

Improvements

The tenant of an apartment or a house may wish to make certain improvements on the premises during the term of occupancy. Normally, if improvements are easily removable, such as carpeting, they would remain the property of the tenant. Some improvements, however, may not be quite so portable. For example, a tenant may install built-in bookcases or a wet bar. Unless the tenant and the landlord have agreed in advance, improvements of this sort might be claimed by the landlord as his property. If any improvements are to be made in the premises, the landlord and the tenant should agree, before the improvements are made, who will have the benefit on the termination of the lease.

Amending the Lease

Even though a lease is a binding legal contract, it can be amended at any time on mutual agreement of the landlord and tenant. (The same holds true in a purchase contract for a house or condominium.) If the parties do agree to any amendments in the contract, changes can be accomplished. Proper consideration (payment) is made between the parties, and the amendment is properly signed by both parties. Any of the clauses noted above could thus be inserted into a lease agreement even after the agreement has originally been signed and occupancy has been taken. Whether or not to include any amendments on the lease is a matter of bargaining, and if one party is giving up certain rights, the other party will naturally want to receive certain other rights in exchange. Before any rights or obligations are exchanged, legal advice should be sought on the specific consequences of such actions.

TENANT'S INSURANCE

The landlord must be insured with respect to damage to the building, such as by fire. But you, as tenant, are responsible for insuring your own possessions. See Chapter 10 for a discussion of tenant's insurance. If the building is extensively damaged by a fire or other catastrophe, you may not be able to occupy your apartment. In arranging for your own tenant's insurance, determine whether you will be provided with any form of reimbursement for added living expenses you may incur for temporary quarters until the building is ready for occupancy.

RENTING MONTH TO MONTH

Not all tenants have a written lease. Many people occupy dwellings on a month-to-month basis without the benefit of any written documents. This, in effect, is a one-month lease. It allows the landlord to alter the terms by giving one month's notice. It also allows the tenant to vacate by giving one month's notice. Laws may differ from state to state on precisely what the rights of the parties are on a month-to-month lease. Generally, a landlord wishing to raise rents or a tenant wishing to move out must give at least one month's notice from the start of any month of their respective intentions to do so. For example, if a tenant wishes to vacate on March 1, he should give proper notice to the landlord no later than the preceding February 1. If this is done, the rental obligation will cease after February, as will the right to occupy the apartment. If, though, notice isn't given until, say, February 10, the landlord might technically be able to hold the person on as a tenant and expect the rental due for the month of March.

LEASING AND BUYING: A COMBINATION

There can be situations in which an individual becomes a tenant and then an owner. She may have a lease with an option to buy or with a first refusal to buy.

A Lease with an Option to Buy

A lease with an option to purchase puts the parties in the following status: As tenants they have the right to occupy the premises for the stated time and for the stated rental. At any time during their tenancy, they have the right to notify the owner of their intent to purchase the property at a previously agreed price. During the period of tenancy, the owner cannot sell the property to any other party, unless the tenants agree to release their option to buy.

Here's an example. The Greens lease a house at $1000 per month with an option to buy the house for $100,000. They may exercise their right to buy at any time during their tenancy, but at least thirty days before the end of the lease. If they wish to exercise their option, they must give the owner the proper notice and enter into a sales agreement. If they fail to give the proper notice within the allotted time, their option will expire, and they will no longer have the right to purchase at the agreed price.

By entering into a lease with an option to buy, the owner of the premises is taking the property off the market for at least the term of the lease. He has no assurance that the tenant will in fact buy the property, and he may be forgoing an opportunity to lease or sell the property to others at a better rental or purchase price. Thus, the owner of the property can well be expected to charge a premium for the lease and perhaps for the purchase as well. In other words, although the property might normally rent for $900 per month, he may charge $1000 per month. Also, the property might normally have a market value of $97,000, and he may put an asking price of $100,000 on it.

Depending on individual circumstances, a lease with an option to buy can be a very desirable arrangement for certain individuals. In exchange for the extra rental or purchase price that may have to be paid, a considerable measure of flexibility can be obtained. The arrangement can also eliminate the need for making a second move, the cost of which may well offset the extra price being paid on the lease or purchase.

A Lease with a Right of First Refusal

A lease with a right of first refusal to purchase is another alternative that should be considered. Under a lease with a right of first refusal to purchase, the owner is still free to offer the property for sale to others during the term of the tenancy, subject, however, to the right of the tenant to meet or beat any bona fide offer that the owner may acquire. Here's how such an arrangement might work. The tenant and the owner agree on a $1000 per month rental, and a $100,000 purchase price after one year. The tenant is not obliged to purchase at all but may do so at this price if the property is still available at the time. During the period of the tenancy, the landlord has the right to offer the property for sale to anyone at all. If another would-be buyer offers $105,000, the tenant then has the express right to meet or beat that $105,000 offer within a period of, say, ten days after he's been notified by the landlord of the offer. If the tenant wishes to meet the offer, he can become the owner. If the tenant does not wish to meet the offer, he must give up the property.

In the case of a lease with a first refusal to purchase, the landlord is not taking the property off the market, as he does under a lease with an option to purchase. Thus, the landlord might be less inclined to charge a premium price for either the rental or the purchase. The tenant under such an arrangement, however, does run the risk of not being able to buy the property at the desired price. The trade-off is having a possibly lower rent and purchase price versus a possible inability to buy the property. This has to be carefully evaluated.

RENTAL LAWS

Virtually every city has ordinances pertaining to health and safety measures in multiple-residence dwellings. These ordinances require landlords to maintain proper levels of sanitation, structural soundness, adequacy of plumbing and wiring, and precautions against fire. Such ordinances may vary considerably from city to city. If tenants feel that their rights have been violated with respect to these health and safety ordinances, they should notify the landlord. If a violation of an ordinance is not corrected, the appropriate city offices should be notified. Rent control laws and condominium-conversion laws have come into being in great profusion in recent years. These laws are designed to protect the interests of tenants, and you should become aware of any such laws that exist in your community.

Rent Control

Rent control laws, in general, impose limits on the amount of rent increases that a landlord can impose on a tenant. A brief summary of the major aspects of the rent control law of the city of Los Angeles will give you an idea of how a typical law works to protect the tenants.

In Los Angeles, the rent control ordinance covers virtually all multiple-dwelling rental units, but it does exclude so-called luxury units: apartments that were renting for more than $750 at the time the ordinance went into effect in 1978. For these luxury units, landlords are free to increase rents as they wish, subject to the law of supply and demand in the marketplace.

For all rental units covered by the law, landlords are permitted to increase the rent only once each year. The amount by which the rent can be increased each year is determined annually by the agency that oversees the city's rent control law. There are some exceptions to this limitation. If a tenant voluntarily moves out of an apartment, the landlord can set the rent for a new tenant at whatever level he wishes. If a $400-a-month apartment is vacated, the landlord can charge a new tenant $500 or more per month, if he can find a tenant willing to pay the price. A landlord is also permitted to increase the rent if he provides certain additional services to the tenant, such as additional garage space, an air-conditioning unit, and various improvements to the premises.

Perhaps as important as the limitation on rental increases is the provision in the Los Angeles ordinance that a landlord cannot evict a tenant without good cause, such as failure to pay rent or violation of the rules and regulations of the building. In effect, a tenant who pays the rent and obeys the regulations can remain in the apartment indefinitely on a month-to-month basis and is protected against rent increases within the stated limits.

Needless to say, landlords do not like such rent control ordinances and point to such restrictions as reason for their cutting back on services to the tenants.

Condominium-Conversion Laws

Leonard owns a ten-unit apartment house, which he wants to sell for $300,000. But the economy is weak, and he has a hard time finding anyone who wishes to make the investment. Leonard then has a clever idea. Instead of looking for a single buyer for the whole building, why not convert the building into condominiums and sell each unit separately for $40,000 each? It may take some additional paper work, but he figures he will probably be able to dispose of the building faster and at a much better price: $400,000 instead of $300,000.

Leonard is planning what is known as condominium conversion: apartments being converted into individual condominiums. Conversions can be bad for the current tenants, particularly if they can not come up with the necessary down payment. They would thus be forced to move out. On the other hand, many tenants find it an attractive opportunity, enabling them to convert their non–tax-deductible rent into substantially tax-deductible mortgage payments.

Condominium-conversion laws have been passed to protect the former type of tenant: the ones who find themselves dispossessed of their living quarters, often because of greedy and inconsiderate landlords. Condominium-conversion ordinances typically require at least a majority approval of existing tenants before a landlord can convert the property into condominiums. The ordinance may also require approval of the city, which may not be easy to obtain depending on the supply and demand of existing rental units in the city.

If you are a tenant, you may someday have to face the possibility of having your apartment converted into a condominium. If that time arrives, you should consider the alternatives: What advantages would there be to you to become an owner and what advantages to remain a tenant, even if it means having to move. The chapters in this book on buying and financing a house offer guidelines to help you make a prudent decision.

A Guide for Renters

If you're comparing rental dwellings, this checklist will help you determine the respective advantages and disadvantages of various sites. The cheapest rent doesn't necessarily mean the best dwelling. If you choose one place and find you're unhappy with it, bear in mind the cost, energy, and effort involved in finding another place and making the move.

Item	Dwelling A	Dwelling B	Dwelling C
☐ Monthly rent			
☐ Month-to-month or lease? If lease, for how long?			
☐ If lease, do you have options to renew? At what rental?			
☐ Total amount of deposits required (security, cleaning)			
☐ Will deposits earn interest? Rate?			
☐ Estimated miles traveled per month to work, school, routine shopping			
☐ Estimated travel cost per month			
☐ Is there a resident manager to handle problems?			
☐ Other tenants' opinions of building management			
☐ General condition of building, grounds, your specific unit			
☐ Are pets allowed?			
☐ Is the building governed by any local rent control ordinance? If so, what is the extent of your protection?			
☐ Extra amenities available: pool, rec room, parking, laundry, storage area			
☐ Security provisions: doorman, access to entryway, lighting			

Look Before You Lease

Renting an apartment (or house) on a month-to-month basis does not constitute a particularly heavy commitment on your part. If things don't work out, you can leave upon giving thirty days' notice in the proper fashion.

But signing a lease for a year or two can involve thousands of dollars, and if things don't work out you could be caught in a costly hassle or have to endure considerable inconvenience. To avoid these problems, take the following precautions before you sign a lease:

☐ Determine whether there are objectionable noises from adjoining apartments. There may be little you can do to silence a tuba-playing neighbor once you've moved in. It might be a sign to look elsewhere.

☐ Check with other tenants in the building to learn how the landlord adjusts complaints, makes needed repairs, and otherwise fulfills obligations under the lease.

☐ A rapidly growing phenomenon is condominium renting. You rent a single unit owned by an individual, rather than rent from a landlord who owns the whole building. In many such cases the owner has purchased the unit as an investment and is renting it out until she can later sell it at a profit. The owner may reside in another city or may simply not be concerned with the ongoing welfare of her tenants. In situations like this, overall management of the building is diluted, and there can be considerable difficulty in maintaining tenant satisfaction. A committee of absentee owners simply cannot maintain the same level of efficiency as can an on-premises landlord or management company. If you're faced with these possibilities, be forewarned accordingly.

☐ Learn the landlord's policies with respect to returning security deposits. If he's reputed to be slow, nit-picky, or argumentative, be prepared to exert your legal rights to insure getting back whatever you're entitled to within the proper time limits set forth in your state's (or city's) laws.

CHAPTER 12

Selling a Home

Perhaps the only transaction more complicated than buying a home is selling a home. Indeed, many people often find themselves doing both simultaneously. When selling a home—or even when vacating a leased dwelling—there are so many personal details to attend to that many of the important financial aspects of the matter are overlooked. This can be a costly error. This chapter will point out these important financial aspects and will prepare you to deal with them. They include the following:

- Setting the proper price and terms for the sale of your home
- Getting your money's worth from your real estate agent
- Investing the necessary time and money to bring the best possible offers from would-be buyers of your home
- How to take advantage of tax laws that apply when you sell your home and when you move
- How to get out of a leased dwelling in the proper fashion

Selling your home—be it a house, a condominium, or a cooperative—can be a very leisurely activity or a very hectic one. It's leisurely if you have all the time in the world, if you have not made a commitment to move into another dwelling until you've sold your existing one, or if you're not under pressure to commence a new job in a different location. These situations are the exceptions rather than the rule. Most often selling a home is hectic: You've already committed to a new dwelling, either by choice or because of a change in job, and you feel that you must sell your home by a certain date or risk having to make payments on two dwellings.

Time can be a costly pressure. Under the crush of a deadline you are likely to accept a lower price than the house might otherwise bring. And you're liable to make other mistakes—financial or legal—that you could later regret. It's easy to say that you should allow yourself ample time to sell your house. But it's not always that easy, particularly when a job transfer occurs.

If a job transfer causes you to move, your first step should be toward your personnel office to find out what assistance your employer offers with respect to the sale of your home and your moving expenses. Many employers provide financial and legal assistance in such cases. But you may have to ask for it. If you're changing jobs to go with a new employer and a move is necessitated, determine what assistance the new employer offers with respect to the relocation.

WHAT IS YOUR HOME WORTH?

Your home is worth just what a willing buyer is prepared to pay for it. Not one penny more.

It's easy, though, to get caught in a trap of thinking your home is worth much more than it really is. For example, one of your next-door neighbors recently put her house on the market, with an asking price of $150,000. Your house is identical to hers, if not actually bigger and better. So, you decide, if she's asking $150,000 for her house, then my house must be worth at least that much if not more. Right? Wrong. The fact that she is asking $150,000 for her house doesn't mean that she'll get it. In fact, her house might only be worth $120,000 or maybe even less. And yours may be worth no more than hers in the final analysis.

Overpricing your house can be a costly mistake, because it can delay a sale of the house. And every month that goes by during which the house is not sold means your costs are mounting: mortgage payments, property insurance, maintenance and upkeep. There are other considerations to deal with as well: anxiety, security problems, vandalism, and other dilemmas associated with being an absentee owner. These concerns can quickly make you an anxious seller. (Reread the discussion on the anxious seller in Chapter 8.)

Setting the Price

For the reasons discussed above, setting a realistic price for your home is the first and most important order of business. A realistic price reflects many factors, some of which are not easy to calculate. Factors to consider are the condition of the home itself, the condition of the neighborhood, how anxious you are to sell, how much "paper" you're willing to carry, whether your existing mortgage is assumable, and the availability of new financing at the time you are selling.

Condition of the House.   Are you trying to sell what real estate people call a "move-in gem" or a "fixer-upper"? You must put yourself in the shoes of would-be buyers and see the house as they see it. Is it visually appealing, is it structurally safe, is it mechanically sound? The more positive the answers to these questions, the higher the price you can ask and get.

Condition of the Neighborhood.   Is the general neighborhood in a state of improvement or decline? There's not much you can do about it if it's in a state of decline except to be ready to accept a lower price than you otherwise might have hoped for. You have to anticipate that a prudent buyer will recognize the trend of the general neighborhood and structure his offer to you accordingly. What about the immediate vicinity of your home? If your surrounding neighbors' houses are eyesores, this can have a negative effect on the value of your home. It might be worth a diplomatic chat with any such neighbors to urge them to correct the eyesores. It might even be worth your chipping in to help them do some cleaning in order to help you get a better price on your house.

How Much of a Buyer's Mortgage Are You Willing to Carry? If a potential buyer does not have as much cash down payment as you're asking, you may well have to consider taking an IOU (in the form of a second mortgage) in order to get your asking price. This is discussed in more detail later in the chapter, but it must be considered as an element of setting your price in the first place.

How Anxious Are You to Sell? In this respect price and time work hand in hand. The more time you have, the higher price you can afford to ask, with the knowledge that you can always lower the asking price as your ultimate deadline gets closer. When time is of the essence, you can't afford the luxury of overreaching on your price. The more critical the time factor, the closer to the actual market your pricing must be.

Is Your Existing Mortgage Assumable? An assumable mortgage, particularly one whose interest rate is lower than the current market rate, can be one of the most attractive features of the deal you are offering. You can't afford to guess whether the mortgage is assumable. The assumability of any mortgage depends, of course, on the credit-worthiness of the party who wishes to assume the mortgage. Further, the lender may have reserved the right to alter the interest rate if the mortgage is assumed. You should determine with as much certainty as possible what the terms and conditions would be if a buyer assumes your mortgage.

Is Financing Available? It could be to your advantage to visit with local mortgage lenders to determine what kind of financing they would offer on the sale of your house. Not only can this help you set a realistic price, but it can also help facilitate a sale to a buyer who is seeking new financing.

Seeking Comparable Sales

After taking into account all of the factors discussed above, perhaps the best way to determine a proper price is to seek comparable sales in the past few months. Try to find houses similar to yours that have recently sold, and determine the selling price. Your best source of information would probably be local real estate brokers. Any firsthand information you can gather on your own from friends and neighbors will also be helpful. But be certain that you determine the actual *selling* price of any comparable properties not the *asking* price. As noted earlier, there can be a big difference between the two.

When you do seek comparable recent sales, make sure the houses you're comparing are truly comparable. They should be as similar as possible to yours in size, configuration, condition, and amenities. The checklist in Table 12-1 will help you evaluate comparables in your neighborhood.

Table 12-1 **Comparable Housing Sales**

		Comparable homes		
Characteristic	*Your home*	*A*	*B*	*C*
1. Location (midblock, corner, cul-de-sac, etc.)	_____	_____	_____	_____
2. Traffic flow (light, medium, heavy)	_____	_____	_____	_____
3. Access to mass transit	_____	_____	_____	_____
4. Access to freeways	_____	_____	_____	_____
5. Access to shopping	_____	_____	_____	_____
6. Lot size	_____	_____	_____	_____
7. Square footage (house)	_____	_____	_____	_____
8. Number of bedrooms, baths	_____	_____	_____	_____
9. Year built	_____	_____	_____	_____
10. Condition	_____	_____	_____	_____
11. Extra amenities (pool, etc.)	_____	_____	_____	_____
12. Asking price (original)	_____	_____	_____	_____
13. Selling price	_____	_____	_____	_____
14. Time on market	_____	_____	_____	_____
15. Other pros and cons	_____	_____	_____	_____

CONDOMINIUM AND COOPERATIVE RESTRICTIONS

If you are selling a condominium or your interest in a cooperative building, you may be restricted in your ability to sell. Any such restrictions are contained in the condominium or cooperative master agreement. You may, for example, be required to offer your unit back to the other owners at a fixed price, or at a price to be agreed upon, before you can offer it to the public at large. Examine the master agreement closely with the help of a lawyer if necessary to determine what restrictions, if any, you must comply with.

REAL ESTATE AGENTS

Does it pay to use a real estate agent to sell your house, or should you try to sell it on your own and save the commission costs? Real estate commissions on the sale of a house average about 6 percent. On a $100,000 sale, the commission would be $6000.

If time and money are no object to you as a seller, you might want to try, for a limited time, to sell it on your own. But sooner or later, except in rare cases, time and money will be of concern to you. If you've made arrangements to move into another dwelling, and you haven't sold your old home before you take oc-cupancy of the new one, you'll be faced with the double-payment problem men-tioned earlier. It only takes a few months of these double payments to quickly equalize what the real estate commission might have been.

If you try to sell your home on your own, give yourself a time limit: If you haven't received any acceptable offers within that time limit, it might be best to turn to real estate professionals for assistance.

Let's see what a real estate agent can do for you as a seller.

☐ *Market and pricing.*   A good agent knows the condition of the market in your general neighborhood and can help you set a realistic price in accordance with the pricing criteria mentioned earlier.

☐ *Financing.*   A good agent will be familiar with financing capabilities in your community at the time you are interested in selling. She will have regular contact with mortgage lenders and will know what kind of down payments, interest rates, and other conditions apply currently. She should also be able to assist a potential buyer in obtaining financing.

☐ *Advertising.*   Are you prepared to write—and pay for—effective advertising that will lure buyers to your home? These are among the duties of the real estate agent, and you can test their effectiveness in creating good advertising by scouring the classified ads in search of advertising that you find particularly appealing.

☐ *Showing your home.*   A real estate agent should be ready, willing, and able to show your home to prospective buyers at any time. You might not be able to do this because of your work commitments. Further, the agent should be able to separate casual lookers from serious buyers and save you time accord-ingly.

☐ *Sales force.*   Not only will the individual agent be working for you, but so will all of the other members of the sales force of the firm. Thus you multiply the number of potential sources of buyers.

☐ *Multiple listing service.*   In many communities most real estate firms belong to the multiple listing service, which publishes a directory of all houses for sale through real estate agents in the community. If your home is listed in the multiple listing directory, virtually every agent in town will be capable of acting as a salesperson for you. If a firm other than the one with whom you've contracted brings in a buyer, the commission will be split between the firms, with your own agent getting a specified share of the commission.

□ *Negotiating.* As you'll note from the earlier chapter on buying a house (Chapter 8), a buyer who is working with a real estate agent has a skilled negotiator at her side. The same goes for a seller who is working with an agent. You may be skilled at whatever you do, but you may not be skilled at the fine art of negotiating a price on the sale of a house. In this respect alone, a good agent can prove worthwhile.

□ *Objectivity.* It's only natural for homeowners to become sentimentally, if not emotionally, involved in their home. The decor, the furniture layout, the traffic patterns—all of these are your own creation and are important to you. But to a would-be buyer, it may all look like a hodgepodge. It's much easier for a real estate agent to take an unbiased view of the property and convince a buyer that everything can be altered to suit the buyer's own tastes and desires. You can't be your own best salesperson if you would take offense at a potential buyer's turning up her nose at your own creations. The real estate agent can overcome this problem and can help earn her commission in the process.

Finding a Good Agent

As in acquiring any other kind of professional help, it's important that you determine the reputation and integrity of any particular real estate agent, as well as the firm that she works for. Gather personal references from other people who have used the services of that individual and her firm. How were they to deal with on a personal level and on a professional level? How would former clients rate their performance with respect to the creativity and the placement of advertising; their availability to show houses; their negotiating skills; their access to financial markets; their willingness to stick to their guns even if a particular property doesn't seem to attract potential buyers? You should also check with the local county Board of Realtors to learn whether the individual and firm are in good standing. Check also with the State Board of Licensing that controls real estate brokers and sales agents to determine that their license requirements have been met and maintained.

As you interview potential real estate agents, you will discuss the price that they feel they can obtain for your house. When you do, beware of a practice known as *highballing.* An agent, overanxious to get the listing, may lead you to believe that she can deliver a buyer at a much higher price than you might have expected. You could thus be lured into signing a long-term exclusive agreement with an agent whose actual performance may be far less than what you would have wanted. The real estate industry has a code of ethics designed to protect the public, but as in any industry, abuses will occur. And once you've signed a listing contract with a real estate firm, you have little recourse if its staff doesn't live up to your expectations.

The Listing Contract

Normally, a real estate agent will require you to sign an exclusive listing contract that will bind you to his firm for as long as the contract states. Six months is a normal minimum term in many communities. In addition to the length of time the agreement is to run, the contract will set forth your asking price. But there is no assurance whatsoever that the agent will be able to deliver a buyer willing to pay that price. Thus, the asking price stated in the listing contract is not binding on anyone. It's merely a target toward which the agent will be shooting.

In a standard listing contract, you, the seller, are responsible for paying a commission to the agent if the agent brings in a buyer ready, willing, and able to pay your asking price. If such a buyer is brought in, and you have changed your mind and don't want to sell to that buyer, you will still be responsible for paying the commission to the agent. If another firm other than the one you're dealing with brings in the ultimate buyer, your own agent will still get a portion of the commission.

Negotiating the Commission

Generally, the real estate agent states what commission she expects to receive, but it can be worth your while to negotiate for a lower commission. Nothing ventured, nothing gained. If it appears that the house will be easy to sell because of its condition, the location, the asking price, or other factors, the agent might be willing to accept a lower commission. On the other hand, if it appears that the house will be difficult to sell, the agent may seek a higher than customary commission. Whatever commission is decided upon, it will be due and payable upon the final closing of the transaction. If a listing contract expires without the agent having brought in a buyer, you are then free to contract with any other agent or to renegotiate an extension of the contract with the original agent.

PREPARING YOUR HOME FOR SALE

If you want to sell your home as quickly as possible and at the best possible price, it may be worth spending some money and energy putting the house in the best possible condition to attract and convince buyers. Some of these expenses can be deducted from any profit you realize, thus cutting your tax liability. Consider the following suggestions.

The Exterior

The exterior appearance of the house and grounds is vitally important. Many potential buyers will cruise around the area, and their first impression of the outside will stick in their minds. Even a house that is elegant inside can scare away buyers if the outside looks shabby. Make sure your lawn is kept in proper trim and that hedges, bushes, and other foliage are properly cared for. Depending on the time of year, you might want to plant seasonal flowers to give the property a better appearance. Be sure your gutters and downspouts are all properly placed. A few gallons of paint to touch up exterior trim can be very important. Homeowners often neglect to notice some of the signs of wear and tear on their houses because they have become accustomed to them. Ask some friends over to give you their honest opinion of what might need improvement to aid sales potential. Get rid of all debris or unsightly matter around the house. Winter in northern climates adds a visual problem to any house. Be certain that snow is shoveled off the drives and walkways and that icicles are removed from overhangs. If winter days tend to be gray and dull in your area, talk to an electrician about some exterior lighting, which can improve the visual qualities of the exteriors, particularly in the late afternoon hours when many prospects are likely to call.

If there are any signs that indicate that you aren't keeping the outside of the house in good shape, a prospective buyer may well suspect that there are problems lurking inside as well.

The Interior

A potential buyer entering your home should get the impression that it is bright and cheery, light and airy. To give a bright and cheerful impression during the daylight hours, raise the shades and open the blinds and curtains. If there is a room, such as a den or study, that you want to have appear particularly cozy, the reverse might be true. Try various combinations of natural and artificial light to achieve the best effect for each room.

The Kitchen.   The kitchen may be the most important room to many buyers. Do what you have to do to make it sparkle. Stock a supply of kitchen deodorant: We often fail to notice odors in our kitchens because we're accustomed to them, but they could be displeasing to a prospect. Freshen the air as well as the physical aspects of the room.

Touching Up.   Any buyer examining a house will be constantly thinking, "How much will we have to spend to put the place in the kind of shape we want it to be in?" Your real estate agent can help you determine where touching up might improve the salability of the house. For example, some rooms could benefit from a painting, particularly if they are currently painted with a very strong color. Light neutral colors tend to please more buyers. Items such as dirt smudges on the woodwork or torn window screens can leave a decidedly negative impression on buyers, and they are so simple to correct.

Closets and Storage Space.   Cluttered closets, basement, and attic will discourage buyers. Before you commence showing your house, scour these areas thoroughly.

Get rid of everything you don't need. Give whatever you can to charities—you can get handsome income tax deductions by doing so—and throw away anything you can't give away. Otherwise, you'll just end up having to pay to have it moved to your new location. To keep your closets looking as spacious as possible, remove all nonessentials and nonseasonal clothing.

Mechanical Parts.   Assume that any serious buyer will sooner or later check to see that everything in the house is in proper working order. To minimize troubles in this regard, make sure that everything does work properly: electrical circuits, light switches, plugs, doorbells, plumbing, windows, furnace, air conditioning, and so on. Call a plumber to correct any rattles, knocks, or other annoying noises that may ring through the house when water is running. Invest in a can of lubricating oil to eliminate any creaking doors and loosen any stuck windows.

Design.   Examine the major rooms in the house to see how minor changes of furniture or lighting might improve the rooms' appearance. You may be able to enhance the appearance of the house with throw pillows, scatter rugs, and other decorative pieces that you may be able to acquire at reasonably low cost.

Leaks and Other Damages.   If prospective buyers see signs of leaking—either on the ceilings or around sinks, toilets, tubs, or showers—they will immediately start tallying up many hundreds of dollars in repair bills to correct a problem, which they assume still exists. If a leak has long since been repaired, but evidence of it still shows on the surface, get it covered up. If the leak still exists, get it corrected. If nothing else, any sign of a leak gives a buyer a better bargaining position.

WHAT FINANCING TO OFFER

The availability of financing is as important to the buyer as is the asking price. If interest rates are high at the time you put your house on the market, you should be prepared to explore a wide range of creative financing possibilities, always with the advice of a good real estate agent and a lawyer. Chapter 9 explores some of these creative financing possibilities.

Is Your Mortgage Assumable?

As noted earlier, you should determine as quickly as possible whether your mortgage can be assumed and under what conditions. If your mortgage is not assumable, you should inquire of local lenders what types of financing plans might be available to a credit-worthy buyer. Take these steps before you start showing the house; let your real estate agent be your guide.

Strategies for Success

Should You Refinance before You Sell Your Home?

You plan to put your house on the market, with an asking price of $150,000. You only owe $60,000 on your home loan. Your loan can be assumed by a credit-worthy buyer. Would it pay to refinance your home loan up to, say, $125,000, in order to make it easier for a potential buyer to make a deal with you? Refinancing can cost a few thousand dollars. Can you recoup this cost in your selling price? If your home doesn't sell soon after you refinance, you'll have to make payments on the much larger loan. Can you recoup these expenses in your selling price? Seek the advice of your real estate agent and lender. If the housing market is brisk, refinancing before you sell can help get a buyer into the fold at relatively little risk to you. In a slow market the reverse might be true. Know the costs before you proceed.

Will You Carry a Mortgage?

Whether by choice or by necessity, you may find yourself having to take a buyer's IOU rather than cash. This will be in the form of a first or second mortgage, which should be drawn up by a lawyer. If it is necessary for you to carry the buyer's promise to pay, negotiate an interest rate as close to the current going interest rate through conventional lenders as possible. It is also advisable to keep the duration of such mortgages at a minimum. Try to get the buyer to accept a term of three years or less. At the end of this time the buyer would be responsible for obtaining new financing on his own. If a buyer insists on a longer repayment program, you should negotiate a higher interest rate as consideration for granting the extra time.

All of these negotiations will, of course, be dependent on your level of anxiety to sell. The more anxious you are to sell, the less room you'll have to negotiate the terms of any paper you may be taking back.

TAX IMPLICATIONS

If you sell your home at a profit, the profit may be subject to income taxes in the year in which you sell. If you sell your property and suffer a loss, the loss is not deductible. But there are important tax provisions that can allow you to postpone the payment of taxes or eliminate them altogether. As with most tax laws, the specific regulations that apply to these situations can be very complex, and professional assistance is advisable.

You have to assume that the Internal Revenue Service will be aware of the fact that you've moved simply by virtue of the new address on your next year's tax return. Your move, of course, may not necessarily mean that you have sold a residence. You may have moved from a rental unit or you may not actually have sold your house. But if you have sold a house, the pertinent facts must be reported on your tax return.

There are two types of tax breaks that can benefit sellers of homes: (1) the rollover, which is available to sellers of any age, and (2) the exclusion, which is available only to sellers aged fifty-five and over.

The Rollover

If you sell your house at a profit, the tax on the profit may be postponed if, within twenty-four months from the date of sale, you buy and occupy another principal residence the cost of which equals or exceeds the "adjusted sales price" of the old residence. The twenty-four-month time limit works in both directions: You can buy the new house as much as twenty-four months before or twenty-four months after the date you sell your old house.

If the purchase price of your new residence is less than the sales price of the old residence, a portion of the profit will be taxable during that year. If you do not purchase a new principal residence—if, for instance, you move into an apartment—the profit will be taxable during the year in which you sold. See current IRS regulations for their specific definitions of the gain that is subject to taxes. If you qualify for a rollover, you should complete form 2119 and attach it to your income tax return.

The Exclusion

If either spouse is fifty-five years of age at the time you sell your home at a profit, you can exclude up to $125,000 worth of profit from taxation altogether. In order to qualify for this exclusion of taxation, you must have owned and occupied the house as your principal residence for at least three of the five years preceding the day of sale.

The exclusion is a once-in-a-lifetime privilege. But the rollover can be used over and over again, until such time as you sell your home and do not purchase another one, at which time the taxes will become due on all aggregate profits realized in prior years.

The matter can be quite complex and professional tax counseling should be sought. For example, The Renaldis bought a home twenty years ago and sold it five years ago at a profit of $70,000. They bought another home at that time and thus took advantage of the rollover to postpone the payment of taxes on the $70,000 profit. Today, with Mr. Renaldi past the age of fifty-five, they are selling their current home and will realize a profit of $60,000. Their total accumulated profit on the two homes is thus $130,000. If they are now planning on buying another home of equal or greater value than their current home, they can choose between the rollover and the exclusion. If they choose the rollover, the tax on the accumulated $130,000 profit will continue to be postponed until such time as they sell their new home and do not buy another one. At that time, they can choose the exclusion if they wish.

If they choose the exclusion now, then $125,000 of the $130,000 will be excluded from taxation, and the remaining $5000 will be subject to taxation. It would make sense for them to choose this alternative if they were not buying another house. But if they were buying another house, they would have to carefully estimate what the future might hold for them with respect to a potential profit on the sale of the new house.

If, instead of selling your house, you convert it to a rental property, different tax rules apply. If you rent it for a limited period of time—such as one year—and then sell it, it may still be considered your principal residence and the rollover or exclusion rules may still apply. However, if you convert it to an ongoing income property for an indefinite period of time, the Internal Revenue Service may consider that it is no longer your personal residence, and upon a sale the taxes would be payable on any profit during the year of sale.

As a result of the Tax Reform Act of 1986, the tax rate on the profit you realize on the sale of a home is higher than it previously had been. For this reason it's imperative that you take advantage of any and all opportunities to reduce the taxable profit. Check current IRS regulations carefully to determine what expenses you've made or might make in your home that can legally reduce the amount of profit and thus reduce the amount of tax. Since there are so many tax ramifications involved in the sale of a home, it's wise to make use of a professional tax counselor before you enter into any final sales contracts.

Moving Expenses and Their Tax Treatment

Whether you're buying or selling a house, you're going to be moving. Moving involves many important considerations. Whether you decide to hire a moving company or do it yourself will probably depend on the number of household goods you'll be moving, the distance, and the time of year (a do-it-yourself move during the snowy season can involve more travail than you'd expect).

If your move is within the boundaries of your state, the moving company will not be controlled by the Interstate Commerce Commission. Customarily, such moves (intrastate) are charged on an hourly basis, plus time and materials for any packing that you hire the mover to do for you.

Generally, interstate moves of equal weight and equal distance will cost roughly the same with most moving companies. There may be important differences in the overall cost of the move based on the amount of packing and unpacking you wish the movers to do. These rates vary from company to company. You may wish to pack your own nonbreakables and have the moving company pack the more fragile items, such as glassware, china, lamps, and so on.

Representatives of moving companies can give you estimates on the cost of your move, but bear in mind that these are only estimates and not generally firm bids. The actual cost can't be determined until the van is loaded and weighed prior to its departure. Moving-company representatives are required to give you Interstate Commerce Commission information that spells out your rights as a shipper of household goods. Be certain to read and understand the information in this document, as it informs you about your rights and the recourse you have if something goes wrong.

Strategies for Success

Right Timing for Your Move Can Save Money

If you're lucky enough to choose the time you want to move, you can save money in the process. Most moving takes place during the summer months when school is out. A summer move can mean a tough (and costly) time getting movers to meet your schedule or renting a move-it-yourself vehicle. Moving in winter, especially in northern climates has its own dangers: icy roads, snowstorms, and the like. If you have the luxury of choosing when you move, spring and fall are the best times. If you have children, a fall or spring move necessitates taking them out of school. If they're young enough, it might not matter. If you have teenagers, it could pose some problems. Discuss the situation with teachers at both the new and old schools. If you *can't* choose your own moving time, at least try to book the moving company as far in advance as possible. Thus you'll have more time to schedule other aspects of your move in the most economical way.

A major portion of your moving expenses (for which you are not reimbursed by your employer) may be tax deductible. Because moving expenses can amount to a considerable sum of money, you should keep a careful record of all such expenses and take advantage of whatever the law allows. In order to deduct moving expenses, you must meet two tests: the distance test and the work test.

The Distance Test. As illustrated by Figure 12-1, measure the distance between your former home and your former place of work. Let's call this distance A and say it's ten miles. Now measure the distance between your former home and your new place of work. Let's call this distance B and say it's fifty miles. The law requires that the difference between distance B and distance A be at least thirty-five miles. If it is, you pass the distance test. Note that the distance test does not refer to the location of your new *residence* but rather to the location of your new *place of work*.

The Work Test. During the twelve-month period immediately following your move, you must be employed full time for at least thirty-nine weeks in order to pass the work test. If you're self-employed, you must be employed full time for at

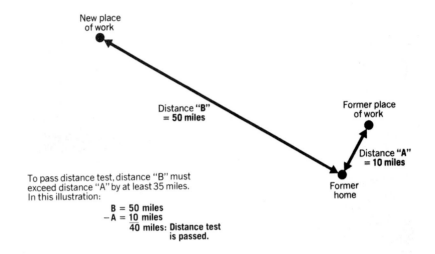

New place
of work

Distance "B"
= 50 miles

Former place
of work

Distance "A"
= 10 miles

To pass distance test, distance "B" must
exceed distance "A" by at least 35 miles.
In this illustration:

Former
home

$$B = 50 \text{ miles}$$
$$-A = 10 \text{ miles}$$
$$40 \text{ miles: Distance test}$$
$$\text{is passed.}$$

Figure 12-1 Distance test.

least thirty-nine weeks during the first twelve months immediately following the move, and you must also be employed full time for at least seventy-eight weeks of the twenty-four-month period immediately following the move.

If you meet both the distance test and the work test, the following expenses of your move may be deductible, in whole or in part. Check current IRS regulations to determine what limits there are to these deductions: travel expenses, including meals and lodging while en route from your old residence to your new residence; the cost of moving your household goods; the cost of house-hunting trips; the cost of temporary quarters at your new location if needed; some of the costs involved in selling your former residence or settling your lease at your old location.

TERMINATING A LEASE

Tenants don't have to worry about all of the ramifications of a sale of a residence. (This fact alone is why many people prefer to remain tenants indefinitely.) But there are a number of things to consider even if you have been renting, be it an apartment, a mobile home, or a house.

As far in advance of your leaving as possible, read your lease carefully. Be certain that you know when the lease terminates. Watch out for any clause that would create an automatic renewal of the lease. Such a clause may read, "Unless either party gives notice to the other in writing of his intention to cancel this lease, the lease will automatically renew for another year upon [date]." This simply means that if you don't want the lease to renew automatically, you must give proper notice to the landlord in writing before a certain date. If you fail to do this, the landlord can technically hold you liable for another year's rent.

If you have given the landlord a security deposit, what does the lease state about getting it back? Many states have laws that stipulate when and under what conditions a landlord is to return a tenant's rental deposit. Know in advance what your rights are in this regard so that you won't have to forfeit any money.

If you're planning to move before your lease has expired, does your lease give you the right to sublet the apartment? If you do sublet, you should be certain that the subtenants are responsible. They should sign an agreement assuming all of your obligations under the lease, including the obligation to repair at their own expense any damages they may cause.

If you wish to move far in advance of the termination date and either you don't wish to or cannot sublet, you should discuss a settlement price with the landlord. You can, of course, simply move out, continue to pay your rent, and hope that the landlord will rerent your apartment quickly. Generally, the law puts some burden on the landlord to try to rerent as quickly as possible, but you can't always depend on the landlord to be diligent in this respect.

If you are renting any appliances or furniture or have any services under contract for an apartment or a rented house, be certain to examine the rental documents. For example, if you have leased the furniture or large appliances, you'll want to be certain that you can terminate these contracts concurrently with leaving the apartment.

If you are paying your own utilities, arrange well in advance to have all utility meters read as of your final day of occupancy. Ask the utility companies—telephone, electric, gas, water—to bill you for the final reading, and be sure that the landlord understands that the meters are to be returned to his name following your departure.

If you suspect that there may be *any* question whatsoever regarding the condition in which you are leaving the house or apartment, settle it with the landlord *before* you leave. Go over the property with the landlord, and be certain that he agrees that everything is as it should be. Then ask the landlord to sign a brief letter stating that everything is in the proper condition.

Renters are entitled to the same tax deductions for moving expenses as are homeowners, provided they meet the same distance and work tests. The cost of settling your lease obligation with your landlord if you move before the end of the lease can be included as one of the deductible expenses.

A Guide for the Home Seller

This checklist should help you *set* and *get* the best possible price for your home. It may cost you some money to complete some of the items, but the expense could return itself many times over in a better price and in a faster sale. You may need the assistance of a real estate agent. Some of the information needed can be found at your local tax assessor's office or at your county recorder's office.

- [ ] What has been the *actual* selling price of *comparable* homes in your area within the past few months?

- [ ] How long were these homes on the market before they sold?

- [ ] How does the actual selling price of these homes compare with the prices that the sellers were originally asking?

- [ ] Based on these comparable sales, what do you realistically think your home should sell for? (Take into account all plus and minus factors that your home may have relative to the comparables.)

- [ ] How will your home appear to a would-be buyer? Ask some friends, and your real estate agent to give you an honest opinion of the following:

    Exterior (paint, trim, landscaping)
    Entry (lighting, odors, a sense of clutter or of orderliness)
    Kitchen (cleanliness, odors) (Does everything work the way it should?)
    Closets, other storage areas (Cluttered, or clean and spacious looking?)
    Bathrooms (squeaky clean is a *must*)
    Other rooms (lighting, odors, traffic flow, condition of flooring and walls)
    Mechanical elements (heater, appliances) (Does everything work properly without offensive noises or odors?)

It's very difficult to see your own home as others might see it. Prospective buyers can be very persnickety, and first impressions of items such as those listed above can make the difference between a ''thanks but no thanks'' and a ''let's talk about the price.''

Moving-Day Headaches

Selling a home, or leaving an apartment, invariably involves one activity that many people regard with fear and loathing: moving day.

All major moving companies offer abundant literature on how you can to take the pain out of moving by doing your own packing, by completing a proper inventory of your goods, by keeping the children out of your hair, and so on. Helpful though this literature may be, it may not prepare you for some of the common and uncommon pitfalls of moving, including

- ☐ *The lowball estimate.* An overzealous sales representative from a moving company may give you an estimate on the cost of the move that is much lower than what you've received from other companies. This could be due to an honest error on the part of the salesperson; it could be due to your failure to disclose everything that you had planned to move; or it could be an intentional ploy by the salesperson to win your business. Remember, an estimate is just an estimate. The total cost of the move won't be known until everything is packed and the van is weighed.

- ☐ *"Bumping."* This term describes the practice whereby four burly 200-pound moving men sit in the back of the moving van while it's being weighed. And you pay for it. It may be a rare occurrence, but it can be costly. Interstate Commerce Commission regulations clearly state that you, the shipper, are entitled to be at the weighing of the truck. Your presence at the weighing could save you money.

- ☐ *Schedule demolition.* Often, despite the best intentions, the day of pickup of your goods can be missed. And the day of delivery at your new destination can also be off target. These missed dates can cause chaos, not to mention considerable cost, if you have to live in a motel for a few days waiting for the van to arrive. Moving companies generally can't guarantee pickup and delivery dates unless, in some cases, you reserve exclusive use of a van. Your best protection against these scheduling problems is to anticipate that the worst will happen. Then if everything goes off smoothly, you'll be that much happier.

CHAPTER 13

Financial Institutions

The notorious bank robber Willy Sutton was once asked by a reporter, "Why do you rob banks?" His reply: "That's where the money is."

Sutton's involvement with banks was a lot more clear cut than yours will be. Dealing with banks and other financial institutions, such as savings associations, credit unions, and so on, can be complicated in these rapidly changing days. But the dealings can be worthwhile in terms of handling your money matters and making your money grow. This chapter is designed to acquaint you with how financial institutions work, what they can do for you, and what your rights are as a user of their services. You'll learn about such matters as

□ Which institutions offer what services

□ How checking accounts work, and the advantages and pitfalls in using them

□ How to shop for the services you'll need

□ What laws protect you with regard to financial matters, and how to pursue your rights if they are violated

Suppose you have some money in your hands and you have no immediate need or desire to spend it. What can you do with it? You have many choices. You can put it in your pocket, in the cookie jar, or under your mattress until you do need it. Or you can entrust the money to one of many financial institutions for a variety of purposes.

If you wanted to use the extra money to pay some of your debts, you could open a checking account at a financial institution. Then instead of having to deliver cash to your creditors, you could simply mail them a check to satisfy the debt. The check, in effect, allows the creditor to receive money from your checking account. You may wish to invest the money so that the total sum will assuredly increase until such time as you need it for other purposes. In such a case, you could establish a savings plan at a financial institution.

You may wish to speculate with the money in the hope that it might increase in the future. In this case you could establish an account with a stockbrokerage firm, a type of financial institution. Or you might wish to put the money away for a very long time to provide an assured fund for yourself in later years or for your survivors upon your death. In such a case, you would contract for a life insurance policy with an insurance company, yet another type of financial institution.

On the other hand, suppose you needed money to buy a car or a house, to pay your taxes, to go on a vacation, or for any other purpose. If you couldn't borrow the money you needed from friends or relatives, you would approach a financial institution for the appropriate type of loan.

ROLE OF FINANCIAL INSTITUTIONS

Financial institutions play an important intermediary role in the nation's economy and in your own personal financial situation. At any given time, there are countless individuals (and businesses and governments) who have more money on hand than they need for their immediate purposes. At the same time, there are countless others who do not have the money they need for specific purposes.

Financial institutions act as intermediaries by providing a safe place for people to keep excess money until they need it. At the same time, they supply services and loans to those who seek to borrow at a fair and reasonable cost.

Intermediaries view this activity as a business. They must acquire the raw material (other people's money) at the lowest possible price (competition considered). And they must lend it out on the most prudent basis, taking into account the ability of the borrower to repay the money by the agreed time. In order for intermediaries to survive, they must make a profit. Thus, they must charge the borrowers more for the use of the money than they have to pay the investors entrusting them with their money.

Certain intermediaries may not be acting as a business but as a service to members of an association. The members may have banded together to pool their excess money and provide for the needs of borrowers. Although it isn't important for the association to generate a profit, members must still generate enough income within the operation to pay for personnel and overhead needed to run the operation efficiently. This type of financial institution is typified by credit unions, which commonly represent employees of a specific company or members of a particular trade union.

A Decade of Change

Until the start of the 1980s, there was a clear distinction among the various types of financial institutions. Commercial banks specialized primarily in checking accounts, business loans, and consumer loans. Savings institutions specialized primarily in savings plans and home financing. Stockbrokerage firms specialized primarily in buying and selling stocks, bonds, and other types of investments and speculations. Insurance companies specialized primarily in life insurance products, pension arrangements, and annuities.

Within a decade these distinctions began to blur, and a number of giant financial "supermarkets" came into being. The developing trends, which are far from over, include the following:

- Acquisitions and mergers among different types of financial institutions. Examples include the acquisition by American Express (international banking, credit cards, traveler's checks) of Shearson Lehman (stockbrokerage); the takeover by Prudential Life Insurance of Bache Group (stockbrokerage); the acquisition by Sears (retail, credit cards) of Dean Witter Reynolds Inc. (stockbrokerage); the acquisition by Citicorp (the nation's largest bank) of Diners Club (credit cards).

- The inevitable spread of banking and savings institutions across state lines. Prior to the 1980s, these financial institutions, except in rare instances, were limited to operating within their state or county boundaries. Their expansion beyond these boundaries, whether through legislation, holding companies, acquisitions, mergers, or even electronic terminals, foretells the further development of the nationwide giants.

- Development of competing services by specific institutions. Stockbrokerage firms have created cash-management accounts, which provide all-in-one checking/investing/borrowing capability for their customers. Banks and savings institutions, in retaliation, have moved to set up stockbrokerage and other types of investment services. Money market mutual funds offer checking account privileges. Insurance companies offer investment programs combined with check-writing privileges. Credit card companies and banks offer life insurance. Savings institutions offer property insurance. And the list goes on. Where it will stop, nobody knows.

These developments have made the financial industry more competitive; thus more choices, more services, and more advantages are available to the *alert* consumer.

TYPES OF FINANCIAL INSTITUTIONS

Since the ultimate size, shape, location, and names of yet-to-be-created future financial supermarkets are as yet unknown, this chapter will concentrate on the basic types of institutions that you would commonly use and that will still remain on a local level even after the national giants have planted their roots. We'll concentrate primarily on institutions offering banking and lending services. The ramifications of stockbrokerage and insurance will be covered in the Chapters 17 and 19, respectively.

Commercial Banks

There are roughly 15,000 commercial banks in the United States. Total assets of these banks are about 2.5 trillion. Commercial banks run the gamut from small country institutions to giant banks in such major cities as New York, Chicago, San Francisco, and Los Angeles. Of all the commercial banks in the United States, the fifty largest control roughly one-third of all deposits; the remaining banks control the other two-thirds.

Commercial banks are often referred to as *full-service institutions*. They offer a broad range of services including checking accounts, savings accounts, trust facilities, and virtually all types of loans.

Subject to the expansionary trends mentioned earlier, commercial banks are generally limited to doing business within their state boundaries. They may be chartered by the state government or by the federal government to operate within a particular state. If a commercial bank is state chartered, it will be controlled and regulated by the State Banking Commission. If a commercial bank is federally chartered, it will be controlled and regulated by the Comptroller of the Currency. If a bank is federally chartered, it will have the word *national* in its name (such as First National Bank), or it will have the initials N.A. (National Association) after its name. Most major banks and many smaller banks are also members of the Federal Reserve System, which exerts additional controls and regulations on the nation's banking industry.

Deposits in commercial banks are insured by the Federal Deposit Insurance Corporation (FDIC) for up to $100,000 per account in the event of the bank's failure. (The amount of insurance per account has increased periodically since the 1960s and could be increased again.) The FDIC is a federal agency that constantly scrutinizes the operations of all banks it insures for the protection of the depositors and the community. All federally insured banks pay an annual premium to the FDIC, and the total is set aside as a reserve to be used to pay off the depositors should a bank be liquidated. In addition to its own funds, the FDIC can call upon the U.S. Treasury Department for additional money to back up its guarantee to depositors. The strength of the FDIC lies not just with its funds but also with its constant surveillance and expertise in determining when banks are in trouble and its swift intervention to prevent financial loss.

In addition to FDIC examination, banks may also be examined by state or federal authorities, depending on their charter. They are also examined by their own internal auditors and commonly by outside independent auditors on orders from the bank's own board of directors. Examinations are generally by surprise and are very rigorous. All cash is counted. All loans are scrutinized in detail, including original credit information, current payment status, and prospects for ultimate full payment. When loans seem to be in jeopardy, the examiners notify the bank officials. If an excess number of loans seems to be in jeopardy, the examiners will instruct the bank to take whatever steps are appropriate to correct the situation. The results of examinations are kept confidential between the examiners and the bank's officials. But examiners will follow up to determine whether the bank has taken necessary corrective steps to keep its operations in healthy condition.

Mutual Savings Banks

Mutual savings banks are few in number. There are about 360 of them located in roughly one dozen states, generally throughout New England and the Northeast, plus Ohio, Minnesota, Oregon, and Washington. But they are substantial in size, controlling almost $160 billion in assets. Mutual savings banks are state chartered and are insured by the Federal Deposit Insurance Corporation, which examines them as it does commercial banks. The major part of the business of mutual savings banks is savings plans and loans on real property—mortgages and home improvement loans. Deregulation in the financial industry, though, has allowed mutual savings banks to extend their scope of business to include checking accounts and various types of consumer loans.

Strategies for Success

Make Sure You Have a Friend at Your Local Bank

Banking can be a very impersonal matter. More and more people are doing a lot of their banking with automatic teller machines, telephone-computer hookups, and mail. Most of your banking needs can be handled in this manner: ordinary deposits, withdrawals, and the like. But it's a very sound strategy to have a friend at the bank—preferably an officer—who knows you and who can lend a hand if you have any problems or concerns. You might have a mix-up with a credit card statement or a checking account balance. Or you may need an emergency loan in a hurry. This friend can help you in such circumstances. Prepare a financial statement to help expedite loan requests, and discuss your financial status with your banking friend once a year or so. And be prepared: Some day your friend will be transferred to another branch. Have another friend waiting in the wings.

Savings and Loan Associations

There are about 3000 savings and loan associations throughout the nation. Traditionally they had concentrated the bulk of their business on providing savings plans for investors and mortgage loans for home buyers. In recent years, however, there have been drastic and shocking changes in the savings and loan industry. Government deregulation allowed the institutions to explore new and often very risky ways of putting their depositors' money to work. Hundreds of institutions had poor management, and were victims of fraud in the process of making loans. Deposits are insured by the Federal Savings and Loan Insurance Corporation (see Figure 13-1), and that government agency was drained of all its funds paying off depositors in the hundreds of institutions that failed. While the majority of savings and loans still do remain healthy, the cost of bailing out the failed and failing ones could hit $150 billion by the end of the century. The shape of the industry might never be the same.

**Figure 13-1   Identifying symbols of the Federal Deposit Insurance Corpo-
ration (FDIC) and the Federal Savings and Loan Insurance Corporation
(FSLIC)**

Credit Unions

Because credit unions don't advertise the way commercial banks and savings and
loan associations do, they're not as familiar to the public as the other institutions.
But credit unions are playing an increasingly important role in the American financial
system. They are associations of individuals who have a common bond—who work
for the same employer, belong to the same religious order, or are members of the
same union or trade association. Credit unions are not operated for profit. They are
operated solely for the benefit of their membership, which is open generally to all
individuals who meet their requirements.

Credit unions accept savings accounts and may pay slightly higher interest than
other institutions. This is possible because they do not have the profit motive, are
generally located in very modest quarters, and do not have to pay any federal
income taxes. Credit unions in some areas may make loans to their members at a
rate slightly more favorable than that charged elsewhere. Loans are usually of the
installment variety.

There are currently about 15,000 credit unions throughout the United States,
supported by over fifty million members. Their assets total roughly $125 billion.
In recent years, credit unions have been gaining the authority to offer a form of
checking account, which would add another measure of competition to the overall
banking industry.

Slightly more than two-thirds of all the credit unions are federally chartered,
and the balance are state chartered. Insurance on credit union accounts is available
through the National Credit Union Administration (NCUA).

Consumer Finance, or Small-Loan, Companies

Consumer finance (small-loan) companies are private businesses, operating generally under state licensing, that make small loans available to credit-worthy seekers.

Consumer finance companies do not accept public deposits. They obtain their money by borrowing from larger institutions such as banks and insurance companies. A small number of these companies have branches throughout the entire country, but most are limited to individual states or cities in their sphere of operation.

Merchant Lenders and Credit Card Companies

Technically, merchant lenders and credit card companies are not financial institutions in the same sense as banks and savings and loan associations are. But they do provide a financial service to many millions of Americans: making credit available virtually at the request of the customer. A merchant lender, generally, is a retail or service establishment that will accept a customer's IOU as payment for goods sold or services rendered. In other words, rather than pay cash, the customer can "charge it."

Commonly, the customer will sign an agreement in which she agrees to make payments over a specified period of time with an agreed rate of interest. In effect, the merchant lender is lending the money to the customer to enable the customer to buy the product. Many merchants do this strictly as a convenience for their customers and to be in line with services that their competitors might offer. Often the merchant lender will sell the customer's loan agreement to another financial institution, such as a bank or a consumer finance company, so that it can get its money right away. In some cases the merchant lender will retain the loan agreement, and the customer will make payments directly to the merchant instead of to a third-party institution.

Some companies such as gasoline companies, hotels and motels, and airlines operate nationally. To induce the public to use their services and products, they issue credit cards to credit-worthy applicants. These credit cards allow the users to charge their purchases, thus creating a loan from the issuing company. The loan is repayable based on the terms contained in the original credit card agreement.

Another form of quasi-financial institution is the credit card company: American Express, Diners Club, and Sears' Discover Card are prime examples. They have made arrangements with many thousands of businesses across the nation and around the world to accept their credit cards in lieu of cash. When a purchase is charged by a customer on a credit card, the credit card company makes payment to the specific merchant and then seeks repayment of the amount borrowed by the customer. The credit card company is thus acting strictly as an intermediary between the merchant and the customer. Most commercial banks also issue various forms of credit cards—Visa and MasterCard. When a purchase is made with a bank credit card, the bank pays the merchant and seeks repayment directly from the customer.

Insurance Companies

Insurance companies (life, health, property, etc.) act as financial go-betweens in that they hold your money for you and invest it, waiting until such time as stated risks occur (death, illness, fire, etc.) They also offer some forms of investments, such as annuities. Their specific roles are explained in more detail in Chapter 19.

Financial Planners

A new type of financial institution has emerged in recent years: companies and individuals who perform financial-planning services. Some are independent. Some are associated with insurance, brokerage, and accounting firms. Some perform services on a fee-only basis. Some earn commissions from products (insurance policies, mutual funds, etc.) they sell to their clients. Many are totally reputable. Some are not.

The swift rise of financial planning as a profession has been accompanied by an equally swift rise in abuses. Throughout most of the nation there are few laws governing or licensing financial planners. Virtually anyone can call himself a financial planner, with or without credentials, education, or scruples. If a consumer gets involved with an unscrupulous so-called planner, there will not likely be any governmental agency with which to register a complaint. There will not likely be any recourse for lost money. There could be, in short, a disaster.

More and more major universities are offering programs in financial planning. And there are two entities that specialize in the field: The Institute of Certified Financial Planners (ICFP) based in Denver offers a course leading to a certified financial planner (CFP) designation. And American College in Bryn Mawr, Pennsylvania, offers a course leading to a chartered financial consultant (ChFC) designation. Note that these designations are not sanctioned by governmental licensing agencies; rather, they are in the form of a degree issued by the school. Another entity, the International Association for Financial Planning (IAFP), which is based in Atlanta, has a Registry of Financial Planning Practitioners: some 600 of the more than 24,000 members have met special qualifications of the association.

Many who call themselves planners may be licensed or registered in a related field, such as insurance, real estate, stock brokerage, or accountancy. And, as noted, many have no governmental licensure or registration of any kind.

The confusion in the industry is compounded by the fact that the two main entities, the IAFP in Atlanta and the ICFP in Denver, have been in disagreement regarding the kind of regulation needed. The IAFP has been advocating a self-regulatory board; the ICFP has been advocating mandatory governmental registration for all practitioners. In time this matter of licensing and registration may be resolved, but the burden still lies upon the customer to exert caution in choosing a planner.

If a planner works on a fee-only basis, you must determine what you get for that fee. If a planner earns a commission on products you purchase, you must determine how objective the planner really is: Are you being sold something that's in your best interest or in the planner's best interest? You must, in all cases, shop around, get personal references, compare services, and when in the slightest doubt about the advice and/or sales pitch you've received, get a second opinion, preferably from someone who isn't selling anything.

But, you might ask, if I've read this book carefully and stay up to date, do I need a financial planner? Likely not.

Strategies for Success

What You Should Know about a Financial Planner

Choosing a financial planner is similar to choosing any professional in whom you are putting a great deal of faith. As with a doctor or lawyer, you want to know the financial planner's training, experience, and credentials. Since you need to trust this person, make sure he has impeccable personal references. And make sure that there is the right "chemistry" between you and the planner. Don't confuse personal rapport with a sales pitch. The two can easily be confused. If the planner earns a commission from selling, determine up front just what it is he sells, so you will know when you are being pitched. Be sure that the planner won't object if you seek second opinions on the recommendations he gives you. If the planner works on a fee basis, understand exactly how the fees will be charged from the outset.

Stockbrokerage Firms

Chapters 16 and 17 explain the main services offered by these institutions.

SERVICES AVAILABLE AT FINANCIAL INSTITUTIONS

The following financial services are those commonly found at larger commercial banks. They may also be available at smaller banks, savings and loan associations, mutual savings banks, and credit unions.

1.	Checking accounts	**8.**	Credit Cards
2.	Savings accounts	**9.**	Special checks
3.	Safe-deposit boxes	**10.**	Notarial services
4.	Trust services	**11.**	Electronic banking
5.	Installment loans	**12.**	Collection services
6.	Business loans	**13.**	International banking
7.	Mortgage loans	**14.**	Investment department

Let's now take a closer look at what these services consist of. Note that savings accounts (passbooks and certificates of deposit) are briefly noted here and are discussed in greater length in Chapters 15 and 16. Installment, credit card, and business loans are dealt with in Chapter 14, and mortgages are discussed fully in Chapter 9.

Checking Accounts

It would be both inconvenient and risky if we had to conduct all our financial transactions with cash. It would be inconvenient if for no other reason than the sheer massive volume of cash that would have to be available in all segments of the economy at all times and risky because a loss of cash is irreplaceable. Checks, simply stated, act as a substitute for cash. Checks are more convenient, and the risk of loss is virtually eliminated.

The efficiency of our checking system is founded on a combination of mutual trust and law. We have grown accustomed to accepting these money substitutes as having the value represented; and in those rare cases when the document proves invalid, there are laws that punish those who have violated the law and the trust between the parties.

Using Checking Accounts. Bob lives in Phoenix, Arizona, and works for the Ajax Supermarket. Each day the supermarket gathers up all the money it has collected from its customers and deposits the money in its checking account at the Arizona National Bank. The essential agreement between the bank and the store is as follows: The bank agrees to hold the money safely for the store and to pay out the money to any persons that the store directs them to make payments to. The store will then issue checks to its employees for their wages, checks to the landlord for the rent on the building, checks to suppliers for the food that it obtains from them, and so on.

The checks order the bank to make payment to the holder of the check. This is the essence of the words "pay to the order of" that appear on all checks. The check—the order to pay—must be signed by a properly authorized representative of the store. The bank will have obtained copies of all the authorized signatures permitted on the checks and can compare these signatures with the signatures on the checks if they wish to determine the validity of the order to pay.

Bob's weekly paycheck, after all deductions have been taken out for income taxes, social security, and fringe benefits, is shown in Figure 13-2.

Negotiating a Check. Bob now holds a piece of paper that is worth $250. The piece of paper is a legal document in which the Ajax Supermarket instructs the Arizona National Bank to pay to the order of Bob Rosefsky the sum of $250. The check is thus known as an *order instrument*. How can Bob then translate this piece of paper into real money? He can cash the check, he can deposit the check into his own account, or he can use the check to pay a debt or pay for a purchase.

☐ *Cashing the check.* Bob takes the check to a branch of the Arizona National Bank, identifies himself, and asks for cash in exchange for the check. But before

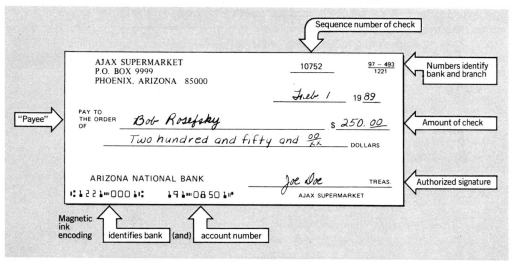

Figure 13-2 Sample check.

the bank will give Bob the cash, they will want him to acknowledge that he has in fact received the money. The bank must do this to prove that it has fulfilled the order given it by the supermarket. Bob acknowledges that he receives the cash by signing his name across the back of the check. This is known as a *blank endorsement.* Bob receives his money; the bank has proof that it has properly fulfilled the order given it. And as the check is processed internally, the supermarket's account with the bank will be reduced by $250 as a result of Bob's cashing the check. (See sample endorsements in Figure 13-3.)

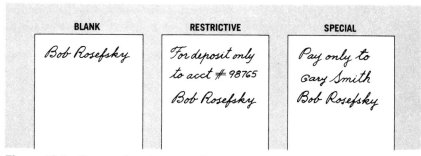

Figure 13-3 Types of endorsements.

Note this important precaution with respect to a blank endorsement: A blank endorsement converts the check from an *order instrument* into a *bearer instrument*. A check containing a blank endorsement can theoretically be cashed by anyone who is the bearer or holder of it. In other words, if Bob endorsed the check in blank when he received it, and if it dropped out of his pocket on the way to the bank and was found by a dishonest person, that dishonest person could likely cash the check and Bob would be out $250. A check should be endorsed in blank only at the time the money is received.

☐ *Depositing the check.* Bob can deposit the check into his own checking account at the Citizens Bank of Phoenix. To do so, he must properly endorse the check and fill out a deposit slip. He may endorse the check in blank, as if he were cashing it. Or, more prudently, he can put a restrictive endorsement on the check. A restrictive endorsement would read, ''For deposit only to acct #007-085844,'' followed by Bob's signature. A restrictive endorsement simply restricts what can be done with the check. In this particular case it can only be deposited to Bob's specific account. If a restrictively endorsed check was lost, a finder would have a very difficult time cashing it.

Figure 13-4 is a sample illustration of a deposit slip. Deposit slips are commonly preprinted with the name and address of the account holder. The person making the deposit writes in the identifying number of the bank upon which the check is drawn—in this case 97-493—and the amount of the deposit, $200—$250 less $50 Bob wants in cash. When the deposit is processed, the receiving bank encodes its own identifying number as well as the identifying number of Bob's account, as shown in the illustration.

Clearing the Check. If Bob does deposit the check in his own bank, his bank technically doesn't know whether the check is any good. They simply have no way of knowing whether the Ajax Supermarket has money in its account when it's time to honor the check. They could thus say to Bob, ''Technically, we can't permit you to take money out against this check until we're sure that it has 'cleared,' that is, has been honored by the bank on which it's drawn, Arizona National.''

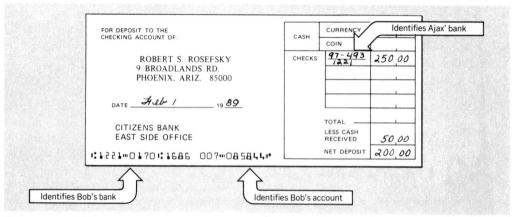

Figure 13-4   Deposit slip.

Bob's bank will actually send the check to the store's bank, where it will be processed. The Arizona National Bank does not notify Bob's bank that the check is good. Bob's bank will know that the check is good and was honored only if they do *not* get it back from the Arizona National Bank. If, in fact, the supermarket does not have enough money in its account to clear the check, the Arizona National Bank will return it to Bob's bank with a note that it was dishonored or that it "bounced," in this case for lack of sufficient funds.

Because both banks are in the same city, it customarily will only take one or two days for the check to go from one bank to the other. Thus, Bob's bank can be reasonably sure that the check has cleared if it hasn't heard otherwise within two or three days—the time it would take for the check to come back. In common practice, Bob's bank knows that he has been depositing these checks from the Ajax Supermarket for many years and that there has never been a problem. Thus, they would probably allow him to draw against the funds without waiting for the check to be cleared by the originating bank.

While a check is in the clearing process, which can be upward of one to two weeks if it is written on a bank in a distant part of the country, the funds are considered "uncollected" by the bank. For example, Bob receives a check for $1000 from his cousin Bernie in Binghamton, New York. Bob deposits it into his account at the Citizens Bank of Phoenix. Bob's bank knows that it will take roughly one week for the check to return to Bernie's bank in Binghamton. If the check is to bounce, it will take another week before Bob's bank finds out about it. Or if the check does not bounce, Bob's bank will still want to wait that additional week to be assured that the check hasn't in fact bounced. Bob's bank thus regards that $1000 as "uncollected funds" for a period of two weeks. But Bob thinks he has $1000 in the bank, and he writes a check for $700 to a local used car dealer as down payment on a car. The car dealer takes Bob's check into Bob's bank the next day, where it bounces. Bob has drawn a check against uncollected funds, and his check will not be honored. Not only will this cost Bob a few dollars for the bounced check fee, but it will also cause him considerable embarrassment.

New laws are emerging that lessen the amount of time banks are allowed to clear checks. Before you plan to draw on a check that you're depositing from an out-of-town bank, ask your banker how long it will take before you can draw against the funds.

Using the Check to Pay Debts or Make Purchases.   Bob owes $250 to his friend Gary in Taos, New Mexico. He wants to use his paycheck to settle his debt to Gary. He thus puts a *special endorsement* on the back of his check, which reads, "Pay to the order of Gary Smith," followed by his signature. A special endorsement gives only the named party the right to collect the amount of the check or to negotiate the check on to a subsequent holder. When Gary receives the check, he endorses it by signing his own name below Bob's signature, and the check will eventually come back to the original bank, where it presumably will be honored.

Although Bob pays off his debt in this fashion, it might have been unwise for him to do so. It would have been better for him to deposit the store's check into his own account and then draw his own check payable directly to Gary. He would ultimately receive back his canceled check and would thus have adequate proof that Gary had received the payment and that the debt was paid. As it is, the store will get the check back, and Bob will have to seek the store's help in verifying that Gary received the money.

Figure 13-3 shows samples of blank, restrictive, and special endorsements as outlined in the foregoing paragraphs.

Stopping Payment on the Check. The treasurer of the Ajax Supermarket learns that the computer has erroneously issued a check to one of the store's meat suppliers. The check is for $500 more than it should be, and the treasurer is concerned that the meat supplier will cash the check and will refuse to refund the excess $500 because there has been an ongoing dispute between them over a previous bill. The treasurer wants to stop the check before the meat supplier can cash it at her bank.

It's literally a race against time. The proper course for the treasurer is to go to the supermarket's bank, Arizona National, and issue a *stop payment order*. He must inform the bank in writing, including such information as the number of the check, the amount of the check, the date it was issued, and to whom it was payable, and then sign the order. This done, the bank will then refuse to allow payment on the check when it is presented. But if the meat supplier gets to the bank first and is able to cash the check, she will have the money in hand, and it will then be a hassle between the supplier and the store to decide who is entitled to the money.

Once a proper stop payment order has been filed with the bank, the bank might be responsible to the store if they make payment on the check in error. Thus, once a stop payment order has been signed, the bank alerts all of its tellers and the appropriate bookkeeper on the Ajax account to refuse payment should the check be presented. If a stop payment order is conducted verbally and the proper documents haven't been signed, the bank might not be responsible if it does pay the check. Banks customarily charge a few dollars for the processing of a stop payment order.

Overdrawing Your Account. We previously noted the problems that can arise when a checking account customer writes checks against uncollected funds. The same costs and embarrassments can occur if one writes checks when there simply isn't enough money in the account to cover the checks. This is a case of being "overdrawn." If a customer overdraws an account too frequently, he could jeopardize his credit standing with the bank. In some instances, a bank may pay a check even though it would overdraw the account. This may occur because the customer is in good standing, has rarely overdrawn, and the overdraft is for a relatively small amount. The bank isn't worried about getting its money, and rather than put the customer to any inconvenience, the bank allows the check to be paid.

In other cases, banks offer overdraft privileges to their customers. If a check overdraws an account, the bank will automatically lend the customer at least enough money to cover the overdraft and will deposit that loaned money into the customer's checking account. The loan must then be repaid at a specified rate of interest. This program can be convenient and eliminate embarrassment, but it can also be at least as costly as basic overdraft charges. It might also act as too great a temptation for the customer who lacks the discipline to keep a checking account properly balanced.

Keeping Track of Your Account. The register, or stub, is where the checking account customer keeps a record of all deposits and checks. The register should be updated immediately with each transaction. One of the most frequent causes of overdrawn accounts and other errors is customer failure to enter deposits and checks. If you neglect to enter a check transaction in your register, you run the risk of forgetting that transaction and subsequently overdrawing. Registers come in several forms. Figure 13-5 shows some sample registers, indicating how transactions are noted in them.

a.

CHECK #	DATE	CHECK ISSUED TO (or description of deposit)	AMOUNT OF CHECK	AMOUNT OF DEPOSIT	BALANCE 139.90
143	2/21	To *Joes Gas Sta* / For *Gas*	7.75		CHECK OR DEP. 7.75 / BAL. 132.15
Dep	2/27	To *(Net Paycheck)* / For		200.00	CHECK OR DEP. 200.00 / BAL. 332.15
144	3/15	To *Electric Co.* / For *Feb. bill*	28.10		CHECK OR DEP. 28.10 / BAL. 304.05
145	3/15	To *Saving & Loan* / For *March pmt*	242.00		CHECK OR DEP. 242.00 / BAL. 62.05

b.

CHECK # 144	DATE 3/5
TO *Electric Co.* *Feb. bill*	
BALANCE	332.15
CHECK	28.10
DEPOSIT	
NEW BAL.	304.05

CHECK # 145	DATE 3/5
TO *Saving & Loan* *March pmt.*	
BALANCE	304.05
CHECK	242.00
DEPOSIT	
NEW BAL.	62.05

Figure 13-5 *(a)* Sample checkbook register.
(b) Sample checkbook stubs.

1. Arrange canceled checks and deposit slips by number or date.
2. Check them off in your checkbook, verifying each amount as you proceed.
3. *Add* to your checkbook any deposits or other credits recorded on this statement that you have not already added.
4. *Subtract* from your checkbook any checks or other charges recorded on this statement that you have not already subtracted.
5. List at right each check you have written that is not yet paid by bank (does not show on statement). Total them, and enter total on line 10.

CHECKS NOT YET PAID		
DATE	#	AMOUNT
3/8	149	52.50
3/9	150	7.50
3/10	151	10.00
TOTAL		70.00

6. List any deposits you have made that do not show on statement, and enter total on line 8.

DEPOSITS NOT YET CREDITED	
DATE	AMOUNT
3/10	100.00
TOTAL	100.00

7. Ending balance as shown on statement.
8. Add total from line 6.
9. Subtotal.
10. Subtract total from line 5.
11. This total should be the same as the balance in your checkbook.

$	182.00
+	100.00
	282.00
–	70.00
$	212.00

Figure 13-6 Sample reconciliation of checking account.

Reconciling Your Account. Periodically—usually monthly—the bank returns a statement to each of its checking account customers. This statement contains an itemized listing of all transactions made on the account and includes all checks written and cleared during the previous month as well as all deposit slips. Thus the customer has written verification of every transaction. The bank also makes a microfilm record of all items, which the customer can refer to if necessary.

The statement also contains instructions for determining that the balance shown by the bank matches the balance shown in the customer's account. This is known as *reconciling the account*. Figure 13-6 illustrates an example of a monthly account reconciliation.

Shopping for Checking Accounts. The distinction between checking accounts and savings accounts has been blurred in recent years. Formerly, checking accounts did not pay interest; only savings accounts did. Now we have checking accounts that pay interest and savings accounts that have check-writing privileges. The Personal Action Checklist at the end of this chapter will help you to decide which of the plans available in your community offer the lowest cost (or highest income) in your individual case. The important matters to consider in shopping for the best account are the following: the minimum balance that you're required to keep in your account in order to earn interest or offset service charges; the number of checks you write each month; and the overall convenience and relationships you can establish by dealing with a particular institution.

Savings Accounts

Savings accounts are available at commercial banks, mutual savings banks, savings and loan associations, and credit unions. Generally, they take one of three forms: passbook accounts, savings certificates of deposit (CDs), and money market accounts.

Unlike checking accounts, where money flows in and out constantly, savings accounts are relatively inactive. They're used as a device to accumulate money over a long period of time.

Financial institutions are willing to pay savings accounts customers for the use of their money. The payment is referred to as *interest*. In effect, customers are lending their money to the institution, and the institution is paying interest for the loan.

Passbook Accounts. The old standard type of savings account is the passbook account. A passbook account may be opened with any amount of money, and the customer may make deposits to or withdrawals from the account as desired. (Some institutions might limit the number of withdrawals permitted in a month or in a quarter, and if the number is exceeded, the institution might levy a modest service charge.) Passbook savings account customers usually receive a small booklet, or passbook, in which each deposit and withdrawal is entered and in which the interest earned on the account is added to the customer's balance. A variation of the passbook account is the statement account, in which a monthly or quarterly statement is mailed to the customer. The statement reflects all transactions in the account for the preceding period.

Certificates of Deposit. Increasing in popularity in recent years is the savings certificate of deposit (CD). This is a contractual agreement between customer and institution whereby the customer agrees to leave a certain sum of money with the bank for a fixed period of time, perhaps as short as seven days or as long as ten years. Certificates generally pay a higher rate of interest to the customer than passbook accounts because the institution is assured that it will have the fixed sum of money available for lending for a known period of time. If a certificate customer wishes to withdraw funds before the agreed time has elapsed, she will suffer a penalty. Check to determine current penalty regulations before you open a certificate account.

Money Market Accounts. Money market accounts are relatively new. They are, in a sense, like a super passbook account. They pay a higher rate of interest than passbooks, but usually require a fairly substantial minimum amount in order to open such an account, perhaps $1000 or more. As a general rule, one can make deposits to or withdrawals from a money market account as desired. Many such accounts impose a service charge if there are too many deposits or withdrawals in a given period of time.

Competition is keen among institutions for savings accounts of all types. Since the advent of deregulation in the 1980s, there are virtually no legal limitations on the interest rates institutions can pay on these accounts. Careful shopping is essential if the saver is to obtain the best deal available at any given time in the community.

Because many consider savings accounts as a form of investment, they are treated more fully in Chapter 16.

Safe-Deposit Boxes

Safe-deposit boxes provide the ultimate security for valuable items and documents that cannot be replaced or duplicated. Financial institutions that rent safe-deposit facilities will make boxes of varying sizes available, generally on a yearly rental basis. The amount of the rent depends on the size of the box. The person or persons renting safe-deposit facilities must sign a signature card at the time the box is rented. Only those persons who have signed the card are permitted entree to the box. A key is given to safe-deposit customers, and it must be presented in addition to signing the entry form. It takes a combination of two keys—the one held by the customer and the one held by the institution—to allow entry into a box. If the customer loses a key, the likelihood is that the institution will have to drill the door open, probably at the customer's expense. Naturally, access to the box is available only during normal banking hours.

Some institutions may offer safe-deposit facilities at a reduced charge for customers who utilize other services.

Trust Services

Trust departments are usually found in larger commercial banks. The basic function of a trust department is to act as a trusted custodian of money or property for customers who require such services.

One very frequent use of trust services arises when an individual dies and directs that property go to his survivors "in trust." He will have established an agreement with the bank to act as trustee of the stated money and property. The trust department will then be responsible for investing the money prudently, for managing property (such as real estate), for selling any securities or properties that it deems proper to sell, for assisting with the necessary tax returns and other accounting matters on behalf of the trust, and for distributing the proceeds in accordance with the wishes of the individual who established the trust. Charges are levied for trust services depending on the total value of assets in the trust and the complexity of instructions that the trust department must follow. See Chapter 21 for further discussion of trusts.

Installment Loans

See Chapter 14 for a full discussion of installment loans.

Mortgage Loans

See Chapter 9 for detailed information on mortgage loans.

Credit Cards

We have already discussed credit cards; see the sections called Merchant Lenders and Credit Card Companies in this chapter.

Special Checks

Traveler's checks provide a safe and convenient means of having funds available when one is traveling, either in the United States, where personal checks may not be acceptable outside your own home community, or particularly in foreign countries, where neither personal checks nor American dollars may be acceptable as exchange. Traveler's checks can be purchased at most financial institutions in denominations of $10, $20, $50, and $100. The common charge is $1 per $100 worth of traveler's checks. If lost, traveler's checks can be replaced at offices of the issuing agencies or by mail as directed in the instructions included with each packet of traveler's checks.

Money orders are a form of check that one purchases at financial institutions (and at U.S. post offices) usually for payment of bills or for any other personal needs. Money orders can be purchased in any denomination. They generally cost more than checks, and one must go to the institution in order to purchase them; thus, they aren't nearly as convenient as a checking account.

If you're entering into an important transaction, such as the sale of your home, and you want to be absolutely certain that the check you receive from the other party will be good, you might want to require that the party give you a *cashier's check* or a *certified check* instead of a normal personal check. A cashier's check is a check drawn on the bank's own funds. A certified check is an individual's check that the bank has certified (in effect, guaranteed) that the funds are indeed in the account. Similarly, you might be required to present a cashier's check or certified check in certain situations. Assuming that you do have adequate funds in your account, the bank can accommodate these requests quickly and at little or no fee, depending on your status as a customer.

Notarial Services

We often have to sign documents requiring that our signature be "notarized." This service is performed by a notary public, and most financial institutions have a notary public on their staff available to serve their customers. The purpose of notarization is to verify that the signature is indeed that of the person indicated. When a signature is to be notarized, the document must be signed in the presence of the notary, and the notary must know that the signer is who he represents himself to be. Many institutions do not charge for notarial services, particularly for their own customers. Notarial services can also be obtained through law firms, governmental offices, insurance agencies, and other businesses.

Electronic Banking

Most institutions throughout the nation have begun installing electronic tellers—machines that offer twenty-four-hour service on a variety of transactions: withdrawals, deposits, loan payments, and transfers from one account to another. Customers wishing to utilize these services are generally issued a plastic card with a secret code number assigned to it, thus preventing anyone except the authorized user from making use of the card.

Collection Services

Business and commercial accounts are more likely to make use of this little-known service. For example, landlords living in distant cities may find it more convenient for tenants to make their rent payments to local banks, which will in turn deposit the payments into the landlords' accounts. They may feel that there's a psychological advantage that gets the rent paid more promptly if the payments are made to a local bank rather than to some distant address. Charges are made in accordance with the volume of service rendered.

International Banking

International banking is predominantly a service for the business executive and is available in larger commercial banks. As U.S. business spreads throughout the world, the need has arisen for banking services to exchange foreign currency for U.S. currency, to establish business contacts in foreign countries, and to assist with the various business negotiations and transactions taking place between U.S. and foreign firms.

Investment Department

As noted earlier, whatever money banks don't lend out to the public or keep in reserve, they invest, usually in high-quality government and corporate bond issues. Many individual investors who seek these types of securities find it more convenient and less costly to acquire them through their bank investment department rather than through stockbrokerage firms. Anyone contemplating investing in government or corporate securities would do well to inquire at their local bank to see whether their investment department can provide service comparable to or better than local brokerage firms.

LAWS GOVERNING FINANCIAL INSTITUTIONS

Financial institutions and the transactions that emanate from them are governed by a complex system of state and federal laws. As noted earlier, each institution is given its original license to operate, either by the state in which it is located or by the federal government. The respective government then generally oversees and regulates the operation of the institution, including periodic audits and examinations to ascertain whether the institution is complying with governmental guidelines. Additional state regulations with which institutions must comply include laws of negotiable instruments (an important aspect of which is the concept of the "holder in due course"), laws of usury, and laws regarding secured transactions. Federal laws with which institutions must comply include the Truth in Lending Law, the the Fair Credit Billing Law, Fair Credit Reporting Law, and the Equal Credit Opportunity Law. Let's examine each of these.

State Laws

Negotiable Instruments. The state negotiable instruments laws refer to instruments, such as checks and promissory notes (IOUs), that are negotiated, that is, sold, exchanged, and otherwise passed from hand to hand. Each state has its own laws of negotiable instruments, but they all tend to be quite similar. In essence, negotiable instruments laws determine what constitutes a valid negotiable instrument and what does not. A check is a good example of a negotiable instrument. It carries an unconditional order to pay a fixed sum of money to the holder, it's dated, and the person who draws the check must sign it. If a check does not contain any of these elements—such as the signature of the drawer—it could be construed as being nonnegotiable and need not be processed in the manner that valid checks are processed. In short, it could be returned to the person who drew the check, and the intended transaction would thus not occur.

Another example would be a promissory note: You buy a TV set from a local appliance dealer. Instead of paying cash for it, you sign a promissory note in which you agree to make payments over a specific period of time. The promissory note is payable directly to the dealer. The dealer in turn sells your promissory note to a local bank or finance company so that he can get his money immediately. You then end up making your payments to the bank. The bank has become a *holder* of your negotiable instrument *in the due course of business*, assuming that the instrument has been properly created and executed. If you had neglected to sign it, the TV dealer would not have been able to sell it to the bank. If the TV dealer had not properly endorsed it, the bank would not have bought it from him.

Assuming that the paper work was all done properly, what would happen if you got the TV set home and found out that it didn't work? You'd want to refuse to make payments to the dealer, but the dealer would simply tell you that he had sold your IOU to the bank. Could you refuse to make payments to the bank? Federal Trade Commission regulations state that, in general, if you, a buyer, have a valid claim or defense against the original dealer, you would have the same claim or defense against the party who subsequently bought your promissory note. In other words, if you could have legally refused to pay the dealer because the TV set was defective, you could just as legally refuse to pay the bank for the same reason. Before you sign any promissory notes involving any such contractual rights, be certain you understand contractual terms that could have a bearing on your obligation to pay.

Usury Laws. Each state has its own laws of usury. The usury laws dictate the maximum rate of interest that can be charged for various types of loans. You should determine what the maximum interest rates allowable for various categories of loans are in your own state. If lenders charge an excessive or usurious rate of interest on loans or on other kinds of financing, they may be subject to penalties. The borrowers or debtors in usurious transactions should determine what their rights are in such cases and take appropriate action.

In most states the laws protecting against usury apply to individuals only. Corporations do not have the same measure of protection when they borrow.

Secured Transactions Laws. You purchase an automobile and arrange for financing through your local bank. In the common transaction, you will sign documents that give the bank the right to take back your car if you fail to make the payments as promised. As a result of your signing these documents and the bank's recording of them in the appropriate governmental office, the bank has what is known as a *security interest* in your new automobile.

By recording the security agreement, the bank has put all other parties on notice that it has a first lien on your car. Years later, when you pay off the loan, the bank should release that security interest by completing and filing the appropriate papers at that time.

Secured transaction laws are slightly different in each state, but they all derive from one uniform recommended law called the Uniform Commercial Code. These state laws describe how a lender goes about protecting his security interest in a property and how he must release that security interest when the loan is eventually paid off. The loan does not dictate when or if a borrower must put up security for a given loan nor how much security should be put up. That's between the borrower and the lender. The law does, however, describe the means by which each party is protected in such a transaction.

Federal Laws

Truth in Lending Law. Congress passed the Truth in Lending Law in July 1969. The main purpose of the Truth in Lending Law (also referred to as *Regulation Z*) is to inform borrowers and consumers of the exact cost of credit so that they can compare costs offered by various credit sources.

The Truth in Lending Law is very broad in scope. It applies to virtually all issuers of credit, including commercial banks, savings and loan associations, credit unions, consumer finance companies, residential mortgage brokers, department stores, automobile dealers, furniture and appliance dealers, artisans (such as electricians and plumbers), and professionals (such as doctors, dentists, and lawyers). If these parties or any others issuing credit to the public extend credit for personal, family, household, or agricultural uses, or for real estate transactions, they must comply with the regulations of the Truth in Lending Law.

The main objective of the Truth in Lending Law is to establish a uniform means of quoting credit costs. Prior to the passage of this law, grantors of credit frequently quoted interest costs in a variety of different forms—add-on, discount, simple, per month, per year, and so on. This variety of quoting costs made it quite difficult for the typical consumer to compare the true costs between one lender or credit grantor and another. It was, in a sense, like trying to compare apples to oranges.

The Truth in Lending Law dictates that any grantor of credit must clearly set forth the *total finance charges* that the customer must pay, directly or indirectly, in order to obtain the desired credit. The finance charges can include any of the following costs: interest, loan fees, finder's fees, service charges, "points" (commonly, the added fees charged in a residential mortgage transaction), appraisal fees, premiums for credit life or health insurance, the cost of any investigation or credit reports.

In addition to stating the total dollar amount of finance charges, the credit grantor must also express the cost in terms of a percentage. This is known as the *annual percentage rate* (APR). The APR formula requires all lenders and credit grantors to quote credit costs using the same mathematics. APR, then, is the pure way of comparing credit costs among different lenders.

The Truth in Lending Law does not fix the interest rate that may be charged on credit. This is decided by the lender and the borrower within the limitations of state usury laws. Figure 13-7 is an example of a typical disclosure statement showing the various aspects of the credit transaction as referred to in the Truth in Lending Law.

If, in order to borrow money, you have to put up your home as collateral for

DISCLOSURE STATEMENT

_____
(BANK)

_____
(OFFICE)

_____
(ADDRESS)

The following disclosures are made pursuant to the Consumer Credit Protection Act by the above-named Bank (herein called Bank) to the Borrower(s) named herein (herein collectively called Borrower) in connection with the proposed loan described herein (herein called Loan):

TRANSACTION: PROPOSED LOAN — NONREAL PROPERTY			
Amount	Security	Purpose	Type of Loan
$ _____ Nonrescindable transaction	Not secured by real property	Consumer or agricultural	

NAMES AND ADDRESSES OF BORROWERS:

1. AMOUNT OF CREDIT (excluding any Prepaid Finance Charge (Item 3) and Required Deposit Balance (Item 4)
   (a) Net loan proceeds $_____
   (b) Charges included in Amount Financed
      (1) Insurance premiums
         Credit life (if not required) $_____
         Credit disability (if not required) $_____
         Property $_____
         Liability $_____
      (2) _____ $_____
      (3) Charges, if any, itemized under Column A of Item 2 $_____
   AMOUNT FINANCED (Total) $_____

2. CERTAIN CHARGES NOT INCLUDED IN FINANCE CHARGE (Item 6)

	A Included in Amount Financed	B Not included in Amount Financed
(a) Fees to public officials for determining, perfecting, releasing or satisfying security		
(1) Recorder	$	$
(2) Secretary of State	$	$
(3) _____	$	$
(b) Fees imposed by law		
(1) License	$	$
(2) Certificate of title	$	$
(3) Registration	$	$
(c) _____	$	$
Total (enter at Item 1(b)(3))	$	

3. FINANCE CHARGES PAID SEPARATELY OR WITHHELD

	A Paid Separately	B Withheld from Loan Proceeds
(a) Loan fee	$	$
(b) Commitment fee	$	$
(c) Appraisal fees	$	$
(d) Investigation fees (_____)	$	$
(e) Credit report fees	$	$
(f) Notary fees	$	$
(g) Document preparation fees	$	$
(h) Insurance premiums Required credit life	$	$
Required credit disability	$	$
(i) _____	$	$
(j) _____	$	$
(k) _____	$	$
Total	$	$

PREPAID FINANCE CHARGE (Col. A plus B) $_____

4. REQUIRED DEPOSIT BALANCE $_____

5. TOTAL PREPAID FINANCE CHARGE AND REQUIRED DEPOSIT BALANCE $_____

6. AMOUNTS INCLUDED IN FINANCE CHARGE
   (a) Interest at ____% per annum on _____ $_____
   (b) Interest added on of $_____ per $100 of Loan per annum $_____
   (c) Flat charge $_____
   (d) _____ $_____
   (e) _____ $_____
   (f) Charges, if any, itemized in Item 3 $_____
   FINANCE CHARGE (Total) $_____

Any interest included in the Finance Charge accrues from date of advance, except that if a series of advances is to be made pursuant to written agreement, interest accrues on each advance from date thereof and has been computed until maturity of the Loan in accordance with the estimated or approximate dates and amounts of advances as furnished by Borrower.

7. TOTAL OF PAYMENTS $_____
   Payable in_____ payment(s) as follows [Note any Balloon Payment(s)]: _____
   _____
   _____
   _____
   _____
   _____
   _____

8. ANNUAL PERCENTAGE RATE _____%

9. LATE PAYMENT CHARGE is payable on any payment in default for____ days in an amount equal to_____

10. PREPAYMENT CREDIT. Upon prepayment of the Loan in full, Borrower will be entitled to a rebate of any unearned (prepaid) (precomputed) interest_____
   _____
   _____

11. PREPAYMENT CHARGE. Upon partial or full prepayment of the Loan_____
   _____
   _____

12. SECURITY. Loan is to be secured by a security agreement covering the property described_____
   _____

and by an assignment of rights under insurance policies thereon as required by Bank, all as described in the security agreement(s). The security agreement(s) (will) (will not) cover (certain) after acquired property, and (will) (will not) secure future and other indebtedness. Loan is to be subject to a lien under Civil Code § 3054 on personal property of Borrower in Bank's possession. Except as may be provided above, Loan is not to be secured as a result of any existing agreement between Bank and any Borrower or other person, any such agreement to the contrary notwithstanding.

INSURANCE

ANY PROPERTY OR LIABILITY INSURANCE TO BE WRITTEN IN CONNECTION WITH THE LOAN MAY BE OBTAINED BY BORROWER THROUGH ANY PERSON OF HIS CHOICE, provided, however, that Bank may for reasonable cause refuse to accept an insurer on any such insurance which is required by Bank. Such insurance may ☐ not be obtained from or through Bank ☐ be obtained through Bank at the cost set forth in a separate Insurance Statement furnished by Bank.

[Complete if credit insurance may be written but is not required] CREDIT LIFE AND CREDIT DISABILITY INSURANCE ARE NOT REQUIRED TO OBTAIN THE LOAN. No charge is to be made for such insurance and none is to be provided unless Borrower to be insured thereunder signs and dates the statement below. If obtained through Bank, the cost for credit life insurance will be $_____ and for credit disability insurance will be $_____

I desire credit ☐ life and ☐ disability insurance.

_____
(DATE)   (SIGNATURE)

●IMPORTANT NOTE: ASTERISK DENOTES THAT AMOUNT INDICATED IS AN ESTIMATE.

Borrower acknowledges reading and receiving a duplicate of this Disclosure Statement and that he has not entered into any agreement with Bank for the making or payment of the Loan; and if the Loan is to be made in a series of advances pursuant to written agreement, approves the Annual Percentage Rate and method of computing the Finance Charge as set forth above, and all the terms of that proposed agreement. THIS IS NOT AN OFFER OR COMMITMENT TO LEND OR TO PROVIDE INSURANCE.

_____   _____
(BANK)   (BORROWER)
By_____
_____   _____
(DATE)   (BORROWER)

TL-4 (7-69 REV)

Figure 13-7 Sample disclosure statement.

the loan, the Truth in Lending Law requires that the lender give you a three-day period in which you can elect to cancel or rescind the transaction by sending proper notice to the lender. (This does not apply in cases where you are borrowing money to buy the home initially.) The purpose of this three-day "cooling-off" period is to protect borrowers who might have second thoughts about a transaction, particularly when they might have received a high-pressure sales pitch or misleading promises. If you do elect to cancel such a transaction and proper notice is given to the lender, you are entitled to a return of any down payment you have given the lender or merchant.

Although the Truth in Lending Law sets forth a means of comparing credit wisely and prudently, it does not necessarily instruct the consumer how to make a decision on which lender to do business with. The cost of credit is not the only factor that must be considered in making a borrowing decision. For example, if a local bank offers an APR slightly higher than an out-of-town credit firm, the borrower might still be better off doing business with the local bank, where other services and considerations may be provided that wouldn't be found at the out-of-town institution.

The Truth in Lending Law also sets forth regulations regarding the use of credit cards, the liability for their unauthorized use, and the means by which credit may be advertised.

Fair Credit Billing Law.   The Fair Credit Billing Law was passed in October 1974 as an amendment to the Truth in Lending Law. It was designed to put an end to the frustration that certain credit customers have when they receive a bill that contains an error and then cannot get the error properly corrected. It pertains to open-end credit—credit arising out of revolving charge accounts, checking overdraft plans, and credit card obligations. It does *not* apply to normal installment loans or purchases that are paid in accordance with a set schedule of installments.

The Fair Credit Billing Law covers only billing errors on your periodic statement. Billing errors are those that might arise as a result of the following: charges that you did not make or charges made by a person not allowed to use your account; charges billed with the wrong description, amount, or date; charges for property or services that you did not accept or that were not delivered as agreed; failures to credit your account for payments or for goods you have returned; accounting errors, such as arithmetic mistakes in computing finance charges; billings for which you request an explanation or written proof of purchase; and failures to mail or deliver a billing statement to your current address provided you gave at least ten days' notice of any change of address.

The Fair Credit Billing Law requires that open-end creditors give a notice summarizing the dispute settlement procedures to all customers who have active accounts or who open new accounts after October 28, 1975. After the first notice, additional copies must be provided to customers every six months.

The dispute settlement procedures regarding a billing error, as outlined by the Federal Trade Commission, are as follows:

1. *How you notify the creditor of a billing error.*   If you think your bill is wrong, or if you need more information about an item on your bill, here's what you must do to preserve your rights under the law. On a sheet of paper separate from the bill, write the following: your name and account number; a description of the error and an explanation of why you think it's an error; a request for whatever added information you may think you need, including a copy of the charge slip; the dollar amount of the suspected error; and any other information you think will help the creditor to identify you or the reason for your complaint or inquiry. Include your address and photocopies of the bill itself and the charge in question.

   Send your billing error notice to the address on the bill listed after the words "Send inquiries to" or similar wording indicating the proper address.

   Mail it as soon as you can, but in any case early enough to reach the creditor within sixty days after the bill was mailed to you.

   Do not simply notify the creditor by telephone. This will not necessarily protect your rights under the law. The proper way to protect your rights is to notify the creditor in writing.

2. *What the creditor must do.*   The creditor must acknowledge all letters pointing out possible errors within thirty days of receipt of such letters, unless the creditor is able to correct your bill during that thirty days. Within ninety days after receiving your letter, the creditor must either correct the error or explain why he, the creditor, believes the bill is correct. Once the creditor has explained the bill, the creditor has no further obligation to you, even though you still believe there is an error, except as provided in item 5 below.

3. *How you are protected from collection and bad credit reports.*   After the creditor has been notified, neither the creditor nor an attorney nor a collection agency may send you collection letters or take other collection action regarding the amount in dispute. But periodic *statements* may be sent to you, and the disputed amount can be applied against your credit limit. You cannot be threatened with damage to your credit rating or sued for the amount in question, nor can the disputed amount be reported to a credit bureau or other creditors as being delinquent until the creditor has answered your inquiry. However, you remain obligated to pay whatever portion of your bill is not in dispute.

4. *What happens if the dispute is settled?*   If it is determined that the creditor has made a mistake on your bill, you will not have to pay any finance charges on any disputed amount. If it turns out that the creditor has not made an error, you may have to pay finance charges on the amount in dispute, and you will have to make up any missed minimum or required payments on the disputed amount.

5. *What happens if the dispute is not settled?*   If the creditor's explanation does not satisfy you and you notify the creditor in writing within ten days after you receive his explanation that you still refuse to pay the disputed amount, the creditor may report you to credit bureaus and other creditors and may pursue regular collection procedures. But the creditor must also report that you do not

think you owe any money, and the creditor must let you know to whom such reports were made. Once the matter has been settled between you and the creditor, the creditor must notify those to whom he had reported you as being delinquent.

6. ***How the creditor can be penalized for not following the procedure.*** If the creditor does not follow these rules, the creditor is not allowed to collect the first $50 of the disputed amount and finance charges, even if the bill turns out to be correct.

7. ***When can you withhold payment for faulty goods or services purchased with a credit card?*** If you have a problem with property or services purchased with a credit card, you may have the right not to pay the remaining amount due on them if you first try, in good faith, to return the item or give the merchant a chance to correct the problem. There are two limitations on this right: (a) you must have bought the item or services in your home state or, if not within your home state, within one hundred miles of your current mailing address; and (b) the purchase price must have been more than $50. However, the two limitations do not apply if the merchant is owned or operated by the creditor or if the creditor mailed you the advertisement for the property or services.

In brief, the Fair Credit Billing Law gives you the right of extensive protection against alleged errors in billing. But you must exercise your rights as they are stated in the law. If you fail to do so, you may have waived those rights.

Fair Credit Reporting Law. The Fair Credit Reporting Law, which went into effect in April 1971, is designed to give access to any information that may be on file at local credit bureaus regarding your own individual credit history. It also enables you to take steps to correct erroneous or outdated material that may be in your file.

It should be noted, contrary to what many people think, that credit-reporting agencies are *not* governmental agencies. They are generally private firms, operating either on their own or as a cooperative of various merchants and lenders within the community. It is their job to accumulate appropriate credit information on individuals and make it available to their respective participating members. Easy access to credit information on the citizens of a community makes it easier and more convenient for credit to be granted to credit-worthy seekers. To this extent, the local credit bureau, as a clearinghouse of information, serves a most valuable purpose. But there have been abuses within the industry, as in any industry, and the Fair Credit Reporting Law was designed to correct these abuses.

Under the Fair Credit Reporting Law, you can, on presenting proper identification, learn the contents of your file at your local credit bureau. The identification requirements are for the borrower's own protection. This aspect of the law would eliminate the chance of a stranger walking into a credit bureau claiming to be you and viewing your credit file.

Regarding erroneous information, you can request the bureau to reinvestigate any items you question. If the information is found to be inaccurate or cannot be verified, it will be deleted. If the reinvestigation doesn't resolve the problem, you can write a brief statement explaining your position, and the statement will be included in all future credit reports. If an item is deleted or a statement added, you can request that the bureau so notify anyone who has received regular credit reports on you during the last six months.

If you've been denied credit during the past thirty days because of a report from the credit bureau or if you've received a collection notice from a department affiliated with the credit bureau, the law states that you're not to be charged for viewing your file. Otherwise a reasonable charge can be imposed for the privilege of viewing your file.

Information in your credit file that is adverse may not be disclosed to creditors after seven years have elapsed, except if you have had a bankruptcy in your past. That information may remain in your file and be available to inquirers for up to fourteen years.

As with the other laws, the Fair Credit Reporting Law gives rights to the individual, but it's up to the individual to see that these rights are obtained when deserved.

Equal Credit Opportunity Law. The Equal Credit Opportunity Law went into effect in October 1975. Essentially, it's designed to prevent any discrimination in the granting of credit regarding sex or marital status of any person applying for credit.

In the most general sense, this law was designed to correct an apparent abuse that often prevented women from receiving credit to which they might otherwise be entitled. Highlights of the law include the following:

- ☐ Creditors must not discriminate against any applicant on the basis of sex or marital status in any phase of a credit transaction.
- ☐ Creditors must not make any statement to any applicant that would discourage a reasonable person from applying for credit because of sex or marital status.
- ☐ Creditors must open separate accounts for husbands and wives if requested and if both are credit-worthy.
- ☐ Creditors must consider alimony and child-support payments as they would any other source of income in assessing credit-worthiness if the applicant wishes to rely on these means of income.
- ☐ Creditors must allow applicants to open or maintain accounts in their birth-given name if they so desire.
- ☐ Creditors must give the reason why credit has been denied or terminated when asked by the applicant.

Fair Debt Collection Practices Law. The Fair Debt Collection Practices Law, which went into effect March 20, 1978, prohibits abusive, deceptive, and unfair debt-collection practices. The law covers personal, family, and household debts, including loans, charge accounts, medical bills, and the like. Here, in brief, is how the law works:

☐ A debt collector may contact you in person or by mail, telephone, or telegram, but it should not be at unusual places or times, such as before 8 A.M. or after 9 P.M. A debt collector may *not* contact you at work if your employer disapproves. A debt collector may contact any other person for the purpose of trying to locate you, but if she does so she may not tell the other person anything other than that she is trying to contact you. If you have an attorney, she must contact only your attorney. The debt collector must not tell anybody else that you owe money, should not talk to any person more than once, should not use a postcard, and should not put anything on an envelope or in a letter to others that identifies the writer as a debt collector.

Table 13-1 **Federal Regulatory Agencies**

Businesses	*Regulatory agencies*
National banks	Comptroller of the Currency Washington, DC 20219
State member banks	Federal Reserve Bank serving the area in which the state member bank is located
Nonmember insured banks	Federal Deposit Insurance Corporation Supervising Examiner for the District in which the nonmember insured bank is located
Savings institutions insured by the FSLIC and members of the FHLB system (except for savings banks insured by FDIC)	The FHLB's Supervisory Agent in the Federal Home Loan Bank District in which the institution is located
Federal credit unions	Regional Office of the National Credit Union Administration serving the area in which the federal credit union is located
Creditors subject to Interstate Commerce Commission	Office of Proceedings Interstate Commerce Commission Washington, DC 20523
Retail, department stores, consumer finance companies, all other creditors, and all nonbank credit card issuers	Federal Trade Commission Washington, DC 20580
Small business investment companies	U.S. Small Business Administration 1441 L Street, NW Washington, DC 20416
Brokers and dealers	Securities and Exchange Commission Washington, DC 20549

☐ Within five days after you are first contacted by a debt collector, she must send you *written notice* telling you the amount of money you owe, the name of the creditor, and what to do if you feel you do not owe the money.

☐ If you feel you do not owe the money, you must inform the debt collector in writing within thirty days after she has first contacted you. She may then not contact you again except (1) to send you proof of the debt, such as a copy of the bill, in which case she can begin collection proceedings again; or (2) to notify you that certain specific action will be taken, but only if, in fact, she usually does take such action. In short, you can stop the debt collector from constantly harassing you if you properly notify her in writing to stop.

☐ A debt collector may not use false, deceptive, threatening, or abusive statements to induce you to pay. She may not threaten to take any legal action which she in fact cannot legally take.

Enforcement of the Federal Laws. Generally, the Federal Trade Commission administers all the foregoing federal laws regarding retail firms, department stores, consumer finance companies, all other creditors, and all nonbank credit card issuers. Table 13-1 indicates which federal agency enforces the various federal laws regarding credit and borrowing.

Earnings and Costs of Checking Accounts

This checklist is designed to help you compare the costs of various checking account plans, particularly those that pay interest. As with so many other of our day-to-day concerns, the lowest price is not always the best price.

Criteria	*Plan A*	*Plan B*	*Plan C*
☐ How much do you have to keep in the account in order to earn interest or in order to avoid charges for your checking account?	_____	_____	_____
☐ Is the amount above an *average* per month (or quarter), or is it a fixed-dollar minimum?	_____	_____	_____
☐ Can you keep the minimum balance in an account other than the checking account itself, such as a savings certificate?	_____	_____	_____
☐ What charges will you incur if your required minimum balance drops below the set level?			
Basic monthly charge?	_____	_____	_____
Charge per check written?	_____	_____	_____
☐ Based on your past history (if you've had a checking account previously), what type of average balance would you expect to keep in your account?			
How many checks would you write per month?	_____	_____	_____
☐ If you've not had a checking account before, estimate your average balance.	_____	_____	_____
☐ Based on estimates above, how much do you expect you'll earn (interest income less monthly charges) with this plan?	_____	_____	_____

Criteria	*Plan A*	*Plan B*	*Plan C*
☐ Business hours of institution?	————	————	————
Open Saturdays?	————	————	————
Automatic teller service available?	————	————	————
☐ Convenience in getting to and from the institution.	————	————	————
☐ Personal feelings about the institution: helpfulness of staff, other services offered, and so forth.	————	————	————

Mistaken Identity

In the mid-1970s a company called Lincoln Thrift and Loan Association, based in Phoenix, Arizona, grew rapidly by offering investors a higher rate of interest than they could get at local banks and savings and loan associations. Investors were told that their accounts were ''insured'' and that the ''insurance'' was overseen by the State of Arizona.

In virtually all respects, Lincoln Thrift looked like a bank (or savings and loan association): it advertised in the same style; it had branches and tellers; and as was the custom then, it gave away gifts for new accounts.

But it was not what it seemed to be.

Shortly before Christmas day in 1975, the roughly 20,000 customers of Lincoln Thrift received shocking news: state authorities had closed the business. It had made an excessive number of bad loans, and there were accusations that the company management had pocketed large sums for its own private use.

And, worst of all, the insurance company that was supposedly protecting the accounts was insolvent too. It was not, as it had appeared, a quasi-governmental agency. The insurance company was owned by the same people who owned the thrift and loan company. If two birds in flight are tied together and you shoot one down, both will fall.

The customers had invested almost $60 million with Lincoln Thrift. For many, it was their life savings. And not a penny of it was actually insured.

It took years for government-appointed trustees to unravel the mess and collect on whatever loans they could. By the early 1980s, customers had finally received about 40¢ for every dollar they had invested. Needless to say, they earned no interest at all during that time. It's not likely that they'll ever collect more than that.

There are many thrift and loan companies throughout the nation. Failures are relatively rare. Lincoln Thrift was an uncommon but gruesome experience.

The facts and the need for caution and prudence speak for themselves.

CHAPTER 14

Credit and Borrowing

Imagine what would happen to our economy if it weren't possible to borrow money. Everything would grind to a halt: People couldn't buy cars, houses, or appliances until they had accumulated enough cash to do so. Similarly, businesses and governments would be hard pressed to create new facilities, purchase needed equipment, expand their ongoing programs.

We live in a credit society. Making wise use of your ability to borrow can enhance your life. Abusing your credit can be very harmful. This chapter explores the wise and unwise uses of credit and explains how credit techniques work. You'll learn the following:

- ☐ How to evaluate how much borrowing you can afford to do and under what circumstances
- ☐ Where to seek the credit you need and how to best assure you'll get the money you need
- ☐ How to structure your borrowing to best suit your ability to repay your loans
- ☐ How to avoid the dangers of credit abuse
- ☐ Where to look for help if you have credit problems

THE MORRIS PLAN

Most of us take the "buy now, pay later" aspect of our economy for granted. But it was not always so. It wasn't until about 1916, with the development of a phenomenon called the Morris Plan, that the individual working person could borrow from banks and other financial institutions. Prior to that, businesses, governments, and wealthy individuals were the predominant borrowers. Their loans were generally on a "demand" or "time" basis. A demand loan was repayable in its entirety upon the demand of the lender. A time loan was repayable after the passage of the stated amount of time. If the borrower wished and if the lender were willing, such loans could be renewed for an additional period of time, once the borrower had paid the interest due. It was generally felt that if working people borrowed on such a basis, they would spend the borrowed funds on goods and services and would not be able to repay the lump sum at the agreed time.

Then, in 1916, a man named Arthur Morris devised a plan that would enable individual working people to borrow money that they needed for immediate purposes. Today, Morris's plan seems commonplace, but it was a revolutionary concept when originally devised.

The key to Morris's idea, which came to be known as the *Morris Plan*, was that a loan could be repaid in monthly installments over a fixed period of time. The Morris Plan was the origin, the grandfather, of the installment loan, the time-payment plan, the revolving charge account, the credit card loan, and all other forms of borrowing that we are accustomed to.

Morris's reasoning was simple enough: Although it might be difficult for the typical worker to repay one large lump sum, if the individual was prudent and well employed, he should be able to set aside a fixed amount each month to apply to the debt. This type of debt would command a higher rate of interest from the borrower, and the lender would have a constant inflow of money as payments were made each month on the loans, thus enabling the lender to keep putting the available money back to work on a constant basis.

From an initial institution in Virginia, the Morris Plan proved itself. Within a few years there were scores of Morris Plan institutions in operation around the country. Commercial banks soon saw the advantages and profits in making such loans, and merchants began to accept the installment IOUs of customers for many products. The "buy now, pay later" years were on their way.

The Morris Plan and all that developed from it proved successful on more than one level. By putting borrowing power into the hands of millions of American workers, more goods could be manufactured and sold. This in turn helped to create more jobs, which in turn created more income for more people. This then enabled a much larger segment of the population to borrow and buy.

Today, there are very few adults in America who do not carry one of the descendants of the Morris Plan with them in their wallets or purses: the credit card. The credit card, in effect, allows holders to write personal installment loans—within limits—whenever and wherever they choose.

WHAT IS CREDIT?

Credit is the ability to borrow. It is *not* a right. It's a *privilege* earned through careful planning and faithful performance. Good credit, properly used, can be a most valuable asset. Wise borrowers will have studied their own financial situation with great care. They will know the difference between needs and luxuries. They will know within pennies their ability to repay. They will know how to approach the lender, what to ask for and what not to ask for, and what to expect. They will resist the temptations that scream out, "Buy me now!" and "Easy credit!"

They will have carefully defined their *access to credit, need for credit*, and *capacity for credit*. And they will keep each in proper perspective and balance. Let's take a closer look at these three important elements of credit.

Access to Credit

Access to credit refers to the amount of credit readily available to you through such means as charge accounts, credit cards, and installment loans. Access to credit is, of course, directly related to lender and merchant willingness to grant credit. This in turn depends on your past performance, income, other debts, work, and the purposes for which you may wish to borrow.

Need for Credit

Credit needs refer to the various needs you may have that can or should be fulfilled through borrowing. Common needs for borrowing include automobile financing; revolving charge accounts at your department stores so that a large clothing purchase, for example, can be paid for over an extended period of time, thus making it easier on the monthly budget; and personal loans for home improvements and emergencies. Note that we are referring to *needs*, not *luxuries*. Most of us would like to obtain certain luxury items and indeed may be able to through the use of credit. But using credit to acquire luxuries, as opposed to using credit to fulfill needs, can be dangerous. If your available credit is used excessively to obtain luxuries, you can cut off your access to credit for the more important needs.

Capacity for Credit

Capacity for credit refers to the amount of borrowing you can realistically handle within your current situation of income and other expenses, as well as your future situation regarding anticipated income and other expenses.

Many people sometimes find themselves having access to more credit than they realistically need. (Or they may have needs for credit that are in excess of their credit capacity.) For example, Charlie and Charlotte estimate that they have access to roughly $15,000 worth of credit. Based on past experience, they're confident that their bank would lend them up to $5000 without collateral if necessary. The sum total of all of their credit cards and charge accounts would allow them to go into additional debt of about $5000. And a representative of a lending firm has told them that the equity in their house would allow them to borrow another $5000— if they were willing to give a second mortgage on the house. Their current credit needs are much more modest. Their automobile is all paid off, and next year they'll need a new one. They estimate that they might need to borrow between $4000 and $5000 for this purpose. Over and above this, their credit needs don't exceed $1000, which they use in their charge accounts to even out the monthly cost of clothing and home necessities.

At present, then, their *capacity* for credit exceeds their credit *needs*. However, in a few years, Charlie and Charlotte's oldest child will be starting college, and they expect to have to borrow quite heavily to meet those costs. At that time, their credit *needs* may exceed their credit *capacity*. They should immediately begin making careful plans to help assure them that they'll be able to borrow what they need when they need it in the future. They would be wise to visit a lending officer at their bank and review their access to credit, their needs for credit, and their credit capacity for the present and for the next three to five years. Such a periodic review is wise for anyone who wants to maintain good control over the wise use of credit.

SOURCES OF CREDIT

Installment loans for a variety of purposes are available at banks, savings and loan associations, credit unions, and consumer finance (small-loan) companies. As a general rule, the cost of borrowing at these various institutions tends to be highest at the consumer finance companies. Interest rates at credit unions tend to be equal to or possibly slightly less than those at banks and savings and loan associations.

Dealer financing is another common source of credit. When you purchase such items as automobiles, furniture, and appliances, the dealer may be able to arrange financing for you. The dealer may extend the loan to you directly or may place your loan with one of the financial institutions mentioned above. When dealers place financing with another institution, it's common for them to get a fee for doing so. Before you accept a dealer financing arrangement, you should compare the cost of such an arrangement with the costs you'd be charged if you dealt directly with a lender of your own choice.

Charge accounts are frequently used as a source of credit. Department stores, for example, approve open-end credit arrangements with credit-worthy customers, allowing them to charge purchases at the store up to a certain maximum limit. They are expected to pay at least a minimum amount each month toward the debt. If they don't pay the charge account debts in full each month, they are charged interest for the balance. This interest charge is usually based on the average amount outstanding in the account during the prior month.

Credit cards have become one of the most popular sources of credit. The most common types of credit cards are those offered by banks and savings and loan associations: MasterCard and Visa. These cards are honored extensively throughout the United States and in foreign countries at all types of retail establishments. "Travel and entertainment" cards (American Express, Diners Club, Carte Blanche) are commonly used for business purposes at hotels and restaurants. Airlines and gasoline companies also issue credit cards for use in obtaining their specific products and services.

If credit card applicants are deemed worthy, they are granted a "line of credit" by the credit card company. That is, a maximum amount is established that they can charge. Card users are then expected to pay at least a certain monthly minimum amount toward their accumulated debt. Any unpaid debt will accrue interest. The manner in which interest on credit card debts is calculated can be very complex. The best way to avoid the matter entirely is to pay your credit card debt in full each month so that no interest accrues against you.

Strategies for Success

Watch Out for Credit Card Scams

Get into the habit of collecting your credit card carbon copies. If a disreputable merchant sees you throw away your copy of the credit card charge, he'll know that he has a good chance of "bumping" (increasing) the amount of your charge, and you'll be without proof to the contrary. Depending on the handwriting, it can be easy to change a 3 to an 8 and a 1 to a 4. Thus a charge of $23 can easily be made to look like $28, or $115 can be made to look like $145. Unless you check your monthly statements carefully and have the original slips to prove the amount of your purchases, you could be out a lot of money in a hurry. Likewise, avoid giving your credit card number to strangers, such as those who might be soliciting sales over the telephone. Credit card scams make billions of dollars for the con artists. Don't let any of that money be yours.

Most issuing institutions also charge an annual fee for the use of the credit card. Interest costs on credit card usage tend to be higher than interest costs on a direct installment loan made at a bank.

Undisciplined use of credit cards and charge accounts tends to create some of the more serious financial problems confronting individuals. It's much easier to pay the minimum monthly amount than to pay off the entire month's charges. But this means that heavy interest costs are added to the debt, and those costs keep mounting over the months (and perhaps even years) while the debt is being paid off. And the ease of using credit cards—at almost any time or any place desired—compounds the problem by adding new debts to the existing debt already charged against the card. Credit cards are an inexpensive convenience when the full month's charges are immediately paid. But they can lead to what's called *plastic poverty* if only the minimum monthly amount is paid. A mountain of debt can be very difficult to pay off and can cause serious disruptions to one's overall financial status.

REPORTING OF CREDIT

The promptness with which you pay your existing debts affects your ability to borrow in the future. Your performance record is known as your *credit history*. Information that makes up your credit history is compiled by a credit bureau. Credit

	☐ SINGLE REFERENCE ☒ IN FILE REPORT ☐ TRADE REPORT
CREDIT BUREAU OF ANYTOWN 1131 MAIN ST. ANYTOWN, ANYSTATE 12345	☐ FULL REPORT ☐ EMPLOY & TRADE REPORT ☐ PREVIOUS RESIDENCE REPORT ☐ OTHER_____

FOR FIRST NATIONAL BANK ANYTOWN, ANYSTATE 12345	Date Received **4/11/86** Date Mailed **4/11/86** In File Since **APRIL 1970** Inquired As: **JOINT ACCOUNT**

CONFIDENTIAL
crediscope® REPORT

Member
Associated Credit Bureaus, Inc.

REPORT ON: LAST NAME	FIRST NAME	INITIAL	SOCIAL SECURITY NUMBER	SPOUSE'S NAME
CONSUMER	ROBERT	G.	123-45-6789	BETTY R.

ADDRESS: CITY	STATE:	ZIP CODE	SINCE:	SPOUSE'S SOCIAL SECURITY NO.
1234 ANY ST. ANYTOWN	ANYSTATE	12333	1973	987-65-4321

PRESENT EMPLOYER:	POSITION HELD:	SINCE:	DATE EMPLOY VERIFIED	EST. MONTHLY INCOME
XYZ CORPORATION	ASST. DEPT. MGR.	10/81	12/81	$ 2500

DATE OF BIRTH	NUMBER OF DEPENDENTS INCLUDING SELF:		OTHER: (EXPLAIN)
5/25/50	4	☒ OWNS OR BUYING HOME ☐ RENTS HOME	☐

FORMER ADDRESS:	CITY:	STATE:	FROM:	TO:
4321 FIRST AVE.	ANYTOWN	ANYSTATE	1970	1973

FORMER EMPLOYER:	POSITION HELD:	FROM:	TO:	EST. MONTHLY INCOME
ABC & ASSOCIATES	SALES PERSON	2/80	9/81	$ 1285

SPOUSE'S EMPLOYER:	POSITION HELD:	SINCE:	DATE EMPLOY VERIFIED	EST. MONTHLY INCOME
BIG CITY DEPT. STORE	CASHIER	4/81	12/81	$ 1200

WHOSE	KIND OF BUSINESS AND ID CODE	DATE REPORTED AND METHOD OF REPORTING	DATE OPENED	DATE OF LAST PAYMENT	HIGHEST CREDIT OR LAST CONTRACT	BALANCE OWING	PAST DUE AMOUNT	NO. OF PAYMENTS	NO. OF MONTHS HISTORY REVIEWED	30-59 DAYS ONLY	60-89 DAYS ONLY	90 DAYS AND OVER	TYPE & TERMS (MANNER OF PAYMENT)	REMARKS
2	CONSUMER'S BANK B 12-345 2/6/86 AUTOMTD.		12/85	1/86	1200	1100	-0-	-0-	2	-0-	-0-	-0-	INSTALLMENT $100/MO.	
3	BIG CITY DEPT. STORE D 54-321 2/10/86 MANUAL		4/81	1/86	300	100	-0-	-0-	12	-0-	-0-	-0-	REVOLVING $ 25/MO.	
1	SUPER CREDIT CARD N 01-234 12/12/85 AUTOMATD.		7/82	11/85	200	100	100	1	12	1	-0-	-0-	OPEN 30-DAY	

PUBLIC RECORD: SMALL CLAIMS CT. CASE #SC1001 PLAINTIFF: ANYWHERE APPLIANCES
AMOUNT $225 PAID 4/4/82
ADDITIONAL INFORMATION: REF. SMALL CLAIMS CT. CASE #SC1001--5/30/82 SUBJECT SAYS CLAIM PAID
UNDER PROTEST. APPLIANCE DID NOT OPERATE PROPERLY.

Figure 14-1 Sample Credit Bureau Report.

bureaus exist in every community for the purpose of gathering information on the credit performance of individuals in that community. (See the discussion in Chapter 13 on the Fair Credit Reporting Law. This federal law controls what credit bureaus can and cannot do and what your rights are with respect to your credit history.)

Figure 14-1 illustrates a typical credit report issued by a credit bureau belonging to the Associated Credit Bureaus, Inc., a national trade association. The form is self-explanatory. Note, however, that in the bottom half of the form, under the heading of Credit History, the numbers in the far left column are explained as follows: (1) indicates the account is the sole responsibility of this individual; (2) indicates that it is a joint account with the spouse contractually liable; (3) indicates that the spouse is an authorized user of this account.

COST OF CREDIT

The fee you pay for the use of someone else's money is called interest. Interest rates are expressed as a percentage of the amount borrowed and for a given period of time.

Fixed-Rate Interest

Simple Interest. If you were borrowing $1000 for one year and the interest rate was 10 percent per year, you would pay a fee of $100 (10 percent of $1000) for the use of the money for a period of one year. If you were borrowing $1000 and the interest rate was expressed as 1 percent per month, you would pay a fee of $10 per month (1 percent of $1000 equals $10), a total over the year of $120 in interest. In these examples, you would have the use of the entire $1000 for the full period, be it one year or one month. This calculation is what is commonly known as *simple interest.*

Loans calculated on a simple-interest basis are loans that are generally repayable in one lump sum at a specific time, such as 30, 60, 90, or 120 days hence. Or the loan may be repayable on the demand of the lender. Businesses generally borrow on a simple-interest basis, and some individuals may also be able to borrow on that basis. (The expression *prime rate* refers to the simple interest rate that banks charge their most credit-worthy borrowers. Prime rate loans in theory are the safest and lowest risk loans that lenders make. Thus, the prime rate is the lowest interest rate that a lender offers. Borrowers who do not have the financial strength and credit-worthiness of prime rate borrowers pay a higher rate of interest. As the prime rate moves up and down, as it tends to do regularly, other interest rates usually follow.)

Of more concern to the average individual is the mode of calculating interest on installment and open-end credit. Installment loans are those that are repayable in equal monthly installments; open-end credit refers to debts generated through charge accounts, credit card accounts, and checking account overdraft accounts. In an open-end account, you are billed for a minimum monthly payment, based on the total amount of the current balance you owe.

308 · CREDIT AND BORROWING

Add-on Interest. Probably the most common way of calculating interest in an installment loan is the add-on method. Here's how it works: You want to borrow $1000 for twelve months, and the rate is 6 percent add-on per year. Your rental fee for the use of the bank's money is 6 percent of $1000 or $60. The lender then adds the $60 to the $1000 worth of principal, making a total of $1060.

The total of $1060 is divided by twelve, giving you twelve equal monthly payments of $88.33 each. Thus, with the add-on loan, you receive the $1000 in cash, and over the course of one year you repay $1060. It sounds like simple interest, but it is really quite different. In the simple interest loan, you have the use of the full $1000 for the full one year. Under the installment method, such as add-on, you have the use of the full $1000 only during the first month of the loan, at the end of which you make your first payment. During the second month, therefore, you have the use of only eleven-twelfths of the money and of proportionately less each month until the final month, when you have the use of only one-twelfth of the money. In effect, then, you are paying $60 rental but you don't have the use of all the money all the time as you would in the simple interest loan. However, you do have the use of whatever it is you obtained with the money you borrowed—a car, an appliance, or whatever.

What if the loan is for more than one year? In the add-on method, the interest rate would be multiplied by the number of years. For example, if you are borrowing $1000 for two years at a 6 percent per-year add-on rate, your total interest obligation would be $120 over the full two-year period: 6 percent ($60) per year times two years equals $120.

Discount Interest. Another way of figuring interest on installment loans is the discount method. Let's use the same example as above: a $1000 loan for 12 months at a 6 percent discount per-year rate. Working from a prefigured chart, the lender notes that 6 percent of $1064 equals $63.84. Let's round this off to $64 for ease in figuring. A promissory note is signed for $1064, and the lender discounts or subtracts the interest, leaving you with $1000 in cash. The $1064 is divided by twelve, giving you twelve equal monthly payments of $88.66. You receive $1000. You repay $1064. Comparing the discount with the add-on method, you can see that the discount results in a slightly higher cost to the borrower and a slightly higher return to the lender. In other words, in the examples above, the 6 percent discount method will cost the borrower $4 more per year than the 6 percent add-on method.

Annual Percentage Rate. If you were shopping for a loan, and one lender quotes you a 10 percent add-on rate, another quotes you a 10 percent discount rate, and still a third quotes you a 10 percent simple interest rate, you'd be very confused. But, thanks to a federal law, the Truth in Lending Law, the confusion is removed. Under the Truth in Lending Law, lenders and grantors of credit may *calculate* their interest rate and other finance charges in any way they want (within the limitations of the state's usury laws). But no matter how the rates are calculated, they must be *expressed* in terms of annual percentage rate (APR). The Federal Trade Com-

Table 14-1   **Converting Add-on Rates to APR**

Term (Months)	Add-on rates (%)			
	5½	6	6½	7
12	10.00[a]	10.90	11.79	12.68
18	10.18	11.08	11.98	12.87
24	10.23	11.13	12.12	12.91
30	10.23	11.12	12.00	12.88
36	10.20	11.08	11.96	12.83
48	10.11	10.97	11.83	12.68
60	10.01	10.85	11.68	12.50

[a]Figures express APR percentages.

mission has prepared extensive tables by which any lender can convert add-on or discount rates to APR terms. Table 14-1 shows the conversion of add-on rates for common installment loans to APR, based on the FTC tables.

For example, a 6 percent per-year add-on rate for a twenty-four-month loan is equal to an APR of 11.13. A 6 percent per-year add-on rate for thirty-six-month loan is equal to an APR of 11.08.

Under the Truth in Lending Law all lenders are required to quote their rates only in terms of APR, even though many of them may still calculate their rates on an add-on or discount basis.

Variable Interest Rate

Most installment loans are written at a fixed rate of interest. If you sign up for a three-year loan at 14 percent APR, the interest rate will not fluctuate for the full three years of the loan.

When variable-rate mortgage loans for home financing became more commonplace in the early 1980s, some lenders announced plans to offer variable-rate installment loans, such as for car purchases, home improvements, and the like. In such cases, the interest rate could vary or ''float'' up and down during the life of the loan. With a floating- or variable-rate installment loan, it would be impossible to know your total interest expense at the time you obtained the loan. It could be more costly than a fixed-rate loan or less costly. You wouldn't know until the end of the term.

Since the life of most installment loans is relatively short (three to five years or less), it's not likely that the floating-rate installment loan will become as common as the variable-rate mortgage loan. But you should be aware of it. For purposes of this chapter, we'll discuss only the fixed-rate loans for which your true cost of credit can be known in advance.

Interest on Open-End Credit

In the typical installment loan, the borrower receives a lump sum of money and pays it back in equal installments. In open-end credit, this is not necessarily the case. If, for example, you have a credit card account and you have not paid all of your charges, you will be carrying an open-end loan. *Open-end* means, in effect, that you can, at will, add to that debt by making additional charges or diminish it by making payments. Because the total balance you owe at any given time can fluctuate almost daily, the APR is normally calculated on the average balance owed throughout the monthly billing period. The APR rate is expressed on the billing statement each month as required by the Truth in Lending Law.

Computing Cost of Credit

The APR gives us the means of comparing true interest rates on various loan quotations. The actual dollar cost of any loan is set forth in the disclosure statement provided to you by the lender. (See Figure 13-7 for a sample disclosure statement.) There can be other financing costs included on the disclosure statement, so for your best protection in comparing loan costs, the complete tally of all the costs involved in any given quotation should be expressed in dollar amounts on the disclosure statement. Use this as your ultimate comparison.

Additional Financing Costs

Many lenders may offer or suggest that the borrower obtain credit insurance as a part of the installment loan transaction. There are two common types of credit insurance: life and health. Credit life insurance will pay off any remaining balance on the loan should the borrower die before the loan is paid off. The borrower's survivors need not, therefore, pay the remaining balance on the loan.

Health insurance guarantees that payments are made in the event the borrower becomes disabled for an extended period of time due to poor health or an accident. Credit health policies may differ from lender to lender regarding the initial waiting period involved before the insurance takes effect. In other words, if the waiting period is fifteen days, you must be disabled for more than fifteen days before the insurance will take effect. Thus if you are disabled for, say, twenty-five days altogether, the insurance will protect you for ten days out of that month. They will, in effect, make roughly one-third of your monthly payment for you.

If your loan does include charges for life or health insurance, the lender, in effect, is lending you the amount of the premium for that insurance in advance.

Deducting Consumer Credit. Prior to 1987, virtually all of the interest that you paid on all of these types of loans could have been deductible on your tax return if you itemized your deductions. The Tax Reform Act of 1986 eliminates the deductibility of consumer interest. Therefore, the cost of borrowing money is greater than it previously was, owing to the loss of this deduction. The deduction did not cease all at once, however. It is being phased out gradually. For tax year 1988, you can deduct 40 percent of your consumer interest expense. For tax year 1989, you can deduct 20 percent of your consumer interest expense. For tax year 1990, 10 percent of your consumer interest expense can be deducted. From 1991 onward, there is no deduction allowed for consumer interest expense unless Congress changes its mind.

Consumer debt generally refers to non–housing-related loans such as car loans, credit card debts, charge accounts, student loans, personal loans, and the like. If you are a homeowner, it may be possible to deduct home improvement loans, tuition loans, and loans for certain medical expenses by including these borrowings in an overall home loan. See your home loan lender and your tax advisor for details.

EARLY REPAYMENT OF LOAN

Loan officers frequently have to resolve a perplexing dispute that arises when customers wish to pay off their installment loans ahead of schedule. Here's a typical situation. Charlie had borrowed $5000 for a thirty-six-month term. The interest cost for the three years was $900, which, when added to the $5000, gave Charlie a total debt of $5900 and monthly payments of $164. Eighteen months have elapsed, and Charlie has accumulated some unexpected funds and wishes to use them to pay off his installment loan. Against the original debt of $5900, Charlie has, during these first eighteen months, made payments totaling $2952, reducing his debt to $2948.

Charlie then figures that since he's halfway through the loan, he should pay half of the interest that he originally committed to, or $450. Subtracting the $450 from the $2948, Charlie calculates that he owes the bank $2498 to wipe the loan off the books. But the bank figures differently. They figure that Charlie is entitled to get back only 25.7 percent of the original $900, or $231. In other words, of the $900 Charlie was originally committed to pay, the bank is charging him 74.3 percent of that amount, or $669. In effect, then, $231 of his original interest commitment would be "rebated" to him. This would make his payoff figure $2717. Charlie is enraged to learn that he owes the bank $219 more than he had expected to. What happened to that $219? The Rule of 78s happened.

Rule of 78s

It was noted earlier that in typical installment loans borrowers have the use of the full original amount borrowed only during the first month of the loan. Then, as they make periodic payments, they have the use of progressively less and less of the original amount of the loan. This is the basis for the so-called Rule of 78s, which determines how each month's payment is broken down into interest and principal.

In installment loans, borrowers commit themselves to pay a certain amount of interest over the term of the loan. If they pay off the full balance of the loan before the full term elapses, borrowers are entitled to get back a portion of their interest cost, plus a portion of any other rebatable charges such as insurance. But borrowers do not get back an amount directly proportional to the amount of time the loan has run. In Charlie's case, he has a thirty-six-month loan, and he pays it off at the end of eighteen months. His interest rebate does not equal one-half of the original amount of interest, even though one-half of the loan has elapsed.

Here's another example of the rule of 78s in action. On a twelve-month loan, Sue has the use of all the money during the first month. She then makes her first payment. During the second month she has the use of only 11/12 of the money. For the third month it becomes 10/12. And so on until the last month when she has the use of only 1/12 of the money.

Because Sue has the use of more money in the earlier months, she has to pay proportionately more for it. Actually, the borrower has the use of twelve times more money in the first month than in the last month.

In the Rule of 78s, the sum of the number of months in a twelve-month loan equals 78 (1 + 2 + 3 + 4 . . . to 12 = 78). During the first month of a twelve-month loan, you're charged with 12/78 of the total interest. During the second month of a twelve-month loan you're charged with an additional 11/78 of the total interest. During the third month of a twelve-month loan, you're charged with an additional 10/78 of the total interest. The last month you are charged with 1/78. The total of the twelve fractions is 78/78 or 100 percent of the total interest.

If, therefore, you paid off a twelve-month loan at the end of six months, you'd be charged for 57/78 of the total interest owed (12 + 11 + 10 + 9 + 8 + 7 = 57). Your rebate would be the remaining 21/78, or about 27 percent of the original interest charged to you. If the original interest had been $60, you'd thus be rebated about $16.

For loans of other than twelve months' duration, the key number becomes the sum total of the number of months. For example, in a twenty-four-month loan, the sum of the numbers 1 through 24 equals 300. During the first month of such a loan, you are charged for 24/300 of the total interest. During the second month, you're charged for 23/300 of the total of the interest. And so it would go throughout the term of the loan. Table 14-2 converts all of these fractions into percentages to enable you to calculate the rebate on loans ranging from twelve to thirty-six months at six-month intervals.

For loans set to run for other terms than those shown in the table, your banker can give you a precise rebate breakdown. A good working knowledge of installment loans and how rebates are figured can be most important in determining when, how, and why you should consolidate loans, refinance them, or pay them off. Here's how you can figure the rebates on any loans included in the table.

1. Determine the total interest you have been charged for the loan.

2. Decide at what point you want to figure the rebate, for instance, after nine months of a twenty-four-month loan. Locate the factor on Table 14-2 for a loan

Table 14-2 Rebate Schedule from the Rule of 78s (Showing Percentage of Finance Charge to Be Rebated)

No. of months loan has run	Original term of loan				
	12 months	*18 months*	*24 months*	*30 months*	*36 months*
1	84.6	89.5	92.0	93.5	94.6
2	70.5	79.5	84.3	87.3	89.3
3	57.7	70.2	77.0	81.3	84.2
4	46.1	61.4	70.0	75.5	79.3
5	35.9	53.2	63.3	69.9	74.5
6	26.9	45.6	57.0	64.5	69.8
7	19.2	38.6	51.0	59.3	65.3
8	12.8	32.2	45.3	54.4	61.0
9	7.7	26.3	40.0	49.7	56.8
10	3.8	21.0	35.0	45.2	52.7
11	1.3	16.4	30.3	40.9	48.8
12	–0–	12.3	26.0	36.8	45.0
13		8.8	22.0	32.9	41.4
14		5.8	18.3	29.2	38.0
15		3.5	15.0	25.8	34.7
16		1.7	12.0	22.6	31.5
17		0.58	9.3	19.6	28.5
18		–0–	7.0	16.8	25.7
19			5.0	14.2	23.0
20			3.3	11.8	20.4
21			2.0	9.7	18.0
22			1.0	7.7	15.8
23			0.33	6.0	13.7
24			–0–	4.5	11.7
25				3.2	9.9
26				2.1	8.3
27				1.3	6.8
28				0.65	5.4
29				0.22	4.2
30				–0–	3.1
31					2.2
32					1.5
33					0.90
34					0.45
35					0.15
36					–0–

that has run nine months. Find where the nine-month row meets the column under the heading 24 Months. That factor is 40 percent, which is the percentage of your interest charge that you will get back or that will be credited to you if you pay off a twenty-four-month loan after nine months have run.

3. Multiply your original interest cost by the rebate percentage to get the actual dollars to be rebated.

4. From your original total debt, subtract the amount of payments made so far. Then subtract the dollar amount of your rebate. The final total is your payoff figure.

Let's look at another example using this formula. You had originally borrowed $2000 repayable in thirty months. The interest cost was $250, making your total debt $2250. Monthly payments are $75. You want to pay off the balance due after nine months. What will your rebate and your payoff amounts be? (The rebate schedule is the same for all interest rates.)

1. The percent of your total original interest that will be rebated to you is 49.7 percent. (See Table 14-2 where the column headed 30 Months (original term of loan) meets the nine-month row (number of months loan has run).

2. Your rebate is $124.25 (49.7 percent of $250).

3. Your payoff figure is $1450.75. From the original total debt of $2250, you subtract $675, representing the nine payments you made at $75 each. From this sum you further subtract the $124.25, that is, your rebate. In other words, your payoff figure is your *original debt* less *payments made to date* less *rebate due you*.

Other rebatable charges, such as insurance premiums, are figured on the same basis. Thus, if you had a life-insurance premium charge on the above loan of $30, you would receive a rebate of that charge of $14.91 (49.7 percent of $30).

Does it make sense to pay off an installment loan early? In the example, above, you presumably found yourself with a windfall of $1450. Even though the loan was only 30 percent paid off (nine months out of thirty), more than half the total interest has been used up. If you use the $1450 to pay off the loan, you'll save about $125, representing the remaining interest you're obliged to pay. If, though, you put that $1450 into a savings account, it will earn roughly $150 over the next twenty-four months.

On the other hand, if you pay off the loan early and put the $75 per month into a savings account—instead of paying it on the loan—you'll build up a comparable nest egg at the end of twenty-one months. Much of the decision depends on your individual human nature. It might be easier to put away the lump sum in a savings account and thus realize a sizable nest egg at the end of the period than to deposit $75 each month into the savings account.

REFINANCING AN INSTALLMENT LOAN

Having the money to pay off an installment loan is a pleasant dilemma rarely faced. Much more frequent is the desire to refinance the loan, perhaps to reduce the monthly payments. The Rule of 78s applies in this situation just as it would in an early payoff. Following the example above, you might wish to refinance the original $2000 loan after nine of the thirty months had elapsed. As the formula indicates, you would have a balance of $1450. Assume that you wished to refinance this balance for a new thirty-six-month term at an 11.08 APR (6 percent add-on). You would have to pay an additional $261 in interest for the new loan. The $261 added to the $1450 remaining payoff figure gives a new debt of $1711 and monthly payments (interest and principal) of $47.53. You thus reduce your monthly payments by almost $30, but in so doing you incur added interest expense and an ongoing debt for fifteen additional months. Whether it's wise to do this would depend on personal circumstances, and refinancing of a debt in such a manner should be done only after consulting a loan officer. To extend the debt could create a bottleneck years down the road when other credit needs arise.

INCREASING AN INSTALLMENT LOAN

As with refinancing, individuals will frequently want to add a new sum of money to their credit line. For example, in the situation above assume that you wish to acquire another $1000. You do not wish to take out a separate new loan but want to add the $1000 to your existing installment loan to run for a period of thirty-six months. Your payoff balance on the original loan is $1450. To this the lender adds the $1000 new money and then must add on the interest. Assuming an 11.08 APR (6 percent add-on), the additional interest would be $441. This would give you a total debt of $2891 with monthly payments of $80.30. For roughly $5 more than you are now paying each month, you have another $1000 cash in hand. But, as with the refinancing, the payment schedule has stretched out for an additional thirty-six months—fifteen months longer than you were otherwise obliged to make payments. And, as with refinancing, adding on to debt in this manner should be done only after adequate consultation.

SHOPPING FOR LOANS

Rate of Interest

A slight difference in the interest rate on an installment loan can have a considerable impact on the overall cost for the term of the loan. Table 14-3 illustrates the effect of varying interest rates on a sampling of different loans.

Table 14-3 **Comparing Interest Costs**

Loan size/length[a]	APR (%)	Add-on (%)	Total interest	Total to be repaid	Monthly payments
$1000/12	10.00	5½	$55	$1055	$87.92
	10.90	6	60	1060	88.33
	11.79	6½	65	1065	88.75
	12.68	7	70	1070	89.33
$2000/24	10.23	5½	$220	$2220	$92.50
	11.13	6	240	2240	93.33
	12.12	6½	260	2260	94.16
	12.91	7	280	2280	95.00
$3000/36	10.20	5½	$495	$3495	$97.08
	11.08	6	540	3540	98.33
	11.96	6½	585	3585	99.58
	12.83	7	630	3630	100.83

[a]Figures for length are in months.

Size of Down Payment

To the extent that you borrow to buy anything, the cost of borrowing can add as much as 10 to 30 percent to the cost of the item. The less you can borrow, the less interest you'll be paying and the lower your monthly payment and overall obligation.

The question may arise: It is better to finance the whole amount of a purchase and put the available down payment dollars into a savings account where it can earn interest? Generally, when you're starting from scratch with an installment loan, before the Rule of 78s comes into play, you probably wouldn't do as well in going for the larger financing. Because a savings account pays less than what you must pay a lender for a loan, you'd probably be better off applying your available cash toward the purchase price and reducing the amount of the loan accordingly.

Table 14-4 illustrates the dollar effect of varying down payments on a specific loan.

Length of Term

The amount of time or term of an installment loan can affect overall costs considerably. The longer the term, the lower the monthly payments and the higher the interest costs. Do the lower payments make up for the higher interest costs? Table 14-5 illustrates the effect of different terms on loans of varying sizes.

Table 14-4 **Effect of Down Payment on Loan Costs on a $3000 Purchase: 11.08% APR (6% Add-on) 36-Month Loan**

Down payment	Amount of loan	Total interest cost	Total to be repaid	Monthly payment
–0–	$3000	$540	$3540	$98.33
$ 300	2700	484	3184	88.44
500	2500	450	2950	81.94
800	2200	396	2596	72.11
1000	2000	360	2360	65.55
1200	1800	326	2126	59.05
1500	1500	270	1770	49.16

There are other basic guidelines helpful in determining how long an installment loan should run. Generally speaking, the life of the loan should not exceed the expected life use of the product or service for which you're borrowing. Also, when one borrows for a recurring need, the loan should be paid off before the need occurs again. Examples of recurring loans include those for the payment of taxes, vacations, winter expenses, or automobiles.

Table 14-5 **The Effect of Different Terms on Loan Costs[a]**

Amount borrowed	Term of loan (months)	Total interest cost	Total to be repaid	Monthly payment
$1000	12	$ 60	$1060	$ 88.33
1000	18	90	1090	60.55
1000	24	120	1120	46.67
1000	30	150	1150	38.33
1000	36	180	1180	32.77
2000	12	240	2240	93.33
2000	18	300	2300	76.67
2000	24	360	2360	65.55
2000	30	420	2420	57.62
2000	36	480	2480	51.67
3000	12	360	3360	140.00
3000	18	540	3540	98.33
3000	24	630	3630	86.42
3000	30	720	3720	77.50
3000	36	900	3900	65.00

[a]All loans are calculated at 6% add-on per year; APR varies according to length of loan.

For example, say you borrow $600 on June 1 for a summer vacation. With a twelve-month loan, you'll be all paid up by the next summer. But with an eighteen-month loan, you'll be paying for this year's vacation well into next fall. If you were to borrow again in June of next year for that year's vacation, you'd have a few hundred dollars of this year's loan still unpaid if you had taken the eighteen-month plan. If you then combined the remaining old balance and the new loan for yet another eighteen-month loan, you could still be paying for part of this year's vacation three years from now. This is an example of "pyramiding," and it can be a dangerous practice.

Car loans should be geared to the time you expect to retain the car. If you trade every two years, for example, your loan should be paid off within that period. Running the loan longer than the life of the car makes the borrower prone to the risk of pyramiding.

Major household items, such as large appliances, might not need replacing for a decade or more. But they should not be financed for as long as they will last. These debts should be eliminated as quickly as your budget will allow in order to make room for other borrowing needs and to keep your interest expenses down. Most lenders won't exceed a few years for such loans anyway, but avoid the temptation of becoming involved in longer plans that might allow for lower monthly payments. The interest cost will be that much higher, and you could still be paying off a loan when you'd rather have that credit capacity available for some other purpose.

One-shot loans, such as those for special events (weddings, special trips, etc.), and other nonrecurring personal needs should also be paid up as quickly as your budget will allow. The needs won't recur, but taking such a loan for too long can clutter up your future borrowing capacity and have you paying more interest than may be wise.

Home improvements, particularly major additions such as patios, pool, extra rooms, and so on, can get a bit tricky. These items can easily run into many thousands of dollars, and common installment financing plans run to five years, occasionally longer. For the most part, these improvements become a part of the house—you won't take them with you when you move. You may recapture all or a better part of the cost when you sell the house.

When these improvements are integral to the house, you might find it better to add the cost to your mortgage if you can. Check with your mortgage lender to evaluate cost and feasibility. For example, a $4000 home improvement loan for five years could entail monthly payments of roughly $83. If you added that same amount to a mortgage that had twenty years left to run, the monthly payments would be about $35. If you expect to be selling the house within about ten years or less, it could be better to add the home improvement costs to your mortgage.

Dos and Don'ts of Shopping for a Loan

The following list of dos and don'ts can help you communicate more effectively with your lender and will help get your loan application processed more efficiently.

1. Do all of your shopping and homework beforehand. Whenever possible, know exactly what you're going to borrow for, how the money will be used, and what the total needs will be.

2. Do make sure all your other credit accounts are up to date before you apply for credit. If necessary, check with each creditor and with your local credit bureau. The federal Fair Credit Reporting Law permits you to see your credit file (there may be a modest fee involved), and it's wise to review your file every few years to make certain it contains no erroneous items. If there are errors, the law stipulates how they can be corrected. If you have credit accounts that are not up to date, it would be wise to update them before you make your application. A credit history showing late accounts may not kill your chances of getting a loan, but it could well cause delays.

3. Do get an idea of the rates charged by various lenders. This can be done quickly, discreetly, and anonymously. Be certain that any quotes you receive are expressed in terms of APR (annual percentage rate). Determine what the total dollar charges are for interest and any other fees the lender may impose.

   In comparing interest rates, remember that the interest rate isn't the only item you're shopping for. You might be able to obtain a more attractive interest rate if you make a larger down payment on the purchase in question, and you may have to inquire whether this is possible. You also might get a more attractive interest rate if you are a customer of the institution in other departments. Service and convenience must also be considered.

4. Do prepare a list of all your other debts, including the name of each creditor, purpose of the loan, original amount borrowed, current amount owed, and the monthly payment. This will make the loan officer's job much easier and your application simpler to process. Divulge all pertinent credit information, even if you think it may not look good. The lender will probably discover it anyway, and if you haven't mentioned difficult accounts, the lender is liable to wonder why. Also, when you've compiled the list of all your debts and payments, double-check that this new debt you're seeking can be properly taken care of within your current and future budget.

5. Do inquire in advance whether the lender has any specific requirements or taboos. Some lenders have strict requirements regarding the borrower's years on the job, period of residence in the community, and minimum down payment for specific purchases.

6. Do be sure to tell the loan officer clearly and specifically just what the money is for. The more concise you are, the more the officer will be able to advise you if it appears you might be going overboard on a certain debt, since loan officers listen to dozens of requests each day.

7. Do make sure your requested time for loan repayment does not exceed the use period of whatever you're borrowing for. If you let the lender know you've considered this, it will demonstrate your prudence and could enhance your application and relationship with the lender.

8. Do be prepared to discuss your budget in detail. The loan officer wants assurance that there will be money available to pay off the loan, and if she doesn't see room in your current budget for the repayment, your request might be declined—and perhaps wisely so. If you plan to trim other expenses to make room for this debt or if you are anticipating a higher income in the future, discuss these factors with the loan officer.

9. Do bring your spouse, if you have one, to complete the application and sign all the necessary papers. Granted, under the federal Equal Credit Opportunity Law it may no longer be necessary for both spouses to sign credit agreements. Although one signature may satisfy many banks, traditional prudence still dictates that debt is a family obligation—morally if not legally—and that both partners should have a full and complete understanding of their involvements.

10. Do seek the loan officer's specific advice on related financial matters. It's part of the loan officer's job, and she might be able to discover and solve other money problems in ways you aren't aware of.

11. Don't try to get a better interest rate by telling a loan officer that you can do better elsewhere. Chances are you'll be told to go ahead and do so. And if you can do better elsewhere, you might as well. It doesn't hurt to ask if rates are flexible, but petty bickering will very likely gain nothing and may well lose a potential ally—the loan officer.

12. Don't caution the loan officer not to check a certain credit reference. If there is a problem or a dispute with one of your other creditors, clear it up in advance. If you raise suspicions in the loan officer's mind, she will undoubtedly take steps to find out what it's all about.

13. Don't act as if you're doing the lender a favor by asking for a loan. And don't make it appear that the lender is doing you one by making you a loan. This is a business deal and should be treated as such by both sides.

14. Don't be disturbed if the loan officer asks you to do your other business such as your savings or checking account, with her institution. This is part of the job. Very often, a loan applicant may be upset by such suggestions, and this can destroy an otherwise good relationship. A simple "I'll be happy to consider it" should suffice if you don't want to change at the moment.

15. Don't fret if the loan officer starts "selling" life or health insurance for your loan. It's very common, and the cost is not unreasonable. If, after you understand the program, you still don't want it, merely decline politely. The loan officer should know that a "hard sell" is not becoming, nor is it liable to win friends or influence people.

16. Don't expect the loan officer to tell you whether your intentions regarding your borrowing are wise. If you aren't sure of the wisdom of your loan, maybe you shouldn't be asking for it.

17. Don't be surprised, however, if the loan officer does volunteer to question your wisdom. You may be absolutely certain in your own mind, but you may have overlooked something. The loan officer is in the business of evaluating personal

financial decisions, and her professional knowledge might enable her to correct or amplify your thinking. The officer might be able to suggest other alternatives, some of which might provide a better solution than the one you're seeking.

18. Don't wait until the last minute to apply for a loan. Anticipate your needs far enough in advance to take care of all the details. If other matters hinge on whether you get the loan, keep the other parties informed of your progress. Careful and thoughtful planning in this regard can prevent serious problems.

19. Don't demand an answer to your application within a certain time. You have a right to have your papers processed promptly, assuming that everything is in order. The lender will make every effort to do so. But delays, such as receiving an incomplete report from the credit bureau, can happen.

    Often, too, an application may have to be considered by the loan committee. The loan officer isn't "passing the buck" when she refers an application to the loan committee. Your request may be for more than she has authority to approve, or she may just want to get other opinions on a puzzling point in the application. The committee can often be very helpful simply by giving the borrower the benefit of all its best collective thinking.

    When you make your application, the officer should be able to give you a fairly good idea of how long it will take to process. Perhaps she can speed it up a bit for you if circumstances warrant. But if you give her a deadline— an "or else"—you might antagonize her.

20. Don't balk if the loan officer asks you for a co-maker or collateral to support a given loan request. She's trying to help you get your loan, but lending policies may require security. You may not want to comply, but rather than argue about it (which won't help matters), ask for an explanation.

    There is often room for compromise. A request for collateral or a co-maker doesn't necessarily mean your credit isn't good. There just might not be enough of it due to your age, job tenure, and so on. Remember, the loan officer doesn't have to ask you for the extra security. She can turn you down flat, but may not want to. It doesn't hurt to inquire if the request for collateral or a co-signer can be altered, so that the co-signer is obliged for only a part of the loan, or the loan is only partly collateralized.

CREDIT ABUSES

Pyramiding

As noted earlier, pyramiding occurs when a loan for a recurring purpose has not been paid off by the time the purpose recurs. Let's look at a specific example.

Otto has been in the habit of trading his cars every three years. He's always taken three-year car loans, so that the loan has been paid off each time he buys a new car. This year a fancy new model catches his eye, and he's determined to buy it. He'll need $5000 over and above his trade-in on his old car, but he can only afford payments of roughly $130 per month. His banker tells him that the interest

Table 14-6 **Effects of Installment Loan Pyramiding**

48-month loans	Amount borrowed	Interest cost	Total debt	Monthly payments	Payoff after 36 months
Otto's first loan	$5,000	$1,200	$ 6,200	$129	$1,477
Second loan, 36 months later	7,477	1,795	9,272	193	2,206
Status after six years	9,206	2,945	12,152	253	2,850

on a three-year loan for $5000 would be $900, making the total debt $5900, and the monthly payments approximately $164. The dealer tells Otto that they can arrange financing for a four-year term and that the payments would only be $129 per month. (The interest would be $1200, making the total debt $6200.) (See Table 14-6.)

Otto prudently realizes that if he's financing the car for four years he should keep the car for that time. Even though this is contrary to his habit, he vows he will do this.

Three years later Otto has dutifully made thirty-six monthly payments of $129 each, reducing his original balance from $6200 to $1477, taking into account the interest rebate he would receive if he paid off the loan at this time (see first row of Table 14-6). An advertisement lures Otto into the automobile dealer's showroom, where he promptly falls in love with yet another brand-new model car. He realizes he shouldn't trade for at least another year, when the existing loan is paid off, but habit and desire get the best of him. Naturally, inflation has boosted the price of the cars; in order to buy the new model, Otto needs $6000 over and above his trade-in. The $6000 is added to the balance on his previous loan, meaning that Otto will have to borrow $7477. In order to afford the monthly payments, he'll have to go for another four-year loan, which means an added interest burden of $1795. This brings the total new debt to $9272, to be paid in forty-eight monthly payments of $193 each (see second row of Table 14-6).

Three years later Otto has made his payments of $193 for thirty-six months, reducing his payoff balance on this loan to $2206 (again taking into account the interest rebate he would receive). Once again, the lure of a new car is too much for Otto to resist. Now, in order to pay off his old balance and come up with the $7000 he'll need for the new model, he has to incur a total debt of $12,152, which includes new interest of $2945. Again, he goes for the four-year loan, which will mean payments of $253 per month (see third row of Table 14-6).

Otto has fallen into a classic case of pyramiding. Nine years after the initial mistake, he still owes a debt of $2850. His total interest expense over this time period has been almost $6000. Had he stayed with three-year loans in the first place, his total interest expense would have been closer to $4000—a difference of $2000 out of his pocket. And he still owes $2850.

The pyramiding trap is equally as dangerous, if not more so, regarding credit cards and charge accounts. For example, an individual runs up $50 in gasoline bills for her car during a month. She charges them on a credit card. At the end of the month the bill comes in and rather than pay the full $50, which isn't necessary if she chooses to let the credit line run, she decides to send in only the minimum payment, say $10.

The same thing happens the next month: $50 worth of gas bills and a $10 payment. And so on throughout the year. Unless the individual comes to her senses, she could be paying for her January gas in December and even well into the following year. The interest costs continue to mount, adding between 15 and 25 percent per year to the cost of the goods so purchased.

The simple way to avoid pyramiding is to remember that an installment loan or an open-end credit account should be eliminated before the need to borrow for the same purpose occurs again.

Ballooning

Which is more appealing: a twelve-month loan for $1000 with monthly payments of $88.33 or the same loan with monthly payments of only $60? The temptation is to take the loan with the smaller monthly payments, but obviously there's a catch. With the smaller monthly payments there will be one very large payment at the end of the loan, for the loan is to run for only twelve months. In this particular case, after making payments for eleven months at $60 each, the borrower will still owe roughly $400 in the twelfth month. This is what's known as a *balloon payment*, and it can be dangerous. If the borrower isn't equipped to meet the large payment, it may be necessary to refinance that payment and incur additional interest costs. Although the Truth in Lending Law requires lenders to disclose the annual percentage rate and the total costs involved in making the loan, there may not be adequate disclosure regarding the size of the monthly payments. Borrowers should make certain that know they whether there are balloon payments at the end of their loans. Unless there are compelling circumstances for a balloon-payment program, prudence generally dictates sticking to the typical repayment budget with equal monthly payments.

Oversecuring

If you were borrowing $1000 to pay for your summer vacation, it would not seem wise to have to put up your car, your house, your bank account, and all of your other assets as security for that loan. Reputable lenders would certainly not require such collateral. But it can happen that some lenders may seek more security than reasonable for certain loans. This security may include a general assignment of your wages and your personal property. If a borrower does pledge these assets to obtain a loan, the legal aspect is that the lender can take action to recover these assets should the loan become delinquent. The individual borrower must determine when collateral is required for a loan and if the collateral is reasonable, proper, and not excessive. If it is excessive, the borrower is putting assets in jeopardy,

---

Strategies for Success

Credit Repair Clinics Can Be Costly Mistakes

You're up to your neck in debt, and the walls seem to be caving in. How can you get out of this jam? You see an ad that promises to help you get rid of your debts and restore your credit to A-1 condition. All they want is an up-front fee of $300, $500, or whatever amount they think they can get from you. They tell you that you should send them the amount of your monthly payments and that they'll parcel it out to your creditors, putting you back on good footing with all of them. You go along with them, and within a month your creditors are hounding you again. Didn't the credit repair clinic pay your creditors the money you gave them? You call the clinic. The operator tells you that that number is no longer in service. Is your money gone for good? Probably. Only some of these outfits operate this way. Be on guard for other, more subtle ways they can separate you from your money. You're most susceptible when you're having credit panic attacks.

---

which could create severe future problems. The borrower should determine exactly what collateral is being given to the lender. If more is being required than seems necessary, the borrower would do well to shop around at other institutions.

Borrowing from Loan Sharks

Despite all the consumer-protection laws and publicized warnings, there will always be loan sharks as long as there are people willing to pay exorbitant fees for borrowed funds. Loan sharks operate outside the limits of the law. Their interest rates are generally far above what the state usury laws allow, and their collection techniques have been well publicized. If anyone becomes involved with a loan shark, he can expect to bear what could be severe consequences. Before entering into such a situation, an individual should consult a banker or attorney to determine the legal methods that may alleviate his debt problems.

Consolidating Loans

The appeal is almost irresistible: "Why suffer along with all those big monthly payments when you can consolidate all your debts into one loan with a much smaller monthly payment?" If a family or an individual has accumulated too much debt, loan consolidation seems a logical and convenient way out of the crisis. It's a line of least resistance too often taken by borrowers not aware of the potential pitfalls. Poorly planned or impulsively embarked on, a consolidation loan can cause more ultimate troubles than the original loans did. Sound, prudent planning might provide other, more suitable alternatives. By using the following example of a loan consolidation program and consulting the interest finders and rebate formulas, you can plan any consolidation and judge its value.

Charlie and Charlotte have the following loans:

1. A car loan, whose original total amount was $3540, including interest of $540. The loan has run for twenty-four months, and has twelve months to go. Monthly payments are $98.33.

2. A home improvement loan that originally totaled $2480, of which interest was $480. The loan has already run for thirty months and has eighteen months to run. The monthly payments are $51.67.

3. A personal loan, originally totaling $1090, of which interest was $90. Twelve months of the loan have already expired with six months still to run. Monthly payments are $60.55.

Table 14-7 illustrates Charlie and Charlotte's debts and how much they would need to pay them all off. Charlie and Charlotte need roughly $2330 to pay off their existing debts. At an interest rate of 11.08 APR (6 percent add-on), they can obtain a loan of that amount for three years, which would entail an added $419 in interest, giving them a total new debt of $2749. Their thirty-six monthly payments would be $76.30 each, compared with the $210.55 they're now paying.

It seems like an easy way out of what to them has become a serious jam. But is it wise? Is it worth it? If they wait just six more months, the personal loan will be all paid off, reducing their monthly payments to $150. In twelve months the car loan will be paid off, reducing their payments to $51.67. And in eighteen months the home improvement loan will be paid, eliminating their monthly payments altogether.

The consolidation loan will have cost them an additional $419 in interest and will require payments of $76.36 for thirty-six more months. During the next thirty-six months Charlie and Charlotte will in all likelihood have new reasons to acquire debt. Rather than consolidating their loans, they might be far better off in the long run if they could simply tighten their belts and continue with their current debt load. It will be lightened considerably in just six months.

Table 14-7 Loan Consolidation: Charlie and Charlotte's Debts

Loan	Current balance	Monthly payment	Months to run	"Payoff" figure now
Car	$1180	$ 98.33	12	$1117
Home improvement	930	51.67	18	860
Personal	363	60.55	6	352
Total		$210.55		$2330

If proper loan planning is done in the beginning, the need for a consolidation loan might never occur. If this need does occur, careful communications with a lending officer are necessary if a sensible consolidation plan is to be arrived at.

CURING OVERINDEBTEDNESS

As the example above indicates, Charlie and Charlotte might be candidates for a severe case of overindebtedness. The problem, if not promptly treated, can lead to serious impairment of one's credit history and can complicate—if not prevent—the ability to obtain credit for many months or possibly years. It can even force them into obtaining credit through sources that specialize in higher risk situations and charge higher interest rates accordingly.

The first symptom of overindebtedness is late payments. Not only do late payments entail late charges, which can be as much as 5 percent of the amount of the payment (the law varies from state to state), but they can also result in a bad rating on your credit history.

Borrowers who *anticipate* that they might be running into a delinquency problem should act *before* the actual delinquency occurs. Borrowers in such straits should visit *in person*, not by phone or by mail, with the creditors in question and explain the overall circumstances. It might be possible to arrange a different payment date that would be more convenient, to remake the loan on more favorable terms, or to get a temporary reduction in payments. It might even be possible to have late charges waived if your reason for delinquency is acceptable to the creditor.

If the borrower has not complied with the terms of the loan agreement, the lender may deem that the borrower is in default. In that case the lender can commence whatever legal remedies have been reserved in the loan agreement. If collateral has been pledged for the loan, the lender can take steps to recover the collateral and sell it to pay off the loan. If a co-signer is involved in the loan, the lender can look to the co-signer for payment. In some instances the lender may be able to attach or garnish the borrower's wages.

Debt-Counseling Services

In many communities, lending institutions cooperate to create a debt-counseling service to assist people in financial trouble. In many communities this is known as the Consumer Credit Counseling Agency. See your banker for more details on such services available in your community. The agency usually contacts your creditors and gets them to hold off on their collection procedures while you make an effort to reorganize your financial matters. You'll have to make a show of good faith by making some regular periodic payments. If the counselors have been successful, these payments will be smaller than what your normal payments would have been.

Be on guard against some commercial firms that offer debt-reduction services. Federal and state consumer-protection agencies have reported numerous cases of such firms charging excessively for their services. In many cases the firms simply disappear with the customers' money, and no debt reduction is accomplished.

If a debt-counseling service of good repute is not available to you or is not capable of helping you, the next step might be to visit with an attorney who can arrange for an *assignment for the benefit of creditors*. This is similar to the services offered by the debt-counseling firms in that it tries to convince creditors to accept a smaller monthly payment until the full debt is paid off.

Bankruptcy

The ultimate way out of overindebtedness is bankruptcy. If you come to this ultimate move, you should seek the aid of an attorney. Bankruptcy is a last resort for solving debt problems, and whatever the reasons for declaring it, bankruptcy can remain on your credit history for as long as ten years.

Many lenders will attempt to rehabilitate a bankrupt family or individual, particularly if the reasons for bankruptcy were beyond their control. But an ex-bankrupt can still find it difficult to obtain the kind of credit needed for his life style. Indeed, bankruptcy often requires individuals to seriously reduce the quality of their life for an extended period of time.

Bankruptcy laws are federal laws, although state laws may apply in determining the property that can be exempted from the bankruptcy proceedings. There are two basic bankruptcy proceedings for individuals: Chapter 13, otherwise known as the *wage-earner plan*, and Chapter 7, often referred to as *straight bankruptcy*.

Chapter 13. Under Chapter 13, the debtor, under the supervision of a referee and the federal bankruptcy court, works out a plan for the repayment of outstanding debts. In effect, this wage-earner plan keeps creditors from getting at your wages and your property while giving you time to work out a timely payment of outstanding debts. (A similar plan for businesses is known as Chapter 11, wherein the business attempts to reorganize its affairs to satisfy its debts while creditors are kept at bay.)

A Chapter 13 proceeding generally carries less stigma than does a Chapter 7 proceeding.

Chapter 7. Chapter 7 bankruptcy is known as *straight bankruptcy*. In this proceeding, your debts are discharged or eliminated altogether. Bankruptcy laws were revised in late 1979 to make it easier for individuals to declare Chapter 7 and to protect more of the debtor's property from the creditors' claims. Under Chapter 7 declaration, certain of the debtor's property can be exempted from creditors' claims. A debtor can choose whether to take the exemption allowed under federal law or exemptions that might be allowed under the state laws. For example, federal law allows a bankrupt couple to exempt up to $15,000 worth of equity in their home plus additional exemptions for personal property, clothing, and automobile. The Chapter 7 bankruptcy can be filed only once every six years. (A debtor can file a new Chapter 13 proceeding once completing payments based on a prior Chapter 13 proceeding.)

Sometimes personal catastrophe requires an individual to undergo a bankruptcy proceeding. Sometimes, however, it is nothing more than the undisciplined use of credit that leaves an individual with little choice but to declare bankruptcy. The public at large has little sympathy for individuals who spend their way into bankruptcy. Know before you proceed that the spectre of bankruptcy will haunt you for years to come.

Discipline

Making wise use of your ability to borrow can enhance your life. Imprudence can result in financial and emotional disaster. The lure of easy money through charge accounts, credit cards, and other "cash-in-a-flash" enticements can become addictive. Younger individuals, less experienced at the complexities of handling a budget, can more easily be trapped in the credit bind. It's at the earliest stages of using credit that a firm sense of discipline must be imposed on oneself. Only you can determine for yourself the amount of debt you're comfortably able to carry, considering your other financial needs and desires. But there is one unshakable rule that will apply to your use of credit: For every dollar you borrow (or charge), you will be adding 15¢ to 25¢ to the cost of your credit purchase. It can be difficult enough to make ends meet without adding such a heavy cost load to your already weighty burdens.

Comparing Loan Costs

It *can* pay to shop around for the best interest rate available on loans—car loans, home improvement loans, and loans for other personal or business needs. Loan sources include banks, savings and loan associations, credit unions, dealers, and some insurance companies. Employers, relatives, and friends might also be sources. This checklist will aid you in comparing the pertinent terms of most common personal loans.

Term	Lender A	Lender B	Lender C
☐ Down payment required	_____	_____	_____
☐ Monthly repayment programs available	_____	_____	_____
☐ Collateral required	_____	_____	_____
☐ Is co-signer required, and if so, when and under what circumstances? Can co-signer be released from the obligation?	_____	_____	_____
☐ Annual percentage rate (APR)	_____	_____	_____
☐ Monthly payments required	_____	_____	_____
☐ Total interest cost for life of loan	_____	_____	_____
☐ Late charges, if any	_____	_____	_____
☐ Will a better APR be offered if you maintain other accounts with the lender? (You'll probably have to ask, but it can be worth it.)	_____	_____	_____
☐ Cost of credit life insurance (if you desire it)	_____	_____	_____
☐ Cost of credit health insurance (if you desire it)	_____	_____	_____
☐ If you pay off the loan early, are rebates of interest based on the Rule of 78s or on some other formula? Ask and compare	_____	_____	_____
☐ For credit cards and charge accounts, what is the APR? Is it based on average prior monthly balance or some other formula? Ask and compare	_____	_____	_____

A Captive Audience

The furniture store advertisement made Fran and Pat very happy: "Easy Credit! No Money Down! Past Credit Problems Are No Problem For Us!"

Fran and Pat wanted to set up housekeeping, and neither of them ever having had any credit before, they feared that they wouldn't be able to buy a stick of furniture on their slender budget.

The Easy Credit store took excellent care of them, including setting up a two-year financing plan to pay for their purchases. They knew the interest rate was exceptionally high, but at least they were able to furnish their apartment as they had wanted to.

They made every payment on time for two years. Then, wanting some additional furniture, they approached a local bank seeking the money. Their hope was to get out from under the excessive interest costs that the furniture store had charged them.

They proudly gave the furniture store as a credit reference. But on checking their file at the local credit bureau, the bank could find no reference to the furniture store loan. The bank turned down Fran and Pat's request. Dejected, they felt they had no choice but to return to the original furniture store and accept their high-interest financing for their additional purchases.

But the loan officer at the bank smelled something fishy, and he did some investigation. He discovered that the furniture store made a practice of never divulging the good payment records of customers. In this way they succeeded in building a captive audience of borrowers: people who were unwary enough to seek credit elsewhere and who felt that the store and the loan company affiliated with it were their only source of borrowing.

The matter was called to the attention of the Federal Trade Commission, and their threat of investigation put a stop to this unfair, but not necessarily illegal, practice. Pat and Fran got their loan from the bank.

"Easy credit" is a myth. If it's that easy to get, it will be very hard to repay: The interest cost will be inordinately high, and collection procedures will be very harsh if payments aren't made promptly.

CHAPTER 15

Making Your Money Grow: An Overview

A question often asked of financial advisors is: "How should I put my money to work?" Astute advisors should ask the following questions: "What do you want your money to do for you? Do you want it to give you a temporary surge of excitement by putting it to work in a risky situation? Do you want it to grow steadily and safely for you over a number of years? How much risk do you want to take? How long can you leave it alone until you need it?" And so on.

Until one's investment objectives are clearly known, it's difficult to establish sensible investment (or speculative) activities. This chapter introduces you to the concepts that must be understood if you are to construct a meaningful program of making your money grow. It will give you an understanding of the following:

- ☐ How different investment opportunities can be compared
- ☐ How the growth of your money can be affected by taxes
- ☐ How to acquire specific investment information and counsel

Further, this chapter will give you a basic foundation to enable you to better understand the more specific investment techniques discussed in subsequent chapters.

TODAY DOLLARS AND TOMORROW DOLLARS

One of the most essential parts of your financial program involves putting away dollars that you don't need today so that they can be available in the future. Some of the many different ways you can go about accumulating Tomorrow Dollars will involve a relatively high degree of risk, others, a relatively low degree. Some ways might offer a relatively comfortable measure of protection against inflation, while others may grant little or none. Some ways may seem simple, others complicated; some require luck, others prudence.

The challenge is to find the right program that will enable you to accumulate the needed amount of Tomorrow Dollars safely, comfortably, and in such a manner that the accumulation program does not interfere with your ability to pursue your current needs and desires.

The relative importance of your own personal future needs and desires is a major factor in shaping what accumulation techniques you choose. In the opening of this book we discussed the importance of establishing future goals, and you were urged to set specific targets subject to the inevitable changes that will occur as you mature and as your needs and objectives change. Now let's examine the specific vehicles you can utilize to help reach your specific destinations.

Automatic Accumulating

In shaping your long-range accumulation program you must remember that some Tomorrow Dollars are being created automatically as a result of other transactions you may be making. For example, a homeowner makes monthly payments on a mortgage. A portion of these payments is applied toward interest on the debt, and a portion is applied to reducing the debt. Eventually, when the house is sold or refinanced, the portion of the payments that were applied to the debt may be recaptured in cash. This recaptured money is commonly referred to as *equity*. It's a form of automatic accumulating.

Another form of automatic accumulating can occur with life insurance. Breadwinners put away Today Dollars to be used by their survivors. In ordinary life insurance policies, the policy will also build certain values that allow the policy owner to either cash in the policy at a later date or borrow against it or convert the values into other forms of insurance. The insured is building these future values as an automatic part of paying the life insurance premium.

Deductions from our paycheck represent another form of accumulation of Tomorrow Dollars. Social security taxes are automatically deducted from the paycheck of everyone covered by the system; in many cases pension and profit-sharing contributions are also deducted. Thus, we are joining with our employers and our government to create a pool of Tomorrow Dollars. We may have little or no control over how these Tomorrow Dollars are being put to use, but we do have some reasonable assurances regarding how much will be available to us at the preestablished time when we're entitled to retrieve them.

Active Accumulating

Active accumulating of Tomorrow Dollars can take two broad forms. First, we can lend our dollars to another person or institution with the understanding that they will pay us interest for the use of our money. This type of accumulating is referred to as *fixed-income investing*, and a savings account is perhaps the most familiar form of accumulating dollars within this category.

A savings account is, in effect, a loan to a financial institution, accompanied by an agreement stating that the institution will pay us "rental" for the use of our money—interest.

We may also make "loans" to governments and corporations. A U.S. savings bond (Series EE bond) is an example of one of the many kinds of loans that we can make to the federal government. Loans made to cities and states are referred to as *municipal bonds*. Loans made to corporations are referred to as *corporate bonds*.

These forms of accumulating Tomorrow Dollars normally carry a high degree of assurance that we will get all of our money back plus the agreed interest at the agreed time. When we entrust our money, we receive a binding legal contract from the debtor that promises to pay us what we are due, regardless of whether the debtor operates efficiently or profitably. If the debtor should fail, the interest and principal due us might be in jeopardy. Although there have been remote instances of corporations and municipalities defaulting on their debts, defaults by the federal government have never happened, nor have insured accounts in federally insured banks and savings institutions ever lost money as a result of the failure of the institution.

When we lend or entrust our money to others in these forms, we're minimizing both the risk of loss and the chance of gain, and in return we're getting a fairly assured program that will take us to our appointed destination on time.

The other broad form of active accumulating of Tomorrow Dollars is buying something that we hope will generate income and also possibly increase in value while we own it. As owners, either in part or in whole, we have a stake in another entity—an equity.

We buy a portion of ownership in a company, hoping that the company will be profitable and that it will distribute a portion of its profits to its owners. We also hope that the company will prosper and that the value of our ownership interest will increase, allowing us to sell it at a profit in the future.

We may invest in real estate, hoping to operate that property so that it shows a profit and further hoping that the property will increase in value and allow us to reap a profit when we sell. Similarly, we may invest in our own business interest where, in addition to earnings and profits, we may also be able to pay ourselves a living. When we invest our money in a piece of ownership of another entity there may be many outside forces that can shape the destiny of our Tomorrow Dollars.

The distinction between lending our money to reliable debtors on the one hand and buying something with our dollars on the other hand is critical. When we lend, we have a binding legal contract that promises us the return of our money plus interest. When we buy something, we are the owners, and we have to take our chances that we can get our money back at any time we wish. What our money will earn for us as owners is also always uncertain. This distinction should always be remembered when you make any plans regarding the accumulation of Tomorrow Dollars.

INVESTMENT CRITERIA

We now examine the main criteria to evaluate when you set forth a program of accumulating Tomorrow Dollars. These criteria include safety (the reward-risk rule), liquidity, yield, pledge value, hedge value, tax implications, and investigation.

Safety: The Reward-Risk Rule

The reward-risk rule is as simple and as powerful as the law of gravity: The bigger the reward you are seeking, the higher the risk you are taking. The more conservative individual would express this rule a bit differently: The safer my money, the less return I'll have to be satisfied with. There's a third and perhaps more elemental way of expressing this rule: In planning a program of savings and investments, much depends on whether the individual would rather eat well or sleep well.

All of the various investment and speculation vehicles discussed in this chapter are explained in greater detail in subsequent chapters.

Liquidity

Liquidity refers to how quickly and conveniently you can retrieve your money and at what cost, if any. Often a price may have to be paid for liquidity. For example, in a regular savings account, you can get all of your money plus accrued interest immediately, simply by making the request in the proper fashion to the institution. But with a savings certificate—in which you have placed your money with the institution for an agreed minimum amount of time—you might have to forfeit a portion of your interest and principal if you want to get your money out right away. But generally the certificate will pay you a higher rate of interest than the regular passbook savings account.

In other words, the passbook savings account is more liquid than the savings certificate, but at a price. The passbook account offers a lower rate of return in exchange for the ability to get your cash out that much more readily.

The need for liquidity varies from portfolio to portfolio. If you're putting the money away for the long term and are confident that you won't need it for an extended period of time, you can afford to give up liquidity in favor of higher return. On the other hand, if you think you'll need the money sooner, you may feel better forgoing the higher return for the chance of being able to get at your money in a hurry. The amount of liquidity that you need or are willing to forgo depends on the nature and timing of your own individual goals.

Yield

Generally, yield refers to how much money your savings or investments will earn for you. For example, if a savings account is paying 6 percent interest per year and you put $100 into the account, you will receive $6 during the first year that your $100 is in the account. Your yield may be expressed as "6 percent" or as "$6 per $100 per year." The term *yield* is often used interchangeably with *return* and *return on investment*.

In making any form of investment, you should determine not only what yield you can expect immediately, but whether that yield will continue, for how long, and what degree of fluctuation it might be subject to.

□ **Bonds.** If you put your money into long-term corporate or government or municipal bonds, you are assured of a constant yield for the amount of time you own the bonds, assuming that the debtor continues to pay the interest promised. The actual face value of the bond may fluctuate up and down while you own it, and you may sell the bond for more or less than what you originally paid for it. But the actual income you receive for the term of your ownership will remain constant. If you buy a government bond for $1000 that promises to pay 8 percent per year, you will receive $80 for each year that you own the bond, regardless of whether the face value of the bond increases or decreases, which it might.

□ **Savings accounts.** Passbook savings accounts might be somewhat subject to minor fluctuations in yield over the years.

□ **Stocks.** If you buy a share of ownership in a company—called a stock—and if that company distributes a portion of its profits to its owners—called a *dividend*—your yield or return is expressed as the amount of dividend dollars you receive. If you pay $100 for a stock and during the first year of your ownership the company pays you $5 in dividends, your yield can be expressed as 5 percent or $5 per $100 per year, based on your purchase price.

Many companies have long histories of dividend payment records, and many also increase their dividends from time to time. Even more companies have erratic dividend payment histories, while some companies pay none at all. If a company runs into hard times, a dividend payment record may suddenly halt. On the other hand, if a company suddenly has a surge in business, it may start to pay dividends unexpectedly. Investing in the stock market, then, offers a broad range of yield possibilities.

□ **Real estate.** An investment in real estate also offers a wide range of yield potential. If you own a property and it's leased for a long term to respectable tenants, and those tenants are responsible for paying escalating costs such as property taxes and utilities, your yield (total income less total expenses) could remain quite constant for long periods of time. On the other hand, if you have less reliable tenants and you as the owner are required to pay those escalating operating costs, your yield could be far less constant and far less satisfactory.

Following the reward-risk rule, you'll find that the more respectable tenants will bargain for and receive a lower rental rate than the less reliable tenants. Although your rental income may therefore be higher from the less respectable tenants, the chances of it ceasing or being eroded by vacancies and added costs are that much greater.

Gain and Loss. It's important to keep a clear distinction between yield and gain or loss. For example, you buy stock for $100 and during the first year of ownership it pays a dividend of $5. But at the end of the year you sell the stock for $120. You have realized a gain of $20 on your investment, plus a dividend of $5, for a total overall increase in your fund of $25. Would this be considered a yield of 25 percent? Technically no. It is indeed an overall gain of 25 percent, but it comes from two different sources—the dividend yield of 5 percent and the increase in value of 20 percent. Similarly, if you sold the stock at year end for $80, you still would have had a dividend yield of 5 percent, but you would have suffered a loss of $20, 20 percent of your original investment.

Generally, in embarking on an investment program, the expected yield is a relatively known quantity, at least with savings accounts, bonds, and stocks with good dividend payment history. The aspect of possible gain or loss, particularly with stocks, is a relatively unknown factor, if not totally unknown. In building toward a specific future goal, a relatively predictable yield can be a far more useful aspect than the relatively unknown gain or loss. Prudent investors should structure their program accordingly.

Strategies for Success

Investment Objectives Should Suit Your Age

A twenty-five-year-old person has more flexibility regarding investing than does a fifty-five- or a sixty-five-year-old person. If younger people make mistakes, they have more *time* and more *psychological resilience* to recover from the mistake than older persons have. Thus the younger person can more easily afford to take risks. As a person gets older, risk taking should gradually decrease. Thus, individuals should define their investment objectives clearly in line with their age. All investment plans should start out by building a solid, risk-free foundation. When people are in their twenties and thirties, a moderate amount of prudent risk can be taken to generate income and capital growth. By the time they are in their forties and fifties, their objectives should tend more toward safety of income and preservation of capital. When they reach the sixties and beyond, preservation of capital, along with reliable income, should be their primary if not exclusive objectives. This is a conservative approach. If you choose to differ, know the risks of doing so.

Pledge Value

You may, from time to time, have an unexpected need for money: to take advantage of a once-in-a-lifetime bargain, to pay pressing bills, to help out someone in need, or to pay for expensive repairs. You may not have the cash on hand, and it thus becomes necessary for you to borrow the needed money. The quickest and sometimes the cheapest way to borrow money is to pledge your investments as collateral for such a loan. The *pledge value* of any investment is a measurement of what percent of the value of the investment you can borrow, how quickly you can get the money, and how much it will cost you.

□ *Savings accounts.* Savings accounts—both passbook and certificate—have the highest level of pledge value among the common types of investments. Most depositors can usually borrow virtually all of the money in their savings account at favorable rates, without any delay. This can be an excellent device for obtaining short-term funds in a hurry and may be preferable to actually invading the savings account or cashing in the certificate.

□ *Stocks.* Because stocks are prone to fluctuation in value, they have a somewhat lower pledge value than savings accounts. The amount you can borrow from your banker against any given stockholdings depends on the quality of the stock itself. You can also borrow from your broker—on a *margin account* (see Chapter 17). In either case, of course, you have to surrender the certificate as collateral for the loan.

□ *Real estate.* High-quality real estate has a high pledge value, but because of the nature of the documentation required in borrowing against real estate, the process can be costly and time consuming. This, in effect, detracts from real estate's otherwise good pledge value.

Hedge Value

Investors must be concerned over the ability of their investments to withstand the effects of inflation. The common expression is "hedging against inflation." This aspect of investing, then, may be called the *hedge value* of an investment.

□ *Savings accounts.* Savings accounts have long been accused of having no protection against inflation because the principal amount invested doesn't grow except for periodic additions of interest to the account. Although it is true that the principal does not increase on its own, there is some protection against inflation because interest rates paid on savings plans tend to rise in line with rising costs. By the same token, interest rates paid on savings plans may also decrease in the face of decreasing costs.

□ *Real estate.* Real estate has long been considered a good hedge against inflation, but again this depends on the nature of the property, the management of the property, and the trend in the community in which the property is located.

□ *Stocks.* Many investors have theorized that the stock market should be a good hedge against inflation. The theory is that as prices rise, the profits of companies also rise. As their profits increase, so should the value of their stock. However, in recent years, stock prices and inflation have not been parallel trends much of the time. Even if it could be proven that the stock market in general provides a good hedge against inflation, this "proof" would be of no value to the individual investor who chooses specific stocks or mutual funds that do not follow the general trend of the stock market.

In short, there is no form of investment or speculation that is a guaranteed hedge against inflation. But there is one very important caution to note regarding the psychology of inflation. Over the years, as inflationary trends have come and gone, thousands of small investors have let themselves be convinced and conned by wily salespeople that inflation was destroying their life savings. Invariably, the salespeople would offer a "better deal." But the better deal was frequently a very risky, if not a downright fraudulent, scheme in which the frightened investors lost all or a portion of their life savings. In other words, the fear of inflation caused them to lose much more money than they might have lost through inflation itself.

Tax Implications

Tax regulations are constantly changing. All investors—large and small—must pay constant attention to the tax implications of the various types of investments available to them. Tax implications divide investments into the following three broad categories:

- ☐ *Taxable investments.* These are investments in which, except as noted below, all of your income is taxed in the year in which it is earned.
- ☐ *Tax-deferred or tax-sheltered investments.* With these investments, the payment of taxes on income earned can be delayed until some future time.
- ☐ *Tax-exempt investments.* All or a substantial portion of your income from these investments is tax free.

Taxable Investments. Income you earn from savings plans and from corporate and U.S. government bonds is subject to taxation. So are dividends earned from investments in stocks. But Congress frequently changes its mind and alters the nature of tax implications on many common investments. For example, prior to the passage of the Tax Reform Act of 1986, dividends received through stock ownership could be partly excluded from taxation. Also profits on the sale of stock (as well as real estate) received favorable tax treatment. The 1986 law eliminated these tax breaks. It may be many years before all of the ramifications and reactions to the Tax Reform Act of 1986 are finally known. It's absolutely essential that investors check current tax regulations with respect to investments before making any firm investment decisions.

Tax-deferred or Tax-sheltered Investments. The best example of a tax-deferred investment is the *individual retirement account*, or IRA, which allows workers to invest money each year for their retirement. The amount they invest in the plan each year can be a form of tax deduction, thus reducing their immediate tax obligation to the government. Furthermore, the earnings on these funds are not taxed each year. However, when the money is withdrawn, which cannot be before age 59½ (without penalty), the taxes on the withdrawn money must then be paid. The presumption is that when money is withdrawn on retirement, the individual investor will be in a much lower tax bracket than at the time the contributions were made. Thus, there can be a considerable tax break. Moreover, all of the money contributed into the fund has been allowed to work without being subject to taxation, which can again make a substantial difference in an overall nest egg over the long term. The Keogh plan, for self-employed individuals, is another example of a tax-deferred investment. IRA and Keogh plans are discussed in more detail in Chapter 20.

In a tax-sheltered investment, some of the income received is offset by some of the expenses incurred in maintaining the investment. The effect is to reduce the amount of income that is subject to taxes. However, when a tax-sheltered investment is later sold, some taxes will become payable. The most common form of tax-sheltered investment is real estate (see Chapter 18 for a more detailed discussion of real estate investing). Because buildings physically depreciate, tax laws allow real estate investors to deduct a depreciation factor from their income. This depreciation factor does not represent an actual loss in value on the building, but rather a paper loss. Indeed, the building may be increasing in value even while the owner is deducting depreciation on his tax return. The depreciation factor offsets income that the building may be earning, thus reducing the amount of taxable income the owner has to pay. When the building is sold, though, the tax payable by the investor on any profit will be affected by the amount of depreciation deducted in earlier years. (Depreciation does not apply with respect to one's residence.)

Although many of the tax benefits from real estate investing survived the Tax Reform Act of 1986, other types of tax-shelter plans (such as leasing and cattle breeding) had their benefits sharply or completely curtailed. As noted above, check current regulations before embarking on any such investments.

Tax-Exempt Investments. When local governments, such as cities and states, borrow money, investors do not have to pay federal income taxes on the interest they receive. These investments are known as *municipal bonds*, and the income the investor receives is referred to as being *tax-exempt*. There are some exceptions, however: (1) As a result of some of the intricacies in the Tax Reform Act of 1986, there are now some municipal bonds that are taxable. You should take care to note the difference before making any investment decisions. (2) If you invest in municipal bonds and sell the bonds at a profit, the profit itself is taxable even though the interest you earned while you owned the bonds is not taxable. (3) If you invest in municipal bonds issued by a government unit outside of your state of residence, the interest earned will be subject to any state income taxes you might have to pay. For example, if a California investor buys a municipal bond issued by the city of San Diego, the interest earned is exempt from both federal and California income taxes. But if that same investor buys a municipal bond issued by the city of Houston, the interest earned is exempt only from federal taxes. He will have to pay California income taxes on that interest. Tax-exempt investments are discussed in greater detail in Chapter 16.

Investigation

"Investigate before you invest" is one of the essential maxims to remember when putting your money to work. An equally important maxim all too frequently overlooked is "investigate before you un-invest." Homework is a necessity before you place your funds in any kind of situation, and there's no form of investment for which homework can't and shouldn't be done. But the homework doesn't stop once you've made the investment.

Knowing when to get out of a situation is as important as knowing when to get in. "But," many say, "I don't want to become a slave to my investment. I don't want to have to worry about it. I just want to be able to put it away and have it grow and deliver what I'm seeking without the worry or the constant checking." All well and good, but beware that such a course may result in a diminished nest egg compared with what it might have been. The decision is up to you as an individual; you don't have to become a fanatic. But you're planting a tree, and you want it to bear the most and the best possible fruit. This involves care, nurturing, and an awareness of all steps you can take to improve your crop. In short, your ability to prosper will depend largely on your willingness to work. And your need to work will be minimized by your initial efforts in understanding how the various forms of investments function and what they can and cannot do for you.

There is more literature published every year on investments than on any other subject with the possible exceptions of dieting and sex. It's impossible to keep up with the outpouring: hundreds of books, thousands of magazines and newspaper articles, tens of thousands of reports and analyses published by stockbrokerage firms and investment advisory firms. Where is one to begin? Following is a selection of useful literature and courses that can assist you in learning more about your investment opportunities.

Books.   Books run the gamut from the "doom and gloom" variety to the "how to get rich overnight" variety. The former tend to preach that the end of the world is rapidly approaching and that unorthodox investments are called for to cope with the calamity. The latter type tend to lure investors toward highly speculative types of portfolios. Between these two extremes there are a number of worthwhile books published each year on basic money management and investment programs. Sample them at your local library or bookstore, and read one or two a year to give yourself some diversity in views and tactics. The problem, in general, with books—including this one—is that there is a considerable amount of time between the writing and the publication, and many of the ideas presented can be outdated before the book is in the stores.

One book that is updated annually is *Dun and Bradstreet's Guide to Your Investments*. It covers a wide range of investment opportunities and is as up to date as publication schedules can allow in the book industry. Specific investment suggestions offered in this guide should be checked for current facts with your banker, stockbroker, or other investment advisor.

Magazines.   *Newsweek* and *U.S. News and World Report*, both weeklies, contain good current information and informative columns on finance and investing. *Forbes* is published every other week and is directed to an audience of businesspeople and investors. It is most highly recommended as a source of specific information and general guidelines on a wide variety of investment techniques. *Financial World*, a weekly, contains in-depth articles on specific stock opportunities and much statistical information. *Fortune* (every two weeks) and *Business Week* (weekly) are both examples of excellent financial journalism, but are directed more to the business-person than to the relatively inexperienced investor. If any of these periodicals prompt you to be interested in a specific investment situation, check with your stockbroker for more detailed information. Also worthwhile are *Money, Changing Times*, and *Barron's*.

Newspapers.   The *Wall Street Journal*, read daily and thoroughly, is the best of all possible tools to keep you alert not only to specific investments but to the state of the economy as well. The business pages of your local newspaper are a necessary supplement to the *Journal*.

Seminars and Courses.   Local community colleges, universities, and financial firms often conduct programs geared to the investor's needs. Such programs will normally be announced in the catalogues published by the schools and in newspaper articles or advertisements. Many seminars conducted by private firms and financial institutions are geared to obtaining clientele or to selling specific investments to attendees. Many of these programs can be extremely expensive. If so, try to find a book that covers the subject just as well for a fraction of the price. If it is the type of program where clientele will be solicited, prepare yourself as you go in for a sales pitch and act accordingly.

Television.   Your television set can be the source of some very good and some very bad investment advice. The national Public Broadcasting System (PBS) and Cable News Network (CNN) offer a variety of worthwhile programs on money and investments. Somewhat in the middle ground are the newly emerging television channels that offer ongoing stock market reports intermingled with advisories. These advisories, in which the host touts a particular form of investment, are often believed by viewers to be objective news presentations. In fact, however, they are extended commercials for the individual salesperson, the product being touted, and the firm being represented. Be certain that you understand the difference between an objective informational presentation and one actually trying to sell something.

The third variety of investment information available on television can be more dangerous than beneficial. This is the ''seminar'' in which the host is attempting to sell an expensive home study course from which you can learn all of the secrets of successful investing in real estate, the stock market, commodities, you name it. Surely you'll get some information for your many hundreds of dollars if you buy these courses. However, if they were truly selling the secrets of success, everybody would know them and they would no longer be secrets. It must be, therefore, that these salespeople are making more money selling you the secrets than they could make by putting the secrets to use. Let the buyer beware of these pitches.

SOURCES OF INVESTABLE FUNDS

All sources of investable funds must be accurately evaluated. Let's look at some of the most common sources.

Inactive Investments

You have little or no control over the inactive investment activities that you're now engaged in, such as building the equity in your home, your life insurance policies, your pension or profit-sharing programs, or your social security. But these funds can become actively investable at some future time, and you must, in line with your goals, determine how much will be available and when. These sources may not materialize for many years, but it's senseless to play guessing games about their amounts. Reasonable estimates, periodically revised, will be needed to help assure that you reach your goals. Check periodically with your employer and with the local office of the Social Security Administration to determine what you can reasonably expect from these respective sources.

Discretionary Income

The major source for active investment funds is your discretionary income—the difference between what you take home in earnings and what you currently spend for all your present needs. "But," say the majority, "I'm just living hand to mouth as it is. By the time everything is deducted from my paycheck and I keep up with rising costs and allow some modest improvements in my life style, there's barely a penny left to put away." Or, as is also said, "There's too much month left at the end of the money." True enough, and in many cases there's little you can do about it. However, a close examination of your current living style, in comparison with your *desired future living style*, is in order. Investable funds can be created by cutting down on current expenditures or by increasing current income. Simply translated, this means additional work and/or belt-tightening. Whether you wish to do either depends on how closely your *existing* investment program meets your targeted goals. If your current program is adequate, there may be no need to either increase your income or tighten your belt. If, though, the development of your nest egg will not be adequate to meet your targeted goals, you may have to consider one of these two steps to expand your discretionary income. The alternative, of course, is to cut down on future goals. But this, perhaps, is the most dangerous course of all.

Consider that the most critical goal for most individuals and families is to have enough income to live in the desired style when work ceases and retirement begins. If, when that time rolls around, you don't have what you had hoped you might have, *you don't get to do it over*. You're locked in. Again, it's up to each individual: How much, if anything, are you willing to sacrifice in your current life style in order to assure a comfortable future life style? When you can give an approximate answer to this question, you'll be more readily able to determine what adjustments you want to make in your current discretionary income.

Inheritances and Gifts.   Other sources of investable funds include inheritances and gifts. This is a touchy area that must be handled delicately, but nevertheless it must be faced. A great many people receive inheritances from parents and other family members, and the amount may be token or may be considerable. It may occur soon, or it may not occur for many, many years. The amount ultimately received can have an important bearing on your own overall plans. If you know or can determine what can reasonably be expected in the way of an inheritance, you may want to adjust your existing investment program or your current life style accordingly.

WHO CAN HELP?

Help is available from a number of sources in structuring a long-range investment program. Financial planners, as noted in Chapter 13, can provide a wide range of assistance. But you must be careful in choosing a financial planner: Many are only concerned with selling you products, and some are overly eager, probably because the sale may be of greater benefit to them than to you. It's essential that you determine at the outset just what products a financial planner is selling. Once you have determined this, you should ask the critical question: If the planner depends on my buying these items for her own income, is she giving me truly objective and valuable advice, or is she just giving me a sales pitch? Some financial planners work on a fee-only basis. They are not inexpensive, but in the long run using their services could prove to be more valuable, particularly if they can direct you to the best possible vehicles for putting your money to work.

Financial planners may claim to be able to service all of your concerns, such as legal, accounting, and taxation, in addition to the basic selection of investments. Be aware that each of these areas requires special expertise. Depending on the nature of your concern, you might be better off seeing a lawyer or accountant if the financial planner does not have the necessary expertise.

Many investors are finding good assistance in handling their money through "families" of mutual funds. Many of the larger mutual fund companies operate a number of different specific funds, each geared toward different investment objectives. They range from the "rock-bound" conservative to the wildly speculative and all points in between. The mutual fund companies provide ample literature explaining what the various specific funds can provide. The attractive feature of the "families" is that it's easy for an investor to switch all or part of his money from one fund to another quickly and at little cost, as circumstances dictate.

When all is said and done, the best financial planner you can find is in your own home—you and your family. Nobody cares more about your financial well-being than you and your family, and you have to be able to sort out all the jargon,

---

Strategies for Success

All Family Members Should Agree on Investment Objectives

It's a tough challenge, but one well worth working toward: All members of your immediate family should be in accord regarding the basic family investment objectives. It can be most counterproductive if, for example, one spouse wants to take heavy risk with the family nest egg and the other wants no risk at all. There's always a happy medium that can be found when both spouses are willing to learn and study, in order to determine what their best course of action would be. Seek the advice of your banker or other trusted financial advisor. If there are older children in the family whose well-being might depend in part on family investments, they should sit in on the deliberations as well.

---

analyze all the proposals, evaluate all the opportunities, and make all the final decisions. Advisors can only advise. You have to take responsibility for your own future, and this requires obtaining the necessary knowledge to know when advisors are right or wrong.

The next chapters examine the most common types of investments available, what they are; how they work; and their respective features regarding yield, liquidity, safety, hedge value, pledge value, tax implications, and investigation.

There are no specific rights or wrongs in structuring an investment portfolio. Each must be tailored to the needs, both present and future, of a particular individual or family. And the portfolio must be structured with the thought that those needs can and probably will change over the years. Thus, although the discussions are presented from a relatively conservative viewpoint, there's ample room for disagreement.

Sources of Your Tomorrow Dollars

Where will the money come from to allow you to meet your future goals? This is an exercise to help make you more aware of the potential sources of your Tomorrow Dollars. Assume that you plan to retire in five years or that there is some other defined goal that you hope to accomplish at that time. Evaluate the following possible sources of money, and see how close you come to meeting your estimated needs. If there is a shortfall, how will you make up the difference?

Source	Lump sum available	Monthly income, if lump sum is invested at 10 percent annual interest
☐ Pension proceeds	_____	_____
☐ Profit-sharing plan	_____	_____
☐ Social security	_____	_____
☐ Equity in your home (after setting aside enough to provide satisfactory living quarters)	_____	_____
☐ Cash or loan value in your life insurance policies	_____	_____
☐ Existing investment programs (savings, bonds, etc.)	_____	_____
☐ Existing speculative programs (stocks, metals, commodities, etc.)	_____	_____
☐ Inheritances realistically expected	_____	_____
☐ Discretionary income (the excess of current income over current expenses, which could be put to work to create a source of Tomorrow Dollars)	_____	_____
☐ Miscellaneous (collections, works of art, etc., that could be sold)	_____	_____

No "Do-Overs"

There's no greater shock than, on nearing retirement, learning that you won't have enough money to live in the manner you'd hoped for. At that age and in those circumstances, you don't get a "do-over." You can't go back ten, twenty, or thirty years and start again to build a nest egg. The following interview illustrates this plight:

> When I finished school I bounced around from job to job for many years. I was out for fun, and the real future seemed too far off to worry about. Then, in my early thirties, I found a job that looked good for the long run. There was no pension plan, but the pay was good, and I was able to live like I wanted to. I still didn't look beyond the following week. I just assumed that I'd always have a good income and that social security would take care of me after that.
>
> Some years later the company offered an investment plan to the employees. If we put in a certain amount each month, they'd add a chunk of their own. They advised us to take advantage of it, to build for our future, but I couldn't see cutting back on my life style by salting away money for ten or twenty years.
>
> Did I mess up! Retirement is just a few years away now, and I don't have a penny to show for all the years I put in with the company. I just checked with the Social Security Administration and found that my monthly check will barely cover the rent on my apartment. What I had thought would be adequate has been chopped into little pieces by inflation.
>
> I really don't know what I'm going to do. The thought of going on welfare just makes me sick. I guess I'll just have to trim my sails and keep on working until they drag me out.
>
> When I was younger I used to like a song that had a line in it: "Let's forget about tomorrow for tomorrow never comes." Back then, that song suited me just fine. But oh how I hate the thought of it today.

Nobody—no employer, no government, no mystical "they"—will take better care of you than you can yourself. If you don't take care of yourself, don't expect anyone else to do it for you.

CHAPTER 16

Making Your Money Grow:
The Money Market

Not too many years ago, average individuals had very few safe choices for investing their money. The most common methods were passbook savings accounts and government savings bonds. Today, however, the choices are many and varied. New techniques are constantly emerging. Confusion reigns. But you need *not* be perplexed by all of the different offerings. You *can* distinguish clearly what each of them offers you. And you *can* choose which is best for you. This is the purpose of this chapter:

□　To describe how different savings techniques work

□　To help you evaluate the opportunities available to you in certificates, bonds, mutual funds, and other situations

□　To acquaint you with certain tax-favored retirement plans

□　And, overall, to help you shape your own investment program using these various devices

Chapter 15 described the two basic ways of making your money grow: (1) lend it to others, in return for which you receive a fee known as *interest*, and (2) buy something (such as stock or real estate) and hope that you can sell it later for more than you paid for it. While you own such an entity, you may also receive a share of the entity's profits, if in fact it is profitable.

There is a critical distinction between the two basic techniques. With the former—lending—you will have an agreement with the borrower (financial institution, corporation, government) stating that you are entitled to have all of your invested money returned, either upon your demand or at some future time. The agreement also states the amount of interest you are to receive. That amount of interest will be either fixed at a certain level or subject to variation. If the interest rate is variable, there may or may not be limits to how high or how low the rate may go. In summary, you are assured of getting all of your money back (assuming that the borrower remains healthy), and you are assured of getting at least some interest.

When you buy something, you do not have assurances of getting all of your money back or getting any return on your money during the period of ownership. If you are fortunate, your investment might increase many times in value. If you are unfortunate, your investment could wither and even disappear altogether. But there is no way of knowing what the future will hold when you make the investment. The distinction between the two techniques could then be most succinctly described as *security* versus *risk*.

A conservative investment philosophy would dictate that you safeguard your future by using secure techniques. Once you have embarked on a well-disciplined plan to create such a foundation for your future security, you might then want to consider using the risk techniques. If you are fortunate, the risk techniques could later enhance your future; if you are unfortunate in your choice of risk investments, your future could suffer.

Let's now explore the various ways of lending your money to assure your future security. In the broad sense, the arena in which you find these opportunities is known as the *money market*.

WHAT IS THE MONEY MARKET?

The money market is not a place but a concept. In a general sense, when IOUs and money change hands, money market transactions have thus taken place. When you open a savings account or buy a savings bond, you have entered into a money market transaction: You have loaned your money to a bank or to the government and you have received their promise to repay you. (In a more technical sense, the money market refers to certain transactions involving short-term government and corporate bonds. See the later discussion on money market mutual funds for more detail.)

There's a wide selection of money market investments. Open-end plans have no fixed time period; money can be deposited and taken out at will; and the rate of interest earned can fluctuate from day to day. Other plans have fixed maturities ranging from as short as a few days to as long as thirty years. These types of plans usually yield a fixed rate of interest payable over the life of the plan. The investor might be limited regarding additional deposits or withdrawals. Also withdrawals of the principal prior to maturity could mean a penalty for the investor.

HOW IS INTEREST FIGURED?

As noted, interest is the fee a borrower pays in order to have the use of someone else's money. Interest is normally expressed as a percentage of the total amount borrowed, calculated on a yearly basis. In other words, if you were to make an investment of $1000 at a 6 percent annual interest rate, you would receive $60 over the course of one year. If you were to remain with that investment for only half a year, you would receive $30 in interest. If you stayed with it for two years, you would receive $120.

Aside from the rate of interest, there are two other aspects in calculating your true return that can have a distinct effect on your overall investment: the compounding of interest and the crediting of interest to your account.

Compounding

The compounding of interest means that the interest you earn stays in your account and begins to earn interest itself. Following the example above, if you earned $60 in interest during the course of one year (on a $1000 investment at a 6 percent annual rate) and you left that $60 in the account, you would then have $1060 to work for you during the second year. During the second year, your $1060 would earn $63.60. And so it would go for future years: You have an ever-increasing amount of money working for you because the interest is left in the account to compound.

In many types of accounts, interest is compounded more frequently than once a year. Quarterly compounding is very common, as is daily compounding. With quarterly compounding, the interest you earn during each quarter of the year is added to your original principal balance. Table 16-1 illustrates this. During the first quarter of the year, with your $1000 investment at 6 percent, you earn $15 (i.e., one-fourth of $60). At the start of the second quarter, you have $1015 working for you, which will earn $15.23. That $15.23 earned during the second quarter is added to the $1015 of principal, thus you have $1030.23 at work for you during the third quarter. With daily compounding, 1/365 of your total annual interest is added to your account each day. As Table 16-1 illustrates, more frequent compounding means a higher return to the investor.

Table 16-1 **Comparison of Compounding Methods: 6% Annual Rate**

Year	Quarter	$1000 Quarterly compounding	Annual compounding
First	First	$1000.00 earns $15.00	
	Second	1015.00 earns 15.23	
	Third	1030.23 earns 15.45	
	Fourth	1045.68 earns 15.69	$1000 earns $60
	Balance at work, end of first year	$1061.37	$1060
Second	First	$1061.37 earns $15.92	
	Second	1077.29 earns 16.15	
	Third	1093.44 earns 16.40	
	Fourth	1109.84 earns 16.64	$1060 earns $63.60
	Balance at work, end of second year	$1126.48	$1123.60

Passbook savings accounts are the most common type of investment in which compounding takes place. But some investments do not offer compounding: Corporate bonds, for example, pay you interest twice a year by check directly from the company. If you don't reinvest the interest on your own, it will not be working for you.

Crediting of Interest to Your Account

Savings plans can differ with respect to the manner in which interest is actually credited to your account. Many institutions will credit you with interest from the day a deposit is made until the day the deposit is withdrawn. For example, if you make a deposit in such an institution on January 15 and withdraw the total balance on December 15, you earn interest for the full eleven months that the money is in the account. However, some institutions use different methods of crediting the interest to your account. For example, an institution might require that the money remain in your account for a full calendar quarter in order to earn interest. Thus, if you make a deposit on January 15, you do not earn any interest for the entire first quarter of the year. You start earning interest at the beginning of the second quarter, April 1. Also, if you withdraw the money on December 15, you forfeit interest for the entire fourth quarter of the year since you are withdrawing it before the end of the full calendar quarter. In such a case, even though your money is in the institution for a full eleven months, you are earning interest for only six months—the second and the third quarters.

Another method of calculating interest uses the low balance in any quarter as the amount on which interest is computed. For example, you start the first quarter of the year with $1000 in your account. On January 15 you withdraw $600 to pay bills until your income tax refund comes in. The refund comes in on February 15, and you put the money back into your account. During the first quarter of the year, you will only be credited for interest on $400, even though you had $1000 in the account for the majority of the time. In a day-of-deposit-to-day-of-withdrawal ac-

Table 16-2 **How Does Your Money Grow? No. 1**

If you invest $1000 per year at this rate of interest (%) . . .	. . . You'll have this much after this number of years[a]			
	5	10	15	20
6	$5,980	$13,970	$24,570	$ 38,990
8	6,340	15,650	29,320	49,420
10	6,710	17,530	34,960	63,000
12	7,120	19,650	41,750	80,700
14	7,540	22,040	49,980	103,770

[a]This table does *not* take into account income taxes on yearly interest earnings.

Table 16-3 **How Does Your Money Grow? No. 2**

If you make a one-time investment of $1000 at this rate of interest (%) . . .	. . . You'll have this much after this number of years[a]			
	5	*10*	*15*	*20*
6	$1,340	$1,790	$2,400	$ 3,210
8	1,470	2,160	3,170	4,660
10	1,610	2,590	4,180	6,720
12	1,760	3,110	5,470	9,650
14	1,960	3,710	7,400	14,960

Example: To better understand the power of compounding, look at where the 10-year column crosses the 10% row. $1000 will have grown to $2590. In other words, your investment will have increased by $1590 over 10 years, or an *average per year* of $159. This means, in effect, that you have enjoyed an *average annual growth* of 15.9%.

[a]This table does *not* take into account income taxes on yearly interest earnings.

count, the interest is calculated on the balance in your account each given day of the quarter, and you don't suffer as you do in the low-balance type of calculation.

Determining the true yield on a money market investment requires more than just examining the rate of interest being paid. You must examine the frequency of compounding and crediting of interest to the account as well. Tables 16-2 and 16-3 illustrate how your money will grow over various periods of time at different rates of interest, compounded annually.

TYPES OF MONEY MARKET INVESTMENTS

The variety of money market investment opportunities is staggering by comparison to just twenty years ago. As borrowers compete ever-more aggressively for investors' dollars, new techniques and new twists on old techniques are emerging at a rapid pace. The selection of opportunities available today might be still broader and more varied than the selection that follows.

Passbook Savings Accounts

A passbook savings account is an open-end agreement between the customer and the financial institution. The customer is free to put in as much money as desired at any given time and can take out as much as desired at any given time. While the money is in the account, it earns interest in accordance with the agreement set forth between the institution and the investor. The institution may reserve the right to alter the interest rate being paid upon giving proper notice to its investors. The form of notice should be set forth in the rules and regulations of the passbook account.

Some institutions may offer special types of passbook accounts that are a cross between a passbook and a time certificate. These accounts have a fixed maturity, but the customer may be able to add or withdraw certain sums from the account periodically.

Financial institutions also offer so-called money market accounts, in addition to passbook accounts. These money market accounts generally require a fairly high minimum deposit—perhaps as much as a few thousand dollars—whereas passbook accounts have little or no minimum requirements. But the money market accounts pay a higher rate of interest than passbook accounts, and they are just as flexible, allowing withdrawals at any time without penalty. Federally insured institutions protect both types of accounts—as well as checking accounts—up to $100,000. It is possible to have more than $100,000 worth of insurance in a given institution if multiple accounts are maintained in different names. Check with your institution for complete up-to-date details on how your account is insured.

Investment Criteria.   The investment criteria for passbook savings and money market accounts are similar. Some of the important features are as follows:

□ **Yield.**   Passbook savings accounts have traditionally given the lowest yield of all money market instruments. To determine the true yield, it's important for the investor to be aware of the annual interest rate payable as well as the frequency of compounding and crediting of interest to the account.

□ **Liquidity.**   Passbook savings accounts and money market accounts are as liquid an investment as one can make short of storing the money in a cookie jar. You can withdraw your entire principal at any time simply by submitting your passbook and the appropriate withdrawal slip. If interest is not credited daily to your passbook account, you could sacrifice some interest if you withdraw the funds prior to the end of the calendar quarter.

□ **Safety.**   Savings accounts insured by the federal government have the highest degree of safety.

□ **Hedge value.**   The interest rates payable on passbook accounts and on money market accounts can rise as inflation boosts costs generally. This doesn't necessarily mean they will rise. If an inflationary trend sets in, investors must pay careful attention to the possible earnings on their savings plans and move to those that offer the best return, all things considered.

□ **Pledge value.**   Savings accounts have a very high degree of pledge value. You can normally borrow up to 90 percent of the total amount in your account at favorable rates by presenting your passbook to a loan officer and signing simple documents.

□ **Tax implications.**   Interest earned on passbook accounts and money market accounts is fully taxable. Check the latest tax regulations.

Certificates of Deposit

Certificates of deposit (or CDs, as they are often called) are fixed contracts for a specific amount of money to run for a specific length of time and to pay a fixed interest rate. A certificate of deposit may be for as short as seven days or for as long as ten years, perhaps even longer. The interest rate payable on any certificate depends on general interest rate conditions at the time the investment is made.

Once a fixed-interest certificate of deposit investment is made, the agreed interest rate is in effect throughout the life of the certificate, even though the general rates may change subsequently. For example, on Monday, you obtain a thirty-month certificate of deposit from a local bank with an interest rate set at 12 percent per annum. You are guaranteed that 12 percent rate for the life of the certificate. On Tuesday, the same bank announces that from that day onward they will pay 11½ percent on all thirty-month certificates. This change will not affect you. It will only affect people who obtain certificates from Tuesday onward until any other change in the interest rate is made. By the same token, if on Tuesday the bank should announce an increase in the certificate rate, you will not be able to take advantage of the higher rate since you committed to a firm contract on Monday at the 12 percent rate.

Some institutions offer certificates with a variable rate of interest. This might entitle you to a higher rate of interest should rates go up during the life of your plan. If the plan does not have a downward limit, it could also mean that you might earn a lower rate of interest than the initial rate, should rates in general turn down.

As a general rule, the longer the life of the certificate, the higher the rate of interest you'll earn. In other words, if a one-year certificate is paying 7 percent, a two-year certificate might pay 8 percent, a three-year certificate close to 9 percent, and so on. Bear in mind, though, that although the longer-term certificates earn a higher rate of interest, your money is tied up that much longer. Thus you are losing some flexibility in your overall financial structure.

Penalties. Since CDs are firm contracts for a set amount of time, you can expect to be penalized if you want to withdraw money from your certificate account before the maturity date. Government regulations have changed from time to time with respect to the total penalty that can be charged. Let's look at an example. You contract with your bank for a twelve-month certificate of deposit for $10,000. The interest rate is fixed at 12 percent. (For purposes of this example we'll not take the compounding of interest into effect.) You are informed when you open the account that the penalty for early withdrawal is three months' worth of interest. Based on the 12 percent interest, you'd be earning $100 worth of interest each month or $1200 for the full year. After two months have elapsed an emergency arises, and you need the $10,000. If you withdraw it from the account, your penalty will be three months' worth of interest or $300—even though so far you have only earned $200. In other words, you'll forfeit the $200 you've already earned, and the extra $100 you owe the bank will be deducted from your $10,000 investment. Check with your bank to determine the penalties currently in effect on early withdrawals.

Renewal.   Commonly, when a CD reaches its maturity, the institution will renew it for another term at the interest rate then prevailing. For example, you have a six-month certificate that was obtained at a 12 percent interest rate. Today the certificate is maturing, and the current interest rate on such certificates is 10 percent. Unless you instruct the institution to the contrary, they will automatically renew your certificate at the 10 percent rate. Some institutions, however, will not automatically renew certificates: They may instead place the funds into a passbook savings account lacking your instructions to the contrary. In such a case you would be likely to earn a much lower rate of interest than what a renewed certificate would have paid. Whether institutions automatically renew certificates or automatically put the proceeds into a passbook account, they will give you a seven-day grace period on the expiration of the original certificate. During that seven days, you will continue to earn interest at the then-prevailing rate. At the end of the seven days, the automatic conversion occurs.

Here is a common problem that arises when you fail to pay attention to the renewal provisions of your certificates. Your six-month certificate matures on the fifteenth of the month. At the end of the seven-day grace period—the twenty-second—your certificate will automatically be renewed for another six months. You have every intention of getting to the bank on or before the twenty-second to take the money out so that you can put it to some other use. But you get distracted and don't get around to doing this until the twenty-third of the month. By this time the certificate has already renewed, and if you now want to take out the money, you will have to pay the penalty as noted above. On a large certificate, a few days' delay can cost hundreds of dollars in lost interest.

Strategies for Success

Use Formula for Safe IRA Investing

How should your IRA money be invested? To the extent that that money is being put away for your retirement, it's not wise to take much risk with it. You want it to *be there* when you need it at retirement time. If you take undue risks with this money, it might *not* be there. Consider, then, this simple formula: forty plus your age equals percent of risk-free investment, that is, the percent of your IRA investment that should be risk free, that should be in federally insured savings, for example. The rest can be put to moderate risk. So if you are thirty years old, 70 percent of your IRA investment should be risk free. The other 30 percent can be put to some moderate risk. If you are fifty years old, 90 percent of your IRA money should be risk free. As noted earlier in more general terms, the older you are, the less risk you should take.

Choices. Deregulation in recent years has made it possible for institutions to offer a virtually infinite assortment of savings certificates. Before the mid-1980s, regulations limited the term of certificates to six months, thirty months, and a few other variations. Now you can obtain a certificate to run as long as you wish. In past years, there was little variety and little problem in making a choice. But now, with such a myriad of choices at hand, making the right decision becomes a complex matter. The list in Table 16-4, used in conjunction with the Personal Action Checklist at the end of this chapter, will help you locate the best deal for your money. As you shop, be certain that you know the extent of insurance on your deposit. If it's less than the full amount offered by the Federal Deposit Insurance Corporation, you must determine exactly what protection, if any, you actually have.

Table 16-4 **Certificate of Deposit Shopping List**

	Institution		
Item	**A**	**B**	**C**
□ *Fixed or variable interest rate?* Many places offer a choice. With the fixed rate, you earn a specific level of interest for the entire term of the certificate. With the variable rate, your interest fluctuates periodically. There's no way of knowing which will be better for you over the long run. The fixed rate is a sure thing. The variable rate is a guessing game: It could do better for you than the fixed. It could do worse.	_____	_____	_____
□ *Frequency of compounding?* How often does interest compound on the certificate? Given two plans with identical *rates*, the one that compounds more frequently will give you a higher return.	_____	_____	_____
□ *Minimum deposit required?* How much must you deposit in order to earn the desired rate of interest? Minimums differ from place to place.	_____	_____	_____
□ *Size breaks?* At many institutions, larger deposits earn higher rates of interest. The breaks may be at $2500, $10,000, $25,000, $100,000. If you can come up with a larger sum of money, you might be able to get a higher return.	_____	_____	_____

Table 16-4 Certificate of Deposit Shopping List (Continued)

Item	Institution A	B	C
☐ *Checking privileges?* Generally, you can't write checks against fixed-term certificates. But most institutions offer interest-earning checking accounts, and many people favor these over standard certificates of deposit. The checking accounts offer a lower rate of interest, but they do offer the flexibility of simple, penalty-free withdrawals.	_____	_____	_____
☐ *"Add-on" privileges?* Will you be able to put additional sums of money into your certificate account? This, if you can do it, might involve a blending of interest rates: combining the original rate with the new rate in effect at the time you make your additional deposit. Add-on privileges offer an extra measure of convenience, particularly for such accounts as IRAs, where annual additions might be made.	_____	_____	_____
☐ *Borrowing privileges?* If you need the money before the certificate matures, you'll have to face a penalty for the early withdrawal. It may be much cheaper for you to borrow against your certificate, rather than cashing it in. Many places offer guaranteed borrowing plans. For example, you can borrow for, say, 1 or 2 percent over what you're earning. Compare borrowing costs with penalty costs.	_____	_____	_____
☐ *Intangibles* Some variables are difficult to judge, perhaps, but they could be important. What other services might the bank offer you? Are you pleased with their manner, their way of doing business? Are they conveniently located? Are they open at convenient hours? Is their personnel friendly, helpful?	_____	_____	_____

Investment Criteria   The following investment criteria for fixed-income securities can help you do some comparison shopping before you invest your money:

☐ *Yield.*   With fixed-income certificates, you are certain of receiving the yield you bargained for by virtue of your contract with the financial institution. Beware, however, of potentially confusing advertising with respect to certificates. Advertising for certificates often quotes two different interest figures: "rate" and "yield," with *rate* being the lower of the two numbers. The rate refers to the actual interest rate that will be paid for the term. For example; if you contract for a $10,000 six-month certificate at a *rate* of 12 percent interest, you'll receive $600 (plus any interim compounding) for your investment (12 percent of $10,000 is $1200, and half of that—six months' worth—is $600). The *yield* means the annualized return you would get if, in fact, you received the same *rate* for a *full one-year* period. However, with a six-month certificate there's no way you can know what your rate will be after the original six-month term, so the *yield* figure gives a true picture only for a one-year certificate.

☐ *Liquidity.*   The liquidity of certificates of deposit is somewhat impaired as a result of the penalty provisions for early withdrawal. It is possible, however, and often advisable to borrow against a certificate rather than cash it in should you have an immediate need for some of the money.

☐ *Safety.*   As with passbook savings accounts, certificates at federally insured institutions are protected by the federal insurance programs up to $100,000 per account. Thus certificates are considered to be at the highest level with respect to safety.

☐ *Hedge value.*   Fixed-rate certificates have no hedge value. Variable-rate certificates can have attractive hedge value.

☐ *Pledge value.*   As with passbook savings accounts, certificates can be used as collateral for borrowing. Many institutions will guarantee a fixed interest rate should you wish to borrow against a certificate. Such an interest rate might be 1 percent over and above what you're receiving on your certificate. In other words, if you are receiving 12 percent interest and you wish to borrow against your certificate, you would have to pay 13 percent per year for borrowing any of your funds. As noted, this could be a cheaper way of getting to your funds than by cashing in the certificate prematurely and suffering a heavy penalty.

☐ *Tax implications.*   Interest income on certificates is fully taxable.

Bonds

Just as you often borrow money to buy a car, to fix up your home, to pay your bills, or to refinance existing older debts, business and governments likewise borrow money for similar needs. They may borrow for a long term (as long as forty years,) or for a short term (a few years or even a few months). When they borrow for a long term, the IOU that they issue is referred to as a *bond*. Short-term IOUs may be referred to as *bills*, *notes*, and, in the case of corporate short-term IOUs, *commercial paper*.

There are three major categories of bonds—federal government, local government, and corporate. And there are three ways that an investor can get involved in bonds: directly, semidirectly, and indirectly.

You can buy various bonds *directly* through a stockbroker and in some cases through the investment department of major banks. You can invest in them *semidirectly* through mutual funds that specialize in various bonds. The mutual funds pool the investments of many individuals and spread them out over a wide assortment of different issues. This is something that the ordinary investor can't do individually.

And although you may not be aware of it, you *already* have *indirect* investments in the bond market. If you have a bank account, an insurance policy, or a pension fund, it's very likely that some of your money is already invested in the bond market. This in itself is a good reason for you to become familiar with the workings of bonds.

Corporate Bonds.   Under the overall heading of corporate bonds are included the IOUs issued by railroads, public utilities (such as local electric and gas companies), and industrial firms (manufacturers and service companies such as airlines and retailing firms). Broadly speaking, there are two classifications of corporate bonds: straight and convertible. The straight bond is a simple long-term IOU of the issuing company, wherein a fixed interest rate is agreed to be paid to the investor. The convertible bond carries with it the right for the holder to convert the bond into shares of that same company's common stock. Convertible bonds, or *convertible debentures* as they're sometimes called, are discussed in more detail later in this chapter.

Corporate bonds can usually be bought in denominations of $1000, and the commission payable to a stockbroker is generally less than when buying stock. If you hold a bond until maturity and it's redeemed directly by the issuer, there'll be no commission to pay.

How to read bond quotations

Many major daily newspapers carry bond quotations, as does the *Wall Street Journal*. *Barron's*, a financial newspaper issued weekly, also contains a full listing of traded corporate bonds.

In bond price quotations, the number quoted is the selling price of the bond expressed as a percentage of its face value. Thus, if a $1000 bond is currently selling for $950, the quotation would appear as "95," which is 95 percent of its face value. Similarly, a bond selling for $985 would be quoted as "98½," which is 98.5 percent of its face value.

For example, in 1965 the XYZ Company borrowed some money from public investors and issued their bonds as IOUs. These bonds contained a promise to pay 6 percent interest per year for thirty years to everyone who bought the bonds, issued in $1000 denominations. The bonds would thus mature in the year 1995, at which time the XYZ Company would pay all holders of the bonds $1000 for each $1000 bond. Over the years, investors traded the bonds back and forth among one another. Because of market conditions, the bond sells today for $950. The quote in the newspaper would look as follows on a day when there was no fluctuation in its price:

Bond	Hi	Low	Last
XYZ 6s 95	95	95	95

This bond would be referred to as the XYZ Company 6s of 95. The 6s refers to the original interest rate that the company agreed to pay (6 percent); the 95 refers to the year of maturity (1995); the three 95 figures refer to the high, low and closing prices for the day. (Remember we said that the price didn't fluctuate on this particular day.)

How bond yields are figured

Bonds have three different yields, and the difference must be clearly understood. (This is equally true for government and municipal bonds.) The following description does not take into account brokerage commissions or income taxes payable on bond interest received.

☐ *Coupon yield.* Referring back to the earlier example of the XYZ 6s of 95, the 6 percent interest that the company originally agreed to pay is known as the *coupon rate*. In other words, the company guarantees that it will pay $60 each year (usually in semiannual installments) to each holder of each $1000 bond. The bond may fluctuate in price up and down, but the holder will continue to get $60 per year for each $1000 bond held, regardless of the price of the bond.

☐ *Current yield.* We noted that the bond was quoted at $950 on a given day. If an investor purchased a $1000 bond for $950 and received $60 per year in interest from the company, the actual *current yield* is 6.3 percent ($60 on $950, which is your actual investment). If, on the other hand, you had paid $1050 for the bond, your *current yield* would be roughly 5.7 percent ($60 is 5.7 percent of $1050, which is your actual investment).

☐ *Yield to maturity.* The third concept of yield is called the *yield to maturity*, and it's a bit more difficult to understand. Say that you buy a bond with a $1000 face value for $950, and you buy it exactly one year before its maturity date. Assume that it's paying the same 6 percent per year as the bond quoted above. When the bond matures one year after your purchase date, you get back the full face amount, $1000. That's $50 more than you paid for it, and the $50 is considered a capital gain. Also, you're going to get the $60 in interest during the year you hold the bond. Altogether you will receive $110 in one year for your $950 investment, or a *yield to maturity* of just over 11.6 percent.

If, however, you purchase the bond five years before maturity date, the $50 gain is prorated over the remaining five years. Thus, you receive the $60 each year in interest plus an eventual extra $50 on redemption, which is equal to an extra $10 on average each year, assuming that you hold the bond until maturity. Your annual average *yield to maturity* is thus approximately $70 each year, about 7.4 percent of your initial $950 investment.

How bonds fluctuate in value

If you buy a good quality bond with a face value of $1000, you will receive your $1000 from the borrowing entity—the government or the corporation—upon the maturity date of the bond. But from the day you buy the bond to the day it matures, its market value can and will fluctuate. In other words, on any given day, the bond might be worth more than you paid for it, or it might be worth less than you paid for it. If you find yourself in a position of having to sell a bond before it reaches maturity, you might have to sell it at a loss, or you might gain a profit. When people talk about the "safety" of bonds, they are referring to the full value redemption at maturity date. In the intervening years, however, the safety factor is subject to two main influences: (1) interest rate movements and (2) the financial condition of the issuing entity.

As a general rule, the market value of a bond moves in the opposite direction of interest rate trends. (The market value of a bond is what you can get for it if you were to sell it at any given time.)

Let's return to the example of the XYZ bonds. When XYZ Company borrowed the money in 1965, conditions were such that it had to pay an interest rate on those bonds of 6 percent, that is, $60 per $1000 per year. Let's say that you bought one such bond at that time. Five years later, in 1970, conditions are such that if XYZ were to borrow at that time, they would have to pay 8 percent interest per $1000 ($80 per $1000 per year). When you originally bought the XYZ bond, you intended to hold on to it for the full thirty years, earning interest as the years went along. But in 1970, you faced a financial emergency, and you found it necessary to sell the bond.

You came to me and said, "Bob, I have a perfectly good $1000 bond from the XYZ Company, paying 6 percent interest per year. I'd like to sell it to you for $1000."

I replied, "Why should I pay you $1000 for that bond when I can buy a brand-new bond from a company of comparable quality that will pay me 8 percent or $80 per year? If I can earn 8 percent on my money today, why should I settle for 6 percent, which is all I would earn if I bought your bond for $1000?"

Obviously dismayed, you answered me, "You mean I invested in this bond in good faith, being told that it was perfectly safe, and now I can't sell it for what I paid for it?"

"Don't be upset. I'll make you an offer. I'll buy your $1000 bond from you for $750. I'll earn $60 a year, which means that on my investment of $750 I'll be earning 8 percent, which is what I can get in the open market by buying a brand-new bond today—8 percent of $750 equals $60.''

Thus, in order to sell your bond, you had to take a $250 beating. However, if interest rates had moved down during the same period of time, you would have been able to sell your bond at a profit. The reality is this: We never know in which direction interest rates will move, how far they will move, or for how long. Thus there is always an element of risk in bond investing, whether you do so directly or indirectly.

There is one type of investment that gets around this problem: the *floating-rate bond*. If the interest rate on a given bond is permitted to move up and down, the principal value will not fluctuate. For example, you invest in a bond that is paying 8 percent interest per year initially. If interest rates move upward to 9 percent, and your bond is allowed to pay you the higher rate of return, your principal value will remain the same. By the same token, if interest rates move down, your principal will remain at the same face value level, and you'll receive a lower yield. In other words, you can't have it both ways: You have to accept either a floating rate of interest or a floating market value in bond investments.

There are a small number of floating-rate bonds available in both the taxable and tax-exempt categories. The most popular ones have been issued by banks, with Citicorp being the leader in the field. There may be limits concerning how high or how low the interest rate on a floating-rate bond can go. If interest rate trends in general exceed these limits, either on the up side or the down side, it is possible that your principal value could also fluctuate. But this is much less likely than with a fixed-rate bond.

The other factor that can affect the market value of a bond is the financial status of the issuing entity. If a company falls on bad times, or if a local government runs into financial difficulties, the marketplace may evaluate the company's bonds as being worth less than their face value because of the problems. For example, will the company be able to earn enough money to pay the interest it owes on its bonds? If the marketplace deems that payments of interest or principal are in jeopardy, the value of the bonds falls. As bonds get to within a few years of maturity date, they are generally less susceptible to these various fluctuations.

Sinking fund and call privileges

When corporations borrow money, they typically do something most individuals and families should be well advised to do. They set up what is called a *sinking fund* out of which they will eventually pay off the bond. They put aside so much money each year toward the eventual redemption of that bond and actually use those monies to pay off the investors, either at maturity or in advance of maturity if market conditions so dictate. For example, a company has issued a bond paying 7 percent interest per year. After the passage of a number of years, the interest rates prevalent throughout the economy have dropped to 6 percent. The company sees an opportunity to refinance the existing IOUs and drop its interest rate from

7 to 6 percent, thus cutting its interest expense considerably. In order to take advantage of this possible occurrence, many bonds have written into them a *call privilege*, which means that the company has the right to call in the existing bonds and pay off the holders at an agreed price.

A would-be investor in corporate bonds should determine what call privilege or protection exists. Because a bond is usually a relatively long term investment, it would be to the investor's advantage to know that the company can't call the bond for at least five to ten years.

Corporate bond ratings

There are thousands of corporate bonds available to investors at any given time. How is one to determine the relative quality of so many bonds? Corporate bonds are rated according to quality by two companies: Standard and Poor's, and Moody's. Both rating systems are very similar, taking into account the basic financial strength of the corporation and its ability to pay the interest on its debts. Highest-rated bonds offer the lowest rate of interest and the lowest risk to investors. Following is a brief summary of the Standard and Poor's ratings:

AAA	Highest-grade obligations
AA	High-grade obligations
A	Upper–medium-grade obligations
BBB	Medium-grade obligations
BB	Lower–medium-grade obligations
B	Speculative obligations
CCC–CC	Outright speculations with the lower rating denoting the more speculative
C	No interest is being paid
DDD–D	All such bonds are in default with the rating indicating the relative salvage value

The ratings companies keep a watch on the financial status of all bond issuers, and if there is a change in the financial strength of a company, its rating will be changed accordingly. For more specific details on the ratings, refer to the monthly rating books published by the two companies, available at stockbrokerage firms and at most local libraries.

Junk bonds

Bonds have historically been considered a safe haven for investors' money since the issuing entities were generally always financially sound. However, there were hundreds, perhaps thousands, of other companies who found the door to the bond market closed to them. They weren't able to raise funds by issuing IOUs because of a variety of reasons: Perhaps their credit-worthiness was not high enough, or perhaps they had not been in business long enough. Maybe their financial affairs were not strong enough or their management was not very well known. Perhaps they had had some bad years.

Nevertheless, among all of these companies there had to be many that were perfectly honorable, reliable, credit-worthy, and able to deliver interest and principal payments as promised. In the mid-1980s, there arose new opportunities to allow many of these companies to borrow money in the bond market, albeit at higher rates of interest than their more credit-worthy or experienced peers. The higher rate of interest was due to the perceived higher level of risk involved in lending money to less "proven" corporations.

As a rule, these corporations were rated BBB or lower. Because of their lower ratings, the instruments of these companies became known as *junk bonds*, despite the fact that many of them were of reasonably good quality. Aggressive marketing by many brokerage firms created tens of billions of dollars' worth of junk bond transactions, including many mutual funds that attracted the dollars of investors seeking higher returns and willing to take somewhat higher risks. Depending on overall conditions in the economy, junk bonds paid roughly 3 to 5 percent more than U.S. treasury bonds. A careful analysis of any given junk bond or mutual fund portfolio of such bonds could reveal a hidden opportunity: a small but well-managed company that is paying a high yield with a relatively low risk.

Junk bonds are subject to the same types of fluctuations as bonds of higher quality. Note that in times of sharp stock market fluctuations, junk bonds are more likely to suffer a sharper downturn than bonds with higher ratings.

Investment criteria

Some of the important investment criteria for corporate bonds are as follows:

- □ **Yield.** With higher-rated companies, you have a very high assurance of receiving the yield (interest payment) that you have bargained for. With lower-rated companies, the yield may be in doubt.

- □ **Liquidity.** The major bond exchanges (New York and American) maintain a ready market for buyers and sellers of bonds. But depending on the specific issue and the number of bonds being bought and sold, it could take from a few minutes to a few days to effect a transaction.

- □ **Safety.** The higher the rating of the bond and the closer it is to maturity, the safer your investment. As noted, bond prices can fluctuate substantially in value, moving in the opposite direction from interest rates.

- □ **Hedge value.** If a bond is bought at or near face value, there is little protection against inflation. As prices move upward—interest rates being among those prices—bonds will likely decrease in value, as noted above. Thus, the hedge value might be considered negative. If, on the other hand, a bond is bought below face value and maturity is approaching, the bond price will move upward as maturity nears, thus offering a measure of protection against rising prices.

☐ *Pledge value.* The amount that one can borrow against bonds and the interest rate paid on such a loan depend on the quality of the bond as determined by the rating services. Generally, well-rated bonds provide ample opportunity for pledging at reasonably favorable interest rates. However, if a bond has decreased in value, the amount that can be borrowed against it will decrease proportionately.

☐ *Tax implications.* Interest earned on corporate bonds is taxable.

U.S. Government Bonds. The federal government is the biggest borrower of all. Federal IOUs range from the common savings bond for as low as $25 to the multimillion-dollar obligations issued frequently by the U.S. Treasury. The federal government even borrows from itself. For example, the Social Security Administration invests its own funds in U.S. Treasury IOUs. Federal government obligations are further broken down into three subcategories: U.S. Treasury borrowings, federal agency borrowings, and savings bonds.

U.S. Treasury

The U.S. Treasury borrows frequently on a short-term, medium-term, and long-term basis. Short-term securities are called *treasury bills*, and their maturities range from three months to one year. Medium-term securities are called *treasury notes*, with maturities ranging from one to seven years. Long-term securities are called *treasury bonds*, with maturities ranging from five to thirty years. Any of these treasury securities can be obtained at a nominal commission through a stockbroker or the investment department of a bank or directly from the Federal Reserve Bank at no commission. The prices and yields of all U.S. Treasury obligations are listed daily in the *Wall Street Journal* in a column titled: "Treasury issues: Bonds, notes, bills."

Federal agency securities

A number of federal government agencies are frequent borrowers of large sums of money. The money they borrow is generally pumped back into the economy to subsidize such things as mortgage loans for home buyers and farm loans for the agricultural industry. Investments are available in a wide range of maturities. Short-term obligations, usually for a year or less, are commonly called *notes*. Medium-term obligations, which may run from one to five years, are commonly referred to as *debentures*. Long-term obligations that run from five to twenty-five years are referred to as *bonds*. Some of the more popularly traded federal agency obligations are issued by the Federal National Mortgage Association, the Federal Home Loan Bank, Banks for Cooperatives, Federal Land Banks, and Federal Intermediate Credit Banks.

The prices and current yields (before commissions) of U.S. Treasury obligations and agency obligations are quoted daily in the *Wall Street Journal* under the heading "Government, agency, and miscellaneous securities."

Savings bonds

Savings bonds are the most commonly known and popular forms of bonds issued by the federal government. They are currently called Series EE and HH bonds. (Savings bonds sold prior to 1980 are Series E and H bonds.) Series EE bonds sold since November 1, 1982, offer a fluctuating rate of interest. This is designed to keep the bonds more competitive with savings programs offered by financial institutions.

The fluctuating rate on the Series EE bonds works as follows: If you buy and hold the bonds for at least five years, you will earn the fluctuating rate of interest or the guaranteed minimum, whichever is greater. In 1987 the guaranteed minimum was set at 6 percent, but this could change in the future. Check before you invest. The fluctuating rate is adjusted every six months, and it's based on 85 percent of the average yield on five-year U.S. treasury securities. In other words, if the average yield on five-year U.S. treasury securities is 10 percent, then the Series EE bonds will pay 8.5 percent for that six-month period.

Series E and EE bonds continue to pay interest for forty years from their dates of issue. Once they have reached forty years of age, they stop paying interest and should be cashed in. Taxes are due on the accrued interest at that time. This is one particular advantage for Series E and EE bonds: The interest you earn is not taxable on your federal income tax return until you cash the bonds in. The interest is also tax-exempt on state and local income tax returns.

Series HH bonds may be acquired in exchange for Series E or EE bonds. In so exchanging your Series E or EE bonds, you can further defer taxation on the accumulated interest until the Series HH bonds are cashed. But interest earned on the Series HH bonds is taxable in the year you receive it. Check with the nearest Savings Bonds Division of the U.S. Treasury for full details on current rates and terms of savings bonds.

Zero coupon bonds

Zero coupon bonds are a new breed of investment. While there are some corporate and municipal zero coupon bonds available, by far the largest quantity on the market are related to U.S. government bonds, thus their inclusion in this section. As noted previously, bonds typically pay interest twice a year, and the face amount is then paid to bondholders on the maturity date of the bonds. With zero coupon bonds, there is no interest paid in the same sense. Rather, the bonds are bought at one price and are then redeemed in the future for a much higher price. In short, these bonds have a coupon yield of zero. The most commonly traded zero coupon bonds are derived from issues of the U.S. Treasury and have been nicknamed by various brokerage firms as CATS (Certificates of Accrual on Treasury Securities) and TIGRs (Treasury Investment Growth Receipts).

Zeros, as they're called, have proven popular because they offer a guaranteed return for a set period of time, and there is no need to bother with reinvestment of your interest earnings. However, the IRS has ruled that although you are not

Table 16-5   **Zero Coupon Bonds: A Sampling of Various Rates and Maturities**

If you invest this much . . .	For this many years . . .	At this yield . . .	You'll have this much at maturity
$5,200	5½	11.85%	$10,000[a]
2,500	11	12	10,000
1,600	13	12	10,000
1,000	19	11.75	10,000

[a]Amounts are rounded off; rates and terms vary.

receiving interest *in hand* each year, you must pay taxes on the accrued interest each year. Thus, zeros might not be advisable for personal accounts that are subject to taxation. But they could be appropriate for IRA and Keogh plans or any other tax-deferred portfolio. Table 16-5 offers examples of zeros and how they grow. Get full details from your stockbroker before you invest in them.

Investment criteria

As we have seen, government bonds can vary considerably. The following investment criteria will help you compare the different types of government bonds.

☐ *Yield.*   On regular government, agency, and zero bonds, you are certain to get the yield you are promised. The yield on Series EE bonds, as noted, will fluctuate, with a minimum guarantee if you hold the bonds for five years. The yield of Series HH bonds is assured and could be boosted by the Treasury.

☐ *Liquidity.*   There is an active market for government, agency, and zero issues, which would allow you to cash in your holding prior to maturity at the going market price, subject to commissions. Series EE and HH bonds may not be cashed in until six months after their date of purchase.

☐ *Safety.*   Government issues are considered to be in the highest safety category. To the ultimate skeptic, it's safe to presume that before the government falls, everything else will have long since fallen.

☐ *Hedge value.*   As with corporate bonds, an investor in long-term government issues has virtually no protection against inflation, assuming that interest rates go up as inflation increases, which is likely. The rate of income is fixed, and higher interest rates will mean lower market values for the bonds, as already discussed. Short-term investors are better able to guard against inflation. If inflation has boosted interest rates, short-term investors can move into higher-yield issues as their older ones mature. Fluctuating-rate Series EE bonds do offer good protection against inflation.

☐ *Pledge value.*   Series E, EE, H, and HH bonds cannot be pledged as security for a loan; thus they have no pledge value. Other government issues can be pledged, usually at a very high percentage of their face values. Generally, government issues would have higher pledge value than corporate issues of comparable size and maturity.

☐ ***Tax implications.*** Government and agency bonds are subject to federal taxation but are exempt from state and local income taxes. Series E and EE bonds are tax-deferred for federal returns, and tax-exempt on state and local income tax returns. The interest Series H and HH bonds earn each year is taxable for that year. Interest earned on zeroes (even though not received by you) is taxable each year; it is tax-deferred if in IRA or Keogh accounts.

Municipal Bonds. States, cities, towns, water districts, school districts, sewer districts, highway authorities, and a variety of other local entities have periodic needs to borrow funds. The interest that these bonds pay has been deemed exempt from federal income tax obligations. This, of course, benefits the local residents of the particular jurisdictions. It makes the cost of building and maintaining schools, roads, sewers, whatever, cheaper than if the holders of the municipal bonds had to pay income taxes on the interest they earn. If the bonds were not tax-exempt, they would have to be issued at a higher interest rate, resulting in higher interest costs being passed along to taxpayers.

There are two major types of municipal bonds: general obligation bonds and revenue bonds. The *general obligation bonds* are backed by the taxing authority of the locality. The *revenue bonds* are backed by the revenues produced by the entity, such as toll roads on a highway authority bond, or water-usage fees on a water-revenue bond.

The Tax Reform Act of 1986 puts limits on the purposes for which municipalities can issue tax-exempt bonds. Many cities and counties were using their tax-exempt borrowing status to attract investment funds. They then would turn the money over to private developers to build housing projects. Congress felt that this was a potential abuse of the tax-exempt borrowing privilege and created quotas as to how much of this type borrowing could be done in the future. Municipalities still borrow for such purposes, but the interest they pay to investors might not be tax-exempt. From 1988 onward, we have had municipal bonds that are *tax-exempt* and municipal bonds that are *taxable*. It's obviously critically important that any investor determine the full and correct status of any such investments before making a commitment.

Tax exemption

The most notable aspect of municipal bonds is that the interest they pay investors is exempt from the investors' federal income taxes. Interest earned is also exempt from state income taxes if the investor lives in the state in which the bond is issued. However, if an investor buys a municipal bond and later sells it at a profit, that profit is subject to full federal and state income taxes.

In comparing a tax-exempt investment with a taxable investment, one must determine how many dollars are left in either case after paying any applicable taxes. Table 16-6 compares tax-exempt yields with taxable yields. For example, a taxpayer

Table 16-6 **Comparison of Yields: Tax-Exempt versus Taxable Securities**

If you are in this tax bracket (1988 and after)	*A tax-exempt yield of*		
	6%	*7%*	*8%*
	Will net you the same as taxable yield of		
15%	6.9%	8.2%	9.4%
28	8.3	9.7	11.3
33	8.8	10.4	11.9

in the 28 percent tax bracket invests $1000 in a tax-exempt security paying 7 percent ($70 per year). If that same investor puts $1000 into a taxable security paying 9.7 percent per year, he earns $97 before federal income taxes. If the $97 is taxed at the 28 percent rate, he owes approximately $27 in taxes, reducing his *after-tax* yield to $70. Thus a taxable yield of 9.7 percent can be the same as a tax-exempt yield of 7 percent. (Numbers have been rounded off, and state income taxes and commission costs have not been included in the example.)

Although tax exemption of municipal bonds is attractive, municipal bonds are not for everyone. Taxpayers in higher brackets can benefit considerably, but taxpayers in lower brackets may not be better off with municipal bonds than with taxable securities, particularly when the commission costs of buying and selling such bonds are taken into account.

Municipal bond quotations

Quotations on the prices and yields of municipal bonds are not available in daily newspapers. An investor would have to contact a stockbroker for specific details on the prices and yields of any municipal bonds.

Municipal bond ratings

Municipal bonds are rated by the same two services that rate corporate bonds, Standard and Poor's and Moody's. As with the corporate bonds, these ratings services examine the financial status of the municipalities, and the ratings compare the relative qualities of the various issues. The formats in both ratings systems are similar. Following is a brief summary of the Standard and Poor's ratings.

AAA	Highest quality
AA	High grade
A	Good grade
BBB	Medium grade
BB	Speculative grade
B	Low grade
D	Default

As with corporate bonds, if the financial condition of a municipality changes, so will its rating. Higher ratings mean a lower return to investors and a lower risk. Check with the ratings services for more specific details.

Investment criteria

The following investment criteria should be considered before purchasing municipal bonds.

☐ **Yield.** In higher-rated municipal bonds you are assured of receiving the yield you bargained for.

Lowest-rated bonds are subject to termination of interest payments and even possible loss of principal. See the Consumer Beware section at the end of this chapter for an example of bonds that had been highly rated and suddenly turned sour, causing huge losses for investors.

☐ **Liquidity.** Trading in municipal bonds is not as active as is trading in stocks and corporate bonds. Thus, investors wishing to sell municipal bonds may have to wait many hours or days (or possibly even weeks in the case of smaller issues) until willing buyers come along. If sellers are eager to get a quick trade, they may have to settle for a lesser price.

☐ **Safety.** As with corporate bonds, the higher the rating of a municipal bond, the higher the safety level. Municipal bonds, like corporate bonds, are subject to the same fluctuations and call privileges. Indeed, the traditionally stable municipal bond market has undergone relatively severe fluctuations in recent years in conjunction with interest rate changes. Thus, long-term investors in municipal bonds must be concerned over getting caught in a long-term downswing in the value of their holdings should interest rates move upward from the time they bought the bonds.

There have been innovations—and more will be created—to protect municipal bond investors from these fluctuations. One type is called the *floating-rate bond*, in which the interest rate floats up and down within set limits, based on U.S. Treasury rates. Because the interest rate floats, the principal balance of the investment should remain relatively stable. Another innovation is the *option tender bond*, in which the holder has the option, or privilege, of cashing in the bond with the original issuer after some years from the date of issue. The investor can cash such bonds in at the original issue price. Check with stockbrokers for more details on these and other innovations in municipal bonds.

☐ **Hedge value.** Municipal bonds offer a rather indirect protection against inflation. Although the bond itself pays a fixed rate of income for as long as one holds it, the tax-exempt factor can be translated into some protection against inflation for the investor whose income is on the rise. As your income increases, you move into ever-higher tax brackets. The higher the tax bracket you're in, the greater the tax advantage the municipal bond affords you.

☐ **Pledge value.** Holders of municipal bonds should be able to borrow against their holdings without much difficulty. The percentage of the total value that they can borrow and the interest rate they'll have to pay will depend on the quality of the issue itself as well as its current price level. The higher the quality, the higher percentage of face value you may be able to borrow.

□ ***Tax implications.*** Except as noted, the interest earned on these securities is exempt from federal income taxes.

Miscellaneous Money Market Investments

Over the last decade, the ingenuity of the financial marketplace has been particularly bright with respect to the creation of new and unusual forms of fixed-income investment. Some of the concepts outlined here have long been the domain of big-money investors. But as the competition for investment dollars has heightened, the concepts have been enlarged to allow the small investor access to these techniques. Over the years, some will capture the public attention, some will fail to, and new techniques will continually be emerging.

Mutual Funds. The mutual fund concept has found great favor with the public at large. Mutual fund companies and stockbrokerage firms pool the investments of many small investors and put that money to work in a variety of ways. The most common types of mutual funds invest in the stock market. These funds are discussed in more detail in Chapter 17. But mutual funds in the money market have grown rapidly in popularity; these funds encompass corporate bonds, municipal bonds, U.S. government bonds, and money market instruments. Before examining each specific type of fund, let's examine some of the main distinctions among mutual funds in general.

□ ***Closed versus open-end funds.*** The vast majority of mutual funds are open-end funds. The managers of the fund are continually buying and selling securities at whatever pace they see fit. Thus the composition of the overall fund is constantly changing. The ability to buy and sell allows the fund managers to adjust to changing market conditions. It also expands the possibility of the managers making wise decisions *and unwise* decisions. Open-end funds are also often known as *managed funds*.

There are also a small number of closed-end funds. These function in much the same way as the open-end funds with respect to buying and selling securities on a continuing basis. However, to invest in a closed-end fund, one buys shares in such funds on the stock market rather than dealing directly with the mutual fund company itself.

Yet another type of pooled investment is the *unit trust*. Unlike investment funds that are constantly buying and selling securities, the unit trust buys a group of securities and holds them until maturity. The income with a unit trust is thus more certain than it is with a managed fund, but the value of each share is susceptible to the ups and downs of the market. Remember, interest rates and bond prices move in opposite directions.

☐ ***Load versus no-load.*** The terms *load* and *no-load* refer to the commission price an investor pays to buy shares in a mutual fund. A load can be as much as 8 or 9 percent of the initial investment. In other words, in a typical 8½ load fund, 8½ percent of the investor's initial investment goes to pay the brokerage commission. On a $1000 investment, $85 goes toward commissions and only $915 goes to work for the investor. A no-load fund implies that there is no commission to pay when acquiring the investment. But there may be other charges incurred over the life of the investment with both load and no-load funds.

☐ ***Maintenance and service charges.*** In addition to the loading commission, mutual funds charge some kind of monthly or annual service fee. Commonly, the service fee is based on a percentage of the fund's assets. Some funds may also take a fee based on the earnings of the fund during the year. These fees may be deducted from the total fund assets or directly from each individual account. Either way, they are an added cost that can affect your yield. Some mutual funds charge a redemption fee when you cash in your shares. Before making your initial investment, you should determine any and all charges that may occur.

☐ ***Fund objectives.*** With fixed-income mutual funds, the most common objective is to generate maximum income for the investors. (The common stock mutual funds' objectives fall into a broader spectrum ranging from income to speculative growth.) But there can be a distinct difference in the level of income and safety sought by various funds. This will largely be a factor of the distribution of the invested assets.

☐ ***Distribution of investments.*** How will a fund invest the money it receives from individual investors? Differences can be considerable. Some funds will go for the highest quality investments available. This will mean the highest possible level of safety for investors but a lower level of income than can be obtained from funds that seek out investments of lesser quality. It's necessary to determine the broad makeup of the portfolios of a number of funds before making an investment decision.

☐ ***Minimum investment required.*** As a broad average the minimum initial investment required in fixed income mutual funds is $1000. There may be a few with a lower initial amount, and there are some with a higher initial required investment. After the initial investment, investors may make additional investments in smaller amounts.

☐ ***Extra privileges.*** Many mutual funds are a part of a family of other mutual funds. The owner of shares in such funds may therefore have the privilege of exchanging all or a portion of their shares for shares in another fund managed by the same investment advisory group. For example, you might switch from a corporate bond fund into a common stock fund or vice versa, at a minimal charge. Reinvestment privileges—whereby your earnings are automatically reinvested in additional shares of the fund—are commonplace, usually at no extra charge. Withdrawal privileges—taking out a fixed amount each month or each quarter—are also available, with some minimal restrictions regarding the amount of withdrawals.

☐ ***Investment criteria.*** The investment criteria of a given fixed-income mutual fund will be approximately the same with regard to yield, liquidity, safety, hedge values, and pledge values as for that specific type of instrument. In other words, a mutual fund that concentrates exclusively on long-term corporate bonds will have the same investment criteria as individual corporate bonds, and so on. There is one important difference, however. The value of the investment criteria depends largely on the investor's own individual ability to interpret changes, trends, and concepts. Theoretically, the professional money managers are better able to do this than individuals. It follows, theoretically, that an investor who is seeking high income may do well, but a professional money manager may be able to do better, and so on.

The mutual fund concept allows investors to spread their risk over many securities rather than place all of their eggs in one basket. But a careful evaluation of the objectives, the management, and the overall risks involved is as necessary with a mutual fund as it is with a single investment and a specific issue. Investors are advised to read a number of prospectuses of various mutual fund offerings so as to distinguish among the various criteria noted above.

Following is a summary of major types of fixed-income mutual funds as well as brief descriptions of additional innovative fixed-income investments.

Corporate bond funds

Corporate bond funds invest in a wide variety of corporate bonds: high-quality, low-quality, long-term, and short-term bonds. The range of possibilities is vast, and it is essential to examine the prospectuses to determine the level of risk and income that an investor can expect.

Tax-exempt municipal funds

Tax-exempt municipal mutual funds invest predominantly in municipal bonds—those whose income payable to investors is exempt from federal income taxes. The range of quality and risk is not as wide as with corporate bonds, but a range does exist. As with buying municipal bonds, investors should be aware that not all of the income will necessarily be exempt from federal income taxes. If, for example, a mutual fund buys a bond and sells it later for a profit, the portion of the profit that is distributed to shareholders is taxable. Further, interest income from a mutual bond fund can be taxable on the local level (state and city). And as the prospectuses for these funds disclose, many funds do not invest 100 percent of their assets in tax-exempt municipals. They reserve the right to invest a small portion in other types of instruments that might be taxable. On the whole, however, the major portion of income on such funds is tax-exempt. It would be wise to check with one's tax advisor to determine if tax-exempt mutual funds make sense in any given individual situation.

Government bond mutual funds

One of the fastest-growing segments of the mutual fund industry has been funds that invest in U.S. government securities, including bills, notes, bonds, and mortgage pools backed by the federal government and its agencies. (See the discussion in Chapter 18 on these mortgage pools.) As a rule, these government funds involve relatively high quality securities, which means they yield a relatively low rate of return to investors but a high level of safety and the peace of mind that goes with it. Investors must always be wary, however, of the fact that bond market prices and interest rates move in opposite directions. Thus, even though these mutual funds are touted as being the ultimate in safety, there is the unavoidable risk of market fluctuation. The bonds in the fund are safe, that is, they will pay 100¢ on the dollar at maturity time. In the interim, there is always the risk of fluctuation that can send the value of an investment down suddenly if interest rates rise.

Another type of government security mutual fund is known as the *enhanced-yield fund*. These funds invest some of the pooled money in interest rate futures, which can produce a somewhat higher yield to investors but which also entail a higher level of risk.

Money market mutual funds

Money market mutual funds have been very popular with investors. They give small investors access to higher rates of return that might not otherwise be available. They also provide a good "parking place" for investment dollars while waiting for better opportunities to appear. Note one important distinction between money market *mutual funds* and money market *accounts*, which are available at banks and savings institutions. The money market accounts are protected by the Federal Deposit Insurance Corporation programs. The money market mutual funds do not have this protection. Otherwise, the accounts function similarly. It's best to compare the current rates of return for these two types of funds before making an investment choice. Following are some of the main features of money market mutual funds:

☐ They are flexible: Investors can get out at any time without penalty.

☐ Returns on these funds will vary from day to day, as interest rates fluctuate. Thus, investors never know what their actual return will be over a long run. (With certificates of deposit, investors are assured a fixed rate for a fixed period of time.)

☐ Fees are reasonably low compared with other types of mutual funds. However, in many funds, the individual broker or salesperson that one deals with may receive little or no commission. This has caused many brokers to shun small investors' business in money market funds. For those brokers who don't shun such business, the next item can prove a problem for investors.

☐ In virtually all money market mutual funds, the investor will be dealing with a salesperson or a stockbroker. Sooner or later that investor should expect to receive a call from the salesperson or broker suggesting that the investor get out of the money market fund and into something else. If the investor isn't prepared for this sales pitch, he may find himself making a switch that could prove profitable or unprofitable. In short, an investor might find himself being wooed from a highly secure position into a speculative position. This is not necessarily bad, but the investor should be aware of the potential before making an investment.

☐ Shares in money market mutual funds are not insured as are bank accounts, but the bulk of money market fund investments are in highly secure instruments such as government issues and bank certificates.

☐ Many large brokerage firms offer to tie in money market investments with checking accounts and credit card availabilities. In effect, a portion of your checking account balance that isn't needed for immediate use can be invested in the brokerage firm's money market fund where it can earn a high rate of interest. The minimum deposits required for such services and the cost of such services should be carefully examined by prospective investors.

Following are some other types of money market investments that may be available to individual investors directly or that may be included in a mutual fund portfolio.

Strategies for Success

Compare Yields Along with Maturities

One basic rule of money market investing is clear: All other things being equal, a security that promises a higher yield also carries a higher risk. But what if all other things are *not* equal? What if they are equal in quality (such as federally insured deposits or U.S. Treasury obligations) and the only difference is their maturity, that is, how long they have to run. There can also be a difference in the yield. Generally, the *longer* the term, the *higher* the yield. But the longer term doesn't always produce that much better a yield to warrant tying up your money for those extra years. Here's a simple example. A three-year obligation of the U.S. Treasury Department offers a yield of 7.9 percent. At the same time, a ten-year Treasury obligation offers a yield of 8.7 percent. Is it worth tying up your money for seven extra years to gain less than 1 percentage point extra in yield? Ask yourself before you take the plunge.

Repurchase Agreements.   Financial institutions often have to borrow large sums of money for very short periods of time—from a few days to a few months. They may borrow from one another, they may borrow from the government (from the Federal Reserve Bank in the case of commercial banks and from the Federal Home Loan Bank in the case of savings and loan associations). Or they may issue what are known as *repurchase agreements*, or *repos*. In a repurchase agreement, a bank will sell securities that it owns to outside investors and will give those outside investors a promise that it will repurchase the securities within a fixed period of time at a higher price than the investors paid for them. For example, Bank X may sell $1 million worth of its own government securities to investor Y. The bank promises to repurchase those securities ninety days later for $1,025,000. That $25,000 represents the lender's profit, which is equal to an annual yield of 10 percent on the invested money.

In many communities, financial institutions have offered small parcels of repurchase agreements to small investors. In other words, instead of selling a single $1 million security to a single investor, it breaks the $1 million down into 1000 pieces worth $1000 each and offers these small pieces to individual investors. Commonly, repurchase agreements in this form run for eighty-nine days or less and pay a yield to investors considerably higher than what their passbook savings accounts will pay. Repurchase agreements are technically not bank accounts and, thus, are not covered by the federal insurance.

Banker's Acceptances.   Say an American company sells a product to a Japanese company for $200,000. The Japanese company gives a written promise to pay for the goods upon delivery, which is expected to be in six months. The American company doesn't want to wait for its money, so it takes the Japanese company's promise to pay to a bank. The bank examines the credentials of the Japanese company and agrees to buy its promise to pay from the American company at a certain price. The bank has thus, in effect, "accepted" the Japanese promise to pay. The bank may then turn around and sell this IOU to investors. The instrument is known as a *banker's acceptance*. In effect, the investor is buying the promise to pay of a foreign company. The investor is secured to the extent that a bank or other financial institution is willing to take the risk itself. Banker's acceptances tend to pay an attractive rate of interest for short-term investments. Some financial institutions have parceled out banker's acceptances in small lots, similar to their technique with repurchase agreements, thus making portions of banker's acceptances available to small investors. Many money market mutual funds also will have banker's acceptances in their portfolios.

Commercial Paper.   When corporations borrow for a long term, as discussed, their promises to pay are called *corporate bonds*. Often, corporations will borrow for a short period of time—such as a few months. Short-term corporate borrowings are referred to as *commercial paper*, and their quality tends to follow the quality of the corporation's bonds. As the bond is rated, so commonly will the commercial paper be rated. See the discussion on bond ratings for more detail. Money market mutual funds frequently carry sizable amounts of commercial paper in their portfolios.

Commodity-Backed Bonds. Commodity-backed bonds are relatively rare but could become commonplace. In a commodity-backed bond, the corporation borrowing money gives the investor a choice of being paid off either in cash or in the particular product that the company makes or sells.

Convertible Bonds. Convertible bonds (sometimes called *convertible debentures*) are corporate bonds that give the owner the right to convert the bonds into common stock of the issuing company. Here's an example: XYZ Corporation issues a convertible bond with a selling price of $1000. The bond pays an interest rate of 10 percent—$100 per year. This rate is fixed for the life of the bond. An owner of the bond has the right to convert her bond into fifty shares of XYZ common stock, which is now selling for $20 per share and paying a $2 per share dividend. Thus, the income from fifty shares of the common stock is $100 per year, the same as the bond. At this point, the $1000 bond and the fifty shares of common stock are equal in value. There would seem to be no point in converting from the bond to the stock. However, an investor may be hopeful that the dividend on the stock could increase, say from $2 to $3 per share. If, in fact, this happens and the investor converts from the bond to the stock, he increases his yield from $100 to $150 per year. The interest rate on the bond is fixed, but since the dividend rate on the stock is not fixed, an investor who is willing to speculate on increased dividends could find convertible bonds profitable.

On the other hand, the bond is eventually going to be worth $1000 upon maturity. The investor knows this for sure. The stock could drop to a much lower level than its conversion value. If an investor does convert, she is taking a chance. The stock could decrease in value, and she could suffer a considerable loss.

During the holding period, prior to a decision to convert, the bond and the stock tend to move up and down on a fairly parallel course. Once the investor has converted from the bond to the stock, she can't convert back to the bond again if her expectations do not work out.

YIELDS ON MONEY MARKET SECURITIES

The Personal Action Checklist at the end of this chapter will help you to compare the current yields on the most common types of money market securities. Since these yields change frequently, you should compare them at the time you are ready to make a specific investment.

Comparing Current Income Opportunities

It's expected that savings opportunities will become more and more competitive as the financial industry gradually adjusts to the congressionally mandated deregulation of interest rates. Whereas in the past, virtually all institutions paid comparable rates of interest, the emerging deregulation is expected to offer the public a mind-boggling assortment of choices. Following are what will be among the more popular choices, along with criteria that can help you evaluate which is best for your specific current situation.

Item	Annual rate (%)	Yield, after compounding and taxes	Maturity	Penalty[a]	Safety[b]
☐ U.S. Treasury issues					
3-month	_____	_____	_____	_____	_____
6-month	_____	_____	_____	_____	_____
12-month	_____	_____	_____	_____	_____
24-month	_____	_____	_____	_____	_____
36-month	_____	_____	_____	_____	_____
☐ U.S. agency issues					
under 1 year to maturity	_____	_____	_____	_____	_____
2 to 5 years to maturity	_____	_____	_____	_____	_____
☐ Certificates of deposit					
6-month	_____	_____	_____	_____	_____
12-month	_____	_____	_____	_____	_____
30-month	_____	_____	_____	_____	_____
48-month	_____	_____	_____	_____	_____
☐ Corporate bonds, commercial paper					
under 3 years to maturity	_____	_____	_____	_____	_____
3 to 6 years to maturity	_____	_____	_____	_____	_____

Item	Annual rate (%)	Yield, after compounding and taxes	Maturity	Penalty[a]	Safety[b]
☐ Special tax-protected investments					
tax-deferred IRA and Keogh					
plans	————	————	————	————	————
tax-exempt municipal notes and					
bonds	————	————	————	————	————
tax-deferred annuities	————	————	————	————	————

[a]Penalty refers to any loss of interest or principal if any principal is withdrawn prior to the maturity of the investment.

[b]Safety refers to the level of security: governmental insurance, quality of the issuing company, and so on. Evaluate as per discussion in this chapter, plus any up-to-date developments that would have a bearing on safety.

"Whoops!!!"

The northwest corner of the United States is an energy-rich area: Raging rivers throughout Washington and Oregon provide inexpensive hydroelectric power. It would not seem to be an area in which anything more than dams needed to be built to create electricity.

Back in the 1960s the idea of building nuclear power plants swept the nation —including the Washington/Oregon area. A group of eighty-eight public utility companies—mostly small, rural, and unsophisticated—decided to build five nuclear power plants in the region—mostly large, expensive, and unnecessary. They called themselves the Washington Public Power Supply System, WPPSS for short. Through some clever but legal maneuvering, they were able to sell tax-exempt bonds to raise the money to build their nuclear power plants. Altogether they raised over $8 billion, making them the largest issuer of municipal bonds in the country at that time.

Bonds were sold to investors large and small. They were highly rated and offered an unusually high return. Brokers assured investors that all of the bonds were perfectly safe, because they were backed by the promise of the eighty-eight utility companies to pay for the power that the plants generated.

Then a funny thing happened. The people who ran WPPSS discovered that if all the nuclear plants were completed, they would be able to generate more electricity than they could sell. That fact, plus the higher than anticipated costs of construction, presented a very dismal picture to the WPPSS people: They couldn't afford to pay off on $2.25 *billion* worth of the bonds that they had issued. They were faced with having to default on those $2.25 billion worth of bonds.

"That'll never happen," the brokers reassured the investors.

Wrong. It did happen, in late 1983. The nickname Whoops proved to be horribly true. It was the biggest municipal bond default in history. And it won't be the last.

CHAPTER 17

Making Your Money Grow:
The Stock Market

This chapter continues our exploration of ways you can make your money grow—hopefully. The stock market involves aspects of risk not found in money market investments. The nature of these risks are not always understood by would-be investors and speculators. If the risks aren't understood, serious damage can be done to your financial well-being. To help you understand and evaluate these risks, we'll examine the following:

□ What makes the stock market tick

□ How to understand the language and the numbers of the stock market

□ What motivates various kinds of people to put their money to work in the stock market, the better to help you identify and understand your own motivations

□ Specific techniques that you can use within the arena of the stock market

□ Evaluating the professional help available to you through stockbrokers

A PERSPECTIVE

From 1982 until late 1987 the stock market enjoyed one of its longest and most powerful upward trends in its history. For five years nothing seemed to be able to dampen the enthusiasm of stock market players: not severe federal deficits, not severe international trade deficits, not ruinous scandals of insider trading, not the gradual but discernible decay of America's industrial power in the world. Speculative fever ran amok not just in the United States but in most of the other major stock exchanges around the world. During this extended period, many new attitudes about the market were shaped, particularly in the younger segments of the population. These attitudes included the following perceptions: The stock market only goes in one direction—up, the stock market is an assured way to wealth, and people are foolish if they put their money to work in any way other than the stock market.

Then on October 19, 1987, the earth shook under Wall Street. The Dow Jones

Industrial Average plummeted by 508 points, its worse single day ever. The after-shocks were felt for months thereafter, and analysts will be debating the causes of the debacle for years. Indeed, the long-term implications of the crash that began in late 1987 may be felt throughout the economy of the nation and the world until the end of the century.

It was the unthinkable, the incredible, and the impossible all rolled into one. In the space of just six and one-half hours, roughly $500 billion worth of what could have been spendable wealth disappeared. The market crash and its long-term aftereffects serve as a grim but real and healthy reminder that speculation has its retribution. The aforementioned attitudes regarding the stock market's invincibility should certainly be recycled into much more modest and realistic versions: The stock market can lead to wealth; it can also lead to poverty.

This chapter is a basic primer on how the stock market functions. It's not intended to predict the future. But there certainly is a new dimension in the stock market's future: As with earthquakes, until one *does* happen, you can always choose to believe that one might *never* occur. Once an earthquake *does* occur and you're in the middle of it, it is permanently etched in your brain. From that moment on, you always know that it *can* happen again. Likewise with the stock market: Until a crash occurs, you can always pretend to believe that one might never occur. But once one occurs, there's no denying that the "impossible" can happen again. Bear this in mind as you consider the basic functions of the stock market as outlined in the balance of this chapter.

STOCK OWNERSHIP: A FORM OF INVESTING

In the previous chapter on money market investing we explored the possibilities of creating future wealth by lending your money to another entity, receiving in turn a promise to pay a fee (interest) for the use of your money, plus the promise to return it at an agreed time. These promises are legally binding obligations of the debtor or institution.

Stock ownership as a form of investment is quite different. With stock ownership, the investor has become a part owner of a business enterprise and has no promise (legal or otherwise) that he will receive any fee for the use of his money or that anyone will be obliged to pay him any or all of his money back at any future time. He is dependent on the profitability of the business venture to generate a return on his investment and to create the possibility of a gain should he later wish to sell the investment.

Lending versus Buying

What's the difference between lending your money to a business (investing in a corporate bond) and buying a portion of ownership in the business (buying stock)? Businesses often need money to develop new products, expand their facilities, buy new equipment, modernize, and finance other job-creating activities. Some of the money needed may come from the profits that the business generates, but this isn't always enough. In order to acquire large sums of money relatively quickly, a business will either borrow from investors (issue corporate bonds) or will sell a portion of itself to investors (issue stock). The former route is frequently referred to as the *debt market*, the latter as the *equity market*.

Regarding its debt, the company has a legal obligation to pay interest to the investors and to return the principal sum at the agreed time. With equity, or stock, the company has no such legal obligation. *If* profits are in fact generated, the company *may* distribute a portion of the profits to the stockholders. The company is under no obligation to buy the stock back from a stockholder. If stockholders want to sell the stock, they look for buyers willing to pay an attractive price.

The important priority to note in comparing debt with stock ownership is that debt service (interest) *must* be paid *before* profits are tallied. Profits are the dollars left over after the business has paid all of its obligations, among which may be the payments due on its debts.

The same holds true when a business is terminated, either voluntarily or otherwise. In such a procedure, commonly called a *liquidation*, everything that the company owns is converted into cash. Out of this pool of cash, all of the company's debts are paid, including any bonds that may be outstanding. What's left over is split up between the stockholders. In other words, creditors have priority over stockholders in liquidation as well as in the day-to-day operation of a business.

The profitability of any kind of business venture depends on a great many factors, including management of the business, nature of the competition, overall ups and downs in the nation's economy as well as in a particular category of industry, and the totally unpredictable quirks and whims of the investing public. It's this last element—the whims and quirks of the investing public—that makes the stock market a series of unending dilemmas. In the stock market, you are not just necessarily betting on how profitably the company can perform; you are also betting on how *other* people think the company might perform.

Primary Market versus Secondary Market

Distinction should be made between the primary or new issues market and the secondary market. The primary market is that aspect of stock trading in which companies raise money from the investing public. Once the money has been raised and shares of ownership in the companies have been issued to the investors, the stock is traded in the secondary market. Only a tiny percentage of all stock transactions are primary market transactions; the vast majority are on the secondary market.

The primary market serves a critically important purpose in the economy of the nation: It provides ready access for companies to raise money for expansion, research, and other worthwhile purposes. The secondary market is often looked upon as little more than a gambling casino. There is, however, an important purpose for the secondary market: Without the secondary market, the primary market could not exist. Businesses could not raise money by selling stock if the investors did not know that they could readily sell their stock at a fair price. Thus, despite the often speculative aspect of the secondary market, our economy would severely flounder without it.

Possibilities *versus* Probabilities

Virtually every transaction in the stock market, every purchase, and every sale of every share, is essentially a disagreement. The sellers want to get out because they don't think the stock offers them satisfactory income or potential any longer. The buyers want to get in because they feel the stock *does* offer satisfactory income or profit potential. In other words, the two parties disagree about the potential of the stock.

The stock market offers a vast spectrum of possibilities. The challenge is to find that small cluster of possibilities that can help achieve your stated objectives. But note the word *possibilities*. For fixed-income investment, we're dealing with the realm of *probabilities*; in the stock market it's *possibilities*.

In your own personal life, you have a spectrum of future needs and desires: some probable and some possible. It's *probable* that you're going to retire some day and need adequate money to live on. It's *possible* that some day you might be in a position to enjoy a trip around the world. Goals that are probable, fixed, or certain need appropriate techniques if they are to be achieved. Those techniques tend to fall into the spectrum of fixed-income investment. You can't afford to take chances when it comes to achieving your fixed and necessary goals. You have to be certain that they will be reached or at least as certain as you can be.

Other goals that are less certain may be appropriately sought after by the *less certain* investment techniques, principally the stock market, *but not until after you have established a disciplined program that you feel confident will put you on the path to achieving your fixed goals.*

In other words, get a reasonable program under way that will take you to your fixed destinations. If you still have funds available to invest after you've put enough away toward those top priorities, you might want to consider the more speculative techniques to help you achieve lesser priority goals—goals that if not achieved will not cause you to really suffer.

For a more vivid comparison of the difference between fixed-income investing and "ownership" investing, let's look at the following scale, which represents the likelihood of achieving stated objectives:

1. Relatively total certainty
2. Fairly certain
3. Highly probable
4. Probable
5. Highly possible
6. Possible

7. Relatively uncertain

8. No degree of certainty

The objective: to put away X dollars today and know that you will have Y dollars at some future date. The risk taken on fixed-income types of investment should fall into the top half of the scale, from one to four. High-quality stocks fall in the middle, from three to six. High-quality stocks are those that have a very strong assurance of continuity of dividends; they are, nonetheless, subject to fluctuations in value, which can have an important bearing on your overall nest egg.

The majority of investments in the stock market fall in the four to seven range, and a considerable number would be in the six to eight range. A small number of lower-rated fixed-income securities might fall into the bottom half of the scale, but the risk in such securities is much more self-evident because of the ongoing ratings of the securities.

For the balance of this chapter, we'll examine in greater detail some of the inner workings of the stock market. In no way at all should any of the discussion be construed as recommendations to buy, sell, or hold any types of securities; it is to help you to determine whether or not the stock market offers the opportunities that will help you meet your goals, to understand how the mechanism works, and to motivate you to do further independent research to find the specific areas that will provide you with the returns you're seeking.

Cautions

As you read and discuss the material on the stock market, bear in mind the following cautions:

1. Aided by sophisticated computers, millions of hours are spent every day studying every movement, jiggle, and quiver of the stock market. Yet no one can predict with any degree of certainty what direction the market as a whole or any individual stock is liable to take even a minute or two from now.

2. There have probably been more statistics compiled about the stock market and more books written about it than any other phenomenon on earth. Yet it continues to be one of the most confusing, mystifying, and frustrating subjects we deal with.

3. The stock market touches our day-to-day life in more ways than we can imagine, yet we are powerless to control it in even the slightest way. Even though you may have never had anything to do directly with the market and don't intend to ever have anything to do with it, it can still affect you. If the company that employs you is traded on the stock market, swings in the value of its stock can affect the future profitability of the company and possibly your future. If your employer or boss is a stock market trader, his success or failure in the market on a day-to-day basis can have an effect on his personality and attitude, which in turn can affect yours. If your pension fund or profit-sharing fund has money invested in the stock market, the investment expertise of those who manage the funds can have a profound bearing on your future.

4. There is no person, no book, no system, no computer that can *assure* you of making money in the stock market. The stock market can play an important function as an integral part of establishing your future security. But unless one approaches it with the proper frame of mind, the proper expertise, and the proper degree of skepticism, its traps and pitfalls can destroy the very best intentions.

HOW BUSINESSES OPERATE

A brief look at how a corporation functions will assist you in understanding the workings of the stock market. A corporation is a legal entity in its own right. Each separate state has its own specific laws governing how a corporation may be created and how it can be run. Like a person, a corporation can own, buy, or sell property; it can be taxed; it can sue and be sued; and it can conduct business.

A corporation is owned by its stockholders. Operating within the framework of applicable laws, the stockholders determine what they wish their corporation to do. But, particularly with corporations that have a great many stockholders, it is cumbersome for the stockholders to meet and consult over every item of corporate business. Thus, the stockholders elect a group of representatives who will act on their behalf in setting basic policy and direction for the corporation. These representatives are referred to as the *directors*.

In turn, the directors will choose a group of individuals to carry out the day-to-day and month-to-month operations of the business. These people are called the *officers* of the corporation. The chief officer of a corporation is commonly called the *president*. (Many large corporations also have other titles of high magnitude that may be equal to or greater in power than the president, such as chief executive officer.) Under the president and answering directly to her is an array of vice presidents, each with their own area of tasks, obligations, and responsibilities. Other officers of the corporation are generally the treasurer, the secretary, and the comptroller, and each of these may have an additional hierarchy of assistants.

The stockholders generally meet once each year, at which time they are informed of the progress and future potential of the corporation. It's at the annual meeting that the stockholders select the directors, who in turn select the officers. If individual stockholders are unable to attend this annual meeting, they receive a *proxy*, a voting authorization on which they can indicate their selection of directors and their choice on a number of issues on which stockholders have been asked to express an opinion or a vote.

Commonly, the board of directors recommends to the stockholders a slate of nominees for the board for the forthcoming year. If ownership has been pleased with the job that management has done, the board's recommendations will usually be followed. If ownership has not been pleased with management's performance, a struggle might ensue. One or more directors may be voted out, and one or more proposed policies may be rejected by the stockholders. It is the rule rather than the exception in most large corporations that the stockholders will comply with the recommendations of the board of directors. Stockholders assume that management knows best, even though there may have been some setbacks during the year, or they may simply not care to express any contrary views when completing their proxy vote. In recent years, though, the annual meetings of many major corporations have been enlivened by sharp discussions between ownership and management regarding corporate responsibility in the fields of discrimination, pollution, and political practices. As a result, many corporations have adopted policies in keeping with stockholder wishes to amend their stance or create a new stance in line with these highly visible public issues.

HOW STOCK MARKETS OPERATE

An individual's share of ownership in a corporation is represented by the stock certificate, which stipulates how many shares the individual owns. The value of each share and thus of one's overall sum total of shares, is determined by a number of factors: profitability of the company, future potential for the company, amount of dividends the company is paying, and what the public at large thinks the share is worth. If stockholders wish to sell their stock, they must find buyers who are willing to pay the asking price. If investors wish to buy stock, they must find willing sellers. In small local corporations, word of mouth may be all that's needed to find a buyer or seller, if one is to be found. But with large corporations, particularly those with hundreds of thousands or millions of shares outstanding, relying on word of mouth would be impractical. If would-be investors in stocks did not feel confident that they could sell their shares quickly and efficiently, they would likely be discouraged from making the investment in the first place.

Thus, throughout the nation and the world, exchanges long ago came into being to provide a ready marketplace for both buyers and sellers. The most familiar is the New York Stock Exchange, located in lower Manhattan, in an area commonly referred to as Wall Street. Other major U.S. exchanges include the American Stock Exchange and the Pacific Stock Exchange.

The stock exchanges are basically a form of auction in which buyers and sellers try to achieve the best buying or selling price. An investor who wishes to buy or sell stock places an order with a local stockbroker who works for a firm who owns a "seat" on an exchange. The order is relayed from the local broker's office to the firm's facilities on the floor of the exchange. In some cases, the brokerage firm may fill the order itself. In other cases, the order may be referred to a "specialist" on the floor of the exchange. Stocks traded on any given exchange are individually represented by specialists whose job it is to match certain buy and sell orders and to keep an orderly marketplace for the stock they represent. In order to do so, they may be required to actually buy or sell stocks from their own account. When the order is filled, word is relayed back to the local brokerage firm, which informs the customer of the results. Written confirmation of the transaction follows shortly thereafter.

The Prospectus

Before a stock can be publicly traded (including on an exchange), it must comply with certain governmental regulations. If a stock is to be sold only to the residents of the specific state in which the company is located, the company must comply with local state regulations. If it is to be traded broadly, beyond state boundaries and across the nation, it must comply with requirements of the federal agency that oversees such matters, the Securities and Exchange Commission (SEC).

Federal regulations require a company to disclose a variety of facts relating to its operation, including the identity and experience of its management, its debts, its legal affairs, its overall financial status, and the potential risks an investor might face in investing in the company. All of this information—usually spelled out at great length in cumbersome legal jargon—is contained in a document called the *prospectus*.

A prospectus is required when a company initially sells its stock or when it issues subsequent securities, including stocks or bonds. Once the initial prospectus has been issued, a company need not issue subsequent ones unless it offers additional securities at a later date. Thus, while the prospectus is an important tool for the investor, if it is substantially out of date (as most are), its value can be diminished. Yet it still might serve as important background material and should not be ignored.

Corporations issue annual reports for the stockholders and for the SEC. These reports contain more up-to-date information than the prospectus. A would-be investor should examine the annual reports and compare them with the original prospectus, if for no other reason than to determine how well the company has met its original objectives.

Mutual funds must also issue a prospectus when they seek investment dollars from the public. The existence of a prospectus for either a mutual fund or a stock can mislead an investor into thinking that the government has somehow given its blessing to the validity and value of a given investment. Nothing could be farther from the truth! On the front cover of each prospectus is the often overlooked statement: ''These securities have not been approved or disapproved by the Securities and Exchange Commission, nor has the Commission passed on the accuracy or adequacy of this prospectus. Any representation to the contrary is a criminal offense.'' This statement means exactly what it says: The government does not in any way stand behind any of the statements made in the prospectus. However, if the prospectus is misleading or inaccurate, the corporation or mutual fund can be subject to criminal prosecution. The prudent investor should make wise use of the prospectus without being misled by it or by any sales pitches claiming governmental approval.

Investor's Insurance

The government does, however, offer one measure of protection to investors through the Securities Investor Protection Corporation (SIPC). When scores of banks folded as a result of the Great Depression in 1929–1935, the government acted to create an insurance program that would prevent a recurrence of such a disaster. The Federal Deposit Insurance Corporation came into being to insure bank depositors against the bank failure. But until 1970, there was no comparable protection for investors who entrusted their funds to stockbrokerage firms. A severe stock market collapse in 1969–1970 caused a number of brokerage firms to fail. Many more firms that were on the brink of imminent failure were absorbed by larger and healthier firms. As a result of the near panic that ensued, the government, in conjunction with the securities industry, took steps to create the SIPC, which would insure investors' accounts for the value of any securities or funds held by their brokerage firm in the event of a failure of such a firm. Most major firms currently provide this protection to their customers, but some smaller firms may not. (*Note* that the insurance does *not* protect against the value of any stock going down.)

Keeping Records

The shares of most major corporations are traded by the hundreds or thousands every business day. It's not uncommon for over 200 million shares of stock to change hands in a single day on the New York Stock Exchange alone. This total volume is made up of many thousands of individual transactions, representing handfuls or major blocks of shares. Smaller corporations whose shares are seldom traded may hire clerical help to administer the necessary paperwork involved in periodically amending the list of stockholders. But most major corporations hire ''transfer agents'' to take care of this burdensome task. Transfer agents are usually affiliated with major banks.

When you buy or sell shares of a stock, the transfer agent is notified accordingly, and your name is either placed on or removed from the list of stockholders of that corporation. As dividends become payable, the transfer agent sees to it that the dividend is transmitted to you or to your account with the stockbroker.

When you buy stock, you have the choice of obtaining the certificate registered in your own name (or in the name of whatever parties you choose as owners, such as husband and wife jointly) or having the broker retain custody of the stock. In the latter case, the stock would be listed ''in street name.'' Technically it is in the broker's name and possession, but he is holding it for your account. Some investors may prefer to have the certificate in their own hands, aware of the fact that they should make proper safekeeping arrangements for it. Other investors prefer the convenience of having it remain in the broker's custody. In such cases investors receive monthly statements from their brokers indicating the status of their accounts and which securities are being held in their name.

Each buy and sell transaction is followed up by a written confirmation that indicates the date of the transaction, the price for which the security was bought or sold, the amount of the broker's commission, and any appropriate taxes, and the net amount due to the broker or to the investor from the broker. These confirmation slips should be retained by the investor, for they contain information helpful in determining future gains or losses on the stock. Confirmation slips also indicate the *settlement date*, which is the day by which the payment must be made and the stock delivered.

Strategies for Success

Shop for Brokerage Commissions and Services

Does it pay to use the services of a so-called full-service stockbroker? Or are you better off using a discount broker? Commissions on stock transactions can vary considerably, and the amount of commission you have to pay a broker can cut deeply into your return. Remember, you pay a commission when you buy stock and when you sell stock. The commission is generally calculated on the number of shares you're trading and the prices of those shares. Full-service brokers can offer you a wide range of research and other advisory materials. Discount brokers simply take your order and execute it, offering few if any frills. Prepare a shopping list of possible transactions. For example, 50 shares at $25 each; 100 shares at $40 each; and 300 shares at $60 each. Call both types of brokers, and ask how much they would charge on these trades. Find out what kind of services they offer and what those services are worth to you. Also check their reputation as part of your comparison shopping.

Executing Orders

Once you have opened an account with a broker by signing the necessary papers, you can execute orders, that is, instruct your broker to buy or sell on your behalf. (If the individual broker with whom you regularly deal is not available at the time you wish to place an order, you can always place an order through another representative of the firm.) Orders to buy or sell stock can take many different forms. Here are the major types:

Market Orders. If you instruct your broker to buy or sell "at the market," she will buy or sell your shares at whatever the going market price is. She should, of course, try to get the best possible price, but it may not be exactly what you had in mind. For example, XYZ is currently selling at $50 per share. You instruct your broker to buy one hundred shares "at the market." At the moment your order reaches the floor, the best possible price for these shares may have risen to $51 per share, which is what you would end up paying. On the other hand, if you instruct your broker to sell your one hundred shares "at the market," the best possible price available when your order reaches the floor might be $49, which is what you'd get. It could also work the other way around. You might be able to buy at a lower price than you had anticipated or sell at a higher price.

Limit Orders. A limit order sets a maximum or minimum price on the sale or purchase of shares. For example, you purchased one hundred shares of XYZ at $50 per share. You have made up your mind that if the price reaches $55 per share, you want to sell and take your profits and that if it drops to $45 per share, you want to sell and cut your losses. You can place a limit order at $55 per share, and this order is executed only when the stock can be sold at $55 per share. If the stock never reaches this level, the limit order is never completed. If you want to buy stock, a limit order can also be used. Say you wish to buy one hundred shares of XYZ if the price drops to $45 per share. You place a limit order with your broker, and if and when XYZ hits $45 per share, your order is executed. If the stock never hits this price, your order won't be executed.

Time Orders. A time order can be attached to a limit order. It adds a time deadline to the limit order. A time order may be for a day or for any number of days. One common type of time order is called a *"good this week" order* (GTW). This order remains in effect until the end of the calendar week. For example, you would like to buy one hundred shares of XYZ for $45 per share, but only if XYZ hits $45 per share before the end of the week. You thus instruct your broker to enter a combined limit order and time order. If XYZ does hit $45 per share before the end of the week, your order is executed. If not, then the stock isn't bought. Another form of time order is called the *open order* or *"good till canceled" order* (GTC). It is a standing order to buy or sell at a fixed price until you, the investor, cancel the order or until it is actually executed at that price.

Fill or Kill Orders. This is an order to buy or sell at a fixed price immediately. For example, you wish to sell one hundred shares of XYZ at $55 per share. With a fill or kill order, if your broker cannot execute immediately at that price, the order is canceled.

Most orders to buy and sell stock are handled by telephone. It's important, therefore, to make certain that your broker has followed your instructions explicitly, particularly concerning the number of shares you're selling or buying, the price at which you wish to buy or sell, and the specific type of order you're placing. These specifics should be repeated between you and the broker, and you both should make immediate written note of them.

STOCK MARKET INVESTORS: WHAT ARE THEY SEEKING?

The vast diversity of stock market investors can be broken down into three broad categories: by objective, by size, and by type.

Investors by Objective

What are investors seeking when they buy stocks? Their motives could be any of the following: short-term growth, long-term growth, income production, and "no foggy idea." Let's look at each in turn.

Short-Term Growth. Investing for short-term growth might be best described as "out to make a fast buck." If this is your objective, you might be as well served by your nearest racetrack or gambling casino as by the stock market. Humorist Will Rogers had some good advice for those who dive into the stock market looking for a fast buck: "It's easy to be successful in the stock market. You just buy stock, and when it goes up you sell it. And if it don't go up, don't buy it."

Long-Term Growth. Long-term growth is a more prudent objective and is more likely to reward the patient investor who has done the necessary homework. Investors whose objectives are long-term growth will analyze industries and specific companies whose long-term future looks healthy and profitable and will select their investments accordingly. If they select wisely and luckily and are willing to wait long enough, they may well realize their objectives.

Income Production. Many investors get involved in the stock market with the main objective of receiving income in the form of dividends. While the dividends they earn might not be as rewarding as what they could have earned in money market investments, there is also the secondary hope that the stocks will increase in value over a period of time.

Investors whose objectives are balanced between growth and income are perhaps the ones who are approaching the market most intelligently. They are the types of investors who set a target for upside potential and downside potential. They might, for example, define their objectives as a 15 percent annual return (after brokerage commissions) on their investments—perhaps 7 percent might come through receipt of dividends and the other 8 percent through increase in the value of the shares. For example, you own some shares of XYZ stock. Say that XYZ Company is selling at $50.00 per share and is paying a $3.50 per-share dividend per year. This is equal to a 7 percent return in the form of dividends. If, during your first year of ownership of XYZ, the price moves from $50.00 to $54.00 per share—an 8 percent increase during the year—you will have realized your 15 percent objective. By the same token, you would also set a downside limit. If XYZ drops to $45.00 per share, you'll get out at that price and thus shelter yourself from any further losses. There are no strict rules to determine what a desirable balance is. Many of your objectives in this area must relate to what can be attained with the same investable dollars in the money market. If you know that you can attain a 15 percent return on a guaranteed money market instrument, then why take a chance on a 15 percent objective in the stock market? You could do better, or you could do worse. But if 15 percent is your aim and you can get it for certain in the money market, it might be best to take it that way and wait to play the stock market another day.

"No Foggy Idea."   Most stock market investors haven't the foggiest idea what their objectives are. They're not sure why they bought what they bought when they bought it. And they have no notion as to when or why they should sell. Their only hope for success in the market is good luck.

Investors by Size

Within the size categories there are individuals and institutions—or, put another way, small investors and large investors. Individual investors (as well as groups of them such as in investment clubs) and small organizations generally trade in small blocks of stock. Blocks of one hundred shares are referred to as *round lots*; blocks of less than one hundred shares are referred to as *odd lots*. The latter type of transaction may carry a slightly higher brokerage commission called the *odd lot differential*.

Large investors, such as pension and profit-sharing funds, mutual funds, trust funds, large corporations, insurance companies, and the like, often trade in very large blocks of many thousands of shares at a time. Large block trades can disrupt the normal flow of supply and demand of shares and can thus cause considerable fluctuations in the price of a given stock at the time that such an order to buy or sell is placed.

Investors by Type

The following are brief descriptions of eight broad categories of investors. They may represent individuals or institutions. They are all together in the market at the same time, all expressing a constant flow of opinions that may be in total accord or total discord with their colleagues. Generally there is enough disagreement to keep most prices on a relatively even keel most of the time. Let's take a closer look at the cast of characters.

Novices.   Novices aren't really sure what they're doing. Their obvious motivation is to "make money," but they're not really certain how or if they will. If they have done any studying at all, it's probably been only superficial; most likely they are involved in the market because of the suggestion of someone else, and they've probably followed the suggestion at its face value. They may fancy themselves as investors, but their real status is more akin to that of blind bettors.

Insiders.   There are three types of insiders: way-insiders, the fringe-insiders, and the pretend-insiders. Way-insiders are on intimate terms with the day-to-day operation of corporations—officers, employees, directors, or major stockholders. They are privy to information not yet available to the public that, when released to the public, can have a good or bad effect on the stock of the companies. They may know, for example, that potentially profitable deals are about to be completed or that sharp losses are about to be announced. If their information is accurate and the announcements have the anticipated effects, they could reap substantial profits or avoid sharp losses by selling out their existing holdings.

Fringe-insiders may have indirect or delayed access to the intimate information available to way-insiders. They may, for example, be stockbrokers for way-insiders or close friends, associates, or relatives. They may be suppliers to or buyers from the companies. They may also be professional advisors (lawyers, accountants) of way-insiders. They are likely to obtain valuable inside information sometime after the way-insiders have obtained it, perhaps learning of the important facts in time to act on their own behalf, perhaps not. They don't really know for sure what will happen, but if they do receive what they believe to be valid insider information, they are very likely to act on it.

Pretend-insiders are another step or two or more removed from fringe-insiders. They are in the "friend of a friend" category. By the time they get the information, the upswing or downswing may have long since occurred, but they won't necessarily be aware of it. Having just obtained what they believe to be valid company secrets, they're still likely to act on the information even though it's long after the fact.

Trading on inside information is illegal. It's not supposed to happen, but it does, and the Securities and Exchange Commission admits that enforcement of insider-information rules is extremely difficult. Even though certain insiders are required to report their buy and sell transactions, it is still very difficult to discover and prove wrongdoing in this area of stock market trading. Illegal though it may be—and successful or unsuccessful though it may be—it does exert a distinct effect on specific stocks and to a lesser extent on the market as a whole.

Hunch Players. Hunch players are generally active traders and possibly seasoned veterans of the stock market. They may be convinced that all the study in the world is for naught because the quirks and whims of fellow investors are imponderable and have more of an effect on the value of any given stock than the true value of the company itself. They'll listen to tipsters avidly, if not actively seeking them out. Much of their trading will be based on what can best be described as hunches: a gut reaction, a voice in the night, an omen.

Theory Traders. Though often mistaken for hunch players, theory traders base their transactions on one or more specific theories that may be directly tied to something as tangible as governmental statistics or as intangible as trends in international currency fluctuations. Though they may be small in number, theory traders can be very influential when their theories prove correct; however, they also have a way of disappearing temporarily when their theories have proven incorrect. Many theory traders will often be found reading stock market advisory newsletters, generally the wellspring of their information and decisions. Because they pay a steep price for these advisory letters, they assume the information has to be correct—otherwise it wouldn't be so expensive.

Sentimentalists. Sentimentalists are well-intentioned investors who place their money in stocks of companies for which they work for or that are located in their hometown. Sentimentality or loyalty will be their primary reason for investing. Emotionally, it's like rooting for the hometown team to win; but rationally, sentimental investing can amount to nothing more than mere speculation.

Technical Analysts. Technical analysts (sometimes called *chartists*) are serious students of the stock market. Essentially, technical analysts closely follow and chart specific short-, medium-, and long-term trends in individual stocks, in groups of stocks, and in the market movement as a whole. Technical analysts, as a group, have come up with a dazzling array of indicators that supposedly give signals to buy and sell. There are market peaks and market troughs; there are bellwether stocks that purportedly lead the way in one direction or another; there are high ratios and low ratios, moving averages, overbought and -sold indexes, and charts that plot every conceivable squiggle a given stock may be subject to. (More detailed information on these various techniques can be obtained through brokers and through the dozens of books available on the subject.)

But in spite of all the information available, the problem is that the meticulously plotted signals of the analysts are often invalidated by the actions of other traders who pay no attention to these signals. Further, the analysts don't necessarily agree with one another regarding which signal means what, and they often come up with conflicting signals.

The Fundamentalists. Fundamentalists are serious investors who have done their homework and who are willing to continue to do the necessary homework. They have learned how to analyze financial statements of companies in which they are interested in investing. They have learned how to seek out the basic sound fundamental value of each company. Fundamentalists are not traders: they're willing to wait years for the fundamental value of the company to prove itself in terms of price appreciation and dividend payments. They realize that their market decisions are subject to the actions of all the other types of investors, but they feel confident that their prudent and rational analyses of the facts at hand will survive the whims and flutters caused by other types of investors.

Fundamentalists know that there's no such thing as a sure thing in the stock market but are willing to take the time necessary to find the best things available. They'll analyze profit-and-loss statements, dividend payment records, the amount the company has earned on its invested capital, profit margins, the ratio of the company's assets to its liabilities and debts, and the trends in the company's overall performance over recent years. They'll have studied the industry as a whole to determine if it is healthy or failing and whether or not it appears to have a chance to grow at a more rapid rate than the economy as a whole. They'll shun advice from tipsters. They won't play hunches, nor will they let sentimentality get the best of them. And they won't subscribe to any theories that are not rooted in accurate financial analyses of the companies they're considering investing in.

Prudent Investors. Prudent investors are the fundamentalists-plus. Plus what? Perhaps plus a bit of technical analyst, for many of the analytical devices can be helpful in the fundamentalist approach. Perhaps also plus a tiny bit of the hunch player, for even the most prudent investor occasionally needs the intestinal fortitude that is second nature to the hunch player to survive unexpected turns for the worse. Prudent investors have most of the following attributes:

☐ They will have a firm, crystal-clear understanding of their current financial situation and overall investment objectives. They will convey this understanding to their stockbrokers and will make joint commitments with their broker to stick with the stated objectives. If prudent investors want the benefit of brokers' expertise, they must give them proper instructions. Without a basic understanding between investors and brokers, both may be groping in the dark. Periodically, with their brokers' aid, prudent investors will review their objectives and determine whether they are still reasonable in view of the unpredictable nature of the stock market.

☐ Prudent investors will clearly define their own role, that is, whether they want to be investors or traders. Investors, broadly speaking, are putting their money to work, and they're willing to let it do the job over the needed span of time. Traders are working on their money and must have the know-how to cope with weekly, daily, and hourly fluctuations and trends. Prudent investors can be a little bit of both, but to do so they must keep their prudent investment funds and speculative trading funds strictly segregated. When the two start to mingle, objectives can get derailed swiftly.

☐ Prudent investors will do their homework. Investment decisions are ultimately the investor's, not the broker's. There are thousands of securities, no two are alike, and no human being can keep track of the fine points of more than a few dozen at a time. Brokers can give investors research tools and opinions, but investors must reach their own conclusions. And sound conclusions require work.

☐ Prudent investors will avoid the natural quirk of human nature that leads one to want to recover losses as quickly as they have occurred. This can lead an investor out of one speculative situation into another.

☐ Prudent investors who find themselves holding stocks at a loss will ask, Would it be consistent with my investment objectives to purchase that same stock today at its current price? If so, they may decide to continue holding the stock. If not, they would look into purchasing other securities more consistent with the stated investment objectives.

☐ Prudent investors will look back to learn from their past mistakes: Why did I buy or sell too soon or too late? Did I listen to a tip? Did I play a hunch? Did I panic? The ability to recognize one's own mistakes and benefit from them is a rare quality, one worth cultivating by the prudent investor who doesn't already possess it.

☐ When prudent investors invest in stock, they will determine, at that time, when they will be likely to sell. They will set limits for themselves and will stick to them, barring unforeseen conditions that may dictate otherwise. They will determine how much of a loss they will be willing to take in order to acquire certain gains. They will be well acquainted with, and willing to abide by, that old maxim of the investment community: Take your profits when you can, and cut your losses when you can.

☐ Prudent investors will be well aware of the value of a good night's sleep. Or, for that matter, of a good day's work. Distractions and frustrations caused by involvement in the stock market can detract from their own personal productivity and pleasure. Whatever gains an investor may be chasing may not, under keen analysis, be worth it in terms of lost time and lost efficiency in other endeavors. In other words, if your involvement with your investment portfolio begins to interfere with your personal life, whatever gains you may achieve may not, in the long run, have been worth it.

☐ Prudent investors will not waste time or money chasing after systems that purport to "beat the market." There are none. And there aren't any books, brokers, newsletters, analysts, chartists, economists, or tipsters who know anything more about where the market is headed than anyone else. If there were, we'd have heard about them long before now.

BASIC STOCK MARKET INFORMATION

The daily trading activity of all of the major stock exchanges is contained in fairly complete detail in the *Wall Street Journal* each day. A number of stocks are traded on more than one exchange, and their listings are contained generally in the larger exchange on which they're traded.

Strategies for Success

Put Your Money Where Your Knowledge Is

You want to take a fling in the stock market, but you don't know where to begin in choosing stocks. How about picking companies that specialize in an area of your own knowledge? For instance, if your field is chemistry, why not choose chemical company stocks? Or if your hobby is photography, consider photographic companies. Perhaps you have a good background in Asian matters. Maybe you should invest in a mutual fund that specializes in Asian companies. This is the basic idea: Put your money where your knowledge is. As somewhat of a specialist, you're better equipped to evaluate the potential of a company or a group of companies that deals in a subject with which you are familiar. It makes sense, doesn't it? At least you have a better chance of success than you might if you knew nothing at all about the company whose stock you chose to buy.

Price Quotations

Many local daily newspapers also carry extensive listings, though many are abbreviated from the full listings used in the *Wall Street Journal*. Figure 17-1 shows a sample New York Stock Exchange listing from the *Wall Street Journal*, and Figure 17-2 gives the accompanying explanatory notes. Let's examine the details more closely. The shaded listing is "AbbtLb," which stands for Abbott Laboratories, a major manufacturer of various health-care products. (All companies traded on the exchange also have a trading symbol. Abbott's is ABT.)

□ *52 Weeks High/Low.* High/low listings indicate that during the previous fifty-two weeks Abbott Laboratories sold at a high of 67 ($67) per share and at a low of 39¾ ($40) per share. (When fractions appear in quotes they are referring to fractions of a dollar. Thus, ⅛ equals 12.5¢; ¼ equals 25¢; and so on.) The purpose of the high/low listings is to give you some idea concerning the stock's recent trading history. The past history has absolutely no bearing on what the future values of the stock might be.

□ *Dividend (Div.).* The dividend column indicates the rate of dividend paid based on the most recent quarterly dividend. It is not necessarily an indication of dividends that will be paid in the future. Abbott Laboratories paid a dividend in the prior year of 1.00, which means $1.00 per share. An investor would have to dig more deeply to determine the likelihood of any company continuing its indicated rate of dividend for the foreseeable future. The *Wall Street Journal* listings do contain some explanatory notes that may bear on the regularity of dividend payments.

□ *Yield (Yld.%).* Yield, which is listed in percentage terms, indicates what you would receive if you bought the stock at its current price (45 ⅝) and received the dividend of $1.00; $1.00 is roughly 22 percent of (45.62). As you look down these sample listings you can see the wide range of yields that the stocks return to investors in the form of dividends.

□ *Price-earnings ratio (P-E ratio).* The price-earnings ratio is arrived at by simple arithmetic, but determining its meaning is a bit more mystic. The specific figure, which is 17 in the case of Abbott Laboratories, is the result of dividing the *price* per share of the stock by the *earnings* per share of the stock. If a company earned $1 million during a year, and it had one million shares of stock outstanding, its earnings per share would be $1. If that same stock were selling for $10 per share, its price-earnings ratio would be 10 to 1 ($10 market price to $1 worth of earnings), or simply 10.

The earnings referred to in the P-E ratio quotes are the actual latest available earnings or the best estimated earnings of the company for a one-year period.

What does the P-E ratio mean? As with other stock market "indicators," it is, at best, a broad and general yardstick, essentially indicating the relative conservatism or speculation involved in a given stock. The lower the P-E ratio, the more conservative the investment; the higher the P-E ratio, the more speculative.

52 Weeks High	52 Weeks Low	Stock	Div.	Yld %	P-E Ratio	Sales 100s	High	Low	Close	Net Chg.
				– A–A–A –						
25⅝	14	AAR s	.36	2.5	13	313	15	14⅛	14½	– ¼
12	8¾	ACM G n	.21e	1.8	...	592	11¾	11⅝	11¾	...
32½	19	AFG s	.16	.7	8	253	22⅜	22¼	22¼	+ ⅛
27	10½	AGS s		...	11	980	13¼	12½	12⅞	+ ⅝
10½	6¼	AMCA		...	...	2	6½	6½	6½	+ ⅛
9⅜	3¼	AM Intl		...	31	649	4⅜	4¼	4⅜	+ ⅛
33¾	17	AM Int pf	2.00	9.9	...	139	20⅜	20⅛	20⅛	– ⅛
65½	26¾	AMR		...	9	4617	31½	29⅞	31½	+ 1½
27½	24⅞	ANR pf	2.67	10.5	...	1	25½	25½	25½	+ ⅜
25	19	ANR pf	2.12	10.3	...	3	20⅝	20⅝	20⅝	+ ⅛
12¼	6⅜	ARX s		...	7	134	7⅛	6⅞	7⅛	...
73½	35⅛	ASA	2.00a	3.9	...	560	51¼	48⅝	51⅛	+ 2½
22⅜	9½	AVX		...	15	167	11⅞	11⅜	11¾	+ ⅜
67	40	AbtLab	1.00	2.2	17	5508	46	43	45⅝	+ 1⅝
28	15⅜	Abitibl g		...	...	124	18⅜	18⅛	18⅜	+ ⅛
16¾	8½	AcmeC	.40	4.1	14	542	10⅛	9⅝	9¾	– ⅛
10½	6⅛	AcmeE	.32b	4.5	25	20	7⅛	7⅛	7⅛	+ ⅛
20	14⅛	AdaEx	3.34e	22.1	...	220	15⅛	14¾	15⅛	+ ⅛
19½	6⅞	AdmM s	.24	2.7	7	181	8¾	8⅛	8¾	+ ¾
35	16⅝	AdvSys		...	12	562	26½	25⅜	26	+ 1
24⅞	7½	AMD		...	...	3715	8⅝	8¼	8⅝	+ ⅛
56¾	29¼	AMD pf	3.00	9.7	...	330	31	30	31	+ 1
11⅞	4⅝	Adobe		...	...	148	5⅛	5	5	– ⅛
20½	15½	Adob pf	1.84	11.2	...	2	16½	16½	16½	– ¼
15	6⅛	Advest	.12a	1.6	6	196	7½	7⅜	7½	+ ⅛
68¼	43⅞	AetnLf	2.76	6.2	6	2261	45	44¼	44⅝	– ¼
83½	33¼	AfilPb s	.40	.9	7	275	44¾	42½	44¾	+ 1½
26⅞	13⅜	Ahmans	.88	6.3	6	1841	14¼	13¾	14	– ⅛
5⅜	1¾	Alleen		...	...	13	2⅛	2⅛	2⅛	...
53⅞	29	AirPrd	1.00	3.0	12	1857	33½	32½	33½	+ ⅞

Figure 17-1 New York Stock Exchange Listing from the *Wall Street Journal.*

EXPLANATORY NOTES

(For New York and American Exchange listed issues)

Sales figures are unofficial.

PE ratios are based on primary per share earnings as reported by the companies for the most recent four quarters. Extraordinary items generally are excluded.

The 52-Week High and Low columns show the highest and the lowest price of the stock in consolidated trading during the preceding 52 weeks plus the current week, but not the current trading day. The 52-week high and low columns are adjusted to reflect stock payouts of 10 percent or more.

u–Indicates a new 52-week high. d–Indicates a new 52-week low.

g–Dividend or earnings in Canadian money. Stock trades in U.S. dollars. No yield or PE shown unless stated in U.S. money. n–New issue in the past 52 weeks. The high-low range begins with the start of trading and does not cover the entire 52 week period. pp–Holder owes installment(s) of purchase price. s–Split or stock dividend of 25 per cent or more in the past 52 weeks. The high-low range is adjusted from the old stock. Dividend begins with the date of split or stock dividend. v–Trading halted on primary market.

Unless otherwide noted, rates of dividends in the foregoing table are annual disbursements based on the last quarterly or semi-annual declaration. Special or extra dividends or payments not designated as regular are identified in the following footnotes.

a–Also extra or extras. b–Annual rate plus stock dividend. c–Liquidating dividend. e–Declared or paid in preceding 12 months. i–Declared or paid after stock dividend or split up. j–Paid this year, dividend omitted, deferred or no action taken at last dividend meeting. k–Declared or paid this year, an accumulative issue with dividends in arrears. r–Declared or paid in preceding 12 months plus stock dividend. t–Paid in stock in preceding 12 months, estimated cash value on ex-dividend or ex-distribution date.

x–Ex-dividend or ex-rights. y–Ex-dividend and sales in full. z–Sales in full.

pf–Preferred. rt–Rights. un–Units. wd–When distributed. wi–When issued. wt–Warrants. ww–With warrants. xw–Without warrants.

vj–In bankruptcy or receivership or being reorganized under the Bankruptcy Act, or securities assumed by such companies.

Figure 17-2 Explanatory notes for New York Stock Exchange Listing from the *Wall Street Journal.*

□ *Sales 100s.* The Sales 100 column indicates the amount of activity in the trading of the stock for the prior day. Abbott Laboratories shows 5508 under this column, which means that a total of 550,800 shares were traded during the prior day. Market analysts will keep an eye on the sales volume of specific stocks, looking for the unusual. If a stock normally has a trading volume within a fairly close range from day to day, and suddenly there seems to be a great surge or a tapering off of activity, this could signal that something out of the ordinary might be happening with the value of the stock. If the stock seems to be moving upward on heavy volume, it would indicate a high degree of buying interest. On the other hand, if the stock moves downward in high volume trading, it would indicate a desire of investors to unload.

□ *High/Low/Close.* The next three columns indicate the high, low, and closing prices per share for the previous day's trading. During the previous day, for example, Abbott Laboratories traded at a high of $46 and a low of $43. It closed out the day at $45.62. During that day a trader might have bought or sold at prices anywhere within that range.

□ *Net change.* Abbott Laboratories closed down 1⅝ ($1.62) from the close of the previous day. In other words, the value of the stock dropped by $1.62 per share from where it had been at its last trade on the prior trading day.

Other Published Listings. More detailed information on specific stocks can be found in *Barron's*, a weekly newspaper, and in the stock guides published monthly and quarterly by Standard and Poor's and Moody's. *Barron's* is commonly available at newsstands, and the stock guides are available at brokerage firms and at most public libraries. The added information consists of historical high and low trading, dividend history and payment dates, the financial status of the company, and a history of its earnings per share. The prudent investor will not rely simply on the daily newspaper quotation but will make extensive use of these more detailed published statistics.

Broker's Quotations. Aided by computers, brokers at local brokerage firms are equipped with video terminals that can display up-to-the-second price fluctuations as well as detailed information on any given quoted stock. In addition, the "ticker tape," now computerized, flashes on a large screen each transaction for each stock that's sold on the respective exchanges.

Stock Market Averages

"How's the market doing?" "Up two." Or you may hear a news broadcaster report, "The market was down nine points today in heavy trading. Analysts attribute the decline to investors' concern over the impending automobile workers' strike."

Dow Jones Industrial Average. What do these cryptic sayings mean? The statements "up two" and "down nine" refer to the daily fluctuations in the Dow Jones

Industrial Average, or DJIA. This is the oldest and most commonly referred to measurement of stock market prices. But it does not reflect the movements of all stocks; rather, it refers only to the movement of thirty major industrial stocks. The Dow Jones Company, which publishes the *Wall Street Journal, Barron's,* and many other financial publications, has historically used these thirty major corporations to reflect the "essence" of the market as a whole. The average is arrived at by tallying the prices of the thirty stocks within the averages and dividing the total by a divisor that takes into account previous stock splits and stock dividends. The divisor is changed from time to time as any of the companies within the group of thirty declares stock splits or stock dividends. Although other companies have devised more broad-based averages over the years, the DJIA has remained the favorite indicator of most investors.

In addition to the Dow Jones Industrial Average, there are two other Dow Jones averages: twenty transportation stocks for the transportation averages and fifteen utility stocks for the utility averages. These, respectively, reflect movements within their respective areas.

Standard and Poor's Stock Price Index.   The Standard and Poor's Corporation maintains an index of 500 major corporations: industrials, utilities, financial, and transportation. All of these stocks are listed on the New York Stock Exchange. Although the Standard and Poor's Index—Industrials (SPII) represents a much broader spectrum of listed securities, it has not achieved the popularity of the DJIA.

The New York Stock Exchange Common Stock Index.   The New York Stock Exchange Common Stock Index is maintained by the New York Stock Exchange itself and covers all of the common stocks listed on the exchange.

Classification of Stocks

Stocks can be classified in a number of ways: by "personality," by objective, and by industry grouping.

☐ **By "personality."**   Vague though the "personality" classification may seem, it can be a worthwhile investment guideline. The basic personalities of stocks are either "blue-chip" or "glamour." Blue-chip stocks are those that are considered to be major, solid companies with relatively stable stock prices and regular histories of dividend payments. In other words, blue-chip stocks are the more conservative of the vast realm of companies. The glamour issues are those that have recently attracted a lot of investor interest, in large measure because they have experienced a high volatility in price, tending toward the upward side. These are the more speculative issues. The price fluctuations are likely to be much more drastic and the payment of dividends more questionable than with the blue-chips.

☐ **By objective.**   For investors whose objective is income, there are income stocks: those that pay a relatively high level of dividend. For investors whose objective is growth, there are growth stocks: those that have recently had spurts in value above and beyond the broad average of stocks as a whole. If you investigate carefully, there is a reasonable assurance that you can find an income stock whose dividend payment level is likely to continue or increase. But there is absolutely no way that you can find a growth stock whose future growth will necessarily match its past growth.

☐ *By industry grouping.*   Despite the profitability (or lack thereof) of any specific company, the value of its stock may be drastically affected by the performance of the overall industrial group into which it falls. For example, a major retailer, such as Sears, may have a very strong financial position. But because of an impending recession, retailers as a whole (of which Sears is one) may have a gloomy outlook. Thus, despite Sears' individual potential, the investment community may frown upon Sears because it belongs to an industrial group whose future is in doubt, at least for the near term.

Many different factors can affect industry groups in one way while not affecting other groups as noticeably. Sharply rising fuel prices can have a negative effect on the airline industry, but perhaps little or no effect on the electronics industry. Rising interest rates can have a negative effect on the construction industry and possibly a positive effect on the banking industry. A severe drought can have a negative effective on the food industry and no effect on the chemical industry. Theoretically, but not necessarily, these external factors will affect each specific company within an industrial group. Following is a sampling of major industrial groups:

Drugs, cosmetics, and health care	Metal producers
Beverages	Electrical
Aerospace	Financial
Chemicals	Automotive
Metal-product manufacturers	Foods
Construction	Electronics
Apparel	Machinery and equipment

Dividends

A dividend is the portion of a company's profit that is paid out to its owners or stockholders. Dividends are commonly paid in cash, but in some instances a corporation may issue additional shares of stock as a form of dividend. This is known as a *stock dividend*, and the recipient of a stock dividend is free to sell these shares for cash or to retain the investment.

The value of a dividend is usually referred to as the *yield*. The yield is the percentage return you're getting on your money, and it's figured very simply by dividing the stock's annual dividend by its price. If a stock is selling at $50 per share and it pays an annual dividend of $2 per share, its *apparent* yield is 4 percent (2 divided by 50 equals 0.04). We use the word *apparent* because the yield does not take into account the commission that you'll have to pay when you buy the stock or when you sell it. The commissions must be considered to come up with a more accurate yield figure.

Further, if you do not hold the stock for at least a full annual cycle, you won't receive the apparent yield. For example, say the above stock paid its dividend quarterly on the first day of January, April, July, and October. It would pay 50¢ for each share four times a year, for a total of $2.00. If you bought the stock on January 2 and sold it during the subsequent December, you'd have received only three of the four dividend payments, or $1.50, even though you had held the stock for almost twelve full months. You would not have received the first dividend, payable on January 1, because you were not a "stockholder of record" on the date called for. In such a case, your yield would be only 3 percent, before the payment of both commissions.

Dividend payments are announced or "declared" by the board of directors of the company at its regular meetings. Here's how it works: At their February meeting, the board of directors of XYZ Company declares that they will pay a dividend on April 1 to "stockholders of record" as of March 5. If you are recorded on the books of the corporation as being a stockholder as of March 5, you'll be entitled to receive the April 1 dividend even though you sell your stock between March 5 and April 1. The reason for the time lag is to give the company enough time to get an accurate list of all its stockholders, in anticipation of the payment date, so that checks can be prepared and other necessary book work done.

Ex-Dividend Date. What if, following the example above, you instructed your broker to buy XYZ stock on March 2? Would you be entitled to the dividend? Probably not. It usually takes four or five days from the time of an order until you are officially registered on the books of a corporation as an owner of the stock. Thus, the stock exchanges, in listing dividends payable on stocks, generally note that a stock is "ex-dividend" about four or five days prior to the *record* date. When a stock is quoted "ex-dividend," it means that if you buy the stock at that time you won't get the next dividend that has been declared by the company. Following along with the example above, XYZ might be quoted as "ex-dividend" on March 1—five days before the record date. Anybody who buys the stock from March 1 onward will not receive the dividend payable in April.

The prudent investor, particularly one bargaining for a known return on invested capital, will pay close attention to the history of dividend payments of any company that he's thinking of investing in. These records can be found in the Moody's and Standard and Poor's guides or can be obtained directly from the broker. Some companies have long histories of regular dividends, many of which increase periodically as earnings increase. Some companies pay no dividends, and other companies pay erratically. Companies that pay small or erratic dividends or no dividends at all tend to fall more into the speculative category of investment. The steady dividend payers are more conservative.

Unlike the movement of a stock's price, which is subject to countless and often indefinable pressures, the dividend payment rate is generally well rooted in the company's earnings and in its willingness to spread those earnings out among its stockholders. Earnings that are not distributed to stockholders are retained within the company (and are referred to as *retained earnings*) for investment within the company itself. These retained earnings may be used as a cushion against troublesome economic times or to create new facilities, which in turn can create new jobs and new products, which can create additional earnings for stockholders.

Commissions

Brokerage commissions are the fees received by brokerage firms for handling your transactions when you buy and sell stock. The commission you pay on any given transaction depends on the number of shares purchased, the price of the shares, and possibly the amount of business you do with a given broker in the course of a year. Full-service brokerage firms, which provide research and other facilities to their customers, charge higher commissions than do discount brokers, which provide very little service other than the execution of orders. Table 17-1 illustrates a range of commissions charged by various types of brokerage firms.

Abuses exist in all industries, and the securities industry is no exception. A common abuse is called *churning*. Churning exists when a broker convinces an investor to continually buy and sell securities, with the net result being large commissions generated for the broker, to the possible detriment of the investor's account. Prudent investors will have committed themselves in all likelihood to ride with their investments for a protracted period of time and likely will not succumb to the intrigues of churning, which demands frequent in and out trading.

Buying Long and Short

When investors buy stocks, hoping for an increase in value as well as receipt of dividends, they are "buying long." This is the most common type of transaction,

Table 17-1 **Sampling of Brokerage Commissions on Stock Transactions**

Type of broker	100 shares at $40 each	300 shares at $30 each
Discount broker A	$42	$ 62
Discount broker B	47	89
Full-service broker A	84	191
Full-service broker B	80	176
Full-service broker C	70	158

constituting the vast majority of all trades on the exchanges. But what if an investor thinks a stock may go down in value? There is a technique called ''selling short'' that enables an investor to seek a profit as a stock declines in value.

Selling short is a sophisticated and risky transaction. Here's how it works. Let's say you think that XYZ, which is now selling at $10 per share, is due to slump in price. You want to ''sell it short'' or bet that it will decline. You borrow 100 shares from your broker and sell them on the open market at the $10 price. You now have $1000 cash in hand (before commissions), and you owe your broker 100 shares of XYZ. If the stock then dips to, say, $6 per share, you in effect buy 100 shares at the going market price for $600 and return the 100 shares to your broker. You took in $1000, then paid out $600, so you're $400 ahead as a result —again, before commissions.

The broker will have obtained the ''borrowed'' stock usually from his firm's supply of customers' stock that they are holding. You, as the short seller, must have cash or unmargined stock in your account before you can initiate a short sale. This is to assure the broker that you have available funds to repay the stock you've borrowed. These funds are effectively tied up during the life of the transaction.

The element of risk involved in short selling can indeed be frightening. On a regular, or long, transaction, your ultimate loss is limited. If you bought XYZ long at $10 per share, and XYZ goes bankrupt, you can lose only the $10 per share. That's it. It can't go any lower than zero.

But if you sell a stock short at $10 per share, and it goes up instead of down, your loss can run on indefinitely. Say you buy 100 shares short at $10, and then the stock runs up to $50 per share. If you want to get out then, you'd have to shell out $5000 to buy enough to pay back your broker the shares you owe him, for a net loss of $4000. If you decide to wait, hoping for a drop, and it goes up another $10 to $60 per share, your loss is even greater. Such run-ups may be rare, but the risk is there.

There's one further problem with selling short: If you're holding stock in a long position, you receive any dividends the stock pays. But if you're in a short position, you are obliged to pay the dividends to the broker since you technically owe him the stock itself. This can add to your losses or cut into your gains. Prudent investors would not be comfortable selling stocks short.

Buying on Margin

Buying on margin is a means of buying stock on credit. The rate of margin varies from time to time, depending on overall economic conditions throughout the nation and the condition of the stock market. The Federal Reserve Board sets the margin rate. If the margin rate is 40 percent, you can buy stock by putting up only 40 percent of the total purchase price. The remaining 60 percent you borrow from the broker using the stock as collateral for the loan. Say that XYZ is selling at $30 per share, and you wish to buy 100 shares. The margin rate at that time is 40 percent. You can thus buy $3000 worth of XYZ by putting up $1200 in cash and borrowing the remaining $1800 from the broker. Let's say further that at that time the interest rate you'll pay your broker on the margin account is 10 percent, which means that during the course of the year you'll owe $180 in interest on the $1800 margin loan.

If XYZ goes to $35 per share at the end of one year, and you sell, you have realized a profit of $500, less the $180 in interest, for a net (before commissions) of $320. But you've only invested $1200 of your own cash at the outset, so your return of $320 is equivalent to a yield of 26.7 percent for the year, not counting commissions or dividends. If you had invested the full $3000 and realized a $500 gain, your rate of return would have been 16.7 percent before commissions. This is what's known as *leverage*. The gain on a sale and the rate of return on the dividends are magnified by the fact that you have less of your own money at work for you.

However, margin buying can be very dangerous, particularly if the stock declines in value. If you had purchased XYZ normally—that is, unmargined—for $3000, and it had dipped to $25 per share, you'd have a loss of $500. But if you had bought it on the margin account, your loss would be increased by the amount of interest you would have to pay on the loan. In the example above, your total loss would come to $680.

Furthermore, if your loan with the broker exceeds the limit, you will get what is known as a *margin call*. For the example above, the amount the broker lends you cannot exceed 60 percent of the market value of the stock. On the $3000 transaction, the margin loan of $1800 was permissible. But if the total value of the stock bought on margin should fall to, say, $2000, the amount of the broker's loan cannot exceed $1200. If this should happen, the broker will call you to tell you to come up with $600 in extra cash or with additional collateral. If you fail to pay this amount, the broker can sell your stock at a loss in order to repay your debt. As a result of these possibilities, trading on margin must be viewed as a highly speculative activity.

Capital Gains

Prior to tax year 1987, if you reaped a profit in the stock market, it would be subject to favorable tax treatment if you had held the stock for a long enough period of time. This treatment was known as the *long-term capital gain* treatment. These gains were taxed at a lower rate than normal income. But the Tax Reform Act of 1986 eliminated the favorable treatment given to stock market profits. However, the subject of preferential treatment for capital gains is being debated continuously, and it is thought that the treatment could eventually be restored. Check current tax regulations to determine the present situation.

Stock Splits and Stock Dividends

Occasionally a company will issue a stock dividend to its stockholders. This may be instead of or in addition to a cash dividend. For example, if a company declares a 10 percent stock dividend, it will give all of its stockholders one share of additional stock for each ten shares already owned. A 100 percent stock dividend means that stockholders will get one new share for every one already owned. In effect, this doubles the amount of shares of stock outstanding. Frequently, companies will continue to pay the same amount of dividend in dollars after a stock dividend. This has the effect of increasing the return to investors, because they have more shares of stock earning dividends for them.

Table 17-2 illustrates the before and after status of a 10 percent stock dividend. In this case, the effect of the stock dividend is to increase the value of the investment and the dividend income assuming that the stock retains its predividend market value.

A company will split its stock when it wishes to get more shares of stock out into the marketplace and also perhaps to bring the price of the stock down into a more attractive range. For example, a two-for-one stock split means that you will end up owning two shares of stock for every one that you had owned originally. Generally, though, when a stock is split, its price will be split accordingly, as will its dividend. If a stock was selling for $50 per share and was paying a $2 per year dividend, it will, after a two-for-one split, probably sell for $25 per share, and the dividend will be $1 per share. Thus, your actual net worth as an owner of that stock will not necessarily have changed as a result of the split. Table 17-3 illustrates the before and after effects of a 100 percent stock split.

A stock split is often taken as a sign of optimism: Investors are eager to buy shares, and when the price has been effectively lowered, more investors will be able to get involved with the company. A buying surge often tends to boost the value of a stock; thus a stock split is viewed by traders as a sign of a possible

Table 17-2 10% Stock Dividend: Before and After

	Before	*After*
You own	100 shares	110 shares
Current value per share	$50	$50
Current total value	$5000	$5500
Annual dividend per share	$5	$5
Total dividend income per year	$500	$550

Table 17-3 100% Stock Split: Before and After

	Before	*After*
You own	100 shares	200 shares
Current price per share	$50	$25
Total value	$5000	$5000
Dividend per share	$5.00	$2.50
Total dividend income per year	$500	$500

upswing in a given stock. Often this is the case, but it is not necessarily so. Sometimes there are rumors of a stock split, but the split may never actually occur. This can cause wild gyrations in the value of a given stock.

Preferred Stocks

Preferred stock is a separate class of stock from common stock, which has been the type under discussion until this point. If a company has bonds outstanding, the bondholders have to be paid before any dividends can be paid to any common stockholders. If a company also has preferred stock outstanding, the holders of the preferred stock also are entitled to preference over the common stockholders. This is the derivation of the name *preferred*. In other words, if a corporation has bonds *and* preferred stock *and* common stock outstanding, the bond holders are first paid the interest due them, then the preferred stockholders are paid their dividends, then the common stockholders receive their dividends. Preferred stock generally pays a higher rate of return on dividends than does common stock, and the preferred stock is less subject to fluctuation than the common stock. For these reasons they tend to appeal more to conservative and relatively sophisticated investors.

Cumulative Preferred Stocks. Most preferred stocks are *cumulative*, which means that unpaid dividends will accumulate, and the preferred shareholders must be paid in full on all back unpaid dividends before common stockholders can be paid any of their dividends. For example, a company has preferred stock outstanding, on which it has set a fixed dividend rate of $3 per share. The dividend rate on its common stock has been $2 per share. The company runs into hard times and for three years pays no dividends. In the fourth year it realizes a healthy profit. Before common stockholders can receive any dividends, the preferred shareholders must be paid $9 for each of their shares for the back accumulated dividends that were not paid.

Callable Preferred Stocks. Some preferred shares will have a *call price*, which means that the company can redeem the preferred shares at a stated price. If the preferred should reach $28 per share and the call price is $25 per share, the owner will suffer a loss if the company does call or redeem the stock. If the call price is above the actual selling price, the owner is in no danger of losing, as long as the call price remains above the selling price. An investor in preferred stock should always determine what call privileges exist regarding the stock. In stock listings, preferreds are indicated by a ''PF'' following the name of the company.

Convertible Preferred Stocks. Like convertible bonds, noted in a previous chapter, convertible preferred stock may be converted into shares of the company's common stock at an agreed ratio. And as with convertible bonds, the price of convertible preferred stock tends to fluctuate in tandem to the common stock, but the fluctuations are generally not as great as with the common stock. Thus, convertible preferreds are considered to offer attractive advantages: a relatively high rate of return on one's investment (from the dividends paid on the preferred stock); a chance to convert into the common stock if the common stock starts to rise rapidly; and a downside cushion of protection since the preferred stock will tend not to drop as rapidly or as deeply as the common stock might if prices begin to fall. Convertibles are a sophisticated area of investing that require further study on the part of any interested student. Ample literature is available from most stockbrokerage firms.

Warrants.   On occasion, when a company is issuing a bond or preferred stock, it may offer *warrants* to purchasers of the bonds or preferred shares as an extra inducement to get them to invest. The warrant entitles investors to purchase shares of common stock at a fixed price for a set period of time. In other words, if the common stock is selling at $20 per share at the time the bonds or preferred shares are issued, the warrant might entitle the holder to acquire a share of common stock at $25. The issuing company will fix the life of the warrant, which may be a few months or a number of years.

Warrants are totally speculative. Owners of warrants do not have any ownership in the corporation unless or until they exercise the warrant—that is, trade it in for the share of stock to which they are entitled. The owner of a warrant receives no dividends and has no voting rights in the company.

Let's look at an example. XYZ issues warrants to buy its stock at $25 a share. You like XYZ, but you don't have $2500 with which to buy 100 shares. You watch XYZ stock move to $27 a share, and you're confident that it will climb to $35 a share within the next twelve months. You buy 100 warrants at $2 per share for a total investment of $200. As the stock of XYZ climbs, so will the value of the warrants. Essentially, for every $1 increase in the value of the stock itself, the warrants will also increase by $1. Thus, if XYZ does reach a higher level, such as $35 a share, the value of the warrant would have increased from your $2 price to $8. You will have reaped a gain without purchasing the stock itself. The warrants do the job for you.

However, there is an ultimate danger with the warrants: They expire at a designated time. Once they expire, they are worthless. If the stock doesn't rise as you had hoped it would, neither does the warrant. Trading in warrants is highly speculative. There are comparable opportunities in trading in stock options, which are explained in the next section.

Stock Options

Trading in stock options is a sophisticated form of investing that can range from highly speculative to staunchly conservative. The volume of stock option trading has expanded phenomenally since the concept was first introduced on major exchanges in the early 1970s. We will now examine the basic concepts of stock option trading, and readers who find the technique appealing will want to seek further information from stockbrokers about specific option-trading possibilities.

Placing a Bet. There are two main ways to gamble at the racetrack. First, you can buy a horse and enter it in races. If your horse wins, you will receive the winner's purse. If the horse never wins, you can recoup some of your investment by selling it, by training it to pull a plow, or by putting it out to stud. In other words, even if your initial gamble never pays off (the horse never wins), the horse still has some residual value.

Second, you can place bets on other people's horses. The life of your bet will be approximately two minutes—the time it takes to run the race. If the horse you bet on wins, you win. If the horse you bet on loses, your betting ticket is instantly and permanently worthless. In short, there is no residual value on the bet.

The situation is very similar in the stock market: There are two basic ways you can gamble. First, you can buy stock and hope that it increases in value. If it does, and you sell the stock, you have won. If the stock does not go up, there is still some residual value in the dividends you will receive and in the selling price you might get for the stock at some later date. Second, you can place a bet that the stock will increase in value. You can do this without actually having to buy the stock itself. You place your bet by buying what is known as an *option*. An option, in effect, is a bet on the stock. And like a bet on a horse, the option has a limited life—upward of nine months at the maximum, after which it will become worthless.

This is a very oversimplified view of stock option trading, but perhaps it will have clarified some of the confusion about what an option is. Option trading is to stock trading what horse betting is to horse owning. Let's take a closer look at how it works.

Calls and Puts. The most common type of option trading is betting that a given stock will increase in value. Technically this is known as a *call option*. It is also possible to bet that a stock will decrease in value. You can place such a bet by buying what is known as a *put option*. For purposes of this discussion and for the sake of clarity, we'll restrict the material to call options.

Option Quotations. Table 17-4 shows how options are quoted in the *Wall Street Journal*. This quotation refers to option trading in the stock of XYZ Company. As the column on the far left indicates, the actual price per share of XYZ common stock closed the prior day at $41 on the New York Stock Exchange. The rest of

Table 17-4 **Option Quotes**

Option NY Close	*Strike Price*	*Jan.*	*Apr.*	*July*
XYZ	35	7	8	9
41	40	3½	4½	5
41	45	2	3	4

the quote illustrates nine potential "bets" that can be placed on the future of XYZ's stock.

Look at the bottom line in the quotation. Let's assume that we are now in late November. You have a hunch that XYZ will rise from its current level of $41 per share to $45 per share by next January. You'd like to bet on your hunch. You can do so by buying the stock itself, but to buy one hundred shares will cost you $4100. Or you can buy an option. As the January column indicates, you can buy January options for $2. Contracts are sold in one-hundred-share lots, so a one-hundred-share option contract would cost you $200.

If you bought one hundred shares of the stock for $4100, and the stock moved up to $4500 by January, you'd have reaped a profit of $400 (before commissions). If you bought a one-hundred-share option contract for $200, and XYZ moved to $45 per share by, say, December, the value of the option would have increased by $4 per share, or $400 for one hundred shares, to roughly $600, and you'd have a $400 profit (again before commissions) on a bet of only $200.

But note this critical difference: If you had bought the stock and the price did *not* rise, you would *still own* the stock *indefinitely*. You'd still be entitled to any dividends that the stock paid. However, with the option, if the bet doesn't work out, the option expires at the established date, and you own nothing after that time.

The cost of your bet is known as the *premium*. The price at which you have the right to buy the stock—$45 in this example—is known as the *strike price*. The expiration is generally the third Friday in the month indicated. (Technically, the option gives you the right to buy the shares of the stock at the strike price. But since the commissions involved in doing so would take a big bite out of your potential profit, most option traders simply sell the option itself to another interested buyer rather than convert their option into the actual shares of the stock.)

Let's say you weren't quite as optimistic about XYZ going to $45 per share by January. But you thought it might reach that level before the following April. In that case, you could buy an option for a premium of $3 per share, or $300 for a one-hundred-share contract. If you wanted to have until July to see whether the price moved up, a one-hundred-share contract would cost $400. The longer the life of the option, the higher the price. This is because you have more time for the stock to reach the desired level. In effect, you're paying an added premium for the extra time.

Buying call options is highly speculative. Once you've bought an option, you receive no dividends on your invested money and the clock is running against you: The option becomes valueless upon the expiration date. It's like the betting ticket on the horse that didn't finish in the money.

Selling Options. Whom do racetrack bettors buy their bets *from*? They buy them from the racetrack owners who have very carefully calculated that they will keep a portion of every bet for their own overhead and profit (not to mention taxes). For every dollar that is bet, the racetrack may pay back only about 80¢ in winnings to the bettors. Over the days and months and years the track knows that it can't lose.

This is why it's better to own a racetrack than to bet at one. And the same philosophy holds true with option trading: It's better to sell options than to buy them.

From whom do option buyers buy their contracts? They buy them from option *sellers*—people who already own the given shares of stock and who are willing to sell them to buyers at a specific price. Referring back to the quotations, let's assume that you purchased one hundred shares of XYZ some time ago for $35 per share. You've been happy with the stock and with the dividends that it has paid, yet you'd be willing to part with the stock if it hit $45 per share, which would mean a $10 per share profit to you.

The option exchanges offer you intriguing possibilities. As the quotations indicate, you, as the owner of XYZ, can sell someone else the right to buy your one hundred shares any time between now and next January, and you'll receive a $200 premium in exchange. Or you can sell an April contract for $300, a July contract for $400. If you sell an option that is never exercised, you get to keep the whole premium. You also get to keep any dividends that are paid on the stock during the life of the option. That's like the racetrack keeping a portion of each bet for its own purposes. If the option is exercised, you must give up your stock at the strike price—$45 per share in the current example. But you have expressed a willingness to do that—to take a $10 per share profit—as part of your overall investment philosophy. If the option is not exercised, you can sell yet another option and keep the premium. If the option is exercised and you give up the stock, you have the $4500 to reinvest as you see fit. (None of these transactions take brokerage commissions into account.)

As this example indicates, selling options can be a sound and secure way for owners of stocks to increase their return substantially without increasing their risk. As long as you are willing to let go of your stock at a fixed higher price than you paid for it, you literally have everything to gain and nothing to lose by selling options on stocks you already own. If you plan to make new investments on stocks for the purpose of selling options against those stocks, you of course take upon yourself the basic risk inherent in any stock investment: the potential fluctuations in value that could work for or against you. Since this discussion was intended as nothing more than a brief overview of option-trading possibilities, interested investors should seek further information of specific techniques from their stockbroker.

Rating the Stocks

Like bonds, stocks are ranked and rated by both Standard and Poor's and Moody's. The following excerpts from the Standard and Poor's explanation of their rating system not only is informational but also serves as a guide to the prudent investor in the quest to determine the relative value of stocks within the broad selection available.

Earnings and dividends rankings for stocks. The relative "quality" of common stocks cannot be measured, as is the quality of bonds, in terms of the degree of protection for principal and dividends. Nevertheless, the investment process obviously involves the assessment of numerous factors—such as product and industry position, the multifaceted aspects of managerial capability, corporate financial policy and resources—that makes some common stocks more highly esteemed than others.

Earnings and dividends performance is the end result of the interplay of these factors, and thus over the long run the record of this performance has a considerable bearing on relative quality. Growth and stability of earnings and dividends are therefore the key elements of Standard and Poor's common stock rankings, which are designed to capsulize the nature of this record in a single symbol. The rankings, however, do not pretend to reflect all other factors, tangible and intangible, that also bear on stock quality.

The Standard and Poor's rankings for common stocks are as follows:

A+	Highest	B	Speculative
A	High	B −	Highly speculative
A−	Good	C	Marginal
B+	Medium	D	In reorganization

Preferred stock ratings, according to Standard and Poor's, represent a "considered judgment of the relative security of dividends but are not indicative of the protection of principal from market fluctuations." These ratings are as follows:

AAA	Prime	BB	Lower-grade
AA	High-grade	B	Speculative
A	Sound	C	Nonpaying
BBB	Medium-grade		

Refer to the respective ratings themselves for more details and information on this important aspect of evaluating one's investment alternatives.

Dividend Reinvestment Plans

Dividends are usually paid to stockholders quarterly. If you own one hundred shares of XYZ, and it is paying a dividend of $5 per share, you will receive a total of $500 in dividends during the year, but you will receive them in quarterly checks of $125 each. This money is yours to do with as you please—to spend or to reinvest. But many investors get lazy about reinvesting their dividend earnings and often find themselves spending these checks on nonessentials. By doing so, they can erode the potential size of their future nest eggs.

Many companies offer an interesting alternative to sending quarterly dividend checks. They offer automatic dividend reinvestment plans in which your dividend is used to purchase additional shares of stock in the company. If an investor has faith in the company and wishes to acquire additional shares at virtually no out-of-pocket cost and with no effort, the dividend reinvestment plan is an ideal way in which to proceed. There are some special advantages to the automatic dividend reinvestment plans depending on the specific company. Brokerage commissions are very low or nonexistent. If the amount of your dividend check is not sufficient to buy a full share of stock, fractional shares can be purchased and added to your account. And some companies even offer a discount on the purchase price as compared with the going market rate that you'd otherwise have to pay.

Companies that offer automatic dividend reinvestment plans will notify stockholders of the availability. To sign up for the plan, the investor merely fills out the simple form the company supplies. From this point on, dividends are reinvested automatically, and customers will receive a quarterly statement of the account. The company will retain the actual additional shares purchased, and the investor can cash them in at any time by notifying the company.

Following is an example of how a dividend reinvestment plan can work. Assume you own 100 shares of XYZ with a value of $50 per share and an annual dividend of $5 per share. Assume for the sake of this illustration that the price of the stock and the amount of the dividend do not vary over the years. As you can see in Table 17-5, in the first year your 100 shares will earn $500 worth of dividends. These dividends in turn will buy ten additional shares of stock, giving you a total of 110 shares going to work for you at the start of the second year. Note that during the fourth year, you would have earned $665.50 in dividends on your original investment of $5000. Your return has increased because you have more shares working for you earning dividends. In essence, then, the automatic dividend reinvestment plan does for your stockholding what compounding interest does for your money market investments.

Table 17-5 **Dividend Reinvestment Plan**

	100 Shares of XYZ, value $50 per share, dividend $5		
Year	*Shares owned, start of year*	*Dividend earned . . .*	*. . . Buys this many new shares . . .*	*. . . Giving you this many total shares by year end*
1	100	$500	10	110
2	110	$550	11	121
3	121	$605	12.1	133.1
4	133.1	$665.50	13.31	146.41

Following is a brief list of some of the companies that have offered dividend reinvestment plans. Check with a stockbroker to determine the current status of available plans.

Allied Chemical	IBM
American Brands	Mobil Corp.
AT&T	Nabisco
Bristol-Meyers	Penney (J.C.)
CBS, Inc.	PepsiCo
Colgate-Palmolive	Pillsbury
DuPont (E.I.)	RCA
Eastman Kodak	Sears
Exxon	Texaco
General Electric	USX
General Motors	Xerox
Goodyear Tire	

Value and Price: The Worth of a Stock

The distinction between *value* and *price* is as important in the stock market as in any other form of commerce. A patch of barren land in the middle of the desert may sell at a very low price, say, $10 an acre, because it seems to have no value. But if there is oil underneath that patch of land, the value can be astronomically high, even though the price was very low.

On the other hand, that same barren patch may have absolutely no value—no oil or anything else hidden beneath it. But a fast-talking salesperson can sell the land to gullible investors, leading them to believe it is a future oil well, a future retirement villa, a potential gold mine, or whatever. In this case, the price may be astronomically high in comparison with the value.

In all of our normal acquisition of the goods we buy, we attempt to make sure that we're getting good value for the money we pay and that value and price are compatible. In the stock market, we have to maintain the same vigil, for very easily the price and value of a stock can take off in opposite directions. We might speculate on a stock with little intrinsic value, but because of a speculative fever the price of the stock may jump and reap a bonanza. Or we may invest in a stock with sturdy and dependable values only to find that a reverse form of speculation has condemned the stock to a severe plunge and our money with it.

There are many factors that can have a direct effect on the *value* of a given stock, and there are many that can have a direct effect on the *price*, although these factors technically have no bearing on the underlying value.

Value. The underlying value of a stock is related to the profitability of the company in selling its product and services to its customers. The essential factors involved are the expertise of management; the cost of its raw materials (which can be affected by weather conditions, labor costs, strikes, and delivery problems); the efficiency in producing its finished product from the raw materials (which can likewise be affected by the foregoing elements of labor, weather, and gremlins); and by the efficiency with which it delivers the finished product to the market, at a price and in a package the public is willing to accept.

Further, with a great many of our major companies now involved in international commerce, international factors must also be considered. These can include fluctuations in currencies between various nations, international politics, trade and tariff regulations, and the same unpredictability regarding weather and labor strife that we have in America but compounded by the distance and difficulty in communicating between the various parties.

Price. Following are some of the important elements that, although they do not affect the underlying value of the company, can have a distinct bearing on the price of the stock.

☐ When a new issue of stock is being offered to the public, the sales tactics of brokerage firms can have a bearing on the price of the stock. Persuasive salespersons pitching to gullible or greedy investors can boost the price of new issues far beyond the true value of the stock. If a new stock is issued when the market is not receptive, even the best salesperson might not be able to prevent a sharp downturn in the value of the stock.

☐ The general health and outlook of the national economy can give a boost to the market as a whole and sometimes to specific stocks, or it can have a depressing effect if the news is bad.

☐ Financial analysts periodically examine major listed companies to determine the true valuation of the company. The reports by the financial analysts are often reacted to vigorously by the investing public. Optimistic reports can have a positive effect on a stock, and pessimistic ones can have a depressing effect. The reports of financial analysts are far from infallible. In determining, or attempting to determine, the true underlying value of a company, they can, by even minor errors or misstatements, have a sharp effect on the price of the stock.

☐ A large investor, such as an institution, might be persuaded to make a substantial investment in a company. A major investment could be a sign of optimism for other investors. On the other hand, if a major investor pulls out of a situation, for whatever reason, this could be construed as a sign of pessimism. There's no way to know what might have persuaded a large investor to get involved or disengaged from a specific situation, but the large block of stock that changes hands is sure to affect the price, at least for a short term.

☐ One of the great imponderables is competition. The threat of formidable competition can have a depressant effect on the stock of a given company; the fading of competition can have a buoyant effect.

☐ The rumor mill is always a potentially troublesome source of information (or misinformation) that can affect the price of a stock. Wall Street is a tight little community, and word can get around very fast. In all likelihood, the day-today ebb and flow of rumors is perhaps one of the most prevalent forces in shaping the daily fluctuations of the market.

MUTUAL FUNDS

Stock market mutual funds pool the dollars of many small investors and place them in a broad portfolio of various stocks. There are hundreds of different stock mutual funds offering a wide variety of choices to the investor. There are *performance funds*, whose objective is to create as rapid a growth pattern as possible. These funds tend to be more speculative, taking chances on stocks that fund management sees as having a quick short-term potential rise. There are growth funds that are geared more to long-term steady growth with less emphasis on dividend income. There are income funds whose primary objective is to generate maximum current dividend income. And there are growth/income funds that attempt to achieve a balance between growth and income factors.

The primary task of investors seeking mutual funds as a vehicle is to determine whether the fund's objectives are in line with their own objectives for short-term growth, long-term growth, income, or a combination of these. These objectives are spelled out in the fund prospectus, which must be read prior to making any investment decision. See the discussion of mutual funds in Chapter 16, in which some of their major features are described in detail.

Once a group of appropriate funds is selected, investors must then review all of the pertinent factors that can shape their investment future: costs involved in buying into the fund, annual charges for management or maintenance, and the history of the fund in meeting its stated objectives.

Sales costs (loading fees) vary considerably with stock mutual funds, from as much as 8½ percent of the investment to as little as zero (no load). Similarly, annual or monthly maintenance and management fees vary considerably. In many cases, the load funds (those with a sales charge) may charge a lesser annual fee than do the no-load funds, and proponents of the load funds claim that this difference over the long pull offsets the initial commission factor. Debate has ranged long and furious over which is better—load funds or no-load funds. Proponents of each side can find specific groups of funds over specific periods of time in which their viewpoint prevailed. There is no simple answer. Like the stock market itself, there's an element of speculation even in choosing one type of fund over another.

Mutual funds are quoted daily in the *Wall Street Journal* as well as in many local daily newspapers, weekly in *Barron's*, and annually in *Forbes* magazine. *Forbes* devotes an entire issue (usually in August) to the mutual fund industry. It rates the funds based on their performance in general up and down markets, giving a perceptive analysis of how various funds have performed during periods of boom and adversity. Another good service is "Investment Companies" by A. Weisenberger.

The daily listings of mutual funds quote the *net asset value* (NAV), the offering price, and the net asset value change. The net asset value of a mutual fund is the actual value per share. It's arrived at by dividing the total assets of the fund by the total number of shares outstanding. If a fund has $10 million in total assets and one million shares are outstanding, the net asset value per share is $10.

The *offering price* is the price that an investor would have to pay for shares in a particular fund. If the fund is a no-load fund, "N.L." will be indicated in the offering price. If the fund is a load fund, the offering price will be higher than the net asset value price, with the difference being the commission charges. For example, a fund may show a net asset value (NAV) of $12.68 and an offering price of $13.86. The investor pays $13.86 for each share, currently carrying an actual market value of $12.68. The difference of $1.18 represents the loading charge. $1.18 is 8½ percent of $13.86. But as a percentage of your money that's actually going to work for you, it is 1.18/12.68, or 9.3 percent.

Another fund shows a net asset value of $7.70 and an offering price of $8.28. The 58¢ difference is the loading charge, which is equal to 7 percent of the dollars invested. A no-load fund sells at the same price per share as the net asset value.

Sales Tactics

Perhaps the most common device accompanying a mutual fund sales presentation is a chart showing how well the fund has performed in past years. Be well aware that for any mutual fund it's possible to find one or more periods of time in which the fund did indeed perform magnificently. But it's also possible to find periods of time in which the fund performed poorly. This information will not likely be presented in the sales pitch. Yet the upward progress that is represented is often considerable enough to strongly tempt otherwise prudent investors.

The bull market of 1982 to 1987 attacted record numbers of investors to mutual funds. The aftermath of the bull market featured mutual fund performance charts showing how well they did during these years. But it's unlikely that you'll ever see graphic evidence of how a fund performed during the 1987 crash. Prudent investors examine a broader time span than what is shown in the sales presentations.

Common Investor Mistakes

The following is a list of the most common mistakes made by mutual fund investors who eventually come to regret having made them.

1. Investors do not know how much of their investment actually goes toward the selling commission. This does not mean to say that commissions are wrong, but an investor should know in advance how much the commission is. If the commission is too high, the prudent investor might prefer to shop for a comparably performing fund that has a lower commission or no commission at all.

2. Investors don't get a clear understanding concerning how their money will be invested. In short, they haven't examined the mutual fund's objectives and do not know whether the given fund invests speculatively or conservatively.

3. Investors don't keep close accounting on their monthly statements. They are not aware from month to month how their investment is performing. Lacking this knowledge, they may not be aware of when it would be a good time to sell the fund or buy more of it.

Mutual Fund ''Families''

As noted in the previous chapter, most major mutual fund companies operate a number of individual funds. These funds run the gamut from those that invest in conservative instruments, such as U.S. government securities, to those that invest in highly speculative options, commodities, and risky stocks. The attractive feature of the fund families is that you can switch from one type of fund to another simply, quickly, and at very low expense. Thus, in shopping for a mutual fund, one should shop for the families as well as for the specific funds within the families, and a clear understanding of the terms and conditions of switching should be known at the outset.

CHOOSING YOUR BROKER

All of the dilemmas discussed above are difficult enough for the advanced investor to cope with, let alone the novice. The choice of the right broker can be an invaluable aid in helping to evaluate the various factors an investor is faced with. There is no assurance that the broker will know the truth or falsity of any given rumor or will be able to evaluate the long-term implications of a new competitor entering the market or an old one leaving it. And a broker can't spend as much time on your account as you might want him to, for he does have other customers. But the good broker, wisely chosen, can direct you to sources of information that can assist you in making a proper decision and can steer you away from unreliable sources.

Choose your broker carefully, remembering at all times that *you* must make the ultimate decisions based on his recommendations and advice. A good broker can be a valuable ally in helping you meet your objectives, but only if you and the broker take the time to state those objectives clearly, and only if he then steadfastly assists you in meeting them.

Remember that a broker, with rare exception, earns his living by executing trades. He gets a commission on each trade, whether you're winning or losing. In other words, if he's going to eat, you've got to trade. If you invest a given sum of money in a given stock and instruct the broker to stash it away and forget about it for five or ten years and then tell him that's all the market investing you plan on doing, it's no wonder he wouldn't regard you as his favorite customer. Granted, he'll make his commission on your initial investment, and if he's still around when you cash in, he'll make another commission on the sale. But meanwhile your money is sitting idle as far as he's concerned, and he knows he's not going to make anything from you.

Naturally, any broker wants his customers to do well because this enhances his own professional image in the community, and each satisfied customer is like a walking, talking billboard. Many brokers can string along a losing customer for a period of time, blaming the continuing losses on market conditions, international news, and a variety of other factors beyond his control. True or not? It depends. There are indeed many factors beyond the control of any brokerage firm; but there are also many that could work to the broker's advantage that are yet overlooked.

The broker may not be keeping close enough tabs on all of his customers' various accounts and may neglect to advise you to buy or sell at an advantageous time. He may be too prone to listening to unfounded rumors and passing them along to his customers. He may not be making adequate use of research materials available in his firm and through other sources. He may be spending too much time hustling and too little time learning. And because there have been all too many lean periods for the brokerage industry in recent years, he may be so worried about where his next meal is coming from that he neglects the application of his own expertise to his customers' needs.

Consider these criteria in choosing your broker: how closely his investment philosophy parallels yours; his reputation for integrity and hard work, which you can learn from other customers who have used his services; the amount and continuity of his schooling, scholarship, and research; his willingness to spend time with you in learning or helping you to set your own goals and to spend time in seeking out the best means of achieving these goals; and finally, faith—something that can't be described, shopped for, or catalogued. It's just got to be there, and you'll know it when it is or isn't.

Playing the "Paper Game" with the Stock Market

The "paper game" is a harmless—and free—way to acquaint yourself with the ups and downs, the trials and tribulations, of the stock market. Play the "paper game" for six months or a year, and you'll have gained a good idea of whether it's the kind of place you want to send your money off to work for you.

The rules of the "paper game" are very simple:

1. Select any ten companies whose stock is traded on the New York Stock Exchange. Pick whichever you like. We'll call this assortment Group A. Make believe that you buy one hundred shares of each.

2. Put a recent listing of the New York Exchange stocks on a wall, and throw ten darts at it. Make believe that you buy one hundred shares of each of the companies nearest whose names the darts landed. We'll call this assortment Group B.

3. Using a tally sheet, as illustrated below, keep track of all your purchases. You may sell Group A stocks whenever you like, but you must pick a replacement. When you sell a Group B stock, you replace it by throwing another dart at the exchange listings.

4. At the end of the designated time—six months or one year—tally how you have done. Compare your Group A success with the success of Group B. How have you fared? Is the stock market a game you'd want to play with real money?

The following tally sheet can be used to keep track of your progress.

	Purchase price	Commission	Sale price	Commission	Dividends	Gain/ loss
Group A stocks						
1.	——	——	——	——	——	——
2.	——	——	——	——	——	——
3.	——	——	——	——	——	——
4.	——	——	——	——	——	——
5.	——	——	——	——	——	——
6.	——	——	——	——	——	——
7.	——	——	——	——	——	——
8.	——	——	——	——	——	——
9.	——	——	——	——	——	——
10.	——	——	——	——	——	——
Group B stocks						
1.	——	——	——	——	——	——
2.	——	——	——	——	——	——
3.	——	——	——	——	——	——
4.	——	——	——	——	——	——
5.	——	——	——	——	——	——
6.	——	——	——	——	——	——
7.	——	——	——	——	——	——
8.	——	——	——	——	——	——
9.	——	——	——	——	——	——
10.	——	——	——	——	——	——

The Great Crash of 1987

It could take years before all the dust settles from the great crash of 1987. Researchers, investigators, and journalists will be sifting through the rubble endlessly looking for clues as to what caused the Dow Jones Industrial Average to lose 508 points in a single day, an historic, all-time record. Were there any criminal culprits? Was there an unforeseen breakdown in the system? Could it happen again?

When the market crashed in 1929—and the downfall in the first few days in that crash was not as severe as it was in 1987—there was little else but buying and selling stocks and buying stocks on credit (margin accounts). In 1987 the simplistic buying and selling of stocks, and even the more sophisticated margin trading, were almost secondary to the exotic side bets that had come into existence in the intervening years. There were puts and calls and index futures. There were exotic "can't lose" gimmicks called *portfolio insurance*. A very high percentage of all the trading going on was generated not by human beings but by computers that were programmed to recognize and react to dozens, perhaps hundreds, of minute signals that theoretically would set off buying or selling transactions that could do nothing but enrich the users of these trading programs.

Many of the workers on Wall Street were very young. During the five-year bull market, from 1982 to 1987, many of the young, business school graduates who were entrusted with tens of billions of dollars of other people's money had never seen a down market. Would they know how to react if and when a down market came along? Did they have the experience to deal with such an event with maturity and judgment? Or would they simply push the panic button?

To the dismay of many investors, they found that they had been lured into side bets wherein they could lose more than they had actually bet. Hundreds of millions of dollars were lost on a technique involving "naked put options." In essence, these were bets that said the market wouldn't go down. Or, if it did go down, it would go down within certain predictable ranges. None of the players of this game could have envisioned the incredible plunge the market did in fact take. Fortunes were lost literally in minutes as players scrambled to get through to their brokers on clogged telephone lines to get them out of these deals.

Was the crash of 1987 incredible, impossible, unpredictable? Yes. Could it happen again? Yes.

CHAPTER 18

Making Your Money Grow: Real Estate and Other Opportunities

Beyond the money market and the stock market, there is a whole galaxy of opportunities for making your money grow (or shrink). Some can be relatively simple and even fun, such as collecting coins, stamps, bubble gum cards, and autographs. Others are much more complex, such as investing in real estate, commodities, a business, or a franchise. Many of these "opportunities" are aggressively sold by smooth-talking salespersons. The naive investor who does not do the necessary homework can end up in trouble. The serious investor who studies hard and realistically evaluates all risks can be successful. After reading this chapter, you should be able to do the following:

☐ Distinguish among the various types of real estate investments

☐ Understand the time and expertise needed to manage real estate investments properly

☐ Recognize the pros and cons of speculating in such things as commodities, precious metals, and gems

☐ Evaluate the true risks and tax implications in any of these varieties of making your money grow

MYTHS AND FACTS ABOUT REAL ESTATE INVESTING

Property values have been increasing at a rapid rate throughout most of the country, and as they increase, the mystique about investing in real estate grows too. Fostered by a myriad of get-rich-quick books and seminars and by the proud boastings of investors who claim to have "made a killing" in real estate, the mystique takes on dangerous proportions for the uninformed would-be real estate investor. Let's first examine some of the myths and some of the facts about investing in real estate.

Myth: Real estate is easy; anybody can make money at it.

Facts: Successful real estate investing always has been and always will be a venture requiring a considerable amount of expertise. As in any kind of investment endeavor, there will always be a handful of lucky ones who make it look easy to others. But those are definitely the exception, not the rule. Real estate is a fast track: Experts profit at the expense of novices. The experts know when to buy, when to sell, how to finance, and how to manage property properly. And even the experts can make mistakes. Expertise in real estate investing can take years to achieve. It requires the ability to deal efficiently and profitably with tenants, tax assessors, lenders, insurance agents, contractors, lawyers, appraisers, and other prospective buyers and sellers. The novice real estate investor, lured by the myth of fast and easy money, is apt to make serious mistakes and incur serious losses.

Myth: Real estate offers an assured return on your investment.

Facts: Real estate investing is very much like the stock market in that there are an infinite number of variables that can, in fact, make an assured return on your investment very questionable: a tenant defaults, seriously curtailing your income. Your furnace or central air-conditioning unit self-destructs, leaving you with a multi-thousand-dollar repair bill. The taxes on real estate in your community double in a short period of time. A visitor to your building trips on a piece of broken flooring material and sues you for five times the amount of your public liability insurance. The neighborhood in which your building is located begins to deteriorate seriously. An unexpected rerouting of traffic makes your building far less attractive to would-be-good-quality tenants. Your city passes a rent-control ordinance.

Events such as these, and countless others, can have a very negative effect on your expected investment return. Any would-be investor in real estate must approach any given project with a keen awareness of the potential unknowns that can drastically affect return.

Myth: Property values always go up.

Facts: The aforementioned factors that can have a negative effect on your hoped-for return can also have a negative effect on the value of the property itself. Real estate is cyclical. There are up periods. There are flat or down periods. And it's impossible to predict the cycles in any community at any given time. Real estate is also subject to the "greater fool" theory. This theory states that if you buy something at whatever price, eventually a greater fool than yourself will come along and buy it from you at an even higher price. The failure of the greater fool theory occurs when property values have gone too high too quickly and the community runs out of greater fools. Then you're stuck.

Always be aware that in any type of investment, winners always boast, but losers are never heard from. This contributes to the myth of profitability in real estate. Winners not only boast, they exaggerate. Losers keep their mouths shut. Thus, you'll hear an excessive amount of good news and a sore lack of bad news from people who have tried their hand in real estate. Be advised accordingly.

Myth: You don't need any money to invest in real estate. You can buy property with "no money down."

Facts: Perhaps more money has been made selling books and seminars on this subject than will ever be made in real estate itself. Sure, you can buy real estate with no money down, if you can find a seller who is willing to part with the property with no down payment. Or you can try to find a lender who is willing to lend you 100 percent of the purchase price. In either case, you're liable to be paying a higher price than the property is worth or a higher interest rate than would be called for in a normal deal. And once the hefty monthly payments begin, you could really be behind the eight ball. The novice real estate investor who tries these techniques is on very risky ground.

Despite these pitfalls, real estate can provide an attractive investment vehicle to individuals who are willing to do the necessary homework and put forth the necessary energy in keeping up with their investments. If the local marketplace is properly researched, if the premises and legal documents are properly scrutinized, and if the required amount of time and patience is devoted to the project, real estate can be very productive over the long run. One of the most attractive aspects of some kinds of real estate investment is the tax deduction that is allowed for the physical depreciation of the building. In a well-structured investment, this factor not only can render the income from the real estate investment free of income taxes but may also shelter the investor's other income from real estate taxes. This factor is discussed in more detail in the section on income-producing real estate.

INVESTING IN REAL ESTATE: TYPES OF OPPORTUNITIES

There are four major types of real estate–related investments plus one type that allows you to invest as part of a group.

- ☐ ***Income-producing real estate.*** You purchase a building with the intent of renting it out to tenants and thereby realizing income. At some later date you may sell the building and realize a profit on the sale as well.

- ☐ ***Vacant-land investing.*** You buy unimproved land with the intent of either developing it, renting it out, or selling it at some future date at a profit.

- ☐ ***Turnover investing.*** You buy a property with the intent of reselling it as soon as possible at a profit. Income is a secondary consideration.

- ☐ ***Mortgage investing.*** You, in effect, lend other people money with the loan being secured by real estate. You don't actually acquire an ownership interest in the property at the time you make the investment, but you might if the borrower defaults. Thus, it's essential that you know the values that apply to the underlying real estate that is collateral for the loan you've made.

☐ *Group ventures.* You pool your money with that of other investors in any or all of the categories above. Group ventures can include real estate investment trusts, syndications, and partnerships.

The whole world is made up of real estate, and opportunity exists in every country in which the free enterprise system is at work. Common sense, however, dictates that the closer to home you invest, the more knowledge and control you will have with respect to your investment. Let us now examine the basic categories of real estate investment.

Income-Producing Real Estate

The primary objective in investing in income-producing real estate is to earn income on your investment and to the extent possible obtain tax sheltering of that income through the depreciation deduction. But, as noted earlier, there are many factors that can affect the flow of income. Let's discuss some of the main factors that must be considered.

Quality and Type of Tenants. In residential property, for example, consider the problems involved in an apartment complex that rents primarily to "the swinging single" crowd, particularly if it's in the vicinity of a university. An owner can expect a relatively high rate of turnover, and with each turnover comes the chance of a vacancy and the possible need to repaint and refurbish each apartment as it's vacated. On the other hand, an apartment complex catering to married couples or older persons might experience a relatively low rate of turnover, thus minimizing the chance for vacancies and the need for refurbishment. Applying the reward-risk rule, which relates as much to real estate as it does to any other form of investment, the properties with the higher chance of turnover and higher refurbishing costs should carry a proportionately higher rent than the more stable properties.

In commercial properties there is a broad spectrum of possible tenants that could occupy any given space, limited only by the landlord's willingness to accept certain types of tenants and zoning ordinances that might control the usage permitted in certain locales. Consider, for example, the possible uses that can occur in a small neighborhood shopping center—a popular type of moderate real estate investment for small or moderate investors. A given space might be occupied by a business or professional firm, such as an insurance agency. It will have relatively little public traffic and will need no special plumbing, electrical, or drainage installations. The same property might be occupied by a coffee shop or a tavern, which could have a high level of public traffic that can contribute to the more rapid deterioration of the premises; in addition, such installations need specialized plumbing, electrical, and drainage connections. Further, these uses could generate smoke and possible fire hazards, which could increase the insurance rates on the building and of the adjoining tenants.

The credit-worthiness of a prospective tenant is not to be overlooked. When entering into a legitimate business venture such as a lease, the landlord can and should check with the local credit bureau to determine the tenant's credit-worthiness. A sloppy credit history might indicate a number of possible actions the landlord should consider: not renting to that particular tenant altogether; asking a higher rent; requiring the tenant find a co-signer to insure payment of the rent, requesting a substantial rental deposit as well as a breakage and cleaning deposit from the tenant to help assure that the rent will be paid.

A tenant who is tardy with rent can cause more than one problem. In addition to the headache and aggravation that the landlord must undergo in collecting overdue rent, the landlord might have to dip into personal funds to meet monthly payments as they fall due.

Strategies for Success

Choose Tenants Wisely for Best Returns

As with any investment, the higher the quality, the lower the risk, and the lower the return. This is as true in real estate as it is in the stock market. Having good tenants in your building means less risk to you: They'll pay their rent on time; their checks won't bounce. Knowing this, you might be willing to take a slightly lower rent in return for fewer headaches. Following are some wise steps to take before signing on a new tenant, either residential or commercial: Get an up-to-date credit check; verify employment; get personal references, including the present landlord; and meet with the prospective tenant personally. If you're a good judge of character, you'll be able to spot a trouble-free tenant from a troublesome one. And remember, the responsible tenant will leave the premises neat and clean. That's less expense for you down the line.

Nature and Quality of the Building. The potential risks and rewards for the landlord are directly related to the quality, location, and nature of the building itself. As in buying a house (Chapter 8), the would-be investor in income-producing real estate must pay explicit attention to all the various mechanical and structural details of the building. If not familiar with building construction, the investor should hire a construction specialist to provide a detailed inspection and report on the building. A building with hidden defects can cause serious and costly problems for the unsuspecting landlord; one in good physical condition will keep risk at a minimum and cut down problems of maintenance, repairs, and replacements. Many investors in real estate are content to take the word of the seller or the real estate agent representing the seller concerning the condition of the building. More prudent investors will determine on their own, with professional assistance, if the building does indeed meet the standards they are seeking.

Location is important to the would-be investor; one must determine whether traffic patterns or changes in adjoining neighborhoods can have an effect on the investment. An attractive gas station, motel, shopping center, or restaurant on a heavily trafficked thoroughfare might seem most appealing. But if a new highway diverts all the traffic away from the street, the result can be disastrous. A neighborhood shopping center might seem to offer attractive possibilities, but when a bigger and better shopping center is constructed a few blocks away, the unaware investor may regret the day he signed the down-payment check.

Prudent real estate investors will check with the local zoning board to determine what uses might be permitted in areas near their properties. They'll check with the traffic and highway agencies to determine what possible changes in traffic routings are anticipated. And they'll check with other real estate firms to learn what new developments are pending within the trading area of the properties they're buying.

The nature of the building must also be considered. Many buildings are limited by their size, shape, and type of construction in the uses to which they can be put. Food franchise buildings often fall into this category; they might prove very unadaptable to other uses should the original tenant move out. On the other hand, some buildings are easily converted to suit many different purposes. The more limited the use of a given building, the more difficult it may be to find tenants and maintain the level of investment return sought.

Property Taxes. Prudent investors will also check with local tax assessors to determine the current situation and likely future trends with respect to property taxes. If it appears that property taxes are likely to be moving sharply upward in the years ahead, they will want to know if they can absorb these taxes and still be on solid ground with respect to their financial projections. For instance, can they expect the tenants to absorb a share of the tax increase? Will the long-term trend of property taxes affect their ability to sell the building profitably in the future?

Utility Costs. All other things being equal, it's better for the landlord if the tenants pay their own utility costs—water, electricity, gas, and heating oil. This can take a lot of financial pressure off the landlord, particularly in areas of climatic extremes where heating or air-conditioning costs can demolish the most carefully planned budget. If a building, either residential or commercial, is not already separately metered for such utilities, the prudent investor will think twice about making the investment. If the landlord pays the utility costs, she can require tenants to pay a pro rata share of any such costs over a certain agreed base amount. Lacking such protection, the landlord is at the mercy of broken thermostats, leaky faucets and toilets, and other costly energy wastes.

Management of the Property. Perhaps the biggest shock that comes to the novice real estate investor is the sudden realization that management of the property can be a time-consuming and vexing matter. When you call your doctor in the middle of the night with a mysterious pain, he'll tell you to take two aspirin tablets and call him back in the morning. When a tenant calls you in the middle of the night to complain of a leaking toilet, you can't just tell him to throw two aspirins into it and call you back in the morning. Management takes time, patience, skill, diplomacy, expertise, and a sense of humor. If you're not handy yourself, you have to find plumbers, electricians, painters, and carpenters you can depend on. When you have a vacancy, you have to be prepared to refurbish the unit so you can show it to prospective tenants, many of whom will never show up at the agreed appointment time.

If the property generates enough income, it might be advisable to hire a professional manager who can deal with all of these matters in a professional way. A good management firm charges from 5 to 8 percent of the rental income, depending on the community and the type of property. A good management firm can be the landlord's best ally; a shoddy management firm can be the landlord's worst enemy. Get personal recommendations before you hire a management firm. If the management firm is also acting as a rental agent, be certain that the firm will screen prospective tenants to your strict standards. Otherwise, it could rent the premises to tenants otherwise unacceptable to you in order to generate its own rental commission in a hurry.

Financing.   The mechanics of financing income property are generally the same as financing one's own home. The investor (unless paying all cash) gives a down payment to the seller of the property and either assumes an existing mortgage or obtains a mortgage loan from outside sources. But here the similarity fades, for the real estate investor must arrange financing geared to her investment objectives: obtaining a satisfactory return on invested capital. If the mortgage payments are so high that, when combined with the other expenses of operating the property, there is no cash flow available to the investor, she is involved in a totally speculative situation—hoping that someday the property will be sold at a substantial profit. Some investors prefer to pay off any mortgage debt as rapidly as possible so that when the debt is finally eliminated, the cash flow on the property will be all that much greater.

The prudent investor, however, will seek a good return on invested capital (the cash down payment) and to that end will attempt to structure the mortgage so that there is adequate cash flow to meet objectives. Clauses in a mortgage that allow the lender to increase the interest, and thus the total monthly payment, can have an obvious effect on the investor's cash flow, and such clauses should be closely scrutinized. If there are interest-rate escalation clauses, the owner will have to be prepared to adjust rents accordingly if she wants to maintain a constant rate of cash flow.

The real estate investor may also need large sums of money at indeterminate future dates in order to accomplish major renovations and repairs. If possible, the investor will negotiate with the mortgage lender to obtain such funds by adding them on to the existing mortgage, hopefully at favorable terms.

A lender considering a mortgage loan application on income property will examine not only the owner's credit-worthiness but the caliber of tenants who currently occupy the building. The owner's ability to make payments on the mortgage is, of course, directly related to the ability of the tenants to make their regular rental payments. The better the tenants, the more favorable terms the borrower should be able to negotiate with the lender. Good tenants will, as noted earlier, be able to bargain for a lower rental from the landlord. The landlord can make up this difference by seeking the most favorable terms on the mortgage payments.

The Lease.   At the heart of any real estate investment is the lease: the agreement between the investor/owner and the tenant/user. Whether the property is commercial, residential, or a combination, the specific terms of the lease can have an important bearing on the investor's overall success. Residential leases tend to be shorter and simpler, usually running for a period of not more than one or two years. Commercial leases can be more complex, and because the property might be usable in many different ways by different tenants, a variety of clauses should be carefully considered by the investor. In either case, residential or commercial, the prudent investor will see to it that an attorney prepares a lease best suited to the investor's interests.

The following are some of the more important terms that should be evaluated, particularly in commercial leases.

Length of the lease

Is there any ideal length of time for a lease? Not really. As noted above, residential leases usually only run for one or two years, sometimes slightly longer. But for commercial leases, it's quite a different story. Tenants will want to know that they have the right to use the property at a fixed rental rate for as long as the property is profitable. If it ceases to be profitable, for whatever reason, tenants will probably want to depart. On the other hand, if landlords feel the space could be rented out more profitably after the passage of time, they may wish to get new tenants or increase the rent.

A preferred situation for tenants is to have a medium-term lease—from three to five years—with options to renew at an agreed rental rate. This offers the tenants both flexibility and fixed overhead. But this might not be to the landlord's advantage. By giving tenants the privilege to renew, the landlord is effectively taking the property off the market for the length of the original term and possibly the period of renewal.

Customarily, where renewal clauses exist, the tenant is obliged to give notice of intention to renew two or three months prior to the expiration of the lease. Technically, the landlord does not know until notice is given whether the space will be available after the expiration of the lease. The landlord can certainly make inquiry, but tenants are not legally obliged to express their intentions to renew or depart until the time stated in the lease agreement. Where there are no renewal privileges, the landlord knows exactly when the premises will be vacated and can begin seeking new tenants with an assurance of when they can take occupancy. Or the landlord can renegotiate the lease with the existing tenant and hope that conditions will permit an equal or better rental on the renewal term.

The landlord should bear in mind that because a tenant has a right of renewal at an agreed rental this does *not* guarantee that the tenant will pay that rental. Renewal date may roll around, and the tenant may want to continue in the space but at a reduced rental. This can put the landlord in a predicament: There's only a relatively short period of time in which to try to find a better tenant for the premises. Working out such problems often comes down to nothing more than plain old hard-nosed bargaining, the outcome of which will generally depend on the condition of the local real estate market at the time. If there's a surplus of tenants looking for space, the landlord is in a better position. Of course, the reverse is also true. There's no way of knowing what these conditions will be like in years ahead, so the parties just have to be prepared to cope with the situation as it arises.

Another factor to consider, particularly in a commercial building, is that having a long-term lease and a good tenant means more security for the lender. The sharp investor will try to translate this security into more favorable financing terms, such as lower interest rates or other beneficial terms.

The rental rate

In most cases, market conditions and tenants' credit-worthiness will determine the probable amount of rent tenants will pay. In commercial rentals, the rent is often expressed in terms of "per square foot." A space of 1000 square feet that rents for $1000 per month, or $12,000 per year, will be quoted as "$12 per square foot per year" or, in some cases, as "$1 per square foot per month."

Commercial rentals are also referred to as *gross* or *net*. In a gross lease the landlord is responsible for virtually all operating costs on the property, including real estate taxes, utilities, maintenance, cleaning, and generally servicing the premises. The tenant having a gross lease pays a higher rental in return for these services. In a net lease, the tenant is responsible for these expenses.

The landlord who wants a minimum of involvement in the management of the building will prefer a net lease. Some tenants may prefer a net lease because they can more directly control the operating expenses on the building. Whether a lease is gross or net, the building must still be properly maintained. A landlord, even with the most perfect net lease, must still see to it that the tenant does all the proper management, maintenance, and repairs that he is required to do under the lease.

Rental payments may be fixed for the term of the lease, or they may escalate upward in line with rising prices or simply by agreement between the parties. In addition to the basic flat rent, commercial leases often have percentage clauses.

A *percentage clause* states that the tenant must pay additional rent to the landlord in an amount equal to an agreed percentage of the volume of business the tenant does. For example, the tenant may be required to pay 6 percent of all gross income in excess of, say, $100,000 per year. In such a case, if the tenant's business does not gross over $100,000 in a year, the percentage clause does not go into effect. But if the tenant generates $150,000 of volume, the percentage lease will require the tenant to pay 6 percent of $50,000, or $3000, in additional rent for that year.

The existence and terms of a percentage clause are a matter of negotiation between the parties. If a landlord feels that a tenant's business prospects are good, the landlord may prefer a lower base rent with a percentage clause. A more conservative landlord may simply prefer a higher base rent and no percentage clause. A percentage lease allows the landlord the right to look at the books and records of the tenant so that the correct amount of the payment can be determined.

Use of the property

The lease stipulates the purposes for which the premises can be used by the tenant or by any subtenants if there is a right of sublease. If, for example, a tenant rents a store property for a retail shoe business, the landlord does not want the tenant or a subtenant to later change the premises to a tavern.

In addition, particularly in a multiple-occupancy situation such as a shopping center, the tenant may request a *noncompetition clause*. Such a clause would prevent the landlord from allowing other spaces in the center to be rented to competitors. The landlord will have to evaluate such a request in light of current market conditions, his eagerness to rent the space, and the rent that the tenant is willing to pay.

Repairs and restorations

The lease should stipulate who is responsible for each and every kind of repair. Customarily, the tenants are responsible for making minor interior repairs, and the landlord is responsible for structural repairs and matters affecting mechanical equipment, such as the heating plant and the air-conditioning unit. Of course, the parties can agree to any combination of who does what and who pays for what. A prudent landlord might prefer that the tenant pay for certain repairs, but the landlord will see to the actual work. By so doing, the landlord can choose the firm to do the repair work and might get a better level of satisfaction than by having the tenant make the choice.

Some leases contain a *restoration clause*, which would require tenants to restore the premises to their original condition. If tenants have made renovations within the premises, they will have to see to it, at their own expense, that the property is brought back to its original condition unless the landlord later agrees otherwise. If a restoration clause is agreed on between the parties, it would be necessary for them to include a careful description of the premises at the time of the start of occupancy (including colored photographs as an added precaution) to assure that the amount of restoration needed is also agreed on.

Default

What if tenants don't live up to the lease agreement? What if they damage the property and do not repair it? Or what if they leave in the middle of a lease and try to escape making further payments? Leases should clearly state that tenants remain responsible for any default, although including such clauses in leases does not necessarily mean that tenants will automatically make good on defaults. Landlords must still pursue their rights, through the courts if necessary, to gain satisfaction.

As a measure of protection against default, the prudent real estate investor will insist upon a rental deposit and a breakage and damage deposit from a tenant. The rental deposit, usually designated as the last month's rent on the lease, assures that the landlord will have at least some cash in hand should the tenant skip. The breakage and damages deposit will protect the landlord to some extent in the event that the tenant neglects to make such repairs. But it should be clearly understood that the amount of the rental deposit and the breakage and damage deposit are not the limit of the tenant's obligation. The tenant will still be obliged to make whatever payments are due over and above the amount of the deposits.

Compounding Your Income. In fixed-income investments your earned interest can be automatically reinvested in your account and go to work for you. This is known as *compounding interest*. The same ends can be accomplished in the stock market, through either a dividend reinvestment plan or a mutual fund that pumps your earnings back into additional shares of the fund. But can you compound your earnings in a real estate investment? In a sense, yes, at least to a certain extent. Prudent real estate investors realize that a portion of their income should be reinvested back into the property, by way of refurbishing and modernization. The net effect of this *should* be to generate higher income from tenants of the property.

It's not as simple or as automatic as the compounded interest on your savings account, and it requires some expertise to know which dollars can generate additional rentals. Investors may prefer to take all income out and invest it in some other fashion, if in fact they are not spending it. But the investor should examine the possibilities of reinvesting the money in the property before making an ultimate decision.

For example, a tenant might agree to an increase of $20 per month if the landlord repaints the premises. The paint job might cost $1000, but the landlord will be getting an additional $240 per year for the balance of the lease.

That's a 24 percent return on the $1000 investment—an attractive situation indeed. The prudent investor will be continually on the alert for ways to increase and compound income by plowing profits back into the property.

Taxes. Before we proceed to analyze how a real estate investment works, it's necessary to understand one of the basic principles of income tax law. Suppose that your taxable income in a given year is $35,000. All of this income came from your employment. (Taxable income is what's left over after all of your deductions and exemptions have been subtracted from your gross income.) You're married and filing a joint return. You are in the 28 percent tax bracket. If you could come up with another deduction of $1000, your taxable income would be reduced to $34,000. At a 28 percent tax rate, the extra deduction would thereby reduce your tax bill by

$280. This is an example, in very oversimplified fashion, of a tax shelter: an outside source that generates a deduction, reducing the tax you would have to pay on the income you earned from work.

Prior to the passage of the Tax Reform Act of 1986, there were many ways to generate such deductions. They were called *tax-shelter investments*, and real estate was one of the most popular. Alas, the Tax Reform Act of 1986 eliminated most of these tax-saving opportunities. But for many investors, ample opportunity to reduce taxes by this means is still available in real estate. *If your adjusted gross income is under $100,000, you can still utilize deductions from real estate investments to offset as much as $25,000 per year worth of income from work.* If your adjusted gross income is between $100,000 and $150,000, you can still achieve a partial deduction. If your adjusted gross income exceeds $150,000, your ability to deduct anything will have been phased out entirely by 1991. The concept of *adjusted gross income* is explained further in Chapter 22.

In brief, then, the attractive tax advantages of real estate investing can still be available to the lower- and middle-income investor. Let's study an example of how these tax advantages can work.

Depreciation deductions: the good news

You purchase and actively manage a small apartment house. The purchase price is $150,000 (see below). You have a down payment of $10,000 and obtain a mortgage of $140,000 payable over twenty years at a fixed rate of 13 percent. Your monthly payments on the mortgage are $1640. The following is the data for the purchase of your real estate investment:

Purchase price	$150,000
Down payment	10,000
Mortgage (13% fixed rate, 20-year term)	140,000
Monthly payments	1,640

For purposes of the "depreciation deduction," which will be explained shortly, the cost basis of the property can be broken down as follows: The land (not depreciable) is valued at $40,000 and the building (depreciable) at $110,000. The depreciation breakdown is:

Land (not depreciable)	$ 40,000	
Building (depreciable)	110,000	
Depreciation period	27.5 years	
$110,000 ÷ 27.5	=	$4,000 depreciation per year

Your operating figures are listed in Table 18-1: Your annual income is $26,400 and annual expenses total $25,680. Your net income, after expenses, is $720. You

Table 18-1 Operating Income and Expenses

Rental income	$2,200 per month	×	12	=	$26,400 per year
Expenses[a]					
Interest	$1,600 per month				
Taxes	100				
Insurance	100				
Maintenance	200				
Miscellaneous	140				
Total expenses	$2,140 per month	×	12	=	$25,680 per year
Net income (rental income − total expenses = net income)					$ 720 per year

[a]Figures are approximate.

invested $10,000 of your own cash, so you are receiving a return of 7.2 percent on your invested money. That's a decent return, but you could earn just as much by putting your money into a savings plan. Then you wouldn't have all the hassle of managing a building. If this is the case, why, then, do people invest in real estate? Because they're after the depreciation deduction.

Buildings physically deteriorate as the years go by. (Despite the physical deterioration, however, buildings might be increasing in value as the years go by.) Tax laws permit investors to show a "loss" on their income tax forms to reflect the supposed physical deterioration of their property. Obviously, this loss is not a real out-of-pocket loss, particularly if the building is appreciating in value. Under the Tax Reform Act of 1986, an investor who owns an income-producing residential property can claim those "losses" over a period of 27½ years. An investor in commercial property can claim losses over a period of 31½ years. The claimed losses must be the same for each year.

The tax law also states that only the building portion of a property is depreciable, not the land portion. The value of your building in our example is $110,000. That's the depreciable portion of the total investment. Dividing 27½ years into the $110,000, we get a $4000 per-year depreciation deduction. In other words, if you were to claim the $4000 deduction each year for 27½ years, you would have written off the entire cost of the building in that time.

For current concerns, you are thus entitled to an annual deduction for depreciation of $4000. Assuming that you are in the 28 percent tax bracket, this deduction will thereby save you $1120 in taxes (28 percent of $4000 equals $1120). The depreciation deduction from the real estate investment allows you to reduce your taxable income from work by $4000. At the 28 percent bracket, this results in a tax savings to you of $1120. Your operating profit of $720, plus your actual cash-in-hand tax savings of $1120, totals $1840. The return on your investment is as follows:

Operating profit	$ 720 per year
Income tax savings	1,120 per year
Return on $10,000 investment	$1,840 (or 18.4% annual return on $10,000)

Thus, $1840 is the actual money you'll have in hand at the end of the year as a result of your real estate investment. The $1840 represents a return of 18.4 percent on your $10,000 cash investment. Is this return big enough to warrant your spending the necessary time in managing the property? Consider also that as the years go by the property increases in value (if you've bought wisely and managed well), so that your ultimate return when you sell the property can be even more handsome.

Tax laws affecting real estate investments (and all other types of investments) have changed frequently in recent years. The tax implications in the example above may be different by the time you make an investment in real estate. It's absolutely essential that you check the tax laws in effect at the time you plan to purchase and that you get professional assistance in analyzing how the current laws will impact on your investment.

Depreciation deductions: the bad news

The depreciation deduction is not all good news. There's a reckoning to be made when you sell your property. Let's return to our example. You paid $150,000 for the building. Now assume that you own the building for ten years and take a depreciation of $4000 for each of those ten years, for a total of $40,000 in depreciation deductions. At the end of ten years you have the opportunity to sell the property for $250,000. Naturally, you'll have to pay a tax on your profit.

What is the extent of your profit? You paid $150,000 and received $250,000 for an apparent profit of $100,000. But you'll have to pay income taxes on more than $100,000. Because you claimed $40,000 in depreciation deductions while you owned the building, the tax law requires that your cost basis be reduced by that amount. In other words, in calculating your profit on the building, you must calculate your cost (for tax purposes) as the original price you paid for the building *minus* any depreciation deductions you have claimed. The original price was $150,000, and you claimed depreciation deductions of $40,000. Thus your cost basis for tax purposes is $110,000. The gain that is subject to income taxes is, then, the difference between your selling price and your cost basis:

$$\$250,000 - \$110,000 = \$140,000$$

In other words, some of the tax advantages that you enjoyed while you owned the building could be taken away from you at the time you sell the building. Again, a careful analysis of tax laws in effect at the time of sale is necessary to help you structure the best terms and the best time for a sale.

Vacant-Land Investing

Investing in vacant or "raw" land can be one of the most extreme forms of speculation. We do hear of "killings" made in land by investors; and we hear statements, such as the one Will Rogers made, "You ought to buy land, cuz they ain't gonna print no more of it." But success in raw land investment, for the most part, remains the province of the skilled professional who has the expertise, the capital, and the selling skills needed to turn a profit most of the time. *Note*, we said "most of the time." Even the skilled professional will have setbacks.

Other forms of investment pay a form of income to investors—interest on fixed-income investments, dividends on stocks, rentals on income properties. But raw land requires investors to be constantly *paying out* money: real estate taxes, public liability insurance, and money for necessary signs and security. Further, investors in raw land have put their capital beyond reach until the land is actually sold. It's extremely difficult to borrow against raw land, and if one does, then the interest expense has to be added to the other expenses.

Whether you are buying land for future building purposes (residence or business) or for a fast turnover to make a quick profit, you should consider the following factors:

"Known" Land. There's a much better chance for success in real estate investment if you're dealing with known land, that is, land that exists in a community with which you're familiar and on which you can get professional estimates from real estate professionals concerning probable future value. Known land also implies that you are certain of the availability of utilities, sewers, roadways, schools, shopping, and other necessary facilities.

"Unknown" Land. Uncounted millions of dollars are lost every year by people who sign contracts and checks to buy parcels of unknown land—generally, land in distant places that is being sold as part of a development program for the creation of a "new city," a resort, or a retirement village. Although there are legitimate developments in all parts of the country, the abuses, intentional or otherwise, that have arisen have been all too frequent. Anyone considering investing in raw land for future personal use, particularly if it's unknown land, must observe the following cautions.

See the land

It's necessary to actually view the land and walk it from corner to corner *before* you sign any documents. The majority of people who have been bilked on such deals haven't done this. Fancy brochures and high-pressure sales pitches lead them to believe that they are getting an idyllic lot in an ongoing development when in fact they may be buying a barren patch of wasteland.

Hire an attorney before you sign anything

The attorney should help you determine whether the land you saw is the land you'll actually be buying. The attorney will also scrutinize the other documents involved and help you ascertain exactly what you can expect for the money you're paying. If you sign documents before you have had legal counsel, it may be too late for the attorney to help you.

Read the property report

If a developer is selling land on an interstate basis—to buyers in many states—federal law requires the provision to prospective buyers of a *property report*. The property report must contain certain information prescribed by the Interstate Land Sales Act, a federal law. If a developer fails to provide the property report within the prescribed time limits, the buyer might be entitled to revoke the contract and obtain a refund.

Obtain an appraisal

It can be wise to get professional help in order to determine the true value of vacant land. The seller's asking price and the true current market value may be far apart, and you don't want to pay more than you reasonably should. A qualified real estate broker or professional appraiser can assist you in learning the true current market value, taking into account the following: recent comparable sales of similar property, existing and future potential traffic patterns in and around the land, future population trends, the stability of the tax base, the scarceness of such land for certain designated uses, and the attractiveness of the terms on which you can buy and later sell the land.

Have the land tested and surveyed

Whether you're planning on building on the land or hoping to sell it to someone else who will, there are certain physical tests that will have to be done sooner or later—the soil test and the percolation test—and two different surveys—the boundary survey and the topographical survey. The *soil test* determines the bearing capacity of the soil. In other words, how much of a building load can the soil withstand? The soil may be compact enough and of the right composition to support a small, one-story cinder-block or brick building, without needing any expensive footing or foundations. On the other hand, the soil may not be proper to support a multistory building without getting into expensive substructures. *Percolation tests* determine the drainage capacity of the land—how much rainfall and moisture the land can absorb without turning into a swamp or a sea of mud. The condition of the ground in this respect can obviously have a bearing on the use of the land and the cost of constructing a building on the land.

Although not technically tests, the boundary survey and the topographical survey will assure a would-be buyer or builder of the true boundaries of the property and of the precise slopes that may exist on the property. If there is, for example, too much slope to the property, a prospective builder might be faced with expensive land-moving costs. These costs could be reflected in the price a buyer is willing to pay for the property.

Prudent investors in raw land might deem it wise to have these tests and surveys made, even before making a purchase, to determine the ultimate usability of the property or the cost of making it most usable to most prospective buyers.

Count the dollars and cents

If you buy a parcel of raw land that doubles in price within the short space of five years, you might break even. Here's the arithmetic. Say that you pay $10,000 in cash for a piece of vacant land. You are forgoing a return on your money of, conservatively, $600 per year. That's how much you could have earned by simply investing the money in a savings certificate insured by the federal government. In addition, you may have the following typical expenses: property taxes, $500; insurance (mainly for public liability to avoid lawsuits if anyone is hurt while crossing the property), $200; signs, advertising, and security, $200. (These figures are just rough estimates, but within the bounds of probability.) Your total annual expenses (including lost interest) are thus $1500, or a total over five years of $7500.

Assume that five years later you are able to sell the property for $20,000. If you have used a real estate agent to find a buyer—which is likely—the agent's commission will be 10 percent of the selling price, or $2000. In addition, you'll probably have expenses related to the sale, particularly legal fees and recording costs that can easily total $500. Your total expenses then are $10,000—$1500 per year for five years, or $7500, plus the $2500 at the time of sale. Your selling price of $20,000 thus results in a net of $10,000. Over a five-year span the property has doubled in value, but you as the investor have only broken even.

This example may be pessimistic, but it's intended to provide you with the kind of ''what if'' arithmetic you would face with such an investment *before* making a decision. The time to evaluate this very clear risk is before making any commitments to invest in raw land. Once the commitment is made, you can't get out of it as you could selling a share of stock or cashing in a savings certificate. You're stuck with it until a buyer comes along, and if that buyer isn't willing to meet your price, you may have to take whatever is offered. And the longer you hold the investment, the more it costs.

Turnover Investing

Probably somewhat more speculative than investing in higher-quality income property and probably less speculative than raw land investing is the purchase of existing homes for subsequent resale. It's a tricky business requiring expertise, hard work, and patience. But many small investors have found handsome profits in such endeavors, so that they have become semi-businesses rather than just investment modes.

Many opportunities exist involving homes that need refurbishing, and these might prove particularly attractive to the investor with repair talents. Such talents will allow you to make reasonably accurate estimates of what renovations might be needed, how much they'll cost, and how much they can boost the potential selling price. A few hundred dollars wisely spent on paint or paneling or flooring, for example, could increase the potential selling price by a thousand dollars or more.

The overall procedure involves seeking out houses that have good underlying basic value but that can be bought for less than the normal market price, perhaps because the owners have had financial difficulties and are anxious to get out. The success of any venture depends on the investor's ability to buy right and to finance right.

Buying Right. Buying right requires the careful evaluation of the neighborhood as well as of the physical structure itself. A run-down house in an area of better homes could command a handsome price if it's spruced up to be on a par with its surroundings. Another run-down house might offer little or no profit potential regardless of how much you do, because the general neighborhood isn't that desirable. Remember that your buyers are looking for location as well as a house, and the selling price is affected accordingly.

There are three ways an investor might find attractive situations to purchase homes that need refurbishing. First, you can scout around privately for people who are hard pressed to sell because of either time or money pressures. The more pressure there is on them, the better the deal you might strike. Word of mouth or simply driving around looking for "for sale" signs are ways of discovering such opportunities. Advertising is another way. The seller may place a classified ad with a tipoff that indicates a good buy; or you, as the investor, can advertise under the "homes wanted" or similar classifications in the want ad pages.

A second way of locating run-down homes for sale is through real estate agents in your area. Make it known to a number of them that you're in the market for such houses, and ask them to contact you if they spot any. Agents might be reluctant to take a listing on run-down houses, but if they know they have a possible buyer, they could put you on to a number of opportunities.

A third likely source of information is banks and savings and loan institutions that have taken back properties on foreclosures and that don't relish owning a lot of unused residential property. This possibility deserves particularly careful attention because you might well find a source of automatic financing when you later sell to another party.

Financing Right. If you've bought right and if you've refurbished correctly, your chances of finding a willing buyer who will pay you the sought-after profit will be greatly enhanced if you can offer the property fully financed. This means that a credit-worthy buyer can step right into a mortgage situation for which you have made prior arrangements. In order to make such arrangements it will be necessary to develop a relationship with a mortgage lending institution or institutions in your community that are willing to cooperate with you in such transactions. As part of the negotiations involved in setting up such a relationship, you may have to guarantee all or part of any given loan that is arranged on behalf of your buyer. Although this can improve your potential profitability in the sale of the house, it does put you on the hook for an extended period, and you should be particularly careful that buyers pay adequate down payments and that their credit history justifies your assuming this possible risk. As noted earlier, many mortgage lenders in the community may have an inventory of used homes that they'd be willing to sell at attractive prices to investors willing to fix them up and offer them for resale. In such cases, they might be willing to cooperate in advance in making commitments for long-term financing to credit-worthy buyers.

The Profit Margin.   Perhaps the biggest challenge in this kind of investment is building enough of a profit margin into the deal to cover your initial expenses, as well as your continuing expenses, and yet not price the property out of the market. Investors must be well aware that once renovations are completed and their properties are on the market, time can start working against them. Every month that goes by in which the houses remain unsold means added costs—interest, taxes, insurance, advertising, and so on. As these costs mount, investors might have to drop the price. As the expenses continue to rise and the asking price continues to drop, investors might succumb to feelings of panic. This is the worst danger. The difference between what they will pay out for the purchase, the renovations, and the continuing expenses and what they'll take in at the time of sale must be most carefully estimated.

A well-structured deal offers the opportunity for substantial profit if a buyer is found in the early months, but as time goes by, profitability rapidly erodes. This risk must be well considered by anyone investing in homes for resale purposes.

Mortgage Investing

Technically, mortgages are not really real estate investments, but many people think of them as such. These investments fall more aptly into the fixed-income category: You're actually buying someone else's IOU with a piece of real estate as security for the IOU. But because you could end up owning the real estate if the borrower defaults on the mortgage payments, it can and perhaps should be considered within the overall category of a real estate investment.

Prudent investors must scrutinize the value of the property as much as they scrutinize the credit-worthiness of the borrower. In effect, they must exercise the same precautions that a bank would in making an original mortgage loan: appraising the property, determining the credit status of the borrower, and seeing to it that there is adequate protection regarding title and property insurance. The assistance of an attorney is necessary for preparing all the required documents, and the cost of the legal service must be taken into account. It's not unusual in private mortgage investing for the costs of legal matters and related documentation to be passed along to the borrower. In addition, the private mortgage lender might be able to impose extra fees or ''points'' in much the same way that institutional lenders do.

Prior to becoming an investor in mortgages, it would be valuable to meet existing mortgage brokers in your community and determine what the current going prices and interest rates are. You might even, as a would-be investor in mortgages, prefer to deal through such brokers before you embark on your own. The mortgage brokers will, in effect, place your money for you in mortgage situations and will take a fee for their services. Most communities have a number of private mortgage brokers who are always looking for funds that they can invest, content to take a service fee for their efforts. You can find them listed in the Yellow Pages of your telephone directory and in the classified section of your newspaper, usually under the heading ''Money to Lend.'' If you do choose to use the services of a mortgage broker, take precautions in advance to assure yourself that the broker is totally reputable. If you turn your money over to a disreputable individual, you might never see your money or the broker again.

A mortgage investment can take one of the following three forms: An existing mortgage can be taken back, a new mortgage can be initiated, or a mortgage can be sold at a discount. Let's take a look at each type of mortgage investment.

"Taking Back" a Mortgage. If you sell property that you own and agree to accept the buyer's IOU in full or partial payment thereof, this is commonly known as *taking back* a mortgage. The buyer of the property becomes obligated to you to make the monthly payments called for in the mortgage agreement. Many people who sell their homes or business properties don't have immediate use for the full proceeds and might prefer to let the money stay in the property as a form of investment.

Initiating a New Mortgage. Initiating a new mortgage is very much like taking back a mortgage, except that instead of taking back a mortgage on a property that you own, you are making a new mortgage loan to an individual who is buying a different property. The interest rate, costs, and added fees that you as an investor can generate out of the deal are subject to negotiation between the parties. Some important cautions are in order, though, if the deal is to be structured to your best advantage.

First, you must determine why the individual is not able to obtain conventional financing through a normal lending institution. If it's because of a weak credit status, you might be asking for trouble. In such cases, you might be able to command a higher interest rate (subject to state usury laws) because you are taking on a higher than normal risk. Or the property buyer may simply not have enough down payment to meet the requirements of the institution, even though the credit status is perfectly acceptable. This is a lesser risk, but one that you should evaluate nonetheless.

Second, you should protect yourself in setting the number of years that the loan will run. Banks measure their mortgage loans in decades, but it's not wise for you to tie up your money that long. You can establish a payment program that is based on a thirty-year payout, for example, but you should reserve the right to have the full amount due and payable in a much shorter period of time, for instance, five or ten years. This matter is subject to negotiation between the parties. The borrower might not like the prospect of having to refinance the loan at the end of five years but may be willing to accept these terms if there is no other choice, especially if, all other things considered, it's still a better deal than can be found elsewhere.

Your documents should be structured so that the borrower (the property owner) cannot sell the property to another party without your express permission. For obvious reasons you would not want the owner to sell the property to a person whose credit status is unacceptable, unless perhaps he remained liable for the debt in case the other party defaulted. A subsequent buyer of the house whose credit history is unacceptable may damage the premises in some way or decrease its value and so jeopardize your investment.

In establishing the interest rate on a new mortgage or a "taken back" mortgage, you might also want to consider what many institutional lenders are doing: They are putting in clauses that permit them to alter the interest rate, when and if interest rates in general throughout the country change. This matter was discussed in more detail in Chapter 9, where it was described from the borrower's viewpoint. As a potential investor in mortgages, consider the same factors, but from the lender's viewpoint.

Buying Mortgages at "Discount." There's an active market in most communities in investing in mortgages at a discount. Let's examine this possibility with an example. Some years ago Murphy bought Johnson's house and Johnson took back a mortgage from Murphy at a 10 percent interest rate. Today Murphy still owes Johnson $40,000 on that mortgage, and payments are to run for another ten years. Johnson needs money now. He can't wait ten years to collect what is owed him. Johnson approaches you to sell you Murphy's IOU. You know that Murphy is very credit-worthy and that the value of the property is more than ample to cover your investment. But comparable investments are available today that will give you a yield of 14 percent. So why would you buy Murphy's IOU, which pays only 10 percent?

You might offer to buy Murphy's IOU at a "discount," that is, for less than the face value. Depending on how anxious Johnson is to get cash, he might be willing to sell you the $40,000 IOU for, say, $30,000. If such a deal is made, you will receive 10 percent on the amount of capital you have at work, and you will also, over the ten-year period, receive an additional $10,000 over and above what you invested. The attractiveness of this kind of investing depends on the original interest rate on the mortgage, the amount of discount you can negotiate, and the true yield that results from the combination of the interest rate and the discount.

Return of Principal. There's one catch to investing in mortgages that investors aren't always aware of. Each monthly payment that you receive contains some interest and some of your own investment that you're getting back. Review the section on mortgage financing in Chapter 9 to refresh your recollection of how this aspect of mortgages works. Since you're receiving a small part of your investment back each month, you have less and less of your original investment working for you as the months go by. Unless you take steps each month to reinvest your principal, your ultimate return won't be as much as you had thought it might be.

For example, you invest $10,000 in a mortgage paying 12 percent interest for ten years. You receive monthly payments of $143.50. Over the full ten years these payments total $17,220. You will have received, therefore, $7,220 more than you had invested. Divide this figure by ten (for ten years), and you come up with an average annual return of $722, which is equal to a 7.22 percent return on your original investment of $10,000. What happened to the 12 percent return that you were expecting? Each month, as you received the checks from the borrower, your original $10,000 investment dwindled, since you were getting some of it back. In short, the whole $10,000 wasn't working for you all the time. In order to have kept it working for you, you would have had to reinvest the principal portion of each monthly payment as you received it. In all likelihood the only way you could invest such small monthly sums safely would be in a passbook savings account where your return would be far lower than 12 percent.

Lending institutions such as banks and savings and loan associations can avoid this problem because, as the money comes in, they are constantly relending all of it. As an individual you can't do this. If you are dealing through mortgage brokers for your mortgage investments, on the other hand, they can pool all of their various investors' payments as they come in and put them back to work in new mortgages. This advantage might offset the fee that you have to pay the broker for keeping your money at work for you at the highest possible yield. But if you do deal with brokers, it is essential that you make certain their records are totally reliable. Their reputation should also be checked most thoroughly before you get involved.

Mortgage Pools.   Instead of just investing in a single mortgage, it is also possible to pool your money with that of other investors in an assortment of numerous mortgages. The most popular program for this type of investing is offered through the Government National Mortgage Association (GNMA, or "Ginnie Mae"), an agency of the U.S. government. Ginnie Mae buys mortgages from lenders (banks, etc.), packages a few dozen into a "pool," and then offers certificates to investors. Each certificate represents a share of ownership in a specific pool of mortgages; the minimum purchase price for a new certificate is $25,000. Ginnie Mae certificates are guaranteed by the U.S. government, which has made them very attractive to investors.

As a Ginnie Mae investor, you receive monthly checks, just as if you owned a single mortgage. The problem of return of principal, as noted above, also exists with Ginnie Mae investments: If you don't reinvest each monthly payment as you receive it, it ceases to work for you. However, many major stockbrokerage firms have created mutual funds that invest in Ginnie Mae certificates. Shares in these funds can be obtained for as little as $1000, and they do offer automatic reinvestment of your monthly income.

Other government-related programs offer similar forms of mortgage pool investing: the Federal Home Loan Mortgage Corporation ("Freddie Mac") offers participation certificates (PCs) and collateralized mortgage obligations (CMOs), and the Federal National Mortgage Association (''Fannie Mae'') offers mortgage-backed securities (MBSs). Get full details on these plans from stockbrokers. And be certain to shop around, since prices and terms can differ from place to place.

Group Investing

There are two ways that small investors can pool their money with that of other small investors to get involved in real estate and take advantage of the depreciation laws discussed earlier.

Syndication. Syndication is one means of group investing. Usually, a promoter or syndicator will embark on a single major project such as an apartment complex or a shopping center. Shares will be parceled out in denominations of $5000, $10,000, and so on to small investors who wish to become involved in the project. The promoter will likely take a fee for efforts in organizing the syndicate and may also share in the profits of the project. These syndicates are usually structured so that the promoters reserve to themselves all control over the management of the funds and the property, and the investors have no say in the matter.

Real estate syndications will often take the form of a limited partnership in which individual small investors are known as *limited partners* and the promoters are known as *general partners*. Syndications and limited partnerships are not without risks—indeed, in many cases the risks can be very high. Often, unwary or gullible investors will allow themselves to believe grossly exaggerated profit and income potentials on such deals, only to find that such rewards never materialize. The prudent investor in a syndication will take every precaution, including viewing and appraising the property, making certain that all legal documents are in order, and determining the reputation and reliability of the organizers of the syndication or partnership.

Real Estate Investment Trusts (REITs). These are specialized forms of investment programs set up under the federal tax laws to allow small investors access to the real estate investment market. A REIT is like a mutual fund. It will pool the money of small investors to acquire a variety of real estate investments, and as long as it adheres to Internal Revenue Service regulations, it can pass its profits, income, and depreciation deductions along to individual investors. The REITs tend to be much larger and more broadly based than syndicates, which usually restrict their deals to one or a few individual properties. REITs are available in shares of stock comparable to buying stock in a company itself. Since REIT shares are sold on stock exchanges, not only is the value of REITs affected by the income and profitability of the real estate interests they own, but they are also subject, to some extent, to the whims of the stock market. Because of this, the REITs lose much of their element of certainty for prudent investors.

Excessive speculation by many REITs during the 1970s caused many of them to go bankrupt and others to incur severe losses for investors. In the 1980s, the REITs began to benefit from a stronger stock market and generally improving conditions in the overall real estate market. But the Tax Reform Act of 1986 and the market crash of 1987 again injected elements of uncertainty into the REIT market. Potential investors should carefully examine the prospectus of a REIT to determine the nature and type of investments they are making and what the potential returns are.

Private Partnerships. Because so many real estate investments require a fairly large down payment, an individual might wish to seek one or more partners on a particular venture. However, there are obvious problems. All of the individuals involved must be firmly committed to the same long-term objectives. For example, investment partners must determine how much of the income will be pumped back into the property for refurbishing and modernization. They must determine who will be responsible for managerial duties, bookkeeping, taking care of tenant problems, and handling all other matters relating to the investment.

If one or more partners want to sell out, will they be required to offer the share to the other partners first, and if so, on what terms? What kind of vote will it take to determine whether the property should be sold or refinanced?

The natural human tendency is not to worry about such matters until they arise. This can be foolhardy, for nothing can stand between friends and business associates more distinctly than disagreements over money. All possible items of dispute, including those noted above, should be reduced to a binding contract among the parties at the inception of the deal. A contract can't eliminate the disputes, but it can minimize them.

To Learn More

If you contemplate becoming seriously involved in real estate investing, it would be advisable for you to take the courses and exams given in your state leading up to the licensing as a salesperson and as a broker. Check with your local County Board of Realtors to determine how these courses of instructions can be obtained.

INVESTING IN SMALL BUSINESSES

Existing Businesses

Many people will come across opportunities to invest in small local existing businesses, becoming involved as a "silent partner," an "active partner," or as the sole proprietor by actually buying the business outright. An existing business may be seeking fresh capital for expansion or renovation or for the purchase of machinery or other equipment. Owners may prefer to seek private financing rather than bank financing so as to cut down on the interest cost. They might prefer to offer a share of the profits to an investor rather than be obliged to pay interest on a loan. Or they may wish to sell all or a part of their interest for a variety of reasons: retirement, illness, wanting to move on to something new, or getting out from under a bad situation.

In any of the instances above, a would-be investor in a going business must do extensive and detailed investigation and will need the assistance of a lawyer and an accountant. Here is a checklist of matters that the prudent investor must examine with the aid of those professional assistants.

How Will Funds Be Used? If the business is seeking funds for expansion, renovation, or new equipment, how specifically will the funds be put to use? What are the prospects of the new capital being able to generate added profits? Often, small businesses will overexpand, anticipating substantial additional business when little or none actually results. Or the cost of the expansion will be too great to permit increased profits. There's a high level of risk in such investments, and the would-be investor should turn to outside sources for help. The local office of the Small Business Administration can direct you to sources of information on specific types of businesses, how they function, and how profitable they might be. Such background information would be advisable for the prudent investor in any kind of business investment situation.

Why Is a Business Being Sold? If all or a part of a business is being sold, you must determine the reasons for the sale. Is it a genuine case of retirement, illness, dissatisfaction with an associate, or lack of a successor? Or is there some problem that might not be visible on the surface? With the aid of your accountant, you should examine at least three years of the business's operating statements, as well as three years of its federal and state income tax returns. You should attempt to trace the flow of income and expenses to determine whether you can spot any trends that could indicate danger ahead.

You should obtain a credit report on the business and on the principal owners to determine if they have been meeting their obligations. These obligations would include the payment to suppliers, lease payments, utilities, and taxes. If you spot any pattern of delinquency in meeting obligations, you might be looking at a danger sign. The pattern might indicate, for example, that the owners have been subsidizing the business out of their own pockets, and these subsidies might not show up in the business's operating statement. The owners may have considered such transactions to be private loans to themselves and not entered them in their books. Although you as a buyer would not necessarily have to repay these loans, you would find, in short order, that the business was not capable of maintaining itself without further subsidy from you.

Other reasons for selling a business might include threat of future competition. Owners may be aware of plans for a major shopping center near the retail outlet and want to sell out while the selling is good rather than risk being wiped out by the competition. Local realtors in the area might be familiar with such pending plans, and they could aid you in making your long-term projections concerning the future profitability of the business. In addition to competition, there are other developments that might affect your investment, such as changes in highway routings, nearby construction projects whose noise and dirt could be troublesome for an extended period of time, or zoning changes that could permit uses of land and buildings near your premises that would be incompatible with your business.

If you're considering investing in a business that relies on a particular product for its success (such as a brand-name item that the business may have a territorial exclusive on), determine whether the particular product will continue to be available to you and if its price will be relatively predictable.

Determine whether there are any claims or lawsuits pending against the business, such as tax liens, claims for refunds, or lawsuits arising out of unpaid obligations or damages suffered by individuals for which there is no insurance to cover the cost. Also, find out whether the business has maintained a good record with the local Better Business Bureau and any other consumer-protection agencies in the community. You don't want to discover after the fact that a business has a bad public image, which can seriously detract from your investment. Determine whether the business has met all of its federal, state, and local government obligations including proper payment of federal and state withholding taxes, unemployment insurance taxes, workmen's compensation insurance premiums, and all necessary filings regarding its business status with all appropriate agencies.

"Goodwill." If you will be replacing the existing owners in the day-to-day operation of the business, either totally or partially, you'll want to determine how much of the business's success (or lack thereof) may be due to the owners' presence. Do they, for example, have a large loyal following that may disappear when they're no longer there on a day-to-day basis? Such a situation could jeopardize your investment. On the other hand, you might be able to determine that the existing owners have a bad public image and that by replacing them the business can actually improve, thus enhancing your investment.

The Lease. Your attorney should review the lease on the premises to determine how well protected you are. How long does the lease run, and what kind of renewal options do you have? What provisions are there for increases in the basic rent or in the cost of utilities, property taxes, and maintenance? To what extent will you be responsible for repairs? Will there be any percentage clauses requiring you to pay a portion of your gross business volume to the landlord as additional rent? If a landlord owns additional space, for example, in a shopping center, do you have any rights to expand into such space should you so desire, and if so, at what cost? Further, are you protected against the landlord allowing your competitors to rent space near you in the same center?

How Much to Pay for a Going Business. There are many elements to consider when determining how much of an investment is justifiable in an existing business. There is the hope for expanded profits as the business enlarges and improves in its efficiency. There is a hope for a profit on a later resale. There is the matter of a salary that one might gain from becoming active in the business. But the ultimate question is: What kind of return will you get on your invested capital? The potential increased profits and the potential profit on a later sale are speculative, and the prudent investor will not be satisfied with mere hopes and promises. The question of a salary is not truly an investment concern. If you do earn a salary from becoming involved in the business, theoretically you'll be giving up some other form of earning to take over the tasks of running the business. If you're moonlighting while retaining your existing work, it's true that you'll have increased your income as a result of your involvement, but you can always moonlight without making a substantial investment in an existing business.

Thus, the question of return on investment becomes all-important, and this can be arrived at, with the help of your accountant, by examining the books closely to determine how much money is left after all expenses, including the business's own taxes and any salary paid to you, have been paid.

Depending on economic times, America's major corporations have an average return on invested capital per year ranging between 10 and 15 percent. If a local business investment doesn't generate at least 10 percent, you might do better to look elsewhere for a source of investing your funds. If the business promises a return of greater than 15 percent, there may be undue risks attached to the investment.

The Legal Documents. With the aid of your lawyer, you will enter into a contractual agreement with the seller or borrower. The contract will spell out all of the rights and obligations of the parties, particularly regarding the ongoing management of the business. The contract will stipulate how any profits are to be split and how any losses are to be made up. The contract should also give you protection if you later determine that the seller or borrower made misrepresentations to you about the business.

If by becoming involved in the business you are becoming liable for any of the business's debts, you should make arrangements with the creditors so that the extent of your obligation is clearly understood. You should also see to it that you are properly protected as an individual regarding the business's lease on its premises, as well as on all insurance policies relating to the operation of the business, including fire and public liability insurance. If the business provides group health, life, or other insurance, and if it provides a pension or profit-sharing plan, you should also see to it that all documents are in order to protect you to the extent that you and your associate have agreed on. These things will not take care of themselves. Many documents may have to be amended to assure that you are getting what you have bargained for and what you're entitled to.

New Businesses

Starting up a business from scratch, either on your own or through such means as a franchise arrangement, does not fall into the investment category at all. It's pure speculation. There can be no assurance whatsoever of your getting any kind of return on the money you put into such a venture. You could reap a bonanza, and you could go broke in short order.

It's one thing to dive into an *existing* business where there is some record of the business's success available for your examination: established clientele, patients, customers, and so on. But to start from scratch, where you have nothing on which to base even estimates, can be extremely hazardous.

Some major national franchises, on the order of McDonald's, Kentucky Fried Chicken, and the like, have indeed produced many successful investor/restaurateur/operators. But for each McDonald's there were dozens of "Beauty Burgers" that proved to be a disaster for one and all. Of course, each new franchise operation that comes along envisions itself as the next McDonald's, and they sell as such to the would-be investors. This is where dreams are turned into nightmares. Proceed, if you must, with complete awareness of the risks that you face, and remember that salespersons representing these franchises are trying to sell you something on which they will make a profit. There's no assurance that you too will make a profit or ever see your money again.

If you're starting up your own business from scratch, be well aware that, on average, it takes from two to three years before a typical new business venture begins seeing a profit. This is not a casual warning but a fact of life. Many businesses will fail because they were not adequately capitalized at the outset. The owner may have gotten an overdose of glamour and failed to see the realities of running a business.

In any kind of new business venture, the efforts of your legal, insurance, and accounting advisors are essential before you proceed with any expenditure of funds. And bear in mind this simple but important caution: If you're prepared to risk it all on a new business venture, you have to be prepared to lose it all.

GAMBLING IN COMMODITIES

Like raw land and new business ventures, the commodity market represents a form of pure speculation. It's one of the most volatile, unpredictable, and high-pressure gambling devices yet devised. Next to a commodity exchange, a Las Vegas casino might seem tame by comparison.

There's an old saying: "If you want to make a small fortune in the commodities market, start with a big fortune." This is no joke! Horror stories abound from investors—some sophisticated, but most naive—who have been lured into the commodities market with the hopes of fast profits. Part of the extremely speculative nature of the commodities market involves the fact that your "bet" has a time limit to it. If you purchase a contract or an option on a given commodity, there's a time limit to that bet. In effect, if your horse hasn't finished in the money within the set period of time, you lose your bet altogether. In the stock market, you can own a stock as long as you like and wait for it to hit whatever target price you have in mind as long as you like. You can live with the stock for years and years as it goes through its ups and downs. But with futures contracts and options contracts, when the expiration date arrives, your betting ticket becomes worthless.

Further, your bet can be won or lost because of many unpredictable influences, such as weather conditions, political events, shifts in economic trends, wars (either starting or ending), and changing consumer sentiments. Not the least of your concerns should be the honesty and integrity (or lack thereof) of your commodity broker. The commodities industry was shamed in early 1989 when an FBI investigation revealed cheating schemes whereby commodity firms bilked investors out of millions of dollars. Table 18-2 lists a small sampling of some items that are traded in the commodities markets, as well as exchanges where the betting can be done.

Commodity Funds

If the commodities market intrigues you, but the high level of risk frightens you, you might find commodity funds more to your liking. Commodity funds pool small investors' money and bet it on a diversified selection of commodities. In effect, commodity funds act like mutual funds, but technically they are a form of limited partnership.

Commodity funds can be somewhat less risky than direct speculations in commodities because of the diversification that is probably not available to

Table 18-2 **Commodities and Exchanges**

Commodities	*Exchanges*
Grains and seeds (corn, oats, soybeans, wheat, etc.)	Chicago Board of Trade
Livestock and meat (cattle, hogs, pork bellies, etc.)	Chicago Mercantile Exchange
Food and fibers (cocoa, coffee, sugar, etc.)	Coffee, Sugar and Cocoa Exchange
Metals (copper, gold, silver, platinum, palladium)	New York Commodity Exchange; International Monetary Market; New York Mercantile Exchange; Chicago Board of Trade
Petroleum products (crude oil, heating oil, gasoline)	New York Mercantile Exchange
Financial (British pound, Canadian dollar, Japanese yen, German mark), U.S. treasury bonds and notes	International Monetary Market; Chicago Board of Trade
Stock market indices (Standard and Poor's 500 Index, New York Stock Exchange Index)	Chicago Mercantile Exchange; New York Futures Exchange

individuals speculating on their own. Further, or at least it is hoped, professional management of the fund should be capable of making better decisions than individuals would be.

Commodity funds also purport to offer individuals better protection against the margin calls than they would have on their own. A substantial amount of commodity trading is done on "margin": Investors put up only a small percentage of the total cost of the contract that they're buying. If the price of the commodity drops, investors either must sell their contract at a loss or come up with additional money to protect their interest. The effect of this is that investors in commodities can lose more than their original investment. Review the section on margin buying in Chapter 17 for more details on the mechanics of such trading.

The commodity funds set aside a substantial portion of their overall assets to meet such margin demands, thus insulating the individual investors from having to come up with more money. This means that not all of your invested money is going to work in commodity contracts; the part that is set aside by the fund will be put to work in more stable investments such as U.S. government securities where they can earn interest until needed for margin calls.

Commodity fund investors should be wary of the costs and commissions that they will incur by investing in these funds. It's not unusual for total costs, including management fees, brokerage commissions, and incentive fees, to total as much as 20 to 30 percent per year. This means that the investor won't make any money at all until after the fund has earned enough to cover these fees.

The prospectus of any commodity fund should be read thoroughly before an investment decision is made. In examining the prospectus, the investor should determine the extent of diversification of the funds' assets, the experience of the portfolio manager, and the ability to get your money out when you want it.

Foreign Commodities and Currencies

Speculating on various foreign currencies in the commodities market (see Table 18-2) is similar to investing in U.S. commodities and every bit as risky if not more so. There are many other ways that Americans can also invest or speculate in the many economic facets of other nations.

Bank Accounts in Foreign Countries. American investors often open bank accounts in other nations, particularly Canada and Mexico. They might be lured by attractive interest rates, or they might be planning on spending time in those other nations and want the convenience of having accounts in place to minimize the task of converting U.S. dollars into local currency. If you're doing this for the latter reason, it can make sense. If you're simply hoping to earn a higher rate of interest abroad than you can obtain at home, you must take into account a number of factors that can be unpredictable: the future exchange rate of the U.S. dollar versus the other currency; the tax laws of the other nation; and the possible devaluation of the other currency while you have a substantial investment in it.

In order to open a bank account in the currency of another nation, you have to convert your U.S. dollars to, for example, pounds. Whenever you want to retrieve some of the money to spend it in the United States, you have to convert it from pounds back to U.S. dollars. These currency exchanges will cost something, and their costs could offset much of the seemingly attractive rate of interest that you had hoped to earn. Tax laws in the other nation might require that a portion of your earnings be withheld to pay taxes in that nation. This can cause you some complicated bookkeeping and filing of tax forms. With respect to the possibility of devaluation, your investment can be immediately diminished in value if, for example, the other nation unilaterally declares that its currency is worth less per U.S. dollar today than it was yesterday. Another fact you should consider is that in the United States your bank deposits enjoy the protection of the Federal Deposit Insurance Corporation programs. Would you enjoy the same protection if your investments were in the banks of another nation?

Foreign Stocks and Mutual Funds. A very small number of stocks in foreign companies can be bought and sold in U.S. stock exchanges using a device called an *American depository receipt* (ADR). Major U.S. banks buy a supply of shares of particular foreign companies and hold the shares in an escrow account for the benefit of American investors who have purchased the ADRs. As an owner of ADRs, you're just as subject to market fluctuations as you would be if you owned the stock directly.

The mutual fund industry has enjoyed very strong sales records in foreign mutual funds. Most major American mutual fund companies offer a variety of funds specializing in foreign regions or specific nations. By investing in these funds, you get the benefit of supposedly expert analysis and advice in choosing the particular stocks. Note well, though, that foreign stock exchanges can be even more volatile than U.S. stock exchanges, and their rules and regulations may be less understandable to you as an investor. If investing in mutual funds of American companies poses a risk, investing in mutual funds of foreign companies poses an even greater risk if for no other reason than that access to knowledge about such companies is not as readily available as it is to domestic companies.

SPECULATING IN PRECIOUS METALS

Gold and silver (and to a similar extent, platinum) are nothing more than blatant and extremely risky speculations. This was made clear at the start of the 1980s, and matters aren't likely to change for the rest of the century. In the early months of 1980, gold soared from a level of about $250 an ounce a year earlier to over $825 an ounce. At the same time, silver reached $50 an ounce from its earlier level of about $10 an ounce. In early 1982, gold had plummeted to under $330 an ounce—a loss of more than 60 percent to those who had bought it at its peak. And there were many who had done so. The silver debacle was much more swift. One wealthy Texas family, the Hunts, had virtually cornered the silver market in early

1980, borrowing heavily to do so. When their ability to repay those debts came into doubt, the price of silver plunged by 80 percent within just a few months. Many small investors were wiped out.

The gold-price roller coaster continued through the mid-1980s. From 1984 to 1987 the price stabilized in the range of $450 to $500 per ounce. In the late 1980s the turmoil began anew, prompted by the stock market crash of October 1987, and by worldwide concerns over the United States' budget and trade deficits. In late 1988 and early 1989 inflation worries began to nag at the American consciousness. According to many gold touts, that should have been a signal for the price of gold to rise. Instead, the price plunged to below $400 an ounce.

Would-be investors in precious metals would be well advised to remember why investing in gold in particular, and other metals secondarily, became tarnished.

Widespread abuses and fraudulent dealings scared many people away from buying metals (see the Consumer Beware section at the end of this chapter). Metal prices no longer seemed to respond to the signals that had set price moves just a few years earlier, signals such as world crises, inflationary trends, and interest rate movements. Many of the so-called gold bugs—commentators and analysts who touted the metals—began to lose their loyal followers because of bad advice. Perhaps the most crushing blow came from the Internal Revenue Service: As of July 1, 1983, bullion dealers were required to report all sales transactions of $10 or more to the IRS. Those who had been using metals trading to hide profits from the IRS would thus be exposed, and trading fell off sharply. The speculative fever could return at any time, and when it does many more innocents will get burned.

A Losing Proposition

If you bought gold for, say, $500, and the price soared by 50 percent over a three-year span to $750, and you then sold it, you would have made a bad deal! Here's the arithmetic that most gold buyers overlook: When you buy or sell gold, you have to pay sales commissions and possibly sales taxes and assay costs. (A buyer may demand an assay, which is a test to determine whether the metal is really gold, and to what extent.) It's not unreasonable to expect these costs to be 10 percent when you buy and 10 percent when you sell. Thus, in the example given, you would pay $50 when you bought and $75 when you sold, for a total of $125. Subtracting these costs from the $750 selling price, you end up with $625.

On the other hand, if you invested your $500 in a guaranteed savings plan paying 10 percent interest with no commissions to pay, your money would grow to over $650 over a three-year span. In short, because of the costs of buying gold and because your money isn't earning anything for you while you own the gold, you would, as in this example, be better off with the old tried and true savings plan.

The example given above is based on the assumption that you had bought real gold! Sadly, the gold marketplace is ridden with fraudulent dealers who pass off gold-plated lead, counterfeit coins, and phony contracts for future delivery in quantities that may never be determined fully. The same precautions apply equally to silver and platinum.

If you must speculate in precious metals, it is imperative that you deal only with firms whose reputations are totally reliable. Particularly avoid dealing with strangers over the telephone or through the mail. Whomever you deal with, keep in mind the following standards of measurement and use them to be certain that you're getting what you bargained for:

Gold and silver are weighed in troy ounces. There are 31 grams to a troy ounce; and there are 480 grains to a troy ounce. It can be dangerous to confuse grains and grams and troy ounces.

What is referred to as pure gold is known as 24-karat gold. Anything less than 24-karat gold means that gold is mixed with another metal. Thus, 18-karat gold is 75 percent real pure gold and 25 percent other metal; 12-karat gold is 50 percent pure gold and 50 percent other metal. Similarly, what is referred to as *sterling silver* is not pure silver, but rather roughly 92.5 percent silver and the rest other metal.

The prices for these metals that are commonly quoted do not refer to a single ounce but to a much larger quantity. This price is known as the *spot price*, and gold is quoted in 100 troy-ounce lots, silver in 5000 troy-ounce lots. You would, then, expect to pay a higher price per ounce for quantities under the spot level.

Where to Speculate

There are a number of ways you can get into commodity investing. Again caution is urged.

□   *Commodity exchanges.*   You can bet on the future value of precious metals on a number of commodity exchanges. Gold is traded on the New York Commodity Exchange and the International Monetary Market (part of the Chicago Mercantile Exchange). Platinum is traded on the New York Mercantile Exchange. Silver is traded on the New York Commodity Exchange and the Chicago Board of Trade. Most major stockbrokerage firms can place these bets for you.

□   *Mining companies.*   Rather than buy the metals themselves, you can buy stock in the companies that mine them. Again, stockbrokerage firms can handle the transactions for you. Mining stocks can be every bit as speculative as the metals themselves, but many do pay dividends so that your money is earning something for you as long as you own the stock.

□   *Certificates.*   Some large banks have gotten into the precious metals business. They will buy and hold for you a certain sum of gold and silver and will give you a certificate representing your interest in the metals. They will, of course, charge appropriate fees for these services.

□   *Coins.*   Many nations, including the United States, have minted gold coins over the years. Some of them are older and, if in good condition, may have collector value over and above the gold value itself. To determine the true value of any such investment, you should seek the assistance of a reputable coin dealer. Many other gold coins that have been recently minted, such as the South African Krugerrand, the Canadian Maple Leaf, and the American Arts Commemorative Medallion offered through the post office, can serve as investments as well. Any potential collector value of these coins is questionable at best and is probably not realizable for many years. All coins are also subject to counterfeiting.

☐ *Jewelry.* All gold jewelry manufactured in the United States is by law required to have the correct karat content stamped on the piece. But this law is not rigidly enforced. The best protection is to deal with reputable jewelers. Speculating in gold by way of jewelry purchases is probably the least feasible in terms of making money, for you will pay the dealer's markup plus the cost of any artistry that has gone into making the piece. It's unlikely that you'd be able to recapture those costs unless the value of gold itself triples or quadruples within a fairly short period of time. But at least jewelry can be worn, and if you appreciate that aspect of it, you'll receive at least some ego benefits, if not financial benefits.

One final caution: Trading in gold and silver—except on the commodity exchanges—is virtually totally unregulated. This means you'll have no governmental agency to turn to for help if you find you've been bilked.

DEALING IN STRATEGIC METALS

Strategic metals, in the broad sense, include such things as cobalt, manganese, iridium, molybdenum, and chromium. These are metals that, at least currently, are considered important to our national defense and industrial production, but that we must import from other countries in large quantities. Advances in technology could render some currently strategic metals not so strategic in the future; and other insignificant metals and chemicals could become very important in the future.

As with the precious metals, the strategic metals are often touted as easy paths to getting rich quick by the same kinds of promoters who push gold and silver. As with gold and silver, the strategic metals investments are highly speculative and subject to the same kind of self-fulfilling prophecy. Speculators who have the good luck to get in right and get out right might make fast money. But investing in strategic metals is not for the prudent investor who wants to build a solid foundation.

Stockbrokers can direct you to all of the speculations available in the field of strategic metals, such as companies which mine the metals. And the same precautions hold true for strategics as for the precious metals: Deal only with people whose reputations are totally reliable, and not with strangers. This means only that you have less chance of being defrauded, not that you'll have a better chance of making a profit.

TRADING IN GEMSTONES

Speculating in metals might almost seem prudent when compared with speculating in gemstones. Trading in gemstones without the assistance of a totally reliable professional (jeweler or gemologist) is absolutely foolhardy. The most popular form of gemstone speculation has been in diamonds. But speculation in colored gemstones (rubies, emeralds, and sapphires primarily) has become popular as well. These speculative opportunities are not restricted to big-money investors. Many plans are devised to appeal to small and medium-sized investors. And many of these plans are rife with danger.

Gemstones are as unlike one another as snowflakes. If you examined 1000 diamonds (or emeralds or rubies or sapphires), it's highly doubtful that you would find any two alike. They can vary not only in size and color but in basic quality, from priceless to pure junk. If you buy any gemstone sight unseen, you could be getting the junk. To buy any gemstone without first having it independently appraised by a reputable jeweler or gemologist is extremely hazardous.

Whether it's your intent to speculate in gemstones or to acquire them as jewelry pieces, you should be aware of the characteristics that contribute to their value or lack thereof. Diamonds are considered to be the most easily appraised of all gemstones. Colored gemstones are more difficult to accurately appraise because of the wider range of colors and chemical compositions in them. But even with diamonds, experts can vary by as much as 10 to 20 percent in their estimate of value.

Diamonds are evaluated in accordance with the four "Cs." Colored gemstones use similar formulas. The four Cs are color, clarity, cut, and carat weight.

□ *Color.* Diamonds can range in color from the highly regarded "pure blue-white" to murky yellows. The better the color, the higher the value. Gemologists can grade the color of a diamond by use of a spectroscope. Even slight differences in the color grade can make a substantial difference in the value of a given stone.

□ *Cut.* Raw diamonds (in the rough) are cut into various sizes and shapes. The more highly valued cuts are those that permit the maximum brilliance of light to refract through the stone. The depth of the stone and the faceting contribute to brilliance or lack thereof. The shape of the finished stone can also bear on its value. Common shapes are emerald cut (rectangular), oval cut, square cut, round cut, and marquise (pointed oval). The perfection and proportion of the cut can make a stone worth more or less. Further, some shapes are more popular than others for jewelry purposes, and this too can affect the value. Gemologists can measure the preciseness of the cut of any diamond and grade it numerically.

□ *Clarity.* When looked at under a magnifying glass or microscope, impurities in a diamond will appear. (Some may even be visible to the naked eye.) The highest clarity diamonds are those with the fewest imperfections or flaws. Clarity is also measured numerically by gemologists.

☐ *Carat weight.* There's a lot of confusion between *karat* and *carat*. *Karat*, as noted above in the discussion on gold, measures the percentage of pure gold in a given item. *Carat* is an actual unit of weight. Thus, a diamond might weigh—on an actual scale—one carat, two carats, and so on. A carat is divided into one hundred points. Thus, a twenty-five-point diamond is equal to one-quarter of a carat. As between two diamonds equal in color, cut, and clarity, the heavier one (carat weight) will be the more valuable. But a one-carat stone of high quality in terms of color, cut, and clarity could be worth vastly more than a three-carat stone whose cut, color, or clarity is poor. Also, a single stone is worth more than an aggregate of smaller stones of equal quality and total weight. Thus, a single one-carat stone is worth more than four twenty-five-point stones of equal quality.

These are the basic guidelines for determining the value of gemstones. *Proceed at your own risk.*

COLLECTING COLLECTIBLES

The possibilities in the realm of collectibles are limitless: from old comic books to Chinese jade, from antique buttons to hubcaps, and everything in between. Whether prudent investment or wild speculation, the field of collectibles offers a measure of personal satisfaction in the hobby aspects of the endeavor. Thus it is difficult to evaluate the financial considerations of collecting: If you get enough pleasure out of accumulating beer cans, movie posters, or original Picasso oil paintings, then perhaps the money doesn't matter.

But whether your objectives in collecting are personal, financial, or any combination thereof, there are some basic precautions to observe lest you be separated from too much money needlessly.

☐ Coins and stamps are the most popular forms of collectibles. There is abundant information published on both of these areas, and the novice should take advantage of this literature. Before buying and before selling, the most current price lists should be consulted. If major transactions are contemplated, an outside appraisal can be inexpensive insurance to protect a large investment.

☐ Many forms of collectibles cannot readily be converted into cash. The more exotic the items, the fewer potential buyers there may be. Finding a buyer for a collection or part of a collection may require considerable time and expense —such as advertising in specialized publications that deal with a particular type of items (antique magazines, etc.).

☐ Lacking ready buyers, such as are commonly available in the areas of coins and stamps, collectors of such things as art may have to turn to dealers and galleries in order to convert their collectibles into cash. A dealer is likely to pay only about half of the item's retail value, and this could mean a loss to the collector. On the other hand, some dealers might be willing to take an item on consignment. They won't promise you any price, but they'll offer it to their clientele and take a commission for their effort. The commission may range from 10 to 25 percent. If they're not successful in selling it, you take it back. If any valuables are left with any kind of dealer on consignment, an agreement should be entered into setting forth the nature of the consignment and the responsibility in case the item is damaged, lost, or stolen.

☐ Many collectibles go through fads. They may be hot one year, cold the next. If you get involved in a fad collectible that is on the wane, you could end up a big loser. But if you're lucky enough to get in on the rise, you could be a big winner. The gambling element is evident.

☐ All collectibles require some level of expertise. Much of this expertise can be acquired by studying; much of it only by trial and error. Before embarking on a program of collectibles, therefore, do whatever studying you can. Then proceed with caution until you feel confident of your ability to know when and what to buy and when and what to sell.

Strategies for Success

Beware of Unregulated Businesses

Stock markets and banks are strictly regulated by the government. If something goes wrong, you *might* have an ally in the state or federal government to help you unravel the problem. But in many other areas of investment opportunity, governmental regulation might range from slim to nonexistent. Simply stated, this means that if something goes wrong, you're on your own. You might have no recourse to any official agency. Generally speaking, franchising, distributorships, precious metals, and limited partnerships have relatively little governmental regulation. Even where regulation does exist, the road to recovery via the government can be long and tortuous. Before you send away your money, know who's out there to help you get it back if things go wrong.

LEASING EQUIPMENT

Equipment leasing is very much like real estate investing, except that instead of buying buildings and leasing them to tenants, you buy equipment and lease it to users. Here's how equipment leasing works: Someone you know needs a particular piece of equipment—an automobile, a typewriter, store fixtures, power tools, and so on. He doesn't have the cash to buy the equipment and doesn't want to finance it. You buy the equipment and lease it to him. The rental he pays you is taxable income to you. As the owner of the equipment, you can take some depreciation deduction on your tax return to offset some of the taxable income that you receive in the form of rental of the equipment. If the numbers are right (and you'll likely need an accountant's advice at the outset), and the risk seems reasonable, proceed accordingly. Deal with people you know. Check the credit of any individual to whom you are leasing equipment. Have a lawyer draw up a simple lease agreement between yourself and the user to protect your interests.

Be aware that equipment leasing does not have the appeal it used to have prior to the passage of the Tax Reform Act of 1986. That tax law severely limited the tax breaks one could obtain through equipment leasing. Now, for the most part, an equipment lease deal has to stand on its own merits, without your being able to take much advantage of the tax breaks formerly available. Proceed with caution and with the help of a tax advisor.

INVESTING IN TV "OPPORTUNITIES"

Hardly a day goes by that yet another get-rich-quick scheme isn't offered on the tube in the form of a seminar, a lecture, a classroom full of "eager students," or some other such sales gimmick. Popular subjects for these spiels have been real estate, the stock market, mail-order distributorships, and a variety of cleverly disguised pyramid schemes. If anyone makes money from these so-called investments, it's the cable TV operator and the promoter, likely not the person who spends many hundreds of dollars for the learn-at-home self-study kit. There can be valid information contained in these kits, whether it is on audio cassette or in printed form. But putting the information to use is never as easy as the TV pitch makes you think it is. Nor are the "students" in the TV seminar classroom as honest or as eager as they seem to be. They may well be hired actors performing a role for a day's pay rather than satisfied investors who have already gotten rich from the product. These self-promoting TV programs are virtually unregulated and can easily prey on the naive and gullible individual trying to find a new career or investment opportunity. They should be approached with the utmost caution. And note well: The money-back guarantees that are generally offered are often worthless. Many companies do not honor their guarantees. This has been the case all too often, leaving customers out many hundreds of dollars with no recourse to anyone to get their money back.

PRIVATE LENDING

While not generally thought of as such, lending money to individuals or businesses is a form of investment. Whether they approach you or you approach them, the same precautions are in order: Establish terms (interest rate, repayment date, etc.) that will be fair and reasonable. Check the credit of the borrower to determine the level of risk you are undertaking. If you feel that the borrower's signature alone on the promissory note does not adequately protect you, seek either collateral or a co-signer for the loan. Be certain that you know the financial status of the borrower: What other debts does she have? What kind of income sources does she have? And, all things considered, from what sources will she be able to make repayment on the loan? Have a properly drawn promissory note signed by the borrower, setting forth all the appropriate terms including your rights should the borrower default on the payments. A lawyer is the right person to do this for you.

In short, take all the same precautions that a bank would take on the making of a loan. If you find yourself faced with the prospect of making a private loan, a chat with your own banker could be helpful to make sure you protect yourself adequately. In addition to having the banker show you the specifics of the loan procedure, it might be wise to inquire whether the banker would be willing to make the loan or to buy the loan from you should you later wish to sell the borrower's IOU. If the banker balks at either prospect, there is probably some flaw in the loan that you might want to know about. Are you willing to take a risk that the bank would not?

KNOWLEDGE

Whether you're investing in the money market, the stock market, the real estate market, any of these assorted miscellaneous investments/speculations, or any new things that may come along, the best investment of all is your own investment in knowledge. The world of money is changing at an increasingly rapid pace: Taxes, interest rates, governmental regulations, the emergence of new techniques are all in a state of flux. Further, your own individual circumstances are also changing. You can't afford to ignore this outpouring of new information. If you want to make your money grow, you must fertilize it. And knowledge is the best fertilizer.

Income Property Evaluator

Before undertaking an investment in income property, a careful analysis must be made of both the cash-flow situation and the condition of the property. The following analysis sheet will help get you started. Further analysis as to the specific investment advantages should be done with the help of your accountant and real estate agent.

- ☐ What is the general condition of the building, including foundation, walls, roof, landscaping?
- ☐ Are the plumbing, heating, air conditioning, electrical system, elevators, and appliances all in working order?
- ☐ What is the current rental income (all sources)?
- ☐ Are there any controls on raising rentals?
- ☐ How much is the potential rental income within twelve, twenty-four, and thirty-six months?
- ☐ How much are the current operating expenses?
- ☐ Do leases provide that tenants absorb any portion of operating expenses?
- ☐ What is the potential total operating expenses within twelve, twenty-four, and thirty-six months (allow for likely increases in property taxes, insurance, maintenance, etc.)?
- ☐ Are property taxes comparable with similar buildings in the area? Can taxes be cut by protesting the assessment?
- ☐ What are the general condition of immediate neighborhood and future trends that might affect it?
- ☐ Are nearby traffic patterns likely to remain stable, or might they be changed? If changed, how will that affect the property?
- ☐ Can the existing mortgage be assumed by buyer? At what interest rate?
- ☐ What is the cost of interest for new financing, if needed?
- ☐ What type of secondary financing will be needed?
- ☐ Will the seller make secondary financing available? At what interest rate? Terms?
- ☐ What is the estimated management time and money needed to run the property efficiently (in hours and dollars per week)?

"By the Time You Get This I'll Be Gone"

From 1981 to late 1983, a Los Angeles–based company called Bullion Reserve of North America attracted tens of millions of dollars from thousands of investors across the country. The investors were buying gold—or thought they were buying gold—which was to have been placed in safe keeping for them in underground storage vaults in Utah. In September of 1983, Bullion Reserve crashed. The underground vaults were empty. Total losses to investors may never be fully known, but they could reach as much as $100 million. On September 28, 1983, Alan Saxon, aged thirty-nine, head of Bullion Reserve, was found dead in his swank beachfront condominium: a suicide. Following are brief excerpts from a tape recording he left his wife. The full transcript of the tape, submitted as evidence at a coroner's inquest on February 27, 1984, is part of the public record in Los Angeles County.

Susan, by the time you get this tape I'll be gone. I'm sorry that I had to leave you. . . . Aside from already giving you all my arguments why I couldn't possibly live somewhere else, the worst would be living with the memory of everybody that I—everybody who lost money. It's bad enough living with it every day for the past few weeks, answering letters from people who said they had their life savings with Bullion Reserve and they trusted us . . . Without the possibility of repaying them, how can I live with myself? . . .

The reason the company is going out of business is because (of) commodity trading . . . staggering losses in commodity trading . . . It's a classic case . . . As late as May 28 of this year I had over six million in various commodity accounts. That's all gone now, lost all that. Lost most of it in the first few days of June . . .

You know, the weird thing is I always used to joke that I wanted two great years, and you know the first day I started commodity trading was August 17, 1981. . . . So, I've had my two great years . . . How many people got to live like me . . . Can't say I didn't live, huh?

It's going to be a lot easier to do this than you think, a lot easier. Say goodbye to the kids for me . . . I'm not leaving messages for anybody else. . . . Goodbye.

Life, Health, and Income Insurance

In order to protect that which you work for, you must take steps to minimize the risks that everyone faces in day-to-day life: loss of life, serious medical problems, and loss of income. All of the best financial planning in the world can be for naught if these steps toward self-protection are not taken. Unfortunately, some of these steps involve dealing with salespersons, and this is not a favorite activity of most people. But this chapter will help you learn what you need to know to best deal with the sales part of the insurance industry, so that you can best protect yourself and your family for the near and long term.

The purpose of this chapter is not to sell you insurance; rather it's designed to enable you to do the following:

☐ Understand how life, health, and income insurance policies work

☐ Distinguish among different types of policies, their benefits, and their costs

☐ Gain a working knowledge of the jargon and language of insurance policies so that you can communicate effectively with sales personnel

☐ Determine how much of what type of insurance you do need as a part of your overall protection plan

☐ Be aware and take advantage of insurance programs available through various governmental agencies

COPING WITH RISK

Life is full of surprises—risks—that we don't adequately anticipate or prepare for. Some of these risks we accept willingly: driving a car, taking on a new job, investing or betting our money. Others may be strictly a matter of fate: illness, natural disaster, an employer going bankrupt.

In earlier chapters we examined automobile insurance and homeowner's (and tenant's) insurance. These types of insurance reimburse us for damages suffered to our cars and our dwellings and also reimburse persons who suffer losses arising from automobile accidents and accidents in the home. We may never suffer losses with respect to our car or our dwelling, but we still need the insurance to protect us "just in case." Likewise with health and income insurance: We may never be ill, and we may never suffer a loss of income due to illness, accident, or other unforeseen causes. But we still need insurance should the unforeseen occur.

Life insurance is designed to provide money to the survivors of an insured person when that person dies. That is an event that will certainly occur, but we never know when. If the breadwinner of a young and growing family dies prematurely, life insurance will, in effect, reimburse the survivors for lost earnings, thus enabling them to continue to live in relative comfort and security. If an insured person dies at or after the normal life-expectancy age, the proceeds of the insurance may be needed to pay estate taxes, to provide support for a surviving spouse, to allow the insured's business to continue, or to simply add to the wealth of the survivors. Now let's take a look at the basic mechanics of life insurance, but first of insurance in general as a device to protect us against risk.

BUYING PROTECTION AGAINST RISK

Insurance is protection against risk; this is what insurance is all about. For example, on an average day, 1000 skiers will run a slope, and one will end up in the hospital. The cost of hospitalization may be $1000. You never know whether that injured skier will be you or one of the 999 others. If it should be you, it will cost you $1000. But if each skier chipped in $1 to cover the cost of that day's accident—whomever it might happen to—you have eliminated your risk at a very insignificant cost. For the price of $1, you may have saved yourself $1000. You may run the slope 1000 times and never be hurt, but actual experience indicates that this isn't likely.

If all the skiers aren't willing to chip into a mutual kitty to protect themselves, some enterprising business executive will offer to make the arrangements for them. The entrepreneur will point out the risks that each skier faces, will arrange to collect and hold all the money in safekeeping, and will see to it that the proceeds are paid out to the injured parties as the injuries occur. For this service, the businessperson is entitled to a fee; thus, instead of charging $1 per skier, he may charge $1.05 or $1.10—whatever he and the skiers agree the service is worth. In so doing, the agent is acting as a one-person insurance company.

This, in a nutshell, is how the insurance industry operates. The insurance company determines the probability of risk in many given situations, such as a house burning down, an automobile crashing, a person dying before the normal life expectancy, and so on. The company will further determine how much money it must collect from each individual to properly protect those individuals should the stated risk occur. The money is invested prudently, so that the fund can grow, until it comes time to pay benefits to people who have suffered the risks. These calculations are known as the *actuarial phase* of insurance. The money that's taken in from each individual is called a *premium*, and the money paid out to individuals who do suffer the stated risks is called *benefits*. The portion of each premium dollar set aside to pay future benefits is called the *reserve*.

Part of each premium dollar that is received by the insurance company is used to pay the agents for their work in selling the insurance to the public. Part of it is also set aside to pay for the buildings that the insurance company occupies, the machines and computers they need, the clerical help, the supplies, the advertising, and the educational material.

When an individual or a business enters into an agreement with an insurance company regarding a specific risk, the parties sign a contract that sets forth all the specific rights, duties, and obligations of the parties. This contract is called an *insurance policy*. Its specific details are discussed later.

LIFE INSURANCE

Why Buy Life Insurance?

Victor is forty years old with a wife and two teenage children. He's in good health and makes about $25,000 per year with good prospects for improvement. He wants to be certain that his children have a good college education, but meeting his monthly mortgage payments hasn't allowed him to put much money aside for college expenses. Even though Victor's life expectancy is about thirty-five more years, he's very much aware of the possibility—however remote—that he could die tomorrow. Contemplating this possibility, Victor thinks, "If I did die suddenly, where would the money come from to keep my family reasonably comfortable and provide for the college education? I'd need an immediate nest egg of about $100,000. If they invested the money wisely, the income and some of the principal could take care of their needs for quite a long time. But right now I'd have trouble raising the price of a Big Mac let alone $100,000."

How can Victor resolve this dilemma? He might be lucky enough to beat multimillion-to-one odds and win a lottery. Or he could start stashing money away in a savings plan; at the rate of $100 per month, he'd have accomplished his goal in just under twenty-five years. These aren't very satisfactory solutions.

To solve his problem, Victor needs an immediate and guaranteed way to create an umbrella of protection for his family. This is the main purpose of life insurance. Life insurance can be created instantly or, more correctly, in the simple few weeks it takes to process an application. Rather than take chances on a lottery ticket or wait decades for a savings fund to build up, Victor can create the level of protection that he wants immediately through life insurance.

Further, the protection is guaranteed as long as the premiums on the policy are paid. Victor might also be prompted to consider the desirability of life insurance for his spouse and children. If his wife works, and if the family is dependent on her income to maintain their standard of living, it might be wise for the family to consider insuring her life as well to provide a source of income that would be lost in the event of her premature death. In some cases, insurance on the life of a nonworking spouse can be utilized to pay the costs of a terminal illness if those costs are not covered by a health-insurance plan; and if the spouse's estate is subject to estate taxes, life insurance proceeds can also be used to pay the taxes in lieu of having to sell other assets to cover the estate tax. The primary objective of a family's life insurance portfolio should be the replacement of a source of income in the event of the breadwinner's death.

On learning how his dilemma can be solved, Victor is likely to ask, "Can I afford to do it?" But a more appropriate question might be, "Can I afford *not* to do it?" The material that follows will help you answer these questions and will give you guidelines that will be useful in establishing any life insurance program you deem suitable for your own needs.

Basic Elements of Life Insurance

Simply put, a life insurance policy is a contract between an individual and an insurance company. The individual agrees to pay premiums, in return for which the insurance company guarantees to pay a certain amount of money to the beneficiaries named in the contract upon the death of the insured party. But not so simply put, life insurance policies are as different as snowflakes. There are over 1800 life insurance companies in the United States, and virtually all of them offer a wide array of different types of policies. Further, the mathematics of life insurance can differ widely depending on the age of the insured when the policy is purchased, the amount of coverage, the type of coverage, and the specific terms of the contract. Perhaps the most visible common thread that runs through all life insurance contracts is the fact that the younger you are when you initiate a contract, the lower your annual costs will be. Let us now examine some of the major diversities in life insurance.

Kinds of Companies: Stock and Mutual.
There are basically two different kinds of life insurance companies: stock companies and mutual companies. Stock companies are owned by stockholders, in much the same fashion as stockholders own other companies such as General Motors, American Telephone and Telegraph, and so on. The stockholders of these companies elect the board of directors to run the company. If the company is run profitably, the stockholders of those companies will likely receive dividends on their stock, again in much the same way as stockholders of industrial companies.

Mutual companies, on the other hand, are in effect owned by their policyholders. The policyholders elect the board of directors, who manage the company. In a mutual company, where the premium income exceeds the expenses (benefits paid and other expenses) by a certain amount, the policyholders/owners will receive back a portion of the excess needed to meet expenses. These sums are also referred to as *dividends*, but they are technically not the same thing as dividends received on common stock.

"Par" and "Nonpar" Policies

The kinds of policies issued by mutual companies, wherein dividends are paid to policyholders, are referred to as *participating policies*—the policyholders participate in a distribution of excess income over expenses. Stock companies generally do not pay such dividends to their policyholders. Their policies are referred to as *nonparticipating*. In some instances, however, stock companies do issue participating policies. Participating and nonparticipating policies are commonly referred to as *par* and *nonpar*, respectively.

The difference between stock and mutual companies may be better understood by referring back to the earlier example of the skiers. The skiers who banded together on their own to chip in $1 for each run formed a kind of mutual company. The skiers who declined to do this on their own and were approached by an outside business executive who would do it for them took part in a stock company.

Premiums on par policies are customarily higher than premiums on nonpar policies, all other things being equal. But the owner of a par policy has the hope of receiving dividends each year that may be used to offset the cost of the premium. Very possibly the amount of dividends received by a par policyholder could reduce the out-of-pocket cost of insurance to a lower level than what an equal nonpar policy would cost. For example, an individual shopping for a life insurance policy may find that two policies of equal face value, one par and one nonpar, have annual premiums of $300 and $250. If, over a period of time, the par policy pays a dividend of $60 per year, the par policy will end up being less expensive than the nonpar policy. But insurance companies cannot give any guarantee of what dividends will be paid in any given year. It depends on their actual experience of premium dollars received and expense and benefit dollars paid out.

How Is Life Insurance Acquired?   Life insurance is generally acquired in one of three ways: group plans, private plans, and credit plans.

Group Plans

Group life insurance is designed for large groups of people in similar circumstances. Your employer, for example, may provide a group life insurance plan for all employees who meet the necessary requirements of tenure on the job. Group insurance may also be issued to members of social organizations, professional organizations, and unions. Frequently, group life insurance is issued in relatively small amounts, and the insured individuals may not be required to take physical examinations to prove the state of their health. The group insurance policy will cover all eligible employees, and each participating individual will receive a copy of the master policy or an outline of it. In some cases, the employer or union may pay the premiums for all of the individuals; in other cases, such as with professional associations, each individual pays the premiums.

When individuals cease to be members of the group, the insurance may terminate. But in many cases it's possible for them to make arrangements to continue the coverage, provided they make the necessary premium payments on their own.

Because administration costs on a group policy can be much lower than those connected with many individual policies, the premium cost to the insured individuals in a group plan is generally lower than what it would be in a private plan.

Private plans

Private insurance is contracted for directly between the individual and the insurance company. Depending on the issuing company and the amount of insurance involved, a physical examination of the insured may be required.

Credit plans

When you borrow money, the lender may offer you a program of life insurance that is designed to pay off any balance on the loan should you die before the loan is paid off. This is available in mortgage loans as well as in small personal installment loans, such as for an automobile or home improvements. The amount of the insurance coverage decreases as the balance on the loan decreases. (This is known as *decreasing term insurance*.) In a long-term mortgage, the insured will generally make payments on the policy each year. In the short-term installment loans, the insured will generally pay the full premium in one lump sum at the inception of the loan. Frequently, the amount of the insurance premium is added to the amount of the loan so that the insured is not out-of-pocket anything at the outset.

Types of Life Insurance.   Basic types of life insurance are generally either permanent or temporary. *Permanent insurance* is designed to run permanently, that is, for the life of the insured individual. This type of insurance is commonly known as *ordinary insurance* or *straight insurance* or *whole life insurance*.

Temporary insurance is designed to run for a specific period of time, such as one year, five years, or ten years. This is known as *term insurance*. At the end of the term specified in the contract, the insurance ceases. However, in renewable term policies the insured has the right to renew for an additional term; however, it will be at a different premium rate. Term policies may also be convertible to ordinary policies. *Universal life insurance* offers a variety of flexible features: The face amount of the policy and the amount of annual premium can be adjusted by the owner of the policy, within limits.

Another type of life insurance contract is the *annuity*, wherein the insured is guaranteed a fixed monthly payment, which will begin at a specified time and will last for the agreed length of time. Let's take a closer look at these various types of life insurance.

Permanent Insurance

Permanent insurance is a lifetime contract. You agree to pay a fixed premium, and the insurance company agrees to deliver a stated sum of money upon your death or, in certain cases, at some earlier time. If the money is to become payable at a date prior to death, the insured may elect to receive it in a lump sum at that date or may elect to have the company pay in periodic installments, which would include an agreed amount of interest. The insurance company can also hold the money (paying interest on it) for as long as the insured lives and then pay it to the beneficiaries. The rate of interest that an insurance company will pay on monies held for the benefit of the insured or survivors is specifically set forth in the contract.

In addition to the benefits payable on the death of the insured (or earlier, if called for), the permanent policy will also build up *cash values*, also referred to as *nonforfeiture values*. These values permit the insured to terminate the policy and obtain either cash or some other form of insurance if desired at some later time. These values are discussed in more detail later.

Examples of permanent insurance include the following:

1. You agree to pay the stated premiums for, say, twenty years. At the end of this period the policy will be "paid up"—the full face value will be payable on death, and you don't have to pay any more premiums. This policy would be referred to as a *limited pay plan* or, in this case, *twenty-pay life*: Twenty years of payments pays it up in full.
2. You agree to pay the stated premiums for the remainder of your life. Upon death, the full face value will be payable. This policy would be referred to as a *whole life policy*.
3. You agree to make certain premium payments, and the full face value then becomes available to you in cash at a stated age, say sixty-five. If you don't elect to take the cash, you can exercise other options, as noted above, such as installment payments or having the company hold it for you plus interest for later payment to yourself or to your beneficiaries in the case of your death. Such a policy is of the endowment species and might be referred to as *endowment at age sixty-five*.

The amount of premiums for these various policies will differ considerably. For example, in the "twenty-pay life" policy, the insurance company must accumulate from the insured all the premiums it will need to make the necessary payments on the death of the insured. It only has twenty years in which to do so, even though the life expectancy of the individual may be much longer. Consequently, the insurance company must charge a higher premium for this kind of insurance than it would for whole life, for it has fewer years in which to accumulate the needed funds.

In *endowment policies*, the full face value becomes payable to the insured parties when they reach a specific age. The person may live many years after that. In such a case, the insurance company has fewer years in which to accumulate the needed funds in which to pay off the face value than it would on a whole life policy, so again it must command a higher premium to meet its own obligations.

Term insurance

Term insurance is "pure" insurance. You obtain a fixed amount of protection at a fixed annual price for a limited amount of time. For example, a twenty-five-year-old might be able to obtain a term policy for $25,000 for five years at an annual premium of $100 per year. Most term policies are renewable, that is, the individual can renew the protection for an additional term, but at a higher annual premium, since the insured is older. Thus, the twenty-five-year-old, on reaching thirty, might find that his $25,000 worth of protection will now cost him $120 per year. To renew for another five-year term at age thirty-five, the annual premium might go to $150 per year. As he gets older still, the cost of his annual premiums will increase at greater rates upon each renewal.

With rare exceptions, term insurance policies do not build up any of the cash or nonforfeiture values found in permanent policies. However, many term insurance policies contain a right to convert to a permanent insurance policy at stated times. Depending on the company and the amount of insurance, the insured may or may not have to take a physical examination, either upon initiating or renewing the term policy or on converting it to a permanent policy.

Because term insurance does not have any cash value buildup as a rule, it is the least expensive among all forms regarding initial out-of-pocket premium expenses. But as term insurance is renewed at ever-increasing ages—and thereby at ever-increasing rates—the ultimate out-of-pocket expenses can reach, and possibly exceed, those of permanent life.

As indicated earlier, another and still cheaper form of term insurance is decreasing term insurance, which accompanies mortgage and installment loans. Such insurance is cheaper because the amount of actual insurance decreases each year as the balance on the loan decreases.

Universal life insurance

Universal life insurance is a relative newcomer to the field. Basically, it's a variation of whole life insurance. Cash values in whole life insurance policies build up at a rather slow pace. In the early 1980s, when interest rates were very high, the life insurance industry found itself losing the battle for investment dollars to the high-flying securities that were paying perhaps double or triple the rate of return that one could earn through the cash value buildup in life insurance policies.

Universal life policies were created largely to compete with securities investments. During times when interest rates are high, universal policies can be very attractive since your premium dollars are invested at higher rates of return, and those returns are in large part credited to you. When interest rates are lower, the universal policies are not as attractive. In general, the universal policy allows the owner to make adjustments in the amount of coverage and the amount of premium to be paid. Quite clearly, universal life mixes investment features with insurance features. If the investment side of the contract does not perform well, there can be negative implications for the insurance side. If you are relatively sophisticated in the structuring of your investment and insurance programs, universal life may play a worthwhile role. But for the relatively unsophisticated individual, the complexities and variabilities of universal life may render it not the best product for your needs.

Annuities

An annuity is designed to provide a source of income to an individual who purchases such a contract. This individual is called the *annuitant*. The buyer of an annuity contract pays money to the insurance company either in one lump sum or in periodic payments over a number of months or years. The insurance company then agrees to pay back to the contract holder a sum of money each month for an agreed amount of time. The sum of money may be fixed in the contract (a fixed-dollar annuity) or may vary (a variable annuity), but there is a guaranteed minimum. With a fixed-dollar annuity the funds are invested conservatively, predominantly in government and corporate bonds as well as mortgages. In the variable annuity, a substantial portion of the money is invested in the stock market. The theory is that the stock market can provide protection against inflation. If the theory works, the annuitant may get more back than she might have received under a fixed-dollar annuity. Here's a brief description of the common types of payment programs available with annuities.

☐ *A straight life annuity.*   In a straight life annuity, once you have made your payments, you will begin to receive the agreed monthly sum at the agreed date. The payments last for as long as you live. If an annuitant dies one month after the payments have commenced, no further payments will be made to any party. If the annuitant lives far beyond the normal life expectancy, she will continue to receive the monthly payments from the insurance company, even if they have to pay out much more than they received at the outset from the annuitant. The company, in effect, is taking the risk that the annuitant will live no longer than the life expectancy.

☐ *Annuity with installments certain.*   An annuity that is set up to provide monthly payments for a fixed period of time—perhaps ten or twenty years—is called an *annuity with installments certain*. If an annuitant dies before the agreed time has elapsed, the beneficiary will continue to receive the payments until the term finally elapses.

☐ *Refund annuities.*   If an annuitant dies before receiving back all the money paid in, then the beneficiary will get back the balance still due. It may be in installments or in one lump sum, depending on the agreement between the parties.

☐ *Joint and survivor annuity.*   This type of annuity can cover two people, such as a husband and a wife. When one dies, the other continues to receive the payments until the agreed fund or the length of time has been exhausted.

The tax treatment of the cash value buildup in insurance and annuity contracts has been the subject of sharp debate in Congress during the late 1980s. The extent to which these buildups are taxable or tax-deferred can have an important bearing on the overall financial value of any given contract. The tax laws are subject to ongoing change. It's essential that you check with your insurance agent and your tax advisor to determine the current and likely future tax treatments of any such plans before you commit yourself to a plan.

Parties to an Insurance Policy.   There can be as many as five parties involved in an insurance policy contract: the owner of the policy, the person whose life is insured, the beneficiary, the contingent beneficiary, and the company itself. The roles of each of these five parties are important to an overall understanding of life insurance. Let's take a closer look at each of them.

The insured

This is the person whose life is insured by the policy. It is on the death of the insured that the proceeds are paid. The insured may also be the owner of the policy, but it is possible for the insured and the owner to be different parties.

The owner

The owner is perhaps the most important person referred to in the policy, for it is the owner who has the power to exercise various options within the policy, including naming and changing the beneficiary and making loans against the policy or cashing in the policy.

Consider Harold and Esther Klein. Harold applies for a life insurance policy on himself and retains ownership in his own name. He names Esther as the beneficiary. In this case, Harold is both the insured and the owner. Harold could also make application for the policy with himself as the insured and Esther as the owner. Alternatively Harold could name himself initially as both insured and owner, but at some later point decide to transfer ownership to Esther.

Here are other examples of the owner and the insured not being the same party: Arthur is a valuable employee, so his boss takes out a policy on Arthur's life payable to the company. The premium is also paid by the company. This is to protect the company in the event of Arthur's death—it would alleviate, for example, the cost of training a replacement and the expense of getting along temporarily without Arthur's services. This is generally known as *key man insurance*. The company is the owner of the policy, and Arthur is the insured.

Jose needs a loan from his bank. The bank, in conjunction with making a loan, may offer Jose a life insurance policy, with the proceeds payable to the bank in the event of Jose's death. As discussed earlier, this is known as *credit life insurance*. In such a case, the bank is the owner of the policy and Jose is the insured. (The bank will also be named as the beneficiary of the policy.)

The owner has important powers regarding an insurance policy. The owner can assign the policy to a creditor. For example, Jose, instead of buying a new credit life policy, assigns an existing policy to the bank to protect the bank in the event of his death before the loan is paid off. Should Jose die before the loan is paid off, the bank will receive the proceeds of the policy; should Jose default on the loan before his death, the bank would have the right to take whatever cash values exist in the policy. (An assignment is valid only if the insurance company has been properly notified and has accepted the assignment.)

The owner, and only the owner, can change the beneficiary of the policy, assuming that that right has been reserved in the original policy; transfer ownership to another party (this might be wise in certain instances of estate planning); exercise the nonforfeiture provisions in the policy; and dictate the manner in which the face amount will be payable to the beneficiary, where a choice exists. It is only the owner who can make these changes, and they must be done in accord with the insurance company's stipulations in the contract. The insured cannot exercise these powers unless the insured is also the owner. If Harold conveys an insurance policy on his own life to Esther as the owner—either as a result of an estate planning recommendation or as a gift or any other reason—then it is Esther, and Esther only, who can exercise the various rights granted in the policy. As long as Harold retains ownership, only he can exercise these rights.

The beneficiary

The beneficiary is the one who receives the stated payments to be made on the death of the insured. The choice of the beneficiary is up to the owner of the policy, who, as noted above, may be the same party as the insured. The beneficiary may be one or more persons, a charity, a business concern, or the estate of the insured.

The contingent beneficiary

There is always the possibility that the originally named beneficiary will die before the insured. The owner of the policy can name a contingent beneficiary, who will take the place of the original beneficiary if the beneficiary dies before the insured. If no contingent beneficiaries are named, the terms of the policy will probably set forth how the proceeds will then be distributed. As with the original beneficiary, the contingent beneficiary can also be one or more persons, a charity, a business concern, the estate of the insured, or any other recipient the owner wishes to name.

The company

The company is, of course, the insurance company with whom you are entering into the contract. You, as the insurance buyer, will deal with a representative of the company—either an agent connected directly with the company or an independent agent who may represent a number of various companies. Once you have entered into the contract, you may or may not see that agent again. It all depends on the level of service the agent wishes to provide and the prospective sales he may feel he can generate from you and your family. Generally, the agent is the primary representative of the company as far as the insured is concerned and the party to whom the insured should turn when any question arises. Some companies maintain service offices in communities throughout the nation to handle questions, problems, and complaints. Otherwise, you turn to the agent directly.

The Life Insurance Contract and Its Clauses.   A life insurance policy is a legally binding contract once it has been properly signed by the necessary parties—the owner and the company. The policy, as a legal contract, sets forth all the rights, duties, and obligations of the parties to the contract. The only way the contract can be amended is by agreement between the parties. If an agreement is reached, it must be set forth in writing and attached to the policy. Changes to a policy for life insurance—or any other kind of insurance policy—are called *endorsements* or *riders*.

The application

An important part of a policy itself is the application, which is the questionnaire that the applicant for the insurance must fill in to have the policy issued. The application contains pertinent information about the individual applying for insurance, including medical data. If the application contains false or misleading information and the insurance company issues the policy not knowing this, the policy might later be voided if the insurance company does learn the truth. For example, an individual applying for life insurance may have recently had a severe heart attack but states that she is in perfectly good health. If she can somehow prevent the insurance company from learning of her physical condition and the policy is granted, she has entered into the agreement on false premises, and the policy might be voided if the company learns of the circumstances within the stated time limit.

Insurance companies go to considerable lengths to assure that they will not be defrauded. Physical examinations will be conducted, and interviews of neighbors may be undertaken to learn an individual's personal habits. All doctors that the applicant has seen in the past few years may be questioned by the insurance company to determine the reason for seeing these doctors.

In recent years, an organization known as the Medical Information Bureau (MIB) has assisted the insurance industry in minimizing fraudulent applications. Currently, in most cases, when individuals apply for life, health, or disability insurance, they will sign a statement giving the insurance company permission to relay all health information to the Medical Information Bureau and seek out any information that may exist there relative to the individual's health.

Recent statistics reveal that of all applications made for life insurance in the United States, only 3 percent are declined. Eighty-five percent of all applications have policies issued at the standard risk levels, and 4 percent of the applications have policies issued at extra risk levels. (Extra risk policies may be issued in cases where there is an obvious health problem but not one so great that the company will refuse the coverage. They will accept coverage, but usually at a higher premium level or in some cases, particularly in health-insurance policies, will exclude certain physical conditions.) Eight percent of all applications are approved by the company but are not accepted by the applicants.

Face amount or face value

The face amount or face value of the policy is the amount of money due the beneficiary on the death of the insured. The face amount is set forth on the policy, and it is what we usually refer to when we talk about the amount of an insurance policy. For example, if we say a "$10,000 life insurance policy," we're talking about the face value of the policy.

It is possible that the beneficiary could receive more or less than the original face value. The beneficiary may receive more than face value if a double indemnity clause was activated in the policy. The beneficiary may also receive more than the face value if the owner had applied dividends that he or she had received toward the purchase of additional insurance.

The face value might be decreased if the owner has borrowed against the policy and has not paid off these loans. In some policies, the face value may change (usually decreasing) when the insured reaches a stated age.

Double indemnity or accidental death benefit

A double indemnity clause, which is generally available at an additional premium, provides for the payment of double the face amount in the event of accidental death as opposed to natural death.

Incontestable clause

Commonly, the insurance company will have a set period of time, usually two years, during which it must take issue with any suspected false or misleading information contained in the application. During that initial two-year period, a company may contest statements made by the applicant and can void the policy if improper statements were made. But once the two years have elapsed, the company can no longer contest any statements.

Guaranteed insurability

Some policies will, for an additional premium, guarantee you the right to increase the face value of the policy within certain limits and within fixed times, regardless of your health. The cost of obtaining this guarantee should be carefully evaluated.

Premium and mode of payments

The policy contract spells out how much the premiums are on the policy and how they can be made. The policyholder may elect to pay premiums annually, semiannually, quarterly, or monthly. The more frequent the mode of payment, the more costly it will be for both the insurance company and the insured. Monthly or quarterly payments might be more convenient to an individual's budget, but the individual should be aware of the probable added cost in paying more frequently than once a year.

Lapse, grace period, and reinstatement

The general agreement in a life insurance policy is that the company will pay the face value to the beneficiary as long as the policy remains "in force." The term *in force* means that the owner of the policy has continued to make premium payments regularly and without fail. If a policyholder does not meet premium obligations, the policy can lapse. When a policy lapses, it is terminated. There is no more insurance.

Unless financial circumstances leave little or no alternative, it can be most imprudent to let a policy lapse. Money paid in up to the date of lapse will be forfeited, and when that individual wishes to obtain life insurance at a later time, it will cost more because of increased age. In some cases, because of the onset of physical problems, the person may not be able to get the insurance at all.

Lapsing of policies is not in the best interests of insurance companies either. They stay in business because of the continuity of insurance programs, not their termination. The insurance industry has structured the typical life insurance policy so that a lapse does not occur that easily or that automatically.

If a premium is not paid by the stated due date, the policyholder will have a "grace period" of usually thirty-one days, during which the payment can still be made to continue the policy in force without any penalty.

If payment still has not been made by the end of the grace period, many permanent policies have an automatic cash loan provision. If cash values have already begun to build up in the policy and there is enough to cover the payment of one premium, the company will automatically borrow against these values and use the proceeds to pay the premium and thus continue the policy in force for another period.

Even after a lapse has occurred, the policyholder has a limited time within which to exercise the so-called rights to reinstate the policy. If a policyholder wishes to reinstate the policy, the individual may have to take a new physical examination or may simply have to sign a statement about health conditions. The approach taken depends on the amount of the face value and the company's general regulations in that regard. If the company is satisfied about the state of the insured's health and if the person pays all back premiums and any interest owing thereon, the policy can then be reinstated.

Waiver of premium

At a slight additional cost to most life insurance policies, a premium waiver provision can be included in the policy. It provides that if the insured is totally disabled, the need to make premium payments will be waived. In other words, the insurance can continue in force, without the insured having to make premium payments during the period of disability. It's like a miniature disability income policy built into the life insurance policy itself. But note that the definition of "totally disabled" may differ from policy to policy. It might, for example, be defined as "unable to work in a job for which you were trained" or "unable to work at all." The difference can be important.

Conversion values

Conversion (or nonforfeiture) values become available to policyholders under permanent life insurance policies. The amount of the values builds up as you pay your premiums over the years, but the rate of buildup will vary from policy to policy. In shopping for an insurance policy, the prudent individual will carefully compare the rate of growth and relative size of these values. Policy A may have a lower premium than policy B for the same face value. Thus, policy A may seem to be the better value. But policy B may have a higher level of conversion values, which could be of considerable importance to the policyholder many years later. Thus, what you get for your premium dollar isn't just the face value of the policy. These other values must be considered most carefully.

Here's how conversion values work. If you cease paying your premiums by choice or otherwise, these conversion values will allow you to convert your policy into a number of alternative plans.

□ *Cashing in.* You can cash in the policy. You then receive the amount of cash set forth in the cash value table (the cash value is usually the same as the loan value).

□ *Borrowing.* You can borrow against the policy, usually up to the amount stipulated in the loan value table. For policies issued before the mid-1960s, a policyholder usually can borrow at the very attractive rate of 5 percent per year. Policies issued in more recent years will carry a higher borrowing rate, but it still might be a very attractive rate compared with what one would have to pay for a simple interest loan at a lending institution.

Borrowing against a life insurance policy may be quick and convenient and inexpensive, but it's not always prudent. The act of borrowing is simple: Notify the company of your wishes, sign the appropriate papers, and receive a check shortly thereafter. Repayment is up to you: You need not repay the principal at all, but you must pay interest annually. If you do not repay the principal, the face value will be diminished by the amount of the outstanding loan at the time of the insured's death. For example, if the face value on a given policy was $10,000 and the owner borrowed $1000 against it, then died before repaying the loan, the beneficiary would receive only $9000.

From time to time, it might pay you to borrow against your life insurance values. For example, if you can borrow against your policy at a 7 percent annual interest rate, and you can invest these borrowed dollars at, say, 10 percent, the 3 percent differential is profit in your pocket. If you invest conservatively, you will still be protecting your family, since the investment itself would be available to them in the event of your death. However, if you speculate with that borrowed money, and the speculation turns sour, you could not only be incurring added costs, but jeopardizing the well-being of your survivors.

If you borrow against your life insurance policy to pay a consumer debt (buy a car, pay off debts, etc.), remember that the deductibility of the interest on your tax return will be phased out by 1991: only 20 percent is deductible for tax year 1989, 10 percent for tax year 1990, and none for 1991 and thereafter, unless Congress changes its mind. (In 1987 and 1988, 65 and 40 percent, respectively, of interest paid on consumer debt was deductible.) If you borrow for home improvements, business purposes, or investment purposes, the interest might be deductible in full. Check with your tax advisor for full details.

☐ *Converting to extended term insurance.*   You can convert your existing pro-gram to extended term insurance. With such insurance, you will be covered for the same original face value of the policy, but only for a *limited period of time* rather than for the rest of your life, had you continued the policy in force.

☐ *Converting to paid-up insurance.*   You can also convert your policy to "paid-up insurance." If you cease paying premiums, you can still be covered for a *portion* of the face value for as long as the original policy would have protected you.

☐ *Automatic premium loan.*   The automatic premium loan provision, as noted earlier, allows the company to borrow against your loan values automatically in order to make premium payments that you have neglected to make.

Nonforfeiture tables

Each policy contains a *table of nonforfeiture values* that indicates the precise level of these values at specific points. Table 19-1 is an abbreviated sample of the normally much longer table of nonforfeiture values. Nonforfeiture values are based on the age of the insured at the time the policy is taken out. Values will vary from company to company and from one type of policy to another.

Here's how the tables work. The face amount of the insurance policy is $10,000, and the age of the insured at the time the policy was taken out was twenty-five. At the end of the tenth policy year (when the insured is thirty-five), the policy will have $1340 worth of cash/loan values. This means the insured can stop making payments, cash in the policy, terminating the insurance altogether, and have $1340 cash in hand. Or the insured can borrow that much against the policy at the interest rate stated in the policy and otherwise continue the policy in force by continuing to pay annual premiums.

If the owner wishes to convert to paid-up insurance, at the end of the tenth policy year, the individual has the right to convert to a permanent policy with a face value of $2900. This means that the owner no longer need pay any premiums; the face value of the policy is now $2900. The last column in Table 19-1 indicates

Table 19-1   **Nonforfeiture Values: Sample Policy, $10,000 Face Value**

End of policy year	Cash/ loan value	Paid-up insurance	Extended term
5	$ 590	$1410	14 years, 48 days
10	1340	2900	20 years, 310 days
15	2100	4130	22 years, 288 days
20	2890	5180	22 years, 303 days

the extended term insurance provisions. At the end of ten years this individual could convert to extended term, in which case coverage would be for the full face amount ($10,000) for 20 years and 310 days. At the end of that time, the coverage would cease altogether.

In order to take advantage of any of the nonforfeiture provisions, the insurance company should be notified of your intention, and you should receive documentation that verifies exactly what steps you're taking. It would be advisable in any case to discuss the ramifications of making such a move with your insurance agent and any other financial advisors before you actually proceed.

Dividend options

Earlier in this chapter we noted that some types of life insurance policies—particularly those issued by mutual life insurance companies—pay dividends to policyholders. If you own such a policy, you'll probably have a number of choices as to the manner in which the dividends are paid. You may wish to receive the dividends in cash to do with as you please; you may want to apply the dividends toward the next premium due on the insurance policy; you may let the premium "ride" with the insurance company where it will draw a rate of interest set forth in the insurance policy; or you may use the dividends to purchase additional life insurance.

An annual statement from your insurance company will indicate what dividends are payable to you and will instruct you how to choose the mode in which the dividends will be applied. If you have any questions, discuss the matter with your agent.

Settlement options

Policyholders may also have options concerning the manner in which the payment of proceeds will be made. These are called *settlement options*. The following options are available concerning the manner of settlement payment: paying the entire face amount in one lump sum to the beneficiaries; paying periodic payments, including interest, to the beneficiaries; paying interest only to the named beneficiary, with a lump sum payable to a subsequent beneficiary on the death of the primary beneficiary. As a rule, the owner of the policy can choose the settlement option. In some cases, a beneficiary might also be able to select an option. Each policy spells out exactly what options are available and how to go about choosing and changing them.

Life Insurance: Who Needs It?

When we're hungry, we go to the market and buy the food we need. We don't have to wait for someone to tell us that our stomachs need refilling. Not so with life insurance. The need is not as clear-cut. Indeed, contemplating the need for life insurance reminds us of our own mortality, and it's no surprise that human nature would short circuit such thoughts.

With life insurance, many of us have to be told of the need, but we frequently

---

Strategies for Success

Keep Life Insurance and Investments Separate

Life insurance and investments fulfill two very different purposes. Life insurance provides a source of money when a breadwinner dies. Investing provides a source of money when a breadwinner wants to stop working or wants to acquire goods or services out of the ordinary. Each has—or should have—it's own target, focus, and goal. Many insurance programs have investment features, which makes it all too easy to confuse the life insurance side with the investing side. It's better to keep a crisply separate view of each. If you let them get too mingled, you could end up with too much on one side, too little on the other side, and more risk on either side than you should reasonably be taking. You can help maintain the separation if you deal with one person for your life insurance needs and with another for your investment activities.

---

don't take any action to satisfy that need until a representative of an insurance company comes knocking at our door offering us a package of insurance programs. The problem is further compounded by the fact that the agent may talk in terms that we don't fully understand.

Despite these negative aspects, sound personal financial planning demands that life insurance be at least carefully investigated as a part of one's overall financial foundation. Not everyone needs life insurance, but you should at least examine how life insurance can function with respect to your own long-term needs and objectives.

Who needs life insurance? In short, if you want to protect or enhance the financial welfare of anyone who is dependent on you and if your existing assets aren't adequate to provide the desired level of protection, you need life insurance. That is, you need it if you want to get the job done quickly and assuredly.

The extent of your need can be more easily determined if the possible times of death are examined. These times can be prematurely or in accordance with normal life expectations. Life insurance may also be needed to resolve estate tax and business situations.

In the Event of Premature Death. If a young breadwinner dies unexpectedly, how will the family survive? Let's look at an example. Jonathan has two children, aged ten and twelve. He wants to be sure that there is enough money for his spouse and children to live comfortably, as well as to provide basic college education for the children. A term insurance program designed to run for fifteen or twenty years will provide the umbrella of protection that's needed. Or Jonathan might prefer permanent insurance, which will cost more at the outset but will likely cost less many years down the road. His choice would depend on the money he has to use for life insurance. A combination of the two approaches might work best for him.

Remember, every family is unique. What's right for one family might not be right for another. One must evaluate the situation one's family would face in the event of the premature death of the breadwinner and act accordingly.

In the Event of Normal Death.   Once the children are grown and most major obligations have been taken care of, the need for life insurance diminishes. Many families, though, prefer to maintain a continuing program of life insurance in order to provide a major inheritance for the survivors. This, of course, is a personal decision that must be structured based on the amount of money available to put toward this purpose.

When Heirs Are Facing Taxes.   Chapter 21 will help you determine whether your heirs are facing the prospect of federal estate taxes on your death. If they are, life insurance can commonly be used to assist survivors in meeting that tax obligation. Life insurance provides instant cash to meet such debts. Lacking the needed cash, survivors might be faced with having to sell other assets—house, investments—in order to pay the taxes. Having to sell off these assets, particularly if they produce income, could provide a hardship for the survivors. Life insurance eliminates the need to sell off other assets.

When Businesses Need Protection.   Similarly, business interests can be protected by life insurance. If, for example, you are the sole proprietor or a partner in a small business, your death could cause the business to have to terminate. If, however, there are life insurance proceeds payable to the business, those proceeds, which are not taxable to the recipient, could be used to hire a replacement for you so that the business could keep running or could provide a fund of cash to allow for an orderly liquidation of the business. Either way, your survivors can be protected by an immediate infusion of cash into the business.

How Much Insurance Is Needed?

The first task in evaluating how much insurance is needed by any individual is to determine, as noted earlier, who is going to be protected by the insurance program and to what extent? These are your goals, and you must define them most specifically in order to reach dollar figures. For example, do you want to insure that the children will have at least 50 percent of their college tuition guaranteed in the event of your premature death? 75 percent? 100 percent? Should they be on their own after that? Or do you want them to have a nest egg to help get them started in their chosen career? These are individual questions that only you can answer.

Now comes the time for some thoughtful arithmetic. You must determine, as accurately as possible, the following:

1. What might be the possible extent of your "final" expenses? These include expenses arising as a result of death and possible uninsured costs of a terminal illness, burial expenses, estate taxes, and a certain sum to help survivors get

through the early difficult time of adjustment. In evaluating these matters, one must also take into account the extent of one's health-insurance coverage for a costly terminal illness—an item of considerable expense. If you feel you're amply protected against such costs through your health-insurance program, you need not necessarily include them as part of your life insurance planning.

2. How much existing debt—mortgages, personal loans, and so on—might the survivors have to pay? Obviously, the amount of your indebtedness can fluctuate considerably from year to year. If you don't now own a house, you won't have to worry about a mortgage being paid off. But if you buy a house tomorrow, there will be a sizable debt that will eventually have to be paid. And if you don't want the family to sell the house to eliminate the debt, you might wish to cover such contingencies through life insurance. Careful planning will cover existing debts, with flexibility retained to increase or decrease as future circumstances warrant.

3. How much per year will the survivors need to maintain themselves in whatever style of living you and they feel would be suitable? Looking at this question in terms of the husband/breadwinner, consideration must be given to the possibilities of the wife remarrying, of her going to work, of children going to work, of other potential sources of income materializing or failing to materialize. Elimination of the husband's own cost of living—food, clothing, recreation, and so on—must also be evaluated. It would probably be simplest to base estimates on a continuation of the current life style, with allowance for possible upward or downward adjustments.

4. Beyond the immediate annual cost of living, estimate the extraordinary expenses that survivors will face and how much of these expenses you want to assure them of being able to meet. Such expenses might include education, weddings, having a stake to go into business on their own, and so on.

5. For how many years would you want them to continue your particular life style on a worry-free basis?

6. What benefits will be provided by social security? A visit with the nearest office of the Social Security Administration can provide this information.

7. Inventory all current assets, paying particular attention to current market value, potential future value, liquidity (how easily and at what cost the assets can be converted into cash), and the earning potential of any assets. Outline a program showing when certain assets could or should be converted to cash to meet family needs. Such a program should also show which nonearning assets might be converted to earning ones. (For example, should that vacant lot you bought for speculation or as a site for your future summer home be sold and the money put to work as an earning asset?)

8. Evaluate what other realistic sources of income there might be in the future, such as inheritances or scholarships. You can't count on these sources materializing, but you should be aware of the possibility.

9. Evaluate current life insurance programs, including group plans and any others. Determine what the proceeds could earn annually if they were conservatively invested, and determine how long the proceeds would last if the principal were invaded by a certain amount each year. (The savings charts in Chapter 16 can assist you with this.) Evaluate all your other assets in the same manner. This information might not be easy to compile, and you may want the help of an accountant, or perhaps your insurance agent could assist you impartially and objectively. Even though it may be difficult to obtain, this information is essential for an intelligent plan to evolve.

A Case History.   When you've surveyed your data, the gaps can be measured, and the alternatives for filling those gaps can come into focus. Let's examine a fairly simple case to illustrate the basic type of thinking you should go through to estimate your own life insurance needs.

Phillip is married, has a twelve-year-old child, and earns $2000 a month after taxes. His wife does not work but is capable of doing so should the need arise. Phillip's current financial status is as follows:

☐   He owns his home, which has a current market value of $90,000. He owes $60,000 on a mortgage with monthly payments of $620.

☐   He has $5000 in a savings plan.

☐   He has $10,000 in the profit-sharing plan at work. This could be payable immediately to his survivors in the event of his death.

☐   He owns two cars, both used, with a current total value of $8000.

☐   He has a life insurance policy with a face value of $45,000.

☐   His debts, in addition to his mortgage, consist of bank loans totaling $5000. Monthly payments are $300.

Phillip has estimated what his family's financial status would be if he were to die suddenly. His existing health and burial insurance would take care of all of his final expenses. He has no estate taxes to be concerned about. His wife and child would need approximately $1720 a month for living expenses: mortgage payment, $620; bank loan payments, $300; other living expenses, $500; and taxes and miscellaneous expenses, $300.

If Phillip were to die now, he would not want his wife to sell the house. She could, though, make use of the savings account, the profit-sharing plan, and the life insurance proceeds, all of which would total $60,000. Phillip and his insurance agent, using Table 20-5 in the next chapter, calculate very conservatively that if the $60,000 were invested at 7 percent per year, before income tax considerations, it would generate interest earnings of only $360 per month. If Phillip's widow were to embark on a ten-year program of dipping into the principal, Table 20-5 indicates that the $60,000 could generate an income of $696 per month. A fifteen-year dipping

Table 19-2 **Income Sources**

Source	Interest only[a]	10-year payout	15-year payout
From existing $60,000	$360	$ 696	$ 538
From extra $100,000	585	1160	896
Total income available	$945	$1856	$1434

[a]The amount of the principal always remains intact.

plan would give her an income of $538 per month. These figures are summarized in Table 19-2. In order to provide enough for his wife and child to be comfortable, Phillip agrees that he needs an additional $100,000 in life insurance. This amount, if invested in accordance with the program in Table 20-5, would provide an additional $1160 per month for a ten-year period, at the end of which time the sum would be depleted. Combining the $696 from the existing $60,000 nest egg plus the $1160 per month from the new insurance to be acquired will provide Phillip's survivors with a grand total of $1856 per month.

After ten years, when the entire nest egg is gone, the child will have completed college and be on her own. The house will have increased in value considerably, and the mortgage on the house will have decreased considerably. Phillip's wife will be left with a substantial equity in the home, which she can sell to create a sizable nest egg for her living expenses.

The calculations above do not take into account some very important other elements. They do not take into account money that can be earned by Phillip's widow and child from their own work. Nor do they take into account social security benefits that will be paid. Based on current rough estimates, which are all that is available from the Social Security Administration, Phillip's widow could receive about $1100 per month until the child reaches the age of sixteen. Further, Phillip's widow can resume receiving social security benefits when she herself reaches the age of sixty. All of this income can be banked to create an even greater security blanket for the survivors. The wife might choose to return to work herself and embark on a fifteen-year dipping plan, which would give her an income of $1434 per month. This amount plus her earnings from work might be a more satisfactory program for her.

Phillip's situation is a relatively uncomplicated one. If he were concerned about such matters as estate taxes, creating a substantial college tuition fund, protecting a business interest, or any other matter beyond the ordinary, his need for insurance would have been much greater. Now, having solved the relatively uncomplicated matter of how much insurance he needs, Phillip must tackle the far more perplexing matter of what kind of insurance to buy.

What Kind of Insurance to Buy

Buying life insurance is a lot like buying a car. You can choose a subcompact with no frills, or you can go lavish and splurge on a fancy sedan with all the trimmings. The sticker price isn't always the determining factor in what you will buy. If you need a car just to hop back and forth to the office or the shopping center, the subcompact might certainly make the most sense. But if you're a salesperson who travels all the time and expects to be driving thousands of miles every week, it may well be worth the added price to buy the luxury car so that the physical comfort of the automobile reduces the wear and tear on your body. There's no easy answer.

Life insurance is just as complicated. You, or Phillip, could go for the stripped-down term policy or for a "loaded" whole life policy. Both have pluses, both have minuses.

Consumerists and the life insurance industry have been arguing bitterly for years about the relative costs and comparisons of features of life insurance policies. The matter is extraordinarily complicated. The whole issue is made even more muddy by the basic underlying argument between term insurance advocates and whole life insurance advocates. But mind boggling though it is, some life insurance shopping is essential before you embark on a plan of your own.

For an excellent starting point, refer to the June 1986, July 1986, and August 1986 issues of *Consumer Reports*, which should be available at your local public library. These issues contain an extended special report analyzing life insurance policies, companies, and costs. Bear in mind, though, that by the time you read these reports, many of the companies may have changed their price structures. Nevertheless, the reports will give you some beginning guidelines to choosing companies and policies.

By way of briefly excerpting these reports, Tables 19-3 and 19-4 illustrate the high and low initial premiums on a variety of policies. The differences of premium costs for seemingly equal policies are, you're likely to agree, astonishing. These tables illustrate the differences only in the initial premium on the given policies, that is, the premium paid during the first year. With the whole life policies, the

Table 19-3   **Term Policies (Nonpar)**

Insured's age	Insured's gender	Policy amount	Amount of initial premium	
			Low range	*High range*
25	Male	$50,000 (nonpar)	$ 58–$90	$151–$367
25	Female	$50,000 (nonpar)	$ 58–$90	$153–$329
35	Male	$50,000 (nonpar)	$ 64–$117	$170–$429
35	Female	$50,000 (nonpar)	$ 64–$110	$161–$384
45	Male	$50,000 (nonpar)	$107–$223	$293–$511
45	Female	$50,000 (nonpar)	$ 99–$137	$245–$445

Table 19-4 **Whole Life (Cash Value) Policies (Par)**

Insured's age	Insured's gender	Policy amount	Amount of initial premium	
			Low range	High range
25	Male	$50,000 (par)	$164–$302	$ 524–$588
25	Female	$50,000 (par)	$164–$258	$ 492–$569
35	Male	$50,000 (par)	$346–$456	$ 819–$1001
35	Female	$50,000 (par)	$311–$401	$ 715–$930
45	Male	$50,000 (par)	$545–$636	$1343–$1707
45	Female	$50,000 (par)	$477–$636	$1248–$1582

premium remains the same for the life of the policy. Insurance company analysts maintain that premium cost alone is not enough upon which to base a wise shopping decision. They have projected other methods of determining the true value, one of the main ones being the *cost adjusted method*. This method assumes that you will terminate the policy after a number of years, and it evaluates the cash you'd have on hand after that time, taking into account premiums you've paid over the years. This method might be valid if in fact everybody did terminate their policies at that time, but obviously not everyone does.

It's not the province of this book to tell you which insurance policy to buy any more than it is to tell you which automobile to buy. You've been shown the tools to use to evaluate insurance programs, and the homework and shopping are up to you. To try to do battle with the analysts would not leave room in this book for any other subjects to be discussed. You will be helped, not so much by charts and graphs and complicated analyses of cost comparisons, but by a good agent, whose value will be discussed shortly.

Prudent insurance buyers make sure that they have chosen a company whose reputation is established. If a would-be buyer has any questions or doubts the stability of any given insurance company, reference should be made to *Best's Insurance Reports* and *Best's Recommended Life Insurance Companies*, which are available at most major libraries. Reference might also be made to the insurance department in your state.

Life Insurance

There is no such thing as a typical insurance agent. An insurance agent's training might range from minimal to the rigorous demands of the courses leading to the CLU (chartered life underwriter) designation. His experience might encompass weeks or decades. His income level can range from paltry to six figures. And his personality, sales techniques, and sense of ethics can run the full spectrum of human potential. Many agents will try to get your business, but if you find the right agent, you've made a valuable catch. But how do you know what to look for? Before we get into a shopping list, let's take a quick look at some of the dilemmas in the industry.

Dilemma No. 1. The insurance agent makes his living by selling insurance policies. Proper counseling may be of equal or greater value to you than the policy itself, but the agent doesn't make a penny unless a sale is made. Needless to say, good counseling can produce a good sale, but it might not.

An agent, therefore, takes a calculated risk on how much time to spend with any given prospect in counseling sessions. This can result in counseling and selling efforts becoming intermingled, to the point where you might not be able to tell them apart. With the agent's help, you should define your protection goals and recognize the gaps between what you have and what you need, and what various alternatives there are that can help you fill these gaps to reach your goals. These items are the subject of counseling. Once you've reached this stage, it's time to get into the specifics of various policies.

If the agent is not willing to take the time you need to understand your goals, you might not be getting the service you need. And the agent might not take the time unless there's a sure sale in sight. This dilemma is perhaps best resolved by open and frank communications at the outset: ''Mr. Agent, this is what I have to learn from you before I will even consider doing business with you. If you're willing to teach me what I think I have to know, I may well be a customer, but there's no guarantee. If you're willing to proceed on those terms, fine. If not, perhaps it would be best if we didn't waste each other's time.''

Dilemma No. 2. With rare exception, people closer to the top of the economic ladder have better access to more sophisticated insurance counseling than those closer to the bottom. This, for better or worse, is the way of our world. It might take an agent the same amount of time or more to sell a $10,000 policy to a working family as it would to sell a $100,000 policy to an executive. The monetary rewards for these two policies are obviously drastically different. Further, the agent who is going for the big sale will probably have to be better equipped to handle the more sophisticated problems wealthy prospects will have. People on the lower rungs of the economic ladder also need more sound advice, but it may be more difficult for them to get it. The more individuals learn about life insurance, the better able they are to take advantage of whatever advice is given and the better prepared to seek and understand the more sophisticated advice that could be of greater value.

Dilemma No. 3. Each of us has so many dollars to spend. Some of these dollars will be spent on our current needs and some will be put away to cover future needs and desires. There are many institutions that would like to take care of our future dollars for us—insurance companies, mutual funds, banks, savings institutions, stockbrokers. They all make their living by putting our future dollars to use until we need them, and the competition is keen to get access to these dollars.

In varying degrees, each of these giant industries has become envious of the success of the others. Some segments of the life insurance industry have reacted, for example, by putting mutual funds in the same attaché case as their insurance policies. The funds might be good, so might the policies. Mixing them together too much may not be.

With all these financial industries competing with one another for our future dollars, it's essential that we keep a clear distinction between insuring and investing. Each has its separate set of purposes and goal-fulfillment abilities. Insurance offers certainty; some forms of investment offer a measure of certainty, others offer little more than possibility.

Keeping these dilemmas firmly in mind, what then do you look for in an insurance agent? As in choosing any professional advisor, you must have trust in the agent's ability, confidence in her training, and knowledge of her integrity. You don't usually get these on a hunch or a first impression, though it's not impossible. Personal familiarity, recommendations from others, and reputation in the community are indicators. The individual who comes on with a hard sell after the first "how do you do?" may have the same program to offer you as the agent who holds back until after the proper rapport has been established. The choice is up to you.

What are the agent's credentials, background, training, and prior experience? Does the agent represent only one company, or does she, as is the case with independent agents, represent the products of a number of different companies? These are important factors to determine and evaluate. It is, of course, possible for an eager-to-get-established novice to serve you just as well as an old pro. But the "perennial job hopper" is liable to leave you with some loose ends hanging.

Chartered Life Underwriters.   In evaluating an agent's credentials, the question of whether he is a CLU (chartered life underwriter) might arise. A CLU is an insurance agent who has been through a rigorous course of instruction to better equip him to serve the public and make a living. Only a small percentage of agents are CLUs. The time and educational requirements may scare off many from pursuing the credential. These educational requirements include five separate courses on economics, taxes, estate planning and conservation, corporate law, contract law, pensions and profit-sharing plans, accounting, and the technical aspects of life insurance itself. Each course requires about sixty hours of classroom work, plus abundant outside homework. On completing the courses, each agent must then pass a four-hour written exam on each of the five subjects.

CLUs don't have any product or secret policies to offer you that other agents don't have, but they do possess the education that might enable them to better determine their clients' needs and find the right policies to satisfy those needs. (Certainly, there are many fine agents who do not have the CLU designation who can serve their clients' needs most adequately.) However, CLUs are individuals who have invested hundreds of hours of their own time to become more expert in their own field. This fact alone might cause many insurance shoppers to lean in favor of doing business with a CLU.

Remember that insurance agents, CLUs or not, cannot make a living unless they sell policies. The amount of time they can give to counseling any client is limited. But the *quality* of counseling is important, perhaps more so than the amount of time given it. This might well be where the CLU has another edge.

A major portion of your efforts must be directed to meeting and evaluating a number of prospective agents. The difference between *choosing* an agent and *being chosen* by an agent can be very important. The selection process is up to you, and if you make the most of it, you'll get the most from it. This may seem an undue amount of work simply to buy an insurance policy. But remember that you are not buying a simple product that you'll use today and be done with tomorrow. You're striving to build a structure that will shelter you and your family for many years. If it's built right, it will last, it will perform, and it will have been worth the time and the money involved.

INSURANCE WHEN THE RISK MAY NOT OCCUR

There is a very distinct and important difference between life insurance and the other common forms of personal insurance. With life insurance, as long as the policy remains in force, the company must pay the agreed benefits to the designated beneficiary upon the death of the insured. There is no question that the risk being insured against—the death of the insured—will occur. Because of the broad base of statistical information available, the insurance company is able to make a reasonably accurate estimate as to when that date will probably be. And the insurance company knows precisely how much it must then pay.

With the other common forms of personal insurance—health, income, property, and public liability—the risk that is being insured against may not occur. If it does, it might occur tomorrow or ten years from now. When it does occur, the company may have to pay a token amount to the insured or a moderate or substantial sum. There may even be a dispute as to whether anything should be paid at all.

With life insurance, you know for certain that a fixed sum of money will be available to you or your beneficiaries. With the other forms of insurance, the money you pay out may never be seen again. Human nature may lead us to think—perhaps dangerously so—that these kinds of risks will occur to others but never to us. We thus think that we will never be out of pocket as a result of such occurrences, and perhaps we should therefore keep our costs for such insurance to a minimum.

In many respects, the potential losses that can be suffered as a result of risks relating to health, income, property, and public liability can be far more devastating than when a breadwinner dies leaving no life insurance. Vague and unpredictable though these risks may be, it would indeed be imprudent to fail to acquire the appropriate level of protection that can prevent a financial disaster.

The basic mechanics are generally the same for life insurance and the other forms of personal insurance. A contract (policy) is entered into between the insured party and the insurance company. The contract sets forth all of the rights and obligations of the parties, including the stated risks that are insured, as well as precise definitions of all the appropriate terms in the policy that can have a bearing on the rights of the parties. The insurance company holds and invests the premium dollars until claims have to be paid.

But the claim procedures with these other forms of personal insurance can often be much more complicated than with life insurance. When an insured individual dies, the company is notified of the death and makes the payment. But in the other forms of insurance, there may be many questions about the status of the insured or of the injured parties, and the extent of damages suffered may be subject to question.

Presenting a claim for payment with these various types of personal insurance may require filling out numerous and extensive forms. The information you submit on the forms may be subject to further investigation by the insurance company to determine the validity of the claims. Although the vast majority of all claims are clearly defined in insurance contracts and are paid in accordance with the company's obligations, there is a continuing burden on the insured individual to comply with the requirements for getting satisfaction and for seeing to it that the full measure of the claim is clearly stated and received.

HEALTH INSURANCE

The average American family might spend as much in a given year on hot dogs and breakfast cereals as it spends (directly or via fringe benefits) on health insurance. If the hot dogs are too fatty or the cereal is nonnutritive, nobody will suffer any great loss. But if money spent on health insurance—either privately or through an employer—isn't wisely planned and maintained, the results can be catastrophic.

The Gap

Currently, out of every $3 spent on private health care and health-care insurance premiums, only about $1 is returned to the public in the form of health-care insurance benefits. The other $2 is lost. This is in spite of the fact that close to 90 percent of the working population is covered by one or more plans of health insurance.

Why should there be such a tremendous gap between what we pay for medical expenses and protective insurance and what we get back in insurance benefits? Many individuals simply prefer to take their chances that they will not be exposed to risk, rather than spend a lot of money for insurance protection. Others may think they are protected by an existing health-insurance program when in fact they are far less protected than they believe. Many people are adequately protected for minor and probable medical expenses but are unprotected for the major catastrophic expenses. Many insurance policies do not increase their benefits at the same rate that health and medical expenses have been skyrocketing in recent years.

One of the single most frequent causes for financial distress is poor health and the lack of proper protection against medical expenses. Many segments of the population have been so poorly protected that the government has intervened—at enormous expense to taxpayers—to provide forms of basic medical care for those segments. Medicare is designed to take care of a substantial portion of medical expenses for the elderly; Medicaid, as administered by the various states and supported by the federal government, does the same service for those economically distressed. Further, for many years, the federal government has been debating the merits of a form of national health insurance to protect the population at large.

Whether or not the government sees fit to close the medical expense gaps for those who don't do this on their own, the prudent individual and family will see that their welfare is protected by designing and maintaining a sensible health-insurance plan.

Case Histories

The following case histories illustrate some typical situations wherein people learn the hard way about the coverage gap in their health-insurance programs.

Arthur's Case History. Arthur considered himself in the peak of health and never paid much attention to the sick-pay policies of his employer. It wasn't until a co-worker suffered an injury and was laid up for four months that he realized how vulnerable he was. Through his co-worker he learned that the employer would provide full pay for the first two weeks of any disability, then half pay for another month and a half, then nothing. After two months of disability, the co-worker had ceased to receive any income, and the total cost of his disability and recuperation put his family into a critical financial bind.

Arthur was thus a ripe prospect for an advertisement that offered "$200 a week extra cash when you're hospitalized . . . and $100 a week when you are recuperating at home!" Those were the two-inch-high letters that caught his eye. He skimmed over the small print in the advertisement, for it seemed too complicated. He bought the policy, and even though he had ten days in which to return it if he wasn't satisfied, the small print in the policy also seemed too complicated. He retained the policy, assured that he was protected come what may.

A freak accident landed him in the hospital with a broken hip a few months later. Arthur was hospitalized for three weeks and sent in his claim for $600. He received a check shortly thereafter. This was in addition to the sick-pay benefits he was receiving from his employer.

But he was in for a long siege of convalescence and rehabilitation and wasn't able to return to work for ten weeks after he left the hospital. Three weeks after leaving the hospital he submitted another claim for the $100 per week that was due him, and again he got a check immediately.

Now the sick-pay benefits from his employment were near an end, but Arthur was not aware that his insurance policy benefits were also at an end. After another month, Arthur filed a claim for his $100 per week, but this time the insurance company notified him that he was entitled to no more benefits.

The small print that he had skimmed over and had not understood explained that the recuperative benefits were payable for no longer than the time he spent in the hospital. Three weeks in the hospital would entitle him to three weeks of at-home benefits. But no more. He had thought that the benefits would be payable for as long as any recuperation lasted, but the policy said otherwise. The remaining weeks of recuperation, with no source of income at all, made a serious dent in Arthur's savings account.

Brian's Case History. Brian was a bright business executive who was keenly aware of his family's need for protection against medical expenses. Ten years earlier, he had carefully shopped around and had obtained a comprehensive medical-insurance program. He filed the policy away, satisfied that he had insulated himself from any problem in the medical expense field, particularly major catastrophes. And he was fortunate, for ten years elapsed with no major health-care obligations. He dutifully paid his premiums, but, being a busy man, never took the time to review the coverage offered by the policy, even though he was aware that medical costs were steadily rising.

Then his wife developed some strange intestinal pains, and the siege began— tests, X-rays, specialists, surgery, hospitals, drugs, postoperative care, nurses, consultations, more drugs, more X-rays, more tests, more nurses. But Brian never had a worry about getting it all paid for.

Finally, the doctor pronounced his wife cured, and Brian started to add up the bills. His ten-year-old policy had provided $50 a day toward the hospital room. That had seemed ample ten years ago, but today the cost was in excess of $500 a day. The surgical schedule in the policy allowed $300 for the needed operation, but the surgeon's bill now was $1200. And so it went throughout all of the specific items Brian had to pay.

The insurance company paid fully and promptly, but the total payments that Brian received were only a fraction of the total bills. Brian realized too late what a costly error he had made by not periodically reviewing and updating his policy. For the sake of a few minutes every few years, he could have saved many thousands of dollars that were now gone forever.

Cora's Case History. Cora was widowed a few years ago, and though she was left with adequate income, she had no protection against medical expenses. Cora was not yet old enough to be eligible for Medicare, but she was old enough to believe what her friends told her about the cost and difficulty of obtaining health insurance at her age. She inquired of a few agents and found, indeed, that what her friends said was true. It was a costly proposition to acquire adequate protection, and she feared dipping into her limited sources of income to obtain that protection.

Like Arthur, she was ripe for the lure of an advertisement offering a medical insurance plan that "required no medical exam . . . absolutely no age limit." Cora mailed in the coupon attached to the ad, and a few days later was visited by an aggressive sales agent who, after scaring her with tales of what might happen to her, sold her a medical and hospital expense plan that, he said, would give her all the protection she might need.

Time passed, and an old kidney ailment came back to haunt Cora. She had all but forgotten about the condition, since she thought it had been cured many years ago. She submitted her claim to the insurance company and was shocked to learn that they would not pay her anything. She was told that preexisting conditions weren't covered in the policy. Any condition that developed after she had acquired the insurance policy would be covered but none that had existed previously and recurred would be covered. Cora had been totally unaware of this clause. As a gesture of goodwill, the insurance company offered to return all the premiums she had paid. But that was a small token compared with the medical expenses she had incurred. Her assets drained by the uninsured illness, Cora had to turn to public welfare.

Big Print Small Print

The big print giveth and the small print taketh away. As the case histories illustrate, a clear understanding of precisely what the insurance contract states is essential if an individual is to have protection. And this requires reading and understanding the small print. If the small print is too garbled by legal mumbo jumbo, seek the assistance of the insurance agent, your family doctor, and any friends or associates who may be helpful. Sadly, many documents—particularly insurance policies— that we must understand to protect our financial situations are not worded in the language of the common person but in the language of the lawyer. To an extent this is necessary, for the wording must clearly define the legal obligations and rights of the parties. Some companies have attempted to present the contractual matters in a more easily understandable format, but not enough are doing so. Even when they are, the client does not always take the time to read beyond the big print to see what the small print says and means.

The big print says, "We will pay you up to $5000 if you are hospitalized because of illness or accident." But the small print says, "Payments shall not exceed $500 in any given year."

The big print says, "No more worries about surgical expense! We will pay you up to $10,000 on your surgical bills." The small print says, in effect, that the $10,000 is the outside maximum payable over the entire life of the contract. Any single claims are subject to a precise schedule of benefits, which may provide payments well below the actual costs. Furthermore, coverage may be for the surgeon's bill only and not cover such things as anesthetic, operating room fees, assistant surgeon, surgical nurse, and recuperative costs.

The big print says, "This policy is guaranteed renewable!" The small print says, "Guaranteed renewable to age sixty-five only, and annual renewals will be made at premium rates in effect at the time of renewal."

The Basic Elements of Health Insurance

Before we delve into the specifics of different kinds of medical costs and the forms of insurance you can obtain, it is necessary to have an overall understanding of the workings of the contracts themselves.

The Health-Care Insurance Contract. The following precautions are necessary, when purchasing insurance for health care and reviewing your contract:

□ Compare a number of plans in detail: For how much and how long are you covered? What exceptions or exclusions or limitations are there? What will the premium costs be? Only by doing this can you really get an accurate comparison of what the policies will offer you.

□ Examine the policy carefully before you buy it. If an agent won't provide you with a copy of the policy being sold, you can find other agents who will. Without a copy of the policy, you are buying big print but getting small print.

□ Examine the policy after you buy it. Conditions may have been imposed on the contract as a result of information contained in your application.

□ Before you buy any policy, determine what actual current costs are in your area for various forms of medical care. This can be done with a few phone calls—to your local medical society, your doctor, and a local hospital. If the policy benefits aren't in line with actual costs, you'll find yourself footing the balance of the bill on your own.

□ Review policies periodically, whether they are group, Blue Cross/Blue Shield, or individual. Old policies can be out of touch with current costs and may need updating or supplementing. Many policies contain riders that permit you to increase your limits from time to time. You may want to take advantage of these rights

□ Remember that it is the policy itself and not what the sales agent says that spells out the obligations of the insurance company. If, later on, the company refuses to pay a claim, you'll get nowhere if you tell them, "But the agent said. . . ."

□ Be well aware that the policy that seems the cheapest isn't always the best.

□ Don't be fooled by some of the wording and language that may appear in mail order or promotional insurance advertisements. Many private companies will attempt to lure buyers by using slogans, replicas, and names that sound like government-sponsored programs. Examples may include such wording as "Medi-Care," "Veterans Insurance Division," "Armed Forces Policy," and so on. Envelopes may be created to resemble official U.S. government envelopes. Plans offered by these companies may be legitimate, but the sales approach is less than ethical, and you could end up paying for far more than what you are actually getting. If you have any questions, check out the reputation of the insurance company. One source of such information is *Best's* directory, a rating service that is probably available at your local library. Your local agent may also have a copy and may be able to help you in deciphering the language in *Best's*. Other information sources include your state insurance department, your local Better Business Bureau, the National Council of Better Business Bureaus, and the Bureau of Deceptive Practices of the Federal Trade Commission (Washington, D.C.).

Health-Care Costs and Risks. The first step in building a sound program of protection is to determine precisely what your existing health-care insurance coverage consists of. If you are protected under a group plan at work, the personnel office at your place of employment should be able to help you understand the precise limits of your coverage.

If you are privately insured, you may have to depend on your agent for help in understanding the details. If a policy—be it group or private—has not been updated within the last year or two, or if it does not contain automatic escalation clauses that increase the benefits in line with increasing costs, it will likely be necessary to amend your policy or find supplemental policies that will bring your level of coverage up to a par with current actual costs. In addition to determining what existing coverage you have, you'll also want to evaluate what this coverage is costing you and how much more you can afford for added protection. Health-care costs and risks you'll be facing can be broken down into three ranges: minor, heavier, heaviest.

Minor Expenses

In the first range are the necessary minor expenses: periodic checkups for all family members, the inevitable smattering of doctor bills for injuries and common illnesses, prescriptions, first aid, and the like. Do you need insurance to cover these relatively minor predictable costs? Are you just swapping dollars with the insurance company—dollars that might better be spent protecting you against the major, unpredictable, possibly crippling costs? No two individuals are alike. Some may prefer to budget these costs in their normal expense program. Others may want the security of insurance even though, over the long pull, it's possible that they may be spending more on premiums than they will get back in benefits. In any event, it's worth looking at your current program to determine whether you are covered for expenses that you'd rather take your chances on and save the administration costs that go to the insurance company.

Heavier Expenses

The second range of health-care costs involve the heavier, less predictable situations that entail hospitalization, extensive doctor bills, and surgery. These situations, in turn, can lead to loss of income due to the length of disability. In addition to out-of-pocket medical expenses and lost income, the convalescent expenses connected with such medical situations can be considerable.

Heaviest Expenses

Major diseases and injuries can entail expenses that swiftly mount into the many thousands of dollars. The initial expense is often followed by protracted periods of disability in which no work can be done and no income received. In addition to conditions that threaten life itself, many impose limitations on one's ability to work and otherwise function normally in society. It is this area of health-care problems—often referred to as *catastrophic*—that has been the primary focus of recent government attention looking to establish some form of federal protection for the public against such costs.

Slightly more than half of the American population has adequate or good protection against catastrophic medical costs. The balance is unprotected or has less than adequate protection.

Although it's logical to assume that a major disability to the family breadwinner would be most damaging (largely due to loss of income), a similar fate befalling any individual can be nearly as severe.

The difficulty in predicting potential costs increases from the first level of health care (the necessary minor expenses) up to this highest level. Fortunately, the health-care insurance industry in America has devised a variety of programs that can be tailored to fit our available budgets and help us achieve the necessary circle of protection we're seeking.

Basic Hospital, Surgical, and Physician Insurance. These three forms of insurance protection cover three different areas of medical costs. Frequently, they are lumped together in one type of basic policy, such as in group programs and Blue Cross/Blue Shield programs. If an individual has more than one plan, such as a group plan at work plus a private plan, care must be taken to determine that coverage does not overlap or, in other words, that you are not protected for the same expense twice. Some policies will not pay you benefits if you have received benefits from another policy. Further, duplication of coverage means that you're paying more in premiums than you need to.

Hospital insurance

Hospital insurance is designed to reimburse you for hospital expenses: room and board, nursing, minor supplies, and perhaps X-rays, tests, and medications. The major item—room and board—may be limited to a maximum amount per day for a maximum number of days. The other items may also be limited to specific dollar amounts. In evaluating the adequacy of hospital insurance, you must take into account the following:

☐ What are the actual going rates at hospitals in your area, particularly the one you'd use if the need arose? What are the costs for a private room, a semiprivate room, and a ward? What about emergency room costs? Intensive-care unit costs? To what extent would the proposed insurance plan cover these costs?

☐ Do your local hospitals anticipate raising their rates and, if so, to what levels? It can be assumed that hospital expenses will increase in the future. If you want complete coverage, does your plan contain provisions that allow you to increase the benefits for hospital care? Would it make sense to pay an added premium to obtain higher coverages if such coverages can in fact be obtained?

□ Is the hospital you'd use covered under the proposed insurance plan? Some hospitals may be excluded from certain kinds of insurance policies, and you must determine this in advance.

□ Must you be an inpatient in order to be covered? That is, do you actually have to be registered in the hospital as a patient? Is there coverage for emergency room treatment and for outpatient visits?

□ For how many days of hospital stay are you fully covered?

□ Are you covered for any cause that may put you in the hospital, or are there exclusions? For example, mental disorders may not be covered, even if you are hospitalized.

□ Are there extra benefits for intensive care? These costs can be considerable, and not all policies will protect an individual against intensive-care confinement. If the policy offers optional intensive-care coverage, what is the cost, and what are the limitations?

□ Must you be in the hospital for a minimum number of days in order to be covered, or are you covered from the very first day? This type of clause is generally referred to as a *waiting period*. Bear in mind that the average hospital stay is only about eight days. If there is a waiting period that leaves you unprotected for the first six or seven days, you'll recover very little for an eight-day stay, and you'll actually be out of pocket for the days during the waiting period.

□ What limitations are there for such miscellaneous expenses as X-rays, radiation treatments, lab tests, nurses, anesthesia, oxygen, traction gear, plasma, ambulance costs, drugs, and medications? How does the protection offered by the policy actually compare with current going costs for these items?

□ What benefits are payable, if any, for nursing care? Benefits may cover only a certain number of hours per day of nursing care, or they may offer twenty-four hour coverage. There also might be limitations on the hourly amount payable for nursing care regardless of the number of hours and other limitations regarding the type of nurse that you'll be reimbursed for.

Surgical insurance

Surgical insurance pays for surgeon's fees and related expenses such as anesthesia, operating room fees, and assistant surgeons. Surgical policies may also provide some coverage for postoperative care and follow-up surgery if needed. Surgical benefits are usually tied to a specific schedule, and related expenses are often expressed as a percentage of the fee allowable to the surgeon. For example, a surgeon may be allowed as much as $400 for a specific type of surgery. The policy may further state that an assistant surgeon will be paid up to, say, 15 percent of the surgeon's fee, which would mean that $60 would be payable toward the fees of the assistant surgeon. In analyzing the surgery-insurance aspect of your protection program, you must consider the following:

□ What are the current going rates for various surgical services in your area? For comparison purposes, ask your family doctor or your local medical society for approximate surgical fees for some of the most frequent surgical procedures, such as stitching lacerations, setting fractures, setting dislocations, tonsillectomies, appendectomies, hysterectomies, and childbirth. How do the surgical benefits of the insurance policy compare with actual current costs?

□ A surgical procedure may require more than one incision. Or you may have two more operations through the same incision. Determine what the extent of coverage would be in such cases. If an incision has to be reopened for further surgery related to the original cause, would this be partially or totally covered in your policy?

□ How much is allowed for the cost of an assistant surgeon, anesthetist, surgical nurses, and operating room fees, and do the benefits payable compare with the current costs in your area?

□ In order for surgery to be covered in your policy, must the surgery be done in the hospital? Some minor surgery may be done in a doctor's office, and this may or may not qualify for coverage under the policy. Further, a great deal of surgery is now being performed in ambulatory-care facilities. These are not hospitals, but they are equipped with virtually all surgical facilities and are designed so that the patient spends a minimum amount of time in them. It's a fairly new phenomenon, and you must determine whether any older policy or a new policy will provide coverage for surgery conducted in such situations.

□ In many policies, the surgical schedule may be connected with the room rate schedule for the hospital portion of the policy. In other words, you would be entitled to a higher schedule of surgical fees if you select a higher schedule of room-rate protection. Do you have the right to increase the surgical benefits at any time in the future? If so, to what limits?

Physician insurance

Generally, physician insurance, also called *basic medical insurance*, is designed to pay doctor bills for hospital visits, office visits, and house calls. There may be a dollar limit per visit and there may be a limit to the number of visits that will be paid for. All plans differ. In determining the breadth of coverage offered by your physician insurance, you must determine the following:

□ What are the actual going rates for doctors' visits in your area, including office visits, house calls, hospital calls, "overtime" visits (such as nights, weekends, and holidays), and telephone consultations? Consider the costs involved, not just with your regular doctor but with specialists as well in such areas as pediatrics; ear, nose, throat; internal medicine; eye; skin; obstetrics and gynecology; and surgical (for nonsurgical consultations).

□ How much will your plan pay for each type of visit with each type of doctor, and how many visits will be paid for per family per illness or accident, and per year? There may be limitations in all these respects. Two seemingly identical policies may pay the same amount per doctor visit, but one may be much more strictly limited in the number of visits that will be covered during a given period of time.

□ Will you receive benefits for diagnostic as well as for treatment calls?

□ Are there any limitations concerning the type of doctors that you'll be covered for? For example, will you be covered for visits with chiropractors, osteopaths, podiatrists? To what extent would you be covered for eyeglasses and for prescriptions?

□ What about dental coverage? In recent years, dental protection has increased considerably, particularly in group policies. Although a group policy is something that's made available to you and your only choice is to accept or reject it, many people want supplementary insurance beyond what their group policy offers for both dental and medical purposes. Thus, it's important to understand what even a group policy will provide regarding these professional services.

Major Medical Insurance

A major medical policy—or "major med" as it's frequently called—is designed to protect you against the major, unexpected, and catastrophic medical expenses that seem to be so commonplace. The basic philosophy behind major med insurance is that you, the insured, will pay some of the minor costs on your own (either out of pocket or through the basic hospital/physician/surgery protection), and the major med coverage will then pay all or a substantial portion of the heavier costs. The initial costs that you yourself absorb are referred to as the *deductible*. For example, a major med policy may have a $500 deductible per family per year. This would mean that the major med coverage would not come into effect until after the family had paid $500 worth of eligible expenses during that year. In such a case, if one individual used up the deductible, then all of the other family members would be eligible for the major med protection.

Another form of deductible might be, for example, $100 per person per year. In such a case, any member of the family would become eligible for the major medical coverage after incurring $100 worth of eligible expenses during the year. But the other members of the family would not become eligible until *each of them* had accumulated expenses up to the deductible amount. Once the deductible is met, the typical major med policy will pay 80 percent of all additional costs, and the insured will have to pay the other 20 percent. (Some major med policies may split this on a 90/10 basis, and a few might even pick up 100 percent of all costs over and above the deductible.)

Most major med policies will also have schedules for room rates and for surgical benefits similar to those contained in the basic policies. The company's obligation to pay, say, 80 percent over and above the deductible may be limited by these specific room rates and surgical benefit schedules. If a major med policy has a $50-a-day limit on hospital rooms, that's all it will pay, even though the policy otherwise states that it will pay 80 percent of your costs over and above the deductible, Where specifically excluded, the hospital room and surgical benefits will not fall into that 80 percent payment obligation of the insurance company. Many policyholders overlook this very important clause and are distressed to learn that the major medical plan has not paid all that they thought it would.

There is also a maximum ceiling—a top limit of total expenses that the policy will pay. If, for example, the maximum is $25,000, then that's all the company will pay, and the insured will have to absorb any costs exceeding this amount.

How it works

Here's an example of how a typical major medical policy works. The policy calls for an annual deductible of $500, with the company then paying 80 percent of all qualifying expenses above the $500 deductible, up to a total of $25,000.

The insured party, Mr. Ramez, has a sixty-day hospital stay resulting from a severe heart condition. His total expenses are $26,000, including hospital room and board, X-rays, private nurse, cardiologist fees, physicians' fees, lab tests, and so on. Mr. Ramez has to pay the first $500 of expenses, and the insurance company pays 80 percent of the next $25,500, or $20,400, subject to room-rate and surgical-rate limits. Mr. Ramez has to pay the remaining 20 percent, or $5100. The total out-of-pocket costs for Mr. Ramez are $5600—the initial $500 deductible and the remaining 20 percent of the excess over the deductible, which was $5100.

Mr. Ramez has now eaten into the maximum benefits payable under the policy, reducing his available protection by $20,400: from $25,000, the original limit, to $4600.

If Mr. Ramez had a basic protection package—surgical/hospital/physician—in addition to the major medical plan, that would have reimbursed him for a portion of the $5600 he was out of pocket. But the limitations in the basic plan might not have protected him adequately for the major portion of the total expenses.

Depending on the type of policy, the costs, and the family's financial circumstances, it might be advisable for some families to forgo the basic coverage and use those premium dollars to pay for a sound major medical insurance program.

Some homework is essential in buying a good major med policy. From company to company and even within the same company, the coverage can vary widely. Here are some of the factors to consider and compare when shopping for a major med plan:

☐ How much is the deductible? Does the deductible apply per family or per person? What expenses can be applied toward the deductible and what expenses cannot?

☐ Does the deductible run for the full year regardless of the claims that may be made against the policy? Or does a new deductible start after each claim is paid? The latter situation might provide far less coverage, particularly if one person has more than one claim in a given year.

☐ How much above the deductible will the company pay—70, 80, 90, 100 percent? This can make a considerable difference both in the level of protection you're receiving and in the premium you'll pay for the coverage.

□ What is the maximum amount that the company will pay, and is it per person, per family, per claim, per year? If the maximum is used up, does it terminate the policy altogether? In some policies the maximum can be replenished over a period of time, thus allowing continued coverage.

□ How much expense can you afford without major medical insurance? Determine the maximum limits on your basic insurance plan, and talk with your doctor to get an idea of the possible costs involved in major situations, such as heart disease, cancer, lung disease, and the effects of major fractures or other disabling accidents. How prepared are you, between your existing assets and your existing basic insurance, to stand the cost of any such major medical catastrophe?

□ How long does the "benefit period" run? The benefit period is the amount of time that benefits will be payable once the deductible has been covered. For example, a major med policy may state that the benefit period will run for one year. This means that if you incur medical expenses, the policy will pay benefits owing to you for up to one year. At the end of the one-year period, you must accumulate a new deductible before a new benefit period will begin to run again.

General Health-Insurance Provisions

There are a number of provisions that can appear in any of the foregoing insurance policies that can affect your rights. They should be given careful attention when choosing a policy. The more important of these provisions are the following:

□ *Maternity benefits.* If you do have maternity benefits, what is covered and what is not? How much of a waiting period is there before maternity benefits will be payable? Maternity benefits may be optional, and obviously if you anticipate the birth of children, you'd want to take advantage of the insurance protection. If you've had coverage for maternity benefits in an ongoing policy, and you have reached a point of not having any more children, you should look into deleting that area of coverage from your policy because it can be costly. How will complications arising from pregnancy be treated—under obstetrical surgery benefits, under maternity benefits, or as regular sickness benefits?

□ *Dependents.* To what extent are dependents, particularly children, covered? If children are born to you or adopted by you after your plan has begun, will they be covered and to what extent? If you have children now who may be incapacitated—mentally or physically—will they be covered by the plan, with what limitations, and up to what age? Until what age are children generally covered under your policies? Once they have passed that age, will they be permitted to continue coverage either on their own or under your wing, by the payment of an additional premium?

□ *Waiver of premium.* As in life insurance policies, if you become totally disabled, a waiver of premium clause will protect you: There will be no need to make premium payments during the period of such disability. Do your health-care insurance plans carry such a provision, and if so, at what cost?

☐ *Termination.* Termination of employment can be particularly important in group health-insurance situations. If you leave the job, presumably your protection under the group plan would cease. Will the insurance company allow you to maintain your protection individually once you have left, and if so at what cost? The extent of coverage offered by group plans can differ widely. If you have comprehensive coverage under an existing group plan, and you are anticipating changing jobs, will your new employer offer you comparable coverage? If not, you'll probably want to supplement the group coverage with a private plan. The costs of doing this should be anticipated before a job change occurs, since the cost can be considerable and may offset what seems to be a higher earning level at a new job. If you leave one employer, federal law may give you the right to continue your group health-care coverage that you had been receiving from that employer. Know your rights under the law.

☐ *Preexisting conditions.* As Cora's case history illustrated, many policies will not provide coverage for conditions that have already been known to exist. Some policies will permit coverage of these preexisting conditions after the passage of time, sometimes one year, but more likely two years. If you do have any known preexisting conditions that are even remotely likely to recur, this clause can be critical to your overall protection package.

☐ *Excluded or rated risks.* Many policies will not provide coverage for certain stated risks, such as injuries occurring during acts of war or riots. Other policies may exclude coverage from more likely risks, such as the onset of mental illness and the costs connected thereto. Still other plans might offer full protection, but at a higher premium cost if the individual is deemed to be risk-prone either as a result of a preexisting condition or as a result of occupation. These specifications should be clearly understood before entering into a policy agreement.

☐ *Renewability and cancelability.* If a policy is guaranteed noncancelable and renewable, you have the right to renew it on its expiration. If a policy is cancelable by the company, or if you do not have a right to renew, the insurance company could terminate your insurance at the end of the policy term or could renew at a higher rate than you had been paying. In a guaranteed renewable policy, though, the rate can be increased only if the entire class of insured have had their rates increased. The company cannot single out just you for an increase. Generally, policies that are noncancelable and guaranteed renewable cost more than those that can be canceled or denied renewal. You're paying more money for the assurance of continued protection, but that expense may well be worth as much as any other facet of your health-care insurance policy.

☐ *Grace period, lapse, and reinstatement.* If you don't pay your premium on the due date, is there a grace period during which you can still pay the premium and continue coverage? Is there a penalty? If the policy does lapse, what rights, if any, are there to have the policy reinstated? If a policy has lapsed, the insurance company may examine your recent medical history as a stipulation for permitting reinstatement. If they determine that you have suffered certain conditions, they may allow reinstatement only if those conditions or recurrence of them are excluded from coverage. Consequently, it can be most imprudent to allow a health-care insurance program to lapse, particularly if such a condition has occurred during the time you've been covered.

Other Forms of Health-Insurance Protection

In addition to the basic forms of medical insurance, there are other modes of protection that may be available. One—the health maintenance organization (HMO)—can offer a fairly comprehensive package. Others, such as workers' compensation, offer only a limited level of coverage.

Health Maintenance Organizations (HMOs).   HMOs are a form of prepaid medical-care facility. Instead of paying premiums to an insurance company and then being reimbursed later, if and when medical expenses occur, with the HMO you pay in advance a fixed amount each month, for which you are entitled to a broad range of medical services. Generally, you use the doctors and facilities provided by the HMO rather than choosing your own. Preventive medicine is at the heart of the philosophy behind HMOs—regular checkups for all family members are covered by the overall fee you pay. It is hoped that major expenses can be avoided by early diagnosis and treatment of various diseases. HMOs have their own schedules of how much treatment is provided for what types of need; additional fees may be payable to the HMO for treatment and care beyond the normal maintenance programs.

The HMO phenomenon has grown rapidly in recent years. There are roughly thirty million people registered with HMOs and close to 700 different plans are available throughout the nation. Many employers have switched their health fringe benefits from group insurance policies to HMO membership for their eligible workers.

If you are choosing an HMO on your own, visit the facilities, talk to the staff, get recommendations from other people who are enrolled in the HMO, and check with the state agency that regulates HMOs in your state to obtain their opinion of the financial stability of the organization.

Workers' Compensation.   If you are injured at work or if you contract an illness related to your work, you will likely be protected by state workers' compensation laws. These laws provide a fixed schedule of benefits for medical care and certain disability income benefits, as well as rehabilitation expense reimbursements. Each individual should consult the employer's personnel office where to determine the extent of coverage provided by workers' compensation.

Medicare.   Medicare is a health-insurance program administered by the Social Security Administration designed to protect citizens sixty-five years of age and over. The costs of and the benefits provided by Medicare are amended from time to time, and anyone currently eligible for Medicare, or soon to become eligible, should check with the local office of the Social Security Administration to determine what current costs and benefits are. There are two aspects of Medicare: hospital insurance (the basic plan), and medical insurance (supplementary plan). These are referred to as "Part A" and "Part B," respectively. Persons eligible for Medicare must pay an initial deductible amount with Part A and a monthly premium in order to be protected by the medical-insurance coverage, Part B. Part A, after the deductible has been paid, covers the bulk of the cost of hospital services and extended-care facilities, including rooms, meals, nursing, and certain drugs and supplies. Part B is designed to defray the costs of doctors' services, as well as those related to medical needs, for such things as X-rays, various equipment, laboratory fees, and so on. Medicare covers a major percentage of these various expenses, but the insured may be responsible for a certain percentage as well. Part A, the hospital-ization insurance, is also limited to a specific number of days.

Many older citizens have had the mistaken belief that Medicare is the ultimate protection for them against health-care expenses in their later years. Although Medicare does cover a substantial portion of normal medical expenses, many people have found themselves still heavily burdened by costs not covered by the program. A number of supplemental programs are available through major insurance com-panies, and any existing or prospective Medicare recipients should explore the advisability of obtaining some supplemental protection. A new law passed in 1988 extends Medicare coverage for "catastrophic" medical problems. Care must be taken to determine how extensive this coverage is; supplemental protection might still be needed.

Do not mistake comprehensive supplemental health-care programs for the often heavily promoted hospital supplemental programs, which offer "tax-free cash while you're in the hospital." These programs offer cash payments only during periods of hospitalization, usually on a per-day basis. The lure of "$1200 a month cash while you're in the hospital" may seem attractive, but it's far less so when you realize that you're being paid only $40 per day and that if there's a waiting period of, say, six days, and you end up in the hospital for eight days, you'll end up with only $80 in benefits, a far cry from $1200. These hospital supplemental plans can fill a very minor portion of the gap, but they should not be relied on as being any form of full-fledged comprehensive protection.

Medical Coverage in Homeowner's and Automobile Insurance. Homeowner's and automobile insurance may contain medical payment plans that will reimburse you for certain medical expenses if guests are injured in your home or anyone is injured in your automobile. The amount of such protection may be minimal or extensive, depending on the premium you're willing to pay in your homeowner's or auto-insurance policies. Although they provide only a limited health-protection plan, they can fill small gaps and should not be overlooked as part of your overall package.

"Dread Disease" Insurance. Some health-care insurance companies have, in recent years, offered "dread disease" policies to protect you against costs incurred by such scourges as cancer. Numerous reports of scare tactics in the marketing of this type of insurance have prompted many state insurance departments to investigate these plans. In evaluating any such plans, you should determine whether the coverage offered duplicates what you already have in your major medical program. Also determine whether you can obtain the same coverage offered by the dread disease plan by expanding the limits of your major medical coverage, perhaps at a lower cost.

Health-Care Insurance Agents

As with life insurance, the agent who handles your health-care insurance program can be a valuable ally in determining the coverage gaps that you face and in presenting a variety of ways by which these gaps can be covered within the budget you have available. If you're covered only by a group plan, it would be advisable for you to meet with a representative of the company carrying the plan to obtain assistance in judging the extent of protection offered and in ascertaining the gaps that remain.

The same general suggestions regarding a life insurance agent hold true with health insurance and the other forms of personal insurance. The agent who is willing to take the time to study your needs, who can communicate clearly and simply, and who is staffed to provide the measure of service you expect for the dollars you're paying is a most important professional within your overall financial structure.

DISABILITY INCOME INSURANCE

How long could you get by without any income? One week? One month? Six months? A year? What other sources could you rely on for funds to live on? Your savings account? Your investments? The equity in your home? Friends, relatives, or institutions willing to lend you money?

Income can be lost in one of four ways: quitting your job, being fired, being laid off, or being laid up due to physical disabilities. With the possible exception of quitting your job, all of these occurrences are totally unpredictable. Loss of work because of a physical disability can mean more than simply lost income. With the disability may come added expenses of rehabilitation, recuperation, medicine and drugs, nursing, and other miscellaneous medical costs. Further, there can be intangible costs: the psychological depression that the laid-up breadwinner may suffer, the extra demands imposed on other members of the family, the natural worry over what prospects the future holds.

Existing Programs

There are a number of existing programs that give a moderate degree of protection against lost income. But for many people these programs won't be enough, and they will want to examine the opportunities offered by companies selling private disability income insurance. Before we delve into the specifics of this kind of personal insurance, let's briefly examine some of the other ongoing programs that may already be protecting your income.

Sick-Pay Plans.   The sick-pay plan at your place of employment should be examined to determine the level of protection it offers. Some employers have a set policy on how much sick pay they will provide for ill or injured employees. Others, particularly in smaller concerns, may "play it by ear" when an employee is unable to work due to physical disability. It would be sheer folly not to take the time to learn what your employer's program is regarding sick pay, for this is the core of your basic income-protection plan. A private plan, should you acquire one, must be tailored around and built on the foundation of your employer's sick-pay program.

Workers' Compensation.   Workers' compensation offers a measure of disability income to workers who are injured on the job or who contract an illness that is job related. But, needless to say, you could be physically disabled from causes not related to your work, in which case workers' compensation would be of no help to you. Through your personnel office, determine what workers' compensation benefits for disability income would be, because this, along with the sick-pay plan, is an important consideration in structuring any private plan for your ultimate protection.

Social Security.   If you become totally disabled—that is, "unable to engage in any substantial gainful activity," according to law—you may be eligible for monthly benefits under the Social Security Administration. You can obtain more specific details from the local office of the Social Security Administration.

Unemployment Insurance.   Unemployment insurance offers a measure of income if you are laid off from work. Your state Unemployment Office can assist you in learning what benefits are payable and for how long. You will be expected to seek out other work if you are receiving unemployment benefits, and you may waive your rights to the benefits if you do not comply with state regulations.

Waiver of Premium Clauses.   Waiver of premium provisions in your policies for life and health insurance can protect you, at least to the extent of those obligations. If you are disabled and unable to work, the premiums for these policies would be automatically paid for you. This is only a minimal level of protection, but it would at least assure that these important payments are being met so that you do not further jeopardize your overall financial situation.

Credit Health Insurance.   Credit health insurance is similar to credit life insurance, which is obtained in conjunction with a loan to pay off the loan in the event of the borrower's death. With credit health insurance, if you are disabled and unable to work, the loan payments will be made for you during the period of disability. The same protection may be available with your home mortgage. The cost of such insurance and the benefits that are available vary from lender to lender. If you believe this is valuable protection, you should determine the costs and the benefits available from various sources at the time you are negotiating the loans.

Evaluating Your Needs

In order to determine how much, if any, disability income insurance you may need, you must evaluate the foregoing sources of protection as well as the other personal sources of available income. These latter sources include the ability of other family members to work and generate income; the size of your personal savings and investments and how much you'd be willing to dip into them and for how long; other assets that may be converted into cash such as the equity in your house, the cash values in your life insurance, plus vested rights in profit-sharing and pension funds that you may be able to get access to; part-time or temporary work that you yourself could do that could help reduce the strain; and loans or gifts from family, friends, and associates.

Some of these sources you may dip into without hesitation. Others you might not want to utilize until all else failed. This is an individual matter that you must examine and resolve yourself. Once you have made a reasonable determination of outside sources of supplementary income, you can begin to examine closely the benefits available from private disability income policies.

Strategies for Success

Who is Covered by Your Group Health Plan?

It can be dangerous to assume that all of your dependents are covered by your group health-insurance plan. The best strategy is to check with your personnel office or the insurance company to be certain you know who is covered. The best course of all would be to highlight the actual language in the policy itself, so there's no question about just who the policy covers. For example, your plan might cover children only until they reach the age of twenty-one. But some plans might continue to cover children until the age of twenty-three, provided they are full-time students. What if your children are too old to be covered, but you still want to provide them with health-insurance protection? Ask your company if you can pay separately—hopefully at group rate—to keep them covered by your policy.

Private Disability Income Insurance

Like life insurance and health insurance, disability income insurance is available in a vast variety of sizes and shapes. You may obtain an individual policy directly through a company, or you may obtain a policy on a group basis, such as through a professional association, a union, or a trade group. Depending on your age, your occupation, and your income, you may be required to take a physical examination for a policy to be approved. The cost of the disability income policy can also vary depending on your age, income, and occupation.

The Waiting Period. One of the most important factors in shaping a disability income policy is the waiting period—the amount of time that you have to be disabled before the insurance will begin to pay benefits. It's possible to obtain a policy that will begin payment of benefits on the very first day of disability due to accident. Or you might obtain a policy with a waiting period of fifteen, thirty, sixty, ninety days or even longer. Waiting periods may differ for accidental disability and disability caused by illness (usually a seven-day minimum wait). Obviously, the shorter the waiting period, the higher the premium, for the company will become obliged to pay you all that much sooner. This is why it's so important to know what your sick-pay plan is at work. If your sick-pay plan will cover you fully or substantially for, say thirty days, there's not much point in beginning the disability plan until after thirty days of disability have elapsed. You can do so, of course, but you'll be paying a substantially higher premium, and you may not recover in disability benefits what the premium will cost you. Once your sick-pay benefits have been exhausted, you might want to look to your ready sources of other income before you begin the disability plan. If your sick-pay plan will last thirty days and readily available other sources can provide for another thirty days' worth of income, it might make sense to have the disability plan begin after sixty days from the date of the disabling incident.

Total and Partial Disability. Disability income policies agree to pay you a flat fixed monthly amount in the event that you are totally disabled. Should you be partially disabled, the company will pay you a portion, usually half, of the full total disability benefit. The definition of total disability can be very important. If, in order to receive total disability benefits, you must be totally unable to perform *any kind* of work, it may be more difficult to obtain such benefits. Many people who become disabled are unable to perform their normal job but still may be able to perform other jobs on a limited basis.

If the definition of total disability states that you are not able to perform *your own specific tasks*, you might be more readily able to obtain total disability benefits. In this case it would not matter that you could perform other duties. The important distinction is whether you can perform your own normal duties in order to be considered totally disabled.

You should also determine whether the policy requires you to be either bed-ridden, home-bound, or under the care of a physician in order to maintain continuing benefits, whether total or partial. As with all insurance, the more liberal the benefits, the higher the premiums. You're probably getting more protection, thus you're paying extra dollars for the desired security.

How Much Protection? Once the disability payments begin, how long will they continue? One year? Five years? Ten years? Lifetime? Policies may differ widely in this respect, as will the cost of the policy. There may also be maximum limitations on how much the policy will pay you over a lifetime. Many income disability policies will cease paying benefits or will curtail the benefits once you have reached age sixty-five, even though you may still be working. Naturally, when you do cease work, it can be expected that the disability income policy will also cease, since it's designed to protect you against lost income.

Benefits that you receive from a disability income policy are not subject to income taxes. Thus, it's not necessary for you to try to obtain a monthly benefit that's equal to your actual income.

Some disability income policies will offer extra benefits in the event of a loss of a limb or limbs or loss of eyesight. Some will also offer death benefits.

All things considered, a sound program of disability income protection is similar to a sound program of medical-expense protection. You may determine that you'd be better off taking your own chances on short-term minor disabilities and using the available premium dollars to amply protect yourself against the major long-term crippling disabilities. As with other forms of personal insurance, the right agent will help you evaluate your needs and illustrate the alternatives you have for protecting yourself against the probable risks.

NURSING HOME INSURANCE

There comes a time in the lives of many people when they are no longer able to care for themselves. This is a possibility that no one can ignore. Whether it occurs with respect to your parents or yourself, the need to live in a nursing home must be anticipated as far in advance as possible. The annual cost of nursing home care can range from $30,000 to $40,000 at the low end to $60,000 to $70,000 or more at the upper end. Not many senior citizens have this kind of disposable income. And if they had to dip into their nest egg to come up with that much money, the nest egg would disappear very quickly.

Nursing home insurance is a new phenomenon. Very few companies offer it, but it's well worth seeking out if you are prudent enough to be concerned about your long-term future or that of any other members of your family who could be in serious financial condition without such protection.

Nursing home insurance pays a daily benefit to the insured that can range from as little as $20 to $30 a day to more than $100 a day. In most cases, the higher benefits can be enough to cover virtually all of the costs of living in the nursing home. Depending on the plan you choose, the benefits can be payable for as long as six years (longer in limited cases); there are also lesser benefits paid for home-care coverage after an individual has been in a nursing home. Most policies have a waiting period (usually about twenty days) before coverage begins; that is, benefits don't begin until after you've been in the nursing home for the requisite waiting period. In some cases, benefits can be payable even if the individual has not been previously hospitalized.

The critical element in obtaining nursing home insurance is that the earlier you embark on such a plan, the less expensive it will be on a yearly basis. Sample policies indicate that a fifty-five-year-old person beginning a nursing home insurance plan will pay approximately $400 per year for average protection. If that person waits to begin the plan until age sixty-five, the annual premium is closer to $800. If a plan is not commenced until the individual is seventy-five years of age, the premium can be as much as $2000 to $3000 per year or more. Does it pay to begin a nursing home insurance plan when you are fifty-five, though you may never need the coverage or, if you do need it, not until you are in your sixties or seventies? Your desire for peace of mind is a determining factor on this critical question. At the very least, you owe it to yourself to begin looking into such plans at the earliest possible time, whether for yourself or for elderly members of your family.

Life Insurance: A Comparison

Shopping for life insurance can be very confusing. Companies differ. Specific policies differ. Insurance agents differ. Decisions are often made on the basis of the personality of the agent or on the "name-brand" reputation of the company. These aren't necessarily improper decisions, but close attention must, of course, be paid to the actual coverage you're obtaining and its cost. The following comparison chart will help you keep a close eye on the numbers themselves.

Item	*Policy A*	*Policy B*	*Policy C*
☐ Annual premium for a $10,000 straight life policy at your current age	_____	_____	_____
☐ Participating or nonparticipating	_____	_____	_____
☐ If participating, what would have been the dividend paid during the past year?	_____	_____	_____
☐ If participating, what is the company's estimate of dividend for the coming year?	_____	_____	_____
☐ If dividends are left to accumulate with the company, what interest rate will they earn?	_____	_____	_____
☐ Total premium cost over the next ten years (excluding dividends, since their actual amount won't be known until each year occurs)	_____	_____	_____
☐ At the end of ten years, what will be your Cash/loan value?	_____	_____	_____
Paid-up conversion value?	_____	_____	_____
Extended term conversion value?	_____	_____	_____
☐ Total premium cost over next twenty years	_____	_____	_____
☐ At the end of twenty years, what will be your Cash/loan value?	_____	_____	_____
Paid-up conversion value?	_____	_____	_____
Extended term conversion value?	_____	_____	_____
☐ At what interest rate can you borrow against the policy?	_____	_____	_____

Ask the help of the respective agents in analyzing and evaluating the difference you find in these numbers. What special features might justify higher costs or lower values?

An Experiment with Mail-Order Insurance

Health and disability insurance are heavily marketed through the mail via ads in newspapers and on television. As an experiment, I responded to a number of mail-order insurance offerings. My survey was not scientific, but the results were convincing. You might want to try a survey of your own before you commit yourself to buying health or disability insurance through the mail.

Inquiry No. 1. Eight weeks after sending in the coupon I had still received no reply. Had I really been in need of the insurance or had I suffered any malady that could have given rise to a claim, I would have been out of luck.

Inquiry No. 2. I received a policy by return mail, and the bills for it started flowing in. It was a disability income policy, and I compared it in detail with other plans received directly from agents. The agents' plans all offered far broader coverage for about the same cost.

Inquiry No. 3. I never received a policy from the company, but I did receive bills urging me to pay the premium before my ''valuable coverage'' (whatever that may have been) lapsed and left me unprotected.

Inquiry No. 4. In response to the coupon, an agent called on me without an appointment. He was personable and tried to be helpful but would not talk about any of the limitations on the policy unless I asked him directly. He seemed surprised that I knew to ask such pertinent questions, and in some cases he wasn't sure of the answers. He had no literature to leave with me and said there was absolutely no way for me to see a sample policy unless I signed up with him. Then he said I would have ten days to cancel if I wanted to. His main concern was to sign me up on the spot. Can't blame him for trying.

Even with a cancellation privilege, insurance is not a product to be bought sight unseen. All too often one doesn't exert the effort to cancel an inadequate policy, and the risk is then that you think you're protected when in fact you are drastically underprotected.

CHAPTER 20

Financial Planning for Later Years

Inside every person there's an echo of ten or twenty or thirty years ago, when the younger self did something very right—or very wrong—and that action now has a very distinct effect on the older self. "If only I hadn't let that fast-talking salesperson con me into that bum of a deal with my whole life's savings." "If only I had started to salt away money for retirement when I was thirty, instead of now, when I'm sixty." "If only I had paid attention to my pension benefits before I quit that job in a huff." So it goes.

Your years of financial maturity may seem far off, but the planning you do now and the actions you take now can have a most decisive effect on your security, or lack thereof, when that time does come. This chapter is intended to motivate you to think of the eventuality of that day and to ignite an awareness of the following:

☐ Your housing needs as your family begins to diminish

☐ Your sources of income when work ceases

☐ Your legal rights under your pension plan

☐ Your capabilities of combating inflation

☐ Your responsibilities to your future self and to your future family and how you will meet them

☐ Your Individual Retirement Account and other pension and profit-sharing plans and how best to take advantage of them

REACHING FINANCIAL MATURITY

There comes a time—it's different for everyone—when we reach a plateau that might be referred to as "financial maturity." This time, particularly for families, generally coincides with those years when children have grown up and moved out on their own. It's a period when we find ourselves looking at our personal and financial affairs from a new perspective. Many of our needs have changed, and many previously long-term, vague goals now begin to come into sharper focus.

As we reach financial maturity our needs and attitudes toward a great many important financial matters are in a state of change. These matters include housing, investing, insurance, use of leisure time, and the ultimate direction of our working career. Many of the financial decisions we make in our twenties and thirties can have a profound bearing on our ability to fulfill goals during the mature years. Thus, thinking about and making plans for the years of financial maturity should begin at the earliest possible time.

The most dangerous course is to totally ignore the future. We live in an age of instant gratification, and we are constantly urged and teased into buying things for the here and now. If we succumb to such urges excessively, we can end up ruining tomorrow for the sake of today. Tomorrow *will* come, and we must be ready for it.

Let's take a close look at some of the major elements of financial planning for the later years, so that alternate choices can be properly envisioned and anticipated. We can only conjure with possibilities and probabilities; specific solutions are strictly the concern of each individual and family.

HOUSING

Mature families must face the decision about where they should live out their old age. There are many factors that contribute to this decision: "This is the old homestead. This is where we raised our family. This is where we feel comfortable. It's almost all paid for, why should we move?" Or, "Without the children, we don't need this house to rattle around in any longer. Do we sell or do we stay, and what are the ramifications of either choice? If we sell, do we find another place in our present community, or do we move to a new community? Do we find another house? A condominium? An apartment?"

Our housing requirements are often drastically altered with the onset of financial maturity, and our personal feelings may easily stand between us and many thousands of dollars that could help provide added security and comfort in the years beyond.

The dilemma is simple enough: retaining the old "family homestead" with its comforts and its memories or exchanging it for another dwelling that may be more practical and economical.

Most homeowning couples in their forties and fifties will have substantial equity in their homes. In addition to what they have paid in on their mortgage debt, the value of the property itself will probably have increased considerably. But as long as the equity is tied up in the house, it's not working for them—except to provide a roof over their head. They may be perfectly content with that roof and not wish for any other pleasures the equity may be able to buy. However, by selling or refinancing the house, they could have the means to provide personal satisfactions previously unavailable because their money was tied up in the property. In addition to equity dollars, sufficient thought must be given to the costs involved in maintaining a home.

Furthermore, one of the main financial advantages in homeownership—the deductibility of mortgage interest and real estate taxes—may be of far less value to you in the later years, particularly on retirement, than they had been in the earlier years. All these considerations must be carefully evaluated.

Let's examine the case of the Johnson family to see what alternatives faced them. The basic thinking in this example can be used to determine the specific dollar advantages in almost any other situation.

Mr. and Mrs. Johnson are in their midfifties. Their children have moved out on their own, and the large family home they purchased fifteen years ago is now far too big for just the two of them. They've started to think seriously about retirement—planned for ten years hence—and they realize that their home represents their single biggest asset as well as their single largest monthly expense. They are puzzled about whether they should keep the house or sell it. And if they sell it, should they rent a dwelling or buy another?

Their house originally cost them $75,000. When they bought it, they paid $15,000 as a down payment and obtained a thirty-year mortgage for $60,000 at 8 percent interest. The monthly payments on the mortgage totaled $440. Today, with fifteen years yet to pay on the mortgage, they still owe roughly $48,000.

If the Johnsons sold their house today, they could get $150,000, after selling expenses such as brokerage commissions. Thus, if they were to sell it and pay off their existing mortgage, they would have a $102,000 cash-in-hand nest egg to do with as they please. (Since the Johnsons would presumably be fifty-five or older at the time they sold the house, up to $125,000 of profit on the sale would be excluded from taxation. See Chapter 12 for a more detailed explanation of this tax situation.) In addition to their current mortgage expense of $440, they have real estate taxes averaging $120 per month, property insurance costs of $40 per month, utility costs averaging $120 per month, and maintenance expenses averaging $80 per month. Their total outlay for shelter is, therefore, $800 per month.

Staying as Is

Let's assume that the Johnsons are willing to spend $800 per month for their basic shelter. They realize that inflation will boost their property taxes, insurance, utilities, and maintenance costs. But because they have a fixed-rate mortgage, the monthly mortgage payment will not be affected by inflation. Table 20-1 illustrates the approximate effect of inflation on their monthly housing outlay ten and fifteen years from now.

They realize that they can only guess at the long-term impact of inflation, but for purposes of this exercise, they have assumed that inflation will double these costs in fifteen years. If the Johnsons decide to remain in the house indefinitely, their outlay will have crept up to $970 ten years from now, the time at which Mr. Johnson plans to retire. Anticipating that his wages will continue to increase between

Table 20-1 **Monthly Housing Outlay: Existing Home**

Expense	Now	In 10 years	In 15 years
Mortgage	$440	$440	–0–
Property taxes	120	200	240
Insurance	40	70	80
Utilities	80	130	160
Maintenance	80	130	160
Total	$800	$970	$640

now and retirement, he has no worries about being able to handle the increased monthly housing outlay. Fifteen years from now, the mortgage will be all paid off, and as Table 20-1 indicates, their monthly outlay will drop to about $640.

Staying put seems to be the simplest course for the Johnsons, for it would involve no need to sell their home and look for another dwelling, nor would they have to worry about any financial manipulations. But is staying put the best course for them? What are their other choices?

Becoming Renters

If the Johnsons sold the house now, they could rent either an apartment or another house. Instead of spending the $800 per month on the mortgage and housing expenses, they could apply it toward their rental. By selling, they'd also have $102,000 in cash to spend or invest as they saw fit. If they couldn't find a rental situation for $800 a month that pleased them, they could invest the $102,000 and use some of the income from that investment toward their rental.

If, for example, they invested the $102,000 in a plan that yielded 8 percent after taxes, that would generate $680 per month income for them. That, added to their current monthly housing outlay of $800, would allow them to spend $1480 per month on rent. And they would always have their $102,000 nest egg intact to do with as they pleased in the future.

If the rental increased on their apartment, it's fair to assume that the available yields on a $102,000 investment would also increase proportionately, thus allowing them to maintain a fairly level standard of housing over the long term.

Buying Another Dwelling

Another alternative would be to *buy* another dwelling—house, town house, or condominium—with the proceeds of the sale on their existing home. Let's say that the Johnsons find a new but smaller dwelling with a $100,000 price tag. They put $40,000 of their total $102,000 nest egg toward a down payment on the new house and sign up for a $60,000 mortgage for fifteen years at 12 percent. The new monthly mortgage payments would be $720. Let's assume that the taxes, insurance, utilities, and maintenance costs would be lower in their new dwelling because it's a more modest property.

Assume that the new monthly expenses are $100 for property taxes, $30 for insurance, $60 for utilities, and $60 for maintenance. This brings the grand monthly total outlay to $970—$170 more than they have currently been paying. Table 20-2 illustrates what their current outlay in a new smaller house would be for the present and for ten and fifteen years hence.

Remember that the Johnsons have $62,000 left over from the sale of their previous house. Assume that they put that to work in an investment that will earn them 8 percent after taxes, roughly $410 per month. They can apply this income toward their housing expense and still leave the $62,000 nest egg intact for future use. Table 20-3 shows the net housing cost for the Johnsons in their new home, assuming that they apply the income from their investment toward these costs.

Currently the Johnsons' net housing costs are $240 per month less than what they now have budgeted for housing ($800 minus $560 equals $240). They could, if they wish, begin an additional investment program with that $240 per month and create an even larger nest egg for their retirement years.

Table 20-2 **Monthly Housing Outlay: New, Smaller House**

Expense	*Now*	*In 10 years*[a]	*In 15 years*[a]
Mortgage	$720	$ 720	0
Property taxes	100	160	200
Insurance	30	50	60
Utilities	60	100	120
Maintenance	60	100	120
Total	$970	$1130	$500

[a]The projections are based on an approximate annual inflation rate of 6 percent for property taxes, insurance, utilities, and maintenance costs.

Table 20-3 **Net Housing Costs: New, Smaller House**

Item	*Now*	*In 10 years*	*In 15 years*
Base costs (from Table 20-2)	$970	$1130	$500
Income from $62,000 investment	410	410	410
Net housing cost, after applying investment income	$560	$ 720	$ 90

What About Refinancing?

If the Johnsons decided to stay put for the time being, would it make sense for them to refinance their existing mortgage? Unless the current interest rates are equal to or less than the original 8 percent interest rate on their existing mortgage, a refinancing at this time would be of relatively little benefit. Assume they were to refinance their existing $48,000 mortgage for a new period of thirty years at 12 percent interest per year. Their monthly mortgage payments would actually *increase* by about $54 per month, to $493 per month. Obviously, there's no advantage to such a move. However, if they wait another five years, the balance on their existing mortgage will have dropped to about $38,000. If they refinance this amount at that time for a new thirty-year term at 12 percent interest, their monthly mortgage payments would then drop to about $390 per month, or $50 per month less than what they are currently paying. Individual circumstances will vary, as will interest rates, and careful calculations will be necessary to determine the value of refinancing at any particular time.

Profit Potential

The Johnsons face yet another perplexity in trying to reach a decision: What profit potential might they be giving up if they sell their existing house? The house has doubled in value in the past fifteen years. Will it double again in the next fifteen years? If they sell now and become renters, would they then be giving up a veritable small fortune that they could reap in the future by selling later? On the other hand, if they sell now and buy another house, what is the profit potential on that other house? Could it be more or less than the potential on the existing house?

If the Johnsons are risk takers, they might prefer to hold on to their existing house and take their chances on what the future housing market might bring. If they are more conservative, they might prefer to establish a workable plan that will ignore the unknown elements and give them a greater sense of security for the years to come.

There is no rule of thumb as to which choice is best for any given family. But there are choices to be made, and these choices should be evaluated clearly, with professional help, wherever uncertainty emerges.

INVESTING

Our investment attitudes and tactics will likely undergo a considerable change as we reach the plateau of financial maturity. Until now, we've been concerned with generating capital to meet the heavy expenses of housing, educating the children, and other family needs. Now, with these needs substantially accomplished, we turn to the philosophy of preservation of capital. While we were younger, we could afford to make mistakes and still recoup. Now we may be at an age when the specter of a financial loss via investments is more fearsome: We may have neither the time nor the ability to recoup.

The advantages of fixed-income investing, as opposed to more speculative forms, become clearer. Although many individuals are just reaching their peak earning years at this stage, the feasibility of taking risks is diminishing. We simply have less time to recover from a poor risk. Anticipating some future time when work may cease, we begin to realize the importance of preserving our capital so that there will be adequate funds available. This does not imply that all attempts to generate capital in more speculative modes should be abandoned altogether. But the risk factor must be examined more closely and should be considered with much more respect than it may have been a decade or two earlier.

A portfolio of fixed-income investments to preserve capital can take many shapes. Perhaps the line of least resistance is to take whatever lump sum you may have accumulated and put it into a long-term high-yielding bond or savings certificate and forget about it for as many years as it has to run. This minimizes the need to have your nose buried in the *Wall Street Journal*, keeping tabs on your capital, and constantly looking for better opportunities. If you're locked into a given situation, you may regret it later if better opportunities do present themselves. On the other hand, nothing better may come along, and you'll be very content to ride it out with your locked-in situation.

But the prudent investor in the mature years must be aware of the value of liquidity and flexibility. To obtain liquidity and flexibility in the fixed-income portfolio, one must consider the advantages of building a portfolio based on *staggered maturities*: Instead of investing a whole lump sum for one long period, the investor would break up the lump sum into perhaps three or four or five nearly equal segments and invest them for different lengths. For example, you have a $10,000 lump sum that you want to put into fixed-income securities. Consider breaking it into four equal parts of $2500 each and investing each of the four segments for a different maturity: one segment for one year, one for two years, one for three years, and one for four years. Within each time span, you can take advantage of the highest-yielding security available. Then as each segment matures, starting in one year, you can redirect that money into whatever is best at that time, considering safety and yield.

With a portfolio like this, you'd have one-quarter of your total nest egg roll over every year. In some years you might have to take a lesser yield than you had previously been earning on that segment because of a drop in overall interest rates. In other years you might be able to obtain a better return. With a program of staggered maturities (not exceeding a five- or six-year maximum), you're going to have a higher degree of control and liquidity with your nest egg, which could bring you a greater sense of satisfaction and financial return.

Overall, as noted in Chapter 16 in the discussion on fixed-income investing, the fixed-income portfolio allows you to predict with a reasonable degree of certainty how much money you will have available at any given future point. By sticking to fixed-income investments with shorter maturities, you can avoid the problem of being caught in a long-term downtrend of prices on such fixed-income securities as bonds. If you need to tap your nest egg, you will have minimized any worry that the value will have shrunk because of fluctuations in these securities.

INSURANCE

Financial maturity brings accompanying changes in our insurance program. We may have had a life insurance program designed to protect our family in the event of the premature death of the breadwinner. Now the family is on its own, and we may have far better uses for these premium dollars. Moreover, because age renders us more susceptible to the risks of injury and illness, we must be increasingly concerned with our ability to cope with such circumstances both psychologically and financially.

Life insurance programs begun when one is in the twenties and thirties can have a most important effect on one's financial status in the fifties and sixties. If young people are willing to sacrifice a bit of current pleasures for the sake of greater security and comfort in the future, they can create a life insurance program that will serve well in the later years. In Chapter 19, we examined some of the deliberations and alternatives facing young people in choosing various kinds of life insurance programs. Let's now look at the effect of one particular choice decades later.

When Sally was thirty, she embarked on a straight life insurance program by buying a policy with a face value of $50,000. Her annual premium for this life insurance protection was $653. From the very first day the policy was issued, Sally and her family had the peace of mind in knowing that $50,000 would be payable to the family in the event of her death. Sally has lived a full and healthy life, and today, twenty years later, she is pleased to observe the nonforfeiture values in her life insurance program.

Table 20-4 illustrates the status of Sally's policy (see Chapter 19 for a more detailed explanation of how these nonforfeiture values work). When Sally is fifty, and the policy is twenty years old, Sally looks at her life insurance needs quite differently than she did when she commenced the policy. Her children are grown now, and there is not as much need for immediate cash to take care of her family in the event of her death.

At age fifty, Sally will have paid premiums totaling $13,060. The policy now has a cash surrender value of $14,450. In other words, Sally can cash in the policy and receive back *more* than what she paid in. If she invests the $14,450 at 8 percent per year, she will have a return of $1156 per year, leaving her $14,450 nest egg intact. The net result of having purchased this type of policy is that for the past twenty years Sally has guaranteed her family a substantial lump sum of money—$50,000—in the event of her premature death. Now, instead of being out of pocket $653 for premiums each year, she can have an added income of $1156 per year plus a cash nest egg of $14,450. If she cashes in the policy, the $50,000 coverage will terminate. Sally may also elect to borrow the $14,450 from the company. On

Table 20-4 **Sally's Life Insurance**

| | | Nonforfeiture values[a] | | |
At age	Total premiums paid to date	Cash/loan value	Paid-up insurance	Extended term
50	$13,060	$14,450	$28,550	19 years, 103 days
65	22,855	27,550	39,950	14 years, 160 days

[a] Policies will differ with respect to these values.

an older policy such as Sally's, this can be done at an interest rate of 5 percent. Sally can then turn around and invest the borrowed funds at, say, 8 percent, and the difference between what she earns at 8 percent and what she pays at 5 percent will be money in her pocket. In the meantime, choosing this alternative, the policy will remain in force, except that in the event of her death, the proceeds payable will be the face value of the policy minus any loans outstanding against the policy.

Sally's other alternatives are to convert the policy to a paid-up or an extended-term status. If she chooses the paid-up method, she can cease paying the annual $653 premium and will have a life insurance policy with a face value of $28,550, paid up for the rest of her life. She doesn't have to pay any more premiums, and, on her death, her survivors will receive that sum. If she converts to extended term insurance, she will be able to stop paying premiums and still be insured for the full $50,000 face value for a period of 19 years, 103 days—until she's almost seventy.

What if Sally continues to pay on the policy and keep it in force until she reaches age sixty-five? She will have paid in a total of $22,855 in premiums, and she will have a cash value of $27,550. The other conversion values for this age are given in Table 20-4.

The important thing is that the thirty-year-old Sally did in fact create the program that the fifty-year-old Sally or the sixty-five-year-old Sally can now either continue or convert to suit current needs. The young woman created a liquid and flexible package that the older one can benefit from.

Health insurance is also important. Many individuals reach retirement age and find that leaving their job means the cessation of a group insurance plan that had given them the protection they've needed throughout their working years. Individuals covered by group medical plans should, at the earliest possible time, investigate what alternatives for health insurance are available upon retirement and determine if the health insurance is continued after their retirement. If it is, they should find out the cost, if any. If it isn't, it's necessary to find out what kind of supplemental coverage is available and at what cost. Nursing home insurance (see Chapter 19) should also be explored, and Medicare should also be carefully investigated in terms of eligibility, amount of coverage, and cost. One should determine if there's a need for supplemental coverage in addition to what Medicare provides. The earlier these matters are looked into, the better off the individual will be.

ACTIVITIES AND IDLENESS

Our personal activities and leisure pleasures may undergo substantial alteration when we reach financial maturity. Much of our free time in our younger years may have been devoted to family affairs or community activities. We may also find that our contemporaries are shifting from old patterns into new ones, and there's a natural need to pursue various interests jointly with friends.

One very serious problem arises from neglecting to develop outside interests that will provide a measure of satisfaction and constructiveness in later years. In spite of all the money one may have accumulated, the loneliness, boredom, and helplessness that can attack are overpowering.

TO WORK OR TO RETIRE?

As financial maturity begins, so starts our thinking about how long we wish to continue working. This might be the most drastic change of all. If you intend to continue working, either voluntarily or out of necessity, what kind of employment might be available to someone with your skills, desires, experience, and needs? If mandatory retirement is not in your future, when will you voluntarily want to begin to taper off and how quickly? Will you want to take some new direction in your career, albeit at a later age? Will you want to try that certain something that you've always wished you could do? The earlier you can start shaping these thoughts into something tangible the better. If you anticipate a work activity that will take some investment on your part, the earlier you can start setting aside the necessary funds the better you'll be able to accomplish your desires. If no investment will be needed, you'll have all that much more time to establish extra reserve funds to see you through should the business venture not work out.

OLDER SINGLE PERSONS

Single individuals reaching financial maturity have some slightly different considerations from those of the married person. (By ''single individuals,'' we're referring generally to people who do not have families dependent on them and do not plan to have one in the future.) Single individuals might easily justify spending more of their disposable income on personal pleasures than married persons. But single persons must be every bit as aware as married persons of the impending future and should avoid developing spendthrift habits that could be regretted later on.

Regarding insurance, single individuals probably have fewer concerns and fewer budgetary obligations. Singles who do not have families dependent on them have obviously little need for life insurance and can allocate those dollars elsewhere. To the extent that single individuals want to leave an inheritance to anyone, life insurance does provide a good vehicle for this purpose, as it does for married persons. But if insurance is simply for the welfare of surviving dependents, the singles may choose to do without such protection.

Many singles may have life insurance policies acquired many years ago. If the original need for the insurance has diminished, they might do well to examine the conversion privileges in the policies, as noted earlier in the case of Sally.

In health and disability insurance, singles have some other matters to be concerned about. Being alone, only one person's health has to be insured. This can represent a savings on premiums compared with what the couple and the family will pay. But if disability strikes, singles can be at a disadvantage—long-term convalescence can be a costly and time-consuming proposition. With couples, the well spouses can assume many of the obligations and duties that single individuals have to pay someone to do. Housekeeping, shopping, nursing care, and the like must be considered, and the costs can run high. It's essential for singles to maintain comprehensive insurance for protection in the event of long-term disabilities.

Singles facing long-term disabilities may be involved in some problems that need a lawyer's attention. For example, if single individuals are unable to act on their own behalf, for whatever reason, someone they trust should be allowed to step into their shoes and take care of their important matters. These matters could be as simple as writing or endorsing checks or as complex as selling a home. The *power of attorney* can be a valuable tool for singles, particularly in the event of an extended disability.

A power of attorney need not be given just to a lawyer; it can be granted to anyone the individual chooses. But a lawyer should definitely draw up the documents. The power of attorney can be limited to specifically stated acts or can be general in scope. A general power of attorney is very broad and should be entered into only in the most compelling circumstances. A lawyer can supply more details.

FINANCIAL ARRANGEMENTS FOR LATER YEARS

How much will you have to live on when your active working career tapers off or ceases altogether?

Before you take a closer look at some of the specific details involved in planning your retirement budget, we must discuss one very frequently made comment: "Whatever we have to live on won't be enough because inflation will eat away at it."

We occasionally hear horror stories of elderly people forced to turn to public welfare or to pet food in order to survive during their later years. Such stories may be true and sad indeed, but they represent only an extremely small fraction of all those who have entered their later years. The vast majority of the elderly are able to live comfortably and contentedly within their fixed income. The prudent individual who has planned properly and saved scrupulously should not have these fears.

Fighting Inflation

Inflation can be a specter, particularly if the ability to work has diminished or disappeared. But it can be coped with. Upon reaching the later years, many individuals reduce their living expenses and thus blunt the effects of inflation. Moving to smaller quarters, moderating clothing needs, and having only one car can sharply reduce financial needs. Many families will have paid off the mortgage on their home, and many will terminate or convert existing life insurance programs. These steps can create additional spendable dollars previously applied toward these purposes.

Beyond what a family or individuals do unconsciously to meet their diminished needs, they might also take some conscious steps to cut back so that their disposable income can still provide satisfaction. A review of any budget can reveal minor excesses that can be reduced or curtailed without materially affecting their life style.

The effects of inflation can also be blunted on the income side. Social security payments are scheduled to increase in line with Consumer Price Index fluctuations, and many pensions also have escalation clauses tied to rising prices. Furthermore, as costs move upward, so inevitably do yields available on secure fixed-income investments. If inflation starts to nibble away at a nest egg, shifting into higher-yielding investments can offset the inflationary bite.

Strategies for Success

Calculate Your Own Personal Inflation Factor

One of the most frightening things to would-be retirees is the unknown impact that inflation might have on their financial structure. The reality is that most senior citizens are not as susceptible to being damaged by high inflation as are younger people. More mature families have fewer inflation-sensitive expenses to worry about than younger families: They have no more children to feed, clothe, shelter, and educate; they are likely to have one car instead of two; their home loan is probably much smaller; and so on. Put your mind at ease and help your future planning by calculating your own inflation factor. Consider which of your expenses are really subject to inflation and how much the higher earnings on your savings (also brought on by inflation) will offset the increased cost of living. Don't fret needlessly. Inflation might not be as bad for seniors as the general statistics indicate.

Shaping the Budget

There are two primary sources of sustenance that must be considered in detail: *income* and *principal*. Income is money received from all sources such as social security, pensions, investments, and work. Principal is accumulated money working for you that may be dipped into for living purposes as the need arises. Until individuals or families determine how much they want to spend, they can't adequately determine how much, if any, principal will meet their needs. The obvious and prudent approach is for them to attempt to live off income and keep principal in reserve until needed. A careful review of their savings and investment program is necessary. How much principal do they have? How well is it protected? Can they count on the projected income from principal? If not, how can they restructure their investment program to offer better protection?

Sources of Income.   The farther you are from a termination of work, the more difficult it will be to get specific figures on the sources of income that will be available. But at least ten or fifteen years before you anticipate retirement, you should begin to obtain some estimates of what might be expected. As the date approaches, you should check with regularity—at least every second year, tapering down to every year—in order to focus more clearly on the ultimate income figures. One very sad mistake is to conjure up in one's own mind what these income sources might be—those who guess too high can be grievously disappointed. The proper way to go about this is to check with the specific sources and get their most reasonable conclusions as to the true amount of dollars that will become available.

☐ *Social security.*   Social security payments are increased periodically as the Consumer Price Index increases. Because there is absolutely no way of knowing what those fluctuations might be in the future, there is no way of predicting what your ultimate social security check might be. But a visit to the local office of the Social Security Administration can be helpful in instructing you about probable trends. The closer you get to actual retirement, the more closely the Social Security Administration can estimate your income.

☐ *Pensions and profit-sharing plans.*   Visit with the administrator of your employer's pension or profit-sharing plan to determine as closely as possible what money you may have coming from these sources. What options do you have with these funds? Will you be paid a fixed monthly amount and, if so, for how long? Will you be able to obtain a lump-sum payment; what will it be; when can you get it? Will payments continue beyond the death of the working spouse and be available to the surviving spouse and, if so, for how long? The Pension Reform Law, passed in 1974, makes many provisions for the benefit of pensioners-to-be. This law, as updated by the Tax Reform Act of 1986, is discussed later in this chapter; the Individual Retirement Account and other pension and profit-sharing plans are also discussed later in this chapter.

☐ *Investments.*   As retirement nears and the ability to earn income from work diminishes, you'll seek to further insure that a fixed amount will be available to meet your needs. The trend toward fixed-income investments becomes more pronounced under these circumstances, and the more you solidify such a program, the more clearly you'll be able to see the kind of return that you can expect once you have retired. The greater your need to know what your investment income sources will be, the more motivated you will become to create a portfolio that clearly defines the sources.

☐ ***Employment.*** Many people continue to work long after they are eligible to retire. They may go into business for themselves or take a full- or part-time job out of either choice or necessity. But the farther away you are from retirement, the more difficult it is to predict how much postretirement income you might earn from working or for how long it might continue. With the earning potential from work so unpredictable, it would be prudent not to rely upon any such income for your basic support and well-being. It would be better to consider any such income as "icing on the cake" to provide for extra comforts and leisure activities during retirement.

Due to peculiarities in the income tax laws and regulations of the Social Security Administration, it is possible for some people to end up with more spendable income—after taxes—once they have retired compared with before retirement. For example, when Bernie and Flora were both sixty-four, they had a total income from their jobs of $20,000 per year. After all taxes and voluntary pension contributions were taken into account, they were left with a net spendable income of $12,500. The following year they retired. Just to keep busy, they took part-time jobs, from which they earned $3000 during their first year of retirement. They received an additional $3000 in that year from a pension plan, and $7200 from social security. The social security income was not taxable. Considering all taxes on their sources of income, Bernie and Flora ended up with a net spendable income of $13,000 during their first year of retirement, even though their actual income from work was a fraction of what it had been during their working years. In other words, they had more spendable money after retirement than they had while they were still working.

Postretirement income from work can also be affected by regulations of the Social Security Administration, which can reduce your benefits if you earn more than a set amount during a given year from work. Anyone planning to work after starting to receive social security benefits must determine immediately what the effect of the earnings will be on benefits. Furthermore, since 1984, part of your social security benefits could be taxable if your income from all sources exceeds the following levels: $25,000 for persons filing a single return and $32,000 for persons filing a joint return, in accordance with IRS definitions. Income from all sources includes social security benefits and interest earned on tax-exempt investments. However, these regulations that curtail and tax social security benefits serve to penalize senior citizens who wish to remain productive members of society or who have invested wisely and well during their working years. The laws are subject to change, and you should determine what impact these regulations can have on your own specific situation.

Sources of Principal. The sources of principal providing future spendable dollars may be easier to estimate than income sources, particularly if an investment portfolio includes fixed-income investments. The potential principal sources are the following:

□ *Equity in your home.*   As noted earlier in this chapter, many people sell their existing home or refinance an existing mortgage to get access to the dollars they've been paying in over the years on their mortgage. This equity can represent a substantial portion of their future nest egg and should be estimated as carefully as possible and as far in advance as feasible.

□ *Life insurance values.*   Individuals with conversion values in their life insurance policies should determine precisely what these values currently are and what they will be in future years, assuming premium payments are continued until a conversion is made. Personal circumstances will dictate whether to continue the protection of the life insurance in full, convert it to one of the other forms of life insurance, or retrieve the cash that's available.

□ *Pension and profit-sharing funds.*   If lump-sum distributions are available instead of monthly payments, these should be counted in your overall sources of principal. See the discussion later in this chapter on lump-sum pension and profit-sharing distributions.

□ *Business interests.*   If you have an interest in a business, either wholly or partially, how might it be converted into investable funds and at what time? How can you best sell out your business or professional interest and on what terms? Anyone in these circumstances must recognize when a business or professional practice is at peak potential and reach a decision as to how much energy should be devoted to the business compared with other pursuits. A common problem arises when a business owner begins to feel a diminution in energies regarding operation of the business. As energies diminish, so can profitability and, in turn, the opportunity to reap the best possible price on a sale of the business. The sad end result can be that the business falls far short of being able to provide for the needs of the owner at the time of retirement because the ability to sell it has been so negatively affected.

Prudent planning may dictate that when business owners or professionals recognize the peak potential in their occupation, they should immediately begin to consider the feasibility of a gradual phase-out. This generally would involve selling the business to a younger successor or turning over the reins to a family member.

□ *Existing investment portfolio.*   Your investment portfolio includes all money you now have invested. Some of it currently may not be offering any return— you are hoping for a gain in value to realize your ultimate rewards. As retirement approaches, you may deem it advisable to convert these nonearning assets into earning situations where you can specifically gauge how much will be available to you at future points.

□ *Potential inheritances.*   Realistically, try to estimate inheritances from family members in the foreseeable future. Will the funds be in cash, securities, property, or some other form? Will they be earning assets or nonearning assets, and what would be involved in converting them into situations best suited to your personal needs? For example, you might inherit a parcel of income-producing real estate. Although this could generate an attractive measure of income, you might not want to continue ownership of the building. It might be a great distance away from where you live, or you simply may not have the desire or expertise to deal with income-producing real estate. What are the prospects of selling the building, and what sacrifice, if any, would be made in your income picture if you convert the property into cash or other securities? These considerations apply to any inherited assets, except perhaps cash.

How Much Income and for How Long? Most of us face the ultimate dilemma in the later years: to have enough money available to live within a desired framework for an *indeterminate* time and to possess the security of having sufficient funds to take care of virtually any contingency. Life expectancy and health factors are unknown quantities, but the amount of money available should be known. If, after work has ceased, you can live comfortably on income alone, your later years should be relatively worry free. The dilemma is compounded in the many situations when principal has to be invaded, minimally or substantially, to provide for necessities and contingencies.

In many cases, it's necessary for a life style to be trimmed in order to conserve enough principal to guarantee future comforts and necessities. Temptations to dip into principal should be yielded to *only* after careful consideration. When the principal is reduced, so is your earning power.

Let's say that you have a nest egg soundly invested, and you want to dip into it to increase your monthly spending money. First you need to determine how much and for how long you can dip into the nest egg before you deplete it? As Table 20-5 shows, starting with a nest egg of $30,000, you could withdraw $269 per month for fifteen years. At the end of fifteen years, you would have depleted the nest egg. Or you could withdraw $179 per month indefinitely and always have the original nest egg intact. (In the latter case you are withdrawing only the interest earned by your investment.)

Pension and Profit-Sharing Plans

For many U.S. workers, pension and profit-sharing plans comprise the bulk of their retirement nest egg. Understanding how these plans work and the laws regarding them are of utmost importance in order to receive maximum benefits.

Pension Reform Law. In September 1974, Congress passed the Employee Retirement Income Security Act of 1974, more commonly known as the Pension Reform Law or ERISA. The purpose of the law was to correct abuses in the administration of pension funds that resulted in pensioners being deprived of monies that were due them. The administration of the law is under the jurisdiction of two

Table 20-5 **Dipping into Your Nest Egg**

Starting with a lump sum[a] of . . .	*. . . You can withdraw this much each month, for the stated number of years, reducing the lump sum to zero . . .*				*. . . Or you can withdraw this much each month and always have the original nest egg intact.*
	10 years	*15 years*	*20 years*	*25 years*	
$ 10,000	$ 116	$ 89	$ 77	$ 70	$ 59
15,000	174	134	116	106	88
20,000	232	179	155	141	118
25,000	290	224	193	176	142
30,000	348	269	232	212	179
40,000	464	359	310	282	237
50,000	580	448	386	352	285
60,000	696	538	464	424	360
80,000	928	718	620	564	467
100,000	1160	896	772	704	585

[a]These figures are based on an interest rate of 7% per year, compounded quarterly, before income tax considerations.

governmental agencies—the Internal Revenue Service and the U.S. Department of Labor. Both agencies produce regulations and guidelines, and the courts undoubtedly will be interpreting these regulations and guidelines for years to come, so specific elements of the law are being modified. The following discussion is intended to acquaint you with the overall concepts. Persons accumulating pension benefits subject to ERISA should determine from their employer exactly what their benefits will be and what their rights are under the law as it becomes amended.

The law is aimed at those pension funds that are "qualified" under the Internal Revenue Service regulations. Qualified pension funds, generally, are those that allow the employer tax deductions for the cost of contributions and that allow the employee receiving the benefits not to have to report the contributions as income until the money in the fund is later withdrawn. About fifty million Americans are thus covered by the blanket protection of the law regarding pensions.

The Pension Reform Law does *not* require any company to start a pension plan. But if a company does begin one, it must meet the requirements of the law. Further, the law does *not* stipulate how much money an employer should pay in pension benefits for employees nor how much, if any, an employee should contribute. But the law does establish that once promises are made regarding pension contributions, those promises must be kept.

The Tax Reform Act of 1986, in conjunction with regulations of the Social Security Administration, have an impact on when retirees will be entitled to full benefits from their pension plans. The Tax Reform Act of 1986 states that employees must be at least sixty-five years of age before they can receive 100 percent of the pension benefits. If they want to retire earlier, the pay-out must be the same as used by the Social Security Administration. For example, the regulations of the Social Security Administration say that individuals are entitled to 80 percent of full benefits if they want to begin receiving benefits at age sixty-two. Thus, if employees want to retire at age sixty-two, they would only be entitled to 80 percent of what otherwise would be forthcoming from the employer's pension plan at age sixty-five. Thus, as with social security benefits, early retirees get smaller pensions because they start receiving their benefits sooner.

Furthermore, the law sets forth a gradual increase in that minimum retirement age, again in line with the Social Security Administration's formula. For individuals born before January 1, 1938, the retirement age—at which you are entitled to full benefits—is sixty-five. If you were born after December 31, 1937, and before January 1, 1945, the retirement age is sixty-six. And if you were born after December 31, 1944, the retirement age is sixty-seven. Check the current regulations of the Social Security Administration to determine how will these requirements affect you.

If your employer does not have a pension or profit-sharing plan, you should still be aware of the benefits available under the law. You may change jobs and go to a company that does have a pension plan, or people close to you may be affected by the law, and your awareness of its benefits can be helpful to them.

The Pension Reform Law attempts to correct abuses in the following areas.

□ **Vesting.** Vesting refers to the time when your benefits are "locked up" or guaranteed as a result of the time you've spent on the job. Say you've worked for a company for many years and you leave, either to change jobs or to retire. When you try to collect your pension, you're told that you hadn't been on the job long enough to receive a full pension, that is, you hadn't worked long enough to have rights "vested" in your behalf.

The Pension Reform Law is designed to eliminate the problem of when you are entitled to how much money. To better understand what this means, let's follow the basic steps involved in obtaining pension benefits from a company.

First you must become eligible to participate in the plan. The law states that any employee who is at least twenty-five years old with at least one year on the payroll must be taken into the pension plan if the company has one. Once you become eligible, the company credits a certain sum to your pension or profit-sharing account each year until you either leave the company or retire. The next step in receiving the benefits is *vesting*, or locking up whatever accrued benefits have been set aside in your name.

The Tax Reform Act of 1986 gives employers two basic options with regard to vesting programs for their employees who are covered by their plans. These choices took effect in 1989. The first option is a gradual schedule that requires workers who are eligible for the plan to be 20 percent vested after three years. Workers receive an additional 20 percent vesting each year after the third year. Thus they are 100 percent vested after seven years. Table 20-6 illustrates this vesting schedule. In the table it is assumed that the employer is contributing $500 per year to the eligible employees' pension fund. For example, employees must be 20 percent vested after three years of eligibility in the plan. At the end of three years, the employer has put $1500 into each employee's plan. Being 20 percent vested means that 20 percent of the amount that has so far been contributed to the plan is now vested for each employee (20 percent of $1500 equals $300). In other words, at some future time, employees who have worked three years will be entitled to receive at least $300 unconditionally. If employees quit after three years of service, nothing further will be contributed to their plan. If they remain on the job, their vesting will increase yearly in accordance with Table 20-6.

The second vesting option is all-at-once vesting. Before the Tax Reform Act of 1986, an employer did not have to vest anything at all until after ten years of eligible service by an employee. The Tax Reform Act of 1986 accelerates the all-at-once vesting option from ten to five years. In other words, after five years of eligible service to an employer who has made this choice, employees are 100 percent vested in whatever money has up to this time been contributed to the plan on their behalf. If employees quit after four years, eleven months, and twenty-nine days, they will not become vested at all.

Employers may choose more rapid vesting schedules if they wish. Union pension plans can still keep ten-year vesting schedules.

These vesting options do not mean that you're entitled to a full pension once you've achieved full vesting. You may have to wait until you actually retire before any of the funds are available. In certain cases, an employer may be willing to pass on the vested funds to an employee in the event of an earlier termination. This must be determined directly with each employer in any specific individual case.

Note also that these vesting requirements refer to the *employer's* contribution to the pension fund. If you are making your own contributions, either directly or through payroll deductions, you are fully and immediately vested regarding these contributions.

Table 20-6 **Vesting: First Option**

Year	Total amount contributed	Amount vested (%)	Dollars vested
1	$ 500	–0–	–0–
2	1000	–0–	–0–
3	1500	20	$ 300
4	2000	40	800
5	2500	60	1500
6	3000	80	2400
7	3500	100	3500

An employer's plan must state which vesting alternative is being used. The employer must keep records of every employee's service and vesting. Each employee is entitled to a yearly statement from an employer concerning vesting and accrued benefit status. You must consult your employer to determine exactly what your benefits are under this important aspect of the Pension Reform Law.

☐ *Funding.*   Funding refers to putting enough money into the pension fund to meet the future promises to pay the benefits. Say that XYZ Company has ten employees in its pension plan. By reasonable estimates, these employees will each receive pension benefits of $50,000 over their lifetime after retirement. Let's assume that all ten employees retire on the same day and that they all request a single lump-sum distribution of their benefits. On this mass retirement day, therefore, the XYZ pension fund should theoretically have at least $500,000 in it.

But what if the XYZ pension fund only has $200,000 in it? Why might this be so? Perhaps through some bookkeeping shenanigans, some imprudent investment, or a simple shortfall in the amount contributed, the company has missed the mark considerably. What then happens to the ten employees? Do they split up the $200,000 into lumps of $20,000 each and sit there in amazement wondering what happened to them?

The Pension Reform Law attempts to correct this possible abuse. It imposes very stringent requirements on all pension funds to put away the amount that they, according to reasonable expectations, will need to meet the targeted promises. Despite the rigid requirements of the Pension Reform Law, a company may still violate the law and not properly fund enough money to meet its obligations. You may not discover this until the time for your retirement at which point, of course, it's too late.

☐ *Folding.*   A company for whom you've worked could also fold after you've already started receiving your pension benefits, thus putting your benefits in jeopardy. The Pension Reform Law has created an insurance program that will guarantee retirees at least a *portion* of their benefits if their company folds. The law established the Pension Benefit Guarantee Corporation (PBGC) to administer this program.

This insurance program is intended to provide for benefits that are *vested*. If you become entitled to your benefits under the PBGC, the *most* you can receive is $750 a month. The actual amount you will receive depends on your highest paid five consecutive years while working for the company. The $750 limit is subject to change depending on future changes in the Cost-of-Living Index. In effect, the PBGC is like a safety net under the overall pension programs throughout America. But don't rely on it to the exclusion of any other safety nets that you might provide on your own through individual initiative and planning.

☐ *Reporting.*   The law has created these benefits and protections for the individual worker, but how is the average individual supposed to learn about them and keep up to date with them? The law has seen to this as well. Every eligible participant in a plan must be given a description of the plan plus a periodic summary of the plan "written in a manner calculated to be understood by the average plan participant." This summary must explain in detail the participant's rights and obligations under the plan. Additionally, the company must maintain open access to the latest annual report on the plan, and related documents must be available for examination by participating employees.

The written explanation shouldn't be treated lightly. You should study the booklet when you get it and ask questions if you don't understand. Sound financial planning requires that you know the exact status of your pension rights at all times.

☐ ***Managing.*** The law sets stringent guidelines for the management of pension funds. It sets forth fiduciary duties, the punishment for their breach, prohibited transactions, and steps to avoid conflicts of interest between the respective parties. In short, it can be expected that the investment philosophy of pension funds will become much more conservative to comply with this requirement of the Pension Reform Law.

Nevertheless, much of the investment strategy of a given pension fund is left to the discretion of the manager of the fund. During the bull stock market of 1982–1987, many pension fund managers had huge investments in the stock market, and the stock market performed exceedingly well for them. Indeed, in a great many pension funds, the employers found that the stock market was performing so well that their companies did not have to put any fresh cash into the pension funds in order to meet their future promises. In other words, the pension funds were growing by virtue of the increasing values of stocks, thus eliminating the need to put corporate cash into the plans each year.

The stock market crash of late 1987 brought a grim reminder to many pension fund managers around the country: The stock market can't be depended on forever. In fact, it can turn on you and change gains into losses. The 1987 market crash altered the investment strategies of many pension funds. Many companies that did not have to put corporate money into the plans prior to the 1987 crash are reconsidering doing so if the stock market performance does not satisfy the pension plan's growth needs. Using corporate cash might affect the amount of money available for stockholder dividends, wage increases, or new research facilities. The need to generate fresh cash for pension plans could thus cut into a business's ultimate profitability and ability to compete.

Employees have a stake in how their pension money is invested, although they may not have a very strong voice in that regard. If you feel that your company's pension plan is taking too many risks in its investment philosophy, you and your co-employees might want to voice your opinion to management accordingly. If you belong to a union, your union might be able to do this for you. Investment managers of pension funds who make serious errors can be punished under the law. But this won't help the employees who, as recipients of the pension fund, find that they're getting less than they are entitled to. The time to voice your concerns is *before* the mistakes are made, not afterward.

Do-It-Yourself Pensions   No company, no government, no union can take better care of your future than you yourself can. The sooner you begin taking better care of your own financial future, the better off you will be. Pension and profit-sharing plans may hold the promise of future security. But you might leave the company, the company might fold, or the plan might suffer losses as a result of unwise investment stategies. Social security has provided more than a safety net for much of the generation now in or near retirement. But by the way the system was structured in the late 1980s, it appeared that most participants then in their forties and younger will not likely get as much social security as they put into it. Of course, this situation is always subject to change by Congress. But until changes are made, it might be foolhardy for people in the younger generations to even think of relying on social security as more than a token portion of their overall retirement income. And, as pointed out previously, Congress has already begun to tax social security benefits—a trend that could increase as years go by.

Do-it-yourself retirement planning is made possible by a variety of plans that offer attractive advantages to those who participate: the Individual Retirement Account (IRA) plan, the 401(k) plan, the SEP plan, and the Keogh plan. The latter plan is for the self-employed.

Individual retirement accounts

The IRA plan is the most common. Here's how it works, particularly as it has been affected by the Tax Reform Act of 1986. In order to be eligible for an IRA, you must have income from employment. Income from investments or pensions does not qualify. If you have less than $2000 income from work in a given year, the amount you can put into an IRA investment is equal to the amount of income you had from work. In other words, if you earn $1500 from work in a given year, you are eligible to invest as much as $1500 that year in an IRA. If your income from work is more than $2000 in a given year, the most you can put into an IRA for that year is $2000. (If you have a nonworking spouse, you can invest up to $2250 in an IRA covering both parties.) If both spouses in a family have more than $2000 income from work each in a given year, they can invest up to $4000 each year in their IRAs. You can put in less than these amounts if you wish. Or you can put in nothing in a given year if you wish. There's no minimum requirement, only a maximum limitation.

There are two major income tax advantages to IRA plans. The first advantage is that your earnings in your IRA plan are tax-deferred: You don't pay income taxes on your IRA earnings until such time as you cash in your plan and spend the money for your own purposes. This means that every dollar your IRA earns goes back to work for you. None of it goes to pay taxes. This tax-deferred feature applies to *all* IRA accounts, old and new, both before and after the passage of the Tax Reform Act of 1986.

The second major advantage to the IRA plan is limited to certain individuals. Prior to the Tax Reform Act of 1986, the amount invested in an IRA each year was tax deductible. For example, you as a married taxpayer filed a joint return.

Your income was $30,000. This put you in the 28 percent tax bracket. You invested $2000 in an IRA, and the amount of your income subject to income taxes was reduced by $2000. In other words, you were taxed on $28,000 instead of $30,000. In the 28 percent bracket, this meant an immediate tax savings to you of $560 for that year. The attractiveness of this advantage was clear. Prior to the Tax Reform Act of 1986, this advantage was available to all workers. But as a result of the Act, this advantage is now limited to certain people.

If you are *not* covered by a retirement or profit-sharing plan at work, you can still claim the deduction for your IRA investment each year. But if you are covered by such a plan at work, your right to claim the annual deduction is determined by how much you and your spouse earn. If either you or your spouse are covered by a retirement or profit-sharing plan at work, you can still claim the *full* deduction for your annual IRA investment if your joint adjusted gross income (before the IRA deduction) is *under* $40,000. If, under the same circumstances, your joint adjusted gross income is more than $50,000, neither you nor your spouse can deduct the IRA investment. If your adjusted gross income falls between $40,000 and $50,000, the amount of the deduction is reduced. For people filing single returns, the lower and upper limits for adjusted gross income are $25,000 and $35,000, respectively. Table 20-7 illustrates the amount of deduction available if your income falls *between* these limits.

For example, you have a profit-sharing plan at work. If you file a single return, and your adjusted gross income is $29,000, you can claim an IRA deduction of 60 percent of the amount of your investment for the year. In other words, if you invest $1000, you can claim a deduction of $600. If you invest $2000, you can claim a deduction of $1200. Let's say that you file a joint return, and you and your spouse's adjusted gross income is $47,000. You can claim an IRA deduction of 30 percent

Table 20-7 **IRA Deductions**

File single return (adjusted gross income)	File joint return (adjusted gross income)	Deduction limit (% of IRA investment)
$25,000	$40,000	100%
26,000	41,000	90
27,000	42,000	80
28,000	43,000	70
29,000	44,000	60
30,000	45,000	50
31,000	46,000	40
32,000	47,000	30
33,000	48,000	20
34,000	49,000	10
35,000	50,000	–0–

of the amount you invest. If you invest $1000, you can claim a deduction of $300. If you invest $2000, you can claim a $600 deduction.

If you find that you can take all or most of the annual deduction for your IRA investment, it's generally wise to put as much away in an IRA plan as you can comfortably afford. If you're not eligible for the annual deduction, you'll have to decide whether the IRA plan is beneficial to you over the long pull. Without the annual deduction, your only benefit is the tax-deferred income. But your money will be tied up for many years in order to earn the tax-deferred income. You should carefully analyze your situation each year. Also, unless or until the law changes, under current conditions an individual might be eligible for the deduction one year and ineligible the next. It can change from year to year as your marital status changes, as your income changes, and as the law itself might change.

The law states that if you withdraw your IRA money before you reach age 59½, you must pay a penalty to the government equal to 10 percent of the amount withdrawn. In addition, you'll have to pay whatever income taxes are due on that withdrawn money. (You might also have to pay a penalty to the bank or mutual fund where your money was invested if, in fact, they have a penalty clause restricting how much you can withdraw and when.) The law also requires that you begin withdrawing money from your IRA plan after you have reached the age of 70½. The Internal Revenue Service publishes detailed documents explaining exactly how these withdrawals work. The Tax Reform Act of 1986 offers one possible advantage: It can make it possible to avoid the 10 percent penalty payable to the government if you take out IRA money before you reach age 59½. To avoid the penalty you must arrange with your bank or broker or mutual fund to pay you the funds on an annuity basis, that is, equal monthly payments (or other equal periodic payments) over your lifetime. This can allow persons under 59½ to have penalty-free access to their IRA money, although it should be noted that the income taxes will still be payable on any such money withdrawn.

401(k) plans

401(k) plans are available only to employees of companies that offer the plans. (The name of the plan is derived from the section of the tax law that created the plan.) If you participate in a 401(k) plan, a certain portion of your wages is placed in an investment program offered by the employer. These wages are not taxable to you until you later withdraw the funds. The earnings are also tax-deferred. You generally have a choice of investment programs. Common choices include a guaranteed-income plan, similar to a savings program; a mutual fund plan that invests in a variety of stocks; and a plan that invests in the stock of your company. It's generally possible to mix and match among the different plans, and you can usually change your mix at certain intervals. It's also common that your company will chip in a certain amount of its money for your benefit. For example, for every dollar that you put in of your own, the company might put in another 25¢ or 50¢. Under the Tax Reform Act of 1986, the amount you can put into a 401(k) plan is limited to $7000 per year. Your employer can contribute over and above this amount to your account, subject to the limits of the law. The maximum employee investment can be increased in later years as inflation increases.

Withdrawals from a 401(k) plan are similar to, but slightly more liberal than, the withdrawal restrictions on IRA plans. It might also be possible to get your funds out at an early age in the event of death, disability, or financial hardship. Withdrawals from 401(k) plans are controlled both by the employer's plan and by tax regulations.

A 401(k) plan can be very advantageous, particularly if the employer is contributing money on your behalf over and above what you are putting in.

SEP plans

A relatively uncommon form of do-it-yourself retirement program is the Simplified Employee Pension (SEP). This concept was designed for small companies that did not want to endure the trouble of all of the paper work involved in a major pension or profit-sharing plan. SEPs operate similarly to IRAs. The employer can make contributions to IRAs that the workers maintain on their own. And workers can also make their own contributions. Employers who don't have pension plans might be interested in setting up this type of pension plan. Both the employer and the employees can benefit.

Keogh plans

Keogh plans are available to self-employed individuals. The maximum amount of an annual Keogh investment is $30,000 or 25 percent of income from work, whichever is less. For example, a self-employed individual earns $80,000 in a year. The maximum Keogh investment allowed this person is 25 percent of $80,000, or $20,000. Another self-employed individual who earns $200,000 in one year is only allowed to put in a maximum Keogh investment of $30,000 for that year. Keogh investments are tax deductible to the participant. If self-employed individuals have employees, they must make contributions on behalf of certain of those employees. Earnings on Keogh plans are tax-deferred. Withdrawals from Keogh plans are similar to those of IRAs: There's a penalty for withdrawals made before age 59½, and a withdrawal program must begin by age 70½. Keogh plans do have further complexities involving the types of plans that can be set up and how much can be contributed to each one. It's advisable for individuals contemplating a Keogh plan to get professional assistance from their own tax advisor or from the institution in which they're opening the plan.

Setting up your plan

IRAs, Keoghs, and SEPs can be set up relatively simply at banks, savings institutions, stockbrokerage firms, mutual fund companies, and insurance companies. The Keogh plan will require more paper work than the IRA. An IRA or Keogh participant should shop around to determine what types of plans are available. IRA and Keogh investments are for retirement purposes and should not be a subject of speculation. Stockbrokerage firms offer IRA and Keogh plans that can be self-directed by the participants. That is, you can instruct the broker as to how your money is to be put to work. But be aware that if undue risk is taken, it can have a hazardous effect on your retirement nest egg.

Note that you do not have to keep your IRA or Keogh investments with the same institution forever. The law allows you to move it from one place to another periodically without penalty. Check current regulations to determine how this can be done. If you do wish to relocate your IRA or Keogh investment, be well aware that it can take the bank or brokerage firm many weeks to accomplish all of the necessary paper work. Thus, plan well in advance to give them notice that you plan to do this so that the paper work will be ready. Also, if you do actually relocate your funds, be certain to keep copies of every document connected with the transfer. In the event the Internal Revenue Service ever asks what happened to your IRA money, you can prove that you simply transferred it to a different institution and did not withdraw it.

Strategies for Success

Do Early Estimates of Tax Impact on Pensions?

If you or your parents are within range of retirement, you should start as far in advance as possible to estimate the impact that taxes can have on your pension. It might be easy to calculate your retirement benefits—social security, pension, profit sharing, IRA, etc.—in the *gross* amount. But it's the *net* amount, the amount *after* taxes, that's important. If you set up a retirement budget based on the gross amount, you're in for some unhappy surprises after the tax collectors have done their job. Indeed, tax matters regarding retirement income can be so complex that a session or two with a tax counselor is advisable. The sooner you do it, the quicker you can build a realistic retirement budget.

Pensions and Taxes.　When you receive your pension, all or a portion of the money could be subject to income taxes. The portion that your employer contributed on your behalf will likely be taxable. Any sums which you contributed on your own will likely have already been taxed in the year in which you earned the money and thus won't be taxable when you receive it in your pension check. It would be nice to think that upon retirement tax matters became easier, but the complexities of taxation on pensions is something that regrettably must be dealt with by all.

You may be given the choice of receiving pension or profit-sharing benefits in (1) a lump sum, or (2) a long-term program of monthly payments. This choice can be made at retirement time or, in many cases, when workers are still young, particularly when a profit-sharing program is disbursed to the workers.

If you are given such a choice, some very careful arithmetic is required—perhaps with the help of an accountant—to determine what is the best long-term program for you. How you handle such a decision can mean the difference of many thousands of dollars either in your pocket or in the tax collector's pocket.

The first choice that has to be made is between the lump-sum payment and the monthly plan. Choosing the lump-sum pay-out means you will get all that you're entitled to in one check. The monthly pay-out plans can take a variety of forms: You might receive one fixed amount per month for as long as you live, and upon your death payments stop. Or you could opt for one of a variety of plans that provide you with a lesser amount per month, with continuing benefits payable to your survivors after your death. Your choice should be based on your individual needs. Here is an example of the type of arithmetic you can do to help determine the best choice.

Let's assume that you are given a choice between a $50,000 lump-sum payment or $400 per month until your death, after which payments cease. If you chose the lump-sum payment, and if you invest the $50,000 at an 8 percent annual rate of return, you would receive an income of $333 per month (before income taxes). And you would always have the $50,000 nest egg available to you should you ever need it. On the other hand, should you choose the $400 per month (again, before income taxes), you will indeed be receiving a slightly higher monthly income, but there is nothing at all left after your death. Also, while you're still alive, there is no nest egg into which you can dip, should the need arise. Based on this example, which is reasonably typical of the type of choices people have, you might find that if you are ready, willing, and able to handle the investment of your own money, you could do better over the long run by choosing the lump-sum payment instead of the monthly payments. Get professional assistance before you do make the choice.

If you do choose the lump-sum payment, there are two possible devices that can minimize or delay the income taxes payable on that lump sum: the *IRA rollover account* and the *forward averaging device*. The first option works as follows: If you receive a lump-sum payment from a pension or profit-sharing plan, you can, within sixty days of receipt of the money, reinvest the money in an account designated as your IRA rollover account. By so doing, you postpone the payment of income taxes on the lump sum until you withdraw the money to spend for your own purposes. Furthermore, by putting the money into an IRA rollover account, investment earnings are tax-deferred until you withdraw them. The IRA rollover account is generally preferred by people who do not need the funds for current spending purposes. The second option, the forward averaging device, is generally preferred by individuals who do need the money to spend currently. By using the forward averaging formula, you pay your income taxes on the lump sum that you have received in the year in which you receive it, but at a much lower rate than normal income taxes would dictate. The forward averaging reduces your tax by calculating the tax as if you had received the lump-sum payment over a five-year span. (There is an exception to this rule: If you were at least fifty years of age on January 1, 1986, you can choose between a ten-year averaging formula using 1986 tax rates or the five-year averaging formula using the tax rates in effect during the year in which you get your lump-sum distribution.) You must meet current IRS eligibility formulas in order to claim the forward averaging device.

One Final Caution.   The laws referred to in this chapter can be of great assistance to people who are covered by pension and profit-sharing plans at work. But half of the U.S. work force—fifty to sixty million individuals—are not covered by any kind of pension or profit-sharing plan. They must depend on their own sense of discipline to put away money for their own future. The government is not there to help them; and there is no employer or union that's putting money away for them. They are on their own, and, as noted earlier, if they are in the younger generations, they should not expect to live on social security. They should take advantage of the IRA concept as much as possible, as well as any other new do-it-yourself programs that may be created by Congress. For the sake of those who are not covered by an employer or union pension plan, recall the admonition stated earlier in this chapter: No company, no government, no union can take better care of your future than you yourself can. If you don't take care of yourself, no one else will do it for you.

Estimating Retirement Costs

Even though retirement may be a long way off for you, this exercise can help you envision changes in your financial situation once your working career has ceased. Assume you'll be retiring within the next few years. Estimate the changes in your income and expenses once you're retired. This will help you shape a workable budget for your retirement—something most people don't do until it's too late.

Item	Now	Then
☐ After-tax income from work	_____	_____
☐ After-tax income from investments	_____	_____
☐ Social security income	_____	_____
☐ Pension, profit-sharing, IRA, or Keogh income (assume lump sum is invested at 10 percent annual income, and you're taking out only the income)	_____	_____
☐ Lump sum from any of the above, on hand for whenever you need it	_____	_____
☐ Housing expenses, assuming you stay where you are	_____	_____
☐ Housing expenses, assuming you move to smaller quarters	_____	_____
☐ Extra income resulting from net gain on sale of home, after setting aside any down payment needed for purchase of new home	_____	_____
☐ Transportation expenses (consider particularly that the "going-to-work" car may no longer be needed or will be used much less)	_____	_____
☐ Clothing expenses	_____	_____
☐ Food, both at home and out, considering work lunches	_____	_____
☐ Entertainment	_____	_____
☐ Insurance premiums (life, health, disability; retirement and Medicare often change one's insurance program considerably)	_____	_____

Excerpts from a Survey of Recent Retirees

"When I was thirty my employer told me that my pension plan would provide $511 per month at age sixty-five. That plus my social security seemed enough to meet all my needs and allow my wife and me to have a leisurely and comfortable life at retirement. I left it at that and didn't make any other plans. We spent what we earned and lived well.

"Then came the blow. I was made to retire at age sixty-two at a $405 per-month pension benefit. And times have changed! Not only am I getting more than $100 less than I expected, but the money I am getting doesn't go very far at all. If I had my life to live over again, I'd have anticipated this possibility and would have salted away some of my earnings in an investment program."

_____

"I retired from my dental practice ten years ago, at age sixty-two. We had no children, and quite honestly I never became involved in any hobbies or activities. Now I'm paying the price. . . . The worst part of retirement is too much time on your hands. Retirees should have hobbies or sports interests consistent with their health. The worst habit is getting bored and turning to the bottle."

_____

"Think young and resolve to be independent as long as you're able. Neither your children nor any organization owes you anything. If you think you've reached the age where now someone will take care of you, you're sadly mistaken. If you haven't long ago accepted the fact that only you are responsible for your future, then you're in for a rude awakening."

_____

"Don't expect to be missed for long by former business associates and do not visit them unless invited. You should be realistic and accept the loss of clout gracefully."

_____

"The best advice is for the couple to get as mentally close together as when they were first married and to remember that they cannot enjoy leisure without doing some work, nor can they enjoy pleasure without having some pain."

CHAPTER 21

Estate Planning

One of the most important—and most overlooked—aspects of personal financial concern is estate planning. It's important because it goes right to the heart of your financial structure while you are living, as well as upon your death. And it's overlooked because people don't like to think about their own mortality, let alone make plans regarding it. Further, when people do investigate estate planning for their own purposes, they are often mystified and put off by the strange language and concepts that prevail in the field.

This chapter examines the jargon and the tools used in the field of estate planning and the many considerations that must be taken into account in establishing a sound and sensible estate plan. One of the most commonly used devices in estate planning is the *last will and testament*, commonly called a *will*. (To minimize confusion between the word *will* used in this sense and other uses of the word, such as "I *will* follow my lawyer's advice," it is typeset WILL throughout this chapter when meant in the former sense.)

- What a WILL is and how it works
- Who are the various parties involved in an overall estate-planning program and what their roles are
- Specific things that you can accomplish and the problems that you can avoid with a properly prepared estate plan
- The ramifications of the federal estate tax and how best to deal with the tax
- How you can, and should, utilize professional help in the creation of a sound estate plan

UNEXPECTED PROBLEMS

Barlow was thirty-seven years old, in good health, and financially self-sufficient. All was well with him. Well, almost all.

Barlow's elderly widowed mother lived with him. She was in failing health but relatively happy that she could live out her remaining days in comfort, close to her son and three beloved grandchildren. But this arrangement deeply troubled Barlow's wife, who was otherwise devoted to her husband and children. The wife was extremely bitter about having the mother live with them. She felt that it was an intrusion on her privacy and a negative influence on the children. Perhaps most important, she felt that the money Barlow had to spend for his mother's care was money that could have been spent by the wife for her own benefit. Barlow and his wife fought frequently and angrily over this issue. The wife had often expressed her preference that, given the choice, she would have the mother sent to the dismal county home for the aged in order to get rid of the whole problem.

Every Saturday morning, Barlow would play three sets of tennis with his old childhood friend, Murray. Murray was decidedly overweight, and Barlow constantly chided him that their Saturday morning exercise was the only thing that was keeping the obese Murray from an early grave. On one Saturday, with Barlow leading three games to one in the second set, Murray raced to the baseline to return a high lob. In midstep, he suddenly clutched at his chest, emitted a loud moan, and fell to the ground. He was declared dead on arrival at the emergency room, a victim of cardiac arrest.

It was weeks before Barlow recovered from the shock of his close friend's death. But one of the first things he was prompted to do when order returned to his life was to ask his lawyer one simple question: "Do I need a WILL?"

"Not necessarily," the lawyer responded.

"But I thought everyone should have a WILL," Barlow said perplexedly.

"If someone dies without a WILL," the lawyer responded, "the state in which he lives will determine how his wealth and property are to be distributed. This is what's known as the law of *intestacy*."

"What would happen to my wealth and property if *I* died without a WILL?" Barlow asked.

"Under the laws of our state—and each state has its own separate laws on this matter—your wife and children would split whatever there was. Your mother would get nothing," the lawyer noted.

Barlow felt a cold chill go through his body. Under these circumstances, he felt certain that his wife would immediately deliver his mother to the county home for the aged and that the wife would likely embark on a spending spree that could quickly erode the funds he had set aside for his children's college education.

Barlow expressed these fears to his lawyer, who in turn suggested that Barlow quickly embark upon an estate plan.

"Let us begin," said Barlow. "I had thought that such matters were best left to the later years. But I have learned now, the hard way, that it's time to do what's right."

This chapter is intended to acquaint you with the rudiments of estate planning. *It is not by any means a guide to preparing one's own estate plan.* But with the understanding that can be obtained by reading this material, you will be capable of discussing your own personal estate planning matters with your lawyer, who is the properly qualified party for tending to the problems of estate planning.

THE ESTATE

While people are living, their *estate* refers to all that they own, less all of their debts. When they die, their estates become legal entities in their own right. When John Doe dies, the "estate of John Doe" comes into existence. This estate becomes the legal machinery that pays the estate taxes, distributes the property and money, and carries out all other legal wishes of the decedent.

If the decedent has executed the proper legal documents, most commonly a WILL, the activities of the estate will be carried out by the *executor* (or executrix), a person or an institution named by the decedent to carry out these functions. If the person has died without a WILL, the state in which the individual resides at the time of death will name an administrator (or administratrix), who will be responsible for carrying out the laws of intestacy of that state as they apply to the individual's estate.

What Is Estate Planning?

Estate planning, simply stated, is the development of a program that will insure that any individual's last wishes are carried out regarding the estate. We have two primary choices in distributing our estate. The first choice is to take steps on our own to insure that our wishes are *clearly stated*, that they will be *carried out*, and that they will receive the *full protection of the courts*. There are many devices to establish the desired program. The most common is the preparation of a WILL. Other devices include life insurance, gifts, trusts, and simply spending it all, leaving nothing behind.

The second choice is to do nothing, in which case the laws of the state of residency at the time of death will determine the distribution of any estate.

In order to make a sensible choice between the two alternatives, we really have to understand the effects of each choice. If we exercise the first choice and see that it's done properly, we can determine who will get what and who will attend to the fulfillment of our wishes. On the other hand, if we choose not to take steps on our own, we owe it to ourselves and our families to know what the state laws are regarding distribution of an estate when there has been no other legal distribution set forth by the individual.

Each state has its own laws concerning this, known as *laws of intestacy*. All state laws are somewhat similar, yet different. Individuals must determine what the state laws of intestacy are and how they might affect them.

Table 21-1 illustrates some examples of how the law of intestacy can work in different states.

Rights Involved in Estate Planning

Rooted deeply in our legal tradition and its English origins are the rights of individuals to determine what will happen to their accumulated wealth upon their death.

Table 21-1 **Who Gets What If You Die Without a Will (Intestate)?**

State	Situation A: *You're survived by spouse and children, but no parents*[a]	Situation B: *You're survived by spouse and parents, but no children*
1	Spouse gets ½; Children get ½.	Spouse gets all; Parents get nothing.
2	Spouse gets ⅓; Children get ⅔.	Spouse gets ½; Parents get ½.
3	Spouse gets first $50,000, plus ½ of any balance; Children get remainder.	Spouse gets first $50,000, plus ½ of any balance; Parents get remainder.
Your state	???	???

[a]Further differences exist under differing survival conditions: for example, if no spouse survives and only parents survive, and so forth.

Our freedom is not total in this respect, but it is precious enough to take the fullest possible advantage of. Over the years, certain limitations have been placed on the overall freedom to distribute our accumulated wealth as we wish. For example, it was long ago determined that the federal government and some state governments would have a right to a certain share of our wealth. When the estate itself, as a legal entity, is required to pay taxes, these taxes are known as *estate taxes*. The federal government levies estate taxes—though the Tax Reform Law of 1981 has eliminated the federal estate taxation from all but a very small percentage of estates. Further, many states levy estate taxes. In some states, those who *inherit* may become liable to pay taxes to the state. These are known as *inheritance taxes*.

Our wishes may be limited because they are contrary to public policy. For example, a court may not carry out the wishes of a deceased person who leaves money to an individual on the condition that the individual marry or divorce a certain person or change religions or do or refrain from doing other things that society at large would deem improper or immoral.

Another form of limitation exists regarding surviving spouses. Laws differ from state to state in this respect, but, generally speaking, a surviving spouse has a right to at least a certain minimum portion of the deceased spouse's estate. If, for example, the laws of a specific state proclaim that a surviving spouse is entitled to at least one-third of the deceased spouse's estate, and the deceased spouse has expressed in his WILL that his widow will receive only 25 percent of the estate, the surviving widow has a "right of election against the WILL." In effect, she can disclaim that portion of the WILL that gives her only 25 percent, and, if everything else has been done in proper legal fashion, the spouse will then be entitled to the minimum allowed by the state, or one-third.

The overriding limitation on our freedom to distribute our wealth as we wish is that we must do so in accordance with the law. If we want the full protection of the courts, we have to play the game by the established rules.

The most obvious purpose of an estate plan is to determine who will get our money and property after our death. But there are other important purposes. In addition to distributing property, the legal documents of the estate plan can establish who will be responsible for carrying out the wishes of the deceased. If the individual has not named a party to do so, the courts will appoint one.

The proper use of an estate plan can minimize taxes; it can name guardians of orphaned children or other individuals previously under the guardianship of the deceased; and it can set forth specific instructions, such as funeral and burial procedures.

Deceased individuals will never know the difference once dead, but they can live with a greater degree of peace of mind knowing that these wishes will be carried out because of a proper estate plan.

Language of Estate Planning

The language of estate planning contains many strange words and phrases. Some people call it legal "mumbo jumbo." Lawyers bandy these strange words about freely, not knowing whether their clients understand the meanings. To better understand the concepts of estate planning and to better prepare yourself to work with your own lawyer on your own plan, it's necessary that you grasp the meanings of the most common bits of jargon. Some of the more important terms used in estate planning are defined below.

Testator/Testatrix.   The testator/testatrix is the person who makes out a WILL. When you ask your attorney to prepare your WILL for you, you are regarded as the testator or testatrix.

Decedent.   A decedent is a person who has died. The testator eventually becomes the decedent.

Beneficiary.   A beneficiary is one who receives an inheritance in the estate of a decedent. For example, your WILL may say, "I leave my summer cottage to my sister Melba." Melba is thus a beneficiary of a portion of your estate, namely, your summer cottage. But what if Melba should die before you? In your WILL, or in other estate documents, you can name a contingent beneficiary. A *contingent beneficiary* is one who takes the place of a named beneficiary who has already died. For example, "My summer cottage shall go to my sister Melba, and if she dies before I do, it shall go to my other sister, Lucy." In this case, Melba is your beneficiary, and Lucy becomes your contingent beneficiary in the event that Melba dies before you do. Had you not named a contingent beneficiary, the summer cottage may have passed through Melba's estate, to whomever she may have named to receive whatever she might have owned.

Bequest (Legacy). A bequest is the specific property or money given to a beneficiary. In the example above, the bequest consists of the summer cottage.

Life Estate. A life estate is a form of bequest with some strings attached. To create a life estate, the WILL might read, "My summer cottage shall go to my sister Melba for as long as she lives, and on her death it shall go to the Boy Scouts of America, Chapter 123." In other words, Melba has the use of the cottage for her life, but she has no right to pass it on to anyone else on her death; at that time it will go the local Boy Scout chapter. You have given her a life estate in the summer cottage, and you have further directed who shall get it after her death.

Executor/Executrix. An executor/executrix is a person (or an institution) one names in a WILL to handle the affairs of the estate. Generally, the executor will be granted broad powers to carry out the directions of the WILL. For example, the executor commonly will be given the power to buy and sell properties and securities and to do whatever else may be needed to carry out the wishes of the deceased as closely as possible. The executor may be entitled to receive a fee, but it is possible to arrange for an executor to serve without a fee. This will all depend on personal circumstances. The testator may request or require that the executor post a bond. This is a form of insurance that will protect the estate from financial harm at the hands of the executor.

The duties involved in executing the WILL can be considerable. In addition to following the specific wishes of the decedent, there may also be responsibilities of a more personal nature to the family members. In all likelihood, the executor will need the assistance of a lawyer and an accountant in fulfilling all the needs of the estate, which can include the payment of estate taxes and income taxes when the estate has earned income on investments or properties prior to the disbursement of the funds to the ultimate beneficiaries. If an executor is unable or unwilling to fulfill the duties, the court will generally appoint a successor.

Administrator/Administratrix. If an individual dies without a WILL, the court will appoint a person or an institution to handle the affairs of the estate. This person is called the administrator/administratrix. Duties are similar to those of an executor, and the question of fees and bonds will probably be determined by the court.

Probate. Probate is a court proceeding in which the validity of a WILL is established. The term *probate* comes from a Latin word meaning "to prove" or "to examine and find good." If the WILL is properly drawn and executed and no one challenges its terms, the court will direct that the terms of the WILL be carried out. If a challenge arises that can't be settled by the parties, the WILL is thus "contested," and additional court proceedings might be needed.

As with other matters relating to the distribution of an estate, the laws of probate can differ from state to state. Generally, the attorney for the estate, acting in conjunction with the executor, will request that the appropriate court commence the probate proceedings. All potential heirs will have been notified and will be given the opportunity to accept or challenge the WILL as written. Would-be heirs who wish to challenge an otherwise valid WILL will have to do so at their own expense, which can be considerable.

A challenge to a WILL, or a contest, can be a most bitter and costly struggle. Even the most carefully planned and painstakingly drawn estate plan cannot guarantee that an outside party will not challenge it. But the chances of an outside party succeeding in such a challenge will be drastically reduced by virtue of the professional expertise that has gone into creating the plan.

Probate procedures are constructed so that frivolous claims or challenges will be quickly dismissed. In order for a challenge to be successful, the challenging party must have fairly clear and convincing proof that all or part of a WILL was invalid or that the WILL being probated was not in fact the last WILL of the decedent.

THE WILL

A WILL is the most common form of device utilized in the formation of an estate plan. A simple WILL, which is adequate for most individuals, can be prepared quickly and inexpensively.

In a sense, a WILL is a form of contract: It is a legally binding document that sets forth certain rights and responsibilities of the parties and cannot be changed without the consent of at least the person who drew up the WILL. If testators have had their WILLS prepared in full compliance with the laws of their state, then, on their death, the executors have the responsibility for carrying out the stated wishes in the WILL, and the state courts are responsible for seeing to it that the rights of the survivors are given the full protection of the law. The major clauses of a WILL that set forth primary responsibilities and rights are as follows.

The Introductory Clause

The introductory clause is generally the opening clause of a WILL and should clearly and unmistakably state, "This is my last WILL and testament," or, "My WILL is as follows." It is essential that this clause establish that you are creating the WILL and that the document is in fact your WILL. If both you and the document are not clearly identified as to who and what they are, it's conceivable that another party might claim that this is not your actual WILL. For example, an individual might intend to create a WILL by writing a personal letter to his spouse, his children, or his attorney. He does not clearly identify the letter as being his purported WILL. In the letter he disinherits one of his children. After his death, the letter is introduced as being his actual WILL. The disinherited child, who would stand to gain considerably if there were no WILL (and the property passed through the laws of intestacy, which would assure each child a certain percentage of the estate) attacks the letter claiming that it is not in fact the true WILL of the deceased. The court will probably uphold the disinherited child, thus invalidating the purported WILL and requiring that the property pass through intestacy.

Revocation of Prior Wills

If an individual is creating a WILL and has previously made another WILL, she should, assuming these are her wishes, clearly revoke the entire prior WILL by stating so clearly in the new WILL. If she does not do this, it's possible that the prior WILL or at least portions thereof might be included in the probate with her new WILL. If there are two WILLS, the latter one will generally control, except to the extent that the specific provision of the two WILLS are consistent with each other. But even this can cause unnecessary complications, which can be avoided by a clear revocation of the former WILL.

For example, a testator prepares a WILL in which she leaves a bequest of $10,000 to each of her grandchildren. At the time she drew the WILL she had two grandchildren. Many years later, she draws another WILL, but does not clearly revoke the earlier WILL. The new WILL contains the same clause giving $10,000 to each of her grandchildren. But now she has eight grandchildren, which means a total bequest to them all of $80,000. This is now a very substantial portion of her total estate. The question may well arise as to whether only the original two grandchildren were entitled to the $10,000 bequest or whether all eight are entitled to it. If all eight are entitled to it, other heirs might receive much less. The actual wording of the old WILL and the new WILL, perhaps with the assistance of the court in interpreting the clauses, will ultimately determine who gets what. But the example illustrates how confusion and disagreement can result when there are two WILLS that may convey the same intentions, but each with a substantially different effect on the overall estate.

Debts and Final Expenses

Before your survivors can receive their share of your estate, the remaining debts, funeral expenses, and taxes must be paid. Commonly, a testator will include a clause in his WILL instructing the executor to make all these appropriate payments. But even if there is no such clause, the executor will still be required to make them.

Each individual state law sets forth the *priority* of who gets what and in what order. If your state laws require that a "widow's allowance" be paid, this generally is the item of first priority. This is not the widow's ultimate share of the estate but is usually a minimum allowance to enable her to get by for at least a short time. After the widow's allowance, the priorities generally run as follows: funeral expenses; expenses of a final illness; estate and other taxes due to the United States; state taxes; taxes of other political subdivisions within the state, such as cities and counties; other debts owed by the decedent.

Creditors of the estate must generally file a claim against the estate if they wish to be paid. The executor may determine, or the testator may have instructed the executor accordingly, that certain claims are not valid. A testator cannot invalidate legitimate claims against her estate by simply stating in the WILL that those claims are not valid. However, if claims are in fact invalid or even questionable, the executor's powers might result in eliminating such claims or minimizing them, particularly if the creditor does not wish to press the matter with the executor and the courts.

If, after all debts, taxes, funeral costs, and final illness expenses are paid, there is enough left in the estate to make payments to the survivors, such payments are then made in accordance with the legacy clauses, which are discussed next. If, however, these debts and expenses consume all that there is in the estate, the survivors may receive nothing. In such a case, the estate is considered to be *insolvent.*

Legacy or Bequest Clauses

Legacy (bequest) clauses determine which of your survivors gets how much. Broadly speaking, there are four ways in which property can pass on death to the survivors: through joint ownership with right of survivorship; through a specific bequest; through a general bequest; and through the residuary. If property is owned in joint names—such as a home or a savings account—the property will pass to the survivor of the two joint owners on death, assuming that the ownership had been structured in that form. The WILL need not necessarily specify such matters, but it would probably be advantageous to make note of these items in the WILL to avoid possible misunderstanding.

A specific bequest or legacy will refer to a particular item or security. For example, a testator may bequeath to a child ''my stamp collection which is located in safe-deposit box 1234 at the Fifth National Bank.'' The collection will pass to the survivor on the death of the testator, assuming that the testator still owns it at the time of death. If he no longer owns it, then obviously it cannot pass, and the gift will dissolve. The heir will receive nothing in its place unless the testator has specifically instructed the substitution of other items of value, or money, should he no longer own the collection. Further, if the subject of a specific bequest is not free and clear—if it has been pledged, for example, as collateral for a loan—the heir will receive that property subject to the debt against it and will be responsible for paying off the debt unless the testator has instructed that the heir is to receive it free and clear. For example, the stamp collection may have been pledged as collateral for a loan. The collection is worth $10,000, and the balance on the loan is $2000. If the testator has not stated that the heir is to receive it free and clear, the heir can be responsible for paying the $2000 owed. If the testator has instructed that the heir should receive it free and clear, however, the $2000 debt will be paid out of other estate resources.

General legacies are those payable out of the general assets of the estate. Commonly, general legacies are in the form of cash, such as ''I bequeath to my housekeeper, Marsha Margolis, the sum of $3000.''

After all property has passed through either joint ownership, specific legacies, or general legacies, everything that's left is called the *residual.* Commonly, this will represent the bulk of many estates. A typical residual clause might read as follows: ''All the rest, remainder, and residual of my estate I hereby bequeath to my wife and children, to be divided equally among them.'' There may be further detailed instructions concerning the manner and timing of such distributions, including the possibility of trusts that would parcel out the payments over a specific period of time.

In planning a WILL program, it's essential that the testator and attorney discuss all these various provisions for distribution in detail. Further, as individual circumstances change over the years, these clauses should be reviewed to determine that the bequests are still what the testator wishes; and if the subjects of specific bequests are no longer owned by the testator, provisions should be made as desired for the proper substitution.

Other elements of who gets what—and who doesn't—may include clauses of disinheritance; clauses that set forth a preference among various heirs; gifts to charitable causes; and clauses that release individuals from debts owed to the decedent.

Survivorship Clauses

Though rare, it can happen that a husband and wife will be killed in a common disaster, such as an automobile accident or an airplane crash. Each of their WILLS should have been created with this possibility in mind, particularly if there are minor children. The couple will want to determine who will be the guardians of the children in the event of such a disaster. If estate taxes are of concern to the couple, a survivorship clause should also set forth the sequence of the deaths (who is to have been presumed to have died first) in such a way as to minimize the effect of estate taxes.

Appointment Clauses

In this clause the testator will appoint the person or institution who will be the executor of the estate. Where personal circumstances dictate, a testator may also want to name an attorney for the estate to act in conjunction with the executor.

If other individuals—such as minor children or elderly parents—are dependent on the testator, the testator should also name the guardian for such individuals. This guardian will have the duties, responsibilities, and fee, if any, that are specified in this appointment clause.

It's common for one spouse to name the other spouse as executor (or executrix). The testator wants to know that someone who is deeply concerned with the welfare of the survivors will be in charge of carrying out the duties of the executor. It should be noted, however, that the duties of the executor can be rigorous and demanding; the more complicated the estate, the more exacting the duties. A surviving spouse may not be equipped to handle many of the duties; thus, many prudent individuals will name an institution, such as a trust department of a bank, as a co-executor. The institution is fully staffed and capable of carrying out the specific legal and accounting responsibilities of the executorship. In cases of substantial estates, such a co-executor should prove to be well worth the fees. The testator, in naming this co-executor, has the added peace of mind of knowing that the burden on the surviving spouse will be minimized; the personal concern will remain, with the added expertise of the financial institution.

The Execution

The final clauses of a WILL are very important. They are called the *testimonium clause* and the *attestation clause*. The testimonium clause contains language in which testators express that they are signing the documents as their true last WILL and testament, as of the specific date on which the documents are executed. The attestation clause contains language in which the witnesses to the WILL agree that they have witnessed the signing of the WILL in one another's presence and in the presence of the testator on the specific date.

The combination of these two clauses should serve as ample proof that the document is in fact the last WILL and testament of the testator, that the document has been properly signed, and that the witnesses can verify all of this.

The execution of a WILL is a ritual that should follow the letter of the law. Each state's law determines how many witnesses should attest to the signing of the WILL by the testator. It is generally imprudent for any individual who may receive a share of the estate—either as a family member or as a recipient of a specific or general bequest—to act as a witness at the signing of the WILL.

In addition to the signing and witnessing at the end of the WILL, the attorney may have the testator and each witness sign or initial each separate page of the WILL. This may help serve as added proof that the WILL that is finally presented for probate is the true and complete total WILL of the testator.

Until the WILL is finally signed and witnessed, it is not in fact valid. Any attempt to cut short the execution procedure might open the doors to anyone with thoughts of contesting the WILL if this person can prove that the WILL was not properly signed or witnessed by the appropriate parties.

Changing a Will

Prudent individuals should review their WILLS and overall estate plans at least every three years. Depending on the extent of change in the testators' circumstances, revisions may or may not be called for. Following are the common circumstances that might dictate the need to amend a WILL or any other portion of an estate plan:

☐ If you move to a different state, your WILL should be reviewed. Remember that the law of WILLS and estate distribution are state laws, and there can be slight or significant differences from one state to another. A change in state residence could therefore have a slight or significant impact on an estate plan. You won't know until you've had your plan reviewed by an attorney in your new state of residence.

☐ Changes in your family circumstances might dictate the need to alter a WILL. Children may have grown up and moved out on their own. If one child has been particularly affluent and another has suffered economically, you might want to make provision to assist the less fortunate child. You may wish to add or delete charitable contributions, to amend your funeral and burial instructions, or to add or delete specific bequests that you have made to individuals. There is a myriad of other possibilities. Testators must see to it that changes are covered in the proper legal fashion.

☐ If there have been substantial changes in your assets and liabilities, a review of your WILL might indicate that changes are in order. If you have acquired substantially greater wealth since the original drawing of the WILL, this may dictate different modes of distribution to your heirs. If your estate has been diminished by financial reversals, appropriate changes might also be in order.

☐ If heirs named in your WILL have died before you, you might want to review the effect that would have on the distribution of your estate.

☐ If an executor or guardian named in the WILL has died or has become incapable of acting in the desired capacity, or if you simply no longer wish to have that person representing your interests, an amendment to your WILL would be in order.

☐ If tax laws change regarding estates, a review of your WILL would most certainly be in order. The changes wrought by the Tax Reform Laws of 1976 and 1981 have a sweeping effect on millions of estate plans already in existence. Virtually all estate plans and WILLs prepared prior to the effective date of these tax laws should be at least reviewed by an attorney, and changes should be made where called for.

A WILL can be legally changed in one of two ways: It can be totally revoked by a brand-new WILL, in which case the brand-new WILL should expressly state that the former WILL is totally revoked, or minor changes can be effected by means of a brief document called a *codicil*.

A WILL *cannot* be legally amended by crossing out or adding words, by removing or adding pages, or by making erasures. A codicil should be drawn by an attorney and should be executed and witnessed in the same fashion as the original WILL. The codicil should then be attached to the WILL. If a WILL is amended in any way other than the creation of a new WILL or the creation of a properly executed codicil, it's all that much easier for anyone who wishes to contest the WILL to be successful. Further, a court might not admit to probate a WILL that has been changed by hand. Such improper changes could conceivably invalidate the entire WILL and could render the estate subject to the laws of intestacy. In short, testators should not destroy all that they have created in the estate plan by making changes unless they are made in the proper, legally prescribed fashion.

Once a WILL has been drawn and executed, it's common for the attorney to keep the original in a safe or a fireproof file. You should keep a copy or two for your own reference, and if you've named a bank or other institution as executor or co-executor, the proper people there should also receive a copy for their files.

Uncommon Wills

Occasionally a court will receive for probate a WILL that has been prepared by the testator in his own handwriting. It may or may not have the appropriate number of witnesses. A WILL that's prepared in the handwriting of the testator is called a *holographic WILL*. Some states permit the probate of holographic WILLS under certain circumstances, but such WILLS are definitely not substitutes for WILLS prepared under proper legal guidelines. The courts recognize that individuals may be in dire circumstances and unable to acquire the proper legal counsel to prepare a totally valid WILL. Thus, allowances are made for the occasional probate of a holographic WILL.

In more extreme cases, a WILL may be spoken by the dying individual to another party or parties. Such a WILL, oral or spoken, is referred to as a *noncupative WILL*. It's allowed only by some states and then only under strictly defined conditions.

Neither a holographic WILL nor a noncupative WILL should be relied on as a substitute for a properly prepared WILL. A court may find such a WILL invalid and could throw the entire estate into a situation of intestacy. Where at all possible, proper legal assistance should be sought in creating a WILL.

In addition to the common WILL, there are other means whereby one may pass wealth to heirs and other generations. A trust is a ''strings attached'' way of passing money or property to another party.

THE TRUST

For example, you have the sum of $10,000 that you would like eventually to pass to your son, who is now twenty-five years old. But you're concerned that he might run through that money imprudently. You thus decide that until he reaches the age of forty, he should be entitled only to the income that the $10,000 will generate through investments. When he reaches forty, he can have the entire amount. In order to accomplish this, you create a trust.

To be sure that your wishes are carried out without further concern on your part, you make an arrangement, for example, with your bank to administer the trust. The bank then becomes the *trustee*. You deposit the $10,000 with the bank, which then agrees to invest it prudently and pay out the income to your son until he reaches the age of forty, at which time he will be paid the full principal amount.

This example is an oversimplified view of the creation and function of a trust, but it's intended to make the point that passing money by trust is not an outright transfer. There are, as noted, strings attached. The trust agreement itself can stipulate just how much the beneficiary (your son) will get at what time and under what circumstances.

In the foregoing case, both parties involved in the trust are still living. This would be called an *inter vivos trust*, or a trust between the living. A trust can also be established in one's WILL to take effect upon death. Instead of property passing outright to the beneficiary of the WILL, it may go in trust. For example, you might leave $10,000 in your WILL in trust for your son until he reaches the age of forty, with the full amount payable to him on that date. Where a trust is established in one's WILL to take effect on death, it's referred to as a *testamentary trust*. A trust can be revocable or irrevocable. A *revocable trust* is one that can be revoked or canceled. An *irrevocable trust* may not be canceled; it is permanent.

Under certain circumstances, trust arrangements may be desirable in place of a WILL or may be used in conjunction with a WILL. There is no fixed rule—it all depends on individual circumstances.

The law of trusts is complicated. A great deal can be accomplished with trusts, both in the control of property and in the minimization of estate taxes. An attempt at a do-it-yourself trust might be even more foolhardy than a do-it-yourself WILL because of the added complexities of the trust laws.

The trustee is the person or firm having the duty of carrying out the directions of the trust. The trust document, which is a form of contract, spells out the trustee's powers and responsibilities. Many people prefer to use a financial institution as a trustee instead of an individual. Bank trust departments are operated by professionals, and there is an assurance of permanence. Such permanence has obvious advantages if a trust is designed to continue for many years. As with naming executors in a WILL, an individual might prefer to name both a corporate trustee (such as a bank) and a person close to the family as co-trustees.

GIFTS

Making gifts of money or property is another form or way of distributing one's estate. Gifts have long been popular with more wealthy individuals as a means of cutting down on their potential estate tax liability. By making gifts prior to death, money or property may escape taxation, wholly or partly. The overall desirability or feasibility of making gifts a part of an estate plan should be discussed in detail with professional advisors.

INSURANCE

For a great many families, life insurance is the predominant way of passing wealth from one generation to the next. Indeed, in families of lesser means, a life insurance program may be the only form of estate planning necessary. But it would be imprudent to rely on the existence of life insurance policies as a substitute for sound estate planning. Even the most modest estates should attempt a review with the proper professionals to determine what will occur on the death of each individual.

Insurance can pass money from one generation to another, but it may not assure that the parties who need the money most or who are most entitled to it will get what the testator wishes. For example, an individual may have little estate other than life insurance policies, and if her children are named as beneficiaries, her widower may not receive what he needs for his own survival. If the children aren't willing or able to help him, he could be in dire straits. On the other hand, the widower could be the sole beneficiary of the life insurance policies, and the children could thus be deprived of funds that their mother wished them to have. These matters should be discussed with a life insurance agent in conjunction with an attorney and accountant.

Strategies for Success

Be Aware of Life Insurance Settlement Options

It is commonly thought that when someone who has life insurance dies, the insurance company pays a lump sum of money to the beneficiary of the life insurance policy. This is generally the case, but it need not be. The owner of a life insurance policy can choose from a number of options—called *settlement options*—that determine how the life insurance money is distributed. One wise and simple estate planning strategy is to know what these options are and to use them when appropriate. For example, a husband might feel that his beneficiaries (wife and children) are not sufficiently able to handle the large sum of money that the insurance proceeds would be. So he might choose a settlement option wherein the insurance company would pay the money out over a period of time, including some interest, rather than in one lump sum. Do you know what options your policies offer?

JOINT NAMES

Putting property in joint names, such as husband and wife, often seems a simple and attractive way to insure that the surviving spouse will receive everything in the event of the other spouse's death. This may be true in many cases, but it can subject the total value of the estate to estate taxes that could have been avoided and may prevent the money from ultimately going where the couple had wished it to go. For families of more modest means, a joint-names program might suffice in many cases. It's not safe to make any assumptions about the ultimate distribution of an estate wherein everything is owned jointly. The advice of a competent attorney is still essential.

OTHER USES OF ESTATE PLANNING

At the beginning of this chapter, you were introduced to Barlow and his problems. Barlow followed his lawyer's advice and created an estate plan to pass his accumulated wealth and property to those he wished to have it. In addition to the distribution of wealth, Barlow also provided that his mother should remain in his home until it became no longer medically feasible for her to do so. He also established a trust program by which his wife and children would receive their inheritance over a period of years rather than in one lump sum. This arrangement, Barlow felt, would protect the interests of all concerned. Having thus created his estate plan, Barlow achieved a peace of mind that had eluded him for some time.

As Barlow's situation indicates, there are purposes of estate planning other than the distribution of one's accumulated wealth and property. An estate plan can be utilized to provide care for others, to manage money, to assure a continued life style for the survivors, and to minimize taxation.

If you go about planning your estate in the wrong way, you may fail to achieve what you want your estate plan to accomplish. Let's take a closer look using another example.

Strategies for Success

Beware of Do-It-Yourself Estate Planning

You want to save some money on legal fees, so you buy a book on how to write your own WILL, or you copy your cousin Elmer's WILL for your own, because you and he "tend to think alike," or you just buy some blank WILL forms at the local stationery store and fill in the blanks. Making your own WILL in such ways can be a *big* mistake. Estate planning is necessarily a complex matter. Shortcuts can mean that the wrong people can be cut short if you make a mistake in the do-it-yourself process. The proper estate plan, created by properly trained people, can help assure that the courts of your state will see to it that your wishes are carried out. If your do-it-yourself attempt isn't legally correct, chaos could result. You don't want that, do you?

THE WRONG WAY

Rita was a wealthy widow with two sons, Jeremy and Roger. Jeremy had taken over the family business and was dutiful, loyal, and devoted to his mother. Roger, on the other hand, had had a bitter argument with his mother many years before and had run off to Paris. He had been there ever since, earning his living as a jazz guitarist. Rita had long ago vowed that Roger would "never get a penny from me."

One reason for Rita's wealth was that she carefully watched every penny that she spent. Thus it was that when she was ready to create an estate plan, she shunned the expense of a lawyer. Rather, she went to a local stationery store where, for $2, she bought a blank WILL form and proceeded to fill it out herself, leaving her entire estate to Jeremy. The blank WILL indicated that there were to be two witnesses to Rita's signature. But since Rita didn't want anyone other than Jeremy to know of her WILL, she had only Jeremy sign as a witness.

When Rita died, Roger was shocked to learn that he had been disinherited by his mother. Roger asked his lawyer to look into the matter, and after doing so, the lawyer recommended that Roger contest the WILL. If the WILL could be proved invalid, then Rita's estate would be divided equally between Jeremy and Roger. The lawyer pointed out that there had been only one witness, whereas the state law requires two witnesses. Further, the only witness, Jeremy, was the heir to the entire estate, and this threw another cloud over the validity of the WILL.

Under such circumstances, Roger could have an excellent chance of having the WILL invalidated, thereby upsetting Rita's intent to disinherit him. By saving a small sum on legal fees, Rita allowed half of her wealth to go where she had not intended it to go.

THE RIGHT WAY

There is really only one proper way in which a desired estate plan should be implemented: with the aid of a capable lawyer. Any attempts—repeat, *any attempts*—at do-it-yourself estate planning can be fraught with danger. Last wishes may not be carried out as expressed; taxes may have to be paid when they could have been avoided; and survivors could be left in a variety of predicaments that could have been avoided.

Thus, a lawyer, particularly one specializing in estate matters, is *the best* qualified party to tend to the problems of estate planning. The lawyer may see fit to call in other professionals—bankers, insurance agents, accountants—as the need arises.

The first necessary step in the creation of an estate plan is a visit with the chosen lawyer. During this initial meeting, you should disclose all of your assets and liabilities and, most important, your estate-planning objectives. The lawyer will then be able to determine what estate-planning documents might be best suited to achieving your stated objectives.

What Should an Estate Plan Accomplish?

Four main objectives should be kept in mind when creating or amending any estate plan.

1. To establish the proper liquidity and distribution of assets
2. To establish a program of sound management of assets

3. To provide for the assured continuation of a family's life style in the event of death, disability, or retirement

4. To minimize taxation. Three aspects of taxation must be taken into account: the federal gift and estate taxes that would come out of the overall estate assets; the taxes that the heirs may ultimately have to pay on inherited property; and, perhaps of slightly lesser concern, the income taxes that the estate may have to pay, if it has had earnings before the ultimate distribution of the assets to the heirs.

Let's now take a closer look at each objective.

Distribution and Liquidity. Distribution of one's assets and the liquidity of those assets go hand in hand. *Distribution* refers to "who gets what." Regardless of the size of your estate, you want to be certain that it will be distributed in the fashion you desire. *Liquidity* refers to the ability to put cash on the table as quickly as possible and with as little expense as possible. The more liquid one's assets, the easier it will be for everybody to get whatever it is they are to have. The most important reasons for having liquidity are to be able to provide for the immediate needs of one's survivors—spouse, children, and so on—and to be able to pay any estate taxes when they are due.

Mike's case illustrates the dangers in failing to make adequate provision for proper distribution and liquidity in one's estate.

Mike was a good provider, or so he had thought. Twenty years ago, when he was forty, Mike made some major changes in his life. He gave up his job as a plumber, and with a partner, Willy, he opened up a wholesale plumbing-supply firm. His only child, Maryanne, was soon to be married, so Mike and his wife, Sybil, decided to sell their home and buy an apartment house. They would live in one of the apartments. Mike also borrowed heavily to buy a large tract of vacant land fifteen miles outside the city. He was confident that the city would grow in that direction, and that in ten to fifteen years this land would be extremely valuable as a site for a shopping center and new housing.

All of these things accomplished, Mike took one further step. He visited a lawyer to have a WILL prepared. For reasons that Mike had long since forgotten, he left the land to his wife, Sybil; the apartment house to his daughter, Maryanne; and his interest in the plumbing-supply business to be divided equally between Sybil and Maryanne.

Twenty years later, the status of Mike's estate is as follows:

☐ Mike and Willy worked hard at their business and it prospered. Mike, with an easy and outgoing personality, was the "Mr. Outside" of the business. He took care of the sales, the customer relations, and the good will of the venture. Willy, on the other hand, was the "Mr. Inside." He took care of the books, the inventory, and the detail work, which Mike preferred not to handle. Both of them drew a decent wage from the business, and except for an occasional bonus, they pumped all of the profits back into the business. They were constantly improving their leased store and warehouse, updating their equipment, and expanding their lines. Twenty years after having begun the business, Mike was proud that he could draw a salary of $40,000 a year, upon which he and his wife could live comfortably. He was even more proud of the fact that he valued his share of the business at $200,000.

☐ The apartment house also proved to be a good investment. It was a well-built building located in a desirable part of town. While it generated good rental income, Mike preferred to reinvest much of the income in improving the building rather than spending it for his own personal purposes. Today, after all expenses, the apartment house was generating $20,000 a year income, and if Mike wanted to sell it, he could reap $200,000 after all selling costs. He and his wife continued to live in the same apartment.

☐ The vacant land didn't fare as well as Mike had hoped for, but his potential profit was still substantial. An anticipated highway was never built, and the community growth was not as rapid as Mike had expected. Had those things taken place, the land today might have been worth in excess of half a million dollars. Nonetheless, as the community grew, Mike felt that the land could now be sold in various parcels to net him $300,000.

☐ Mike had no other assets of any consequence. All available income from the business and the apartment house were reinvested back into those entities, and Mike felt that his growing wealth precluded the need for any life insurance.

☐ Daughter Maryanne's lot was not a happy one. She and her husband moved out of state, and while their marriage was basically happy, their financial situation was constantly in chaos. Mike had given them some financial help and guidance early in their marriage, but nothing seemed to change their wasteful, spendthrift ways. Many years ago, Mike had given up. He would no longer help them, and Maryanne felt very bitter and angry toward her parents because of this.

☐ Mike was a wealthy man—at least on paper. His net worth exceeded $700,000. But in the twenty years since he had drawn his original WILL, he had never taken the time to reexamine it or change it in any way.

A costly failure to plan

In spite of Mike's apparent wealth, his distribution of assets and lack of liquidity resulted in terrible turmoil upon his death. The problems Sybil faced were as follows:

☐ An appraisal of the plumbing-supply business verified that, at the time of Mike's death, his interest was indeed worth $200,000. But no buyer could be found. Willy had become very difficult to deal with and without Mike's talents, the profitability of the business quickly declined. The income that Mike had been bringing home quickly shriveled to a fraction of what it had been. And that was the money that Sybil needed to live on.

☐ The apartment house had been willed to Maryanne, and she took the opportunity to get her revenge against her parents. She expressed her intention to sell the property as quickly as she could and pocket the profits. She told her mother that she could remain as a tenant in the building, but she'd have to pay rent like everyone else.

☐ In desperation, Sybil looked to the vacant land as her source of salvation. But in her grief, confusion, and anxiety, she was to be easily taken advantage of by any potential buyer. Given enough time and clear-headedness, she could have sold the land for a gain of $200,000. But under the circumstances, Sybil found herself accepting an offer for half that amount. And after paying the capital-gains taxes on the profit from the sale of the land, her nest egg was reduced even further.

Alternatives?

Mike's greatest error was his failure to review and update his estate plan. Had he done so periodically, he could have corrected the problems: total lack of liquidity and a distribution plan that gave the wrong things to the wrong people.

What else could Mike have done? He could have worked out an arrangement with Willy whereby Willy would buy out Mike's interest in the event of Mike's death. This could have been accomplished through a plan known as *key man life insurance*. It would work like this: Each partner would have his life insured for an agreed amount, say, $200,000 in Mike's case. In the event of either partner's death, the life insurance proceeds would be paid to that partner's survivors, and the other partner would then gain the dead partner's interest in the business. In Mike's case, Willy would have ended up with total control of the business to do with as he pleased, and Sybil would have ended up with $200,000 cash to do with as she pleased.

By giving the apartment house to Sybil instead of Maryanne, Mike could have assured Sybil of the continuing rental income as well as a place to live rent free.

It would have cost Mike relatively little to implement these or other alternatives. He, of course, is not around to feel the brunt of his planning errors. But his wife will have to live with them for the rest of her life.

Management of Estate Assets.   The bulk of Ned's estate consisted of life insurance and stocks. By the time Ned reached his mid forties, he had accumulated a large enough estate to provide for his family in a most comfortable style, including education for the children and total peace of mind for his wife in the event he should die suddenly, as he unfortunately did.

Ned's plan had been carefully prepared, but he had made one major miscalculation. When left on her own, Ned's wife proved to be a very poor manager of money. Between her grief at having become a widow at such a young age and her lack of familiarity with the specifics of investments, Ned's estate was wiped out within a few short years.

Ned had at one time thought that because there was a sizable sum involved, he should arrange to have it flow through some form of managed program whereby the money would be allocated to the family as needed. But because of his faith in his wife and because of the cost involved in a managed program, he didn't do so.

Proper management of assets in an estate is a factor all too often overlooked, as is the distributional plan discussed in the case of Mike. Tales are legion of widows and children who have squandered money, been bilked, or were ill-advised.

The prudent individual planning an estate program must be aware of the need for sound management of assets for as long as the survivors will have use or need of those assets. Management can be accomplished in a number of ways. Assets can flow through a trust arrangement whereby income is paid to the survivors, and they can further have a right to tap the principal as and if the need arises for specific purposes. Insurance policies can be arranged so that the money is paid out over an extended period rather than in one lump sum. Similar extended withdrawal plans can be set up with annuities, mutual funds, and pension and profit-sharing plans. Whether a management program is set up formally, as through a life insurance company or a trust, or whether it's established by common consent among the parties, there is still no substitute for a basic knowledge on the part of family members about the nature of the assets of the estate, an awareness of the pitfalls that can jeopardize those assets, and a cool collected head to keep things on an even keel, particularly during the difficult early months and years following the death of the breadwinner. In short, education and knowledge are essential for a sound management plan.

As with all other elements of estate planning, the matter of management must be reviewed from time to time and amended as needed.

Assurance of Continued Life Style. Olive worked out a fine estate plan, taking into account all the foregoing questions of distribution and management of assets. But her mistake came in viewing the estate plan as something that commenced at the time of death. Her primary concern—the concern of many—was to provide ample funds so that her family could continue to live in their accustomed manner upon her death.

But she erred in failing to provide for that same life style while she was still living. When Olive first fell ill, her business associates continued to pay her a full salary for a number of months even though she was contributing nothing to the business. All her medical expenses were paid by a very comprehensive health-insurance program. But after several months, her associates came to her and said they'd have to reduce her salary since the business was hurting by her continued sick-pay benefits and the loss of her energies.

Olive could understand this and consented to it, feeling that she would soon be on the road to full recovery and at full earnings. But it didn't work out that way. A few months later her associates told her sadly that they would have to cut her salary down to a minimum level, and a few months after that it was terminated completely. Even though her medical expenses continued to be paid, there was no income, and Olive had to start dipping into her reserves.

Her illness lingered, and when she died three years later, the bulk of her estate had been used up. Her heirs received virtually nothing. Olive's case illustrates a most tangible problem that has very intangible solutions: an otherwise adequate estate demolished by unforeseen events. In Olive's specific case, a solid program of life and disability insurance could have provided ample protection and allowed her to leave her estate much more intact. Those are insurable risks, but other occurrences are less insurable. A portfolio of investments can suddenly turn sour —stocks, real estate, business interests. The need to support elderly or disabled family members can drain one's assets suddenly and sharply.

Prudent individuals will insure against all foreseeable risks, within reason, without becoming "insurance poor." And they will further structure their portfolio of investments and business relationships to at least minimize the chaos that could result from unforeseen catastrophes.

Perhaps most important is to communicate with family members about the size and extent of the estate and what they can expect from it. They should be prepared for the contingencies they will face, realizing that the more knowledgeable they are, the better they will be able to cope on their own.

Minimizing Taxes. Carl had no worries about estate taxes. Two years ago, when he had his WILL prepared, his lawyer told him that his estate was not large enough to incur any estate taxes. At that time, Carl's total wealth was approximately $350,000: the equity in his house, which was worth $180,000; his investments valued at $120,000; his vested rights in a pension fund worth $30,000; and his personal property worth $20,000. Carl signed his WILL, content that all his wealth would go as directed to his wife and children and that none would go to the government.

But a lot can happen in a short period of time. Carl's wife ran off with Roger, a jazz guitarist from Paris, and Carl sued for divorce. His wife didn't contest the divorce—she was content to let Carl keep everything, including the three children. Furthermore, and unbeknownst to Carl, his great-aunt Trudy had fallen critically ill and had included Carl in her WILL.

The $40,000 hangover

On January 2 Carl awakened groggily. He had suffered through the previous day with a massive hangover due to overindulgence on New Year's Eve. Now that headache was gone, but a worse one awaited him in his mailbox. There he found two letters. One was from his lawyer informing him that the divorce proceedings had become final. The other was from a lawyer in Vermont telling him that his Aunt Trudy had died and that Carl was now the proud owner of one-third of Aunt Trudy's Vermont dairy farm, with his interest worth approximately $400,000.

The good news quickly turned to bad when Carl telephoned his lawyer to discuss these matters. "Alas," said the lawyer, "the value of the inheritance boosts your total worth to $750,000, and the divorce means that you can no longer take advantage of the important estate tax savings device known as the *marital deduction*. In other words," the lawyer cautioned, "if you were to die today, your estate would owe federal estate taxes of about $40,000."

Carl was dumbfounded. "How can that be?" he gasped. "When I went to bed last night, I could have died in my sleep and not owed Uncle Sam anything. Now I wake up in the morning, and my estate could be in debt for $40,000 if I died today!"

Carl's lawyer then proceeded to explain to him how estate taxes work and what can be done to minimize them or avoid them. What the lawyer told Carl is substantially what follows in the rest of this chapter.

HOW ESTATE TAXES WORK

Very few estates will be subjected to estate taxes. But as Carl's case illustrates, an obligation to pay these taxes can arise unexpectedly. Or, more likely, the obligation to pay taxes can arise more gradually as one's wealth increases over the years due to inflation (such as in the value of one's house), appreciation in the value of one's investment portfolio, the addition of life insurance and pension benefits to one's net worth, and so on. If you are in your twenties or thirties today, your estate may seem too small to cause you concern about estate taxes. But as you reach your forties, fifties, and sixties, your total wealth will likely increase by many times its current value, thus exposing you to estate taxation.

Sound financial planning dictates that continued attention be paid to one's potential estate tax liability. With proper advance planning, the costly bite of estate taxes can indeed be minimized.

Three Kinds of Taxes

Three possible kinds of taxes can arise when a person dies. They are as follows:

1. **Estate taxes.**   When people die, their estates become legal entities. If the estates are large enough, the federal government will levy a tax on their value. The tax is to be paid out of the estates' assets, generally before anything is distributed to the survivors. It often happens that an estate will have to sell investments or other property in order to pay the federal estate taxes. The federal estate tax is the biggest of all possible taxes arising on one's death, and it is the tax that will be discussed in greater detail in the sections that follow. In addition to the federal estate tax, some states also levy an estate tax.

2. **Inheritance taxes.**   Some states levy an inheritance tax. This is a tax that is paid by those who receive inheritances. The basic difference between estate taxes and inheritance taxes are as follows: Estate taxes are paid out of the assets of the estate *before* anything is distributed to the heirs. Inheritance taxes are paid by the heirs *after* the estate has been distributed.

3. **Income taxes.**   Many months, if not years, can elapse before an estate is distributed to all of the heirs. During that time, the assets of the estate may be invested and receive income. In such cases, the income received is subject to income taxes. A separate return must be filed for any such income earned by

an estate. An inheritance that you receive is not subject to income taxes. If, say, you receive $10,000 from Uncle Willy's estate, the $10,000 is not considered taxable income to you. If you invest that $10,000 and earn $1000 a year in interest, however, the $1000 income is subject to income taxes on your own personal return. If you receive property as an inheritance and you later sell that property at a profit, the profit is subject to income taxation.

Federal Estate Tax.   The following discussion incorporates the extensive changes in estate and gift-tax laws that were in effect in 1988. Tax laws are always subject to change. Check the current law for the most up-to-date situation.

Beulah died in 1988. At the time of her death, Beulah owned a substantial interest in the family business and had a portfolio of investments that she had received as an inheritance from her parents. The total value of all assets that Beulah owned, including her personal effects, was $830,000.

Beulah's funeral expenses and the costs of administering her estate totaled $20,000. In her will, Beulah had made a charitable bequest to the Red Cross of $10,000 and a bequest to her husband of $50,000. The balance of her estate was distributed equally among her three children.

A few months later, after all the paper work and proceedings were completed, Beulah's accountant notified her heirs that Beulah's estate owed $55,000 in federal estate taxes.

Table 21-2 illustrates how Beulah's estate tax was arrived at. Each of the following items are listed in the table:

1. The *gross estate* consists of everything that an individual owns or that is owed to the individual. This can include assets that may have been in joint names and that pass directly to the survivor of the jointly owned property. In Beulah's case, as noted, the *gross estate* totals $830,000.

2. Certain *deductible expenses* are subtracted from the *gross estate*. These items can include funeral expenses, the costs of administering the estate, certain debts of the deceased person, and charitable bequests. In Beulah's case, these *deductible expenses* total $30,000.

Table 21-2 **Beulah's Estate**

1. *Gross estate*	$830,000
2. Less *deductible expenses and contributions*	− 30,000
3. *Adjusted gross estate*	800,000
4. Less *marital deduction*	− 50,000
5. *Taxable transfers*	750,000
6. *Tentative tax on $750,000 =*	$248,300
7. Less *credit*	− 192,800
8. *Tax due*	$ 55,500

3. After subtracting the *deductible expenses* from the *gross estate*, we arrive at the *adjusted gross estate*, which in Beulah's case is $800,000.

4. The *marital deduction* is one of the most important ways of reducing estate taxes. The *marital deduction* consists of that portion of an estate that is left, in proper legal fashion, to one's surviving spouse. For deaths occurring in 1982 or after, there is generally no limit to the amount of *marital deduction* that can pass from one spouse to the other. This applies whether the transfer of wealth occurs before death or upon death. Note that gifts or bequests made to other family members, such as children or parents, do *not* qualify for the *marital deduction*. Only gifts or bequests made to the spouse qualify.

   Beulah could have made a bequest to her husband of her entire estate, but for reasons of her own choosing she only stipulated a $50,000 bequest.

5. Subtracting the *marital deduction* from the *adjusted gross estate* gives us the *taxable transfers*. This is the amount that is finally subject to the federal estate tax, and in Beulah's case it is $750,000. This is the amount upon which the *tentative tax* is calculated in accordance with Table 21-3.

6. Beulah's *taxable transfers* total $750,000. According to Table 21-3, the *tentative tax* due on that amount is $248,300.

7. All estates are entitled to a *credit* against the *tentative tax* due. In 1987 and later, the credit allowable is $192,800. (See Table 21-4.)

Table 21-3 **Federal Estate and Gift Tax Rates**

Taxable transfers (via gift or estate, after all proper expenses, deductions, marital deduction)	Tax due (before credit)
Under $10,000	18 percent of Taxable Transfers
$ 10,000 to $ 20,000	$ 1,800 plus 20% of excess over $ 10,000
20,000 to 40,000	3,800 plus 22% of excess over 20,000
40,000 to 60,000	8,200 plus 24% of excess over 40,000
60,000 to 80,000	13,000 plus 26% of excess over 60,000
80,000 to 100,000	18,200 plus 28% of excess over 80,000
100,000 to 150,000	23,800 plus 30% of excess over 100,000
150,000 to 250,000	38,800 plus 32% of excess over 150,000
250,000 to 500,000	70,800 plus 34% of excess over 250,000
500,000 to 750,000	155,800 plus 37% of excess over 500,000
750,000 to 1,000,000	248,300 plus 39% of excess over 750,000
	For taxable transfers in excess of $1,000,000 the maximum tax rate will increase up to a limit of 50% to 55%.

Table 21-4 **Credit and Exempt Equivalents**

Year	Credit	Exempt equivalent
1982	$ 62,800	$225,000
1983	79,300	275,000
1984	96,300	325,000
1985	121,800	400,000
1986	155,800	500,000
1987 and later	192,800	600,000

8. Subtracting the allowable *credit* from the *tentative tax*, we arrive at a *tax due* of $55,000. The federal estate tax return is to be filed within nine months of the individual's death. Extensions for payment can be arranged with the Internal Revenue Service.

Credit against taxes

The credit against taxes means, in a nutshell, that for all deaths occurring in 1987 and after, an estate with taxable transfers of less than $600,000 will not be subject to federal estate taxes. Put another way: If, after taking into account all proper deductions, gifts to spouses, and any other steps that can reduce one's estate tax liability, there is less than $600,000 remaining, the estate will not have to pay federal estate taxes.

Cutting Beulah's estate tax

If Beulah had made a bequest to her husband in the proper legal fashion of $200,000, her estate would not have had to pay any estate taxes. Why? Because such a bequest, qualifying for the marital deduction, would have reduced her taxable transfers to $600,000, and the tax due thereon would have been totally offset by the credit. It would thus seem a simple matter for virtually anyone to eliminate possible estate taxes by making a large enough marital deduction bequest to their surviving spouse to reduce the taxable transfers to a point where they would be offset by the credit.

However, it isn't always necessarily best to give the largest possible marital deduction to the surviving spouse. Much depends on individual circumstances, but the larger the marital deduction to the surviving spouse, the bigger the potential estate tax on the surviving spouse's estate after death. We'll examine the implications of the "second" estate tax—that on the surviving spouse's estate—shortly.

Giving it away

Beulah could also have eliminated the whole tax problem by giving away all or part of her wealth while she was still alive. As of 1988, individuals can make gifts to as many persons as they wish, but if the gifts exceed $10,000 per recipient per year, the amount in excess of $10,000 is subject to taxation at the same rates as the estate tax rates. If both spouses join in making gifts, the annual amount that can be given per recipient without incurring tax liability is $20,000.

An estate that might otherwise be subject to taxation can be reduced considerably by making gifts over a period of years. Naturally, one does not want to make gifts imprudently, and the advice of your estate-planning lawyer should be sought before embarking on any program of gifts, whether to minors or to others.

Taxes on the second estate

In doing the estate planning necessary to minimize the federal estate tax, it's important to pay attention to the potential tax on a surviving spouse's estate. This problem is likely to arise only in estates of very substantial value, but it's a potential problem that everyone should be aware of.

Here's a simple example: Mr. and Mrs. Jameston have a combined estate worth $1 million. In his will, Mr. Jameston leaves the entire amount to his wife. This eliminates the estate tax from Mr. Jameston's estate. He has made the maximum marital deduction gift to his spouse, reducing his taxable estate to zero. However, now Mrs. Jameston has the $1 million and no spouse. She is not entitled to a marital deduction unless she remarries. If she does not remarry and still has the $1 million in her estate at the time of her death, her estate will owe a federal estate tax of $153,000. (Taxable transfers of $1 million would result in a tentative tax of $345,800. This is reduced by the credit of $192,800, leaving a final tax due of $153,000. (See Tables 21-3 and 21-4.)

If, instead of leaving the entire $1 million to his wife, Mr. Jameston had left her $600,000, they could have avoided the estate tax altogether on both estates. By leaving his wife $600,000, Mr. Jameston's taxable transfers would have been reduced to $400,000, putting them in the exempt category (below $600,000). And if Mrs. Jameston's $600,000 was still intact at the time of her death, she would also fall into the exempt category. The other $400,000 in Mr. Jameston's original estate could have been distributed in a variety of other ways.

Persons facing a potential problem on second estate taxation certainly do need the advice of capable counsel at the earliest possible time.

YOU MAY HAVE MORE THAN YOU KNOW

"What does all this have to do with me?" you may be asking. "All these huge amounts of money are more than what I'll ever expect to see in my life."

Not necessarily. Your total estate could reach dimensions that you might not dream of today. The value of your home, your life insurance, your pension benefits, and any inheritances you may receive can boost an otherwise untaxable estate into taxable status more quickly than you might think.

Further, while your own estate might not approach taxable ranges for many years, your parents or other family members might now be in a potentially taxable situation. Their lack of planning could expose their estate to taxes, which could, in turn, diminish your inheritance. Open and frank conversation among family members is always desirable on matters such as this, particularly when it involves retaining one's acquired wealth within the family unit, as opposed to sending it to the government.

With these thoughts in mind, let's briefly review some of the ways in which estate taxes can be minimized.

TAX-AVOIDANCE DEVICES

Estate planning specialists often recommend one, or a combination, of the following devices to minimize estate taxation. Individual circumstances, along with the advice of professionals, will help one determine what is best in any given individual case.

- ☐ Giving gifts has already been mentioned as a means of reducing one's estate and thereby the taxes thereon. Gifts may be either outright or in trust. When a gift is made in trust, the recipient may not be able to have full access to the gift until some future time. It may be possible for the donor of the gift to receive income that the gift generates. For example, a father may give a child, in trust, a gift of stock. The child may not be able to sell the stock until he or she reaches age twenty-one. In the meantime, the dividends payable on the stock may still be received by the father. If a gift made in trust is revocable—that is, the donor has the right to take the gift back—the gift may still be considered to be part of the donor's estate.

- ☐ Life insurance is a common way of passing wealth from one generation to another. A father may take out a life insurance policy and name his children as beneficiaries of the policy. If the father retains *ownership* in the policy, the value of the policy can be taxed as part of his estate. If the ownership of the policy resides in the wife or the children, however, the value of the policy will not be taxed in the estate of the father.

- ☐ Private annuities are a fairly complicated arrangement, usually between members of a family, whereby a child will purchase an asset from the parent, with a promise to pay for the purchase over an extended number of years. Such a plan, when properly constructed, has the effect of taking the value of the asset out of the estate of the parent. A private annuity should be entered into only upon the advice of legal and tax counsel.

- ☐ Ownership of properties in joint names will not necessarily relieve one's estate from taxation, though it may simplify the administration of an estate and thereby cut down on administrative costs.

IT'S NEVER TOO EARLY

While estate planning is commonly thought of as an activity for senior citizens, you are never too young to consider the importance and benefits of estate planning. Thought should be given to estate planning when an individual marries and as children are born. Then, periodically, as the family grows, further consideration and review should be given to a plan at least every few years. As the family structure changes, so does the need for reviewing the plan. In addition to the financial benefits that can result from sound estate planning, the peace of mind that can be achieved cannot be denied.

Distribution of Your Estate

Estate planning, properly done, should involve an attorney with expertise in the field. The assistance of an accountant and a life insurance agent can also be worthwhile. Even though federal estate taxes affect only a very small percentage of the population, there are still many important matters that must be resolved. Who will get what? How liquid are your assets? What provisions have you made to take care of the immediate and long-term needs of your survivors?

The following checklist is designed to motivate you to commence a proper program of estate planning. It is based on the assumption that you will die tomorrow. You should acquaint yourself with your state's law of intestacy to learn what would happen if you died without a WILL or other satisfactory distribution arrangements (trusts, for example).

Your assets	*Value*	*Who would get what?*
☐ Your home	————	————
☐ Your personal possessions	————	————
☐ Proceeds of pension or profit-sharing plans	————	————
☐ Proceeds of life insurance policies	————	————
☐ Any debts owed you	————	————
☐ Your investment portfolio, specifically:		
Stocks	————	————
Bonds	————	————
Savings accounts	————	————
Real estate	————	————
Collections	————	————
Other	————	————
☐ Any business interests you may have	————	————

Living Trusts: Proceed with Caution

A relatively new device for estate planning has grown in popularity in recent years. It's known as the *living trust*, and for certain families it can provide a number of advantages. In oversimplified terms, the living trust arrangement requires that you transfer your assets now, while you are living, into a trust arrangement. The trust, not you individually, will thus become the technical legal owner of your assets. Since these assets are technically no longer a part of your estate but rather are owned by the trust, they can pass to your designated heirs without having to go through the often costly and time-consuming probate proceedings. In short, given the right circumstances, a living trust can expedite the distribution of your assets to your heirs, at a possibly lower ultimate cost than might be incurred through the probate proceedings.

But the initial cost of creating a living trust, plus the ongoing cost of maintaining it and updating it as needed, can be considerable. A living trust is *not* for everyone! Larger and more complicated estates are more likely to benefit from a living trust arrangement than are smaller and less complicated estates. If your estate truly does not warrant having a living trust established, and you do so anyway, you are likely to expose yourself and your heirs to greater costs and complications than you otherwise might have wanted.

A living trust should be compared with all other possible alternative methods of estate planning, and you should get the advice of a trusted and objective attorney who is a specialist in estate-planning affairs. If you have the slightest doubt about the wisdom of one method over another, seek a second opinion without delay.

CHAPTER 22

Income Taxes

You can't get away from income taxes. Virtually every facet of your financial affairs is affected in one way or another by the federal income tax: when you borrow, when you invest, when you set up a record-keeping program, when you plan for your retirement, and when you do your day-to-day budgeting. These matters and many others are affected by income tax implications.

In 1986 Congress passed a sweeping Tax Reform Act. It was supposed to make federal income taxes simpler. It did not. It necessitated many new and complicated forms, calculations, phase-ins, and phase-outs that will last for years. The Tax Reform Act of 1986 was the fourth major overhaul of income tax laws in a ten-year period. It certainly will not be the last. And as the laws change, so, perhaps, must your own financial plans if you want to take advantage of what the law allows or escape any disadvantages that the law may impose.

This chapter is not intended to be step-by-step guide to filing your tax return. That information—in much more expanded form—is available in a variety of commercial publications. Rather, this chapter is designed to do the following:

- [ ] Give you a basic understanding of how the income tax laws work
- [ ] Illustrate the strategies and decisions you can and should consider in order to keep your taxes at a minimum
- [ ] Acquaint you with audit procedures and how to deal with them

BE PREPARED

As you read this chapter you should have at hand the most current copies of the basic income tax forms, particularly the 1040 form and the schedules that accompany it. These forms are included in the instruction package the Internal Revenue Service mails to all taxpayers each January. They are also available year-round at local IRS offices and during the first few months of each year at most banks, savings associations, and post offices.

Specific examples of tax situations and sample illustrations of segments of the tax forms are included in this chapter for the purpose of giving you a general understanding of the laws and the forms. For the year in which you are studying this chapter or doing your return, you must determine the current laws and how they apply to the current forms.

This chapter discusses federal income taxes. Most states and a few cities also levy income taxes on their citizens. State and city tax formats generally follow the federal format, so this chapter will also be helpful to you in understanding your local income tax situation.

IMPORTANCE OF KNOWING ABOUT INCOME TAXES

Let's look at a few examples to illustrate the importance of understanding income tax laws.

☐ In order for both Ralph and Marcia to work, they had to hire a babysitter to take care of their two small children. Like many people, they hated to do the work connected with filing their federal income tax return. To minimize that work, they went to a tax-preparation service that was offering to complete returns for a price far lower than other services. You get what you pay for: The cheap service neglected to ask Ralph and Marcia if they had child-care expenses. And Ralph and Marcia didn't know the difference. Had they known the facts, they could have cut their tax bill by over $1000 by claiming the child-care expenses as a credit against their tax!

☐ Jan moved from Detroit to Los Angeles to take a better job. Her new employer paid one-half of her moving expenses, and Jan paid the other half out of her own pocket. She was so pleased with the new job that she didn't give a second thought to paying some of her own moving expenses. And when it came time to file her tax return, she overlooked the fact that she could have claimed those moving expenses as a deduction to her income. This could have cut her tax bill by many hundreds of dollars, and it would have taken only a few minutes to enter the necessary information on the form.

☐ Karl was a machinist. His boss required that Karl provide certain of his own tools needed for the job, as well as his own work clothes. The boss didn't reimburse Karl for these expenses, but Karl was otherwise happy with the job and didn't mind the expense. Nor did he pay attention to the tax laws, which could have allowed him a deduction for part of the unreimbursed cost of the tools and work clothes. By not claiming the deduction, Karl paid much more in income taxes than he'd actually had to.

☐ Brent was a traveling salesman. He returned from the road every Friday afternoon and spent two or three hours sitting at his dining room table filling out his expense vouchers and doing other paper work associated with his job. Another salesperson had once told him that if he did work at home, he could claim a deduction on his tax return for the expense of having an office in his home. Brent thus figured that the use of his dining room table for a few hours each week was worth $2400 a year in deductible expense. Without seeking other advice, he claimed $2400 on his tax return, which resulted in a tax savings of over $800. But Brent was more than a little dismayed when an auditor for the Internal Revenue Service called him in for a visit: the expense was being disallowed as an *improper deduction*, for it did not meet the very stringent guidelines for claiming office-at-home expenses. Brent had to pay up accordingly, plus interest and penalty.

□ Much to his surprise, Joel received an inheritance of $2000 upon the death of a long-lost uncle. Wanting to be perfectly legal and forthright about this windfall, Joel included it, but did not identify its source, as "other income" on his tax return. By doing so he increased his taxes by $600. But, he figured, he was still better off by $1400, and the IRS couldn't claim he was hiding income. In fact, the IRS assumed that the unspecified $2000 was legally taxable income, and they gladly accepted the extra $600 from Joel. But if Joel had done his homework before completing his tax return, he would have learned that inheritances are *nontaxable income*. He should *not* have reported it, and he should *not* have paid the tax. If he later realized his mistake, he could have filed an *amended return* and gotten back the overpayment. But he never did realize the mistake. Nor did the government.

PERVASIVENESS OF TAXES IN OUR LIVES

The examples above illustrate just a few of the hundreds of common situations in which income taxes raise an issue. And as the examples show, many people could be paying more in income taxes than they really have to. Or they may be courting costly problems by *not* paying the taxes they really do owe. With hundreds, perhaps even thousands, of dollars at stake in your own tax return, it's essential that you make yourself aware of all the possible ways to keep your taxes at the legal minimum. A professional tax preparer can help you gain this awareness to some extent, but you only spend a few hours a year doing the taxes. The preparer may not think to ask about, and you may not remember, all of the transactions you conducted during the year that could have tax consequences.

Your awareness of the tax laws will help you to be a better record keeper and a better manager of your financial affairs. The preparer can only work with the information you provide. It's up to you to know which transactions have tax implications and to collect the necessary documentation that will enable you to support whatever claims you make on your return.

The income tax structure also requires that you make a number of important choices, such as which form to file, which filing status to choose, whether you should itemize your deductions, and so on. Making the wrong choice could mean paying higher taxes than necessary or running into a hassle with the IRS. If you make a choice that favors the government, you can *not* necessarily assume that they'll correct the matter for you. For example, if you choose not to itemize your deductions, when in fact doing so would lower your taxes, the IRS will not come back to you with the suggestion that you itemize. They'll gladly accept the extra taxes you've paid.

Let's examine the basic workings of the income tax structure and the ways in which you can make the correct decisions to legally minimize your taxes.

BASIC CONCEPT OF INCOME TAXES

Your assignment, should you choose to accept it, is to take advantage of all the ways you can to legally reduce your taxable income and the taxes thereon. Should you choose not to accept it, you'll pay more taxes than you may have to. When you glance at the tax forms, you may think that this is an impossible mission. It isn't, if you're willing to do a reasonable amount of disciplined homework, for which you can be amply rewarded.

Following, in brief, are the steps you'll take. We'll examine each one in more detail later.

1. Tally all your income that is subject to taxes. (Do not include income that is not subject to taxes, such as inheritances or life insurance proceeds that you might have received, for example.)

2. Reduce that total by the proper legal methods—adjustments, deductions, and exemptions.

3. Then figure the lowest possible tax by choosing the right filing status and claiming all proper credits.

Let's look at an oversimplified example of how the income taxes are calculated in accordance with these three steps. Table 22-1 illustrates the case of Glenda and Mac.

Step 1: Glenda and Mac have a total of $40,000 of income for the year. Of this amount, $2000 is tax-exempt income from an investment and $38,000 is income from work and other taxable sources. Thus, their total income that is subject to taxation is $38,000.

Step 2: All the legal subtractions are now calculated. Glenda and Mac have $3000 in adjustments as a result of their eligible individual IRA account investments. They have deductions totaling $5000 for the year. In this particular year, each exemption is worth $1950. Glenda and Mac have two children, so they are entitled to a total of four exemptions, or $7800. Their deductions and exemptions total $15,800. This leaves them with $22,200 of income on which taxes must be paid.

Step 3: Glenda and Mac's proper filing status is as a married couple filing jointly. For their filing status, the tax on $22,200 for the year in question is $3330. Further, Glenda and Mac have paid for child care in order for them to work, which

Table 22-1 **Glenda and Mac's Income Taxes**

Step		
1. Income subject to taxation:		$38,000
2. Less Adjustments	$3,000	
Deductions	5,000	
Exemptions	7,800	
Total		15,800
Income on which taxes must be paid		$22,200
3. Tax on $22,200 at 15% rate	$3,330	
Child-care credit	− 330	
Net tax due	$3,000	
Withheld during year	3,100	
Refund due Glenda and Mac	$100	

entitles them to a credit of $330. This credit is subtracted from the tax due. This leaves them with a net tax due of $3000. During the year, Glenda and Mac have had a total of $3100 withheld from their pay for federal income taxes—$100 more than they owe in taxes, so they are entitled to a refund of $100.

We'll now take a closer look at how these specific steps are taken on the actual tax forms. Bear in mind that the tax laws and forms can change from year to year, thus this discussion must be general in nature.

Before proceeding you should complete the Personal Action Checklist at the end of this chapter. It's designed to help you update many of the important specifics of the tax forms and laws. You'll be better enable to understand how your own personal tax situation is to be calculated if you complete the checklist first.

WHO MUST FILE?

Your first step, of course, is to determine whether you are legally required to file an income tax return for the past year. This will depend on three main factors: the amount of gross income you received during the year; whether you are married; and whether you or your spouse is over the age of sixty-five. Depending on your age and marital status, there are different levels of gross income at which you will be required to file a return. You may not owe any taxes; indeed, you might be entitled to a refund. But you must file a return if you fall within the legal requirements. Determine what the minimum income requirements are for the current tax year. (If you've completed the Personal Action Checklist at the end of this chapter, you will have obtained this information as well as other specific data that are likely to change from year to year.)

There are a few other circumstances under which you might be required to file a return:

□ If you are claimed as a dependent on someone else's tax return, such as your parents', you may be required to file your own tax return if you had a certain amount of *unearned* income during the year. (Unearned income is generally income from investments as opposed to earned income, which is income from work.)

□ Even if your income for the year falls below the aforementioned minimum levels, you'll have to file a return if you owe certain other taxes outside the normal realm of income taxes. Such other taxes might include taxes on a distribution from an IRA account or social security taxes on tips that you didn't report to your employer.

□ If you are self-employed, either full time or part time, you will have to file a tax return if your net earnings from self-employment exceed the fixed amount. This is so regardless of your age or marital status. Self-employed persons must also pay self-employment tax on the self-employment income. This is comparable to the social security tax that regular employees have withheld from their wages.

There are some circumstances when you may not be *required* to file a tax return, but *should* file one. For instance, you may not have earned enough income to be required to pay taxes, but you did have income taxes withheld from your pay. If you file a tax return, you will be entitled to a refund of the taxes that were withheld from your pay. If you don't file a return, even though you're not required to, don't expect a refund.

Check specific IRS instructions for the current year to determine the exact filing requirements as well as to clarify any other matters discussed in this chapter.

Strategies for Success

Do Your Own Income Taxes

If not every year, then at least every second or third year you should do your own income taxes. Yes, it can be a burden, one that you'd just as soon avoid by paying someone else to do it for you. But because income taxes play such an important role in so many of our financial matters, you would better serve yourself by being knowledgeable about how income taxes work. And you can best get that knowledge by preparing your own returns. Doing so will keep you more aware of not only current tax regulations but changes that are slated to occur in the tax laws. By anticipating changes, you can make better decisions regarding such matters as investing, borrowing, and making certain major purchases. If you *don't* do your own taxes at least once every few years, you could make costly financial decisions.

WHICH FORM SHOULD YOU USE?

There are three forms that individuals can use to file their returns: the 1040EZ, the 1040A, and the 1040. The 1040EZ is by far the simplest to use, but it can only be used if you are single, claim only one exemption, and have taxable income of less than $50,000 (not more than $400 of which can be from interest income). The 1040A, often called the *short form*, is available to every filing status but cannot be used if you want to itemize your deductions.

To take full advantage of all the tax-cutting devices available—itemizing deductions and using all possible credits—you should use the 1040 form, often called the *long form*. For the balance of this chapter we'll be referring to the long form provisions.

Filing Status

The first important choice you have to make in preparing your return is with respect to your filing status. The segment on the form looks like this:

Filing Status

1 _____ Single
2 _____ Married filing joint return
3 _____ Married filing separate return
4 _____ Head of household
5 _____ Qualifying widow(er) with dependent child

As you can see, there are five possible choices. Many taxpayers can qualify for more than one status, but choosing the wrong one can result in higher taxes.

Married Taxpayers. Married taxpayers can choose to file separate returns or they can file together on a joint return. With very few exceptions, it will be to their benefit to file a joint return. If you aren't sure whether it's better to file jointly or separately, calculate the tax both ways and choose whichever is the lower tax.

If you were legally married on the last day of the year, you are considered to have been married for the whole year. If your spouse died at any time during the year, you also are considered to have been married for the whole year.

If married persons do choose to file separately, they both must do the same with respect to their deductions. They both must either itemize their deductions, or they both must use the "standard deductions." One spouse can't go one way and the other spouse the other way. This is often considered the disadvantage of filing separately.

There is a possible exception to this general rule: Even though you may be technically still married, if you live with your dependent child apart from your spouse, you may be considered unmarried if you meet certain tests. In such cases, you could file as a single taxpayer or as a head of household, and you will not have to itemize your deductions even if your spouse does, or you may itemize your deductions even if your spouse does not. In order to qualify for this unusual status, you must meet all four of the following tests: (1) You must file a separate return; (2) you must pay more than half the costs of keeping up your home for the tax year; (3) your spouse did not live in your home at any time during the tax year; (4) your home was, for more than six months of the year, the principal home of your child or stepchild, whom you can claim as a dependent. If you can satisfy these four tests, you can file as a single person. If your home in test (4) was your child's principal home for the *whole* year, and all the other tests are met, you can then file as a "head of household," in which case your tax rate will be less than as a single person.

Unmarried Taxpayers. Unmarried taxpayers may be able to choose from the other three filing statuses: single, head of household, and qualifying widow(er) with dependent child. Of these three choices, the single status will pay the highest tax, followed by the head of household and the qualifying widow(er). In one recent year, for example, individuals with a taxable income of $24,000 would have paid the following taxes, depending on their status:

Single	$4400
Head of household	3613
Qualifying widow(er)	3600

As you can see, choosing the correct legal status can make a considerable difference in the amount of taxes you'll have to pay.

Head of household

If you can qualify for this status, your tax rate will be lower than the single status or than the married-filing-a-separate-return status. In order to qualify you have to be unmarried on the last day of the year, and you must have paid more than half the costs of keeping up a home that was the principal home for the *whole* year for any relatives whom you can claim as a dependent (see the later discussion on who qualifies as a dependent). These relatives can include your married children or grandchildren; your grandparents; your brothers and sisters; your in-laws; and your blood-related aunts, uncles, nieces, and nephews. Note that these family members must *actually* have lived with you.

You can also qualify if unmarried children or grandchildren lived with you, even though they may not be technically your dependents. Further, you can qualify if your mother or father were your dependents, even though they did not actually live with you.

Check the current IRS instructions for the definitions of "keeping up a home," the "cost of keeping up a home," and other specific pertinent definitions and requirements.

Qualifying widows and widowers

People who qualify for this status pay at the same tax rate as married couples who file a joint return. This is the lowest rate of the five different statuses. If your spouse died in a preceding year, you can file as a qualifying widow or widower if you were entitled to file a joint return with your spouse for the year of death, *and* you did not remarry before the end of the current tax year. You must *also* have a child, stepchild, or foster child who qualifies as your dependent for the year, and you must have paid more than half the costs of keeping up your home, which had to be the principal home of that child for the whole year.

Exemptions and Dependents

As was noted earlier, for every exemption you can legally claim, you are allowed to reduce your income that is subject to taxation. For tax year 1988, each personal exemption was $1950; for 1989 $2000. After the 1988 tax year, the exemption is to be adjusted yearly for inflation. (Individuals in high tax brackets may lose the benefit of all or part of the personal exemptions if their income exceeds approximately $150,000 for joint filers, $90,000 for single filers, and $124,000 for heads of households. These amounts are subject to change.) Check current regulations for the year in which you are filing.

The section of the 1040 form where this information is requested looks like this:

Exemptions

☐ Yourself
☐ Spouse

First names of dependent children who lived with you_____

_____

Total boxes checked ☐

Total children listed ☐

Other dependents

Name	Relationship	No. of months lived in your home	Did dep. have income of $ or more?	Did you provide more than $\frac{1}{2}$ of dep. support?	Total other dependents ☐
_____	_____	_____	_____	_____	
_____	_____	_____	_____	_____	
_____	_____	_____	_____	_____	

Add numbers entered in boxes above ☐

Obviously, the more exemptions you can legally claim, the lower your taxes will be. You are entitled to claim one exemption for yourself and, if you are married, you can claim one exemption for your spouse. You can claim an exemption for a spouse even if the spouse died during the year.

In addition to yourself and your spouse, you may claim additional exemptions for every person who is your legal dependent. For the most part, children are the most commonly claimed dependents. But you are not limited just to children. Other persons, related or not, may qualify as dependents if all necessary tests are met. (Employed persons such as housekeepers, maids, and servants cannot be claimed as dependents.)

In order for persons to qualify as dependents, they must meet *all* of the following five tests:

1. The support test
2. The gross income test
3. The member of household or relationship test
4. The citizenship test
5. The joint return test

Let's take a brief look at each requirement. Check current regulations to determine the full extent of the tests.

1. *The support test.*   You must provide more than half of the dependent's total support during the calendar year.

2. *The gross income test.*   Generally, you may not claim a person as a dependent if that person had gross income during the year in excess of the amount of the personal exemption. (Tax-exempt income such as social security payments is not included in gross income.) There are two main exceptions to this rule. The gross income test can be ignored if the person you claim as a dependent is your child and is either under nineteen or is a full-time student, in accordance with IRS definitions. In other words, if your child was under nineteen and earned over the legal maximum gross income for the year, that child can still be claimed as a dependent. Similarly, if the child was over nineteen and earned more than the permitted maximum but was a full-time student, the child can still be claimed as a dependent.

3. *The member of household or relationship test.*   Provided the other tests are met, a person who lives with you for the entire year and is a member of the household can qualify as a dependent, even though that person is not related to you.

Further, certain relatives can qualify as dependents even if they do not live with you, provided they meet all the other tests. These relatives can include children and grandchildren, parents and grandparents, brothers, sisters, step-family, and in-laws.

4. *The citizenship test.* To qualify as a dependent, the person must be a U.S. citizen or a resident of Canada or Mexico for some part of the calendar year in which your tax year begins.

5. *The joint return test.* If the person you wish to claim as a dependent has filed a joint return with a spouse, you cannot claim that person as a dependent. For example, you supported your daughter for the entire year while her husband was in the Armed Forces. The couple files a joint return. Even though your daughter may meet all the other tests, you may not claim her as a dependent.

The tax regulations are very specific as to what constitutes support of a dependent. Some expenses qualify while others do not. Check current regulations to be certain that you are proper in claiming your dependents. Note also that you cannot claim a partial dependent. Either someone meets the test or they don't.

Income

You must declare all of your income that is legally taxable and you must, as noted earlier, take care *not* to report any income that is *not* taxable. The *income* section of the 1040 form looks like this:

Income		
	Wages, salaries, tips, etc.	_____
Please attach	Interest income	_____
Copy B of your	Dividends	_____
Forms W-2 here.	Alimony received	_____
	Business income (or loss)	_____
	Capital gain (or loss)	_____
	Pensions, annuities, rents, royalties, partnerships, etc.	_____
	Other income (state nature and source)	_____
	Total Income	_____

The sample form does *not* contain all of the possible income items. It has been abbreviated to include the more common types of income only. Check current regulations and forms to determine the full extent of reportable income.

Taxable Income on 1040 Form. Let's take a more detailed look at each of these items of taxable income.

Wages, salaries, tips, etc.

For most taxpayers, this is the major source of taxable income. Early in the year, employees receive copies of W-2 forms from their employer. These forms summarize the total amount of income earned during the taxable year and indicate how much of these earnings have been withheld by the employer to pay income taxes, social security taxes, state income taxes, and any other withholdings that are required or voluntary. The amount of total income that shows on your W-2 form should be inserted on this line, and a copy of the W-2 should be attached to this part of your form when you mail it in.

Interest income

On the line asking for your interest income you place the total of all taxable interest you've earned during the year. The current form will dictate whether you are required to itemize all the sources of income on a separate schedule. Taxable interest generally includes interest you earn on regular deposits with banks, savings and loans, and credit unions (including interest-bearing checking accounts and certificates of deposit); also interest earned on mortgages, trust deeds, promissory notes, corporate bonds, and U.S. government bonds (except for Series E and EE savings bonds). With Series E or EE bonds you have the option of declaring the interest earned in a given year and paying taxes on it during that year or of deferring the taxation until you later cash the bonds.

Some types of interest earned are tax-exempt. The interest you earn from municipal bonds or mutual funds that invest in municipal bonds is exempt from federal income taxes. If you own municipal bonds that are issued by a local governmental unit in your state of residency, the interest you earn would also be exempt from state income taxes. However, if you sell municipal bonds or funds at a profit, the profit is fully taxable. Interest earned on U.S. obligations is exempt from state income taxes.

Some types of interest earned are not taxable in the year in which you earned it but will be taxable in some future year. This is known as *tax-deferred income*. It includes interest earned from annuity plans, IRA plans, Keogh plans, and other pension and profit-sharing programs.

The effects of tax-deferred earnings can be very attractive, since all of your earnings remain in your account to work for you. Let's look at a simple example: Say you have an account of $1000 earning 10 percent per year, or $100. In a normally taxable situation, a taxpayer in the 28 percent bracket would have to pay $28 in taxes out of the $100 earned. That would leave $1072 in the account after one year.

In a tax-deferred account, though, the entire $100 would be added to the $1000,

Table 22-2 **$1000 Earning 10% Per Year**

	Taxable account	*Tax-deferred account*
After		
1 year	$1072	$1100
2 years	1149	1210
3 years	1232	1331
4 years	1321	1464
5 years	1416	1610

which would leave $1100 in the account after one year. Table 22-2 traces a taxable and a tax-deferred account, using the above example.

Dividend income

On the line requesting your dividend income you insert the total value of dividends you've received during the year. This includes dividends you receive on common stocks, mutual fund shares, and those that have been reinvested in shares of common stock or a mutual fund. If the total amount of dividends you've received exceeds a certain limit, the form will indicate that you are to itemize all dividend income on a separate schedule.

Tax laws state that any party who pays you more than $10 per year in interest or dividends must prepare a form 1099 that indicates the amount paid to you. A copy of this form is sent to you, and a copy is sent to the IRS. You should therefore assume that the IRS knows you received that particular amount of money. Should you fail to report it on your tax return, you can expect to be questioned by the IRS.

Alimony received

Alimony payments that you receive are considered fully taxable income. However, child-support money received is not considered taxable income. See current regulations for definitions of taxable alimony.

Separately Scheduled Income. If you receive certain other types of income, you will be required to complete additional detailed schedules. These types of income include business income, capital gains, and other miscellaneous types of income.

Business income or loss (Schedule C)

If you ran your own business, part time or full time, as a sole proprietor, you are required to complete Schedule C and show the income or loss from that business on the appropriate income line on the form. (If you operated the business as a partnership or a corporation, you'll have to file the appropriate partnership or corporate income forms.)

Capital gains and losses (Schedule D)

The regulations on capital gains and losses have been changed by Congress probably more often than any other aspect of the entire tax law. And, if tradition means anything in Washington, the regulations on capital gains and losses will continue to be changed in the future.

The concept of capital gains and losses applies to the sale of capital assets, which in general are investments such as stocks, bonds, and real estate, among other things. If you sell these assets at a profit, you have realized a *capital gain*. If you sell these assets at a loss, you have realized a *capital loss*. Prior to the Tax Reform Act of 1986, there were different tax treatments for capital gains and losses, depending on how long you had owned the capital asset. In years prior to the Tax Reform Act of 1986, the so-called holding period varied from six to twelve months and back to six months again. If you held capital assets for less than the then-designated holding period, the gain or loss from selling the assets was considered a short-term capital gain or loss. If you held the capital assets for longer than the then-designated holding period, it was considered a long-term capital gain or loss. And throughout the years prior to the 1986 law changes, the tax *rate* on capital gains varied as well.

The Tax Reform Act of 1986 effectively removed the tax advantages of the capital-gains concept. Since tax year 1988, capital gains, whether long-term or short-term, have been taxed at the same rate as ordinary income. In other words, if you sell stock and realize a profit, the profit is taxed at the same rate as your earnings from work or the interest you receive on your savings account. This meant that for 1988 and after, taxes on capital gains for most investors can be as high as 28 to 33 percent. Prior to the Tax Reform Act of 1986, the maximum tax on long-term capital gains was 20 percent.

It is always possible that Congress will restore some tax advantages for capital gains. If you are holding capital assets for future sale, you should consider the possibility of favorable changes in the tax laws before you sell such assets. If a restoration of the tax advantages for capital gains seems to be in the offing, it might pay to delay selling certain capital assets until the benefits are in fact restored.

In the meantime, it appears that it will still be necessary to separately schedule capital gains and losses when completing your tax return each year. Schedule D is the traditional schedule used for this purpose. Note, too, that your state income tax regulations may have different requirements with regard to capital gains. This may necessitate additional record keeping on your part.

There is one advantage created for investors as a result of the Tax Reform Act of 1986: All or a part of your net investment *losses*—whether short-term or long-term—can be subtracted from your otherwise taxable income. The maximum amount you can subtract is $3000 each year. For example, in 1990 you have investment gains of $2000 and investment losses of $7000, for a *net* loss during the year of $5000. On your 1990 federal tax return, you can reduce your otherwise taxable income by $3000 as a result of this loss provision. Assuming that in 1991 you have no investment transactions at all, you can, for that year, subtract the remaining

$2000 worth of 1990 losses from your 1991 income. Check to see if these regulations are still in effect at the time you file your annual return.

Miscellaneous taxable income

There are many types of income, other than those noted above, that are taxable. Included are the following:

☐ Fees for services you perform such as serving as a member of a jury, an election precinct official, a notary public, an executor or administrator of an estate, to name a few.

☐ Property you receive through barter. If you receive property in exchange for your services, you must include as income the fair market value of the property on the date you received it. If you receive the services of another person in exchange for your services, the fair market value of these services is also taxable.

☐ Gambling winnings are taxable income. However, you can deduct gambling losses during the year up to the extent of your winnings. Winnings from lotteries and raffles are considered gambling winnings. If you win property other than cash, the fair market value of the property must be counted as taxable income.

☐ Prizes and awards received as a result of drawings, television or radio programs, beauty contests, and the like are taxable. So are awards and bonuses that you receive from your employer for your good work or your suggestions. As with gambling winnings, prizes in the form of property must be included in taxable income at their fair market value.

☐ Part or all of any unemployment insurance benefits that you receive might be taxable income. See the instructions in the form 1040 for specific details on the formula that determines how much, if any, of your unemployment insurance benefits are taxable.

It should be noted that this discussion on types of taxable income does not include all types; it is rather a sampling of the most common types of taxable income. You should refer to the 1040 instructions and your professional tax preparer to determine whether you have any taxable income over and above what has been mentioned here.

Nontaxable Income. You may receive nontaxable money from various sources. These items should not be reported on the income part of your 1040 form. Following is a sampling of the more common types of nontaxable income. As with the taxable items, you should check the 1040 instructions for more specific details as to revisions in the law.

☐ **Interest income.** As noted earlier, *some* types of interest income may be excludable, including interest received on tax-exempt bonds and interest which is otherwise excludable because of specific regulations in the tax laws.

☐ *Accident and health-insurance proceeds.* Payments that you receive for the following are exempt from tax: workers' compensation payments; Black Lung benefit payments; Federal Employees Compensation Act benefits; damages received for injury or illness; benefits received under an accident or health-insurance policy for which you paid the premiums; disability benefits received for loss of income; compensation received for permanent loss of a part of your body or a function of your body; and reimbursement for medical care.

☐ *Gifts and inheritances.* Gifts and inheritances are not considered income. But if the cash or property you receive as a gift or inheritance generates income for you, the income that is generated is taxable. If a gift or inheritance is paid to a trust fund instead of to you, the income you receive from the trust fund may be taxable to you.

☐ *Life insurance proceeds.* Payments made because of the death of the insured person are generally not taxable. There are some possible exceptions: If someone else turned an insurance policy on their life over to you and you paid a price for the transfer of that policy, then proceeds payable to you as beneficiary may be taxable to you. Also, if proceeds of a life insurance policy are paid out in monthly installments and those monthly installments include interest from the insurance company, the interest portion of the monthly payments are taxable to you.

☐ *Social security benefits.* Social security isn't generally taxable, unless your income from all sources exceeds $25,000 (single returns) or $32,000 (joint returns).

☐ *Scholarships, fellowships, and grants.* Generally, money received in the form of scholarships, fellowships, and grants is not taxable if you are a candidate for a degree. There are, however, numerous technical exceptions, and you should check the IRS regulations to be certain that you do report any portion of such income that may be taxable.

☐ *Prizes and awards.* These may be tax free if you meet certain requirements: The prize must be awarded in recognition of your past accomplishments in religious, charitable, scientific, educational, artistic, literary, or civic fields. In order for such monies to qualify as nontaxable income, you must also not have entered the contest on your own; rather you must have been selected as a possible recipient without any volunteering on your part. And you must not be required to perform future services as a condition of receiving the prize. Athletic awards do not qualify for tax-exempt status.

Total Income. In completing this portion of your 1040 form, you add up all the items that are considered taxable income. Be sure not to include items that are excludable from taxation. From this total income figure you now begin the subtractions.

Adjustments to Income

This is the first main category of expenses that can be used to reduce your total income figure. Items included in the adjustments category are often referred to as *deductions*. But technically they are not deductions. You are entitled to claim these adjustment items even if you do not itemize your deductions. (See later discussion on itemized deductions.) The most common types of adjustments will appear on your 1040 form in the following manner:

Adjustments to Income

Payments to IRA plans	————
Payments to Keogh plans	————
Alimony paid	————
Total Adjustments	————

You may be required to fill out separate schedules or forms with respect to the claiming of some of the adjustments. The current 1040 will instruct you accordingly. Here's a brief rundown of these more common adjustment items.

Payments to IRA Plans.   If you qualify, you might be able to claim an adjustment to your income for the money you invest in an IRA plan. Chapter 20 explains in detail who can qualify for this deduction, either in whole or in part.

Payments to Keogh Plans.   If you have income from self-employment, you're eligible to take part in a Keogh plan, which can entitle you to an adjustment to your income. Chapter 20 has details on how Keogh plans work. If you're eligible, you can reduce your income taxes considerably by taking advantage of either an IRA plan or a Keogh plan.

Moving Expenses.   Prior to the Tax Reform Act of 1986, if you moved to change jobs or start a new job, you could have been entitled to claim some of your moving costs as an adjustment. As a result of the 1986 law, moving expenses must now be claimed as an itemized deduction. See the section on itemized deductions for more details. Also, the adjustment for married couples when both work has been eliminated by the Tax Reform Act of 1986.

Alimony Paid.   As noted in the income section, alimony received is taxable income. On the other hand, alimony that is paid is an adjustment that can be used to reduce your total income.

Adjusted Gross Income.   At this point you will total your adjustments and subtract them from the total income. The result is the "adjusted gross income."

The amount of your adjusted gross income can be important: The amount you can claim for some of the itemized deductions is keyed to a formula involving your adjusted gross income. These formulas are explained with respect to each deduction to which they apply.

Deductions

The tax law, in general, has identified certain types of expenses as being "deductible" from your income. These expenses include those for medical purposes, charitable contributions, taxes that you've paid, interest that you've paid, casualty or theft losses that you've suffered, and other expenses that are related to your ability to generate income.

Standard Deduction.   Whether or not you have actually incurred such expenses, the law allows you to claim a certain fixed amount of deductions anyway. This fixed amount is known as the *standard deduction*. The amount of the standard deduction depends on your filing status. Table 22-3 indicates the scheduled standard deduction for different filing statuses that came into effect in 1988. (Double-check to determine if these numbers have changed for any year in which you file a return.) Let's look at an example. Assume that during the year the Slavkins do not incur even one penny's expense for any of the deductible items: They have no deductible medical expenses, no home loan interest to pay, no state income taxes to pay, and they make no charitable contributions. Even though they have not incurred any expenses of a deductible nature, they are still entitled to claim a $5000 standard deduction for that year, which reduces their otherwise taxable income accordingly.

To Itemize or Not to Itemize?   If you have, in fact, spent *more* on deductible items than the standard deduction allows, you are entitled to claim all of those expenses as deductions. But you must itemize each and every one of them, and you must have proper evidence that you did in fact incur such expenses.

The choice is yours: You can take the easy route and claim the standard deduction, in which case you won't have to keep records of all the particular expenses; or you can keep all the proper records and tally up the deductible expenses to see what you actually did pay for such items. If your true deductible expenses

Table 22-3   **Standard Deduction**

Filing status	1988 and after
Married, filing jointly	$5,000
Married, filing separately	2,500
Head of Household	4,400
Single	3,000

exceed the standard deduction amount, it will pay you to itemize. The only way you can tell is to know for sure what your itemized expenses are. Many taxpayers take the shortcut of the standard deduction, when in fact, had they itemized, they would have saved tens, hundreds, or even thousands of dollars.

How do you decide whether you should itemize or not? If you are a homeowner, it's very likely that you will have deductible expenses in excess of the standard deduction amount. For most homeowners, the interest expense on their mortgage and their real estate taxes alone will be close to, if not more than, the standard deduction amount.

If you're not a homeowner, you'll have to do some more careful estimating of your deductible expenses. Unless you have paid very high state income taxes or have other unusually high deductions, it's much less likely that you will benefit from itemizing your deductions as a nonhomeowner. Nevertheless, it's worth a quick survey of possibly deductible expenses to see if itemizing your deductions is advisable.

The following discussion will help familiarize you with the types of expenses that are deductible. The more familiar you become with these expenses, the more readily you'll make note of them throughout the year in your checkbook or otherwise so that you will be aware of them as deductible items when you're filling out your tax return. By so doing, you'll begin to find the process of itemizing that much simpler.

If you do itemize your deductions, you will be required to complete Schedule A of the 1040 form. An abbreviated example of Schedule A is shown. Note that this form is subject to change from year to year. Use the current form, and check current regulations to be certain you are claiming all proper deductions in the proper form.

Types of Deductions. Following is a brief explanation of the common deductions that are listed on Schedule A, plus many of the allowable deductions that are not specifically listed on Schedule A. The latter are listed under Miscellaneous Deductions, on Schedule A.

Medical and dental expenses

The Tax Reform Act of 1986 states that you can claim a deduction for your nonreimbursed medical expenses to the extent those expenses exceed 7½ percent of your adjusted gross income. In other words, if your adjusted gross income (as determined by the formulas on the previous pages) is $40,000, you can claim a deduction for nonreimbursed medical expenses in excess of $3000. That is to say, you cannot deduct anything for the first $3000 of medical expenses. If your expenses are in excess of $3000, the excess can be deducted, subject to current regulations. (Self-employed persons were scheduled to be able to deduct 25 percent of their health-care insurance premiums until 1990. Check current regulations for specific details.)

Schedule A—Itemized Deductions

Medical and Dental Expenses

(follow formula on current version of Schedule A to arrive at proper deductions)

TOTAL MEDICAL _____

Taxes

State and local income _____
Real estate _____
Personal property _____
Other (itemize) _____

_____ _____
_____ _____
_____ _____

TOTAL TAXES _____

Interest Expense

Home mortgage _____
Credit and charge cards _____
Other (itemize) _____

_____ _____
_____ _____
_____ _____

TOTAL INTEREST _____

Contributions

Cash contributions _____
Other than cash _____
TOTAL CONTRIBUTIONS _____

Casualty or Theft Losses

Follow instructions on current version of Schedule A. Complete and attach form 4684 to your return. _____

Miscellaneous Deductions

Union dues _____
Other (itemize) _____

_____ _____
_____ _____
_____ _____

TOTAL MISCELLANEOUS DEDUCTIONS _____

Summary of Itemized Deductions:

Total medical _____
Total taxes _____
Total interest _____
Total casualty _____
Total miscellaneous _____
TOTAL DEDUCTIONS _____

Taxes

The Tax Reform Act of 1986 allows you to deduct the following taxes: local (state, city) income taxes that you pay; real estate taxes that you pay on property that you own; and personal property taxes that you pay. Taxes that are *not* deductible include the following: sales taxes, utility taxes, federal income taxes, fines, penalties, and so-called sin taxes (taxes on tobacco and alcohol products).

Interest expense

The deductibility of interest expenses will become one of the most complicated aspects of the income tax law. Prior to the Tax Reform Act of 1986, virtually all interest was deductible by those who paid it. But as a result of the 1986 law, individuals must keep track of four different types of interest that they pay. Each type is subject to its own rules regarding deductibility. Let's look at each of these four types of interest:

☐ **Consumer interest.** Part of the interest that you paid for "consumer debt" used to be deductible. This deduction will have been completely phased out after 1990. Consumer debt, in general, includes credit card debt, charge account debt, car loans, and personal loans. For tax year 1988 you were able to claim a deduction of 40 percent of your consumer interest. In other words, if you had $1000 of consumer interest expense in 1988, you could have claimed a deduction of $400. For tax year 1989 you were only allowed to deduct 20 percent of your consumer interest. For tax year 1990 the allowed deduction was set at 10 percent. For all tax years after 1990, none of your consumer interest is deductible. Of course, Congress may change its mind and reinstate this deduction. Be sure you check current regulations.

☐ **Home loan interest.** Interest on home loans is either fully deductible or partially deductible, depending on the date the loan was made and the purposes of the loan. If your home loan was taken out on or before August 16, 1986, all of the interest on the loan is deductible, regardless of the size of the loan or the purpose for which the loan was obtained. But for loans written after that date, there are restrictions regarding how much interest is deductible: The amount of interest you can deduct is related to the original purchase price of the home plus allowable improvements. (If you have financed certain educational or medical expenses as a part of your home loan, the interest on those expenses may also be deductible.)

For example, you bought your home in 1980 for $40,000, using $10,000 as a down payment and taking a loan of $30,000. In 1981 you added on a room at a cost of $5000. In 1985 your home had increased in value to $65,000, so you refinanced your loan in 1985 to a total of $55,000. Since you had completed this refinancing before the cutoff date of August 16, 1986, you can continue to deduct all of your interest on the full $55,000 debt. But if you had refinanced the original loan after August 16, 1986, you could only deduct interest on the debt of $45,000—the original cost of the home ($40,000) plus the cost of the improvements ($5000). (See specific current regulations for full details on this complex area, plus the most current regulations on deductibility of interest for second home loans and dollar limits on the deductibility of interest on home equity loans.)

☐ *Investment interest.* Interest paid on loans relating to investments is deductible, within limitations relative to the amount of investment income you receive.

☐ *Business interest.* If you borrow money for legitimate business purposes, the interest on such loans continues to be fully deductible.

The entire matter of the deductibility of interest can be made even more complex when an individual borrows for a variety of purposes. For example, assume you borrow $10,000 against a life insurance policy, and you use the money in part to pay off an existing car loan, in part for your business needs, and in part to improve your home. Various portions of the interest you pay may or may not be deductible in any given year. Tax laws expect you to be able to track the interest paid for debts of various purposes and to claim deductions accordingly.

Contributions

If you itemize your deductions, you can deduct your charitable contributions made to properly qualified charitable organizations. (See IRS regulations for definitions of qualified charities and for certain limitations that may apply with respect to the maximum amount you can deduct in a given year.) Contributions may be cash or property. If you give property such as clothing or books, the deduction should be an amount equal to the then fair market value of such property. In order to justify the charitable deductions, you should have proper documentation and appraisals. If you are actively involved in a charitable organization, you cannot deduct the value of your time contributed to the organization, but you can deduct out-of-pocket expenses that you incur on behalf of the charity.

Casualty or theft losses

If you suffer a sudden and unexpected loss or casualty, you can deduct the value of the loss provided you meet the following requirements: (a) the amount of each separate casualty or theft loss is more than $100; *and* (b) the total amount of *all* losses during the year is more than 10 percent of your adjusted gross income for that year. For example, your adjusted gross income is $25,000, and you suffer a casualty loss of $2000. You *cannot* claim this loss as a deduction, since it is *less* than 10 percent of your adjusted gross income. But if you had a loss of $3000, you could claim a deduction. How much? First you must subtract the $100 noted above; then you must subtract the 10 percent of your adjusted gross income: $3000 less $100 less $2500 equals a deduction of $400.

Deductible casualty losses may result from a number of different causes, including fire, hurricanes, tornadoes, floods, storms, sonic booms, and vandalism. Nondeductible casualties include car accidents when your own negligence caused the accident; breakage of household items such as china and glassware under normal conditions of use; damage done by a family pet; damage caused by termites, moths, plant disease; damage caused by progressive deterioration of your property.

Theft losses include those arising from burglary, robbery, larceny, and embezzlement. However, simply misplacing or losing money or property may not be considered a deductible theft loss.

Miscellaneous deductions

In addition to the deductions listed above, there are other expenses that are deductible, at least in part. These fall under the general category of miscellaneous deductions.

Subject to specific IRS definitions of each of the following items, here are the major miscellaneous expenses that might be claimed as deductions that are subject to the limitations following the list:

☐ Fees for investment advice

☐ Fees for investment management

☐ Fees for administration of trusts

☐ Legal expenses relating to the collection of income

☐ Subscriptions to publications on investing

☐ Rental costs for safe-deposit boxes, to the extent the box is used to store investment-related items

☐ Cost of tax advice and preparation of tax returns

☐ Appraisal costs relating to a casualty loss or a charitable contribution

☐ Unreimbursed employee business expense

☐ Continuing education expenses

☐ Business use of your residence

☐ Literature relating to your job or profession

☐ Dues to unions or business-related associations

☐ Work uniforms and tools

☐ Certain costs related to seeking a new job

(If you are self-employed, many of these expenses might be business-related expenses that can be fully deductible on Schedule C.)

The Tax Reform Act of 1986 imposes a new formula for calculating these miscellaneous deductions. Let's call it the *2 percent rule*. The rule states that qualifying expenses can be deducted only to the extent that they exceed 2 percent of your adjusted gross income for the year. For example, you have an adjusted gross income of $30,000, 2 percent of which is $600. Assume you tally up $1000 worth of miscellaneous deductions. On your return you can only claim $400, the extent to which your miscellaneous deductions exceed the 2 percent ($600) level.

If your adjusted gross income for the year was $40,000, 2 percent of which is $800, you could claim any miscellaneous deductions exceeding $800. In other words, if your total miscellaneous deductions for the year were $1000, you could only claim a deduction on your return of $200.

Nondeductible items

If you claim deductions that aren't legal, the IRS will disallow them. If this happens, you will have to pay back taxes that you thought you had previously avoided. You might also have to pay interest and penalties. Following is a brief list of some nondeductible items that are often erroneously claimed as deductions:

☐ Commuting to and from work

☐ Life insurance premiums

☐ Property-insurance premiums

☐ Hobby expenses

☐ Social security taxes

☐ Attorney fees not relating to producing and collecting income

☐ Home-related expenses such as allowances for children, clothing, utility expenses, and school tuition

☐ Home repair and maintenance expenses

☐ Losses you might suffer on the sale of your house or personal effects

Tax regulations and definitions are always subject to change. Check the latest tax guidelines for specific details on any and all matters pertaining to deductions.

Total Deductions.   Total all of your expenses that are deductible. If the allowable deductions exceed the current amount allowed for the standard deduction, you should itemize your deductions. If the itemized deductions do not exceed the standard deduction, you should claim the standard deduction.

Tax Computation

We've now reached the point where the tax can be calculated. Table 22-4 illustrates the tax rates in effect for years 1988 and after. (These rates are always subject to change so check current rates at the time you file a return.)

Earlier in this chapter we read about Glenda and Mac and their tax picture. Refer back to Table 22-1. You'll see that Glenda and Mac have an income of $22,200 on which taxes are to be paid. We can determine the amount of taxes they must pay from Table 22-4, under the joint returns column. Glenda and Mac's income being less than $29,750, they are taxed at a flat 15 percent rate. Fifteen percent of $22,200 is $3330.

What if Glenda and Mac had instead a taxable income of $30,750? Look at the next row in the joint returns column of Table 22-4. Their tax would be $4463

Table 22-4 **Tax Rates, 1988 and After**

Single returns		Joint returns	
Taxable income	Tax	Taxable income	Tax
Up to $17,850	$0 plus 15%	Up to $29,750	$0 plus 15%
$17,851 to $43,150	$2,678 plus 28%	$29,751 to $71,900	$4,463 plus 28%
$43,151 to $100,480	$9,759 plus 33%	$71,901 to $171,090	$16,265 plus 33%
$100,481 and over	$28,678 plus 28%	$171,091 and over	$48,998 plus 28%

plus 28 percent of any excess over $29,750. In this example, the income exceeds $29,750 by $1000. Thus their taxes would be calculated as follows: $4,463 plus $280 (28 percent of $1000) equals $4743.

This is essentially how taxes are calculated using the tax tables provided by the Internal Revenue Service.

Credits against Income Taxes.   Glenda and Mac spend money for child care so they can both work. If you have such expenses, you may be entitled to a credit against your taxes (see IRS instructions). In Glenda and Mac's case, the credit amounts to $330, reducing their tax bill in our first example to $3000.

Other Taxes and Payments

Follow IRS instructions on the 1040 form to determine whether you owe any taxes over and above the income taxes. If you had self-employment income during the year, you will owe additional self-employment taxes. (These are taxes in lieu of social security taxes, which your employer would have paid and deducted on your behalf.) On the other hand, if you had more than one employer during the year, more than the necessary amount of social security taxes may have been paid or deducted on your behalf, and you can claim a refund for the excess paid. The amount of tax withheld from your pay and the amount of any estimated tax payments you've made on your own are then deducted from the tax due. The final difference is then either payable by you or refundable to you. This net amount is entered in the section entitled Refund or Balance Due. The return should then be signed and dated by yourself and your spouse and by the paid preparer, if you used one. Mail the return and a check for any balance you owe to the IRS in accordance with current instructions.

Estimated Taxes.   In all likelihood, most, if not all, of your taxes due will have been paid during the year as a result of money withheld from your earnings for that purpose. However, if you have earnings from which there has been nothing withheld for taxes, you may have to pay what is known as the *estimated tax.* This is payable quarterly, in conjunction with filing form 1040ES. If your withholding has been large enough to cover all taxes due, you might not have to bother with the estimated tax. Check current regulations to determine who must pay this tax and what the penalties are for failing to do so.

Alternative Minimum Tax. The alternative minimum tax (AMT) is designed to make certain that earners in high income tax brackets pay at least a certain minimum amount of tax. Less than one-half of 1 percent of all taxpayers have to deal with this thorny problem. Be on the lookout for AMT implications if you have claimed depreciation deductions on an accelerated basis, if you have invested in tax shelters, if you have incentive stock options, or if you have contributed to charity property that has appreciated in value.

TAX-CUTTING STRATEGIES

As mentioned previously in this chapter, if you don't claim all of the exemptions, adjustments, deductions, and credits to which you are entitled, the Internal Revenue Service won't do it for you. Throughout the year, it's your job to make certain that you keep track of all these items and incorporate them into your tax return. Similarly, you must seek out other tax-cutting strategies and take advantage of them. The government will not hand them to you. Following are examples of some of these basic strategies.

Strategy 1: Tax-Exempt or Tax-Deferred Income

To the extent feasible in your own personal circumstances, take advantage of opportunities to earn tax-exempt or tax-deferred income. There are two major areas in which this can be done: your investment program and at work.

Tax-Exempt Income. You can earn tax-exempt income by investing in municipal bonds or in mutual funds that specialize in municipal bonds. See Chapter 16 for a detailed discussion of these techniques.

Tax-Deferred Income. Tax-deferred investment income is available through tax-deferred annuities. These annuities are obtainable through insurance companies, commonly in conjunction with stockbrokerage firms. In such plans you invest a lump sum of money, and the company agrees to pay you a fixed amount of interest for a specific period of time. The interest rate is subject to modification after the initial period has elapsed. Further, certain employees, such as those of tax-exempt groups and schools, are allowed to purchase retirement annuities on a month-to-month basis. In such a plan, a portion of one's pay is used to purchase a retirement annuity, and the amount used to purchase the plan, via payroll deduction, is not subject to income taxes in the year in which it was earned. The income, however, is subject to taxes when it is withdrawn upon retirement.

Some of your income from work may also be considered as having a tax-deferred status. This is particularly so with funds contributed to pension and profit-sharing plans. Your employer may contribute certain sums of money each year to a pension or profit-sharing plan on your behalf. In effect, the employer is paying you a form of future income: You won't have the use of the money until some future time, but in the meantime you don't have to pay income taxes on it during the years in which the money is credited to your account. In addition to pension and profit-sharing plans, some individual employees might find it worthwhile to establish a tax-deferred compensation program that would delay payment for work done until some future year. The object of any tax-deferred compensation plan is to delay the payment of taxes on income from work into a future year when the taxpayer will be in a lower tax bracket, such as upon retirement.

A relatively new device that allows you to earn tax-deferred income is the so-called *salary reduction* or 401(k) plan. If your employer offers this plan, a portion of your income may be invested instead of being paid to you. This income and its earnings are tax-deferred, as might any contributions your employer has also made to the plan.

Individual Retirement Accounts (IRAs) and Keogh plans can be ideal ways to defer taxes on income both from work and from investments. See Chapter 20 for a detailed discussion of these plans. To the extent you are eligible, you should take advantage of these plans.

U.S. Series EE savings bonds also offer the opportunity to earn tax-deferred income. With these bonds you have an option: You can pay income taxes on the interest you earn each year from the bonds, or you can delay paying taxes on interest earned until you ultimately cash in the bonds. The latter choice means, in effect, that you can defer taxes on the interest income from Series EE bonds for as long as the bonds are earning interest for you.

Strategy 2: Tax Withholding and the W-4 Form

Suppose someone advised you to embark on an investment plan of $90 per month, and you were guaranteed to earn no interest at all. At the end of the year you would get back the $1080 that you had paid in and not a penny more. You'd think such advice was rather absurd, wouldn't you?

The fact is that tens of millions of people do just that. Of the more than one hundred million individual tax returns filed annually, over 80 percent get a refund from the government. The average refund check is about $1000. Some are for much less; some are for much more. The reason these taxpayers get a refund check is that they have had more of their pay withheld by the employer than was really necessary to meet their annual tax obligation. The government holds those excess payments for the full year and then returns them to taxpayers in the form of refund checks once the taxpayers file their returns for the year.

Employers are required to withhold from workers' pay checks enough to meet their tax obligations for the year. Employers estimate the amount they must withhold for each pay period based on information that the employees provide on their W-4 forms, which they complete when they start work with an employer. W-4 forms establish the number of allowances employees are claiming. The *more* allowances employees claim, the *less* is withheld from their pay.

What qualifies as an allowance? Most commonly, each exemption you claim on your tax return is equal to one allowance. In other words, if you claim four exemptions, you can also claim four allowances on your W-4 form. You are entitled to claim additional allowances over and above the number of exemptions. For example, if you itemize your deductions, you are entitled to claim additional allowances. If you are entitled to certain credits against your tax, you are entitled to claim additional allowances. There are also additional allowances that can be claimed relative to your work and marital status.

W-4 forms, which are available at your employer's personnel office, contain a work sheet that will assist you in calculating the correct number of allowances to claim. If you claim fewer allowances than you're legally entitled to, more money than necessary will be withheld from your pay. The basic strategy, then, is this: See to it that your W-4 form reflects the correct number of allowances to which you are entitled. This should result in just the right amount being withheld from your pay—not too much, not too little. If you have been having too much withheld from your pay, a proper adjustment in your W-4 form can fatten your weekly paycheck. Then, rather than sending excess money to the government where it earns no interest all year long, you'll have that money to invest or spend as you see fit.

Strategy 3: Shifting Deductions and Income

As each calendar year draws to a close, you should try to estimate your likely tax liability for the year compared with what it might be next year. The reason for doing this is to try to determine whether it would make sense to shift income or deductions from one year to the next in order to cut your tax bill. The overall strategy behind such moves is to claim deductions in years in which you'd be more highly taxed and to receive income in years when you'd be taxed less.

For example, if tax rates are scheduled to be lower next year (as is sometimes the case), it would make sense in many cases to delay year-end income from December of the current year into January of the next year. Reason? It will be taxed at a lower rate next year, and you'll save money accordingly. By the same token, given the same circumstances, it also makes sense to accelerate deductions. This means making deductible expenses this year that you'd otherwise make next year. A deduction is worth more to you in a higher tax year than it is in a lower tax year.

On the other hand, it may happen that tax rates are scheduled to go *up* next year, or that your *income* is likely to *increase* substantially next year. In either of those cases, the reverse of the above strategies may be worthwhile. In other words, you might want to accelerate income (take it this year instead of next year) and delay paying deductible expenses.

Shifting incomes or deductions need span only a few weeks—from late December into early January. If much more time than that is involved, shifting may become counterproductive since the loss of use of your money for more than a few weeks might offset the value of the shifted income or deductions.

Examples of shifting income include year-end bonuses that could be declared or paid in early January instead of late December; payment for fees or services; sales that result in capital gains. Examples of deductions that can be shifted from one year to the next at year-end include charitable contributions; payment of state income taxes and local property taxes; interest expenses; medical and dental expenses that you'd otherwise put off paying until next year but that you can pay this year.

If tax rates are *not* scheduled to change from this year to next year, and you know nearing year-end that your income will be *lower* next year than it was this year, the same strategies as noted above can be worth seeking out. A drop in income from one year to the next can occur in many ways: A pay cut is in the offing; a spouse who was working may stop working; or you may have had an exceptionally high income this year due to bonuses, commissions, or capital gains, which are not likely to be repeated next year.

Shifting Income to Children. Regulations set forth by the Tax Reform Act of 1986 make it possible for a family with children to cut its income taxes somewhat by making gifts to children of income-producing assets. The tax savings is based on the general assumption that children do not earn as much income as their parents and are thus taxed in lower brackets or are not taxed at all.

In a given year, the first $500 of investment income received by each child is free of income tax. The second $500 of investment income received by each child is taxed at the child's tax rate, not the parents' tax rate. If a child is *under* fourteen years of age, any investment income over $1000 received by each child in a given year is taxed at the parents' tax rate, if the parents' tax rate is higher than the child's tax rate. If a child is fourteen years of age or older, investment income in excess of $1000 a year continues to be taxed at the child's tax rate.

Here's an example of how the savings can work: You have a savings account of $6000 earning 8 percent ($480) per year. If you make a gift of this account to your child, the $480 of income (assuming it's the only income the child has) escapes federal income taxes. If the account remains in your name, you have to pay income taxes on the earnings each year, from $100 to $150.

Different rules apply to the taxation of income received by children from work. (Prior to the Tax Reform Act of 1986, tax benefits in shifting assets to children were much more liberal. If you had embarked on a plan prior to the enactment of the 1986 law, be certain that you now become aware of the new regulations in this area.)

Strategy 4: Tax Shelters

Prior to the passage of the Tax Reform Act of 1986 there was a very aggressive phenomenon in the financial world known as the *tax-shelter industry*. It was possible, in those days, to invest money in a variety of schemes and reduce your income taxes as a result of deductions and credits created by the schemes. Some of these investment plans were legitimate and worthwhile. But many of them were extremely risky, and many were outright fraudulent. Review the section in Chapter 18 on real estate investing to get an idea of how these plans worked. As the discussion in that chapter illustrates, there is still some possibility of legitimate tax shelters in real estate investing. But with rare exceptions—some oil and gas drilling plans—the Tax Reform Act of 1986 effectively slammed the door on the tax breaks that had been available through tax shelters.

However, despite all of Congress's continuing efforts to close all tax loopholes and keep them closed, new loopholes are constantly being created. And as new loopholes are found, new sales schemes are created to lure your dollars. Then, when the clamor against these new loopholes gets loud enough, Congress will close them up. And so the cycle goes.

At any given time, there may be tax advantages available in a variety of investments and speculative schemes. It's up to the prudent investor and sensible taxpayer to examine any such opportunities thoroughly; to exercise caution with respect to the enthusiasm of the salesperson; and to proceed with the knowledge that today's tax break could be eliminated tomorrow. If you do claim deductions or credits arising out of what the IRS would consider a tax-shelter scheme, you increase your chances of being audited by the IRS. We'll examine that phenomenon more in the remainder of this chapter.

FILING TAX RETURNS

What happens if you are not able to file your return by the due date, or if you discover that a return that you did file was incorrect? The law does allow you an opportunity to get an extension on your filing date, and it also allows you to correct a return already filed if the need arises.

Filing Extensions

Regulations in recent years have allowed taxpayers an automatic four-month extension for the filing of their individual returns. (Check to see if current regulations are still the same.) In order to obtain the automatic four-month extension, you must file a form 4868 with the Internal Revenue Service. This form must be filed by the regular due date (April 15) with the IRS center in your area. Note that the extension of the time to file your return is *not* an extension of the time to pay the taxes. Your taxes must be paid at the time you file the extension form. You can incur a penalty if you've not paid your taxes by the time you file for the extension. Interest charges on late payments may also be imposed.

If you need more time beyond the automatic four-month extension, you may be able to get an additional extension of time to file if you have a very good reason. You can apply for an additional extension by sending a letter to the Internal Revenue Service stating your reasons or by filing form 2688. If this request for additional time to file is not granted, the Internal Revenue Service will expect the filing of your return almost immediately after they have notified you of the rejection of your application.

Amending Tax Returns

Once you've filed your return for any given year, you can amend it later if you determine that you owe the government or that they owe you a refund because you didn't claim exemptions, adjustments, deductions, or credits to which you were legally entitled. The proper form to use to amend your return is a 1040X. Follow the 1040X instructions carefully, and be certain to attach any forms or schedules that are needed to explain the changes.

The law allows you ample time to file an amended return. You have three years from the date you filed your original return or two years from the time you paid your tax, whichever is later, to file the amendment.

IRS EXAMINATIONS AND AUDITS

For about 95 percent of all individual taxpayers, the year's concerns end with the filing of their tax returns and the payment of any taxes due (or the receipt of any refund owed). But for the other 5 percent, the struggle is not over: About half of them will hear from the Internal Revenue Service with respect to arithmetic errors made on their return, and the other half will be subjected to some form of examination or audit.

When errors in arithmetic are involved, taxpayers will hear relatively quickly. But it may be two years, three years, or even longer before some audits are announced and resolved. Under the law, the Internal Revenue Service has three years from the date you file a return to assess additional taxes if proper reason exists to do so. If you have failed to report a substantial item of income, the IRS has six years from the filing of your return to claim back taxes. If someone has filed a return with false or fraudulent information intending to evade taxes or if someone has failed to file a return at all, there is no time limit on when the IRS can pursue its claim. But taxpayers are not totally at the mercy of the IRS. The law sets forth very clear-cut rights for all taxpayers to appeal and protest decisions that go against them. Let's examine what happens once your return is filed.

Initial Screenings

All returns are checked clerically to determine that the arithmetic is correct and to make certain that the returns and any checks attached thereto have been properly completed and signed. If a mistake in arithmetic is discovered, the IRS will re-calculate the amount of tax due and will send you either a refund for the amount overpaid or a bill for the amount you owe them. If other corrections are needed (for example, you forgot to sign your return), you will be notified accordingly.

A further screening is conducted to determine whether there are errors in the return with respect to deductions, exemptions, and the like. These are some of the most common areas in which errors are found:

□ You have excluded from income more dividends (or interest) than the law allows.

□ You have claimed deductions for medical expenses without taking into account the stated limitations in the law.

□ You have claimed a partial exemption.

□ Perhaps most important, your reported income does not match the W-2 form your employer has provided or the 1099 forms that have been provided by various brokers, dealers, and financial institutions. Anyone who pays you interest or dividends of more than $10 during the year or anyone through whom you have sold stock, bonds, precious metals, and similar items, must report those transactions to the IRS on 1099 forms. You're to be sent copies of all such 1099 forms in January of each year, covering the prior year. The IRS will cross-check the information it receives on 1099 forms with the information that you report. If you have failed to report any of these forms of income, it would be wise to assume that the IRS will know about it.

If the IRS finds errors in these or other reporting areas, you will be notified by mail of the correction. If you disagree with their findings, you can ask for a meeting with an IRS representative or you can submit whatever information is necessary to support your claim. As noted earlier, matters such as these may be resolved fairly quickly after the filing of your return. But once such matters are resolved, that does not mean you're off the hook with respect to a more detailed audit.

Selection for Audit

In recent years the IRS has been auditing about 2 percent of all individual returns filed. While on the surface this would indicate that your chances of being audited in a given year are only one in fifty, bear in mind that that chance occurs every year, and sooner or later the law of averages is likely to catch up with you.

Out of approximately one hundred million returns filed each year, how does the IRS select the two to three million returns for actual auditing? Figure 22-1 illustrates the approximate breakdown of reasons the IRS uses to choose returns for auditing.

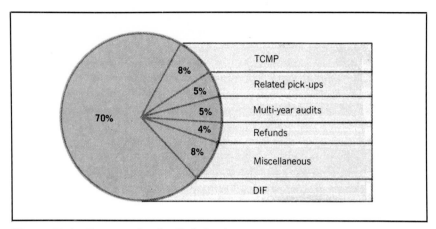

Figure 22-1   Reasons for Audit Selection

Discriminate Income Function (DIF).   About 70 percent of the returns chosen for audit are selected by the Discriminate Income Function (DIF). Returns are examined by computers, and specific elements of the return are scored. These elements include your total income, your adjusted gross income, your deductions, your adjustments, your credits. Based on past statistical evidence, agents can determine which returns—by virtue of the scoring—have the greatest potential for recovering additional taxes through an audit. This is known as *audit potential*. The IRS does not divulge the specifics of how each item is scored, but in general terms

---

Strategies for Success

Bugged by an Auditor? Ask for a New One

Most income tax auditing takes place by mail. There's only a very remote chance that you'll have to deal face to face with an IRS auditor. If you do have to meet with an agent and if there is enough money at stake, you might well want to have a professional accompany you. Tensions can be high and personalities can clash when auditor meets taxpayer. Many taxpayers may feel intimidated, "stressed out" by the mere fact of an audit. This can impair one's ability to best present one's own position. If you do feel uncomfortable with the auditor assigned to your case, you *can* ask to have that auditor replaced by another one. Talk to the local IRS supervisor and present your request. There's no guarantee that you'll like the new one either, but at least there is an opportunity to cut the tension. It can work in your favor. But you have to ask.

it would seem to be tempting an audit if one's tax bill was too low relative to the gross income declared, and so on.

Once a return has been selected by the DIF process, an examiner will scrutinize it to see if errors exist or if improper avoidance techniques have been used. The majority of DIF audits are conducted via correspondence. You may, for example, receive a letter requesting that you send photostats of checks, receipts, or other evidence to support your specific claims. If you can provide such evidence, the audit may be ended quickly. If you are unable to provide the evidence, an additional tax will be payable.

If the audit isn't conducted via correspondence, you may be requested to appear at the local IRS office. In some cases, the audit can be scheduled at your place of business or home, particularly if the records involved are extensive or if the matter is very complex.

Taxpayer Compliance Measurement Program (TCMP). About 8 percent of all returns chosen for audit are selected via the Taxpayer Compliance Measurement Program (TCMP). This is a random selection by the IRS computers and/or agents and is considered to be a much more comprehensive and thorough review of your overall situation. A TCMP audit can be very detailed and time consuming even if you have nothing at all to hide. The purposes of the TCMP are to police the voluntary-compliance aspects of the law and to unearth more statistical data to support the DIF program.

Related Pickups. About 5 percent of the returns chosen for auditing are based on "related pickups." If, for instance, your business partner is chosen for audit, you might also be chosen; the questionable deductions claimed by the one partner might be suspect with regard to the other partner. Further, if you have not reported all the income that your W-2 and 1099 forms show you actually received, this could be cause for an audit under this category.

Multi-Year Audits. About 5 percent of the returns selected for audit are chosen because more than one of your returns is in question. For example, if you had reported deductions from a real estate investment in your 1987 return and in years prior to that, you might be audited not just for your 1987 return, but for your 1985 and 1986 returns as well.

Refunds. About 4 percent of all taxpayers who claim refunds on their returns are audited if for no other reason than to verify the facts that would allow a refund.

Miscellaneous. The remaining audits are done for a variety of reasons, which can include the seeking of verification on capital-gains transactions, appraisals of charitable contributions, appraisals of casualty losses, and so forth. The IRS also exchanges tax information with state taxing authorities, and a mismatch of information between your state return and your federal return may also prompt an audit in this miscellaneous category.

Audit Red Flags. Aside from the aforementioned procedures by which returns are chosen for audit, the following are generally regarded as being common "red flags" that will prompt an IRS audit of your return:

- ☐ An individual return with income over $50,000, particularly if you have claimed deductions through a tax-shelter arrangement
- ☐ Excessive deductions claimed for travel and entertainment expenses
- ☐ Deductions claimed for the expense of maintaining an office in your home
- ☐ Losses arising out of what the IRS determines to be a "hobby," even though you determine such activity to be an ongoing business

Audit Strategies You Can Use

Perhaps no other phenomenon in our modern society has gotten more critical reviews than an IRS audit. Perhaps, subconsciously or otherwise, the government has tried to instill a fear in us all of the audit procedure. In so doing, they would hope to encourage taxpayers to be as honest and forthright as possible in preparing their returns to avoid a possible audit. Whatever the psychological foundation for our fear of audits, the fact is that most audits really do not have to be feared, particularly if your return is an honest one and you have the documentation necessary to back up your claims.

Bear in mind if you are called in for an office audit that you are dealing with another human being. That human being is there to do a job. The auditing agent has the same day-to-day cares and concerns that you do: meeting the monthly house payment, putting groceries on the table, worrying about personal matters, and so on. Very likely you will be treated in much the same way that you treat the auditing agent. If you are surly, don't be surprised if you are met with surliness. If you are pleasant, cooperative, and polite, chances are better that you'll be met with those same traits. If you arrive with your documents in well-organized fashion, you're going to make the agent's job that much easier, which in turn could make your examination that much easier. There is, of course, no guarantee that these techniques will work, but if they don't, you can ask to see the agent's supervisor and request that another agent take over the examination.

If a reasonably small amount of money is involved, you may feel comfortable in handling the audit proceedings on your own. If, however, through the initial correspondence or through the initial office visit, it appears that a substantial amount of money might become involved, it would be wise to consider hiring an accountant or tax attorney to assist you with the proceedings. If you have had a professional or a tax preparer establish your return initially, that person would be the likely candidate to assist you with the audit.

An audit proceeding is a legal entanglement. Your legal rights and the government's legal rights are in apparent opposition. As in any legal entanglement, you must determine what your likely overall costs will be in terms of money, time, and annoyance. Only you can determine the relative values of these items. If you feel that your case is weak, it might be better to resolve the matter quickly, pay the tax due (or a lesser negotiated amount if you're able to do so), and save yourself future time and energy that would be involved if you pursued the matter. On the other hand, if you feel that your case is strong and there is enough money involved, you might deem it worthwhile to fight the matter all the way. You have to determine for yourself what compromises are in order. The IRS looks at the matter in much the same way: The agent's time and energy must be evaluated in line with the hoped-for amount of back taxes that can be recovered. Thus, negotiations are always a possibility. But a good negotiator will let the other side make the first proposal.

Audit Strategies the IRS Will Use

The value of any employee is measured by performance. An auditing agent of the IRS is expected to produce tax revenues as efficiently as possible. The IRS denies that there is any ''quota'' as to how much agents should produce; but good agents will justify their employment and promotions by producing as much revenue as possible in the most cost-efficient way. It might safely be presumed, then, that a good agent, considering a delinquent tax of, say, $500, might be willing to accept a lesser amount—perhaps $350—on the spot rather than try to go for the whole $500 over a protracted period of protests and appeals. In short, negotiations are possible, and your success will be in direct proportion to the strength of your case and your ability to recognize the weak points in the agent's case.

But be assured that an efficient agent will probe quickly and deeply to determine just what your strengths and weaknesses may be. Following, for example, are some of the interrogation guidelines that an agent might use.

☐ With respect to claims for charitable deductions, the agent will attempt to determine whether the payments were actually made to qualified charitable organizations; if property was contributed, as opposed to cash, the agent will seek to verify the true fair market value of the property at the time it was given and will determine whether the giver retains any control over the property, which could disqualify it from being a true contribution.

☐ With respect to claimed deductions for interest payments, the agent will ascertain whether the interest payments were made on a valid, existing debt that you, the taxpayer, owed. This may necessitate your providing copies of all the documents relating to the loan agreement.

☐ With respect to deductions claimed for taxes paid, the agent will determine whether the tax is in fact of the type deductible in accordance with the present rules and regulations.

☐ With respect to claims for medical deductions, the agent will seek to determine whether any insurance reimbursement has been made to you or is expected by you. The agent will also probe to be certain that amounts that you've claimed as child-care expenses aren't also claimed as medical expenses.

☐ If a deduction is claimed for a casualty or theft loss, the agent will attempt to determine that a theft or casualty loss has actually occurred and that your loss was the direct result of such an occurrence. The agent will also determine whether insurance proceeds have been received by you or are expected by you.

☐ If you claim a deduction for educational purposes, it will be the agent's job to determine if your expenses were primarily incurred for the purpose of maintaining or improving skills or for meeting express requirements for retaining your job status. This may necessitate evidence from your employer.

☐ If you've claimed alimony expenses as an adjustment to your income, you can expect that the agent will request a copy of the underlying divorce documents for inspection.

☐ One of the major sources of back taxes arises with respect to claims for travel and entertainment deductions. If you've claimed what seem to be excessive expenses in that regard, the agent will seek to reconcile the amount of your claimed deduction by asking you to prepare an analysis of the cash you had available to you to make the payments you've claimed to have made. The agent can ask you to take into account the totals of all monies you have received from work, expense accounts, investments, and savings, less your estimated expenses for personal living and investing. The difference, at least in part, will be an amount that you theoretically could have spent for travel and entertainment. If that amount of cash available does not jibe with the amount of deductions you've claimed, you could be in for a back tax assessment.

The examples above of IRS auditing tactics are just a random sampling of the *preliminary* probes that you should expect the agent to make. If you are armed with all of the necessary documentation at the initial meeting, you might be able to bring the audit to a swift conclusion. If you're not prepared to document your claims immediately, the agent will normally give you a reasonable amount of time to collect the necessary documents and will schedule a future meeting at which the matter should be resolved.

Resolving an Audit: You Agree

If you and the agent agree on the findings at your initial meeting—which could take less than an hour—ask the agent to tell you how much in additional taxes you will owe. You will then be asked to sign a form stipulating the content of the agreement, and shortly thereafter you will receive a written report plus a bill for whatever taxes you may owe, plus any interest or penalties that have been agreed upon. Note that if you sign the agreement you waive your rights to appeal in the future. If paying the back taxes in one lump sum will cause a hardship for you, you can ask the agent to put the payments on an installment plan. You have to ask for this as it's unlikely that they'll volunteer it. But it is possible in specific cases to work out an installment arrangement.

Resolving an Audit: You Disagree

If you are unable to settle the matter in the IRS office audit, you should immediately ask for a written copy of your legal rights under such circumstances. Where disagreement occurs, you can ask for an immediate meeting with a supervisor, with the hopes that such a meeting might result in a more favorable compromise. If you don't reach an agreement with the supervisor, the agent will then send you a report explaining the additional tax liability. You then have the right to request a conference at the district level to see if the matter can be resolved. If a settlement still isn't reached at the conference level, you'll then receive a Notice of Deficiency, which is commonly referred to as a *ninety-day letter*. In this letter the government notifies you that you will be assessed the additional tax owed ninety days from the date the letter was mailed. If you still believe that your case is valid, you have ninety days in which to choose one of three courses to further your appeal:

☐ You can file a petition with the Tax Court.

☐ You can pay the tax that the government claims is due and then file a refund claim for it. Once the refund claim has been turned down, you then sue for your refund in either a federal district court or the court of claims.

☐ If the amount of tax is $5000 or less, you can proceed in the relatively new Small Claims Division of the Tax Court.

The first two choices are more suitable for claims involving substantial sums of money, and you'll likely need professional representation. In the Small Claims Division, however, procedures are relatively informal, and in many instances you can plead your own case. Small Claims Division cases are heard by commissioners instead of judges, and the proceedings move much more rapidly than in the more formal court system. It's likely that a case may be settled before it is actually heard. But once a decision is reached, whether by settlement or by judgment, the decision is final, and there are no further appeals to be had.

As with all tax matters, rules and regulations are subject to change from time to time. If you find yourself involved in a tax dispute, make certain that you know your rights as they currently exist.

Your Best Protection

There is nothing that can insulate you better from the rigors of a tax audit than an accurate return accompanied by all proper documentation for all claims made. If you have these in hand, an audit should be nothing more than a minor inconvenience every few years. Lacking either a correct return or the proper documentation, an audit can become a costly source of stress—not only will you have to pay back taxes plus possible interest and penalties; the proceedings can also interfere with your normal ability to generate your income and live a peaceable day-to-day life. It may seem tempting to put some extra money in your pocket by avoiding taxes improperly or evading taxes illegally. But the consequences of doing so can ultimately be more costly than you may think.

Updating Tax Information

You should complete this checklist *before* you read Chapter 22. The information you will gather in completing the checklist will enable you to gain a clear focus of the general information in the chapter and the specific information needed to complete the current year's tax returns.

The information you need to complete this checklist is available in the most recent IRS instructions for the 1040 form as well as in the most recent IRS Publication 17, *Your Federal Income Tax*.

Fill in the blanks as they apply to the current tax year:

☐ *Who must file a return?* You must file a return if you are single, under sixty-five, and had a gross income of $ _____ for the year; if you are single, sixty-five or over, and had a gross income of $ _____ for the year; if you are married, both spouses under sixty-five, and had a combined gross income for the year of $ _____ ; if you are married, one spouse is sixty-five or older, and had a gross income of $ _____ . If you are self-employed (part time or full time), you must file if you had net earnings from self-employment of $ _____ or more.

☐ *Exemptions.* The value of each exemption for the current year is $ _____ . Generally, if you wish to claim someone as a dependent, that person's gross income for the year may not exceed $ _____ . (See exceptions for children and full-time students.)

☐ *Standard deduction.* For married persons filing jointly and for qualifying widow(er)s: $ _____ ; for singles or heads of household: $ _____ ; for married persons filing separately: $ _____ .

☐ *Itemized deductions.* Estimate your own actual expenses for the year, subject to the tax law limitations in effect for the year: medical and dental expenses that are not reimbursed by insurance, employer, or otherwise $ _____ ; taxes paid for which deductions are allowable $ _____ ; interest paid, including home mortgage, and other debts for which interest is deductible $ _____ ; charitable contributions $ _____ ; casualty or theft losses not reimbursed by insurance or otherwise $ _____ ; other deductions $ _____ .

See text and IRS instructions for specific details. If total of proper itemized deductions exceeds the standard deduction for your filing status, you should itemize your deductions.

Some Tax ''Helpers'' Can Harm You

Every year without fail—usually between Super Bowl Day and Groundhog Day— the landscape in every city and town becomes littered with Income Tax Preparation signs. At the same time, newsstands are overloaded with books offering do-it-yourself guidelines for completing your own tax returns.

Care should be taken in choosing either a tax preparer or a book. With respect to the preparers, beware of high-sounding promises that they can ''guarantee'' you lower taxes. The most any preparer can guarantee you is an accurate return, based on the information you supply. Preparers can't create deductions where none legally exist. They must follow the same rules that you must.

Compare their prices carefully. Some advertise very low prices, but these prices might be only for the simplest of forms. The extras can add up quickly. Determine, as best you can before you commit yourself, what the *total* price will be for the service.

Fly-by-night preparers have been a problem, both for the public and for the IRS. Some have filed false or erroneous returns, leaving the taxpayer to answer to the IRS. Others have pocketed their customer's tax payment or refund checks and disappeared into the night.

Tax-preparation services can be helpful, but you must use care in selecting one. How long has it been in business? What personal recommendations can you get from satisfied customers? Don't overlook the regular full-time accountants who don't advertise. They may be no more expensive than the seasonal services, and they're available to assist you all year.

As for the books, some of them are nothing more than reprints of official IRS books that you can obtain at little or no cost from the nearest IRS office. Worthwhile books include J. K. Lasser's *Your Income Tax*, published by Simon and Schuster, and the H & R Block annual tax guide. The Lasser book is very comprehensive; the Block book offers an easy step-by-step guide to completing the returns.

Preparers and books aside, though, nobody can help you better than yourself: Your ongoing knowledge of and attention to the income tax laws is your best assurance of keeping your taxes as low as possible.

Appendix

CONSUMER GRIPES

In our nation of roughly 250,000,000 people, we conduct uncounted billions of money transactions every day. We do it with machines: pay phones, parking meters, robot bankers, video games, juke boxes, and devices that vend everything from the daily newspaper to a steaming hot meal. We do it with people: bank tellers, store clerks, and restaurant cashiers. We do it through the mail: paying bills by check, ordering goods, and settling up our taxes. And, in growing numbers, we're even doing it by computers that talk to one another by telephone.

We have come to take it for granted that virtually all of these transactions will flow smoothly virtually all of the time. And indeed they do. We rarely, if ever, voice a word of thanks to the people who designed the intricate machines, to the bookkeepers who post our accounts correctly, to the shipping clerks who send out the exact goods that were ordered, to the technicians who keep the mammoth computers running efficiently.

But when something goes wrong—against *us*—the air turns purple with swear words and vows of vengeance! (When was the last time you complained if a vending machine gave you two candy bars instead of one, or a store undercharged you for a purchase, or a waiter added a bill wrong in your favor?)

Though the occurrences may be statistically rare, things *do* go wrong now and then, and there's nothing more frustrating than the feeling that you've been short-changed or ripped off.

This appendix is designed to help you cope with such moments. First, some advice on how to *prevent* things from going wrong in the first place. Then some guidelines and contacts help you *correct* matters when things do go wrong.

PREVENTIVE MEDICINE

The following tips, ranging from simple to fairly complicated, can help keep money troubles away from your door. The more complicated efforts can be well worth your involvement when a substantial amount of money is at stake.

Handling Money

Whenever you receive money, for example, cashing a check or getting change from paying a bill, count the money immediately in front of the person who gave it to you. If you turn away from the cashier for just a few seconds and then claim you were shortchanged, you're likely to lose a war of words. And money. The time to claim an error is immediately.

Also, if you pay for a purchase with a large bill—say you're giving a $20 bill for a purchase of just a few dollars—take a second to note the first few numbers on the serial of the bill. If you then get change back for a $10 instead of a $20, you'll have some instant evidence that you gave the clerk a $20: Recite those few numbers.

Signing Charge Slips

Always be certain that the charges on a credit card slip are added up properly. If the clerk hasn't filled in the total, you do it. Unscrupulous merchants can insert a higher total than is proper, and you may never catch the difference. You're doubly courting trouble if that unscrupulous merchant sees you throw away your copy of the charge. Then he'll know you won't have a record of the correct amount, and he'll be even more tempted to raise the total, even if it was already filled in. (For example, the shopkeeper might change the number 3 to an 8.)

Also, don't let a merchant make more than one stamping of your credit card. If an error is made on the first stamping, be certain that the charge slip is totally torn up so that it can't be used. Best bet, tear it up yourself.

Checking Monthly Statements

Probably the single biggest source of frustration with bank accounts arises because customers neglect to do the monthly reconciliation on their checking accounts. The frequent results of carrying the wrong checking account balance are bounced checks, added costs, embarrassment, and possibly even bad marks on your credit rating. Ten to twenty minutes per month of reconciling your account can avoid such problems. Do the same with all of your credit card and charge account statements.

Also, if you deposit an out-of-town check in your checking account, ask your banker how long you may have to wait before they'll allow you to draw out money against that check. It may be as much as a few weeks. If they know you well enough, they may not restrict you at all. If you don't ask, you won't receive.

Refund Policies

Know before you buy exactly what any store's refund policies will be. The law may not necessarily entitle you to a refund if you bought defective or unsatisfactory goods. Merchants concerned with public goodwill should have a fairly liberal refund policy, under reasonable circumstances. But many will give you only an exchange privilege or a credit instead of an outright cash refund. In some instances, such as an "as-is" sale, there may be no privileges of any kind.

Determine, too, how long you have to get a refund, a credit, or an exchange. Be certain you keep whatever documents you may need, such as sales slip, credit card slip, and so forth. Find out if you lose your refund privileges if you use a product.

Cancellation (Recision) Privileges

Some transactions may give the buyer the right to cancel, or rescind, a deal, even after papers have been signed. This may be because of a law (federal or state) or simply by agreement between buyer and seller. If you do have such privileges, know *precisely* what you must do to exercise them, by when, in what form, and under what circumstances. Get it all *in writing*. If you then do wish to exercise the privilege, be certain that you do it in *precisely* the right way.

Money-Back Guarantees

Promises of money-back guarantees can be classic cases of "the big print giveth, the small print taketh away." Under what circumstances will you get your money back? Will you get it all back? Or will you forfeit some of it? There's no substitute for knowing your contractual rights.

Mail-Order Buying

Though as huge and as generally efficient as the mail-order industry is, it's still the primary cause of consumer complaints, according to the Council of Better Business Bureaus. There's one important rule to keep in mind: The better you know the people you're dealing with, the better chance you have of being satisfied or of getting satisfaction should things go wrong. In other words, if you can buy through local merchants, you've got someone to complain to if things go wrong. If you're dealing with a mail-order house hundreds or thousands of miles away, you're just another number in their computer. Let the buyer beware and shop accordingly.

Warranties

Part of shopping for a product requires that you also know the terms of any warranty that may come with the product. You should know these terms *before* you buy. Cost and annoyance can be considerable when you're told, "Sorry, that isn't covered under the warranty." Do your homework, particularly with respect to such big-ticket items as appliances, cars, houses, and home improvements.

Patience

If a situation gives off signals of sounding "too good to be true" or if it makes you think you're getting the "deal of the century" (particularly if you sign *right now* on the dotted line), you're likely courting trouble with Snake Oil Sam. If he gets your money, you're likely to never see it again. Keep your impulsive nature in hand. Resist the lures and the temptations of Sam's persuasions.

"But What If"

If an advertisement or a salesperson tells you that a product or a service will provide certain results, you tend to believe such representations. Then nagging frustration sets in if you don't get what you expected out of the product or service. It's nice to be trusting, but it can get you into trouble. The remedy: Ask the salesperson, "But what if . . . ?"

For example, the salesperson tells you, "This shirt will not shrink." *You* must ask, "But what if it does?"

The delivery clerk promises you, "This package is guaranteed to arrive by tomorrow noon." Again, *you* must ask, "But what if it doesn't?"

"You pay me $X, and I'll see to it that your roof stops leaking . . . your transmission stops slipping . . . your septic tank stops overflowing . . . the ghosts disappear from your TV reception. . . ." *You must ask*, "But what if . . . ?"

In short, know your rights and your recourses *before* you get involved in any kind of situation that could prove "iffy." If your rights and recourses aren't clearly spelled out, you may find you don't have any.

Get It in Writing

As a general rule, spoken (oral) statements by a salesperson will prove meaningless in a dispute. If any promises are made with respect to a deal, get them in writing. Have the promises signed by a person who is legally authorized to sign on behalf of the company. Don't assume that the salesperson you're dealing with is legally authorized to sign for the company. Check with the company headquarters to be sure. And get *that* assurance in writing as well. This is particularly important in such major costly deals as buying a home, home improvement contracts, and any other major purchase involving time-payment contracts.

Get Names and Numbers

Know whom you're dealing with, and take notes of price quotes, delivery promises, and so forth. Keep all documents relating to a specific transaction. If a foul-up occurs, it's much easier to track your way to the source of the problem if you have all this information.

◻ ***Documentation.*** Gather together every shred of evidence that will support your position: receipts, sales slips, credit card slips, warranties, contracts, letters, memos of phone conversations, cancelled checks, shipping documents, copies of order forms, certified or registered mail receipts, and copies (or summaries) of any appropriate laws that pertain to the matter. Organize these in chronological order, and write a brief diary setting forth the history of the matter as it occurred from day to day. The diary, supported by the specific documents, will allow you to present your position in a clear and logical way.

◻ ***Assertiveness.*** This is no time to pussyfoot around. Your money and your legal rights are at stake, and you must be firm, persuasive, and exacting. You must not allow yourself to be put off, delayed, or shunted from one department to another. Nor is it a time to become wild and ranting. If you're dealing with people who are otherwise reasonable, and you come on like a vengeful tiger, you could thwart or delay your chances for recovery.

Setting Your Targets

An essential part of your battle plan is to focus on the *who*, the *what*, the *when*, and the *how* of your complaint.

◻ ***Who?*** To whom should you address your complaint? Unless the company has a specific office to deal with consumer problems, you should aim for the highest person in authority: the owner, the president, the branch manager.

◻ ***What?*** What are you seeking? Do you want your money back? Do you want a replacement? Do you just want an apology? Are you seeking damages? Be specific. Structure your presentation accordingly.

◻ ***When?*** When should you commence seeking satisfaction? Immediately, if not sooner. Waiting only serves to blur memories, to cloud facts, to erode your position.

◻ ***How?*** How should you present your case? In person, if at all possible. The next best way is by combination of letter and telephone. If you are able to visit personally, then the meeting should be summarized in writing as soon thereafter as possible.

The Plan of Attack

Actually rehearse what you're going to say or write. Do a rough draft of a letter. Jot down notes to guide you through a personal meeting. Be organized, thorough, and precise.

Here are samples of letters, illustrating possible right ways and wrong ways of handling money disputes. You might find them helpful in structuring your own letters or personal presentations.

Research, Research, Research!

The less you know the people you're dealing with, the greater the need for research *before* you commit yourself to spending any money. The time to check with the Better Business Bureau or governmental Consumer Protection Bureau is *before* the transaction, not after it. If you're dealing with a business located in another city check with the BBB and the governmental agencies in that other city as well as your own. To the extent possible, get personal references from other customers, clients, or patients *before* you get involved. If a transaction has legal, tax, or financing ramifications, check them out with a lawyer, an accountant, or a banker *before* you get involved. Doing research before a transaction is relatively quick and cheap. Trying to dig out from under a transaction that has gone sour (partly because of lack of research) is time consuming, painful, and expensive.

Let's examine some of the things you can do to minimize the waste of time, the pain, and the cost that can occur when things do go wrong.

DIGGING OUT FROM UNDER

The range of things that can go wrong is roughly as follows: On the one hand, it could have been a plain simple goof on the part of the seller or institution. If you're dealing with reasonable and reputable people, the matter should be simply and swiftly corrected by a personal visit, a phone call, or a letter. On the other hand, you could be the victim of an out-and-out fraud, with little if any hope for satisfaction.

Or the problem could fall anywhere between the two extremes. This portion of the Appendix will give you some suggestions to help you dig yourself out from under a bad situation. After your initial contact with the other party—following these suggestions—you should have a fairly good idea of what to expect in the way of settlement: Did you get a prompt and courteous promise of satisfaction, did you get a runaround, or did you get something in between?

Very early in the struggle you must evaluate for yourself just what kind of uphill battle you're facing. Some battles require you to spend more time, energy, and money than the matter is really worth. This is a personal decision that you'll have to reach on your own. There is no rule of thumb that holds the right answer. This in no way means to imply that you should ever just walk away from a rough situation. You may have to cope with the fact that you won't get your money back. But such matters should never go unreported to the appropriate authorities. You may be out some money, but by reporting the matter you can help others avoid falling into the same trap.

Arming for Battle

Your chances of winning are all that much greater if you have the following weapons in your arsenal.

WRONG

To whom it may concern:

  I recently bought a jacket at your store. The very first time I wore it three of the seams split. I brought the jacket back to the store, and one of the clerks told me that I must have caused the rips myself by twisting and turning too much. He told me any tailor can fix it.

  I don't think this is right. I think your store should somehow take care of this. I've been a customer of yours for a long time.

  Hoping to hear from you soon.

  Sincerely,

*(**Wrong!** This could go to the janitor, who isn't at all concerned.)*

*(**Wrong!** Be specific so they can trace the sale and respond with more detail.)*

*(**Wrong!** You've indicated that you're easy to push around.)*

*(**Wrong!** Don't "think"; assert!)*

*(**Wrong!** Don't "hope"; propose a specific time by which the matter is to be resolved.)*

RIGHT

Mr. R.J. Klorf
President
Klorf Klothing

Dear Mr. Klorf:

  Last Friday, May 16, I bought a jacket at your store. Enclosed is a copy of the sales slip. I was taken care of by Mr. Thneffy, who has been very helpful to me in my past dealings at Klorf Klothing. He assured me that the jacket was of very fine construction. His word, I'm sure you'll agree, carries with it the fine reputation of your store.

  To my dismay, three seams ripped the first time I wore the jacket. It appears that there were some flaws in the manufacturing process, and I know it's customary for retailers to have recourse to the manufacturer in such cases.

  I brought the jacket back in on Saturday, May 17. Mr. Thneffy was not in, so I spoke to a Mr. Gleebaw, who told me he was just a trainee. I was very dismayed when he told me, in less than polite fashion, that the rips were my own fault and that I should get the jacket repaired at my own expense. All the other senior personnel were busy at the moment, and I was on a tight schedule,

*(**Right!** Go directly to the problem solver.)*
*(**Right!** Specifics help Klorf get to the heart of the matter.)*

*(**Right!** Get to his soft spot: the store's personnel and reputation. But do so diplomatically.)*

*(**Right!** Show that you know Klorf needn't be out of pocket to correct the matter.)*

*(**Right!** It may be your word against Gleebaw's, but a sensitive businessman will side with his customers and will appreciate knowing of misbehavior on the part his employees, particularly trainees.)*

so I decided to deal directly with you on the matter.

I'm sure that you would not agree with such handling of any customer, let alone a long established one. This runs contrary to your store's fine reputation, which I'm certain you wish to maintain.

I'd simply like to have the jacket properly repaired or replaced. If that's not possible, I expect a prompt refund. I shall come into the store at about noon on May 23 to resolve the matter. If you can't meet with me personally, I'll assume that you'll have instructed someone else to take care of me.

Sincerely,

*(**Right!** Shows that you're being reasonable, that you've tried to not bother him.)*
*(**Right!** You know that he can't disagree.)*

*(**Right!** Stroke him a bit.)*
*(**Right!** He'll get the message.)*

*(**Right!** Again, you're being reasonable, yet assertive.)*

*(**Right!** Don't leave things hanging. He'd like to resolve it as quickly as you would.)*

This was an innocent enough situation, which might have been resolved even with the Wrong letter. But why take a chance when you can take the more assertive approach and resolve the problem that much more swiftly and satisfactorily? The next set of letters illustrates a situation that probably could have been avoided in the first place had proper precautions been taken.

WRONG

To the Keep Kool Pool Company:

It's been almost four months since I gave your salesman my check for $2000 as a down payment for the installation of a swimming pool in my backyard. He promised me that work would begin no later than June 15. It's now August 10, and no work has begun. My check was cashed a long time ago. Frankly, we're getting tired of waiting. When can we expect the work to begin? Please respond by return mail.

Sincerely,

RIGHT

In accordance with our contract dated April 25, work was to have begun on our pool not later than June 15. It is now June 20, and work has not begun. This is to notify you that if work has not commenced in earnest by June 25 we will hold you in default on the contract. In such case our deposit will be immediately refunded and the contract will be voided. If the matter is not taken care of one way or the other, we will report the entire incident to the Better Business Bureau, to the State Consumer Protection Bureau, and to the State Contractors Licensing Board, as well as to our attorney, for prompt action.

Sincerely,

The situation, as the facts in the Wrong letter imply, smacks of fraud, negligence, or a combination of the two on the part of Keep Kool Company. The buyers have obviously waited far too long to take action and have been indecisive in seeking a solution. The Right letter takes the bull by the horns, which is often necessary in cases such as this. What steps could Keep Kool customers have taken to have avoided this problem in the first place?

Whether you attack a problem in person, by phone, or by mail, the elements in these letters should help you to avoid losing tactics and to make the most of the assertive winning tactics.

WHERE TO GET HELP

Following is a listing of various state, federal, and private sources of help in consumer/money problems.

State Agencies

Listed herein are the main consumer affairs agencies for each state. Most states also have numerous other agencies dealing with such matters as banking, insurance, motor vehicles, occupational licensing, real estate, employment, health, and safety. Further, many of these agencies may have regional branches, depending on the state. The central agency may be able to help you, or it may direct you to one of the other agencies. Bear in mind that all governmental agencies are limited by budget and by the law as to how much they can help you. As a general rule, they will not act as your attorney in aiding you in getting your money back or in defending you against claims of creditors. Before you place reliance on any governmental agency, inquire as to just what can and cannot be expected of them.

Alabama

Governor's Office of Consumer
  Protection
138 Adams Ave.
Montgomery, AL 36130
(205) 832-5936; (800) 392-5658

Alaska

Office of the Attorney General
420 L St., Suite 100
Anchorage, AK 99501
(907) 276-3550

Arizona

Economic Protection Division
Department of Law
200 State Capitol Bldg.
Phoenix, AZ 85007
(602) 255-5763

Arkansas

Consumer Protection Agency
Justice Bldg.
Little Rock, AR 72201
(501) 371-2341; (800) 482-8982

California

Department of Consumer Affairs
1020 N St.
Sacramento, CA 95814
(916) 445-0660; (800) 952-5210

Colorado

Office of the Attorney General
1525 Sherman St., Third floor
Denver, CO 80203
(303) 839-3611

Connecticut

Department of Consumer
    Protection
State Office Building
Hartford, CT 06115
(203) 566-4999; (800) 842-2649

Delaware

Consumer Affairs Division
820 N. French St.
Wilmington, DE 19801
(302) 571-3250

District of Columbia

D.C. Office of Consumer
    Protection
1407 L St. NW
Washington, DC 20005
(202) 727-1308

Florida

Division of Consumer Services
110 May Bldg.
Tallahassee, FL 32304
(904) 488-2221; (800) 342-2176

Georgia

Governor's Office of Consumer
    Affairs
225 Peachtree St. NE
Atlanta, GA 30303
(404) 656-4900; (800) 282-4900

Hawaii

Consumer Protection Office
250 S. King St., P.O. Box 3767
Honolulu, HI 96811
(800) 548-2560

Idaho

Consumer Protection Division
State Capitol
Boise, ID 83720
(208) 834-2400; (800) 632-5937

Illinois

Consumer Advocate Office
160 N. LaSalle St. Room 2010
Chicago, IL 60601
(312) 793-2754

Indiana

Consumer Protection Division
215 State House
Indianapolis, IN 46204
(317) 633-6496; (800) 382-5516

Iowa

Consumer Protection Division
1209 E. Court
Des Moines, IA 50319
(515) 281-5926

Kansas

Consumer Protection Division
Kansas Judicial Center
310 W. 10th St.
Topeka, KS 66612
(913) 296-3751

Kentucky

Consumer Protection Division
Frankfort, KY 40601
(502) 564-6607; (800) 372-2960

Louisiana

Governor's Office of Consumer
  Protection
P.O. Box 44091
Baton Rouge, LA 70804
(504) 925-4401; (800) 272-9868

Maine

Consumer and Anti-Trust Division
State Office Building, Room 505
Augusta, ME
(207) 289-3716

Maryland

Consumer Protection Division
131 E. Redwood St.
Baltimore, MD 21202
(301) 383-5344

Massachusetts

Executive Office of Consumer
  Affairs
McCormack Bldg., One Ashburton
  Place
Boston, MA 02108
(617) 727-7755

Michigan

Consumer Protection Division
670 Law Bldg.
Lansing, MI 48913
(517) 373-1140

Minnesota

Consumer Protection Division
102 State Capitol
St. Paul, MN
(612) 296-3353

Mississippi

Consumer Protection Division
Justice Bldg. P.O. Box 220
Jackson, MS 39205
(601) 354-7130

Missouri

Consumer Protection Division
Supreme Court Bldg.
P.O. Box 899
Jefferson City, MO 65102
(314) 751-3321

Montana

Consumer Affairs Division
805 N. Main St.
Helena, MT 59601
(406) 449-3163

Nebraska

Consumer Protection Division
State House
Lincoln, NE 68509
(402) 471-2682

Nevada

Consumer Affairs Division
2501 E. Sahara Ave., 3rd floor
Las Vegas, NV 89158
(702) 386-5293

New Hampshire

Consumer Protection Division
Statehouse Annex
Concord, NH 03301
(603) 271-3641

New Jersey

Division of Consumer Affairs
1100 Raymond Blvd. Room 504
Newark, NJ 07102
(201) 648-4010

New Mexico

Consumer and Economic Crime
  Division
P.O. Box 1508
Santa Fe, NM 87501
(505) 827-5521

New York

Consumer Protection Board
99 Washington Ave.
Albany, NY 12210
(518) 474-8583

North Carolina

Consumer Protection Division
Justice Bldg. P.O. Box 629
Raleigh, NC 27602
(919) 733-7741

North Dakota

Consumer Fraud Division
State Capitol,
1102 S. Washington St.
Bismarck, ND 58501
(701) 224-3404; (800) 472-2600

Ohio

Consumer Frauds and Crimes
  Section
30 E. Broad St.
Columbus, OH 43215
(614) 466-8831

Oklahoma

Department of Consumer Affairs
Jim Thorpe Bldg., Room 460
Oklahoma City, OK 73105
(405) 521-3653

Oregon

Consumer Protection Division
520 S.W. Yamhill St.
Portland, OR 97204
(503) 229-5522

Pennsylvania

Bureau of Consumer Protection
301 Market St., 9th Floor
Harrisburg, PA 17101
(717) 787-9707

Rhode Island

Rhode Island Consumers Council
365 Broadway
Providence, RI 02909
(401) 277-2764

South Carolina

Office of Citizens Service
State House, P.O. Box 11450
Columbia, SC 29211
(803) 758-3261

South Dakota

Department of Commerce and
  Consumer Affairs
State Capitol
Pierre, SD 57501
(605) 773-3177

Tennessee

Division of Consumer Affairs
Ellington Agriculture Center,
  P.O. Box 40627
Melrose Station
Nashville, TN 37204
(615) 741-1461; (800) 342-8385

Texas

Consumer Protection Division
P.O. Box 12548, Capitol Station
Austin, TX 78711
(512) 475-3288

Utah

Division of Consumer Affairs
330 E. Fourth South
Salt Lake City, UT 84111
(801) 533-6441

Vermont

Consumer Protection Division
109 State St.
Montpelier, VT 05602
(802) 828-3171; (800) 642-5149

Virginia

Division of Consumer Council
11 S. 12th St., Suite 308
Richmond, VA 23219
(804) 786-4075

Washington

Consumer Protection and
Anti-Trust Division
1366 Dexter Horton Bldg.
Seattle, WA 98104
(206) 464-7744; (800) 552-0700

West Virginia

Consumer Protection Division
3412 Staunton Ave. SE
Charleston, WV 25305
(304) 348-8986

Wisconsin

Office of Consumer Protection
State Capitol
Madison, WI 53702
(608) 266-1852

Wyoming

Assistant Attorney General
123 Capitol Bldg.
Cheyenne, WY 82002
(307) 777-7841

Federal Agencies

Look in the White Pages of your telephone directory under U.S. government for specific offices that may have branches in your area. Following is a listing of major federal agencies that oversee matters discussed in this book. Contact them for information and for referral to the regional office nearest you.

□ **Commodity Futures Trading Commission.** Information and complaints regarding firms trading in commodity futures. 2033 K St. NW, Washington, DC 20581. (800) 424-9383.

□ **Consumer Product Safety Commission.** Information and complaints about consumer products. (800) 658-8326.

□ **Equal Employment Opportunity Commission.** Discrimination in employment. (202) 634-7040.

- [] *Federal Deposit Insurance Corporation.* Inquiries and complaints about state-chartered banks that are examined by the agency. (202) 389-4512.

- [] *Federal Home Loan Bank Board.* Inquiries and complaints about savings and loan associations covered by the Federal Savings and Loan Insurance Corporation (FSLIC). (202) 377-6000.

- [] *Federal Reserve System.* Oversees member banks; also has responsibilities with respect to Fair Credit Reporting Law and Truth in Lending Law. (202) 454-3204. Similarly, the *Comptroller of the Currency* oversees federally chartered banks. (202) 447-1600.

- [] *General Services Administration.* Operates the Consumer Information Center, which offers numerous documents of consumer interest. For a free catalogue of publications, write to Consumer Information, Pueblo, CO 81009. The GSA also operates many federal information centers around the country. These centers can help refer you to appropriate governmental agencies relative to your problems. Check the White Pages in your telephone directory under U.S. government, or call (202) 755-8660.

- [] *Interstate Commerce Commission.* Regulates household moving companies, bus and rail companies. For information and complaints, call (800) 244-9312.

- [] *National Credit Union Administration.* Information and complaints regarding federally chartered credit unions. (202) 492-7715.

- [] *Pension Benefit Guaranty Corporation.* Pension insura⁻ e matters, IRA information. (202) 254-4817. Check also the U.S. Depart of Labor office nearest you.

- [] *Federal Trade Commission.* Deceptive advertising, unfair business practices, consumer protection. Check for regional office nearest you, or call (202) 523-3625.

- [] *U.S. Postal Service.* Mail fraud, mail-order transactions. Consumer Advocate's Office. (202) 245-4514.

- [] *Securities and Exchange Commission.* Stock markets, investment in and trading of securities. Complaints and inquiries to Office of Consumer Affairs, SEC, Washington, DC 20549. (202) 523-3952.

Private Agencies. Some of these private and professional associations may deal only with complaints involving members. It might, then, be a wise precaution to learn if a particular company or professional is a member of the appropriate association before you get involved.

- [] *Better Business Bureau.* Check your telephone directory for local bureau. For location of bureaus in other cities, contact the *Council of Better Business Bureaus*, 1150 17th St. NW, Washington, DC 20036; (202) 862-1200. Inquiries, complaints, and arbitration services.

- [] *Local Media.* Many newspapers and radio and television stations offer consumer-assistance services. They can alert you to potential problems before you get involved and in some cases can help you get satisfaction from an otherwise bad deal.

☐ *Association of Home Appliance Manufacturers.* Offers a Consumer Action Panel, which investigates complaints about most major home appliances. 20 N. Wacker Drive, Chicago, IL 60606. (312) 984-5858.

☐ *American Movers Conference.* Investigates complaints about interstate home-moving companies. 1117 N. 19th St., Suite 806, Arlington, VA 22209. (800) 336-3094.

☐ *American Society of Travel Agents.* Handles complaints, inquiries about travel agencies. 711 Fifth Ave., New York, NY 10022. (212) 486-0700.

☐ *Blue Cross/Blue Shield Associations.* May be able to help resolve problems and complaints that couldn't be solved at the local level, regarding payment of hospital and related bills. 1700 Pennsylvania Ave. NW, Washington, DC 20006. (202) 785-7932.

☐ *Direct Mail Marketing Association.* Complaints on mail-order problems. Can also have your name deleted from certain mailing lists, on your request. 6 E. 43rd St., New York, NY 10017. (212) 689-4977.

☐ *Direct Selling Association.* Complaints on door-to-door selling, home sales "parties." 1730 M St. NW, Suite 610, Washington, DC 20036. (202) 293-5760.

☐ *Electronic Industries Association.* Consumer Affairs Department handles complaints on radios, television sets, stereos, etc. 2001 I St. NW, Washington, DC 20006. (202) 457-4900.

☐ *National Association of Security Dealers.* Complaints regarding stockbrokers, security sales. 1735 K St. NW, Washington, DC 20006. (202) 833-7200.

☐ *National Home Study Council.* Complaints regarding mail-order correspondence courses. 1601 18th St. NW, Washington, DC 20009. (202) 234-5100.

☐ *Professional Associations.* If dealings go wrong with local professionals, such as doctors, lawyers, accountants, real estate agents, your first and best line of attack is the local city, county, or state association. Check your telephone directory for location. Recourse to the respective national association might also be helpful. Major ones include:

—*American Medical Association.* 535 N. Dearborn St., Chicago, IL 60610. (312) 751-6000.

—*American Dental Association.* 211 E. Chicago Ave., Chicago, IL (312) 440-2500.

—*National Society of Public Accountants.* 1717 Pennsylvania Ave. NW, Washington, DC 20006. (202) 298-9040.

—*American Bar Association.* 1155 E. 60th St., Chicago, IL 60637. (312) 947-3885.

—*National Association of Realtors.* 430 Michigan Ave., Chicago, IL 60611. (312) 440-8000.

Glossary

Numbers in parentheses indicate chapter references. Words are defined in the context in which they are used in the text. *Italicized* words within the definitions are separately defined within the Glossary.

Acquisition costs (9)   Expenses that a borrower will have to pay in obtaining a home financing loan. Generally payable to the lender, these expenses can include legal fees, appraisal fees, and *points*.

Add-on interest (14)   One method of calculating *interest* costs in an *installment loan*. For example, if one borrows $1000 for one year at 10 percent add-on interest, the interest cost—$100—is added on to the amount borrowed, making the total debt $1100. Dividing $1100 by twelve results in monthly payments of $91.67.

Adjustments (8)   In a real estate transaction, the pro-rating between buyer and seller of any prepaid expenses (such as property taxes) that the seller has incurred prior to the *closing*.

Adjustments to income (22)   In the calculation of one's income taxes, a main category of expenses that can be used to reduce the amount of income that is subject to taxation.

Administrator/administratrix (21)   A court-appointed person responsible for handling the *estate* of a person who died without a *will*.

Age Discrimination in Employment (2)   A federal law that protects workers between the ages of forty and sixty-five with respect to hiring and firing problems because of their age.

Amended tax return (22)   A tax return that may be filed after the original return was filed to correct errors in the original return.

Annual percentage rate (APR) (14)   The interest rate that the federal government requires be disclosed to borrowers in most installment loan transactions. The APR is designed to offer an accurate comparison of interest costs on different loan offerings.

Annuity (19)   A type of investment with an insurance company that guarantees the investor a fixed monthly income for a specific period of time.

Assessment (10)   A percentage of the market value of a parcel of real estate, used to establish the property taxes on that parcel.

Assets (3)   The total value of everything you own, plus everything owed to you.

Assumable mortgage (9)   A *mortgage* that allows future credit-worthy buyers of the property to take over responsibility of paying the existing loan.

Attestation clause (21)   A clause in a *will* in which the witnesses to the will confirm that they have performed their duties in accordance with the law.

Audit (22)   The procedure in which the Internal Revenue Service examines in detail one's income tax return.

Bait and switch (5)   An illegal selling scheme in which a seller offers a product at an unreasonably low price (the ''bait''). A would-be buyer, lured by the bait, is then ''switched'' to a higher-priced item.

Balloon clause (9)   A provision in a loan agreement (mortgage or installment) that allows the lender to demand full payment of the loan at a set point in time.

Banker's acceptance (16)   A form of investment that arises when a bank holds a foreign company's promissory note (IOU) and sells portions of that note to investors.

Bankruptcy proceedings (14)   Federal court proceedings in which the debts of individuals or companies can be wiped out or in which the court may instruct creditors to hold off in their attempts to collect debts due them from the bankrupt person or company.

Beneficiary (19, 21)   One who receives an inheritance from the *estate* of a *decedent*; also, one who receives the proceeds of a *life insurance policy* on the death of the insured person.

Benefits (19)   Money received from an insurance company when the insured party suffers a loss that is covered by the insurance policy.

Bequest (21)   The specific property or money given to a *beneficiary* from the *estate* of a *decedent*.

Blue-chip stock (17)   *Stock* of a company considered to have high investment quality: relatively stable prices and strong dividend payment history.

Bond (16)   A long-term debt instrument.

Buying down (9)   A type of ''creative'' home financing whereby the seller pays part of the interest charges for the buyer for a specified period of time.

Call option (17)   A contract that gives the owner the right to buy one hundred shares of a given common *stock* at a predetermined price (the ''strike price'') at any time until a fixed future date.

Call privilege (16)   The right of a *corporation* or other issuer of debt to pay off the holders of the debt at an agreed price prior to the scheduled maturity of the debt.

Cashier's check (13)   A check drawn on a bank's own account.

Cash management account (13)   A type of account offered by stockbrokerage firms that provides a combination of checking, investing, and borrowing capabilities for its customers.

Certificate of deposit (13, 16)   A contractual investment with a financial institution wherein the investor agrees to deposit a fixed sum of money for a fixed amount of time in return for a guaranteed interest rate.

Certified check (13)   An individual (or business) check that has been guaranteed by the bank upon which it is drawn, that is, the funds are guaranteed to be available when the check is presented for payment.

Churning (17)   An improper practice wherein stockbrokers create excessive trading in customers' accounts to generate commissions for themselves.

Civil Rights Act (2)   See *Fair Employment Practices Law*.

Closing (8)   In a real estate transaction, the event at which the transfer of *deeds*, money, and promises-to-pay takes place.

Codicil (21)   A document that, when properly executed, amends a *will*.

Co-insurance clause (10)   A provision in most property-insurance policies that states that the insured party will receive full replacement value for losses only if the premises are insured for a stated percentage (usually 80 percent) of full value.

Collision insurance (6)   Coverage for the insured's auto for damages resulting from a collision with another vehicle or object.

Commercial paper (16)   An instrument of short-term debt issued by a *corporation*.

Commodity-backed bond (16)   A corporate debt that allows the holder (investor) a choice of being paid off either in cash or in the particular product (commodity) that the company makes or sells.

Commodities (18)   A variety of products (such as cattle, wheat, precious metals, etc.) whose future values are subject to fluctuation. Commodity markets offer the opportunity to speculate in those future values. (Also known as "futures trading.")

Compounding of interest (16)   Occurs when the *interest* you earn stays in your account and begins to earn interest itself.

Comprehensive insurance (6)   Coverage for the insured's auto for damages resulting from occurrences other than collision, such as fire and theft.

Condominium (8)   An owned dwelling unit that is part of a multiple-unit structure.

Condominium conversion (8, 11)   The act of modifying the form of ownership of a multiple-unit building from single ownership of the entire structure to individual ownership of each specific unit within the entire structure.

Contingent beneficiary (19)   One who takes the place of an original *beneficiary* (in a *will* or *insurance policy*) should the original beneficiary die before the *testator* or the insured.

Cooperative (8)   A type of housing arrangement wherein each resident owns a percentage of the total building and has an agreement with all the owners for the right to use a specific unit in the building for his own dwelling.

Corporation (16)   A legal entity created under state law for the purpose of conducting a stated business. A corporation is owned by its stockholders, who in turn elect a board of directors to set the ongoing policies of the corporation. The directors in turn select officers to run the day-to-day affairs of the corporation.

Corporate bond (16)   A long-term debt instrument issued by a *corporation*. Some bonds may contain a *call privilege*. Some bonds are convertible, that is, the owner has the right to convert the bond into *stock* of the same company, upon stated terms and conditions.

Co-signer (14)   One who jointly signs a credit agreement with the principal borrower. The co-signer must pay the debt if the borrower fails to do so.

Creative financing (9)   A general term describing home financing arrangements that are privately negotiated between seller and buyer, with or without the participation of outside lenders or investors.

Credit bureau (14)   A nongovernmental organization that collects and distributes credit information. Merchants and lenders use this information to make decisions on granting credit to those who apply.

Credit capacity (14)   The amount of borrowing consumers can realistically handle, considering their current and future income and expenses.

Credit health insurance (14)   A form of health insurance that will pay loan payments if an insured borrower is disabled due to health or accident.

Credit history (14)   The record of one's credit activity, as maintained by the local *credit bureau*.

Credit life insurance (14)   A form of life insurance that will pay off any balance due on an installment loan should the borrower die before the loan is otherwise paid.

Credit union (13)   A type of financial institution that is owned by individuals who have a common bond, such as the employees of a company or governmental agency.

Debt-counseling service (14)   An agency that assists creditors who are having financial troubles.

Decedent (21)   One who has died.

Decreasing term insurance (19)   A type of life insurance; the amount of coverage decreases from year to year.

Deductible (6, 10)   With respect to property-damage insurance (auto, home), the amount that an insured must first pay out of pocket before the insurance company becomes liable. For example, if one suffers a casualty valued at $200 and has a $50 deductible for such occurrences, the insured is responsible for the first $50 and the insurance company will then reimburse $150.

Deductions (22)   Regarding income taxes, a category of expenses that are subtracted from adjusted gross income to lower the amount of income subject to taxation. Taxpayers may claim *itemized deductions* or *standard deductions*.

Deed (8)   A document by which title to real estate passes from the seller to the buyer.

Deficit (1)   The status of a budget (one's financial condition) when more money has been spent than has been taken in, the difference being considered as debt.

Disability income insurance (21)   Insurance that provides some income to a worker who becomes unable to work due to injury or health problems.

Discount interest (14)   A method of calculating *interest* costs in an *installment loan*. For example, if one signs a loan agreement for $1110 for one year at 10 percent discount interest, the interest cost—10 percent of $1110, or $111—is "discounted," or subtracted, from the total IOU, leaving the borrower with $999 cash. Dividing $1110 by twelve results in monthly payments of $92.50. Compare *add-on interest*.

Discretionary income (3, 15)   Extra money available once one's basic needs have been paid for.

Discriminate Income Function (DIF) (22)   A computerized procedure used by the IRS to select tax returns for *audit*. The computer compares various elements of a given return (income, deductions, etc.) and further compares those ratios to average levels for such claims.

Dividend (17)   That portion of a company's profit which the directors vote to pay out to stockholders. Usually paid quarterly.

Double indemnity (19)   A life insurance policy provision that will pay *beneficiaries* double the *face amount* of the policy in the event of the accidental death of the insured.

Dow Jones Industrial Average (17)   The most commonly referred to index of stock prices and their movements. It reflects the prices of thirty major industrial stocks.

Down payment (14)   That portion of the purchase price (of a house, a car, etc.) paid by the buyer in cash at the time of purchase.

Earnest money (8)   A token payment of cash to bind a preliminary agreement between the buyer and seller of a house (or other item).

Easement (8)   The right given to someone to use your land for a specific purpose (to cross over the property, to construct utility lines, etc.).

Eminent domain (10)   A legal concept that permits a local government to acquire or condemn private property when a proven public need for the property exists, for example, to widen a highway, to build a school. Owners of the private property must be adequately paid for their property.

Employee Retirement Income Security Act (ERISA) (2, 20)   A federal law that protects the right of employees with respect to pension and profit-sharing plans. Also known as the Pension Reform Law of 1974.

Endorsement (13)   The writing of one's signature on the back of a check (or other negotiable instrument), thereby acknowledging receipt of the cash or credit indicated on the check. Endorsements may be in blank (signature only); restrictive (limiting how the check may be further negotiated); or special (such as when the funds are to be paid or credited to a third party).

Equal Credit Opportunity Law (13)   A federal law designed to prevent discrimination regarding sex or marital status of individuals applying for credit.

Equity (11)   The difference between what your house (or other property) is currently worth and what you owe on it.

Escrow (9)   A third party who acts as an intermediary in a real estate transaction, seeing to it that the instructions of the parties are complied with; also a sum of money paid monthly to a mortgage lender to pay property insurance premiums and property taxes as they fall due. Also referred to as an escrow account or reserve account.

Estate (21)   The legal entity that comes into being upon the death of a person; that is, upon John's death the estate of John comes into being. Also refers to the net worth of the decedent; that is, John's estate is worth $100,000.

Estate taxes (21)   A federal or state tax on the *estate* of a *decedent*.

Exclusion (12)   An amount of income that is free of income taxes. For example, if the seller of a home is over the age of fifty-five, he may be able to exclude from taxable income up to $125,000 worth of profit on the sale of the home.

Ex-dividend date (17)   A date that determines whether a buyer of *stock* will be entitled to a recently declared *dividend*. One who buys before the ex-dividend date will receive the dividend. One who buys after the ex-dividend date will not receive the dividend.

Executor/executrix (21)   The person or institution designated by a *testator* to carry out the settlement of the testator's *estate*.

Exemptions (22)   With regard to income taxes, the number of persons dependent on the taxpayer, including the taxpayer. For each proper exemption the taxpayer is allowed to reduce income subject to taxes by a fixed amount.

Face amount (face value) (19)   The amount of money that a *life insurance policy* will pay to the *beneficiary* on the death of the insured person.

Fair Credit Billing Law (13)   A federal law that protects the rights of persons who receive erroneous bills from creditors.

Fair Credit Reporting Law (13)   A federal law that gives individuals the right to view their *credit history* and to take steps to have errors corrected.

Fair Debt Collection Practices Law (13)   A federal law that protects debtors from unfair, deceptive, and abusive debt-collection practices.

Fair Employment Practices Law (2)   A federal law designed to prevent job discrimination because of an individual's race, sex, religion, or national origin. Also known as the Civil Rights Act of 1964.

Fair Labor Standards Law (2)   A federal law that protects certain minors with respect to jobs that could be hazardous or detrimental to their well-being.

Federal Deposit Insurance Corporation (FDIC) (13, 16)   The federal agency that insures accounts in commercial banks and mutual savings banks against the failure of the institutions.

Federal Savings and Loan Insurance Corporation (FSLIC) (13, 16)   The federal agency that insures accounts in savings and loan associations against the failure of the institutions.

Filing extension (22)   Available to taxpayers who file the proper form, an added time to file their tax return.

Filing status (22)   One of five categories chosen by taxpayers as a part of completing their returns; the choice of category, which is broadly based on a taxpayer's marital situation, affects the amount of tax payable.

Fill or kill order (17)   An order given to a stockbroker to buy or sell stocks at a specific price, with the understanding that if the order can't be filled immediately at the given price, the order will terminate.

Financing contingency clause (8)   A provision in a contract for the purchase of real estate that allows buyers to be released from their obligation if they are not able to obtain financing at a certain rate of interest by an agreed date.

Fiscal policy (1)   The policy that determines how a government will raise money and for what purposes it will spend it.

Floating-rate bond (16)   A *bond* in which the interest rate payable to holders will fluctuate up and down, usually within set limits and/or in accordance with some outside index.

Foreclosure (9)   The procedure by which a lender can obtain title to property which has been pledged as security for a loan when the borrower has defaulted on that loan.

Foreign exchange (18)   Generally, the currency of other nations. The future values of the currencies of major nations can be bought and sold at commodity exchanges.

Form 1040 (1040A) (22)   The basic forms used to file one's federal income taxes. Taxpayers who wish to claim certain *adjustments, tax credits*, and *itemized deductions* use the 1040 (long form). Taxpayers who do not wish to claim these items use the 1040A (short form).

Fringe benefit (2)   A form of payment to a worker, other than current money, such as insurance protection, pension plans, and profit-sharing plans.

Funding (20)   The placing of money in a pension plan by an employer. Proper funding requires that enough money be placed in the fund to meet future promises to pay benefits to covered employees.

Garnishment (2)   A legal procedure by which a creditor can get access to a debtor's wages to satisfy a debt due the creditor.

General obligation bond (16)   A type of *municipal bond* backed by the taxing authority of the municipality.

Generic products (4)   Grocery, pharmaceutical, and other items with ''plain'' or nonbrand labels.

Glamour stock (17)   *Stock* of a company that the investment community perceives as ''hot'' or as a ''winner.'' Compared with blue-chip stocks, glamour stocks are relatively less stable in their prices and dividend payment records.

Graduated payment plan (9)   A home financing plan that permits the borrower to make lower than usual payments in the first few years, with payments then increasing in the later years.

Gross lease (18)   A commercial lease that requires the landlord to pay for virtually all expenses relating to the property.

Group insurance (2)   One of many kinds of insurance plans (usually life and health) that is offered to members of a group, such as company employees or members of a fraternal organization. Because many individuals are covered under a single master policy, the cost to each insured is less than the same insurance would be if purchased individually.

Group venture (18)   The pooling of money with several investors to purchase real estate (or other investments).

Health Maintenance Organization (HMO) (19)   A prepaid medical-care facility.

Hedge value (15)   Generally, the ability of an investment to withstand the effects of inflation.

Heir (21)   One who receives an interest in the *estate* of a *decedent*.

Highball (6)   A selling technique whereby the salesperson attempts to convince you that your property (trade-in car, house) is worth much more than you thought it was, to lure you into doing business.

Holographic will (21)   A *will* prepared in the handwriting of the *testator*; it is not always valid.

Homeowner's insurance (10)   A form of *insurance policy* that reimburses the owner of a home for losses suffered due to fire, theft, and other causes. Risks covered and cost of policy depend on the type of policy, generally including basic form (the least coverage and cost), broad form (middle range), and comprehensive (highest coverage and cost). See *Tenant's insurance*.

Hospital insurance (21)   A form of *insurance policy* that will reimburse the insured for costs of being hospitalized, including room, board, and other specified services.

Income-producing property (18)   Generally, real estate that is purchased as an investment and from which rental income and depreciation deductions flow to the investor.

Income shifting (22)   The procedure whereby taxpayers in a high tax bracket transfer income-producing assets to low-bracket taxpayers, such as their children, so that the income will be taxed at a lower rate.

Income stocks (17)   Stocks that are expected to pay a high level of dividend income to holders.

Incontestable clause (19)   A provision in an insurance policy that cuts off the rights of the insurance company to challenge statements made in the application after a stated period of time.

Individual Retirement Account (IRA) (20)   A do-it-yourself retirement investment plan with attractive tax benefits, available to all workers.

Inheritance tax (21)   A state tax on individuals who receive inheritances.

Installment loan (14)   A loan that is repayable to the lender in equal monthly amounts, customarily over a period of years.

Insurance policy (19)   A contract made with an insurance company wherein the company agrees to pay money to the named parties if certain events occur, such as the death, illness, or disability of the insured party or the destruction of the insured's property, home, or car.

Interest (14)   The fee paid for the use of another's money.

Intestacy (21)   The status of one who dies without a *will*. In such case, the law of the state in which the decedent resided will determine how the estate is to be distributed.

Itemized deductions (22)   A specific listing of all allowable expenses that can be used to reduce the amount of income subject to taxation.

Keogh plan (20)   A do-it-yourself retirement investment plan with attractive tax benefits, available to self-employed persons.

Land contract (9)   A manner of purchasing real estate wherein the *deed* is not conveyed to the buyer at the *closing*, but rather at some future date, as agreed on by the parties.

Land lease (8)   An arrangement for purchasing real estate wherein the buyer buys only the structure and *leases* the land upon which the structure exists.

Lease (11)   A contract by which the owner of property allows another (the tenant) to use that property for an agreed time and price.

Lease with option to buy (11)   A lease that also gives the tenant the right to purchase the property at an agreed price within certain time limits.

Lease with right of first refusal (11)   A lease during which the tenant is given the right to purchase the property if he is willing to match the terms of any bona fide purchase offer the owner receives from outside parties.

Liability (3)   A debt; an amount of money owed to someone else.

Life insurance policy (19)   An *insurance policy* in which the company promises to pay a fixed sum of money to the *beneficiary* upon the death of the insured (covered) party.

Lien (8)   A legal right obtained by a creditor with respect to property that has been pledged as collateral for a loan made by the creditor to the debtor. Having a lien on the property can allow the creditor to force a sale of the property in order to satisfy the debt. Liens against property can also arise as a result of the debtor's failure to pay taxes, or to pay contractors and artisans who have worked on the property.

Life estate (21)   Bequests wherein recipients have the use of the subject properties only for the remainder of their life, after which the properties pass to others previously named by the original *testators*.

Limit order (17)   An order given to a stockbroker to buy or sell stock within a high or low price range.

Liquidity (15)   Generally, how quickly, conveniently, and cheaply you can retrieve your money from a given investment.

Listing contract (12)   A contract between a seller of real estate and a real estate broker in which the seller gives the broker the exclusive right to try to sell the property for a specific period of time.

Load charge (16)   The sales commission an investor pays when investing in a mutual fund.

Loan consolidation (14)   A procedure whereby one new loan is obtained to pay off numerous smaller loans.

Loss leader (5)   A product offered by a merchant at a lower-than-normal price to lure shoppers to the store.

Major medical insurance (19)   A form of health insurance designed to protect the insured against heavy, even catastrophic, health-care expenses.

Margin investing (17)   Buying *stock* partly with your own funds and partly with funds that you have borrowed from the stockbroker.

Marital deduction (21)   The portion of one's estate that is left, in proper legal fashion, to the surviving spouse. The marital deduction amount reduces the taxable portion of the estate.

Market order (17)   An order given to a stockbroker to buy or sell stock at whatever the going price might be.

Medical payments coverage (6)   A part of one's automobile insurance (optional) that reimburses driver and occupants for limited medical expenses arising from an accident. Also available on homeowner's and tenant's insurance.

Medicare (19)   A health-insurance program administered by the Social Security Administration for the protection of citizens aged sixty-five years old and over.

Monetary policy (1)   That part of a government's program that regulates the amount of money flowing throughout the economy.

Money market fund (16)   *Mutual funds* that specialize in acquiring high interest rate *money market instruments*.

Money market instrument (16)   Generally, short-term, high-quality investments, including *certificates of deposit, bonds, repurchase agreements, commercial paper*, and *banker's acceptances*.

Mortgage (9)   A debt secured by real estate. When one borrows money to pay for a home purchase, the debt is referred to as a first mortgage and/or a purchase money mortgage. In some states this type of debt is known as a trust deed.

Multiple listing (8)   A service offered by subscribing real estate brokers in a given area, wherein all houses and other properties for sale in that area are listed and described in a frequently published directory.

Municipal bond (16)   A debt issued by a local government agency (state, city, county, or subdivisions thereof). Interest earned by investors in such bonds is exempt from federal income taxes.

Mutual fund (16)   A pooling of the money of many investors, which, under professional management, attempts to fulfill stated investment objectives.

National Credit Union Administration (13)   The agency that insures accounts in federally covered credit unions.

National Labor Relations Act (2)   A federal law that regulates relations between employers and labor unions.

Net lease (18)   A type of commercial lease in which the tenant is responsible for most or all of the operating costs of the property.

Net worth (3)   The difference between *assets* and *liabilities*; a measure of one's wealth.

No-fault insurance (6)   A type of automobile insurance required in some states, in which injured parties are paid by their own insurance companies (up to set limits) regardless of who was at fault in the accident.

Noncupative will (21)   A *will* that is spoken by the *testator* to another party; not usually valid.

Nonparticipating policy (19)   A *life insurance policy* in which dividends are not paid to policy holders. (See *Participating policy*.)

Nontaxable income (22)   Money received by a taxpayer that is not subject to income taxes, such as inheritances, life insurance proceeds, and social security payments.

Occupational Safety and Health Act (OSHA) (2)   A federal law that sets health and safety standards for working environments.

Odd lot (17)   A block of less than one hundred shares of *stock*.

Open-end clause (9)   A clause in a *mortgage* that allows the borrower to borrow back up to the original amount of the loan at the original or otherwise agreed interest rate.

Open-end mutual fund (16)   A *mutual fund* in which the portfolio managers may buy and sell securities as their judgment dictates.

Option tender bond (16)   A *bond* that gives the holder the right to cash in the bond at some specified date prior to the scheduled maturity.

Overdraft (13)   The result of writing a check on one's checking account when the amount of the check exceeds the balance in the account.

Participating policy (19)   An insurance policy wherein policy holders participate in annual distributions of excess income generated by the company. These distributions are commonly known as *dividends* and are also called *nonparticipating policies*.

Pension Benefit Guarantee Corporation (PBGC) (20)   A federal insurance program that guarantees retirees a continuation of at least a portion of their promised pension benefits should the company or the pension plan fail.

Pension plan (2)   A fringe benefit offered by many employers, whereby the employer puts aside a sum of money for the benefit of the employee upon retirement. Some plans also allow voluntary contributions by employees.

Pension Reform Law of 1974 (2, 20)   (See *Employee Retirement Income Security Act.*)

Percentage clause (18)   A provision in a commercial lease that states, generally, that the tenant must pay the landlord a certain percentage of the tenant's dollar volume of business, under agreed conditions.

Permanent insurance (19)   Life insurance in which the amount of *premium* paid remains fixed for the life of the policy. Also known as ordinary, straight, or whole life insurance.

Physician insurance (19)   A form of health insurance that pays doctors' bills within stated limits.

Pigeon drop scheme (5)   A fraudulent activity wherein the victim is convinced to part with cash in order to share in what appears to be a large sum of money that the perpetrator says has been found lying on the street. There are many variations of this scheme.

Pledge value (15)   Generally, the ease and cost of borrowing against a particular investment.

Points (9)   Added fees that a lender will charge a borrower, usually in a home financing transaction. One point equals 1 percent of the amount of the loan.

Ponzi scheme (5)   A fraudulent investment activity in which new victims are constantly being lured to participate, and their invested money is used to pay off prior victims. At some point the perpetrator will attempt to disappear with as much money as can be mustered from the victims.

Premium (17, 19)   In option trading, the cost of purchasing a contract. In insurance, the fee paid for coverage provided.

Prepayment clause (9)   A provision in a *mortgage* that determines to what extent the borrower may make advance payments on the loan and what penalties, if any, may also have to be paid as a result.

Price-earnings ratio (P-E ratio) (17)   The price of a given *stock* divided by the per-share earnings of the company. A low ratio tends to indicate a more conservative investment situation. A high ratio tends to indicate a more speculative situation.

Probate (21)   A court proceeding in which the validity of a *will* is proven.

Productivity (1)   A measurement of efficiency.

Profit-sharing plan (2)   A fringe benefit whereby eligible employees receive a share of the company's profits, either annually or, more usually, on retirement.

Prospectus (17)   A document that must be published by *corporations* offering securities, in which certain facts regarding the offering must be disclosed.

Proxy (17)   A write-in ballot used by stockholders of a *corporation* that allows them to vote on the election of directors and other pertinent issues. Used in lieu of personally attending the stockholders' meetings.

Public liability coverage (6, 10)   Insurance that provides legal defense and pays claims if the insured's actions cause bodily harm or property damage to others. Common with automobile, homeowner's, and tenant's insurance policies.

Put option (17)   A contract that gives the holder the right to sell one hundred shares of a given *stock* at a predetermined price and by a given future date.

Pyramiding (14)   A form of credit abuse (largely self-inflicted) that occurs when a loan taken for a recurring purpose (car purchase, vacation) is not fully paid by the time the purpose recurs again and a new loan is needed.

Real estate investment trust (REIT) (18)   A form of *mutual fund* for real estate investments.

Reconciliation (13)   The procedure to determine whether one's checking account balance matches the bank's calculations.

Repurchase agreement (16)   A form of short-term investment; typically, an investor purchases a fractional interest in a pool of government securities from a financial institution. The institution agrees to repurchase the certificate at a higher price within a fixed period of time.

Restrictive covenant (8)   A provision in a *deed* that can control certain things that an owner of real estate can or cannot do on the property.

Revenue bond (16)   A type of *municipal bond* backed by the revenues produced by the entity borrowing the money (e.g., a toll road).

Right of assignment clause (8)   A contractual clause that permits parties to a contract to transfer their interests in the contract to other parties.

Reward-risk rule (15)   An investment adage that correctly states that the greater return you expect on an investment, the greater risk you'll be taking.

Rollover (12, 20)   Regarding the sale of a home, a technique that allows the postponement of taxes otherwise due on a profit from such sale. Also a type of *individual retirement account* that allows postponement of taxes payable on the lump-sum payment of a *pension* or *profit-sharing plan*.

Round lot (17)   A block of one hundred shares of *stock* or one divisible by one hundred.

Rule of 78s (14)   The most common method of calculating the rebate of prepaid interest charges on an *installment loan* when the loan is paid off before its scheduled maturity.

Schedules A and B (22)   Federal income tax forms used in conjunction with the 1040 form for declaring itemized deductions (A) and income from interest and dividends (B).

Securities and Exchange Commission (SEC) (17)   A federal regulatory agency that oversees the trading of *stocks*.

Securities Investor Protection Corporation (SIPC) (17)   A federal agency that insures certain aspects of investors' accounts with brokerage firms in the event of the firm's failure.

Security (14)   A tangible asset that a borrower pledges to a lender in order to obtain a loan. If the borrower defaults, the security may be sold by the lender to satisfy the debt.

Settlement options (19)   Various ways that the proceeds of a life insurance policy can be paid out.

Shared appreciation mortgage (9)   A form of *mortgage* wherein the lender charges the buyer a favorable interest rate in exchange for a share in future profits from the sale of the property.

Shared equity (8)   Two or more individuals or families combine their financial resources to purchase a dwelling for themselves.

Short selling (17)   A speculative technique that, when successful, allows one to profit from the drop in value of shares of *stock*.

Simple interest (14)   One means of calculating loan costs, usually in a loan payable in one lump sum as opposed to installments. The interest cost is expressed as a percent of the amount borrowed, usually on an annual basis. For example: 10 percent annual simple interest on a $1000 loan is $100 for a one-year loan, $50 for a six-month loan, $25 for a three-month loan.

Sinking fund (16)   A reserve account set up by a *corporation*; money is put into the account each year to be used to pay off a debt of the corporation when it falls due.

Sleeping second (9)   A *creative financing* tool involving a second mortgage that is owed by the buyer to the seller but upon which no payments are required for an agreed time.

Standard deduction (22)   For taxpayers who choose not to itemize their deductions, the fixed amount that can be used to reduce the amount of income subject to taxation. The deduction may be taken whether or not the taxpayer actually incurred such expenses.

Stock (17)   Form of ownership of a fractional part of a *corporation*. One owns "shares of stock." Unless otherwise specified, stock is considered "common." Some corporations also issue another class of stock known as "preferred." Owners of preferred shares have a higher claim to company dividends (and assets in the event of liquidation) than owners of common shares.

Stock investment program (2)   A *fringe benefit* in which employees are offered the opportunity to buys shares of *stock* in the company at a lower price than they could on the open market.

Stop payment order (13)   Written instructions to a bank given by the maker of a check ordering the bank not to pay a specific check that the maker issued.

Strike price (17)   The price at which you can buy the underlying *stock* in a *call option* contract.

Surgical insurance (19)   A form of health insurance that reimburses the insured for surgical and related expenses.

Surplus (1)   The status of a budget (one's financial condition) when more money has been taken in than has been spent. (See *Deficit*.)

"Take back a mortgage" (18)   Expression used when the seller of property accepts the buyer's IOU instead of cash. The IOU will be secured by a *mortgage* on the property. (Also referred to as ''take back paper.'')

Takeover operation (6)   A sales technique involving a succession of salespeople, one taking over after the other, at ever-increasing pressure. This scheme is designed to wear down your resistance, especially with automobile sales.

Tax credit (22)   An amount that may be deducted from your computed federal income tax. Every dollar's worth of credit reduces your tax by one dollar.

Tax-deferred investments (15, 20)   Investments whose earnings are not subject to taxation during the year earned, but will be subject to taxation in some later year. (See *Individual retirement account; Keogh plan*.)

Tax-exempt investments (15)   Investments whose earnings are not subject to taxation at any time. (See *Municipal bond*.)

Tax rate (10)   With respect to real property taxes, the factor used to determine the amount payable, usually expressed in terms of dollars per $1000 worth of *assessment* value. For example, a tax rate of $20 per $1000, applied to property assessed at $40,000, results in an annual property tax of $800.

Tax tables (22)   With respect to federal income taxes, the tables from which most taxpayers can determine their taxes due.

Taxable income (22)   In the calculation of taxes payable, the income upon which the tax is figured after having taken into account all proper *deductions, exemptions*, and *adjustments*.

Taxable investments (15)   Investments whose earnings are subject to taxation in the year in which earned.

Taxable transfer (21)   With respect to federal estate and gift taxes, the amount upon which the tax is figured after having taken into account all proper deductions.

Taxpayer Compliance Measurement Program (TCMP) (22)   A random selection by the Internal Revenue Service of tax returns to be audited.

Tenant's insurance (10)   A form of property insurance for those who rent their dwellings. (See *Homeowner's insurance*.)

Term insurance (19)   Also known as temporary insurance; a form of *life insurance* wherein the *premium* cost increases as the age of the insured increases. Policies run for a set number of years, and premiums are increased on renewal of policies. (See *Permanent insurance*.)

Testator/testatrix (21)   A person who makes a *will*.

Testimonium clause (21)   A clause in a *will* in which the *testators* state that they are signing the document as their true last will and testament.

Time order (17)   An order to a stockbroker to buy or sell *stock* subject to a time deadline; usually attached to a *limit order*.

Title insurance (8)   Insurance that will reimburse the insured for losses suffered (within stated limits) should a claim be made against the title of property owned by the insured.

Town house (8)   (Also known as a row house.) A form of dwelling unit adjoined on both sides by similar units.

Treasury bill (16)   A short-term (less than one year) federal government debt instrument, minimum denomination $10,000.

Treasury bond (16)   A long-term (up to twenty years or more) federal government debt instrument.

Treasury note (16)   A medium-term (one to seven years) federal government debt instrument.

Trust (21)   An arrangement, often in complex legal fashion, whereby one person or institution (the trustee) has custody of someone else's (the trustor's) money or property, for ultimate distribution to a named third party (the beneficiary). An inter vivos trust is one that comes into being while the trustor is alive. A testamentary trust is one that comes into being upon the death of the trustor.

Truth in Lending Law (13)   A federal law that, among other things, requires covered lenders to provide a uniform interest rate quotation to borrowers. (See *Annual percentage rate*.)

Turnover investing (18)   With reference to real estate investing, a program of buying property with the intent of reselling it at a profit as soon as possible.

Unemployment insurance (2, 19)   A state-administered insurance program paid for by employers. It provides financial benefits to employees who are laid off.

Uninsured motorist insurance (6)   A form of coverage in automobile insurance policies that protects insured individuals when they are injured in an accident with uninsured drivers.

Unit pricing (4)   The pricing of food and other grocery products expressed in units of measurement (ounces, pounds, etc.), that is, the price per ounce or per unit.

Usury laws (13)   State laws that dictate the maximum rate of interest that can be charged for various types of loans.

Vacation time sharing (7)   An arrangement whereby one buys the right to use a specific dwelling unit (such as at a resort) for one or more specific weeks each year for many years.

Vanity rackets (5)   Various schemes, sometimes fraudulent, in which the promoter offers to ''publish'' your book, song, and so forth for a fee, no matter what the quality of the work.

Variable-rate mortgage (9)   A home financing arrangement in which the interest rate payable by the borrower may fluctuate up or down.

Vesting (20)   The concept that pertains to one's pension benefits becoming irrevocably due; vesting occurs according to a preset schedule.

Waiver of premium (19)   A clause in an insurance contract (usually life, health, or disability plans) that states that if the insured becomes disabled, the need to pay the premiums on the policy will be waived during the period of disability.

Warrant (17)   Sometimes part of a *stock* offering, it allows the holder to purchase shares of the company's stock at a set price for a limited period of time.

W-4 form (22)   A federal tax form in which a worker claims a number of allowances which in turn determine the amount of tax withheld from the worker's pay.

Will (21)   A document that, when properly drawn and executed, assures the protection of the state court over the distribution of the individual's *(testator's) estate*, in accordance with the wishes as expressed in the document.

Workers' compensation (2, 19)   A state-administered health and disability program, paid for by employers, that provides certain benefits to workers who suffer job-related injuries or illnesses.

Yield (15)   Generally expressed as a percentage, the earnings you'll receive from an investment; for example, a return of $5 in one year on an investment of $100 equals a yield of 5 percent.

Zone (10)   A specified area within a community that can only be used for specific purposes, such as residential and commercial.

Index

About the Author

Bob Rosefsky's credentials—as author, educator, and professional consultant—uniquely suit him for the task of creating the definitive work on personal financial matters.

After receiving his B.A. degree from Yale University and his Juris Doctorate from Syracuse University College of Law, he practiced law and worked in banking for several years, dealing with the public as a professional "problem solver." His skills as such led him to a new career in the mass media, where he helped pioneer the newly emerging concept of personal financial planning.

Mr. Rosefsky has written eight books on various financial subjects, including a college textbook, and his advice has been widely syndicated through newspapers, radio, and television. Most recently he has served as "Money Advisor" for ABC's radio and television affiliates in Los Angeles.

His experience as an educator is both innovative and extensive. He has created two college-credit television courses, "You and the Law," and "Personal Finance." The latter has won an Emmy Award as Best Instructional Series and is nationally distributed by the Public Broadcasting System. Tens of thousands of students from all parts of the nation have received credit at their local colleges for these courses.

He has taught Business and Economic Journalism at the University of Southern California, as well as financial planning seminars for University of California, Los Angeles, Extension Program; University of Southern California, College of Continuing Education; and numerous community colleges.

He has served as a member of the Board of Governors of the Society of American Business and Economic Writers and has been honored with the John Hancock Award for Excellence in Financial Journalism.

Bob and his wife have four children and one grandchild. Their home is in Los Angeles, California.